The
UNDERSIDE
of
AMERICAN
HISTORY

Fifth Edition

VOLUME ONE: TO 1877

The
UNDERSIDE
of
AMERICAN
HISTORY

Fifth Edition

VOLUME ONE: TO 1877

Edited by

THOMAS R. FRAZIER

The Bernard M. Baruch College of The City University of New York

HARCOURT BRACE JOVANOVICH, PUBLISHERS

San Diego   New York   Chicago   Austin   Washington, D.C.
London   Sydney   Tokyo   Toronto

Preface

The study of American history in colleges and universities has undergone a profound change in the past several decades. When scholars began to examine the social and economic factors behind the upheaval in American society during the 1960s, the placid picture of an American paradise, idyllic and relatively peaceful, developing its natural and human resources, was shattered. In its place emerged a history of violence and turmoil in which race was pitted against race and class against class in a struggle for scarce resources and the status conferred on those who possessed them.

Most history texts published recently have tried to account for this change and to include material dealing with its emergent themes. Format restrictions and a focus on the "mainstream" of American history, however, have constrained its presentation. The purpose of *The Underside of American History* has been to supplement these more general academic works. The first four editions dealt with groups and themes that traditionally had been ignored or slighted in the existing textbooks: American Indians, blacks, women, the working class, East Asian immigrants, poor whites, the elderly, Mexican-Americans, children, female labor; and the incidence of socialism, peace movements, and revivalism, among other topics. The first volume of this Fifth Edition, in which over three-fourths of the selections are new, continues the concerns of the previous four editions but extends the subject matter to include female servants and slaves, seamen, republican values, political education, new religious movements, Indian wars, and frontier violence. It points out that many of the problems in America today are rooted in the past and suggests that conflict, stress, and repression will continue to characterize much of American society as long as social, economic, and political inequities are not resolved.

The selections are arranged in roughly chronological order: Volume 1 begins with the colonial period and continues through Reconstruction; volume 2 covers mainly the period between Reconstruction and the present. Each volume contains a general introduction that presents the major themes of the readings. In addition, a brief headnote introduces each selection and indicates both its historical context and its significance. An annotated bibliography closes each major part of the collection.

I gratefully acknowledge the advice and assistance of the following historians; their comments and suggestions on each edition of this book have been most helpful: Carol Ruth Berkin of the Baruch College of the City University of New York, Robert Calhoon of the University of North Carolina at Greensboro, Mark T. Carleton of Louisiana State University, William H. Chafe of Duke University, Joseph Conlin of California State University at Chico, Nancy Cott of Yale University, Juan Gómez-Quiñones of the University of California at Los Angeles, John Murrin of Princeton University, Gary B. Nash of the University of California at Los Angeles, David Reimers of New York University, Ronald G. Walters of Johns Hopkins University, and Sean Wilentz of Princeton University.

THOMAS R. FRAZIER

Contents

2

THE NEW NATION   135

3

THE ANTE-BELLUM
NORTH AND SOUTH   259

4

WESTWARD EXPANSION   359

The

UNDERSIDE
of
AMERICAN
HISTORY

Fifth Edition

VOLUME ONE: TO 1877

Introduction

This introduction is intended to provide a broad overview of the following selections, which address often neglected aspects of American history. In these pages, the stress is on the failings of the system, and the focus is not on the victors but the victims. These selections deal with material or episodes from the past that are either left out of or given short shrift in the standard histories: they attempt to redress an imbalance in the existing literature. The result, of course, is not a comprehensive or balanced view of our history. Unless these notes and readings are considered within a larger context, they provide a distorted view of history. They are, however, an essential part of the whole story and must be taken into account in any valid assessment of the American past.

It is natural that the study of the history of the United States should concentrate on the English colonization of North America. It was, after all, the English, not the French or the Spanish, who gained a secure foothold in this part of the New World by the middle of the seventeenth century, and their institutions prevailed in shaping the new society. When the English began settling the eastern seaboard of what was to become the United States, the area was virtually free of European colonization, with the exception of the Dutch settlements in New Netherland (around present-day New York). Thus, they were freed of having to adapt to any established social or religious system. Moreover, they were nearly free of English control, chiefly because of the distance that separated the colonies from the mother country. Left to their own devices, the English concentrated on two goals: surviving in the wilderness—a feat that they accomplished with the help of the Indians already established in the territory—and turning the vast natural resources of the New World to their profit. As the colonists concentrated on building up their strength, they began to consider certain factors as obstacles to their progress.

The "Indian problem" provided the first major test of English policy in the New World. The settlers' way of dealing with these aliens was simply to displace them. The Indians struggled with all the means at their disposal—often with French and Spanish support—to preserve their lives, culture, and land, but they were no match for the technologically more advanced English. Those Indians who survived the initial confrontations with the colonists were forced to retreat southward and westward, and their sporadic attempts at organization and resistance proved futile. One group, the Five Civilized Tribes of the southeast, tried to escape alien status by assimilating to the English way of life. Their efforts were rejected, and they not only remained foreign but were forcibly moved outside the borders of the then existing states. Continually displaced, the Indians were finally removed to reservations on undesirable property, most of it west of the Mississippi River.

A second major threat to the progress of the English in the New World was the chronic shortage of manpower to provide a labor base for economic development. Two major sources of supply were found. First, poor whites from Europe—primarily from England in the seventeenth century—were brought to the New World as indentured servants. Under the popular "headright" system of land distribution, anyone who paid for a passage to the New World received fifty acres of land. Thus, investors could send over settlers, and both parties would benefit from the transaction: the investors would acquire title to large estates and claim most of the profits from the cultivation of the land. The indentured servants worked for a specified number of years in return for their passage and, sometimes, a percentage of the profits. When their terms of service expired, they became freemen with the right to participate in colonial government and to hold land, without sharing profits or paying rents to absentee landlords.

During the first 150 years of settlement, the practice of indentured servitude was a major source of new population for the New World. Moreover, indentured servants were the main labor force in the colonies during most of the seventeenth century. Upon gaining their independence, some of these servants prospered in the New World. Others moved into the yeoman farmer class of the developing society and established small subsistence farms. This latter group never shared in the nation's wealth, and many of these farmers' descendants live in poverty to this day in the foothills of the Appalachian Mountains.

By the end of the seventeenth century, a second and vastly more profitable labor supply had opened up to the colonists—African slaves. The first Africans were involuntary immigrants and, along with the Indians, perpetual aliens in the New World. They were brought to North America in 1619 and arrived in increasing numbers during the next two centuries before the trade was officially banned in 1808. By 1790, when the first federal census was taken, blacks made up 19.3 percent of the total population of the United States. Over fifty thousand blacks were free, yet even they were not permitted to move into the mainstream of American life. Although a few blacks in eastern cities led relatively comfortable lives and attained some economic security, most were unskilled laborers and met with racial discrimination at every turn. In the North, for example, white craftsmen protested against the employment of blacks in the skilled trades, which resulted in the exclusion of blacks from certain crafts. This precedent has continued to the present, with ruinous economic results for the black community.

Any consideration of the oppression suffered by blacks in this country, however, must focus first on plantation slavery in the South. From the beginning, the majority of blacks were southern slaves employed in occupations ranging from skilled craftsman to common field hand. By 1860 almost half of the four million slaves in North America were engaged in cotton production. Relying almost exclusively on imported African labor, nineteenth-century white southerners developed a thriving plantation economy. In the process, they developed a devastating system of chattel slavery—perhaps the most devastating in the modern world in terms of long-range impact. Further, by identifying slavery with color, they set into motion a pattern of color discrimination that has had endless repercussions for American society.

The lives of southern slaves were circumscribed by their masters. Slaves were deprived of education and were given little opportunity for self-improvement and advancement; in some cases, they were even denied the security of family life and religion. In response to this repression, slaves fought to develop a subculture of their own, recovering what they could from their African past, borrowing from the white culture, and drawing on their unique experience in America. More visibly, they protested their condition by rebelling or conspiring to rebel, by running away, and by refusing to cooperate with the system.

Nonetheless, the superior power and efficiency of the slave system effectively limited the experiences of most of the black bondmen. When emancipation came at the conclusion of the Civil War, few of the freedmen were trained in the skills that freedom would require, such as ownership of real property, political participation, and the handling of money. Furthermore, since racial prejudice persisted among even the northern liberators, blacks were given little opportunity during Reconstruction to move into positions of economic independence. In 1877, when the Reconstruction period ended and federal troops were removed from the South, most of the freed blacks who remained were again forced into positions of dependence on white society. The South's recovery from the war, like her earlier rise to economic stability, was achieved at the expense of the black man, who was relegated by law and custom to a position of agricultural serfdom.

A third initial challenge faced by the English in the New World was governmental. How was order to be established and upheld in the vast new territory opened up by colonization? The process was by no means as orderly as some accounts of colonial history suggest. Some of the colonies adapted the English system of representative government; others were ruled indirectly by England through governors or proprietors. When settlers throughout the colonies began to demand a higher degree of self-government, conflict between governors and settlers became commonplace, and violence was often the result. Indeed, violent struggles against the English authorities marked most attempts to establish order in the colonies. Furthermore, in almost every colony serious struggles took place between the settlers in the coastal areas and those in the interior, who quarreled over the distribution of power and benefits and, not least, the system of taxation.

The issue of colonial self-government ultimately led to the struggle for independence. For the most part, the leaders in this fight were the political elite of the colonies and the descendants of the English settlers. When independence was won, it was they who met in Philadelphia in 1787 to shape the American nation.

Although the political genius of the Founding Fathers cannot be questioned, there were grave deficiencies in the outline they drew up for the form of the new nation. In the Constitution of 1787, for example, slavery was given permanent legal status, and Indians were recognized as a people apart from the mass of Americans. A less obvious but perhaps more serious flaw in the legacy of the Founding Fathers was a pattern of thinking not explicitly articulated. That is, many of their ideas seemed to proceed from the assumption that the people of the United States would share the same language, religion, customs, and political and economic institutions. The push toward homogeneity that can be seen in the thought of the earliest American political theorists has been at the root of many of the nation's difficulties for the past two hundred years. Since the first surges of nationalism in the revolutionary era, American leaders have tended to regard any challenge to the political and economic status quo as an alien threat, as something foreign to and incompatible with the American way of life.

For the first century of the new nation's life, many of the so-called alien threats did come from true aliens—either from immigrants or from the domestic aliens who were barred from citizenship, the Indians and the African slaves. Later, even challenges brought by the native-born were frequently considered to be alien-inspired and were suppressed in the name of patriotism. Those who could not or would not conform to the dominant way of life could expect to meet with serious opposition.

The first American political parties were founded on this principle of challenge and opposition. They appeared in the 1790s when James Madison and Thomas Jefferson sought to organize resistance to Alexander Hamilton, President Washington's strongest adviser. Members of the government took the names of Federalists, and their opponents called themselves Republicans. Party strife was rampant from the beginning. One of the Federalist government's first acts was the passage of the flagrantly repressive Alien and Sedition Acts in 1798, an expression of early nativist sentiment, as well as an attempt to stifle Republican opposition. These acts were hotly protested, and by the time they went out of effect in 1801, they had stirred up the first of many furious debates between the nationalists and the advocates of states' rights. Party organization at state and local levels developed rapidly, and the party system in the United States was institutionalized within a few decades.

With the establishment of American democracy came another threat to the dominance of the well-to-do Americans of English descent, this time from the poorer members of the same ethnic group. During the colonial period, harsh penal practices and traditional patterns of deference kept the poor " in their place." With the coming of independence, however, the poor—particularly those in the growing cities—took the revo ary ideology seriously and sought an increased role in the gover iety. New methods of social control, including penal refor anization, were developed to cope with this new c tition for employment kept many of the "deser r quiescent, but the rebellious poor con maintaining an orderly, and hie

In apace. After the
1840s, began to threaten
Prote of the new immi-
gran o rapidly to be dis-
per d. Public programs to
he rst nonexistent. Many
in , juvenile homes, mental
h wing in number and in-
 " Public systems of educa-
 lay behind them, attempted
to way of life, and many immigrant gr , resisted by setting up private
school system foreign, fear that by sheer numbers the immigrant dominant Anglo-Saxon strains of
the American populatio rulent anti-Catholicism—all contributed to the rise of a nativis vement that stretched across almost a century before it finally subsided. In many northeast cities, violent clashes broke out between Protestants and Irish Catholics, provoked primarily by the refusal of the Catholics to accept Protestant indoctrination.

Along with the religious conflicts in the northeast came bitter competition for jobs. By the middle of the nineteenth century, the Industrial Revolution had swept the United States, and the machinery of production had become so efficient that a surplus of unskilled labor existed for the first time in American history. This provided factory owners, members of a rising industrialist class, with the opportunity to stretch hours and reduce wages in the search for greater profits. Wage reductions, in turn, often meant that women and children had to go to work in the mills and mines in order to maintain family incomes at a subsistence level. The struggle of the unskilled worker and the urban factory operative, immigrant or native-born, is one of the major motifs of nineteenth- and twentieth-century American life. Workers were able to improve their conditions only when they organized resistance to the dominant economic policies through national trade unions, which were slow to evolve.

Up to the early 1800s, the dominant sector of Americans had been not only white, Protestant, and English, but also male. Indeed, few women in the Western world have had any direct power or influence over the direction of society until quite recently. In America, as elsewhere, women were schooled only in the domestic arts and social graces, were deprived of the right to vote, were denied participation in politics and public life, and were expected to find fulfillment by living in the shadow of a successful man. In the second quarter of the nineteenth century, however, American women became caught up by the general movement for reform and began to challenge male dominance. Despite stinging denunciations, women called attention to the society's prejudices against "the weaker sex" and began to take leading roles in the religious movements and communitarian social experiments of the day. Some joined with radical male reformers in advocating complete reorganization of society and complete restructuring of religious life. Since male dominance seemed analogous to the structure of traditional religion—in which God, the father, or Jesus, the male child, was the ruler of the church—many women felt that attacking traditional religion was especially in their interest. Some became prophets and seers, and others even founded new religious movements, such as the Shakers.

During this first period of awakening to women's rights, most women remained submissive, apparently content in their traditional roles. But as the leisure of the middle-class woman increased and as servants and machines took on many of her customary household duties, masses of women found themselves hard pressed to reconcile the roles society foisted on them with their own feelings and needs. At the same time, growing industry and commerce provided a new measure of independence for married and unmarried women alike, and the ranks of working women swelled.

By the 1850s, the size of the American nation had increased dramatically. National interest in geographical expansion, combined with the ideology of Manifest Destiny, led to the incorporation of the West Coast into the Union. Settlers sought their fortunes in the West, traveling overland for the most part before the completion of the transcontinental railroad. This covered-wagon migration, so famed in American popular culture, provided new opportunities for land speculation and exploitation for those dissatisfied with their lives in the Middle West.

Though one might expect that the settler's lonely struggle to pacify the wilderness—and the Indians—would have led to a strong sense of individuality, the westward advance carried with it a powerful pressure to conform to the eastern establishment. Perhaps an insecurity of life on the Great Plains and in the Far West lay behind the extravagant attempts to impose on the various western peoples a homogeneity similar to that which prevailed in the East. In any case, geographical expansion became synonymous with the expansion of Anglo-Saxon culture and control.

Predictably, those who suffered most from the settlement and development of the West were the aliens. With the conclusion of the Mexican War in 1847, thousands of persons of Spanish and Spanish-Indian descent suddenly found themselves foreigners living within American territory. "Vigilante" justice all too often held sway in the remote and virtually lawless West, and the Chinese, Mexican Americans, Indians, and other ethnic minorities were the most frequent victims of the summary justice dealt out by the self-appointed citizen groups.

The years between the Mexican War and the Civil War were years of deepening sectional crisis. With every new state admitted to the Union, arguments over slavery grew more pointed and intense. The westward advance continued as a backdrop to civil war and recovery. By the end of the Reconstruction period, the United States stretched from coast to coast, and Protestant-English influence over the whole area was secured. The dominant Americans would continue to strive vainly to convert all whites to their point of view. More successfully, they would continue to exclude all nonwhites from full participation in American life.

The Three Cherokees, came over from the head of the River Savanna to London 1762
(Their Interpreter that was Poisoned.)

1

COLONIAL
AMERICA

Indians, Colonists, and Property Rights

WILLIAM CRONON

When the Europeans landed on the North American continent at the turn of the sixteenth century, the area north of the Rio Grande was inhabited by an estimated ten to twelve million people. Although the explorers first assumed that these people—mistakenly called Indians by Columbus—were members of one cultural group, it soon became clear that they were divided into many separate nations with distinctive cultural traditions. Yet from the beginning, the Europeans viewed these native cultures as inferior to their own, an attitude that shaped European–Native American relations for centuries to come.

In the sixteenth century most of the exploration and conquest of the New World was carried out by the Spanish and the Portuguese. These early adventurers were able to justify their activities by citing the authority of the Pope, who had divided the newly discovered hemisphere between Spain and Portugal with the Line of Demarcation of 1493. The Pope had given the Catholic countries a mandate to take possession of the land and to convert the natives to Christianity. Thus, the conquistadores were usually accompanied by missionaries who sought to convince the conquered populations that Catholicism was the one true religion. During the period of conquest many of the Indian populations from New Mexico through South America overlaid their traditional religions with elements of Christianity.

The situation was very different when major settlement was begun by the English in the seventeenth century. The English intended not only to explore, conquer, and exploit the land but also to settle on it, and the presence of many Indian nations along the eastern seaboard presented a formidable obstacle to their securing control and exclusive ownership of the land.

The British used various means to overcome this obstacle. By allying themselves with one Indian group against another, they were able to capitalize on existing hostilities among various tribes. In addition, instead of converting the Indians to Protestant Christianity, the English used the "heathenism" of the Indians as an excuse for betraying them, arguing that since heathens could not be expected to uphold treaties or agreements, such agreements were invalid from the start. Like the Spanish, the English justified their activities by maintaining their superiority to the Indians. After centuries of scholarship that has absolved the colonists' seizing of Indian lands, we are now developing a new perspective, one that treats the Indian people not as inferior but as different.

In addition to the superior-inferior ideology, conflicting notions of property rights led to cultural and physical conflict between colonists and Indians. William Cronon (Yale University), in his brilliant study of the changing ecology of early New England, includes a chapter on the differing conceptions of property that existed between the English settlers and the native Americans. That chapter, reprinted here, describes the process whereby the European concept of ownership as the *exclusive* right to land evolved in the New World in contrast to the Indians' concept of ownership as the right to *use* available land. As a result of this difference in understanding, the colonists often "bought" what the Indians did not have to "sell."

To take advantage of their land's diversity, Indian villages had to be mobile. This was not difficult as long as a family owned nothing that could not be either stored or transported on a man's or—more probably—a woman's back. Clothing, baskets, fishing equipment, a few tools, mats for wigwams, some corn, beans, and smoked meat: these constituted most of the possessions that individual Indian families maintained during their seasonal migrations. Even in southern New England, where agriculture created larger accumulations of food than existed among the hunter-gatherer peoples of the north, much of the harvest was stored in underground pits to await later visits and was not transported in large quantities. The need for diversity and mobility led New England Indians to avoid acquiring much surplus property, confident as they were that their mobility and skill would supply any need that arose.

This, then, was a solution to the riddle Thomas Morton had posed

INDIANS, COLONISTS, AND PROPERTY RIGHTS   From *Changes in the Land: Indians, Colonists and the Ecology of New England* by William Cronon (New York: Hill & Wang, 1983), pp. 54–81. Reprinted by permission of Farrar, Straus & Giroux, Inc.

his European readers. If English visitors to New England thought it a paradox that Indians seemed to live like paupers in a landscape of great natural wealth, then the problem lay with English eyesight rather than with any real Indian poverty. To those who compared Massachusetts Indians to English beggars, Morton replied, "If our beggers of England should, with so much ease as they, furnish themselves with foode at all seasons, there would not be so many starved in the streets." Indians only *seemed* impoverished, since they were in fact "supplied with all manner of needefull things, for the maintenance of life and lifelyhood." Indeed, said Morton, the leisurely abundance of Indian life suggested that there might be something wrong with *European* notions of wealth: perhaps the English did not know true riches when they saw them. In a passage undoubtedly intended to infuriate his Puritan persecutors, Morton counterposed to the riddle of Indian poverty a riddle of Indian wealth: "Now since it is but foode and rayment that men that live needeth (though not all alike,) why should not the natives of New England be sayd to live richly, having no want of either?"

Why not indeed? It was not a question that sat well with the New England Puritans, who had banished Morton for just such irreverence (not to mention his rival trade with the Indians). Criticism of Indian ways of life was a near-constant element in early colonial writing, and in that criticism we may discover much about how colonists believed land should be used. "The *Indians*," wrote Francis Higginson, "are not able to make use of the one fourth part of the Land, neither have they any setled places, as Townes to dwell in, nor any ground as they challenge for their owne possession, but change their habitation from place to place." A people who moved so much and worked so little did not deserve to lay claim to the land they inhabited. Their supposed failure to "improve" that land was a token not of their chosen way of life but of their laziness. "Much might they benefit themselves," fumed William Wood, "if they were not strong fettered in the chains of idleness; so as that they had rather starve than work, following no employments saving such as are sweetened with more pleasures and profit than pains or care." Few Indians, of course, had actually starved in precolonial times, so Wood's criticism boiled down to an odd tirade against Indians who chose to subsist by labor they found more pleasurable than hateful. (Ironically, this was exactly the kind of life that at least some colonists fantasized for themselves in their visions of the natural bounty of the New World.) Only the crop-planting (and therefore supposedly over-worked) women were exempted from such attacks. As we have seen, the full scorn of English criticism was reserved for Indian males, whose lives were perhaps too close to certain English pastoral and aristocratic fantasies for Calvinists to tolerate. At a time when the royalist Izaak Walton would soon proclaim the virtues of angling and hunting as pastimes, the Puritan objections to these "leisure" activities carried political as well as moral overtones.

More importantly, English colonists could use Indian hunting and gathering as a justification for expropriating Indian land. To European eyes, Indians appeared to squander the resources that were available to them. Indian poverty was the result of Indian waste: underused land, underused natural abundance, underused human labor. In his tract defending "the Lawfulness of Removing Out of England into the Parts of America," the Pilgrim apologist Robert Cushman argued that the Indians were "not industrious, neither have art, science, skill or faculty to use either the land or the commodities of it; but all spoils, rots, and is marred for want of manuring, gathering, ordering, etc." Because the Indians were so few, and "do but run over the grass, as do also the foxes and wild beasts," Cushman declared their land to be "spacious and void," free for English taking.

Colonial theorists like John Winthrop posited two ways of owning land, one natural and one civil. Natural right to the soil had existed "when men held the earth in common every man sowing and feeding where he pleased." This natural ownership had been superseded when individuals began to raise crops, keep cattle, and improve the land by enclosing it; from such actions, Winthrop said, came a superior, civil right of ownership. That these notions of land tenure were ideological and inherently Eurocentric was obvious from the way Winthrop used them: "As for the natives in New England," he write, "they inclose noe Land, neither have any setled habytation, nor any tame Cattle to improve the Land by, and soe have noe other but a Naturall Right to those Countries." By this argument, only the fields planted by Indian women could be claimed as property, with the happy result, as Winthrop said, that "the rest of the country lay open to any that could and would improve it." The land was a *vacuum Domicilium* waiting to be inhabited by a more productive people. "In a vacant soyle," wrote the minister John Cotton, "hee that taketh possession of it, and bestoweth culture and husbandry upon it, his Right it is."

This was, of course, little more than an ideology of conquest conveniently available to justify the occupation of another people's lands. Colonists occasionally admitted as much when they needed to defend their right to lands originally purchased from Indians: in order for Indians legitimately to sell their lands, they had first to own them. Roger Williams, in trying to protect Salem's claim to territory obtained from Indians rather than from the English Crown, argued that the King had committed an "injustice, in giving the Countrey to his *English* Subjects, which belonged to the Native *Indians."* Even if the Indians used their land differently than did the English, Williams said, they nevertheless possessed it by right of first occupancy and by right of the ecological changes they had wrought in it. Whether or not the Indians conducted agriculture, they "hunted all the Countrey over, and for the expedition of their hunting voyages, they burnt up all the underwoods in the Countrey, once or twice a yeare." Burning the woods, according to

Williams, was an improvement that gave the Indians as much right to the soil as the King of England could claim to the royal forests. If the English could invade Indian hunting grounds and claim right of ownership over them because they were unimproved, then the Indians could do likewise in the royal game parks.

It was a fair argument. Williams's opponents could only reply that English game parks were not just hunted but also used for cutting timber and raising cattle; besides, they said, the English King (along with lesser nobles holding such lands) performed other services for the Commonwealth, services which justified his large unpeopled holdings. If these assertions seemed a little lame, designed mainly to refute the technical details of Williams's argument, that was because the core of the dispute lay elsewhere. Few Europeans were willing to recognize that the ways Indians inhabited New England ecosystems were as legitimate as the ways Europeans *intended* to inhabit them. Colonists thus rationalized their conquest of New England: by refusing to extend the rights of property to the Indians, they both trivialized the ecology of Indian life and paved the way for destroying it. "We did not conceive," said Williams's opponents with fine irony, "that it is a just Title to so vast a Continent, to make no other improvement of millions of Acres in it, but onely to burn it up for pastime."

Whether denying or defending Indian rights of land tenure, most English colonists displayed a remarkable indifference to what the Indians themselves thought about the matter. As a result, we have very little direct evidence in colonial records of the New England Indians' conceptions of property. To try to reconstruct these, we must use not only the few early fragments available to us but a variety of evidence drawn from the larger ethnographic literature. Here we must be careful about what we mean by "property," lest we fall into the traps English colonists have set for us. Although ordinary language seems to suggest that property is generally a simple relationship between an individual person and a thing, it is actually a far more complicated social institution which varies widely between cultures. Saying that A owns B is in fact meaningless until the society in which A lives agrees to allow A a certain bundle of rights over B and to impose sanctions against the violation of those rights by anyone else. The classic definition is that of Huntington Cairns: "the property relation is triadic: 'A owns B against C,' where C represents all other individuals." Unless the people I live with recognize that I own something and so give me certain unique claims over it, I do not possess it in any meaningful sense. Moreover, different groups will permit me different bundles of rights over the same object. To define property is thus to represent boundaries between people; equally, it is to articulate at least one set of conscious ecological boundaries between people and things.

This suggests that there are really two issues involved in the problem of Indian property rights. One is individual *ownership*, the way the inhabitants of a particular village conceive of property vis-à-vis each other; and the other is collective *sovereignty*, how everyone in a village conceived of their territory (and political community) vis-à-vis other villages. An individual's or a family's rights to property were defined by the community which recognized those rights, whereas the community's territorial claims were made in opposition to those of other sovereign groups. Distinctions here can inevitably become somewhat artificial. Because kin networks might also have territorial claims—both *within* and *across* villages—even the village is sometimes an arbitrary unit in which to analyze property rights: ownership and sovereignty among Indian peoples could shade into each other in a way Europeans had trouble understanding. For this reason, the nature of Indian political communities is crucial to any discussion of property rights.

A village's right to the territory which it used during the various seasons of the year had to be at least tacitly accepted by other villages or, if not, defended against them. Territorial rights of this kind, which were expressions of the entire group's collective right, tended to be vested in the person of the sachem, the leader in whom the village's political identity at least symbolically inhered. Early English visitors who encountered village sachems tended to exaggerate their authority by comparing them to European kings: Roger Williams and John Josselyn both badly asserted of New England Indians that "their Government is Monarchicall." Comparison might more aptly have been made to the relations between lords and retainers in the early Middle Ages of Europe. In reality, sachems derived their power in many ways: by personal assertiveness; by marrying (if male) several wives to proliferate wealth and kin obligations; by the reciprocal exchange of gifts with followers; and, especially in southern New England, by inheriting it from close kin. Although early documents are silent on this score, kin relations undoubtedly cemented networks both of economic exchange and of political obligation, and it was on these rather than more formal state institutions that sachems based their authority. As William Wood remarked, "The kings have not many laws to command by, nor have they any annual revenues."

Polity had less the abstract character of a monarchy, a country, or even a tribe, than of a relatively fluid set of personal relationships. Although those relationships bore some resemblance to the dynastic politics of early modern Europe—a resemblance several historians have recently emphasized—they were crucially different in not being articulated within a state system. Kinship and personality rather than any alternative institutional structure organized power in Indian communities. Both within and between villages, elaborate kin networks endowed individuals with greater or lesser degrees of power. A sachem—who could be either male or female—asserted authority only in consultation with other powerful individuals in the village. Moreover, the sachem of one village might regularly pay tribute to the sachem of another, thus acknowledging a loose hierarchy between villages and sachems. Such hierarchies might be practically unimportant until some major conflict or external threat arose, whereupon the communities assembled into a larger confederacy until the problem was solved. The result, like Indian subsistence patterns, entailed a good deal more flexibility and movement than Europeans were accustomed to in their political institutions. As the missionary Daniel Gookin indicated, it was a very shifting politics:

> Their sachems have not their men in such subjection, but that frequently their men will leave them upon distaste or harsh dealing, and go and live among other sachems that can protect them: so that their princes endeavour to carry it obligingly and lovingly unto their people, lest they should desert them, and thereby their strength, power, and tribute would be diminished.

Insofar as a village "owned" the land it inhabited, its property was expressed in the sovereignty of the sachem. "Every sachem," wrote Edward Winslow, "knoweth how far the bounds and limits of his own Country extendeth." For all of their differences, a sachem "owned" territory in a manner somewhat analogous to the way a European monarch "owned" an entire European nation: less as personal real estate than as the symbolic possession of a whole people. A sachem's land was coterminous with the area within which a village's economic subsistence and political sanctions were most immediately expressed. In this sovereign sense, villagers were fairly precise about drawing boundaries among their respective territories. When Roger Williams wrote that "the *Natives* are very exact and punctuall in the bounds of their Lands, belonging to this or that Prince or People," he was refuting those who sought to deny that legitimate Indian property rights existed. But the rights of which he spoke were not ones of individual ownership; rather, they were sovereign rights that defined a village's political and ecological territory.

The distinction becomes important in the context of how such territorial rights could be alienated. Williams said that he had "knowne them make bargaine and sale amongst themselves for a small piece, or quantity of Ground," suggesting that Indians were little different from Europeans in their sense of how land could be bought and sold. When two sachems made an agreement to transfer land, however, they did so on behalf of their two political or kinship communities, as a way of determining the customary rights each village would be allowed in a given area. An instructive example of this is the way Roger Williams had to correct John Winthrop's confusion over two islands which Winthrop thought Williams had bought from the Narragansett sachem Miantonomo. Williams had indeed gotten permission to use the islands for grazing hogs—a land transaction of sorts had taken place—but it was emphatically not a purchase. "Be pleased to understand," cautioned Williams, "your great mistake: neither of them were sold properly, for a thousand fathom [of wampum] would not have bought either, by strangers. The truth is, not a penny was demanded for either, and what was paid was only gratuity, though I choose, for better assurance and form, to call it sale." What had been transacted, as Williams clearly understood, was more a diplomatic exchange than an economic one. Miantonomo, like other New England sachems, had no intention of conducting a market in real estate.

That this was so can best be seen by examining how a village's inhabitants conceived of property *within* its territory. Beginning with personal goods, ownership rights were clear: people owned what they made with their own hands. Given the division of labor, the two sexes probably tended to possess the goods that were most closely associated with their respective tasks: women owned baskets, mats, kettles, hoes, and so on, while men owned bows, arrows, hatchets, fishing nets, canoes, and other hunting tools. But even in the case of personal goods, there was little sense either of accumulation or of exclusive use. Goods were owned because they were useful, and if they ceased to be so, or were needed by someone else, they could easily be given away. "Although every proprietor knowes his own," said Thomas Morton, "yet all things, (so long as they will last), are used in common amongst them." Not surprisingly, theft was uncommon in such a world.

This relaxed attitude toward personal possessions was typical throughout New England. Chrétien Le Clercq described it among the Micmac of Nova Scotia by saying that they were "so generous and liberal towards one another that they seem not to have any attachment to the little they possess, for they deprive themselves thereof very willingly and in very good spirit the very moment when they know that their friends have need of it." Europeans often interpreted such actions by emphasizing the supposed generosity of the noble savage, but the Indians' relative indifference to property accumulation is better understood as a corollary of the rest of their political and economic life. Personal goods could be easily replaced, and their accumulation made little sense for the ecological reasons of mobility we have already examined; in addition, gift giving was a crucial lubricant in sustaining power relationships within the community. As Pierre Biard noted, guests thanked their hosts by giving gifts that were expressions of relative social status, and did so "with the expectation that the host will reciprocate, when the guest comes to depart, if the guest is a Sagamore, otherwise not." Willingness to give property away with alacrity was by no means a sign that property did not exist; rather, it was a crucial means for establishing and reproducing one's position in society.

When it came to land, however, there was less reason for gift giving or exchange. Southern New England Indian families enjoyed exclusive use of their planting fields and of the land on which their wigwams stood, and so might be said to have "owned" them. But neither of these were permanent possessions. Wigwams were moved every few months, and planting fields were abandoned after a number of years. Once abandoned, a field returned to brush until it was recleared by someone else, and no effort was made to set permanent boundaries around it that would hold it indefinitely for a single person. What families possessed in their fields was the *use* of them, the crops that were produced by a woman's labor upon them. When lands were traded or sold in the way Williams described, what were exchanged were usufruct rights, acknowledgments by one group that another might use an area for planting or hunting or gathering. Such rights were limited to the period of use, and they did not include many of the privileges Europeans commonly associated with ownership: a user could not (and saw no need to) prevent other village members from trespassing or gathering nonagricultural food on such lands, and had no conception of deriving rent from them. Planting fields were "possessed" by an Indian family only to the extent that it would return to them the following year. In this, they were not radically different in kind from other village lands; it was *European* rather than Indian definitions of land tenure that led the English to recognize agricultural land as the only legitimate Indian property. The Massachusetts Court made its ownership theories quite clear when it declared that "what landes any of the Indians, within this jurisdiction, have by possession of improvement, by subdueing of the same, they have just right thereunto, according to that Gen: I: 28, chap: 9: I, Psa: 115, 16."

The implication was that Indians did *not* own any other kind of land: clam banks, fishing ponds, berry-picking areas, hunting lands, the great bulk of a village's territory. (Since the nonagricultural Indians of the north had *only* these kinds of land, English theories assigned them no property rights at all.) Confusion was easy on this point, not only because of English ideologies, but because the Indians themselves had very flexible definitions of land tenure for such areas. Here again, the concept of usufruct right was crucial, since different groups of people could have different claims on the same tract of land depending on how they used it. Any village member, for instance, had the right to collect edible wild plants, cut birchbark or chestnut for canoes, or gather sedges for mats, wherever these things could be found. No special private right inhered in them. Since village lands were usually organized along a single watershed, the same was true of rivers and the coast: fish and shellfish could generally be taken anywhere, although the nets, harpoons, weirs, and tackle used to catch them—and hence sometimes the right to use the sites where these things were installed—might be owned by an individual or a kin group. Indeed, in the case of extraordinarily plentiful fishing sites—especially major inland waterfalls during the spawning runs—several villages might gather at a single spot to share the wealth. All of them acknowledged a mutual right to use the site for that specific purpose, even though it might otherwise lie within a single village's territory. Property rights, in other words, shifted with ecological use.

Hunting grounds are the most interesting case of this shifting, non-agricultural land tenure. The ecological habits of different animals were so various that their hunting required a wide range of techniques, and rights to land use had to differ accordingly. The migratory birds in the ponds and salt marshes, for example, were so abundant that they could be treated much like fish: whoever killed them owned them, and hunters could range over any tract of land to do so, much like the birds themselves. (In this, Indian practices bore some resemblance to European customs governing the rights of hunters, when in pursuit of game, to cross boundaries which were otherwise legally protected.) Likewise, flocks of turkeys and the deer herds were so abundant in the fall that they were most efficiently hunted by collective drives involving anywhere from twenty to three hundred men. In such cases, the entire village territory was the logical hunting region, to which all those involved in the hunt had an equal right.

The same was not true, on the other hand, of hunting that involved the setting of snares or traps. The animals prey to such techniques were either less numerous, as in the case of winter deer or moose, or sedentary creatures, like the beaver, which lived in fixed locales. These were best hunted by spreading the village population over as broad a territory as possible, and so usufruct rights had to be designed to hold the overlap of trapped areas to a reasonable minimum. Roger Williams described how, after the harvest, ten or twenty men would go with their wives and children to hunting camps which were presumably organized by kin lineage groups. There, he said, "each man takes his bounds of two, three, or foure miles, where hee sets thirty, forty, or fiftie Traps, and baits his Traps with that food the Deere loves, and once in two dayes he walkes his round to view his Traps."

At least for the duration of the winter hunt, the kin group inhabiting a camp probably had a clear if informal usufruct right to the animals caught in its immediate area. Certainly a man (or, in the north, his wife) owned the animals captured in the traps he set, though he might have obligations to share which created *de facto* limits to his claims on them. The collective activities of a camp thus tended to establish a set of rights which at least temporarily divided the village territory into hunting areas. The problem is to know how such rights were allocated, how permanent and exclusive they were, and—most crucially—how much their interaction with the European fur trade altered them. . . . We can conclude that, however exclusive hunting territories originally were and however much the fur trade changed them, they represented a different kind of land use—and so probably a different set of usufruct rights—than planting fields, gathering areas, or fishing sites.

What the Indians owned—or, more precisely, what their villages gave them claim to—was not the land but the things that were on the land during the various seasons of the year. It was a conception of property shared by many of the hunter-gatherer and agricultural peoples of the world, but radically different from that of the invading Europeans. In nothing is this more clear than in the names they attached to their landscape, the great bulk of which related not to possession but to use. In southern New England, some of these names were agricultural. Pokanoket, in Plymouth County, Massachusetts, was "at or near the cleared lands." Anitaash Pond, near New London, Connecticut, meant, literally, "rotten corn," referring to a swampy location where corn could be buried until it blackened to create a favorite Indian delicacy. Mittineag, in Hampden County, Massachusetts, meant "abandoned fields," probably a place where the soil had lost its fertility and a village had moved its summer encampment elsewhere.

Far more abundant than agricultural place-names, however, throughout New England, were names telling where plants could be gathered, shellfish collected, mammals hunted, and fish caught. Abessah, in Bar Harbor, Maine, was the "clam bake place." Wabaquasset, in Providence, Rhode Island, was where Indian women could find "flags or rushes for making mats." Azoiquoneset, also in the Narragansett Bay area, was the "small island where we get pitch," used to make torches for hunting sturgeon at night. The purpose of such names was to turn the landscape into a map which, if studied carefully, literally gave a village's inhabitants the information they needed to sustain themselves. Place-names were used to keep track of beaver dams, the rapids in rivers, oyster banks, egg-gathering spots, cranberry bogs, canoe-repairing places, and so on. Some were explicitly seasonal in their references, just as the Indian use of them was. Seconchqut Village in Dukes County, Massachusetts, was "the late spring or summer place." The Eackhonk River in Rhode Island was named to mark "the end of the fishing place," meaning the inland limit of the spring spawning runs. Unlike the English, who most frequently created arbitrary place-names which either recalled localities in their homeland or gave a place the name of its owner, the Indians used ecological labels to describe how the land could be used.

This is not to say that Indian place-names never made reference to possession or ownership. A variety of sites refer to "the boundary or ending place" which divided the territories of two different Indian villages or groups. One of the more graphic of these was Chabanakongkomuk, in Worcester, Massachusetts, a "boundary fishing place" whose name could be rendered, "You fish on your side, I fish on my side, nobody fish in the middle—no trouble." Such regions between two territories were often sites of trade: thus, Angualsicook meant the "place of barter." Most importantly, they were eventually places marking a boundary with the truly different people from across the sea. The

Awannoa Path in Middlesex County, Connecticut, carried the very suggestive label "Who are you?" as a reference to "Englishmen" or "strangers."

Boundaries between the Indians and these intruding "strangers" differed in fundamental ways from the ones between Indian villages, largely because the two interpreted those boundaries using very different cultural concepts. The difference is best seen in early deeds between the two groups. On July 15, 1636, the fur trader William Pynchon purchased from the Agawam village in central Massachusetts a tract of land extending four or five miles along the Connecticut River in the vicinity of present-day Springfield, leaving one of the earliest Indian deeds in American history to record the transaction. Several things are striking about the document. No fewer than thirteen Indians signed it, two of whom, Commucke and Matanchon, were evidently sachems able to act "for and in the name of al the other Indians" in the village. In defining their claims to the land being sold, they said that they acted "in the name of Cuttonus the rightful owner of Agaam and Quana, and in the Name of his mother Kewenusk the Tamasham or wife of Wenawis, and Niarum the wife of Coa," suggesting that both men and women had rights to the land being transferred. On the Indian side, then, an entire kin group had to concur in an action which thus probably had more to do with sovereignty than ownership.

Moreover, village members evidently conceived of that action in strictly limited terms. Though they gave permission to Pynchon and his associates "for ever to truckle and sel al that ground," they made a number of revealing reservations: in addition to the eighteen coats, eighteen hatchets, eighteen hoes, and eighteen knives they received as payment, they extracted the concessions that

> they shal have and enjoy all that cottinackeesh [planted ground], or ground that is now planted; And have liberty to take Fish and Deer, ground nuts, walnuts akornes and sasachiminesh or a kind of pease.

Understood in terms of the usufruct rights discussed above, it is clear that the Indians conceived of this sale as applying only to very specific uses of the land. They gave up none of their most important hunting and gathering privileges, they retained right to their cornfields, and evidently intended to keep living on the land much as they had done before. The rights they gave Pynchon were apparently to occupy the land jointly with them, to establish a village like their own where cornfields could be planted, to conduct trade there, and perhaps to act as a superior sachem who could negotiate with other villages about the land so long as he continued to recognize the reserved rights of the Agawam village. The Agawam villagers gave up none of their sovereignty over themselves, and relinquished few of their activities on the land. What they conferred on Pynchon was right of ownership identical to their own: not to possess the land as a tradeable commodity, but to use it as an ecological cornucopia. Save for cornfields, no Indian usufruct rights were inherently exclusive, and transactions such as this one had more to do with sharing possession than alienating it.

On the English side, the right "for ever to truckle and sel al that ground" of course carried rather different connotations. In the first place, the transaction was conducted not by a sovereign kin group but by a trading partnership operating under the much larger sovereignty of the Massachusetts Bay Company and the English Crown. None of the three partners who acquired rights to the land—William Pynchon, Henry Smith, or Jehu Burr—was actually present at the transaction, which was conducted for them by several men in their employ. Insofar as we can make a valid distinction, what the Indians perceived as a political negotiation between two sovereign groups the English perceived as an economic transaction wholly within an English jurisdiction. As we have seen, Massachusetts recognized that Indians might have limited natural rights to land, and so provided that such rights could be alienated *under the sanctions of Massachusetts law.* No question of an Indian village's own sanctions could arise, for the simple reason that Indian sovereignty was not recognized. The Massachusetts Bay Company was careful very early to instruct its agents on this point, telling them "to make composition with such of the salvages as did pretend any tytle or lay clayme to any of the land." Indian rights were not real, but pretended, because the land had already been granted the company by the English Crown.

Land purchases like Pynchon's were thus interpreted under English law, and so were understood as a fuller transfer of rights than Indian communities probably ever intended. Certainly Pynchon's deed is unusual in even mentioning rights reserved to the Indians. Later deeds describe exchanges in which English purchasers appeared to obtain complete and final ownership rights, however the Indian sellers may have understood those exchanges. In 1637, for instance, John Winthrop received lands in Ipswich, Massachusetts, from the Indian Maskonomett, who declared that "I doe fully resigne up all my right of the whole towne of Ipswich as farre as the bounds thereof shall goe all the woods meadowes, pastures and broken up grounds unto the said John Winthrop in the name of the rest of the English there planted." Deeds in eastern Massachusetts—when they existed at all—typically took this form, extinguishing all Indian rights and transferring them either to an English purchaser or, as in this case, to an English group with some corporate identity. As the English understood these transactions, what was sold was not a bundle of usufruct rights, applying to a range of different "territories," but the land itself, an abstract area whose bounds in theory remained fixed no matter what the use to which it was put. Once the land was bounded in this new way, a host of ecological changes followed almost inevitably.

European property systems were much like Indian ones in express-ing the ecological purposes to which a people intended to put their land; it is crucial that they not be oversimplified if their contribution to ecological history is to be understood. The popular idea that Euro-peans had private property, while the Indians did not, distorts European notions of property as much as it does Indian ones. The colonists' prop-erty systems, like those of the Indians, involved important distinctions between sovereignty and ownership, between possession by communi-ties and possession by individuals. They too dealt in bundles of cultur-ally defined rights that determined what could and could not be done with land and personal property. Even the fixity they assigned to prop-erty boundaries, the quality which most distinguished them from Indian land systems, was at first fuzzier and less final than one might expect. They varied considerably depending on the region of England from which a group of colonists came, so that every New England town, like every Indian village, had idiosyncratic property customs of its own. All of these elements combined to form what is usually called "the New En-gland land system." The phrase is misleading, since the "system" re-sided primarily at the town level and was in fact many systems, but there were nevertheless common features. . . . Their development was as much a product as a cause of ecological change in colonial New England.

Colonial claims to ownership of land in New England had two po-tential sources: purchases from Indians or grants from the English Crown. The latter tended quickly to absorb the former. The Crown derived its own claim to the region from several sources: Cabot's "discovery" of New England in 1497–98; the failure of Indians adequately to subdue the soil as Genesis I.28 required; and from the King's status—initially a decidedly speculative one—as the first Christian monarch to establish colonies there. Whether or not a colony sought to purchase land from the Indians—something which Plymouth, Connecticut, and Rhode Is-land, in the absence of royal charters, felt compelled as a matter of expediency or ethics to do—all New England colonies ultimately de-rived their political rights of sovereignty from the Crown.

The distinction between sovereignty and ownership is crucial here. When a colony purchased land from Indians, it did so under its own system of sovereignty: whenever ownership rights were deeded and pur-chased, they were immediately incorporated into English rather than Indian law. Indian land sales, operating as they did at the interface of two different sovereignties, one of which had trouble recognizing that the other existed, thus had a potentially paradoxical quality. Because Indians, at least in the beginning, thought they were selling one thing and the English thought they were buying another, it was possible for an Indian village to convey what it regarded as identical and nonexclu-sive usufruct rights to several different English purchasers. Alterna-tively, several different Indian groups might sell to English ones rights to the same tract of land. Uniqueness of title as the English understood it became impossible under such circumstances, so colonies very early tried to regulate the purchase of Indian lands. Within four years of the founding of Massachusetts Bay, the General Court had ordered that "noe person whatsoever shall buy any land of any Indean without leave from the Court." The other colonies soon followed suit. The effect was not only to restrict the right of English individuals to engage in Indian land transactions but—more importantly, given the problem of sovereignty—to limit the rights of Indians to do so as well. Illegal individual sales nevertheless persisted, and titles in some areas became so confused that the Connecticut Court in 1717 made a formal declaration:

> That all lands in this government are holden of the King of Great Britain as the lord of the fee: and that no title to any lands in this Colony can accrue by any purchase made of Indians on pretence of their being native proprietors thereof.

Even by the late seventeenth century, Indian lands were regarded as being entirely within English colonial jurisdiction; indeed, the logic of the situation seemed to indicate that, for Indians to own land at all, it had first to be granted them by the English Crown.

If all colonial lands derived from the Crown, how did this affect the way they were owned and used? As with an Indian sachem, albeit on a larger and more absolute scale, the King did not merely possess land in his own right but also represented in his person the collective sovereignty which defined the system of property rights that operated on that land. In the case of the Massachusetts Bay Company's charter, the King conferred the lands of the grant "as of our manor of Eastgreenewich, in the County of Kent, in free and common Socage, and not in Capite, nor by knightes service." Land tenure as of the manor of East Greenwich put a colony under Kentish legal custom and was the most generous of feudal grants, involving the fewest obligations in relation to the Crown. It was ideally suited to mercantile trading companies, since it allowed easy alienation of the land and did not impose the burden of feudal quitrents on its holders. Both of these features made Kentish tenure attractive to would-be settlers and promoted the early development of a commercial market in land. As opposed to tenure in capite or by knight's service, which carried various civil and military obligations for their holders, free and common socage—in some senses, the least feudal of medieval tenures—conceived of land simply as property carrying an economic rent, a rent which was often negligible. In Massachusetts, the Crown's only claim was to receive one-fifth of all the gold and silver found there. Given New England geology, the burden did not prove onerous.

The royal charter drew a set of boundaries on the New England landscape. Unlike those of the Indians, these were not "boundary or ending places" between the territories of two peoples. Rather, they were defined by lines of latitude—40 and 48 degrees north—that in theory stretched from "sea to sea." Between those lines, the Massachusetts Bay Company was given the right

> To have and to houlde, possesse, and enjoy all and singuler the aforesaid continent, landes, territories, islands, hereditaments, and precincts, seas, waters, fishings, with all and all manner their commodities, royalties, liberties, prehemynences, and profits that should from thenceforth arise from thence, with all and singuler their appurtenances, and every parte and parcell thereof, unto the saide Councell and their successors and assignes for ever.

It was an enormous grant, no doubt in part because the King's personal claim to the territory was so tenuous. For our purposes, its significance lies in the sweeping extent and abstraction of its rights and boundaries, its lack of concern for the claims of existing inhabitants, its emphasis on the land's profits and commodities, and its intention that the land being granted could and would remain so bounded "forever." In all of these ways, it implied conceptions of land tenure drastically different from those of the Indians.

Because the King's grant was so permissive, and gave so little indication as to how land should be allocated within the new colony, the company and its settlers found themselves faced with having to devise their own method for distributing lands. Initially, the company thought to make grants to each shareholder and settler individually, as had been done in Virginia, but this idea was rapidly—though not completely—replaced with grants to groups of settlers acting together as towns. The founding proprietors of each town were collectively granted an average of about six square miles of land, and from then on were more or less free to dispose of that land as they saw fit. In terms of sovereignty, the chief difference between Indian and English villages lay in the formal hierarchy by which the latter derived and maintained their sovereign rights. But in terms of ownership—the way property and usufruct rights were distributed *within* a village—the two differed principally in the ways they intended ecologically to use the land. When the Agawam villagers reserved hunting and gathering rights in their deed to William Pynchon, they revealed how they themselves thought that particular tract of land best used. Likewise, John Winthrop's deed to Ipswich—clearly an English rather than an Indian document—in speaking of "woods meadowes, pastures, and broken up grounds," betrayed the habits of thought of an English agriculturalist who was accustomed to raising crops, building fences, and keeping cattle. Conceptions of land tenure mimicked systems of ecological use.

The proprietors of a new town initially held all land in common. Their first act was to determine what different types of land were present in their territory, types which were understood to be necessary to English farming in terms of the categories mentioned in Winthrop's deed: forested lands for timber and firewood, grassy areas for grazing, salt marshes for cutting hay, potential planting fields, and so on. Like their Indian counterparts, English villages made their first division of land to locate where houses and cornfields should be; unlike the Indians, that division was conducted formally and was intended to be a permanent one, the land passing forever into private hands. Land was allocated to inhabitants using the same biblical philosophy that had justified taking it from the Indians in the first place: individuals should only possess as much land as they were able to subdue and make productive. The anonymous "Essay on the Ordering of Towns" declared that each inhabitant be given "his due proportion, more or lesse according unto his present or apparent future occasion of Imployment." A person with many servants and cattle could "improve" more land than one who had few, and so was granted more land, although the quantities varied from town to town. In this way, the social hierarchy of the English class system was reproduced, albeit in modified form, in the New World. Grants of house lots and planting grounds were followed by grants of pastures, hay meadows, and woodlots, all allocated on the same basis of one's ability to use them.

In these and later grants as well, the passage of land from town commons to individual property was intended to create permanent private rights to it. These rights were never absolute, since both town and colony retained sovereignty and could impose a variety of restrictions on how land might be used. Burning might be prohibited on it during certain seasons of the year. A grant might be contingent on the land being used for a specific purpose—such as the building of a mill—and there was initially a requirement in Massachusetts that all land be improved within three years or its owner would forfeit rights to it. Regulations might forbid land from being sold without the town's permission. But, compared with Indian villages, grants made by New England towns contemplated much more extensive privileges for each individual landholder, with greater protection from trespass and more exclusive rights of use. The "Essay on the Ordering of Towns" saw such private ownership as the best way to promote fullest use of the land: "he that knoweth the benefit of incloseing," it said, "will omit noe dilligence to brenge him selfe into an inclusive condicion, well understanding that one acre inclosed, is much more beneficiall than 5 falling to his share in Common."

Different towns acted differently at first in relation to their common lands, their behavior usually depending on the land practices of the regions of England from which their inhabitants came. Some settlers, like those of Rowley or Sudbury, came from areas with open-field systems, where strong manorial control had been exercised over lands held in common by peasant farmers. They initially re-created such systems in New England, making relatively few small divisions of common holdings, regulating closely who could graze and gather wood on unenclosed land, and not engaging extensively in the buying or selling of real estate. Settlers in towns like Ipswich or Scituate, on the other hand, came from English regions where closed-field systems gave peasant proprietors more experience with owning their lands in severalty. They proved from the start to be much interested in transferring lands from common to private property as rapidly as possible, so that their land divisions were more frequent and involved more land at an earlier date. In these towns, a market in real estate developed very early, both to allow the consolidation of scattered holdings and to facilitate limited speculative profits in land dealings.

In the long run, it was this latter conception of land—as private commodity rather than public commons—that came to typify New England towns. Initial divisions of town lands, with their functional classifications of woodlot and meadow and cornfield, bore a superficial resemblance to Indian usufruct rights, since they seemed to define land in terms of how it was to be used. Once transferred into private hands, however, most such lands became abstract parcels whose legal definition bore no inherent relation to their use: a person owned everything on them, not just specific activities which could be conducted within their boundaries. Whereas the earliest deeds tended to describe land in terms of its topography and use—for instance, as the mowing field between a certain two creeks—later deeds described land in terms of lots held by adjacent owners, and marked territories using the surveyor's abstractions of points of the compass and metes and bounds. Recording systems, astonishingly sloppy in the beginning because there was little English precedent for them, became increasingly formalized so that boundaries could be more precisely defined. Even Indian deeds showed this transformation. The land Pychon purchased from the Agawam village was vaguely defined in terms of cornfields, meadows, and the Connecticut River; an eighteenth-century deed from the same county, on the other hand, transferred rights to two entire townships which it defined precisely but abstractedly as "the full Contents of Six miles in Weadth and Seven miles in length," starting from a specified point.

The uses to which land could be put vanished from such descriptions, and later land divisions increasingly ignored actual topography. What was on the land became largely irrelevant to its legal identity, even though its contents—and the rights to them—might still have great bearing on the price it would bring if sold. Describing land as a fixed parcel with purely arbitrary boundaries made buying and selling it increasingly easy, as did the recording systems—an American innovation—which kept track of such transactions. Indeed, legal descriptions, however abstracted, had little effect on everyday life *until* land was sold. People did not cease to be intimately a part of the land's ecology simply by reason of the language with which their deeds were written. But when it came time to transfer property rights, those deeds allowed the alienation of land as a commodity, an action with important ecological consequences. To the abstraction of legal boundaries was added the abstraction of price, a measurement of property's value assessed on a unitary scale. More than anything else, it was the treatment of land and property as commodities traded at market that distinguished English conceptions of ownership from Indian ones.

To present these arguments in so brief a compass is of course to oversimplify. Western notions of property, commodity, and market underwent a complex development in both Europe and America over the course of the seventeenth and eighteenth centuries, one which did not affect all people or places in the same way or at the same time. Peasant land practices which had their origins in the manorial customs of feudal England were not instantly transformed into full-fledged systems of production for market simply by being transferred to America. Many communities produced only a small margin of surplus beyond their own needs, and historians have often described them as practicing "subsistence agriculture" for this reason. When seventeenth-century New England towns are compared with those of the nineteenth century, with their commercial agriculture, wage workers, and urban and industrialism, the transition between the two may well seem to be that from a subsistence to a capitalist society. Certainly Marxists wedded to a definition of capitalism in terms of relations between labor and capital must have trouble seeing it in the first New England towns. Most early farmers owned their own land, hired few wage laborers, and produced mainly for their own use. Markets were hemmed in by municipal regulations, high transportation costs, and medieval notions of the just price. In none of these ways does it seem reasonable to describe colonial New England as "capitalist."

And yet when colonial towns are compared not with their industrial successors but with their Indian predecessors, they begin to look more like market societies, the seeds of whose capitalist future were already present. The earliest explorers' descriptions of the New England coast had been framed from the start in terms of the land's commodities. Although an earlier English meaning of the word "commodity" had referred simply to articles which were "commodious" and hence useful to people—a definition Indians would readily have understood— that meaning was already becoming archaic by the seventeenth century. In its place was the commodity as an object of commerce, one by definition owned for the sole purpose of being traded away at a profit. ("Profit" was another word that underwent a comparable evolution at about the same time: to its original meaning of the benefits one derived from using a thing was added the gain one made by selling it.) Certain items of the New England landscape—fish, furs, timber, and a few others—were thus selected at once for early entrance into the commercial economy of the North Atlantic. They became valued not for the immediate utility they brought their possessors but for the price they would bring when exchanged at market. In trying to explain ecological changes related to these commodities, we can safely point to market demand as the key causal agent.

The trade in commodities involved over a small group of merchants, but they exercised an influence over the New England economy beyond their numbers. Located principally in the coastal cities, they rapidly came to control shipping and so acted as New England's main link to the Atlantic economy. Because of their small numbers, it might reasonably be argued that the market sector of the New England economy was a tiny isolated segment relatively unconnected to the subsistence production of peasant communities in the towns. Certainly we should make a distinction between ecological changes resulting directly from the activities of merchants and those caused by the less market-oriented activities of farmers. But the farmers had their own involvement in the Atlantic economy, however distant it might have been. Even if they produced only a small surplus for market, they nevertheless used it to buy certain goods from the merchants—manufactured textiles, tropical foodstuffs, guns, metal tools—which were essential elements in their lives. The grain and meat which farmers sold, if not shipped to Caribbean and European markets, were used to supply port cities and the "Invisible trade" of colonial shipping. Not all of this commodity movement was voluntary. Town and colony alike assessed farmers for their landholdings and so siphoned off taxes which were used to run government and conduct trade. Although taxes bore some resemblance to political tributes in Indian societies, the latter were not based on possession of land and did not reinforce the sense that land had an intrinsic money value. Taxes thus had the important effect of forcing a certain degree of colonial production beyond the level of mere "subsistence," and orienting that surplus toward market exchange.

But the most important sense in which it is wrong to describe colonial towns as subsistence communities follows from their inhabitants' belief in "improvement," the concept which was so crucial in their critique of Indian life. The imperative here was not just the biblical injunction to "fill the earth and subdue it." Colonists were moved to transform the soil by the property system that taught them to treat land as capital. Fixed boundaries and the liberties of "free and common socage" assured a family that improvements belonged to them and to their heirs. The existence of commerce, however marginal, led them to see certain things on the land as merchantable commodities. The visible increase in livestock and crops thus translated into an abstract money value that was reflected in tax assessments, in the inventories of estates, and in the growing land market. Even if a colonist never sold an improved piece of property, the increase in its hypothetical value at market was an important aspect of the accumulation of wealth. These tendencies were apparent as early as the 1630s. When English critics claimed that colonists had lost money by moving their wealth to New England, the colonists replied that they had simply transformed that money into physical assets. The author of *New England's First Fruits* declared that the colonists' "estates now lie in houses, lands, horses, cattel, corne, etc. though they have not so much money as they had here [in England], and so cannot make appearance of their wealth to those in *England*, yet they have it still, so that their estates are not lost, but changed." Here was a definition of transformable wealth few pre-colonial Indians would probably have recognized: if labor was not yet an alienated commodity available for increasing capital, land was. "The staple of America at present," wrote the British traveler Thomas Cooper in the late eighteenth century, "consists of Land, and the immediate products of land."

Perhaps the best single summary of this view is John Locke's famous chapter on property in the *Two Treatises of Government*. Locke sought to explain how people came to possess unequal rights to a natural abundance he supposed had originally been held in common; to accomplish this task, he explicitly contrasted the societies of Europe with those of the American Indians. "In the beginning," he said, "all the world was America." In that original state, possession was directly related to the labor one spent in hunting and gathering: one could own whatever one could use before it spoiled. What enabled people to accumulate wealth beyond the limits of natural spoilage was something Locke called "money." Bullionist that he was, he thought of money as gold and silver which could be stored as a source of permanent value without fear of spoiling. But the way he actually used the word, "money" was an odd hybrid between a simple medium of exchange that measured the value of commodities, and *capital*, the surplus whose accumulation was the motor of economic growth. It was capital—the ability to store wealth in the expectation that one could increase its quantity—that set European societies apart from precolonial Indian ones. As Locke said:

> Where there is not something both lasting and scarce, and so valuable to be hoarded up, there Men will not be apt to enlarge their *Possessions of Land*, were it never so rich, never so free for them to take. For I ask, What would a Man value Ten Thousand or a Hundred Thousand Acres of excellent *Land*, ready cultivated, and well stocked too with Cattle, in the middle of the in-land Parts of *America*, where he had no hopes of Commerce with other Parts of the World, to draw *Money* to him by the Sale of the Product? It would not be worth the inclosing, and we should see him give up again to the wild Common of Nature, whatever was more than would supply the Conveniences of Life to be had there for him and his Family.

New England had not returned to the "wild Common of Nature" but had in fact abandoned it. However incomplete Locke's analysis of why that had happened, and however inaccurate his anthropological description of Indian society, his emphasis on the market was sound. It was the attachment of property in land to a marketplace, and the accumulation of its value in a society with institutionalized ways of recognizing abstract wealth (here we need not follow Locke's emphasis on gold and silver), that committed the English in New England to an expanding economy that was ecologically transformative.

Locke carries us full circle back to Thomas Morton's riddle. His characterization of the Indians as being "rich in Land, and poor in all the Comforts of Life," bore a close resemblance to the comparisons of Indians with English beggars which Morton had sought to refute. Locke posed the riddle of Indian poverty as clearly as anyone in the seventeenth century. He described them as a people

> whom Nature having furnished as liberally as any other people, with the materials of Plenty, *i.e.* a fruitful Soil, apt to produce in abundance, what might serve for food, rayment, and delight; yet for want of improving it by labour, have not one hundredth part of the Conveniences we enjoy: And a King of a large fruitful Territory there feeds, lodges, and is clad worse than a day Labourer in *England.*

Because the Indians lacked the incentives of money and commerce, Locke thought, they failed to improve their land and so remained a people devoid of wealth and comfort.

What Locke failed to notice was that the Indians did not recognize themselves as poor. The endless accumulation of capital which he saw as a natural consequence of the human love for wealth made little sense to them. Marshall Sahlins has pointed out that there are in fact two ways to be rich, one of which was rarely recognized by Europeans in the seventeenth century. "Wants," Sahlins says, "may be 'easily satisfied' either by producing much or desiring little." Thomas Morton was almost alone among his contemporaries in realizing that the New England Indians had chosen this second path. As he said, on their own understanding, they "lived richly," and had little in the way of either wants or complaints. Pierre Biard, who also noticed this fact about the Indians, extended it into a critique of *European* ways of life. Indians, he said, went about their daily tasks with great leisure,

> for their days are all nothing but pastime. They are never in a hurry. Quite different from us, who can never do anything without hurry and worry; worry, I say, because our desire tyrannizes over us and banishes peace from our actions.

Historians often read statements like this as myths of the noble savage, and certainly they are attached to that complex of ideas in European thought. But that need not deny their accuracy as decriptions of Indian life. If the Indians considered themselves happy with the fruits of relatively little labor, they were like many peoples of the world as described by modern anthropoligists.

Thomas Morton had posed his riddle knowing full well that his readers would recognize its corollary: if Indians lived richly by wanting little, then might it not be possible that Europeans lived poorly by wanting much? The difference between Indians and Europeans was not that one had property and the other had none; rather, it was that they loved property differently. Timothy Dwight, writing at the beginning of the nineteenth century, lamented the fact that Indians had not yet learned the love of property. "Wherever this can be established," he said, "Indians may be civilized; wherever it cannot, they will still remain Indians." The statement was truer than he probably realized. Speaking strictly in terms of precolonial New England, Indian conceptions of property were central to Indian uses of the land, and Indians could not live as Indians had lived unless the land was owned as Indians had owned it. Conversely, the land could not long remain unchanged if it were owned in a different way. The sweeping alterations of the colonial landscape which Dwight himself so shrewdly described were testimony that a people who loved property little had been overwhelmed by a people who loved it much.

From Indentured Servant to Planter's Wife: White Women in Seventeenth-Century Maryland

LOIS GREEN CARR and LORENA S. WALSH

Although African slavery was to become the most important form of servile labor in North America in the eighteenth and nineteenth centuries, the labor force during the first hundred years of English colonization was made up primarily of indentured servants from England—men, women, and children who sold themselves into temporary bondage in return for passage to the New World. Historians have estimated that one-half to three-fourths of the immigrants to the English colonies in the seventeenth century fit into this category.

In view of the many hazards faced by New World settlers, the reluctance of prosperous tradesmen and skilled craftsmen to journey from Europe to North America is understandable. The three thousand miles that separated America from England, the strangeness of the land, and the danger of conflict with the Indians made the attraction of the New World slight for those comfortable in the old. Apart from a few daring speculators, most of the prosperous immigrants were families seeking religious freedom. These immigrants settled primarily in New England and Pennsylvania.

There was a great demand for new population in America. Laborers were needed to grow food for the colonists and to develop commerce. Additional human resources were necessary to defend the settlements against hostile Indians, as well as against the French and the Spanish.

Fortunately for the development of the colonies, several conditions in the Old World made labor available. Foremost was a growing surplus of population in England. Farmland, which hitherto had been divided into individually owned strips and farmed communally, was increasingly consolidated into large tracts of land, thereby forcing the English peasants to become tenant farmers or to look for new means of livelihood. Industrialization, which might have absorbed these landless peasants, was more than a century away, and city life held little promise for them. Many turned to indentured servitude in the colonies as a solution to their problems, to the relief of both England and America.

Women who became indentured servants were in a particularly advantageous position in the colonies. Since the beginning of the migration to the New World, women had been in short supply. As the following selection by Lois Green Carr (Historian, Historic St. Mary's City) and Lorena S. Walsh (Research Fellow, Colonial Williamsburg) explains, female servants who had served their indenture might expect to have their status significantly elevated by marrying into the farming class. By comparing marriage and childbearing patterns in colonial Maryland and England, the article attempts to evaluate the experience of the migrating women.

F our facts were basic to all human experience in seventeenth-century Maryland. First, for most of the period the great majority of inhabitants had been born in what we now call Britain. Population increase in Maryland did not result primarily from births in the colony before the late 1680s and did not produce a predominantly native population of adults before the first decade of the eighteenth century. Second, immigrant men could not expect to live beyond age forty-three, and 70 percent would die before age fifty. Women may have had even shorter lives. Third, perhaps 85 percent of the immigrants, and practically all the unmarried immigrant women, arrived as indentured servants and consequently married late. Family groups were never predominant in the immigration to Maryland and were a significant part for only a brief time at mid-century. Fourth, many more men

FROM INDENTURED SERVANT TO PLANTER'S WIFE: WHITE WOMEN IN SEVENTEENTH-CENTURY MARYLAND By Lois Green Carr and Lorena S. Walsh, in *William and Mary Quarterly*, 3rd series, Volume 34 (1977), 542–71.

than women immigrated during the whole period. These facts—immigrant predominance, early death, late marriage, and sexual imbalance—created circumstances of social and demographic disruption that deeply affected family and community life.

We need to assess the effects of this disruption on the experience of women in seventeenth-century Maryland. Were women degraded by the hazards of servitude in a society in which everyone had left community and kin behind and in which women were in short supply? Were traditional restraints on social conduct weakened? If so, were women more exploited or more independent and powerful than women who remained in England? Did any differences from English experience which we can observe in the experience of Maryland women survive the transformation from an immigrant to a predominantly native-born society with its own kinship networks and community traditions? The tentative argument put forward here is that the answer to all these questions is Yes. There were degrading aspects of servitude, although these probably did not characterize the lot of most women; there were fewer restraints on social conduct, especially in courtship, than in England; women were less protected but also more powerful than those who remained at home; and at least some of these changes survived the appearance in Maryland of New World creole communities. However, these issues are far from settled, and we shall offer some suggestions as to how they might be further pursued.

Maryland was settled in 1634, but in 1650 there were probably no more than six hundred persons and fewer than two hundred adult women in the province. After that time population growth was steady; in 1704 a census listed 30,437 white persons, of whom 7,163 were adult women. Thus in discussing the experience of white women in seventeenth-century Maryland we are dealing basically with the second half of the century.

Marylanders of that period did not leave letters and diaries to record their New World experience or their relationships to one another. Nevertheless, they left trails in the public records that give us clues. Immigrant lists kept in England and documents of the Maryland courts offer quantifiable evidence about the kinds of people who came and some of the problems they faced in making a new life. Especially valuable are the probate court records. Estate inventories reveal the kinds of activities carried on in the house and on the farm, and wills, which are usually the only personal statements that remain for any man and woman, show something of personal attitudes. This essay relies on the most useful of the immigrant lists and all surviving Maryland court records, but concentrates especially on the surviving records of the lower Western Shore, an early-settled area highly suitable for tobacco. Most of this region comprised four counties: St. Mary's, Calvert, Charles, and Prince George's (formed in 1696 from Calvert and Charles). Inventories from all four counties, wills from St. Mary's and Charles, and court proceedings from Charles and Prince George's provide the major data.

Because immigrants predominated, who they were determined much about the character of Maryland society. The best information so far available comes from lists of indentured servants who left the ports of London, Bristol, and Liverpool. These lists vary in quality, but at the very least they distinguish immigrants by sex and general destination. A place of residence in England is usually given, although it may not represent the immigrant's place of origin; and age and occupation are often noted. These lists reveal several characteristics of immigrants to the Chesapeake and, by inference, to Maryland.

Servants who arrived under indenture included yeomen, husbandmen, farm laborers, artisans, and small tradesmen, as well as many untrained to any special skill. They were young: over half of the men on the London lists of 1683–1684 were aged eighteen to twenty-two. They were seldom under seventeen or over twenty-eight. The women were a little older; the great majority were between eighteen and twenty-five, and half were aged twenty to twenty-one. Most servants contracted for four or five years service, although those under fifteen were to serve at least seven years. These youthful immigrants represented a wide range of English society. All were seeking opportunities they had not found at home.

However, many immigrants—perhaps about half—did not leave England with indentures but paid for their passage by serving according to the custom of the country. Less is known about their social characteristics, but some inferences are possible. From 1661, customary service was set by Maryland laws that required four-year (later five-year) terms for men and women who were twenty-two years or over at arrival and longer terms for those who were younger. A requirement of these laws enables us to determine something about age at arrival of servants who came without indentures. A planter who wished to obtain more than four or five years of service had to take his servant before the county court to have his or her age judged and a written record made. Servants aged over twenty-one were not often registered, there being no incentive for a master to pay court fees for those who would serve the minimum term. Nevertheless, a comparison of the ages of servants under twenty-two recorded in Charles County, 1658–1689, with those under twenty-two on the London list is revealing. Of Charles County male servants (N = 363), 77.1 percent were aged seventeen or under, whereas on the London list (N = 196), 77.6 percent were eighteen or over. Women registered in Charles County court were somewhat older than the men, but among those under twenty-two (N = 107), 5.5 percent were aged twenty-one, whereas on the London list (N = 69), 46.4 percent had reached this age. Evidently, some immigrants who served by custom were younger than those who came indentured, and this age difference probably characterized the two groups as a whole. Servants who were not only very young but had arrived without protection of a written contract were possibly of lower social origins than were servants who came under indenture. The absence of skills among Charles County servants who served by custom supports this supposition.

Whatever their status, one fact about immigrant women is certain: many fewer came than men. Immigrant lists, headright lists, and itemizations of servants in inventories show severe imbalance. On a London immigrant list of 1634–1635 men outnumbered women six to one. From the 1650s at least until the 1680s most sources show a ratio of three to one. From then on, all sources show some, but not great, improvement. Among immigrants from Liverpool over the years 1697–1707 the ratio was just under two and one half to one.

Why did not more women come? Presumably, fewer wished to leave family and community to venture into a wilderness. But perhaps more important, women were not as desirable as men to merchants and planters who were making fortunes raising and marketing tobacco, a crop that requires large amounts of labor. The gradual improvement in the sex ratio among servants toward the end of the century may have been the result of a change in recruiting the needed labor. In the late 1660s the supply of young men willing to emigrate stopped increasing sufficiently to meet the labor demands of a growing Chesapeake population. Merchants who recruited servants for planters turned to other sources, and among these sources were women. They did not crowd the ships arriving in the Chesapeake, but their numbers did increase.

To ask the question another way, why did women come? Doubtless, most came to get a husband, an objective virtually certain of success in a land where women were so far outnumbered. The promotional literature, furthermore, painted bright pictures of the life that awaited men and women once out of their time; and various studies suggest that for a while, at least, the promoters were not being entirely fanciful. Until the 1660s, the expanding economy of Maryland and Virginia offered opportunities well beyond those available in England to men without capital and to the women who became their wives.

Nevertheless, the hazards were also great, and the greatest was untimely death. Newcomers promptly became ill, probably with malaria, and many died. What proportion survived is unclear; so far no one has devised a way of measuring it. Recurrent malaria made the women who survived seasoning less able to withstand other diseases, especially dysentery and influenza. She was especially vulnerable when pregnant. Expectation of life for everyone was low in the Chesapeake, but especially so for women. A woman who had immigrated to Maryland took an extra risk, though perhaps a risk not greater than she might have suffered by moving from her village to London instead.

The majority of women who survived seasoning paid their transportation costs by working for a four- or five-year term of service. The kind of work depended on the status of the family they served. A female servant of a small planter—who through about the 1670s might have had a servant—probably worked at the hoe. Such a man could not afford to buy labor that would not help with the cash crop. In wealthy families women probably were household servants, although some are occasionally listed in inventories of well-to-do planters as living on the quarters—that is, on plantations other than the dwelling plantation. Such women saved men the jobs of preparing food and washing linen but doubtless also worked in the fields. In middling households experience must have varied. Where the number of people to feed and wash for was large, female servants would have had little time to tend the crops.

Tracts that promoted immigration to the Chesapeake region asserted that female servants did not labor in the fields, except "nasty" wenches not fit for other tasks. This implies that most immigrant women expected, or at least hoped, to avoid heavy field work, which English women—at least those above the cottager's status—did not do. What proportion of female servants in Maryland found themselves demeaned by this unaccustomed labor is impossible to say, but this must have been the fate of some. A study of the distribution of female servants among wealth groups in Maryland might shed some light on this question. Nevertheless, we still would not know whether those purchased by the poor or sent to work on a quarter were women whose previous experience suited them for field labor.

An additional risk for the woman who came as a servant was the possibility of bearing a bastard. At least 20 percent of the female servants who came to Charles County between 1658 and 1705 were presented to the county court for this cause. A servant woman could not marry unless someone was willing to pay her master for the term she had left to serve. If a man made her pregnant, she could not marry him unless he could buy her time. Once a woman became free, however, marriage was clearly the usual solution. Only a handful of free women were presented in Charles County for bastardy between 1658 and 1705. Since few free women remained either single or widowed for long, not many were subject to the risk. The hazard of bearing a bastard was a hazard of being a servant.

This high rate of illegitimate pregnancies among servants raises lurid questions. Did men import women for sexual exploitation? Does John Barth's Whore of Dorset have a basis outside his fertile imagination? In our opinion, the answers are clearly No. Servants were economic investments on the part of planters who needed labor. A female servant in a household where there were unmarried men must have both provided and faced temptation, for the pressures were great in a society in which men outnumbered women by three to one. Nevertheless, the servant woman was in the household to work—to help feed and clothe the family and make tobacco. She was not primarily a concubine.

This point could be established more firmly if we knew more about the fathers of the bastards. Often the culprits were fellow servants or men recently freed but too poor to purchase the woman's remaining time. Sometimes the masters were clearly at fault. But often the father is not identified. Some masters surely did exploit their female servants sexually. Nevertheless, masters were infrequently accused of fathering their servants' bastards, and those found guilty were punished as severely as were other men. Community mores did not sanction their misconduct.

A female servant paid dearly for the fault of unmarried pregnancy. She was heavily fined, and if no one would pay her fine, she was whipped. Furthermore, she served an extra twelve to twenty-four months to repay her master for the "trouble of his house" and labor lost, and the fathers often did not share in this payment of damages. On top of all, she might lose the child after weaning unless by then she had become free, for the courts bound out bastard children at very early ages.

English life probably did not offer a comparable hazard to young unmarried female servants. No figures are available to show rates of illegitimacy among those who were subject to the risk, but the female servant was less restricted in England than in the Chesapeake. She did not owe anyone for passage across the Atlantic; hence it was easier for her to marry, supposing she happened to become pregnant while in service. Perhaps, furthermore, her temptations were fewer. She was not 3,000 miles from home and friends, and she lived in a society in which there was no shortage of women. Bastards were born in England in the seventeenth century, but surely not to as many as one-fifth of the female servants.

Some women escaped all or part of their servitude because prospective husbands purchased the remainder of their time. At least one promotional pamphlet published in the 1660s described such purchases as likely, but how often they actually occurred is difficult to determine. Suggestive is a 20 percent difference between the sex ratios found in a Maryland headright sample, 1658–1681, and among servants listed in lower Western Shore inventories for 1658–1679. Some of the discrepancy must reflect the fact that male servants were younger than female servants and therefore served longer terms; hence they had a greater chance of appearing in an inventory. But part of the discrepancy doubtless follows from the purchase of women for wives. Before 1660, when sex ratios were even more unbalanced and the expanding economy enabled men to establish themselves more quickly, even more women may have married before their terms were finished.

Were women sold for wives against their wills? No record says so, but nothing restricted a man from selling his servant to whomever he wished. Perhaps some women were forced into such marriages or accepted them as the least evil. But the man who could afford to purchase a wife—especially a new arrival—was usually already an established landowner. Probably most servant women saw an opportunity in such a marriage. In addition, the shortage of labor gave women some bargaining power. Many masters must have been ready to refuse to sell a woman who was unwilling to marry a would-be purchaser.

If a woman's time was not purchased by a prospective husband, she was virtually certain to find a husband once she was free. Those famous spinsters, Margaret and Mary Brent, were probably almost unique in seventeenth-century Maryland. In the four counties of the lower Western Shore only two of the women who left a probate inventory before the eighteenth century are known to have died single. Comely or homely, strong or weak, any young woman was too valuable to be overlooked, and most could find a man with prospects.

The woman who immigrated to Maryland, survived seasoning and service, and gained her freedom became a planter's wife. She had considerable liberty in making her choice. There were men aplenty, and no fathers or brothers were hovering to monitor her behavior or disapprove her preference. This is the modern way of looking at her situation, of course. Perhaps she missed the protection of a father, a guardian, or kinfolk, and the participation in her decision of a community to which she felt ties. There is some evidence that the absence of kin and the pressures of the sex ratio created conditions of sexual freedom in courtship that were not customary in England. A register of marriages and births for seventeenth-century Somerset County shows that about one-third of the immigrant women whose marriages are recorded were pregnant at the time of the ceremony—nearly twice the rate in English parishes. There is no indication of community objection to this freedom so long as marriage took place. No presentments for bridal pregnancy were made in any of the Maryland courts.

The planter's wife was likely to be in her mid-twenties at marriage. An estimate of minimum age at marriage for servant women can be made from lists of indentured servants who left London over the years 1683–1684 and from age judgments in Maryland county court records. If we assume that the 112 female indentured servants going to Maryland and Virginia whose ages are given in the London lists served full four-year terms, then only 1.8 percent married before age twenty, but 68 percent after age twenty-four. Similarly, if the 141 women whose ages were judged in Charles County between 1666 and 1705 served out their terms according to the custom of the country, none married before age twenty-two, and half were twenty-five or over. When adjustments are made for the ages at which wives may have been purchased, the figures drop, but even so the majority of women waited until at least age twenty-four to marry. Actual age at marriage in Maryland can be found for few seventeenth-century female immigrants, but observations for Charles and Somerset counties place the mean age at about twenty-five.

Because of the age at which an immigrant woman married, the number of children she would bear her husband was small. She had lost up to ten years of her childbearing life—the possibility of perhaps four or five children, given the usual rhythm of childbearing. At the same time, high mortality would reduce both the number of children she would bear over the rest of her life and the number who would live. One partner to a marriage was likely to die within seven years, and the chances were only one in three that a marriage would last ten years. In these circumstances, most women would not bear more than three or four children—not counting those stillborn—to any one husband, plus a posthumous child were she the survivor. The best estimates suggest that nearly a quarter, perhaps more, of the children born alive died during their first year and that 40 to 55 percent would not live to see age twenty. Consequently, one of her children would probably die in infancy, and another one or two would fail to reach adulthood. Wills left in St. Mary's County during the seventeenth century show the results. In 105 families over the years 1660 and 1680 only twelve parents left more than three children behind them, including those conceived but not yet born. The average number was 2.3, nearly always minors, some of whom might die before reaching adulthood.

For the immigrant woman, then, one of the major facts of life was that although she might bear a child about every two years, nearly half would not reach maturity. The social implications of this fact are far-reaching. Because she married late in her childbearing years and because so many of her children would die young, the number who would reach marriageable age might not replace, or might only barely replace, her and her husband or husbands as child-producing members of the society. Consequently, so long as immigrants were heavily predominant in the adult female population, Maryland could not grow much by natural increase. It remained a land of newcomers.

This fact was fundamental to the character of seventeenth-century Maryland society, although its implications have yet to be fully explored. Settlers came from all parts of England and hence from differing traditions—in types of agriculture, forms of landholding and estate management, kinds of building construction, customary contributions to community needs, and family arrangements, including the role of women. The necessities of life in the Chesapeake required all immigrants to make adaptations. But until the native-born became predominant, a securely established Maryland tradition would not guide or restrict the newcomers.

If the immigrant woman had remained in England, she would probably have married at about the same age or perhaps a little later. But the social consequences of marriage at these ages in most parts of England were probably different. More children may have lived to maturity, and even where mortailty was as high newcomers are not likely to have been the main source of population growth. The locally born would still dominate the community, its social organization, and its traditions. However, where there were exceptions, as perhaps in London, late age marriage, combined with high mortality and heavy immigration, may have had consequences in some ways similar to those we have found in Maryland.

A hazard of marriage for seventeenth-century women everywhere was death in childbirth, but this hazard may have been greater than usual in the Chesapeake. Whereas in most societies women tend to outlive men, in this malaria-ridden area it is probable that men outlived women. Hazards of childbirth provide the likely reason that Chesapeake women died so young. Once a woman in the Chesapeake reached forty-five, she tended to outlive men who reached the same age. Darrett and Anita Rutman have found malaria a probable cause of an exceptionally high death rate among pregnant women, who are, it appears, peculiarly vulnerable to that disease.

This argument, however, suggests that immigrant women may have lived longer than their native-born daughters, although among men the opposite was true. Life tables created for men in Maryland show that those native-born who survived to age twenty could expect a life span three to ten years longer than that of immigrants, depending upon the region where they lived. The reason for the improvement was doubtless immunities to local diseases developed in childhood. A native woman developed these immunities, but, as we shall see, she also married earlier than immigrant women usually could and hence had more children. Thus she was more exposed to the hazards of childbirth and may have died a little sooner. Unfortunately, the life tables for immigrant women that would settle this question have so far proved impossible to construct.

However long they lived, immigrant women in Maryland tended to outlive their husbands—in Charles County, for example, by a ratio of two to one. This was possible, despite the fact that women were younger than men at death, because women were also younger than men at marriage. Some women were widowed with no living children, but most were left responsible for two or three. These were often tiny, and nearly always not yet sixteen.

This fact had drastic consequences, given the physical circumstances of life. People lived at a distance from one another, not even in villages, much less towns. The widow had left her kin 3,000 miles across the ocean, and her husband's family was also there. She would have to feed her children and make her own tobacco crop. Though neighbors might help, heavy labor would be required of her if she had no servants, until—what admittedly was usually not difficult—she acquired a new husband.

In this situation dying husbands were understandably anxious about the welfare of their families. Their wills reflected their feelings and tell something of how they regarded their wives. In St. Mary's and Charles counties during the seventeenth century, little more than one-quarter of the men left their widows with no more than the dower the law

Table I
Bequests of Husbands to Wives, St. Mary's and Charles Counties, Maryland, 1640 to 1710

	N	Dower or Less	
	N	N	%
1640s	6	2	34
1650s	24	7	29
1660s	65	18	28
1670s	86	21	24
1680s	64	17	27
1690s	83	23	28
1700s	74	25	34
Totals	402	113	28

Source: Wills, I–XIV, Hall of Records, Annapolis, Md.

required—one-third of his land for her life, plus outright ownership of one-third of his personal property. (See Table I.) If there were no children, a man almost always left his widow his whole estate. Otherwise there were a variety of arrangements. (See Table II.)

During the 1660s, when testators begin to appear in quantity, nearly a fifth of the men who had children left all to their wives, trusting them to see that the children received fair portions. Thus in 1663 John

Table II
Bequests of Husbands to Wives with Children, St. Mary's and Charles Counties, Maryland, 1640 to 1710

	N	All Estate		All or Dwelling Plantation for Life		All or Dwelling Plantation for Widowhood		All or Dwelling Plantation for Minority of Child		More than Dower in Other Form		Dower or Less or Unknown	
		N	%	N	%	N	%	N	%	N	%	N	%
1640s	3	1	33	33								2	67
1650s	16	1	6	2	13	1	6	1	6	4	25	7	44
1660s	45	8	18	8	18	2	4	3	7	9	20	15	33
1670s	61	4	7	21	34	2	3	3	5	13	21	18	30
1680s	52	5	10	19	37	2	4	2	4	11	21	13	25
1690s	69	1	1	31	45	7	10	2	3	10	14	18	26
1700s	62			20	32	6	10	2	3	14	23	20	32
Totals	308	20	6	101	33	20	6	13	4	61	20	93	30

Source: Wills, I–XIV.

Shircliffe willed his whole estate to his wife "towards the maintenance of herself and my children into whose tender care I do Commands them Desireing to see them brought up in the fear of God and the Catholick Religion and Charging them to be Dutiful and obedient to her." As the century progressed, husbands tended instead to give the wife all or a major part of the estate for her life, and to designate how it should be distributed after her death. Either way, the husband put great trust in his widow, considering that he knew she was bound to remarry. Only a handful of men left estates to their wives only for their term of widowhood or until the children came of age. When a man did not leave his wife a life estate, he often gave her land outright or more than her dower third of his movable property. Such bequests were at the expense of his children and showed his concern that his widow should have a maintenance which young children could not supply. A husband usually made his wife his executor and thus responsible for paying his debts and preserving the estate. Only 11 percent deprived their wives of such powers. In many instances, however, men also appointed overseers to assist their wives and to see that their children were not abused or their property embezzled. Danger lay in the fact that a second husband acquired control of all his wife's property, including her life estate in the property of his predecessor. Over half of the husbands who died in the 1650s and 1660s appointed overseers to ensure that their wills were followed. Some trusted to the overseers' "Care and good Conscience for the good of my widow and fatherless children." Others more explicitly made overseers responsible for seeing that "my said child . . . and the other [expected child] (when pleases God to send it) may have their right Proportion of my Said Estate and that the said Children may be bred up Chiefly in the fear of God." A few men—but remarkably few—authorized overseers to remove children from households of stepfathers who abused them or wasted their property. On the whole, the absence of such provisions for the protection of the children points to the husband's overriding concern for the welfare of his widow and to his confidence in her management, regardless of the certainty of her remarriage. Evidently, in the politics of family life women enjoyed great respect.

We have implied that this respect was a product of the experience of immigrants in the Chesapeake. Might it have been instead a reflection of English culture? Little work is yet in print that allows comparison of the provisions for Maryland widows with those made for the widows of English farmers. Possibly, Maryland husbands were making traditional wills which could have been written in the communities they left behind. However, Margaret Spufford's recent study of three Cambridgeshire villages in the late sixteenth century and early seventeenth century suggests a different pattern. In one of these villages, Chippenham, women usually did receive a life interest in the property, but in the other two they did not. If the children were all minors, the widow controlled the property until the oldest son came of age, and then only if she did not remarry. In the majority of cases adult sons were given control of the property with instructions for the support of their mothers. Spufford suggests that the pattern found in Chippenham must have been very exceptional. On the basis of village censuses in six other counties, dating from 1624 to 1724, which show only 3 percent of widowed people heading households that included a married child, she argues that if widows commonly controlled the farm, a higher proportion should have headed such households. However, she also argues that widows with an interest in land would not long remain unmarried. If so, the low percentage may be deceptive. More direct work with wills needs to be done before we can be sure that Maryland husbands and fathers gave their widows greater control of property and family than did their English counterparts.

Maryland men trusted their widows, but this is not to say that many did not express great anxiety about the future of their children. They asked both wives and overseers to see that the children receive "some learning." Robert Sly made his wife sole guardian of his children but admonished her "to take due Care that they be brought up in the true fear of God and instructed in such Literature as may tend to their improvement." Widowers, whose children would be left without any parent, were often the most explicit in prescribing their upbringing. Robert Cole, a middling planter, directed that his children "have such Education in Learning as [to] write and read and Cast accompt I mean my three Sonnes my two daughters to learn to read and sew with their needle and all of them to be keept from Idleness but not to be keept as Comon Servants." John Lawson required his executors to see that his two daughters be reared together, receive learning and sewing instruction, and be "brought up to huswifery." Often present was the fear that orphaned children would be treated as servants and trained only to work in the fields. With stepfathers in mind, many fathers provided that their sons should be independent before the usual age of majority, which for girls was sixteen but for men twenty-one. Sometimes fathers willed that their sons should inherit when they were as young as sixteen, though more often eighteen. The sons could then escape an incompatible stepfather, who could no longer exploit their labor or property. If a son was already close to age sixteen, the father might bind him to his mother until he reached majority or his mother died, whichever came first. If she lived, she could watch out for his welfare, and his labor could contribute to her support. If she died, he and his property would be free from a stepfather's control.

What happened to widows and children if a man died without leaving a will? There was great need for some community institution that could protect children left fatherless or parentless in a society where they usually had no other kin. By the 1660s the probate court and county orphans' courts were supplying this need. If a man left a widow, the probate court—in Maryland a central government agency—usually appointed her or her new husband administrator of the estate with power to pay its creditors under court supervision. Probate procedures provided a large measure of protection. These required an inventory of the movable property and careful accounting of all disbursements, whether or not a man had left a will. William Hollis of Baltimore County, for example, had three stepfathers in seven years, and only the care of the judge or probate prevented the third stepfather from paying the debts of the second with goods that had belonged to William's father. As the judge remarked, William had "an uncareful mother."

Once the property of an intestate had been fully accounted and creditors paid, the county courts appointed a guardian who took charge of the property and gave bond to the children with sureties that he or she would not waste it. If the mother were living, she could be the guardian, or if she had remarried, her new husband would act. Through most of the century bond was waived in these circumstances, but from the 1690s security was required of all guardians, even of mothers. Thereafter the courts might actually take away an orphan's property from a widow or stepfather if she or he could not find sureties—that is, neighbors who judged the parent responsible and hence were willing to risk their own property as security. Children without any parents were assigned new families, who at all times found surety if there were property to manage. If the orphans inherited land, English common law allowed them to choose guardians for themselves at age fourteen—another escape hatch for children in conflict with stepparents. Orphans who had no property, or whose property was insufficient to provide an income that could maintain them, were expected to work for their guardians in return for their maintenance. Every year the county courts were expected to check on the welfare of orphans of intestate parents and remove them or their property from guardians who abused them or misused their estates. From 1681, Maryland law required that a special jury be impaneled once a year to report neighborhood knowledge of mistreatment of orphans and hear complaints.

This form of community surveillance of widows and orphans proved quite effective. In 1696 the assembly declared that orphans of intestates were often better cared for than orphans of testators. From that time forward, orphans' courts were charged with supervision of all orphans and were soon given powers to remove any guardians who were shown false to their trusts, regardless of the arrangements laid down in a will. The assumption was that the deceased parent's main concern was the welfare of the child, and that the orphans' court, as "father to us poor orphans," should implement the parent's intent. In actual fact, the courts never removed children—as opposed to their property—from a household in which the mother was living, except to apprentice them at the mother's request. These powers were mainly exercised over guardians of orphans both of whose parents were dead. The community as well as the husband believed the mother most capable of nurturing his children.

Remarriage was the usual and often the immediate solution for a woman who had lost her husband. The shortage of women made any woman eligible to marry again, and the difficulties of raising a family while running a plantation must have made remarriage necessary for widows who had no son old enough to make tobacco. One indication of the high incidence of remarriage is the fact that there were only sixty women, almost all of them widows, among the 1,735 people who left probate inventories in four southern Maryland counties over the second half of the century. Most other women must have died while married and therefore legally without property to put through probate.

One result of remarriage was the development of complex family structures. Men found themselves responsible for stepchildren as well as their own offspring, and children acquired half-sisters and half-brothers. Sometimes a woman married a second husband who himself had been previously married, and both brought children of former spouses to the new marriage. They then produced children of their own. The possibilities for conflict over the upbringing of children are evident, and crowded living conditions, found even in the households of the wealthy, must have added to family tensions. Luckily, the children of the family very often had the same mother. In Charles County, at least, widows took new husbands three times more often than widowers took new wives. The role of the mother in managing the relationships of half-brothers and half-sisters or stepfathers and stepchildren must have been critical to family harmony.

Early death in this immigrant population thus had broad effects on Maryland society in the seventeenth century. It provided what we might call a pattern of serial polyandry, which enabled more men to marry and to father families than the sex ratios otherwise would have permitted. It produced thousands of orphaned children who had no kin to maintain them or preserve their property, and thus gave rise to an institution almost unknown in England, the orphans' court, which was charged with their protection. And early death, by creating families in which the mother was the unifying element, may have increased her authority within the household.

When the immigrant woman married her first husband, there was usually no property settlement involved, since she was unlikely to have any dowry. But her remarriage was another matter. At the very least, she owned or had a life interest in a third of her former husband's estate. She needed also to think of her children's interests. If she remarried, she would lose control of the property. Consequently, property settlements occasionally appear in the seventeenth-century court records between widows and their future husbands. Sometimes she and her intended signed an agreement whereby he relinquished his rights to the use of her children's portions. Sometimes he deeded to her property which she could dispose of at her pleasure. Whether any of these agreements or gifts would have survived a test in court is unknown. We have not yet found any challenged. Generally speaking, the formal marriage settlements of English law, which bypassed the legal difficulties of the married woman's inability to make a contract with her husband, were not adopted by immigrants, most of whom probably came from levels of English society that did not use these legal formalities.

The wife's dower rights in her husband's estate were a recognition of her role in contributing to his prosperity, whether by the property she had brought to the marriage or by the labor she performed in his household. A woman newly freed from servitude would not bring property, but the benefits of her labor would be great. A man not yet prosperous enough to own a servant might need his wife's help in the fields as well as in the house, especially if he were paying rent or still paying for land. Moreover, food preparation was so time-consuming that even if she worked only at household duties, she saved him time he needed for making tobacco and corn. The corn, for example, had to be pounded in the mortar or ground in a handmill before it could be used to make bread, for there were very few water mills in seventeenth-century Maryland. The wife probably raised vegetables in a kitchen garden; she also milked the cows and made butter and cheese, which might produce a salable surplus. She washed the clothes, and made them if she had the skill. When there were servants to do field work, the wife undoubtedly spent her time entirely in such household tasks. A contract in 1681 expressed such a division of labor. Nicholas Maniere agreed to live on a plantation with his wife and child and a servant. Nicholas and the servant were to work the land; his wife was to "Dresse the Victualls milk the Cowes wash for the servants and Doe allthings necessary for a woman to doe upon the s[ai]d plantation."

We have suggested that wives did field work; the suggestion is supported by occasional direct references in the court records. Mary Castleton, for example, told the judge of probate that "her husband late Deceased in his Life time had Little to sustaine himselfe and Children but what was produced out of ye ground by ye hard Labour of her the said Mary." Household inventories provide indirect evidence. Before about 1680 those of poor men and even middling planters on Maryland's lower Western Shore—the bottom two-thirds of the married decedents—show few signs of household industry, such as appear in equivalent English states. Sheep and woolcards, flax and hackles, and spinning wheels all were a rarity, and such things as candle molds were nonexistent. Women in these households must have been busy at other work. In households with bound labor the wife doubtless was fully occupied preparing the food and washing the clothes for family and hands. But the wife in a household too poor to afford bound labor—the bottom fifth of the married decedent group—might well tend tobacco when she could. Eventually, the profits of her labor might enable the family to buy a servant, making greater profits possible. From such beginnings many families climbed the economic ladder in seventeenth-century Maryland.

The proportion of servantless households must have been larger than is suggested by the inventories of the dead, since young men were less likely to die than old men and had had less time to accumulate property. Well over a fifth of the households of married men on the lower Western Shore may have had no bound labor. Not every wife in such households would necessarily work at the hoe—saved from it by upbringing, ill-health, or the presence of small children who needed her care—but many women performed such work. A lease of 1691, for example, specified that the lessee could farm the amount of land which "he his wife and children can tend."

Stagnation of the tobacco economy, beginning about 1680, produced changes that had some effect on women's economic role. As shown by inventories of the lower Western Shore, home industry increased, especially at the upper ranges of the economic spectrum. In these households women were spinning yarn and knitting it into clothing. The increase in such activity was far less in the households of the bottom fifth, where changes of a different kind may have increased the pressures to grow tobacco. Fewer men at this level could now purchase land, and a portion of their crop went for rent. At this level, more wives than before may have been helping to produce tobacco when they could. And by this time they were often helping as a matter of survival, not as a means of improving the family position.

So far we have considered primarily the experience of immigrant women. What of their daughters? How were their lives affected by the demographic stresses of Chesapeake society?

One of the most important points in which the experience of daughters differed from that of their mothers was the age at which they married. In this woman-short world, the mothers had married as soon as they were eligible, but they had not usually become eligible until they were mature women in their middle twenties. Their daughters were much younger at marriage. A vital register kept in Somerset County shows that some girls married at age twelve and that the mean age at marriage for those born before 1670 was sixteen and a half years.

Were some of these girls actually child brides? It seems unlikely that girls were married before they had become capable of bearing children. Culturally, such a practice would fly in the face of English, indeed Western European, precedent, nobility excepted. Nevertheless, the number of girls who married before age sixteen, the legal age of inheritance for girls, is astonishing. Their English counterparts ordinarily did not marry until their mid to late twenties or early thirties. In other parts of the Chesapeake, historians have found somewhat higher ages at marriage than appear in Somerset, but everywhere in seventeenth-century Maryland and Virginia most native-born women married before they reached age twenty-one. Were such early marriages a result of the absence of fathers? Evidently not. In Somerset, the fathers of very young brides—those under sixteen—were usually living. Evidently, guardians were unlikely to allow such marriages, and this fact suggests that they were not entirely approved. But the shortage of women imposed strong pressures to marry as early as possible.

Not only did native girls marry early, but many of them were pregnant before the ceremony. Bridal pregnancy among native-born women was not as common among immigrants. Nevertheless, in seventeenth-century Somerset County 20 percent of native brides bore children within eight and one half months of marriage. This was a somewhat higher percentage than has been reported from seventeenth-century English parishes.

These facts suggest considerable freedom for girls in selecting a husband. Almost any girl must have had more than one suitor, and evidently many had freedom to spend time with a suitor in a fashion that allowed her to become pregnant. We might suppose that such pregnancies were not incurred until the couple had become betrothed, and that they were consequently an allowable part of courtship, were it not that girls whose fathers were living were usually not the culprits. In Somerset, at least, only 10 percent of the brides with fathers living were pregnant, in contrast to 30 percent of those who were orphans. Since there was only about one year's difference between the mean ages at which orphan and non-orphan girls married, parental supervision rather than age seems to have been the main factor in the differing bridal pregnancy rates.

Native girls married young and bore children young; hence they had more children than immigrant women. This fact ultimately changed composition of the Maryland population. Native-born females began to have enough children to enable couples to replace themselves. These children, furthermore, were divided about evenly between males and females. By the mid-1680s, in all probability the population thus began to grow through reproductive increase, and sexual imbalance began to decline. In 1704 the native-born preponderated in the Maryland assembly for the first time and by then were becoming predominant in the adult population as a whole.

This appearance of a native population was bringing alterations in family life, especially for widows and orphaned minors. They were acquiring kin. St. Mary's and Charles counties wills demonstrate the change. (See Table III.) Before 1680, when nearly all those who died and left families had been immigrants, three-quarters of the men and women who left widows and/or minor children made no mention in their wills of any other kin in Maryland. In the first decade of the eighteenth century, among native-born testators, nearly three-fifths mention other kin, and if we add information from sources other than wills—other probate records, land records, vital registers, and so on—at least 70 percent are found to have had such local connections. This development of local family ties must have been one of the most important events of early Maryland history.

Historians have only recently begun to explore the consequences of

Table III
Resident Kin of Testate Men and Women Who Left Minor Children, St. Mary's and Charles Counties, 1640 to 1710

	Families N	No Kin % Families	Only Wife % Families	Grown Child % Families	Other Kin % Families
			A.		
1640–1669	95	23	43	11	23
1670–1679	76	17	50	7	26
1700–1710	71	6	35[a]	25	34[b]
			B.		
1700–1710					
Immigrant	41	10	37	37	17
Native	30		33[c]	10	57[d]

Notes: [a]If information found in other records is included, the percentage is 30.
    [b]If information found in other records is included, the percentage is 39.
    [c]If information found in other records is included, the percentage is 20.
    [d]If information found in other records is included, the percentage is 70.
    Only 8 testators were natives of Maryland before 1680s; hence no effort has been made to distinguish them from immigrants.
Source: Wills, I–XIV.

the shift from an immigrant to a predominantly native population. We would like to suggest some changes in the position of women that may have resulted from this transition. It is already known that as sexual imbalance disappeared, age at first marriage rose, but it remained lower than it had been for immigrants over the second half of the seventeenth century. At the same time, life expectancy improved, at least for men. The results were longer marriages and more children who reached maturity. In St. Mary's County after 1700, dying men far more often than earlier left children of age to maintain their widows, and widows may have felt less inclination and had less opportunity to remarry.

We may speculate on the social consequences of such changes. More fathers were still alive when their daughters married, and hence would have been able to exercise control over the selection of their sons-in-law. What in the seventeenth century may have been a period of comparative independence for women, both immigrant and native, may have given way to a return to more traditional European social controls over the creation of new families. If so, we might see the results in a decline in bridal pregnancy and perhaps a decline in bastardy.

We may also find the wife losing ground in the household polity, although her economic importance probably remained unimpaired. Indeed, she must have been far more likely than a seventeenth-century immigrant woman to bring property to her marriage. But several changes may have caused women to play a smaller role than before in household decision-making. Women became proportionately more numerous and may have lost bargaining power. Furthermore, as marriages lasted longer, the proportion of households full of stepchidlren and half-brothers and half-sisters united primarily by the mother must have diminished. Finally, when husbands died, more widows would have had children old enough to maintain them and any minor brothers and sisters. There would be less need for women to play a controlling role, as well as less incentive for their husbands to grant it. The provincial marriage of the eighteenth century may have more closely resembled that of England than did the immigrant marriage of the seventeenth century.

If this change occurred, we should find symptoms to measure. There should be fewer gifts from husbands to wives of property put at the wife's disposal. Husbands should less frequently make bequests to wives that provided them with property beyond their dower. A wife might even be restricted to less than her dower, although the law allowed her to choose her dower instead of a bequest. At the same time, children should be commanded to maintain their mothers.

St. Mary's County wills show most of the symptoms, although exhortations of fathers to children to help their mothers are not included. (See Table IV.) But bequests of dower or less increased by a fifth, and widowhood restrictions began to appear. Evidently, as demographic conditions became more normal, St. Mary's County widows began to lose ground to their children, a phenomenon that deserves further study.

Table IV
Bequests of Husbands to Wives with Children, St. Mary's County, Maryland 1710–1777

Date	N	All Estate		All or Dwelling Plantation for Life		All or Dwelling Plantation for Widowhood[a]		More than Dower in Other Form		Dower or Less Unknown[b]	
		n	%	n	%	n	%	n	%	n	%
1710–19	38	1	3	12	32	2	5	10	26	14	37
1720–29	65	4	6	23	35	0	0	15	23	23	35
1730–39	58	2	3	17	29	5	9	9	16	25	43
1740–49	73	1	1	20	27	6	8	10	14	36	49
1750–59	79	2	3	26	33	11	14	8	10	31	39
1760–69	92	2	2	35	38	10	11	5	5	40	43
1770–77	66	1	3	17	26	10	15	12	18	26	39
Totals	471	13	3	150	32	44	9	69	15	195	41

[a] Includes instances of all or dwelling plantation for minority of child (N = 11)
[b] Includes instances of provisions for maintenance or houseroom (N = 5)
Source: Wills XIII–XLI

It is time to issue a warning. Whether or not Maryland women in a creole society lost ground, the argument hinges on an interpretation of English behavior that also requires testing. Either position supposes that women in seventeenth-century Maryland obtained power in the household which wives of English farmers did not enjoy. Much of the evidence for Maryland is drawn from the disposition of property in wills. If English wills show a similar pattern, similar inferences might be drawn about English women. We have already discussed evidence from English wills that supports the view that women in Maryland were favored; but the position of seventeenth-century English women—especially those not of gentle status—has been explored. A finding of little difference between bequests to women in England and in Maryland would greatly weaken the argument that demographic stress created peculiar conditions especially favorable to Maryland women.

If the demography of Maryland produced the effects here described, such effects should also be evident elsewhere in the Chesapeake. The four characteristics of the seventeenth-century Maryland—immigrant predominance, early death, late marriage, and sexual imbalance—are to be found everywhere in the region, at least at first. The timing of the disappearance of these peculiarities may have varied from place to place, depending on date of settlement or rapidity of development, but the effect of their existence upon the experience of women should be clear. Should research in other areas of the Chesapeake fail to find women enjoying the status they achieved on the lower Western Shore of Maryland, then our arguments would have to be reversed.

Work is also needed that will enable historians to compare conditions in Maryland with those in other colonies. Richard S. Dunn's study of the British West Indies also shows demographic disruption. When the status of wives is studied, it should prove similar to that of Maryland women. In contrast were demographic conditions in New England, where immigrants came in family groups, major immigration had ceased by the mid-seventeenth century, sex ratios balanced early, and mortality was low. Under these conditions, demographic disruption must have been both less severe and less prolonged. If New England women achieved status similar to that suggested for women in the Chesapeake, that fact will have to be explained. The dynamics might prove to have been different; or a dynamic we have not identified, common to both areas, might turn out to have been the primary engine of change. And, if women in England shared the status—which we doubt—conditions in the New World may have had secondary importance. The Maryland data established persuasive grounds for a hypothesis, but the evidence is not all in.

The White Indians
of Colonial America

JAMES AXTELL

When the English began to settle in New England, they adopted a variety of attitudes toward the people already living there. While colonial leaders were sure of their own racial superiority, they were unclear about the origins, identity, and character of their Native American neighbors. British estimations of the Indians' place in the world of living things ranged from the possibility of their being the lost tribes of Israel to their forming a "missing link" between the human and animal worlds.

The English generally agreed that the Indians were "savages"—that is, lacking the qualities considered to be characteristic of "civilized" peoples. Some saw them as "noble savages," people who lived in a state of innocence, unsullied by the sins and temptations of the then modern world. Others saw them as dangerous and both physically and culturally threatening.

Regardless of the attitude they held toward the Indian people, most of the political and cultural leaders of the colonies saw the Indians as distinctly inferior. Their confidence in the superiority of English culture led them to believe that no reasonable person of English background could or would "descend" to adopt the Indian way of life. Imagine their surprise, then, when during the colonial period many colonists deserted the established English settlements and became full-fledged members of Indian tribes.

This situation went largely unnoticed by scholars until the ethnohistory of early New England began to be studied. James Axtell (College of William and Mary) has been a pioneer in this emerging area of study. His article reprinted here explores the phenomenon that he calls "white Indians"—that is, European settlers who adopted Indian culture. Recognizing that most of those who did accept Indian ways were initially removed from their colonial homes by force, he describes the process by which they were adopted into Indian communities—adopted so thoroughly that they refused to return to colonial settlements when given the opportunity to do so. A major factor in the Indians' decision to capture and adopt the English into their families was the decrease in population that the tribes suffered through disease and war. Their replacement policy led them to seek out primarily women and children to replenish their ranks. Axtell's explanation of why so many Europeans chose to stay in their adoptive communities is controversial, but clearly all the European settlers in early New England did not view the difference between Indian and English cultures in the same hierarchical fashion as did the colonial leadership.

The English, like their French rivals, began their colonizing ventures in North America with a sincere interest in converting the Indians to Christianity and civilization. Nearly all the colonial charters granted by the English monarchs in the seventeenth century assigned the wish to extend the Christian Church and to redeem savage souls as a principal, if not *the* principal, motive for colonization. This desire was grounded in a set of complementary beliefs about "savagism" and "civilization." First, the English held that the Indians, however benighted, were capable of conversion. "It is not the nature of men," they believed, "but the education of men, which make them barbarous and uncivill." Moreover, the English were confident that the Indians would want to be converted once they were exposed to the superior quality of English life. The strength of these beliefs was reflected in Cotton Mather's astonishment as late as 1721 that

> Tho' they saw a People Arrive among them, who were Clothed in *Habits* of much more Comfort and Splendour, than what there was to be seen in the *Rough Skins* with which they hardly covered themselves; and who had *Houses full of Good Things,* vastly outshining their squalid and dark *Wigwams;* And they saw this People Replenishing their *Fields,* with *Trees* and with *Grains,* and useful *Animals,* which until now they had been wholly Strangers to; yet they did not seem touch'd in the least, with any *Ambition* to come at such Desirable Circumstances, or with any *Curiosity* to enquire after the *Religion* that was attended with them.

THE WHITE INDIANS OF COLONIAL AMERICA   By James Axtell. First appearance in *William and Mary Quarterly*, 3rd series, Volume 32 (1975), 55–88. © 1975 by James Axtell.

The second article of the English faith followed from their fundamental belief in the superiority of civilization, namely, that no civilized
person in possession of his faculties or free from undue restraint would
choose to become an Indian. "For, easy and unconstrained as the savage life is," wrote the Reverend William Smith of Philadelphia, "certainly it could never be put in competition with the blessings of improved
life and the light of religion, by any persons who have had the happiness of enjoying, and the capacity of discerning, them."

And yet, by the close of the colonial period, very few if any Indians
had been transformed into civilized Englishmen. Most of the Indians
who were educated by the English—some contemporaries thought *all* of
them—returned to Indian society at the first opportunity to resume their
Indian identities. On the other hand, large numbers of Englishmen had
chosen to become Indians—by running away from colonial society to
join Indian society, by not trying to escape after being captured, or by
electing to remain with their Indian captors when treaties of peace periodically afforded them the opportunity to return home.

Perhaps the first colonist to recognize the disparity between the
English dream and the American reality was Cadwallader Colden, sur-
veyor-general and member of the king's council of New York. In his
History of the Five Indian Nations of Canada, published in London in
1747, Colden described the Albany peace treaty between the French
and the Iroquois in 1699, when "few of [the French captives] could be
persuaded to return" to Canada. Lest his readers attribute this unusual
behavior to "the Hardships they had endured in their own Country,
under a tyrannical Government and a barren Soil," he quickly added
that "the *English* had as much Difficulty to persuade the People, that
had been taken Prisoners by the *French Indians,* to leave the *Indian*
Manner of living, though no People enjoy more Liberty, and live in
greater Plenty, than the common Inhabitants of *New-York* do." Colden, clearly amazed, elaborated:

> No Arguments, no Intreaties, nor Tears of their Friends and Re-
> lations, could persuade many of them to leave their new *Indian*
> Friends and Acquaintance[s]; several of them that were by the Ca-
> ressings of their Relations persuaded to come Home, in a little
> Time grew tired of our Manner of living, and run away again to
> the *Indians,* and ended their Days with them. On the other Hand,
> *Indian* Children have been carefully educated among the *English,*
> cloathed and taught, yet, I think, there is not one Instance, that
> any of these, after they had Liberty to go among their own People,
> and were come to Age, would remain with the *English,* but re-
> turned to their own Nations, and became as fond of the *Indian*
> Manner of Life as those that knew nothing of a civilized Manner
> of living. What I now tell of Christian Prisoners among *Indians* [he
> concluded his history], relates not only to what happened at
> the Conclusion of this War, but has been found true on many
> other Occasions.

Colden was not alone. Six years later Benjamin Franklin wondered how it was that

> When an Indian Child has been brought up among us, taught our language and habituated to our Customs, yet if he goes to see his relations and make one Indian Ramble with them, there is no perswading him ever to return. [But] when white persons of either sex have been taken prisoners young by the Indians, and lived a while among them, tho' ransomed by their Friends, and treated with all imaginable tenderness to prevail with them to stay among the English, yet in a Short time they become disgusted with our manner of life, and the care and pains that are necessary to support it, and take the first good Opportunity of escaping again into the Woods, from whence there is no reclaiming them.

In short, "thousands of Europeans are Indians," as Hector de Crévecoeur put it, "and we have no examples of even one of those Aborigines having from choice become Europeans!"

The English captives who foiled their countrymen's civilized assumptions by becoming Indians differed little from the general colonial population when they were captured. They were ordinary men, women, and children of yeoman stock, Protestants by faith, a variety of nationalities by birth, English by law, different from their countrymen only in their willingness to risk personal insecurity for the economic opportunities of the frontier. Their was no discernible characteristic or pattern of characteristics that differentiated them from their captive neighbors who eventually rejected Indian life—with one exception. Most of the colonists captured by the Indians and adopted into Indian families were children of both sexes and young women, often the mothers of the captive children. They were, as one captivity narrative observed, the "weak and defenceless."

    The pattern of taking women and children for adoption was consistent throughout the colonial period, but during the first century and one-half of Indian-white conflict, primarily in New England, it coexisted with a larger pattern of captivity that included all white colonists, men as well as women and children. The Canadian Indians who raided New England tended to take captives more for their ransom value than for adoption. When Mrs. James Johnson gave birth to a daughter on the trail to Canada, for example, her captor looked into her makeshift lean-to and "clapped his hands with joy, crying two monies for me, two monies for me." Although the New England legislatures occasionally tried to forbid the use of public moneys for "the Ransoming of Captives," thereby prolonging the Indians' "diabolical kidnapping mode of warfare," ransoms were constantly paid from both public and private funds. These payments became larger as inflation and the Indians' savvy increased. Thus when John and Tamsen Tibbetts redeemed two of their children from the Canadian Indians in 1729, it cost them £105 10s. (1,270 livres). "Being verry Poore," many families in similar situations could ill afford to pay such high premiums even "if they should sell all they have in the world."

When the long peace in the Middle Atlantic colonies collapsed in 1753, the Indians of Pennsylvania, southern New York, and the Ohio country had no Quebec or Montreal in which to sell their human chattels to compassionate French families or anxious English relatives. For this and other reasons they captured English settlers largely to replace members of their own families who had died, often from English musketballs or imported diseases. Consequently, women and children—the "weak and defenceless"—were the prime targets of Indian raids.

According to the pattern of warfare in the Pennsylvania theater, the Indians usually stopped at a French fort with their prisoners before proceeding to their own villages. A young French soldier captured by the English reported that at Fort Duquesne there were "a great number of English Prisoners," the older of whom "they are constantly sending . . . away to Montreal" as prisoners of war, "but that the Indians keep many of the Prisoners amongst them, chiefly young People whom they adopt and bring up in their own way." His intelligence was corroborated by Barbara Leininger and Marie LeRoy, who had been members of a party of two adults and eight children captured in 1755 and taken to Fort Duquesne. There they saw "many other Women and Children, they think an hundred who were carried away from the several provinces of P[ennsylvania] M[aryland] and V[irginia]." When the girls escaped from captivity three years later, they wrote a narrative in German chiefly to acquaint "the inhabitants of this country . . . with the names and circumstances of those prisoners whom we met, at the various places where we were, in the course of our captivity." Of the fifty-two prisoners they had seen, thirty-four were children and fourteen were women, including six mothers with children of their own.

The close of hostilities in Pennsylvania came in 1764 after Col. Henry Bouquet defeated the Indians near Bushy Run and imposed peace. By the articles of agreement reached in October, the Delawares, Shawnees, and Senecas were to deliver up "all the Prisoners in [their] Possession, without any Exception, Englishmen, Frenchmen, Women, and Children, whether adopted in your Tribes, married, or living amongst you, under any Denomination, or Pretence whatever." In the weeks that followed, Bouquet's troops, including "the Relations of [some of] the People [the Indians] have Massacred, or taken Prisoners," encamped on the Muskingum in the heart of the Ohio country to collect the captives. After as many as nine years with the Indians, during which time many children had grown up, 81 "men" and 126 "women and children" were returned. At the same time, a list was prepared of 88 prisoners who still remained in Shawnee towns to the west: 70 were classified as "women and children." Six months later, 44 of these pris-

oners were delivered up to Fort Pitt. When they were captured, all but
4 had been less than sixteen years old, while 37 had been less than
eleven years old.

The Indians obviously chose their captives carefully so as to maximize the chances of acculturating them to Indian life. To judge by the
results, their methods were hard to fault. Even when the English held
the upper hand militarily, they were often embarrassed by the Indians'
educational power. On November 12, 1764, at his camp on the Muskingum, Bouquet lectured the Shawnees who had not delivered all
their captives: "As you are now going to Collect all our *Flesh*, and
Blood, . . . I desire that you will use them with Tenderness, and look
upon them as Brothers, and no longer as Captives." The utter gratui-
tousness of his remark was reflected—no doubt purposely—in the Shawnee speech when the Indians delivered their captives the following spring
at Fort Pitt. "Father—Here is your *Flesh*, and *Blood*. . . . they have
been all tied to us by Adoption, although we now deliver them up to
you. We will always look upon them as Relations, whenever the *Great
Spirit* is pleased that we may visit them. . . . Father—we have taken
as much Care of these Prisoners, as if they were [our] own Flesh, and
blood; they are become unacquainted with your Customs, and manners,
and therefore, Father we request you will use them tender, and kindly,
which will be a means of inducing them to live contentedly with you."

The Indians spoke the truth and the English knew it. Three days
after his speech to the Shawnees, Bouquet had advised Lt.-Gov. Francis
Fauquier of Virginia that the returning captives "ought to be treated by
their Relations with Tenderness and Humanity, till Time and Reason
make them forget their unnatural Attachments, but unless they are closely
watch'd," he admitted, "they will certainly return to the Barbarians."
And indeed they would have, for during a half-century of conflict captives had been returned who, like many of the Ohio prisoners, responded only to Indian names, spoke only Indian dialects, felt comfortable
only in Indian clothes, and in general regarded their white saviors as
barbarians and their deliverance as captivity. Had they not been compelled to return to English society by militarily enforced peace treaties,
the ranks of the white Indians would have been greatly enlarged.

From the moment the Indians surrendered their English prisoners,
the colonists faced a series of difficult problems. The first was the problem of getting the prisoners to remain with the English. When Bouquet
sent the first group of restored captives to Fort Pitt, he ordered his
officers there that "they are to be closely watched and well Secured"
because "most of them, particularly those who have been a long time
among the Indians, will take the first Opportunity to run away." The
young children especially were "so completely savage that they were
brought to the camp tied hand and foot." Fourteen-year-old John
McCullough, who had lived with the Indians for "eight years, four
months, and sixteen days" (by his parents' reckoning), had his legs tied

"under the horses belly" and his arms tied behind his back with his father's garters, but to no avail. He escaped under the cover of night and returned to his Indian family for a year before he was finally carried to Fort Pitt under "strong guard." "Having been accustomed to look upon the Indians as the only connexions they had, having been tenderly treated by them, and speaking their language," explained the Reverend William Smith, the historian of Bouquet's expedition, "it is no wonder that [the children] considered their new state in the light of captivity, and parted from the savages with tears."

Children were not the only reluctant freedmen. "Several women eloped in the night, and ran off to join their Indian friends." Among them undoubtedly were some of the English women who had married Indian men and borne them children, and then had been forced by the English victory either to return with their mixed-blood children to a country of strangers, full of prejudice against Indians, or to risk escaping under English guns to their husbands and adopted culture. For Bouquet had "reduced the Shawanese and Delawares etc. to the most Humiliating Terms of Peace," boasted Gen. Thomas Gage. "He had Obliged them to deliver up even their Own Children born of white women." But even the victorious soldier could understand the dilemma into which these women had been pushed. When Bouquet was informed that the English wife of an Indian chief had eloped in the night with her husband and children, he "requested that no pursuit should be made, as she was happier with her Chief than she would be if restored to her home."

Although most of the returned captives did not try to escape, the emotional torment caused by the separation from their adopted families deeply impressed the colonists. The Indians "delivered up their beloved captives with the utmost reluctance; shed torrents of tears over them, recommending them to the care and protection of the commanding officer." One young woman "cryed and roared when asked to come and begged to Stay a little longer." "Some, who could not make their escape, clung to their savage acquaintance at parting, and continued many days in bitter lamentations, even refusing sustenance." Children "cried as if they should die when they were presented to us." With only small exaggeration an observer on the Muskingum could report that "every captive left the Indians with regret."

Another problem encountered by the English was the difficulty of communicating with the returned captives, a great many of whom had replaced their knowledge of English with an Algonquian or Iroquoian dialect and their baptismal names with Indian or hybrid ones. This immediately raised another problem—that of restoring the captives to their relatives. Sir William Johnson, the superintendent of Indian affairs, "thought it best to advertise them [in the newspapers] immediately, but I believe it will be verry difficult to find the Freinds of some of them, as they are ignorant of their own names, or former places of abode, nay cant speak a word of any language but Indian." The only recourse the English had in such instances was to describe them "more particularly . . . as to their features, Complexion etc. That by the Publication of Such descriptions their Relations, parents or friends may hereafter know and Claim them."

But if several colonial observers were right, a description of the captives' physiognomy was of little help after they had been with the Indians for any length of time. Peter Kalm's foreign eye found it difficult to distinguish European captives from their captors, "except by their color, which is somewhat whiter than that of the Indians," but many colonists could see little or no difference. To his Maine neighbors twelve-year-old John Durell "ever after [his two-year captivity] appeared more like an Indian than a white man." So did John Tarbell. After thirty years among the Indians in Canada, he made a visit to his relatives in Groton "in his Indian dress and with his Indian complexion (for by means of grease and paints but little difference could be discerned)." When O. M. Spencer returned after only eight months with the Shawnees, he was greeted with a newspaper allusion "to [his] looks and manners, as slightly resembling the Indians" and by a gaggle of visitors who exclaimed "in an under tone, 'How much he looks like an Indian!' " Such evidence reinforced the environmentalism of the time, which held that white men "who have incorporated themselves with any of [the Indian] tribes" soon acquire "a great resemblance to the savages, not only in their manners, but in their colour and the expression of the countenance."

The final English problem was perhaps the most embarrassing in its manifestations, and certainly was so in its implications. For many Indians who had adopted white captives, the return of their "own Flesh, and Blood" to the English was unendurable. At the earliest opportunity, after bitter memories of the wars had faded on both sides, they journeyed through the English settlements to visit their estranged children, just as the Shawnee speaker had promised Bouquet they would. Jonathan Hoyt's Indian father visited him so often in Deerfield, sometimes bringing his captive sister, that Hoyt had to petition the Massachusetts General Court for reimbursement for their support. In 1760 Sir William Johnson reported that a Canadian Indian "has been since down to Schenectady to visit one Newkirk of that place, who was some years a Prisoner in his House, and sent home about a year ago with this Indians Sister, who came with her Brother now purely to see Said Newkirk whom she calls her Son and is verry fond of."

Obviously the feelings were mutual. Elizabeth Gilbert, adopted at the age of twelve, "always retained an affection toward John Huston, her Indian father (as she called him), for she remembered his kindness to her when in captivity." Even an adult who had spent less than six months with the Indians honored the chief who had adopted him. In 1799, eleven years after Thomas Ridout's release, his friend and father, Kakinathucca, "accompanied by three more Shawanese chiefs, came to pay me a visit at my house in York town (Toronto). He regarded myself and family with peculiar pleasure, and my wife and children contemplated with great satisfaction the noble and good qualities of this worthy Indian." The bond of affection that had grown in the Indian villages was clearly not an attachment that the English could dismiss as "unnatural."

Children who had been raised by Indian parents from infancy could be excused perhaps for their unwillingness to return, but the adults who displayed a similar reluctance, especially the women who had married Indian men and borne them children, drew another reaction. "For the honour of humanity," wrote William Smith, "we would suppose those persons to have been of the lowest rank, either bred up in ignorance and distressing penury, or who had lived so long with the Indians as to forget all their former connections. For, easy and unconstrained as the savage life is, certainly it could never be put in competition with the blessings of improved life and the light of religion, by any persons who have had the happiness of enjoying, and the capacity of discerning, them." If Smith was struck by the contrast between the visible impact of Indian education and his own cultural assumptions, he never said so.

To find a satisfactory explanation for the extraordinary drawing power of Indian culture, we should begin where the colonists themselves first came under its sway—on the trail to Indian country. For although the Indians were known for their patience, they wasted no time in beginning the education process that would transform their hostile or fearful white captives into affectionate Indian relatives.

Perhaps the first transaction after the Indians had selected their prisoners and hurried them into cover was to replace their hard-heeled shoes with the footwear of the forest—moccasins. These were universally approved by the prisoners, who admitted that they traveled with "abundant more ease" than before. And on more than one occasion the knee-deep snows of northern New England forced the Indians to make snowshoes for their prisoners in order to maintain their pace of twenty-five to thirty miles a day. Such an introduction to the superbly adapted technology of the Indians alone would not convert the English, but it was a beginning.

The lack of substantial food supplies forced the captives to accommodate their stomachs as best they could to Indian trail fare, which ranged from nuts, berries, roots, and parched corn to beaver guts, horse-flank, and semi-raw venison and moose, eaten without the customary English accompaniments of bread or salt. When there was nothing to eat, the Indians would "gird up their loins with a string," a technique that at least one captive found "very useful" when applied to himself. Although their food was often "unsavory" and in short supply, the Indians always shared it equally with the captives, who, being hungry, "relished [it] very well."

Sometimes the lessons learned from the Indians were unexpectedly vital. When Stephen Williams, an eleven-year-old captive from Deer-field, found himself separated from his party on the way to Canada, he halloed for his Indian master. When the boy was found, the Indian threatened to kill him because, as Williams remembered five years later, "the Indians will never allow anybody to Hollow in the woods. Their manner is to make a noise like wolves or any other wild creatures, when they call to one another." The reason, of course, was that they did not wish to be discovered by their enemies. To the young neophyte Indian this was a lesson in survival not soon forgotten.

Two other lessons were equally unexpected but instrumental in pre-paring the captives for even greater surprises when they reached the Indian settlements. Both served to undermine the English horror of the Indians as bloodthirsty fiends who defile "any Woman they take alive" before "putting her to Death." Many redeemed prisoners made a point of insisting that, although they had been completely powerless in cap-tivity, the Indians had never affronted them sexually. Thomas Ridout testified that "during the whole of the time I was with the Indians I never once witnessed an indecent or improper action amongst any of the Indians, whether young or old." Even William Smith admitted that "from every enquiry that has been made, it appears—that no woman thus saved is preserved from base motives, or need fear the violation of her honour." If there had been the least exception, we can be sure that this champion of civilization would have made the most of it.

One reason for the Indians' lack of sexual interest in their female captives was perhaps aesthetic, for the New England Indians, at least, esteemed black the color of beauty. A more fundamental reason derived from the main purpose of taking captives, which was to secure new members for their families and clans. Under the Indians' strong incest taboos, no warrior would attempt to violate his future sister or cousin. "Were he to indulge himself with a captive taken in war, and much more were he to offer violence in order to gratify his lust, he would incur indelible disgrace." Indeed, the taboo seems to have extended to the whole tribe. As George Croghan testified after long acquaintance with the Indians, "they have No [J]uri[s]diction or Laws butt that of Nature yett I have known more than onest thire Councils, order men to be putt to Death for Committing Rapes, wh[ich] is a Crime they Despise." Since murder was a crime to be revenged by the victim's family in its own way and time, rape was the only capital offense pun-ished by the tribe as a whole.

Equally powerful in prohibiting sexual affronts was a religious ethic of strict warrior continence, the breaking of which was thought to bring misfortune or death. "The Indians will not cohabit with women while they are out at war," noted James Adair, a trader among the southeast-ern tribes for thirty years, "they religiously abstain from every kind of intercourse even with their own wives, for the space of three days and nights before they go to war, and so after they return home, because they are to sanctify themselves." When William Fleming and his wife were taken from their bed in 1755, the Indians told him, "he need not be afraid of their abusing his wife, for they would not do it, for fear of offending their God (pointing their hands toward heaven) for the man that affronts his God will surely be killed when he goes to war." Giving the woman a plundered shift and petticoat, the natives turned their backs while she dressed to emphasize the point.

Captive testimony also chipped away at the stereotype of the Indians' cruelty. When Mrs. Isabella M'Coy was taken from Epsom, New Hampshire, in 1747, her neighbors later remembered that "she did indeed find the journey [to Canada] fatiguing, and her fare scanty and precarious. But in her treatment from the Indians, she experienced a very agreeable disappointment. The kindness she received from them was far greater than she had expected from those who were so often distinguished for their cruelties." More frequent still was recognition of the Indians' kindness to children. Thomas Hutchinson told a common story of how "some of the children who were taken at Deerfield, they drew upon slays; at other times they have been known to carry them in their arms or upon their backs to Canada. This tenderness," he noted, "has occasioned the beginning of an affection, which in a few years has been so rivetted, that the parents of the children, who have gone to Canada to seek them, could by no means prevail upon them to leave the Indians and return home." The affections of a four-year-old Pennsylvania boy, who became Old White Chief among the Iroquois, seem to have taken even less time to become "rivetted." "The last I remember of my mother," he recalled in 1836, "she was running, carrying me in her arms. Suddenly she fell to the ground on her face, and I was taken from her. Overwhelmed with fright, I knew nothing more until I opened my eyes to find myself in the lap of an Indian woman. Looking kindly down into my face she smiled on me, and gave me some dried deer's meat and maple sugar. From that hour I believe she loved me as a mother. I am sure I returned to her the affection of a son."

When the returning war parties approached the first Indian village, the educational process took on a new complexion. As one captive explained, "whenever the warriors return from an excursion against an enemy, their return to the tribe or village must be designated by war-like ceremonial; the captives or spoils, which may happen to crown their valor, must be conducted in a triumphant form, and decorated to every possible advantage." Accordingly, the cheek, chin, and forehead of every captive were painted with traditional dashes of vermilion mixed with bear's grease. Belts of wampum were hung around their necks, Indian clothes were substituted for English, and the men and boys had their hair plucked or shaved in Indian fashion. The physical transformation was so effective, said a twenty-six-year-old soldier, "that I began to think I was an Indian." Younger captives were less aware of the small distance between role-playing and real acceptance of the Indian lifestyle. When her captor dressed Frances Slocum, not yet five years old, in "beautiful wampum beads," she remembered at the end of a long and happy life as an Indian that he "made me look, as I thought, very fine. I was much pleased with the beautiful wampum."

The prisoners were then introduced to a "new school" of song and dance. "Little did we expect," remarked an English woman, "that the accomplishment of dancing would ever be taught us, by the savages. But the war dance must now be held; and every prisoner that could move must take its awkward steps. The figure consisted of circular motion round the fire; each sang his own music, and the best dancer was the one most violent in motion." To prepare for the event each captive had rehearsed a short Indian song on the trail. Mrs. Johnson recalled many years later that her song was "danna witchee natchepung; my son's was nar wiscumpton." Nehemiah How could not master the Indian pronunciation, so he was allowed to sing in English "I don't know where I go." In view of the Indians' strong sense of ceremonial propriety, it is small wonder that one captive thought that they "Seem[e]d to be Very much a mind I Should git it perfect."

Upon entering the village the Indians let forth with some distinctive music of their own. "When we came near the main Body of the Enemy," wrote Thomas Brown, a captive soldier from Fort William Henry, "the *Indians* made a Live-Shout, as they call it when they bring in a Prisoner alive (different from the Shout they make when they bring in Scalps, which they call a Dead-Shout)." According to another soldier, "their Voices are so sharp, shrill, loud and deep, that when they join together after one has made his Cry, it makes a most dreadful and horrible Noise, that stupifies the very Senses," a noise that naturally frightened many captives until they learned that it was not their death knell.

They had good reason to think that their end was near when the whole village turned out to form a gauntlet from the entrance to the center of the village and their captors ordered them to run through it. With ax handles, tomahawks, hoop poles, clubs, and switches the Indians flogged the racing captives as if to beat the whiteness out of them. In most villages, significantly, "it was only the more elderly People both Male and Female wh[ic]h rece[iv]ed this Useage—the young prisoners of Both Sexes Escaped without it" or were rescued from any serious harm by one or more villagers, perhaps indicating the Indian perception of the captives' various educability. When ten-year-old John Brickell was knocked down by the blows of his Seneca captors, "a very big Indian came up, and threw the company off me, and took me by the arm, and led me along through the lines with such rapidity that I scarcely touched the ground, and was not once struck after he took me.

The purpose of the gauntlet was the subject of some difference of opinion. A French soldier who had spent several years among the northeastern Indians believed that a prisoner "so unfortunate as to fall in the course of the bastonnade must get up quickly and keep on, or he will be beaten to death on the spot." On the other hand, Pierre de Charlevoix, the learned traveler and historian of Canada, wrote that "even when they seem to strike at random, and to be actuated only by fury, they take care never to touch any part where a blow might prove mortal." Both Frenchmen were primarily describing the Indians' treatment of other Indians and white men. Barbara Leininger and Marie LeRoy drew a somewhat different conclusion from their own treatment. Their welcome at the Indian village of Kittanning, they said, "consisted of three blows each, on the back. They were, however, administered with great mercy. Indeed, we concluded that we were beaten merely in order to keep up an ancient usage, and not with the intention of injuring us."

William Walton came closest to revealing the Indians' intentions in his account of the Gilbert family's captivity. The Indians usually beat the captives with "great Severity," he said, "by way of Revenge for their Relations who have been slain." Since the object of taking captives was to satisfy the Indian families who had lost relatives, the gauntlet served as the first of three initiation rites into Indian society, a purgative ceremony by which the bereaved Indians could exorcise their anger and anguish, and the captives could begin their cultural transformation.

If the first rite tried to beat the whiteness out of the captives, the second tried to wash it out. James Smith's experience was typical.

> The old chief, holding me by the hand, made a long speech, very loud, and when he had done he handed me to three squaws, who led me by the hand down the bank into the river until the water was up to our middle. The squaws then made signs to me to plunge myself into the water, but I did not understand them. I thought that the result of the council was that I should be drowned, and that these young ladies were to be the executioners. They all laid violent hold of me, and I for some time opposed them with all my might, which occasioned loud laughter by the multitude that were on the bank of the river. At length one of the squaws made out to speak a little English (for I believe they began to be afraid of me) and said, "No hurt you." On this I gave myself up to their ladyships, who were as good as their word; for though they plunged me under water and washed and rubbed me severely, yet I could not say they hurt me much.

More than one captive had to receive similar assurance, but their worst fears were being laid to rest.

Symbolically purged of their whiteness by their Indian baptism, the initiates were dressed in new Indian clothes and decorated with feathers, jewelry, and paint. Then, with great solemnity, the village gathered around the council fire, where after a "profound silence" one of the chiefs spoke. Even a hostile captive, Zadock Steele, had to admit that although he could not understand the language spoken, he could "plainly discover a great share of native eloquence." The chief's speech, he said, was "of considerable length, and its effect obviously manifested weight of argument, solemnity of thought, and at least human sensibility." But even this the twenty-two-year-old New Englander could not appreciate on its own terms, for in the next breath he denigrated the ceremony as "an assemblage of barbarism, assuming the appearance of civilization."

A more charitable account was given by James Smith, who through an interpreter was addressed in the following words:

> My son, you are now flesh of our flesh and bone of our bone. By the ceremony that was performed this day, every drop of white blood was washed out of your veins. You are taken into the Caughnewaga [French Mohawk] nation and initiated into a war-like tribe. You are adopted into a great family and now received with great seriousness and solemnity in the room and place of a great man. After what has passed this day you are now one of us by an old strong law and custom. My son, you have now nothing to fear. We are now under the same obligations to love, support and defend you that we are to love and to defend one another. Therefore you are to consider yourself as one of our people.

"At this time," admitted the eighteen-year-old Smith, "I did not believe this fine speech, especially that of the white blood being washed out of me; but since that time I have found that there was much sincerity in said speech; for from that day I never knew them to make any distinction between me and themselves in any respect whatever until I left them . . . we all shared one fate." It is a chord that sounds through nearly every captivity narrative: "They treated me . . . in every way as one of themselves."

When the adoption ceremony had ended, the captive was taken to the wigwam of his new family, who greeted him with a "most dismal howling, crying bitterly, and wringing their hands in all agonies of grief for a deceased relative." "The higher in favour the adopted Prisoners [were] to be placed, the greater Lamentation [was] made over them." After a threnodic memorial to the lost member, which may have "added to the Terror of the Captives," who "imagined it to be no other than a Prelude to inevitable Destruction," the mood suddenly shifted. "I never saw . . . such hug[g]ling and kissing from the women and crying for joy," exclaimed one young recipient. Then an interpreter introduced each member of the new family—in one case "from brother to seventh cousins"—and "they came to me one after another," said another captive, "and shook me by the hand, in token that they considered me to stand in the same relationship to them as the one in whose stead I was placed."

Most young captives assumed the places of Indian sons and daughters, but occasionally the match was not exact. Mary Jemison replaced a brother who had been killed in "Washington's war," while twenty-six-year-old Titus King assumed the unlikely role of a grandfather. Although their sex and age may not always have corresponded, the adopted captives succeeded to all the deceased's rights and obligations—the same dignities, honors, and often the same names. "But the one adopted," reported a French soldier, "must be prudent and wise in his conduct, if he wants to make himself as well liked as the man he is replacing. This seldom fails to occur, because he is continually reminded of the dead man's conduct and good deeds."

So literal could the replacement become at times that no amount of exemplary conduct could alter the captive's reception. Thomas Peart, a twenty-three-year-old Pennsylvanian, was adopted as an uncle in an Iroquois family, but "the old Man, whose Place [he] was to fill, had never been considered by his Family as possessed of any Merit." Accordingly, Peart's dress, although in the Indian style, was "in a meaner Manner, as they did not hold him high in Esteem after his Adoption." Since his heart was not becoming an Indian anyway, and "observing that they treated him just as they had done the old worthless Indian . . . he therefore concluded he would only fill his Predecessor's Station, and used no Endeavours to please them."

When the prisoners had been introduced to all their new relatives and neighbors, the Indians proceeded to shower them with gifts. Luke Swetland, taken from Pennsylvania during the Revolution, was unusually feted with "three hats, five blankets, near twenty pipes, six razors, six knives, several spoons, gun and ammunition, fireworks, several Indian pockets [pouches], one Indian razor, awls, needles, goose quills, paper and many other things of small value"—enough to make him the complete Indian warrior. Most captives, however, settled for a new shirt or dress, a pair of decorated moccasins, and abundant promises of future kindness, which later prompted the captives to acknowledge once again that the Indians were "a[s] good as their word." "All the family was as kind to me," related Thomas Gist, "as if I had realy been the nearest of relation they had in the world." The two women who adopted Mary Jemison were no less loving. "I was ever considered and treated by them as a real sister," she said near the end of a long life with them, "the same as though I had been born of their mother."

Treatment such as this—and it was almost universal—left an indelible mark on every captive, whether or not they eventually returned to English society. Although captives like Mrs. Johnson found their adoption an "unnatural situation," they had to defend the humanity of the practice. "Those who have profited by refinement and education," she argued, "ought to abate part of the prejudice, which prompts them to look with an eye of censure on this untutored race. . . . Do they ever adopt an enemy," she asked, "and salute him by the tender name of brother?" It is not difficult to imagine what effect such feelings must have had in younger people less habituated to English culture, especially those who had lost their own parents.

The formalities, purgations, and initiations were now completed. Only one thing remained for the Indians: by their daily example and instruction to "make an Indian of you," as the Delawares told John Brickell. This required a steady union of two things: the willingness and gratitude of the captives, and the consistent love and trust of the Indians. By the extraordinary ceremonies through which they had passed, most captives had had their worst fears allayed. From a state of apprehension or even terror they had suddenly emerged with their persons intact and a solemn invitation to begin a new life, as full of love, challenge, and satisfaction as any they had known. For "when [the Indians] once determine to give life, they give every thing with it, which, in their apprehension, belongs to it." The sudden release from anxiety into a realm of affirmative possibility must have disposed many captives to accept the Indian way of life.

According to the adopted colonists who recounted the stories of their new lives, Indian life was more than capable of claiming their respect and allegiance, even if they eventually returned to English society. The first indication that the Indians were serious in their professions of equality came when the adopted captives were given freedom of movement within and without the Indian villages. Naturally, the degree of freedom and its timing depended on the captive's willingness to enter into the spirit of Indian life.

Despite his adult years, Thomas Ridout had earned his captor's trust by the third night of their march to the Shawnee villages. Having tied his prisoner with a rope to himself the first two nights, the Indian "never afterwards used this precaution, leaving me at perfect liberty, and frequently during the nights that were frosty and cold," Ridout recalled, "I found his hand over me to examine whether or not I was covered." As soon as seventeen-year-old John Leeth, an Indian trader's clerk, reached his new family's village, "my father gave me and his two [Indian] sons our freedom, with a rifle, two pounds of powder, four pounds of lead, a blanket, shirt, match-coat, pair of leggins, etc. to each, as our freedom dues; and told us to shift for ourselves." Eleven-year-old Benjamin Gilbert, "considered as the [Indian] King's Successor," was of course "entirely freed from Restraint, so that he even began to be delighted with his Manner of Life." Even Zadock Steele, a somewhat reluctant Indian at twenty-two, was "allowed the privilege of visiting any part of the village, in the day time, and was received with marks of fraternal affection, and treated with all the civility an Indian is capable to bestow."

The presence of other white prisoners complicated the trust relationship somewhat. Captives who were previously known to each other, especially from the same family, were not always allowed to converse "much together as [the Indians] imagined they would remember their former Situation, and become less contented with their present Manner of Life." Benjamin Peart, for example, was allowed the frequent company of "Two white Men who had been taken Prisoners, the one from Susquehanna, the other from Minisinks, both in Pennsylvania," even though he was a Pennsylvanian himself. But when he met his captive wife and infant son by chance at Fort Niagara, the Indians "separated them again the same Day, and took [his] Wife about Four Miles Distance."

Captives who were strangers were permitted not only to visit frequently but occasionally to live together. When Thomas Gist suddenly moved from his adopted aunt's house back to her brother's, she "imajined I was affronted," he wrote, and "came and asked me the reason why I had left her, or what injury she or any of the family had done me that I should leave her without so much as leting her know of it. I told her it was the company of my fellow prisoners that drew me to the town. She said that it was not so far but I mite have walked to see them every two or three days, and ask some of them to come and see me those days that I did not chuse to go abroad, and that all such persons as I thought proper to bring to the house should be as welcom[e] as one of the family, and made many promises how kind she would be if I would return. However," boasted the twenty-four-year-old Gist, "I was obstinate and would not." It is not surprising that captives who enjoyed such autonomy were also trusted under the same roof. John Brickell remarked that three white prisoners, "Patton, Johnston, and Mrs. Baker [of Kentucky] had all lived with me in the same house among the Indians, and we were as intimate as brothers and sisters."

Once the captives had earned the basic trust of their Indian families, nothing in Indian life was denied them. When they reached the appropriate age, the Indians offered to find them suitable marriage partners. Understandably, some of the older captives balked at this, sensing that it was calculated to bind them with marital ties to a culture they were otherwise hesitant to accept. When Joseph Gilbert, a forty-one-year-old father and husband, was adopted into a leading family, his new relatives informed him that "if he would marry amongst them, he should enjoy the Privileges which they enjoyed; but this Proposal he was not disposed to comply with, . . . as he was not over anxious to conceal his Dislike to them." Elizabeth Peart, his twenty-year-old married sister, was equally reluctant. During her adoption ceremony "they obliged her to sit down with a young Man an Indian, and the eldest Chieftain of the Family repeating a Jargon of Words to her unintelligible, but which she considered as some form amongst them of Marriage," she was visited with "the most violent agitations, as she was determined, at all events, to oppose any step of this Nature." Marie LeRoy's honor was even more dearly bought. When "it was at length determined by the [Indians] that [she] should marry one of the natives, who had been selected for her," she told a fellow captive that "she would sooner be shot than have him for her husband." Whether her revulsion was directed toward the act itself or toward the particular suitor was not said.

The distinction is pertinent because the weight of evidence suggests that marriage was not compulsory for the captives, and common sense tells us that any form of compulsion would have defeated the Indians' purpose in trying to persuade the captives to adopt their way of life. Mary Jemison, at the time a captive for two years, was unusual in implying that she was forced to marry an Indian. "Not long after the Delawares came to live with us, at Wiishto," she recalled, "my sisters told me that I must go and live with one of them, whose name was She-nin-jee. Not daring to cross them, or disobey their commands, with a great degree of reluctance I went; and Sheninjee and I were married according to Indian custom." Considering the tenderness and kindness with which most captives reported they were treated, it is likely that she was less compelled in reality than in her perception and memory of it.

For even hostile witnesses could not bring themselves to charge that force was ever used to promote marriages. The Puritan minister John Williams said only that "great *essays* [were] made to get [captives] married" among the Canadian Indians by whom he was captured. Elizabeth Hanson and her husband "could by no means obtain from their hands" their sixteen-year-old daughter, "for the squaw, to whom she was given, had a son whom she intended my daughter should in time *be prevailed with to marry*." Mrs. Hanson was probably less concerned that her daughter would be forced to marry an Indian than that she might "in time" want to, for as she acknowledged from her personal experience, "the Indians are very civil towards their captive women, not offering any incivility by any indecent carriage." An observer of the return of the white prisoners to Bouquet spoke for his contemporaries when he reported—with an almost audible sigh of relief—that "there had not been a solitary instance among them of any woman having her delicacy injured by being compelled to marry. They had been left liberty of choice, and those who chose to remain single were not sufferers on that account."

Not only were younger captives and consenting adults under no compulsion, either actual or perceived, to marry, but they enjoyed as wide a latitude of choice as any Indian. When Thomas Gist returned to his Indian aunt's lodge, she was so happy that she "dress'd me as fine as she could, and . . . told me if I wanted a wife she would get a pretty young girl for me." It was in the same spirit of exuberant generosity that Oliver Spencer's adopted mother rewarded his first hunting exploit. "She heard all the particulars of the affair with great satisfaction," he remembered, "and frequently saying, 'Enee, wessah' (this is right, that is good), said I would one day become a great hunter, and placing her forefingers together (by which sign the Indians represent marriage) and then pointing to Sotonegoo" (a thirteen-year-old girl whom Spencer described as "rather homely, but cheerful and good natured, with bright, laughing eyes") "told me that when I should become a man I should have her for a wife." Sotonegoo cannot have been averse to the idea, for when Spencer was redeemed shortly afterward she "sobbed loudly as [he] took her hand, and for the moment deeply affected, bade her farewell."

So free from compulsion were the captives that several married fellow white prisoners. In 1715 the priest of the Jesuit mission at Sault-au-Récollet "married Ignace shoetak8anni [Joseph Rising, aged twenty-one] and Elizabeth T8atog8ach [Abigail Nims, aged fifteen], both English, who wish to remain with the Christian Indians, not only renouncing their nation, but even wishing to live *en sauvages.*" But from the Indians' standpoint, and perhaps from their own, captives such as John Leeth and Thomas Armstrong may have had the best of all possible marriages. After some years with the Indians, Leeth "was married to a young woman, seventeen or eighteen years of age; also a prisoner to the Indians; who had been taken by them when about twenty months old." Armstrong, an adopted Seneca, also married a "full blooded white woman, who like himself had been a captive among the Indians, from infancy, but who unlike him, had not acquired a knowledge of one word of the English language, being essentially Indian in all save blood." Their commitment to each other deepened their commitment to the Indian culture of which they had become equal members.

The captives' social equality was also demonstrated by their being asked to share in the affairs of war and peace, matters of supreme importance to Indian society. When the Senecas who had adopted Thomas Peart decided to "make a War Excursion," they asked him to go with them. But since he was in no mood—and no physical condition—to play the Indian, "he determinately refused them, and was therefore left at Home with the Family." The young Englishman who became Old White Chief was far more eager to defend his new culture, but his origins somewhat limited his military activity. "When I grew to manhood," he recalled, "I went with them [his Iroquois kinsmen] on the warpath against the neighboring tribes, but never against the white settlers, lest by some unlucky accident I might be recognized and claimed by former friends." Other captives—many of them famous renegades— were less cautious. Charlevoix noticed in his travels in Canada that adopted captives "frequently enter into the spirit of the nation, of which they are become members, in such a manner, that they make no difficulty of going to war against their own countrymen." It was behavior such as this that prompted Sir William Johnson to praise Bouquet after his expedition to the Ohio for compelling the Indians to give up every white person, even the "Children born of White Women. That mixed Race," he wrote, referring to first-generation captives as well, "forgetting their Ancestry on one side are found to be the most Inveterate of any, and would greatly Augment their numbers."

It is ironic that the most famous renegade of all should have introduced ten-year-old Oliver Spencer to the ultimate opportunity for an adopted captive. When he had been a captive for less than three weeks, Spencer met Simon Girty, "the very picture of a villain," at a Shawnee village below his own. After various boasts and enquiries, wrote Spencer, "he ended by telling me that I would never see home; but if I should 'turn out to be a good hunter and a brave warrior I might one day be a chief.'" Girty's prediction may not have been meant to tease a small boy with impossible delusions of grandeur, for the Indians of the Northeast readily admitted white captives to their highest councils and offices.

Just after Thomas Ridout was captured on the Ohio, he was surprised to meet an English-speaking "white man, about twenty-two years of age, who had been taken prisoner when a lad and had been adopted, and now was a chief among the Shawanese." He need not have been surprised, for there were many more like him. John Tarbell, the man who visited his Groton relatives in Indian dress, was not only "one of the wealthiest" of the Caughnawagas but "the eldest chief and chief speaker of the tribe." Timothy Rice, formerly of Westborough, Massachusetts, was also made one of the clan chiefs at Caughnawaga, partly by inheritance from his Indian father but largely for "his own Super[io]r Talents" and "war-like Spirit for which he was much celebrated."

Perhaps the most telling evidence of the Indians' receptivity to adopted white leadership comes from Old White Chief, an adopted Iroquois.

> I was made a chief at an early age [he recalled in 1836] and as my sons grew to manhood they also were made chiefs. . . . After my youngest son was made chief I could see, as I thought, that some of the Indians were jealous of the distinction I enjoyed and it gave me uneasiness. This was the first time I ever entertained the thought of leaving my Indian friends. I felt sure that it was displeasing to the Indians to have three of my sons, as well as myself, promoted to the office of chief. My wife was well pleased to leave with me, and my sons said, "Father, we will go wherever you will lead us."
>
> I then broke the subject to some of my Indian relatives, who were very much disturbed at my decision. They immediately called the chiefs and warriors together and laid the plan before them. They gravely deliberated upon the subject for some hours, and then a large majority decided that they would not consent to our leaving. They said, "We cannot give up our son and brother" (meaning myself) "nor our nephews" (meaning my children). "They have lived on our game and grown strong and powerful among us. They are good and true men. We cannot do without them. We cannot give them to the pale faces. We shall grow weak if they leave us. We will give them the best we have left. Let them choose where they will live. No one shall disturb them. We need their wisdom and their strength to help us. If they are in high places, let them be there. We know they will honor us."

"We yielded to their importunity," said the old chief, and "I have never had any reason to regret my decision." In public office as in every sphere of Indian life, the English captives found that the color of their skin was unimportant; only their talent and their inclination of heart mattered.

Understandably, neither their skill nor their loyalty was left to chance. From the moment the captives, especially the young ones, came under their charge, the Indians made a concerted effort to inculcate in them Indian habits of mind and body. If the captives could be taught to think, act, and react like Indians, they would effectively cease to be English and would assume an Indian identity. This was the Indians' goal, toward which they bent every effort in the weeks and months that followed their formal adoption of the white captives.

The educational character of Indian society was recognized by even the most inveterately English captives. Titus King, a twenty-six-year-old New England soldier, spent a year with the Canadian Indians at St. Francis trying—unsuccessfully—to undo their education of "eight of ten young [English] Children." What "an awfull School this [is] for Children," he wrote. "When We See how Quick they will Fall in with the Indians ways, nothing Seems to be more takeing in Six months time they Forsake Father and mother Forgit thir own Land Refuess to Speak there own toungue and Seemin[g]ly be Holley Swollowed up with the Indians." The older the person, of course, the longer it took to become fully Indianized. Mary Jemison, captured at the age of fifteen, took three or four years to forget her natural parents and the home she had once loved. "If I had been taken in infancy," she said, "I should have been contented in my situation." Some captives, commonly those over fifteen or sixteen years old, never made the transition from English to Indian. Twenty-four-year-old Thomas Gist, soldier and son of a famous scout and Indian agent, accommodated himself to his adoption and Indian life for just one year and then made plans to escape. "All curiosity with regard to acting the part of an Indian," he related, "which I could do very well, being th[o]rougherly satisfied, I was determined to be what I really was."

Children, however, took little time to "fall in with the Indians ways." Titus King mentioned six months. The Reverend John Williams witnessed the effects of eight or nine months when he stopped at St. Francis in February 1704. There, he said, "we found several poor children, who had been taken from the eastward [Maine] the summer before; a sight very affecting, they being in habit very much like Indians, and in manners very much symbolizing with them." When young Joseph Nobel visited his captive sister in Montreal, "he still belonged to the St. Francois tribe of Indians, and was dressed remarkably fine, having forty or fifty broaches in his shirt, clasps on his arm, and a great variety of knots and bells about his clothing. He brought his little sister . . . a young fawn, a basket of cranberries, and a lump of sap sugar."

Sometime later he was purchased from the Indians by a French gentleman who promptly "dressed him in the French style; but he never appeared so bold and majestic, so spirited and vivacious, as when arrayed
in his Indian habit and associating with his Indian friends."

The key to any culture is its language, and the young captives were
quick to learn the Indian dialects of their new families. Their retentive
memories and flair for imitation made them ready students, while the
Indian languages, at once oral, concrete, and mythopoeic, lightened
the task. In less than six months ten-year-old Oliver Spencer had "acquired a sufficient knowledge of the Shawnee tongue to understand all
ordinary conversation and, indeed, the greater part of all that I heard
(accompanied, as their conversation and speeches were, with the most
significant gestures)," which enabled him to listen "with much pleasure
and sometimes with deep interest" to his Indian mother tell of battles,
heroes, and history in the long winter evenings. When Jemima Howe
was allowed to visit her four-year-old son at a neighboring Indian village in Canada, he greeted her "in the Indian tongue" with "Mother,
are you come?" He too had been a captive for only six months.

The early weeks of captivity could be disquieting if there were no
English-speaking Indians or prisoners in the village to lend the comfort
of a familiar language while the captives struggled to acquire a strange
one. If a captive's family left for their winter hunting camp before he
could learn their language, he might find himself, like Thomas Gist,
"without any com[p]any that could unders[t]and one word that I spake."
"Thus I continued, near five months," he wrote, "sometimes reading,
other times singing, never melancholy but when alone. . . . About
the first of April (1759) I prevailed on the family to return to town,
and by the last of the month all the Indians and prisoners returned,
when I once more had the pleasure to talk to people that understood
what I said."

Younger captives probably missed the familiarity of English less than
the adult Gist. Certainly they never lacked eager teachers. Mary Jemison recalled that her Seneca sisters were "diligent in teaching me their
language; and to their great satisfaction I soon learned so that I could
understand it readily, and speak it fluently." Even Gist was the recipient of enthusiastic, if informal, instruction from a native speaker. One
of his adopted cousins, who was about five or six years old and his
"favorite in the family," was always "chattering some thing" with him.
"From him," said Gist affectionately, "I learn'd more than from all the
rest, and he learn'd English as fast as [I] did Indian."

As in any school, language was only one of many subjects of instruction. Since the Indians generally assumed that whites were physically inferior to themselves, captive boys were often prepared for the
hardy life of hunters and warriors by a rigorous program of physical
training. John McCullough, aged eight, was put through the traditional
Indian course by his adoptive uncle. "In the beginning of winter,"

McCullough recalled, "he used to raise me by day light every morning, and make me sit down in the creek up to my chin in the cold water, in order to make me hardy as he said, whilst he would sit on the bank smoking his pipe until he thought I had been long enough in the water, he would then bid me to dive. After I came out of the water he would order me not to go near the fire until I would be dry. I was kept at that till the water was frozen over, he would then break the ice for me and send me in as before." As shocking as it may have been to his system, such treatment did nothing to turn him against Indian life. Indeed, he was transparently proud that he had borne up under the strenuous regimen "with the firmness of an Indian." Becoming an Indian was as much a challenge and an adventure for the young colonists as it was a "sore trial," and many of them responded to it with alacrity and zest. Of children their age we should not expect any less.

The captives were taught not only to speak and to endure as Indians but to act as Indians in the daily social and economic life of the community. Naturally, boys were taught the part of men and girls the part of women, and according to most colonial sources—written, it should be noted, predominantly by men—the boys enjoyed the better fate. An Ohio pioneer remembered that the prisoners from his party were "put into different families, the women to hard drudging and the boys to run wild with the young Indians, to amuse themselves with bow and arrow, dabble in the water, or obey any other notion their wild natures might dictate." William Walton, the author of the Gilbert family captivity narrative, also felt that the "Labour and Drudgery" in an Indian family fell to "the Share of the Women." He described fourteen-year-old Abner Gilbert as living a "dronish Indian live, idle and poor, having no other Employ than the gathering of Hickory-Nuts; and although young," Walton insisted, "his Situation was very irksome." Just how irksome the boy found his freedom from colonial farm chores was revealed when the ingenuous Walton related that "Abner, having no useful Employ, amused himself with catching fish in the Lake. . . . Not being of an impatient Disposition," said Walton soberly, "he bore his Captivity without repining."

While most captive boys had "nothing to do, but cut a little wood for the fire," draw water for cooking and drinking, and "shoot Blackbirds that came to eat up the corn," they enjoyed "some leisure" for "hunting and other innocent devertions in the woods." Women and girls, on the other hand, shared the burdens—onerous ones in English eyes—of their Indian counterparts. But Mary Jemison, who had been taught English ways for fifteen years before becoming an Indian, felt that the Indian women's labor "was not severe," their tasks "probably not harder than that [sic] of white women," and their cares "certainly . . . not half as numerous, nor as great." The work of one year was "exactly similar, in almost every respect, to that of the others, without that endless variety that is to be observed in the common labor of the white people. . . . In the summer season, we planted, tended and harvested our corn, and generally had all our children with us; but had no master to oversee or drive us, so that we could work as leisurely as we pleased. . . . In the season of hunting, it was our business, in addition to our cooking, to bring home the game that was taken by the [men], dress it, and carefully preserve the eatable meat, and prepare or dress the skins." "Spinning, weaving, sewing, stocking knitting," and like domestic tasks of colonial women were generally unknown. Unless Jemison was correct, it would be virtually impossible to understand why so many women and girls chose to become Indians. A life of unremitting drudgery, as the English saw it, could certainly hold no attraction for civilized women fresh from frontier farms and villages.

The final and most difficult step in the captives' transition from English to Indian was to acquire the ability to think as Indians, to share unconsciously the values, beliefs, and standards of Indian culture. From an English perspective, this should have been nearly an impossible task for civilized people because they perceived Indian culture as immoral and irreligious and totally antithetical to the civilized life they had known, however briefly. "Certainly," William Smith assumed, "it could never be put in competition with the blessings of improved life and the light of religion." But many captives soon discovered that the English had no monopoly on virtue and that in many ways the Indians were morally superior to the English, more Christian than the Christians.

As early as 1643 Roger Williams had written a book to suggest such a thing, but he could be dismissed as a misguided visionary who let the Narragansetts go to his head. It was more difficult to dismiss someone like John Brickell, who had lived with the Indians for four and one-half years and had no ax to grind with established religion. "The Delawares are the best people to train up children I ever was with," he wrote. "Their leisure hours are, in a great measure, spent in training up their children to observe what they believe to be right. . . . [A]s a nation they may be considered fit examples for many of us Christians to follow. They certainly follow what they are taught to believe right more closely, and I might say more honestly, in general, than we Christians do the divine precepts of our Redeemer. . . . I know I am influenced to good, even at this day," he concluded, "more from what I learned among them, than what I learned among people of my own color." After many decades with them, Mary Jemison insisted that "the moral character of the Indians was . . . uncontaminated. Their fidelity was perfect, and became proverbial; they were strictly honest; they despised deception and falsehood; and chastity was held in high veneration." Even the Tory historian Peter Oliver, who was no friend to the Indians, admitted that "they have a Religion of their own, which, to the eternal Disgrace of many Nations who boast of Politeness, is more influential on their Conduct than that of those who hold them in so great Contempt." To the acute discomfort of the colonists, more than one captive maintained that the Indians were a "far more moral race than the whites."

In the principled school of Indian life the captives experienced a decisive shift in their cultural and personal identities, a shift that often fostered a considerable degree of what might be called "conversion zeal." A French officer reported that "those Prisoners whom the Indians keep with them . . . are often more brutish, boisterous in their Behaviour and loose in their Manners than the Indians," and thought that "they affect that kind of Behaviour thro' Fear of and to recommend themselves to the Indians." Matthew Bunn, a nineteen-year-old soldier, was the object of such behavior when he was enslaved—not adopted—by the Maumee in 1791. "After I had eaten," he related, "they brought me a little prisoner boy, that had been taken about two years before, on the river called Monongahela, though he delighted more in the ways of the savages than in the ways of Christians; he used me worse than any of the Indians, for he would tell me to do this, that, and the other, and if I did not do it, or made any resistance, the Indians would threaten to kill me, and he would kick and cuff me about in such a manner, that I hardly dared to say my soul was my own." What Bunn experienced was the attempt of the new converts to pattern their behavior after their young Indian counterparts, who, a Puritan minister observed, "are as much to be dreaded by captives as those of maturer years, and in many cases much more so; for, unlike cultivated people, they have no restraints upon their mischievous and savage propensities, which they indulge in cruelties."

Although fear undoubtedly accounted for some of the converts' initial behavior, desire to win the approval of their new relatives also played a part. "I have lived in my new habitation about a week," recalled Oliver Spencer, "and having given up all hope of escaping . . . began to regard it as my future home. . . . I strove to be cheerful, and by my ready obedience to ingratiate myself with Cooh-coo-cheeh [his Indian mistress], for whose kindness I felt grateful." A year after James Smith had been adopted, a number of prisoners were brought in by his new kinsmen and a gauntlet formed to welcome them. Smith "went and told them how they were to act" and then "fell into one of the ranks with the Indians, shouting and yelling like them." One middle-aged man's turn came, and "as they were not very severe on him," confessed the new Indian, "as he passed me I hit him with a piece of pumpkin—which pleased the Indians much." If their zeal to emulate the Indians sometimes exceeded their mercy, the captives had nonetheless fulfilled their new families' expectations: they had begun to act as Indians in spirit as well as body. Only time would be necessary to transform their conscious efforts into unconscious habits and complete their cultural conversion.

"By what power does it come to pass," asked Crévecoeur, "that children who have been adopted when young among these people, . . . and even grown persons . . . can never be prevailed on to re-adopt European manners?" Given the malleability of youth, we should not be surprised that children underwent a rather sudden and permanent transition from English to Indian—although we might be pressed to explain why so few Indian children made the transition in the opposite direction. But the adult colonists who became Indians cannot be explained as easily, for the simple reason that they, unlike many of the children, were fully conscious of their cultural identities while they were being subjected to the Indians' assiduous attempts to convert them. Consequently, their cultural metamorphosis involved a large degree of personal choice.

The great majority of white Indians left no explanations for their choice. Forgetting their original language and their past, they simply disappeared into their adopted society. But those captives who returned to write narratives of their experiences left several clues to the motives of those who chose to stay behind. They stayed because they found Indian life to possess a strong sense of community, abundant love, and uncommon integrity—values that the English colonists also honored, if less successfully. But Indian life was attractive for other values—for social equality, mobility, adventure, and, as two adult converts acknowledged, "the most perfect freedom, the ease of living, [and] the absence of those cares and corroding solicitudes which so often prevail with us." As we have learned recently, these were values that were not being realized in the older, increasingly crowded, fragmented, and contentious communities of the Atlantic seaboard, or even in the newer frontier settlements. By contrast, as Crévecoeur said, there must have been in the Indians' "social bond something singularly captivating." Whatever it was, its power had no better measure than the large number of English colonists who became, contrary to the civilized assumptions of their countrymen, white Indians.

Time, Space,
and the Evolution
of Afro-American Society

IRA BERLIN

By the end of the seventeenth century, the English colonies in North America had turned to African slaves and their descendants to solve the problems arising from a chronic shortage of labor. The English adopted for their own use the Spanish system of African enslavement, which had begun early in the sixteenth century in the Caribbean. Indian slavery, too, had been widely practiced in Latin American, to the point of bringing the native Indian populations close to extinction. But in the North American colonies, although Indian captives were frequently enslaved in the early years of colonization, Indian slavery was never economically profitable. As a result, the African became *the* slave in the English colonies.

Slavery, in the sense of lifetime bondage, is an institution as old as human history. Almost every past civilization has had some system of involuntary service that may, with some accuracy, be called slavery. Throughout history, military conquest has been the most common means of enslavement. What distinguished North American slavery, however, was its racial character. By the beginning of the eighteenth century, any African in the English colonies was assumed to be a slave unless he could prove otherwise. Except in exceptional circumstances, not only the original African but his descendants were confined to slave status.

From the earliest days of settlement in North America, the historical record clearly shows that some blacks were free. What it does not show is the process by which African slavery became the widespread institution that it was by 1700. In fact, historians have disagreed on

whether slavery produced racial prejudice or racial prejudice produced slavery—a question that could have vital significance for easing
racial tensions in America today. If, for instance, slavery as an absolute
form of economic inequality led to racial prejudice, then the elimination of economic inequality in the United States might contribute immensely to the elimination of racial prejudice. If, on the other hand,
prejudice preceded slavery, then equal economic opportunity might
not be expected for blacks until the roots of racial prejudice have been
identified and removed.

Historians are only now beginning to explore the nature of slavery
and slave life in the earliest days of English settlement in North America. One of the persistent myths of that period is that Africans imported
to the New World were culturally empty vessels and had to be taught
by the English all those things they would be required to do in their
new life. While this myth is in the process of being exploded, another
problem remains. Most of the studies of slavery treat the institution as
though it were static—the same at all times and in all places. The
article reprinted below, by Ira Berlin, of the University of Maryland,
seriously challenges that position. Using a comparative analysis of three
different geographical sections of colonial America, he shows that over
a period of time three distinct types of Afro-American culture evolved
according to the needs and usages of the three areas. Many of the
subsequent developments in Afro-American history are more fully illuminated by this approach.

T
ime and space are the usual boundaries of historical inquiry.
The last generation of slavery studies in the United States
has largely ignored these critical dimensions but has, instead,
been preoccupied with defining the nature of American slavery, especially as compared with racial bondage elsewhere in the Americas. These
studies have been extraordinarily valuable not only in revealing much
about slave society but also in telling a good deal about free society.
They have been essential to the development of a new understanding
of American life centered on social transformation: the emergence of
bourgeois society in the North with an upward-striving middle class and
an increasingly self-conscious working class and the development of a
plantocracy in the South with a segmented social order and ideals of
interdependence, stability, and hierarchy. But viewing Southern slavery

TIME, SPACE, AND THE EVOLUTION OF AFRO-AMERICAN SOCIETY   By Ira Berlin, in the
American Historical Review, Volume 85 (February 1980), 44–78. Reprinted by permission of the author.

from the point of maturity, dissecting it into component parts, comparing it to other slave societies, and juxtaposing it to free society have produced an essentially static vision of slave culture. This has been especially evident in the studies of Afro-American life. From Stanley M. Elkins's Sambo to John W. Blassingame's Nat-Sambo-Jack typology, scholars of all persuasions have held time constant and ignored the influence of place. Even the most comprehensive recent interpretation of slave life, Eugene D. Genovese's *Roll, Jordan, Roll,* has been more concerned with explicating the dynamic of the patriarchal ideal in the making of Afro-American culture than in explaining its development in time and space. None of the histories written since World War II has equaled the temporal and spatial specificity of U. B. Phillip's *American Negro Slavery.*

Recent interest in the beginnings of slavery on the mainland of British North America, however, has revealed a striking diversity in Afro-American life. During the seventeenth and eighteenth centuries, three distinct slave systems evolved: a Northern nonplantation system and two Southern plantation systems, one around Chesapeake Bay and the other in the Carolina and Georgia lowcountry. Slavery took shape differently in each with important consequences for the growth of black culture and society. The development of these slave societies depended upon the nature of the slave trade and the demographic configurations of blacks and whites as well as upon the diverse character of colonial economy. Thus, while cultural differences between newly arrived Africans and second and third generation Afro-Americans or creoles everywhere provided the basis for social stratification within black society, African-creole differences emerged at different times with different force and even different meaning in the North, the Chesapeake region, and the lowcountry. A careful examination of the diverse development of Afro-American culture in the colonial era yields important clues for an understanding of the full complexity of black society in the centuries that followed.

The nature of slavery and the demographic balance of whites and blacks during the seventeenth and first decades of the eighteenth centuries tended to incorporate Northern blacks into the emerging Euro-American culture, even as whites denied them a place in Northern society. But changes in the character of the slave trading during the middle third of the eighteenth century gave new impetus to African culture and institutions in the Northern colonies. By the American Revolution, Afro-American culture had been integrated into the larger Euro-American one, but black people remained acutely conscious of their African inheritance and freely drew on it in shaping their lives.

Throughout the colonial years, blacks composed a small fraction of the population of New England and the Middle Colonies. Only in New York and Rhode Island did they reach 15 percent of the population. In most Northern colonies the proportion was considerably smaller. At its height the black population totaled 8 percent of the population of New Jersey and less than 4 percent in Massachusetts and Connecticut. But these colony-wide enumerations dilute the presence of blacks and under-estimate the importance of slave labor. In some of the most productive agricultural regions and in the cities, blacks composed a larger share of the population, sometimes constituting as much as one-third of the whole and perhaps one-half of the work force. Although many Northern whites never saw a black slave, others had daily, intimate contact with them. And, although some blacks found it difficult to join together with their former countrymen, others lived in close contact.

The vast majority of Northern blacks lived and worked in the countryside. A few labored in highly capitalized rural industries—tanneries, salt works, and iron furnaces—where they often composed the bulk of the work force, skilled and unskilled. Iron masters, the largest employers of industrial slaves, also were often the largest slaveholders in the North. Pennsylvania iron masters manifested their dependence on slave labor when, in 1727, they petitioned for a reduction in the tariff on slaves so they might keep their furnaces in operation. Bloomeries and forges in other colonies similarly relied on slave labor. But in an overwhelmingly agrarian society only a small proportion of the slave population engaged in industrial labor.

Like most rural whites, most rural blacks toiled as agricultural workers. In southern New England, on Long Island, and in northern New Jersey, which contained the North's densest black populations, slaves tended stock and raised crops for export to the sugar islands. Farmers engaged in provisioning the West Indies with draft animals and foodstuffs were familiar with slavery and had easy access to slaves. Some, like the Barbadian émigrés in northern New Jersey, had migrated from the sugar islands. others, particularly those around Narragansett Bay, styled themselves planters in the West Indian manner. They built great houses, bred race horses, and accumulated slaves, sometimes holding twenty or more bondsmen. But, whatever the aspirations of this commercial gentry, the provisioning trade could not support a plantation regime. Most slaves lived on farms (not plantations), worked at a variety of tasks, and never labored in large gangs. No one in the North suggested that agricultural labor could be done only by black people, a common assertion in the sugar islands and the Carolina lowcountry. In northern New England, the Hudson Valley, and Pennsylvania, the seasonal demands of cereal farming undermined the viability of slavery. For most wheat farmers, as Peter Kalm shrewdly observed, "a Negro or black slave requires too much money at one time," and they relied instead on white indentured servants and free workers to supplement their own labor. Throughout the North's bread basket, even those members of the gentry who could afford the larger capital investment and the concomitant risk that slave ownership entailed generally depended on the labor of indentured servants more than on that of slaves. Fully two-thirds of the bond servants held by the wealthiest farmers in Lancaster and Chester counties, Pennsylvania, were indentured whites rather than chattel blacks. These farmers tended to view their slaves more as status symbols than as agricultural workers. While slaves labored in the fields part of the year, as did nearly everyone, they also spent a large portion of their time working in and around their masters' houses as domestic servants, stable keepers, and gardeners. Significantly, the wills and inventories of Northern slaveholders listed their slaves with other high status objects like clocks and carriages rather than with land or agricultural implements.

The distinct demands of Northern agriculture shaped black life in the countryside. Where the provisioning trade predominated, black men worked as stock minders and herdsmen while black women labored as dairy maids as well as domestics of various kinds. The large number of slaves demanded by the provisioning trade and the ready access to horses and mules it allowed placed black companionship within easy reach of most bondsmen. Such was not always true in the cereal region. Living scattered throughout the countryside on the largest farms and working in the house as often as in the fields, blacks enjoyed neither the mobility nor the autonomy of slaves employed in the provisioning trade. But, if the demands of Northern agriculture affected black life in different ways, almost all rural blacks lived and worked in close proximity to whites. Slaves quickly learned the rudiments of the English language, the Christian religion, the white man's ways. In the North, few rural blacks remained untouched by the larger forces of Euro-American life.

Northern slaves were also disproportionately urban. During the eighteenth century, a fifth to a quarter of the blacks in New York lived in New York City. Portsmouth and Boston contained fully a third of the blacks in New Hampshire and Massachusetts, and nearly half of Rhode Island's black population resided in Newport. Ownership of slaves was almost universal among the urban elite and commonplace among the middling classes as well. On the eve of the Revolution, nearly three-fourths of Boston's wealthiest quartile of propertyholders ranked in the slaveholding class. Fragmentary evidence from earlier in the century suggests that urban slave-ownership had been even more widespread but contracted with the growth of a free working class. Viewed from the top of colonial society, the observation of one visitor that there was "not a house in Boston" that did "not have one or two" slaves might be applied to every Northern city with but slight exaggeration.

Urban slaves generally worked as house servants—cooking, cleaning, tending gardens and stables, and running errands. They lived in back rooms, lofts, closets, and, occasionally, makeshift alley shacks. Under these cramped conditions, few masters held more than one or two slaves. However they might cherish a large retinue of retainers, urban slaveholders rarely had the room to lodge them. Because of the general shortage of space, masters discouraged their slaves from establishing families in the cities. Women with reputations for fecundity found few buyers, and some slaveholders sold their domestics at the first sign of pregnancy. A New York master candidly announced the sale of his cook "because she breeds too fast for her owners to put up with such inconvenience," and others gave away children because they were an unwarranted expense. As a result, black women had few children, and their fertility ratio was generally lower than that of whites. The inability or unwillingness of urban masters to support large households placed a severe strain on black family life. But it also encouraged masters to allow their slaves to live out, hire their own time, and thereby gain a measure of independence and freedom.

Slave hirelings along with those bondsmen owned by merchants, warehouse keepers, and ship chandlers kept Northern cities moving. Working outside their masters' houses, these bondsmen found employment as teamsters, wagoners, and stockmen on the docks and drays and in the warehouses and shops that composed the essential core of the mercantile economy. In addition, many slaves labored in the maritime trades not only as sailors on coasting vessels, but also in the rope walks, shipyards, and sail factories that supported the colonial maritime industry. Generally, the importance of these slaves to the growth of Northern cities increased during the eighteenth century. Urban slavery moved steadily away from the household to the docks, warehouses, and shops, as demonstrated by the growing disproportion of slave men in the urban North. Aside from those skills associated with the maritime trades, however, few slaves entered artisan work. Only a handful could be found in the carriage trades that enjoyed higher status and that offered greater opportunity for an independent livelihood and perhaps the chance to buy freedom.

In the cities as in the countryside, blacks tended to live and work in close proximity to whites. Northern slaves not only gained first-hand knowledge of their masters' world, but they also rubbed elbows with lower-class whites in taverns, cock fights, and fairs where poor people of varying status mingled. If urban life allowed slaves to meet more frequently and enjoy a larger degree of social autonomy than did slavery in the countryside, the cosmopolitan nature of cities speeded the transformation of Africans to Afro-American. Acculturation in the cities of the North was a matter of years, not generations.

For many blacks, the process of cultural transformation was well under way before they stepped off the boat. During the first century of American settlement, few blacks arrived in the North directly from Africa. Although American slavers generally originated in the North, few gave priority to Northern ports. The markets to the south were simply too large and too lucrative. Slaves dribbled into the Northern colonies from the West Indies or the mainland South singly, in twos and threes, or by the score but rarely by the boatload. Some came on special order from merchants or farmers with connections to the West Indian trade. Others arrived on consignment, since few Northern merchants specialized in selling slaves. Many of these were the unsalable "refuse" (as traders contemptuously called them) of larger shipments. Northern slaveholders generally disliked these scourings of the transatlantic trade who, the governor of Massachusetts observed, were "usually the worst servants they have"; they feared that the West Indian re-exports had records of recalcitrance and criminality as well as physical defects. In time, some masters may have come to prefer seasoned slaves because of their knowledge of English, familiarity with work routines, or resistance to New World diseases. But, whatever their preference, Northern colonies could not compete with the wealthier staple-producing colonies for prime African field hands. Before the 1740s, Africans appear to have arrived in the North only when a temporary glut made sale impossible in the West Indies and the mainland South. Even then they did not always remain in the North. When conditions in the plantation colonies changed, merchants re-exported them for a quick profit. The absence of direct importation during the early years and the slow, random, haphazard entry of West Indian creoles shaped the development of black culture in the Northern colonies. While the nature of the slave trade prevented the survival of tribal or even shipboard ties that figured so prominently in Afro-American life in the West Indies and the Lower South, it better prepared blacks to take advantage of the special circumstances of their captivity.

Newly arrived blacks, most already experienced in the New World and familiar with their proscribed status, turned Northern bondage to their advantage where they could. They quickly established a stable family life and, unlike newly imported Africans elsewhere on the continent, increased their numbers by natural means during the first generation. By 1708, the governor of Rhode Island observed that the colony's slaves were "supplied by the offspring of those they have already, which increase daily. . . ." The transplanted creoles also seized the opportunities provided by the complex Northern economy, the relatively close ties of master and slave, and, for many, the independence afforded by urban life. In New Amsterdam, for example, the diverse needs of the Dutch mercantile economy induced the West India Company, the largest slaveholder in the colony, to allow its slaves to live out and work on their own in return for a stipulated amount of labor and an annual tribute. "Half-freedom," as this system came to be called, enlarged black opportunities and allowed for the development of a strong black community. When the West India Company refused to make these privileges hereditary, "half-free" slaves organized and protested, demanding that they be allowed to pass their rights on to their children. Failing that, New Amsterdam slaves pressed their masters in other ways to elevate their children's status. Some, hearing rumors that baptism meant freedom, tried to gain church membership. A Dutch prelate complained that these blacks "wanted nothing else than to deliver their children from bodily slavery, without striving for piety and Christian virtues." Even after the conquering English abolished "half-freedom" and instituted a more rigorous system of racial servitude, blacks continued to use the leverage gained by their prominent role in the city's economy to set standards of treatment well above those in the plantation colonies. Into the eighteenth century, New York slaves informally enjoyed the rights of an earlier era, including the right to hold property of their own. "The Custome of this Country," bristled a frustrated New York master to a West Indian friend, "will not allow us to use our Negroes as you doe in Barbados."

Throughout the North, the same factors that mitigated the harshest features of bondage in New York strengthened the position of slaves in dealing with their masters. Small holdings, close living conditions, and the absence of gang labor drew masters and slaves together. A visitor to Connecticut noted in disgust that slaveowners were "too Indulgent (especially the farmers) to their Slaves, suffering too great a familiarity from them, permitting them to sit at Table and eat with them (as they say to save time) and into the dish goes the black hoof as freely as the white hand." Slaves used knowledge gained at their masters' tables to press for additional privileges: the right to visit friends, live with their families, or hire their own time. One slaveholder reluctantly cancelled the sale of his slaves because of "an invariable indulgence here to permit Slaves of any kind of worth or Character who must change Masters, to choose those Masters," and he could not persuade his slaves "to leave their Country (if I may call it so), their acquaintances & friends." Such indulgences originated not only in the ability of slaves to manipulate their masters to their own benefit, but also from the confidence of slaveholders in their own hegemony. Surety of white dominance, derived from white numerical superiority, complemented the blacks' understanding of how best to bend bondage to their own advantage and to maximize black opportunities within slavery.

During the middle decades of the eighteenth century, the nature of Northern slavery changed dramatically. Growing demand for labor, especially when European wars limited the supply of white indentured servants and when depression sent free workers west in search of new opportunities, increased the importance of slaves in the work force. Between 1732 and 1754, blacks composed fully a third of the immigrants (forced and voluntary) arriving in New York. The new importance of slave labor changed the nature of the slave trade. Merchants who previously took black slaves only on consignment now began to import them directly from Africa, often in large numbers. Before 1741, for example, 70 percent of the slaves arriving in New York originated in the West Indies and other mainland sources and only 30 percent came directly from Africa. After that date, the proportions were reversed. Specializing in the slave trade, African slavers carried many times more slaves than did West Indian traders. Whereas slaves had earlier arrived in small parcels rarely numbering more than a half-dozen, direct shipments from Africa at times now totaled over a hundred and, occasionally, several times that. Slaves increasingly replaced white indentured servants as the chief source of unfree labor not only in the areas that had produced for the provisioning trade, where their pre-eminence had been established earlier in the century, but in the cities as well. In the 1760s, when slave importation into Pennsylvania peaked, blacks composed more than three-quarters of Philadelphia's servant population.

Northern whites generally viewed this new wave of slaves as substitutes for indentured labor. White indentured servants had come as young men without families, and slaves were now imported in much the same way. "For this market they must be young, the younger the better if not quite children," declared a New York merchant. "Males are best." As a result, the sex ratio of the black population, which earlier in the century had been roughly balanced, suddenly swung heavily in favor of men. In Massachusetts, black men outnumbered black women nearly two to one. Elsewhere sex ratios of 130 or more became commonplace. Such sexual imbalance and the proscription of interracial marriage made it increasingly difficult for blacks to enjoy normal family lives. As the birth rate slipped, mortality rates soared, especially in the cities where newly arrived blacks appeared to be concentrated. Since most slaves came without any previous exposure to New World diseases, the harsh Northern winters took an ever higher toll. Blacks died by the score; the crude death rate of Philadelphia and Boston blacks in the 1750s and 1760s was well over sixty per thousand, almost double that of whites. In its demographic outline, Northern slavery at mid-century often bore a closer resemblance to the horrors of the West Indies during the height of a sugar boom than to the relatively benign bondage of the earlier years.

Whites easily recovered from this demographic disaster by again switching to European indentured servants and then to free labor as supplies became available, and, as the influx of slaves subsided, black life also regained its balance. But the transformation of Northern slavery had a lasting influence on the development of Afro-American culture. Although the Northern black population remained predominantly Afro-American after nearly a century of slow importation from the West Indies and steady natural increase, the direct entry of Africans into Northern society reoriented black culture.

Even before the redirection of the Northern slave trade, those few Africans in the Northern colonies often stood apart from the creole majority. While Afro-American slaves established precedents and customs, which they then drew upon to improve their condition, Africans tended to stake all to recapture the world they had lost. Significantly,

Africans, many of whom did not yet speak English and still carried tribal names, composed the majority of the participants in the New York slave insurrection of 1712, even though most of the city's blacks were creoles. The division between Africans and Afro-Americans became more visible as the number of Africans increased after mid-century. Not only did creoles and Africans evince different aspirations, but their life-chances—as reflected in their resistance to disease and their likelihood of establishing a family—also diverged sharply. Greater visibility may have sharpened differences between creoles and Africans, but Africans were too few in number to stand apart for long. Whatever conflicts different life-chances and beliefs created, whites paid such distinctions little heed in incorporating the African minority into their slaveholdings. The propensity of Northern whites to lump blacks together mitigated intraracial differences. Rather than permanently dividing blacks, the entry of Africans into Northern society gave a new direction to Afro-American culture.

Newly arrived Africans reawakened Afro-Americans to their African past by providing direct knowledge of West African society. Creole blacks began to combine their African inheritance into their own evolving culture. In some measure, the easy confidence of Northern whites in their own dominance speeded the syncretization of African and creole culture by allowing blacks to act far more openly than slaves in the plantation colonies. Northern blacks incorporated African culture into their own Afro-American culture not only in the common-place and unconscious way that generally characterizes the transit of culture but also with a high degree of consciousness and deliberateness. They designated their churches "African," and they called themselves "Sons of Africa." They adopted African forms to maximize their freedom, to choose their leaders, and, in general, to give shape to their lives. This new African influence was manifested most fully in Negro election day, a ritual festival of role reversal common throughout West Africa and celebrated openly by blacks in New England and a scattering of places in the Middle Colonies.

The celebration of Negro election day took a variety of forms, but everywhere it was a day of great merrymaking that drew blacks from all over the countryside. "All the various languages of Africa, mixed with broken and ludicrous English, filled the air, accompanied with the music of the fiddle, tambourine, the banjo, [and] drum," recalled an observer of the festival in Newport. Negro election day culminated with the selection of black kings, governors, and judges. These officials sometimes held symbolic power over the whole community and real power over the black community. While the black governors held court, adjudicating minor disputes, the blacks paraded and partied, dressed in their masters' clothes and mounted on their masters' horses. Such role reversal, like similar status inversions in Africa and elsewhere, confirmed rather than challenged the existing order, but it also gave blacks an opportunity to express themselves more fully than the narrow boundaries of slavery ordinarily allowed. Negro election day permitted a seeming release from bondage, and it also provided a mechanism for blacks to recognize and honor their own notables. Most important, it established a framework for the development of black politics. In the places where Negro election day survived into the nineteenth century, its politics shaped the politics within the black community and merged with partisan divisions of American society. Slaves elsewhere in the New World also celebrated this holiday, but whites in the plantation colonies found the implications of role reversal too frightening to allow even symbolically. Northern whites, on the other hand, not only aided election day materially but sometimes joined in themselves. Still, white cooperation was an important but not the crucial element in the rise of Negro election day. Its origin in the 1740s and 1750s suggests how the entry of Africans reoriented Afro-American culture at a formative point in its development.

African acculturation in the Northern colonies at once incorporated blacks into American society and sharpened the memory of their African past and their desire to preserve it. While small numbers and close proximity to whites forced blacks to conform to the forms of the dominant Euro-American culture, the confidence of whites in their own hegemony allowed black slaves a good measure of autonomy. In this context it is not surprising that a black New England sea captain established the first back-to-Africa movement in mainland North America.

Unlike African acculturation in the Northern colonies, the transformation of Africans into Afro-Americans in the Carolina and Georgia lowcountry was a slow, halting process whose effects resonated differently within black society. While creolization created a unified Afro-American population in the North, it left lowcountry blacks deeply divided. A minority lived and worked in close proximity to whites in the cities that lined the rice coast, fully conversant with the most cosmopolitan sector of lowland society. A portion of this urban elite, increasingly light-skinned, pressed for further incorporation into white society, confident they could compete as equals. The mass of black people, however, remained physically separated and psychologically estranged from the Anglo-American world and culturally closer to Africa than any other blacks on continental North America.

The sharp division was not immediately apparent. At first it seemed that African acculturation in the Lower South would follow the Northern pattern. The first blacks arrived in the lowcountry in small groups from the West Indies. Often they accompanied their owners and, like them, frequently immigrated in small family groups. Many had already spent considerable time on the sugar islands, and some had doubtless been born there. Most spoke English, understood European customs and manners, and, as their language skills and family ties suggest, had made the difficult adjustment to the conditions of black life in the New World.

As in the Northern colonies, whites dominated the population of the pioneer Carolina settlement. Until the end of the seventeenth century, they composed better than two-thirds of the settlers. During this period and into the first years of the eighteenth century, most white slaveholders engaged in mixed farming and stock raising for export to the West Indian islands where they had originated. Generally, they lived on small farms, held few slaves, and worked closely with their bond servants. Even when they hated and feared blacks and yearned for the prerogatives of West Indian slave masters, the demands of the primitive, labor-scarce economy frequently placed master and slave face-to-face on opposite sides of a sawbuck. Such direct, equalitarian confrontations tempered white domination and curbed slavery's harshest features.

White dependence on blacks to defend their valuable lowland beachhead reinforced this "sawbuck equality." The threat of invasion by the Spanish and French to the south and Indians to the west hung ominously over the lowcountry during its formative years. To bolster colonial defenses, officials not only drafted slaves in time of war but also regularly enlisted them into the militia. In 1710 Thomas Nairne, a knowledgeable Carolina Indian agent, observed that "enrolled in our Militia [are] a considerabe Number of active, able, Negro Slaves; and Law gives every one of those his freedom, who in Time of an Invasion kills an Enemy." Between the settlement of the Carolinas and the conclusion of the Yamasee War almost fifty years later, black soldiers helped fend off every military threat to the colony. Although only a handful of slaves won their freedom through military service, the continued presence of the armed, militarily experienced slaves weighed heavily on whites. During the Yamasee War, when the governor of Virginia demanded one Negro woman in return for each Virginia soldier sent to defend South Carolina, the beleaguered Carolinians rejected the offer, observing that it was "impracticable to Send Negro Women in their Roomes by reason of the Discontent such Usage would have given their husbands to have their wives taken from them which might have occasioned a Revolt."

The unsettled conditions that made the lowcountry vulnerable to external enemies strengthened the slave's hand in other ways. Confronted by an overbearing master or a particularly onerous assignment, many blacks took to the woods. Truancy was an easy alternative in the thinly settled, heavily forested lowcountry. Forest dangers generally sent truant slaves back to their owners, but the possibility of another flight induced slaveholders to accept them with few questions asked. Some bondsmen, however, took advantage of these circumstances to escape permanently. Maroon colonies existed throughout the lowland swamps and into the backcountry. Maroons lived a hard life, perhaps more difficult than slaves, and few blacks chose to join these outlaw bands. But the ease of escape and the existence of a maroon alternative made masters chary about abusing their slaves.

The transplanted African's intimate knowledge of the subtropical lowlands environment—especially when compared to the Englishman's dense ignorance—magnified white dependence on blacks and enlarged black opportunities within the slave regime. Since the geography, climate, and topography of the lowcountry more closely resembled the West African than the English countryside, African not European technology and agronomy often guided lowland development. From the first, whites depended on blacks to identify useful flora and fauna and to define appropriate methods of production. Blacks, adapting African techniques to the circumstances of the Carolina wilderness, shaped the lowland cattle industry and played a central role in the introduction and development of the region's leading staple. In short, transplanted Englishmen learned as much or more from transplanted Africans as did the former Africans from them. While whites eventually appropriated this knowledge and turned it against black people to rivet tighter the bonds of servitude, white dependence on African know-how operated during those first years to place blacks in managerial as well as menial positions and thereby permitted blacks to gain a larger share of the fruits of the new land than whites might otherwise allow. In such circumstances, white domination made itself felt, but both whites and blacks incorporated much of West African culture into their new way of life.

The structure of the fledgling lowland economy and the demands of stock raising, with deerskins as the dominant "crop" during the initial years of settlement, allowed blacks to stretch white military and economic dependence into generous grants of autonomy. On the small farms and isolated cowpens (hardly plantations by even the most latitudinous definition), rude frontier conditions permitted only perfunctory supervision and the most elementary division of labor. Most units were simply too small to employ overseers, single out specialists, or benefit from the economies of gang labor. White, red, and black laborers of varying legal status worked shoulder to shoulder, participating in the dullest drudgery as well as the most sophisticated undertakings. Rather than skilled artisans or prime field hands, most blacks could best be characterized as jacks-of-all-trades. Since cattle roamed freely through the woods until fattened for market, moreover, black cowboys—suggestively called "cattle chasers"—moved with equal freedom through the countryside, gaining full familiarity with the terrain. The autonomy of the isolated cowpen and the freedom of movement stock raising allowed made a mockery of the total dominance that chattel bondage implied. Slaves set the pace of work, defined standards of workmanship, and divided labor among themselves, doubtless leaving a good measure of time for their own use. The insistence of many hard-pressed frontier slaveowners that their slaves raise their own provisions legitimated this autonomy. By law, slaves had Sunday to themselves. Time allowed for gardening, hunting, and fishing both affirmed slave independence and supplemented the slave diet. It also enabled some industrious blacks to produce a small surplus and to participate in the colony's internal economy, establishing an important precedent for black life in the lowcountry.

Such independence burdened whites. They complained bitterly and frequently about blacks traveling unsupervised through the countryside, congregating in the woods, and visiting Charles Town to carouse, conspire, or worse. Yet knowledge of the countryside and a willingness to take the initiative in hunting down cattle or standing up to Spaniards were precisely the characteristics that whites valued in their slaves. They complained but they accepted. Indeed, to resolve internal disputes within their own community, whites sometimes promoted black participation in the affairs of the colony far beyond the bounds later permitted slaves or even black freemen. "For this last election," grumbled several petitioners in 1706, "Jews, Strangers, Sailors, Servants, Negroes, & almost every French Man in Craven & Berkly County came down to elect, & their votes were taken." Such breaches of what became an iron law of Southern racial policy suggest how the circumstances of the pioneer lowcountry life shrank the social as well as the cultural distance between transplanted Africans and the mélange of European settlers. During the first generations of settlement, Afro-American and Anglo-American culture and society developed along parallel lines with a large degree of overlap.

If the distinction between white and black culture remained small in the lowcountry, so too did differences within black society. The absence of direct importation of African slaves prevented the emergence of African-creole differences; and, since few blacks gained their liberty during those years, differences in status within the black community were almost nonexistent. The small radius of settlement and the ease of water transportation, moreover, placed most blacks within easy reach of Charles Town. A "city" of several dozen rude buildings where the colonial legislature met in a tavern could hardly have impressed slaves as radically different from their own primitive quarters. Town slaves, for their part, doubtless had first-hand familiarity with farm work as few masters could afford the luxury of placing their slaves in livery.

Thus, during the first years of settlement, black life in the lowcountry, like black life in the North, evolved toward a unified Afro-American culture. Although their numbers combined with other circumstances to allow Carolina blacks a larger role in shaping their culture than that enjoyed by blacks in the North, there remained striking similarities in the early development of Afro-American life in both regions. During the last few years of the seventeenth century, however, changes in

economy and society undermined these commonalities and set the development of lowcountry Afro-American life on a distinctive course.

The discovery of exportable staples, first naval stores and then rice and
indigo, transformed the low country as surely as the sugar revolution
transformed the West Indies. Under the pressure of the riches that staple production provided, planters banished the white yeomanry to
the hinterland, consolidated small farms into large plantations, and carved new plantations out of the malaria-ridden swamps. Before long,
black slaves began pouring into the region and, sometime during the
first decade of the eighteenth century, white numerical superiority gave
way to the lowcountry's distinguishing demographic characteristic: the
black majority.

Black numerical dominance grew rapidly during the eighteenth
century. By the 1720s, blacks outnumbered whites by more than two
to one in South Carolina. In the heavily settled plantation parishes
surrounding Charles Town, blacks enjoyed a three to one majority. That
margin grew steadily until the disruptions of the Revolutionary era, but
it again increased thereafter. Georgia, where metropolitan policies reined
planter ambition, remained slaveless until mid-century. Once restrictions on slavery were removed, planters imported blacks in large numbers, giving lowland Georgia counties considerable black majorities.

Direct importation of slaves from Africa provided the impetus to
the growth of the black majority. Some West Indian Afro-Americans
continued to enter the lowcountry, but they shrank to a small fraction
of the whole. As African importation increased, Charles Town took its
place as the largest mainland slave mart and the center of the lowland
slave trade. Almost all of the slaves in Carolina and later in Georgia—
indeed, fully 40 percent of all pre-Revolutionary black arrivals in mainland North America—entered at Charles Town. The enormous number
of slaves allowed slave masters a wide range of choices. Lowcountry
planters developed preferences far beyond the usual demands for healthy
adult and adolescent males and concerned themselves with the regional
and tribal origins of their purchases. Some planters may have based
their choices on long experience and a considered understanding of the
physical and social character of various African nations. But, for the
most part, these preferences were shallow ethnic stereotypes. Coromantees revolted; Angolans ran away; Iboes destroyed themselves. At other
times, lowland planters apparently preferred just those slaves they did
not get, perhaps because all Africans made unsatisfactory slaves and the
unobtainable ones looked better at a distance. Although lowcountry
slave masters desired Gambian people above all others, Angolans composed a far larger proportion of the African arrivals. But, however confused or mistaken in their beliefs, planters held them firmly and, in
some measure, put them into practice. "Gold Coast and Gambia's are
the best, next to them the Windward Coast are prefer'd to Angola's,"

observed a Charles Town merchant in describing the most salable mixture. "There must not be a Callabar amongst them." Planter preferences informed lowcountry slave traders and, to a considerable degree, determined the tribal origins of lowland blacks.

Whatever their origins, rice cultivation shaped the destiny of African people arriving at Charles Town. Although the production of pitch and tar played a pivotal role in the early development of the staple-based economy in South Carolina, rice quickly became the dominant plantation crop. Rice cultivation evolved slowly during the late seventeenth and early eighteenth centuries as planters, aided by knowledgeable blacks, mastered the complex techniques necessary for commercial production. During the first half of the eighteenth century, rice culture was limited to the inland swamps, where slave-built dikes controlled the irrigation of low-lying rice fields. But by mid-century planters had discovered how to regulate the tidal floods to irrigate and drain their fields. Rice production moved to the tidal swamps that lined the region's many rivers and expanded greatly. By the beginning of the nineteenth century, the rice coast stretched from Cape Fear in North Carolina to the Satilla River in Georgia. Throughout the lowcountry, rice was king.

The relatively mild slave regime of the pioneer years disappeared as rice cultivation expanded. Slaves increasingly lived in large units, and they worked in field gangs rather than at a variety of tasks. The strict requirements of rice production set the course of their work. And rice was a hard master. For a large portion of the year, slaves labored knee deep in brackish muck under the hot tropical sun; and, even after the fields were drained, the crops laid-by, and the grain threshed, there were canals to clear and dams to repair. By mid-century planters had also begun to grow indigo on the upland sections of their estates. Indigo complemented rice in its seasonal requirements, and it made even heavier labor demands The ready availability of African imports compounded the new harsh realities of plantation slavery by cheapening black life in the eyes of many masters. As long as the slave trade remained open, they skimped on food, clothing, and medical attention for their slaves, knowing full well that substitutes could be easily had. With the planters' reliance on male African imports, slaves found it increasingly difficult to establish and maintain a normal family life. Brutal working conditions, the disease-ridden lowland environment, and the open slave trade made for a deadly combination. Slave birth rates fell steadily during the middle years of the eighteenth century and mortality rates rose sharply. Between 1730 and 1760, deaths outnumbered births among blacks and only African importation allowed for continued population growth. Not until the eve of the Revolution did the black population begin again to reproduce naturally.

As the lowcountry plantation system took shape, the great slave masters retreated to the cities of the region; their evacuation of the countryside was but another manifestation of the growing social and cultural distance between them and their slaves. The streets of Charles Town, and, later, of Beufort, Georgetown, Savannah, Darien, and Wilmington sprouted great new mansions as planters fled the malarial lowlands and the black majority. By the 1740s, urban life in the lowcountry had become attractive enough that men who made their fortunes in rice and slaves no longer returned home to England in the West Indian tradition. Instead, through intermarriage and business connections, they began to weave their disparate social relations into a close-knit ruling class, whose self-consciousness and pride of place became legendary. Charles Town, as the capital of this new elite, grew rapidly. Between 1720 and 1740 its population doubled, and it nearly doubled again by the eve of the Revolution to stand at about twelve thousand. With its many fine houses, its great churches, its shops packed with luxury goods, Charles Town's prosperity bespoke the maturation of the lowland plantation system and the rise of the planter class.

Planters, ensconced in their new urban mansions, their pockets lined with the riches rice produced, ruled their lowcountry domains through a long chain of command: stewards located in the smaller rice ports, overseers stationed near or on their plantations, and plantation-based black drivers. But their removal from the plantation did not breed the callous indifference of West Indian absenteeism. For one thing, they were no more than a day's boat ride away from their estates. Generally, they resided on their plantations during the non-malarial season. Their physical removal from the direct supervision of slave labor and the leisure their urban residences afforded appear to have sharpened their concern for "their people" and bred a paternalist ideology that at once legitimated their rule and informed all social relations.

The lowcountry plantation system with its urban centers, its black majority, its dependence on "salt-water" slaves transformed black culture and society just as it reshaped the white world. The unified Afro-American culture and society that had evolved during the pioneer years disappeared as rice cultivation spread. In its place a sharp division developed between an increasingly urban creole and a plantation-based African population. The growth of plantation slavery not only set blacks further apart from whites, it also sharply divided blacks.

One branch of black society took shape within the bounds of the region's cities and towns. If planters lived removed from most slaves, they maintained close, intimate relations with some. The masters' great wealth, transient life, and seasonal urban residence placed them in close contact with house servants who kept their estates, boatmen who carried messages and supplies back and forth to their plantations, and urban artisans who made city life not only possible but comfortable. In addition, coastal cities needed large numbers of workers to transport and process the plantation staples, to serve the hundreds of ships that annually visited the lowcountry, and to satisfy the planters' newly acquired taste for luxury goods. Blacks did most of this work. Throughout the eighteenth century they composed more than half the population of Charles Town and other lowcountry ports. Probably nothing arrived or left these cities without some black handling it. Black artisans also played a large role in urban life. Master craftsmen employed them in every variety of work. A visitor to Charles Town found that even barbers "are supported in idleness & ease by their negroes. . . ; & in fact many of the mechaniks bear nothing more of their trade than the name." Although most black artisans labored along the waterfront as shipwrights, ropemakers, and coopers, lowcountry blacks—unlike blacks in Northern cities—also entered the higher trades, working as gold beaters, sliversmiths, and cabinetmakers. In addition, black women gained control over much of the marketing in the lowcountry ports, mediating between slave-grown produce in the countryside and urban consumption. White tradesmen and journeymen periodically protested against slave competition, but planters, master craftsmen, and urban consumers who benefited from black labor and services easily brushed aside these objections.

Mobile, often skilled, and occasionally literate, urban slaves understood the white world. They used their knowledge to improve their position within lowcountry society even while the condition of the mass of black people deteriorated in the wake of the rice revolution. Many urban creoles not only retained the independence of the earlier years but enlarged upon it. They hired their own time, earned wages from "overwork," kept market stalls, and sometimes even opened shops. Some lived apart from their masters and rented houses of their own, paying their owners a portion of their earnings in return for *de facto* freedom. Such liberty enabled a few black people to keep their families intact and perhaps even accumulate property for themselves. The small black communities that developed below the Bluff in Savannah and in Charles Town's Neck confirm the growing independence of urban creoles.

The incongruous prosperity of urban bondsmen jarred whites. By hiring their own time, living apart from their masters, and controlling their own family life, these blacks forcibly and visibly claimed the white man's privileges. Perhaps no aspect of their behavior was as obvious and, hence, as galling as their elaborate dress. While plantation slaves—men and women—worked striped to the waist wearing no more than loin cloths (thereby confirming the white man's image of savagery), urban slaves appropriated their masters' taste for fine clothes and often the clothes themselves. Lowcountry legislators enacted various sumptuary regulations to restrain the slaves' penchant for dressing above their station. The South Carolina Assembly once even considered prohibiting masters from giving their old clothes to their slaves. But hand-me-downs were clearly not the problem as long as slaves earned wages and had easy access to the urban marketplace. Frustrated by the realities of urban slavery, lawmakers passed and repassed the old regulations to little effect. On the eve of the Revolution, a Charles Town Grand Jury continued to bemoan the fact that the "Law for preventing the excessive and costly Apparel of Negroes and other Slaves in this province (especially in *Charles Town*) [was] not being put into Force."

Most of these privileged bondsmen appear to have been creoles with long experience in the New World. Although some Africans entered urban society, the language skills and the mastery of the complex interpersonal relations needed in the cities gave creoles a clear advantage over Africans in securing elevated positions within the growing urban enclaves. To be sure, their special status was far from "equal." No matter how essential their function or intimate their interaction, their relations with whites no longer smacked of the earlier "sawbuck equality." Instead, these relations might better be characterized as paternal, sometimes literally so.

Increasingly during the eighteenth century, blacks gained privileged positions within lowcountry society as a result of intimate, usually sexual, relations with white slave masters. Like slaveholders everywhere, lowland planters assumed that sexual access to slave women was simply another of the master's prerogatives. Perhaps because their origin was West Indian or perhaps because their dual residence separated them from their white wives part of the year, white men established sexual liaisons with black women frequently and openly. Some white men and black women formed stable, long-lasting unions, legitimate in everything but law. More often than other slaveholders on continental British North America, lowcountry planters recognized and provided for their mulatto offspring, and, occasionally, extended legal freedom. South Carolina's small free Negro population, almost totally confined to Charles Town, was largely the product of such relations. Light-skinned people of color enjoyed special standing in the lowcountry ports, as they did in the West Indies, and whites occasionally looked the other way when such creoles passed into the dominant caste. But even when the planters did not grant legal freedom, they usually assured the elevated standing of their mulatto scions by training them for artisan trades or placing them in household positions. If the countryside was "blackened" by African imports, Charles Town and the other lowcountry ports exhibited a mélange of "colored" peoples.

While one branch of black society stood so close to whites that its members sometimes disappeared into the white population, most plantation slaves remained alienated from the world of their masters, physically and culturally. Living in large units often numbering in the hundreds on plantations that they had carved out of the malarial swamps and working under the direction of black drivers, the black majority gained only fleeting knowledge of Anglo-American culture. What they knew did not encourage them to learn more. Instead, they strove to widen the distance between themselves and their captors. In doing so, they too built upon the large degree of autonomy black people had earlier enjoyed.

In the pioneer period, many masters required slaves to raise their own provisions. Slaves regularly kept small gardens and tended barn-yard fowl to maintain themselves, and they often marketed their surplus. Blacks kept these prerogatives with the development of the plantation system. In fact, the growth of lowcountry towns, the increasing specialization in staple production, and the comparative absence of nonslaveholding whites enlarged the market for slave-grown produce. Planters, of course, disliked the independence truck gardening afforded plantation blacks and the tendency of slaves to confuse their owners' produce with their own, but the ease of water transportation and the absence of white supervision made it difficult to prevent.

To keep their slaves on the plantation, some planters traded directly with their bondsmen, bartering manufactured goods for slave produce. Henry Laurens, a planter who described himself as a "factor" for his slaves, exchanged some "very gay Wastcoats which some of the Negro Men may want" for grain at "10 Bushels per Wastcoat." Later, learning that a plantation under his supervision was short of provisions, he authorized the overseer "to purchase of your own Negroes all that you know Lawfully belongs to themselves at the lowest price they will sell it for." As Laurens's notation suggests, planters found benefits in slave participation in the lowcountry's internal economy, but the small profits gained by bartering with their bondsmen only strengthened the slaves' customary right to their garden and barnyard fowl. Early in the nineteenth century, when Charles C. Pinckney decided to produce his own provisions, he purchased breeding stock from his slaves. By the Civil War, lowland slaves controlled considerably personal property—flocks of ducks, pigs, milch cows, and occasionally horses—often the product of stock that had been in their families for generations. For the most part, slave property holding remained small during the eighteenth century. But it helped insulate plantation blacks from the harsh conditions of primitive rice production and provide social distance from their masters' domination.

The task system, a mode of work organization peculiar to the low-country, further strengthened black autonomy. Under the task system, a slave's daily routine was sharply defined: so many rows of rice to be sowed, so much grain to be threshed, or so many lines of canal to be cleared. Such a precise definition of work suggests that city-bound planters found it almost impossible to keep their slaves in the fields from sunup to sundown. With little direct white supervision, slaves and their black foremen conspired to preserve a large portion of the day for their own use, while meeting their masters' minimum work requirements. Struggle over the definition of a task doubtless continued throughout the formative years of the lowcountry plantation system and after, but by the end of the century certain lines had been drawn. Slaves generally left the field sometime in the early afternoon, a practice that protected them from the harsh afternoon sun and allowed them time to tend their own gardens and stock. Like participation in the lowcountry's internal economy, the task system provided slaves with a large measure of control over their own lives.

The autonomy generated by both the task system and truck gardening provided the material basis for lowland black culture. Within the confines of the overwhelmingly black countryside, African culture survived well. The continual arrival of Africans into the lowcountry renewed and refreshed slave knowledge of West African life. In such a setting blacks could hardly lose their past. The distinctive pattern of the lowland slave trade, moreover, heightened the impact of the newly arrived Africans on the evolution of black culture. While slaves dribbled into the North through a multiplicity of ports, they poured into lowcountry through a single city. The large, unicentered slave trade and the large slaveholding units assured the survival not only of the common denominators of West African culture but also many of its particular tribal and national forms. Planter preferences or perhaps the chance ascendancy of one group sometimes allowed specific African cultures to reconstitute themselves within the plantation setting. To be sure, Africans changed in the lowcountry. Even where blacks enjoyed numerical superiority and a considerable degree of autonomy, they could no more transport their culture unchanged than could their masters. But lowcountry blacks incorporated more of West African culture—as reflected in their language, religion, work patterns, and much else—into their new lives than did other black Americans. Throughout the eighteenth century and into the nineteenth, lowcountry blacks continued to work the land, name their children, and communicate through word and song in a manner that openly combined African traditions with the circumstances of plantation life.

The new pattern of creolization that developed following the rice revolution smashed the emerging hemogeneity of black life in the first years of settlement and left lowcountry blacks deeply divided. One branch of black culture evolved in close proximity to whites. Urban, often skilled, well-traveled, and increasingly American-born, creoles knew white society well, and they used their knowledge to better themselves. Some, clearly a well-connected minority, pressed for incorporation into the white world. They urged missionary groups to admit their children to school and later petitioned lawmakers to allow their testimony in court, carefully adding that they did not expect full equality with whites. Plantation slaves shared few of the assimilationist aspirations of urban creoles. By their dress, language, and work routine, they lived in a world apart. Rather than demand incorporation into white society, they yearned only to be left alone. Within the quarter, aided by their numerical dominance, their plantation-based social hierarchy, and their continued contact with Africa, they developed their own distinctive culture, different not only from that of whites but also from the cosmopolitan world of their Afro-American bretheren. To be sure, there were connections between the black majority and the urban creoles. Many—market women, jobbing artisans, and boatmen—moved easily between these two worlds, and most blacks undoubtedly learned something of the other world through chance encounters, occasional visits, and word of mouth. Common white oppression continually shrank the social distance that the distinctive experience created, but by the eve of the Revolution, deep cultural differences separated those blacks who sought to improve their lives through incorporation into the white world and those who determined to disregard the white man's ways. If the movement from African to creole obliterated cultural differences among Northern blacks, creolization fractured black society in the lowcountry.

Cultural distinctions between Africans and Afro-Americans developed in the Chesapeake as well, although the dimension of differences between African and creole tended to be time rather than space. Unlike in the lowcountry, white planters did not promote the creation of a distinctive group whose origins, function, and physical appearance distinguished them from the mass of plantation slaves and offered them hope, however faint, of eventual incorporation into white society. And, compared to the North, African immigration into the Chesapeake came relatively early in the process of cultural transformation. As a result, African-creole differences disappeared with time and a single, unified Afro-American culture slowly emerged in the Chesapeake.

As in the lowcountry, little distinguished black and white laborers during the early years of settlement. Most of the first blacks brought into the Chesapeake region were West Indian creoles who bore English or Spanish surnames and carried records of baptism. Along the James, as along the Cooper, the demands of pioneer life at times operated to strengthen the slaves' bargaining position. Some blacks set the condition of their labor, secured their family life, participated in the region's internal economy, and occasionally bartered for their liberty. This, of course, did not save most black people from the brutal exploitation that almost all propertyless men and women faced as planters squeezed the last pound of profit from the tobacco economy. The blacks' treatment at the hands of planters differed little from that of white bound labor in large measure because it was difficult to treat people more brutally. While the advantages of this peculiar brand of equality may have been lost on its beneficiaries, those blacks who were able to complete their terms of servitude quickly joined whites in the mad scramble for land, servants, and status.

Many did well. During the seventeenth century, black freemen could be found throughout the region owning land, holding servants, and occasionally attaining minor offices. Like whites, they accumulated property, sued their neighbors, and passed their estates to their children. In 1651, Anthony Johnson, the best known of these early Negro freemen, received a two-hundred-and-fifty-acre headright for importing five persons into Virginia. John Johnson, a neighbor and probably a relative, did even better, earning five hundred and fifty acres for bringing eleven persons into the colony. Both men owned substantial farms on the Eastern Shore, held servants, and left their heirs sizable estates. As established members of their communities, they enjoyed the rights of citizens. When a servant claiming his freedom fled Anthony Johnson's plantation and took refuge with a nearby white farmer, Johnson took his neighbor to court and won the return of his servant along with damages against the white man.

The class rather than racial basis of early Chesapeake society enabled many black men to compete successfully for that scarcest of all New World commodities: the affection of white women. Bastardy lists indicated that white female servants ignored the strictures against what white lawmakers labeled "shameful" and "unnatural" acts and joined together with men of their own condition regardless of color. Fragmentary evidence from various parts of seventeenth-century Virginia reveals that approximately one-quarter to one-third of the bastard children born to white women were mulattoes. The commonplace nature of these interracial unions might have been the reason why one justice legally sanctified the marriage of Hester, an English servant woman, to James Tate, a black slave. Some successful, property-owning whites and blacks also intermarried. In Virginia's Northampton county, Francis Payne, a Negro freeman, married a white woman, who later remarried a white man after Payne's death. William Greensted, a white attorney who represented Elizabeth Key, a mulatto woman, in her successful suit for her freedom, later married her. In 1691, when the Virginia General Assembly finally ruled against the practice, some propertied whites found the legislation novel and obnoxious enough to muster a protest.

By the middle of the seventeenth century, Negro freemen sharing and fulfilling the same ideals and aspirations that whites held were no anomaly in the Chesapeake region. An Eastern Shore tax list of 1668 counted nearly a third of black tithables free. If most blacks did not escape the tightening noose of enslavement, they continued to live and work under conditions not much different from white servants. Throughout the seventeenth and into the first decades of the eighteenth century, black and white servants ran away together, slept together, and, upon occasion, stood shoulder to shoulder against the weighty champions of established authority. Thus viewed from the first years of settlement—the relatively small number of backs, their creole origins, and the initial success of some in establishing a place in society—black acculturation in the Chesapeake appeared to be following the nonplantation pattern of the Northern colonies and the pioneer lowcountry.

The emergence of a planter class and its consolidation of power during a series of political crises in the middle years of the seventeenth century transformed black life in the Chesapeake and threatened this pattern of cultural change. Following the legalization of slavery in the

1660s, black slaves slowly but steadily replaced white indentured servants as the main source of plantation labor. By 1700, blacks made up more than half the agricultural work force in Virginia and, since the great planters could best afford to purchase slaves, blacks composed an even larger share of the workers on the largest estates. Increased reliance on slave labor quickly outstripped West Indian supplies. Beginning in the 1680s, Africans entered the region in increasingly large numbers. The proportion of blacks born in Africa grew steadily throughout the waning years of the seventeenth century, so that by the first decade of the eighteenth century, Africans composed some three-quarters of the region's blacks. Unlike the lowcountry, African imports never threatened the Chesapeake's overall white numerical superiority, but by the beginning of the eighteenth century they dominated black society. Some eighty years after the first blacks arrived at Jamestown and some forty years after the legalization of slavery, African importation profoundly transformed black life.

Slave conditions deteriorated as their numbers increased. With an eye for a quick profit, planters in the Chesapeake imported males disproportionately. Generally men outnumbered women more than two to one on Chesapeake slavers. Wildly imbalanced sex ratios undermined black family life. Physically spent and emotionally drained by the rigors of the Middle Passage, African woman had few children. Thus, as in the North and the Carolina lowlands, the black birth rate fell and mortality rate surged upward with the commencement of direct African importation.

The hard facts of life and death in the Chesapeake region distinguished creoles and Africans at the beginning of the eighteenth century. The demands of the tobacco economy enlarged these differences in several ways. Generally, planters placed little trust in newly arrived Africans with their strange tongues and alien customs. While they assigned creoles to artisanal duties on their plantations and to service within their households, they sent Africans to the distant, upland quarters where the slaves did the dull, backbreaking work of clearing the land and tending tobacco. The small size of these specialized upcountry units, their isolation from the mainstream of Chesapeake life, and their rude frontier conditions made these largely male compounds lonely, unhealthy places that narrowed men's vision. The dynamics of creole life, however, broadened black understanding of life in the New World. Traveling freely through the countryside as artisans, watermen, and domestic servants, creoles gained in confidence as they mastered the terrain, perfected their English, and learned about Christianity and other cultural modes that whites equated with civilization. Knowledge of the white world enabled black creoles to manipulate their masters to their own advantage. If Afro-Americans became increasingly knowledgeable about their circumstances and confident of their ability to deal with them, Africans remained provincials, limited by the narrow alternatives of plantation life.

As in the lowcountry and the Northern colonies, Africans in the Chesapeake strove to escape whites, while creoles used their knowledge of white society for their own benefit. These cultural differences, which were reflected in all aspects of black life, can be seen most clearly in the diverse patterns of resistance. Africans ran away toward the back country and isolated swamps. They generally moved in groups that included women and children, despite the hazards such groups entailed for a successful escape. Their purpose was to recreate the only society they knew free from white domination. In 1727, Governor William Gooch of Virginia reported that about a dozen slaves had left a new plantation near the falls of the James River. They headed west and settled near Lexington, built houses, and planted a crop before being retaken. But Afro-Americans ran away alone, usually with the hope of escaping into American society. Moving toward the areas of heaviest settlement, they found refuge in the thick network of black kinship that covered the countryside and sold their labor to white yeomen with few questions asked. While the possibility of passing as free remained small in the years before the Revolution, the creoles' obvious confidence in their ability to integrate themselves into American society stands in stark contrast to that of Africans, who sought first to flee it.

As reflected in the mode of resistance, place of residence, occupation, and much else, Africans and creoles developed distinctive patterns of behavior and belief. To a degree, whites recognized these differences. They stigmatized Africans as "outlandish" and noted how creoles "affect our language, habits, and customs." They played on African-creole differences to divide blacks from each other, and they utilized creole skills to maximize the benefits of slave labor. But this recognition did not elevate creoles over Africans in any lasting way. Over the course of the century following legal enslavement, it had precisely the opposite effect. Chesapeake planters consolidated their class position by asserting white racial unity. In this context, the entry of large numbers of African—as opposed to creole—blacks into the region enlarged racial differences and helped secure planter domination. Thus, as reliance on black labor increased, the opportunities for any black— no matter how fluent in English or conversant with the countryside— to escape bondage and join the scramble for land, servants, and status diminished steadily.

By the middle of the eighteenth century, the size and character of that free Negro population had been significantly altered. Instead of a large minority of the black population, Negro freemen now composed just a small proportion of all blacks, probably not more than 5 percent. Many were cripples and old folks whom planters discarded when they could no longer wring a profit from their labor. While most were of mixed racial origins, few of these free mulattoes of the Chesapeake, in contrast to those of the lowcountry, traced their ancestry to the planter class. Instead, they descended from white servants, frequently women. These impoverished people had little status to offer their children. Indeed, planter-inspired legislation further compromised their liberty by requiring that the offspring of white women and blackmen serve their mother's master for thirty-one years. Those who survived the term could scarcely hope for the opportunities an earlier generation of Negro free-men had enjoyed. The transformation of the free Negro caste in the century between 1660 and 1760 measured the change in Chesapeake society as its organizing principle changed from class to race.

The free Negro's decline reveals how the racial imperatives of Chesapeake society operated to lump all black people together, free and slave, creole and African. In the Chesapeake, planters dared not grant creoles special status at the expense of Africans. Since the Africans would shortly be creoles and since creoles shared so much with whites, distinctions among blacks threatened the racial division that underlay planter domination. In the lowcountry, where geography, economy, and language separated white and black, those few blacks who spoke, dressed, acted, and looked like whites might be allowed some white prerogatives. But, if lowcountry planters could argue that no white man could do the work require to grow rice commercially, no one in the Chesapeake could reasonably deny that whites could grow tobacco. The fundamen-tal unity of Chesapeake life and the long-term instability of African-creole difference pushed blacks together in the white mind and in fact.

During the middle years of the eighteenth century, changes in the Chesapeake economy and society further diminished differences within black society and created a unified Afro-American culture. The success of the tobacco economy enlarged the area of settlement and allowed planters to increase their holdings. The most successful planters, anx-ious to protect themselves from the rigors of the world marketplace, strove for plantation self-sufficiency. The great estates of the Chesa-peake became self-contained enterprises with slaves taking positions as artisans, tradesmen, wagoners, and, sometimes, managers; the planta-tion was "like a Town," as a tutor on Robert Carter's estate observed, "but most of the Inhabitants are black." The increased sophistication of the Chesapeake economy propelled many more blacks into artisanal positions and the larger units of production, tighter pattern of settle-ment, and the greater mobility allowed by the growing network of roads ended the deadening isolation of the upcountry quarter. Bondsmen in-creasingly lived in large groups, and those who did not could generally find black companionship within a few miles' walk. Finally, better food, clothing, and shelter, and perhaps, the development of immunities to New World diseases enabled blacks to live longer, healthier lives.

As part of their drive for self-sufficiency, Chesapeake slaveholders encouraged the development of an indigenous slave population. Spurred by the proved ability of Africans to survive and reproduce and pressed in the international slave market by the superior resources of West In-dian sugar magnates and lowland rice growers, Chesapeake planters strove to correct the sexual imbalance within the black population, perhaps by importing a large proportion of women or lessening the burden of female slaves. Blacks quickly took advantage of this new circumstance and placed their family life on a firmer footing. Husbands and wives petitioned their owners to allow them to reside together on the same quarter and saw to it that their families were fed, beyond their masters' rations. Planters, for their part, were usually receptive to slaves' demands for a secure family life, both because it reflected their own values and because they profited mightily from the addition of slave children. Thomas Jefferson frankly considered "a woman who brings a child every two years as more profitable than the best man on the farm [for] what she produces is an addition to capital, while his labor disappears in mere consumption." Under these circumstances, the black population increased rapidly. Planters relied less and less on African importation and, by the 1740s, most of the growth of the black population came from natural increase. Within a generation, African importation was, for all practical purposes, no longer a significant source of slave labor. In the early 1770s, the period of the greatest importation into the low-country, only five hundred of the five thousand slaves added annually to the black population of Virginia derived directly from Africa.

The establishment of the family marked the re-emergence of Afro-American culture in the Chesapeake. Although Africans continued to enter the region, albeit at a slower pace, the nature of the slave trade minimized their impact on the development of black society in the region. Unlike those in the lowcountry, newly arrived Africans could rarely hope to remain together. Rather than funnel their cargo through a single port, Chesapeake slavers peddled it in small lots at many tobacco landings that lined the bay's extensive perimeter. Planters rarely bought more than a few slaves at a time, and larger purchasers, usually the great planter-merchants, often acted as jobbers, quickly reselling these slaves to backcountry freeholders. The resulting fragmentation sent newly arrived Africans in all directions and prevented the maintenance of tribal or shipboard ties. Chesapeake slaveholders cared little about the origins of their slaves. In their eyes, newly arrived Africans were not Iboes, Coromantees, or Angolans, but "new Negroes." While the unicentered slave trade sustained and strengthened African culture in the lowcountry, the Chesapeake slave trade facilitated the absorption of Africans into the evolving creole society.

Differences between creoles and Africans did not disappear with the creation of a self-sustaining Afro-American population. The creoles' advantages—language skills, familiarity with the countryside, artisanal standing, and knowledge of the plantation routine—continued to propel them into positions of authority within the slave hierarchy. In some ways, the growing complexity of the Chesapeake economy widened the distance between Africans and creoles, at least at first. Most of the skilled and managerial positions within the region's expanding iron industry went to creole blacks as did the artisanal work in flour mills and weaving houses. On some plantations, moreover, artisan and house status became lodged in particular families with parents passing privileged positions on to their children. Increasingly, skilled slaves entered the market economy by selling their own time and earning money from "overwork," thereby gaining a large measure of freedom. For the most part, Africans remained on rude, backwoods plantations tending the broad-leaf weed. Since creole slaves sold at a premium price and most great planters had already established self-sustaining slave forces, small planters purchased nearly all of the newly arrived Africans after mid-century. These upward-striving men generally owned the least developed, most distant farms. Their labor requirements remained primitive compared to the sophisticated division of labor on the self-contained plantation-towns.

Over the long term, however, economic changes sped the integration of Africans into Afro-American society. Under the pressure of a world-wide food shortage, Chesapeake planters turned from the production of tobacco to that of food-stuff, especially wheat. The demands of wheat cultivation transformed the nature of labor in the region. Whereas tobacco farming required season-long labor, wheat farming employed workers steadily only during planting and harvesting. The remainder of the year, laborers had little to do with the crop. At the same time, however, wheat required a larger and more skilled labor force to transport the grain to market and store it, mill it, and reship it as flour, bread, or bulk grain. Economic changes encouraged masters to teach their slaves skills and to hire them out during the slack season. At first, these opportunities went mostly to creoles, but as the wheat economy grew, spurring urbanization and manufacturing, the demands for artisans and hirelings outstripped the creole population. An increasing number of Africans were placed in positions previously reserved for creoles. The process of cultural transformation that earlier in the eighteenth century had taken a generation or more was considerably shorter at mid-century. Africans became Afro-Americans with increasing rapidity as the century wore on, eliminating the differences within black society that African importation had created.

Chesapeake blacks enjoyed considerably less autonomy than their lowcountry counterparts. Resident planters, small units of production, and the presence of large numbers of whites meant that most blacks lived and worked in close proximity to whites. While lowcountry planters fled to coastal cities for a large part of the year, the resident planter was a fixture of Chesapeake life. Small freeholders labored alongside slaves, and great planters prided themselves on regulating all aspects of their far-flung estates through a combination of direct personal supervision and plantation-based overseers. The latter were usually white, drawn from the region's white majority. Those few blacks who achieved managerial positions, moreover, enjoyed considerably less authority than lowland drivers. The presence of numerous nonslaveholding whites cir-

cumscribed black opportunities in other ways as well. While Chesapeake slaves commonly kept gardens and flocks of barnyard animals,
white competitors limited their market and created a variety of social
tensions. If lowcountry masters sometimes encouraged their slaves to
produce nonstaple garden crops, whites in the Chesapeake—slaveholders and nonslaveholders alike—complained that blacks stole more than
they raised and worked to curb the practice. Thus, at every turn, economy and society conspired to constrain black autonomy.

The requirements of tobacco cultivation reinforced the planters'
concern about daily work routine. Whereas the task system insulated
lowcountry blacks against white intervention and maximized black control over their work, the constant attention demanded by tobacco impelled Chesapeake planters to oversee the tedious process of cultivating,
topping, worming, suckering, and curing tobacco. The desire of Chesapeake masters to control their slaves went beyond the supervision of
labor. Believing that slaves depended on them "for every necessity of
life," they intervened in the most intimate aspects of black life. "I hope
you will take care that the Negroes both men and women I sent you
up last always go by the names we gave them," Robert "King" Carter
reminded his steward. "I am sure we repeated them so often . . . that
everyone knew their names & would readily answer to them." Chesapeake planters sought to shape domestic relations, cure physical maladies, and form personalities. However miserably they failed to ensure
black domestic tranquility and reform slave drunkards, paternalism at
close quarters in the Chesapeake had a far more potent influence on
black life than the distant paternalism that developed in the lowcountry. Chesapeake blacks developed no distinct language and rarely utilized African day names for their children. Afro-American culture in
the Chesapeake evolved parallel with Anglo-American culture and with
a considerable measure of congruence.

The diverse development of Afro-American culture during the seventeenth and eighteenth-centuries reveals the importance of time and
place in the study of American slavery. Black people in colonial America shared many things: a common African lineage, a common racial
oppressor, a common desire to create the richest life possible for themselves and their posterity in the most difficult of circumstances. But
these commonalities took different shape and meaning within the diverse
circumstances of the North American mainland. The nature of the slave
trade, the various demographic configurations of whites and blacks, and
the demands of particular staples—to name some of the factors influ-
encing the development of slave society—created at least three distinctive patterns of Afro-American life. Perhaps a finer analysis will reveal
still others.

This diversity did not end with the American Revolution. While
African-creole differences slowly disappeared as the centerpole of black

society with the closing of the slave trade and the steady growth of an Afro-American population, other sources of cohesion and division came to the fore. Differences between freemen and bondsmen, urban and rural folk, skilled and unskilled workers, and browns and blacks united and divided black people, and made black society every bit as variable and diverse during the nineteenth century as in the eighteenth. Indeed the diversity of black life increased substantially during the antebellum years as political changes abolished slavery in some places and strengthened it in others, as demographic changes set in motion by the Great Migration across the Lower South took effect, as the introduction of new crops enlarged the South's repertoire of staples, and as the kaleidoscopic movement of the world market sent the American economy in all directions.

If slave society during the colonial era can be comprehended only through a careful delineation of temporal and spatial differences among Northern, Chesapeake, and lowcountry colonies, a similar division will be necessary for a full understanding of black life in nineteenth-century America. The actions of black people during the American Revolution, the Civil War, and the long years of bondage between these two cataclysmic events cannot be understood merely as a function of the dynamics of slavery or the possibilities of liberty, but must be viewed within the specific social circumstances and cultural traditions of black people. These varied from time to time and from place to place. Thus no matter how complete recent studies of black life appear, they are limited to the extent that they provide a static and singular vision of a dynamic and complex society.

Jack Tar in the Streets: Merchant Seamen in the Politics of Revolutionary America

JESSE LEMISCH

In historical studies of the period of the American Revolution, much emphasis is placed on the activities of the colonial elite, both pro- and anti-British. The organizing and pamphleteering of men such as John Hancock, John Adams, and Patrick Henry loom large in our accounts of the growing opposition to the British treatment of the American colonies. The new mercantile and military legislation that appeared at the end of the French and Indian War angered much of the colonial population and generated various protests aimed at causing the British to alter their new policies. Many of these protests were successful, most notably the resistance to the Stamp Act. But the antagonistic mood of certain American leaders continued, to the point of provoking a military response from the British. The war for independence was under way.

Often overlooked in studies of this period is the role of the common people in the mounting resistance to the British. For mass protests to be effective, they had to be mass. Letters or proclamations representing the views of only a handful of colonial leaders might have been met with deserving scorn from the British authorities. It appears, though, that the British overlooked the popular base of rising colonial discontent. They, as well as many of the colonial elite, held the masses in contempt—considering them merely sheep waiting for the appropriate shepherd to lead them in one direction or another.

In recent decades, students of mass behavior have begun to look at group activity differently. One of the American pioneers in the study of history "from the bottom up" is Jesse Lemisch (State University of

New York at Buffalo). His article on seamen during the revolutionary era, which is reprinted here, demonstrates the value of the new perspective. What we find is not an inchoate crowd but a determined occupational group which had, over the years, developed a deep sense of grievance over the way it was being treated. These men knew who was responsible for the treatment, and in times of crisis, they purposefully attacked their oppressors.

Although the issue of the impressment of seamen was used as a prime reason for the War of 1812, before Lemisch began his studies, little research had been done on the role of impressment in creating mass discontent in the prerevolutionary era. The loyalty American seamen showed to the cause of independence during the war demonstrates that they were clear about who their primary oppressor was and what should be done about that enemy. It is sad to note that seamen in this period were not treated much better by their friends. But that is another story.

Here comes Jack Tar, his bowed legs bracing him as if the very Broadway beneath his feet might begin to pitch and roll. In his dress he is, in the words of a superior, "very nasty and negligent," his black stockings ragged, his long, baggy trousers tarred to make them waterproof. Bred in "that very shambles of language," the merchant marine, he is foul-mouthed, his talk alien and suspect. He is Jolly Jack, a bull in a china shop, always, in his words, "for a Short Life and a Merry one," and, in the concurring words of his superiors, "concerned only for the present . . . incapable of thinking of, or inattentive to, future welfare," "like froward Children not knowing how to judge for themselves."

Clothes don't make the man, nor does language; surely we can do better than these stereotypes. Few have tried. Maritime history, at it has been written, has had to do with the laborer. In that *mischianza* of mystique and elitism, "seaman" has meant Sir Francis Drake, not Jack Tar; the focus has been on trade, exploration, the great navigators, but

JACK TAR IN THE STREETS: MERCHANT SEAMEN IN THE POLITICS OF REVOLUTIONARY AMERICA By Jesse Lemisch, in *William and Mary Quarterly*, 3rd series, Volume 25 (1968), 371–407. © 1968 by Jesse Lemisch. An earlier version of this article was read at a meeting of the Organization of American Historians, Cincinnati, Ohio, April 1966. A grant and a fellowship from the American Council of Learned Societies aided the research.

rarely on the men who sailed the ships. Thus we know very little about Jack. Samuel Eliot Morison is one of the few who have tried to portray the common seaman. In an influential anecdote in *The Maritime History of Massachusetts* Morison has described a "frequent occurrence" in early New England. A farmer's boy, called by the smell or the sight of the sea, suddenly runs off; three years later he returns as a man, marries the hired girl, and lives "happily ever after." This experience, Morison tells us, was "typical of the Massachusetts merchant marine," where the "old salt" was almost non-existent and where there never was "a native deep-sea proletariat." The ships were sailed by wave after wave of "adventure-seeking boys," drawn by high wages and *wanderlust*. If they recovered, they took their earnings, married, and bought a farm; if not, these "young, ambitious seamen culled from the most active element of a pushing race" stayed on and rose to become masters in a merchant marine distinguished from its class-ridden European counterparts by easy mobility.

There is much to support Morison's *tableau*. Even if the mystique of the sea has been no more than mystique, still it has existed and exerted a powerful force. Washington, Franklin, and thousands of others did suffer attacks of "sea fever." Seamen were, as Morison says, young men, averaging in one sample slightly over twenty-four, with many like John Paul Jones who went to sea at thirteen and even some who went at eight. Many of them "hove in hard at the Hause-hole" and became masters of their own vessels; later, while their sons and grandsons added to their wealth, they retired, perhaps to their farms, and wrote proud histories of their successes. Some, like Nicholas Biddle, found the navy a better outlet for their ambitions than the merchant service. Others, following Morison's pattern, quit the sea early and turned to farming. For many there was mobility between generations and between trades. Seamen and landsmen might be distinct classes in Europe, but in America, men such as Albert Gallatin who knew both the Old World and the New found no "material distinction." So Jack Tar seems to have been simply the landsman gone to sea, indistinguishable from his fellows ashore, and, together with them, on his way to prosperity.

If the seaman was a clean young farm-boy on the make—and likely to succeed—why was Josiah Franklin so apprehensive lest young Benjamin "break loose and go to sea"? Why did Josiah fight his son's "strong inclination to go to sea" by frantically trying to make of him a joiner, a bricklayer, a turner, a brazier, a tallow-chandler, a cutler, a printer—anything, so long as it would keep him on land? Why did Washington's uncle suggest that young George would better become a planter or even an apprentice to a tinker, while explicitly urging that he not become a seaman?

"All masters of vessels are warned not to harbor, conceal, or employ him, as they will answer for it, as the law directs." To a fleeing

apprentice, dissatisfied with the "bondage" of work ashore, to a runaway slave, the sea might appear the only real shelter. Men with no
experience at sea tried to pass for seaman and before long discovered
that they had indeed become seamen. Others *were* seamen, apprenticed
in one vessel and fled to another. Still others, deserted soldiers, bail-
jumpers, thieves, and murderers, had gotten into trouble with the law.
And others went to sea entirely unwillingly, originally impressed—perhaps from jail—into the navy, or tricked into the merchant service by
crimps. These were the floaters who drifted and slipped their moorings,
the suicides, the men whose wives—if they had wives—ran off with
other men; the beneficiaries in their wills—when they left wills—were
innkeepers. Hitherto, argued a proponent of a United States navy in
1782, the merchant marine had been "the resource of necessity, accident or indulgence."

The merchant marine was a place full of forces beyond the seaman's
control: death and disease, storms, and fluctuations in employment.
Indeed, the lack of "old salts" in Morison's merchant marine might
reflect a sombre irony: was the average seaman young because mobility
rapidly brought him to another trade or because seamen died young? A
man in jail, said Dr. Johnson, was at least safe from drowning, and he
had more room, better food, and better company. The Quaker John
Woolman was one of the few sensitive enough to see that if the "poor
bewildered sailors" drank and cursed, the fault lay not so much in
themselves as in the harsh environment and the greed of employers.
Nor was the road up through the hawse-hole so easy as Morison asserts.
That the few succeeded tells us nothing of the many; only the successful
left autobiographies. Perhaps the sons of merchants and ship-masters
made it, along with the captain's brother-in-law and those who attended schools of navigation, but what of the "poor lads bound apprentice" who troubled Woolman, those whose wages went to their masters?
What of the seamen in Morison's own Boston who died too poor to
pay taxes and who were a part of what James Henretta has called "the
bottom" of Boston society? What of those who went bankrupt with
such frequency in Rhode Island? Why, at the other end of the colonies,
did Washington's uncle warn that it would be "very difficult" to become
master of a Virginia vessel and not worth trying?

The presence of such men, fugitives and floaters, powerless in a
tough environment, makes *wanderlust* appear an ironic parody of the
motives which made at least some men go to sea. Catch the seaman
when he is not pandering to your romanticism, said former seaman
Frederick Law Olmsted a century later, and he will tell you that he
hates the sight of blue water, he hates his ship, his officers, and his
messmates—and he despises himself. Melville's Ishmael went to sea when
he felt grim, hostile, and suicidal: "It is a way I have of driving off the
spleen." No matter what we make of Ishmael, we cannot possibly make
him into one of Morison's "adventure-seeking boys." Others, perhaps,

but not Ishmael. The feelings of eighteenth-century Americans toward seafaring and seamen, and what evidence we have of the reasons men had for going to sea indicate that there were many like Ishmael in the colonial period, too, who left the land in flight and fear, outcasts, men with little hope of success ashore. These were the dissenters from the American mood. Their goals differed from their fellows ashore; these were the rebels, the men who stayed on to become old salts.

Admiralty law treated seamen in a special way, as "wards." Carl Ubbelohde says that seamen favored the colonial Vice Admiralty Courts as "particular tribunals in case of trouble," and Charles M. Andrews and Richard B. Morris agreed that these courts were "guardians of the rights of the seamen." The benefits of being classified as a "ward" are dubious, but, regardless of the quality of treatment which admiralty law accorded to seamen, it certainly does not follow that, all in all, the colonial seaman was well treated by the law. Indeed, if we broaden our scope to include colonial law generally, we find an extraordinarily harsh collection of laws, all justifying Olmsted's later claim that American seamen "are more wretched, and are governed more by threats of force than any other civilized laborers of the world." There are laws providing for the whipping of disobedient seamen and in one case for their punishment as "seditious"; laws prohibiting seamen in port from leaving their vessels after sundown and from travelling on land without certificates of discharge from this last job; laws empowering "every free white person" to catch runaway seamen. We find other laws, less harsh, some seeming to protect the seaman: laws against extending credit to seamen and against arresting them for debt, and against entertaining them in taverns for more than one hour per day; laws against selling them liquor and prohibiting them from playing with cards or dice; laws waiving imprisonment for seamen convicted of cursing; laws requiring masters to give discharge certificates to their seamen and laws prohibiting hiring without such certificates. Finally, there are laws which clearly do help the seaman: laws requiring masters to provide "good and sufficient diet and accommodation" and providing for redress if the master refused; laws providing punishment for masters who "immoderately beat, wound, or maim" their seamen; laws providing that seamen's contracts be written.

These harsh or at best paternalistic laws add up to a structure whose purpose is to assure a ready supply of cheap, docile labor. Obedience, both at sea and ashore, is the keystone. Charles Beard at his most rigidly mechanistic would doubtless have found the Constitution merely mild stuff alongside this blatantly one-sided class legislation. Today's historians of the classless society would do well to examine the preambles of these laws, written in a more candid age, by legislatures for which, even by Robert Brown's evidence, most seamen could not vote. Again and again these laws aim to inhibit acts of seamen which may do "prejudice to masters and owners of vessels" or constitute a "manifest detriment of . . . trade." The seamen's interests are sacrificed to the merchants', and even the laws which seem friendly to the seaman benefit the master. Laws against giving credit, arresting, and suing aim to keep the seaman available rather than involved in a lawsuit or imprisoned; the certificates and written contracts seek to prevent desertion and to protect the master against what would today be called a "strike"; the laws protecting the seamen against immoderate punishment and requiring adequate food and accommodation are implicitly weak in that they require that dependents make open complaint against their superiors. Sometimes this limitation is made explicit, as in a South Carolina law of 1751 whose stated purpose is "TO DISCOURAGE FRIVO-LOUS AND VEXATIOUS ACTIONS AT LAW BEING BROUGHT BY SEAMEN AGAINST MASTERS AND COMMANDERS."

Thus if we think of Jack Tar as jolly, childlike, irresponsible, and in many ways surprisingly like the Negro stereotype, it is because he was treated so much like a child, a servant, and a slave. What the employer saw as the necessities of an authoritarian profession were written into law and culture: the society that wanted Jack dependent made him that way and then concluded that that was the way he really was.

Thus if we think of Jack Tar as jolly, childlike, irresponsible, and in many ways surprisingly like the Negro stereotype, it is because he was treated so much like a child, a servant, and a slave. What the employer saw as the necessities of an authoritarian profession were written into law and culture: the society that wanted Jack dependent made him that way and then concluded that that was the way he really was.

II

Constantly plagued by short complements, the Royal Navy attempted to solve its manning problems in America, as in England, by impressment. Neil Stout has recently attributed these shortages to "death, illness, crime, and desertion" which were in turn caused largely by rum and by the deliberate enticements of American merchants. Rum and inveiglement certainly took a high toll, but to focus on these two causes of shortages is unfairly to shift the blame for impressment onto its victims. The navy itself caused shortages. Impressment, said Thomas Hutchinson, caused desertion, rather than the other way around. Jack Tar had good reasons for avoiding the navy. It would, a young Virginian was warned, "cut him and staple him and use him like a Negro, or rather, like a dog"; James Otis grieved at the loss of the "flower" of Massachusetts's youth "by ten thousands" to a service which treated them little better than "hewers of wood and drawers of water." Discipline was harsh and sometimes irrational, and punishments were cruel. Water poured into sailors' beds, they went mad, and died of fevers and scurvy. Sickness, Benjamin Franklin noted, was more common in the navy than in the merchant service and more frequently fatal. In a fruitless attempt to prevent desertion, wages were withheld and men shunted about from ship to ship without being paid. But the accumulation of even three or four years' back wages could not keep a man from running. And why should it have? Privateering paid better in wartime, and wages were higher in the merchant service; even laborers ashore were better paid. Thus Stout's claim that the navy was "forced" to press is only as accurate as the claim that the South was forced to enslave Negroes. Those whose sympathies lie with the thousands of victims of this barbaric practice—rather than with naval administrators—will see that the navy pressed because to be in the navy was in some sense to be a slave, and for this we must blame the slave owners rather than the slaves.

Impressment angered and frightened the seamen, but it pervaded and disrupted all society, giving other classes and groups cause to share a common grievance with the press-gang's more direct victims: just about everyone had a relative at sea. Whole cities were crippled. A nighttime operation in New York in 1757 took in eight hundred men, the equivalent of more than one-quarter of the city's adult male population. Impressment and the attendant shortage of men may have been a critical factor in the stagnancy of "the once cherished now depressed, once flourishing now sinking Town of Boston." H.M.S. *Shirley's* log lists at least ninety-two men pressed off Boston in five months of 1745–1746; *Gramont* received seventy-three pressed men in New York in three days in 1758; *Arethusa* took thirty-one in two days off Virginia in 1771. Binges such as these left the communities where they occurred seriously harmed. Preachers' congregations took flight, and merchants complained loudly about the "many Thousands of Pounds of Damage." "Kiss my arse, you dog," shouted the captain as he made off with their men, leaving vessels with their fires still burning, unmanned, finally to be wrecked. They took legislators and slaves, fishermen and servants. Seamen took to the woods or fled town altogether, dreading the appearance of a man-of-war's boat—in the words of one—as a flock of sheep dreaded a wolf's appearance. If they offered to work at all, they demanded inflated wages and refused to sail to ports where there was danger of impressment. "New York and Boston," Benjamin Franklin commented during the French and Indian War, "have so often found the Inconvenience of . . . Station Ships that they are very indifferent about having them: The Pressing of their Men and thereby disappointing Voyages, often hurting their Trade more than the Enemy hurts it." Even a ferryboat operator complained as people shunned the city during a press; food and fuel grew short and their prices rose.

From the very beginning of the history of impressment in America is a tale of venality, deceit, and vindictiveness. Captains kept deserters and dead men on ship's books, pocketing their provision allowances. In

1706 a captain pressed men and literally sold them to short-handed vessels; his midshipman learned the business so well that after his dismissal he became a veritable entrepreneur of impressment, setting up shop in a private sloop. Another commander waited until New York's governor was away to break a no-press agreement and when the governor returned he seriously considered firing on the Queen's ship. In Boston in 1702 the lieutenant-governor *did* fire, responding to merchants' complaints. "Fire and be damn'd," shouted the impressing captain as the shots whistled through his sails. The merchants had complained that the press was illegal under 1697 instructions which required captains and commanders to apply to colonial governors for permission to press. These instructions, a response to complaints of "irregular proceedings of the captains of some of our ships of war in the impressing of seamen," had clearly not put an end to irregularities. In 1708 a Parliament fearful of the disruptive effect of impressment on trade forbade the practice in America. In the sixty-seven years until the repeal in 1775 of this "Act for the Encouragement of the Trade to America" there was great disagreement as to its meaning and indeed as to its very existence. Did the Sixth of Anne, as the act was called, merely prohibit the navy from impressing and leave governors free to do so? At least one governor, feeling "pinioned" under the law, continued impressing while calling it "borrowing." Was the act simply a wartime measure, which expired with the return of peace in 1713? Regardless of the dispute, impressment continued, routine in its regularity, but often spectacular in its effects.

Boston was especially hard-hit by impressment in the 1740's, with frequent incidents throughout the decade and major explosions in 1745 and 1747. Again and again the town meeting and the House of Representatives protested, drumming away at the same themes: impressment was harmful to maritime commerce and to the economic life of the city in general and illegal if not properly authorized. In all this the seaman himself becomes all but invisible. The attitude towards him in the protests is at best neutral and often sharply antagonistic. In 1747 the House of Representatives condemned the violent response of hundreds of seamen to a large-scale press as "a tumultuous riotous assembling of armed Seamen, Servants, Negroes, and others . . . tending to the Destruction of all Government and Order." While acknowledging that the people had reason to protest, the House chose to level *its* protest against "the most audacious Insult" to the governor, Council, and House. And the town meeting, that stronghold of democracy, offered its support to those who took "orderly" steps while expressing its "Abhorence of such Illegal Criminal Proceedings" as those undertaken by the seamen "and other persons of mean and Vile Condition."

Protests such as these reflect at the same time both unity and division in colonial society. All kinds of Americans—both merchants and seamen—opposed impressment, but the town meeting and the House spoke for the merchant, not the seaman. They opposed impressment not for its effect on the seaman but for its effect on commerce. Thus their protests express antagonism to British policy at the same time that they express class division. These two themes continue and develop in American opposition to the impressment in the three decades between the Knowles Riots of 1747 and the Declaration of Independence.

During the French and Indian War the navy competed with privateers for seamen. Boston again protested against impressment, and then considered authorizing the governor to press, "provided said Men be impressed from inward-bound Vessels from Foreign Parts only, and that none of them be Inhabitants of the Province." In 1760 New York's mayor had a naval captain arrested on the complaint of two shipmasters who claimed that he had welched on a deal to exchange two men he had pressed for two others they were willing to furnish. With the return of peace in 1763 admirals and Americans alike had reason to suppose that there would be no more impressment. But the Admiralty's plans for a large new American fleet required otherwise, and impressment began again in the spring of 1764 in New York, where a seven-week hot press was brought to a partial stop by the arrest of one of the two offending captains. In the spring and summer a hunt for men between Maine and Virginia by four naval vessels brought violent responses, including the killing of a marine at New York; another fort, at Newport, fired on another naval vessel.

Along with the divisions there was a certain amount of unity. Seamen who fled after violently resisting impressment could not be found—probably because others sheltered them—and juries would not indict them. Captains were prevented from impressing by the threat of prosecution. And in 1769 lawyer John Adams used the threat of displaying the statute book containing the Sixty of Anne to frighten a special court of Admiralty into declaring the killing of an impressing lieutenant justifiable homicide in necessary self-defense.

There were two kinds of impressment incidents: those in which there was immediate self-defense against impressment, usually at sea, and those in which crowds ashore, consisting in large part of seamen, demonstrated generalized opposition to impressment. This is what the first kind of incident sounded like: a volley of musketry and the air full of language, grapeshot, round shot, hammered shot, double-headed shot, even rocks. "Come into the boat and be damned, you Sorry Son of a Whore or else Ile breake your head, and hold your tongue." Small arms, swords and cutlasses, blunderbusses, clubs and pistols, axes, harpoons, fishgigs, twelve-pounders, six-pounders, half-pounders. "You are a parsill of Raskills." Fired five shots to bring to a snow from North Carolina, pressed four. "You have no right to impress me . . . If you step over that line . . . by the eternal God of Heaven, you are a dead man." "Aye, my lad, I have seen many a brave fellow before now."

Here is hostility and bloodshed, a tradition of antagonism. From the beginning, impressment's most direct victims—the seamen—were its most active opponents. Bernard Bailyn's contention that "not a single murder resulted from the activities of the Revolutionary mobs in America" does not hold up if extended to cover resistance to impressment; there were murders on both sides. Perhaps the great bulk of incidents of this sort must remain forever invisible to the historian, for they often took place out of sight of friendly observers, and the only witness, the navy, kept records which are demonstrably biased and faulty, omitting the taking of thousands of men. But even the visible records provide a great deal of information. This much we know without doubt: seamen did not go peacefully. Their violence was purposeful, and sometimes they were articulate. "I know who you are," said one, as reported by John Adams and supported by Thomas Hutchinson. "You are the lieutenant of a man-of-war, come with a press-gang to deprive me of my liberty. You have no right to impress me. I have retreated from you as far as I can. I can go no farther. I and my companions are determined to stand upon our defence. Stand off." (It was difficult for Englishmen to fail to see impressment in such terms—even a sailor *doing* the pressing could feel shame over "fighting with honest sailors, to deprive them of their liberty.")

Ashore, seamen and others demonstrated their opposition to impressment with the only weapon which the unrepresentative politics of the day offered them—riot. In Boston several thousand people responded to a nighttime impressment sweep of the harbor and docks with three days of rioting beginning in the early hours of November 17, 1747. Thomas Hutchinson reported that "the lower class were beyond measure enraged." Negroes, servants, and hundreds of seamen seized a naval lieutenant, assaulted a sheriff and put his deputy in the stocks, surrounded the governor's house, and stormed the Town House where the General Court was sitting. The rioters demanded the seizure of the impressing officers, the release of the men they had pressed, and execution of a death sentence which had been levied against a member of an earlier press-gang who had been convicted of murder. When the governor fled to Castle William—some called it "abdication"—Commodore Knowles threatened to put down what he called "arrant rebellion" by bombarding the town. The governor, who, for his part, thought the rioting a secret plot of the upper class, was happily surprised when the town meeting expressed its "Abhorence" of the seamen's riot.

After the French and Indian War press riots increased in frequency. Armed mobs of whites and Negroes repeatedly manhandled captains, officers, and crews, threatened their lives, and held them hostage for the men they pressed. Mobs fired at pressing vessels and tried to board them; they threatened to burn one, and they regularly dragged ships' boats to the center of town for ceremonial bonfires. In Newport in June 1765, five hundred seamen, boys, and Negroes rioted after five weeks of impressment. "Sensible" Newporters opposed impressment but nonetheless condemned this "Rabble." In Norfolk in 1767 Captain Jeremiah Morgan retreated, sword in hand, before a mob of armed whites and Negroes. "Good God," he wrote to the governor, "was your Honour and I to prosecute all the Rioters that attacked us belonging to Norfolk there would not be twenty left unhang'd belonging to the Toun." According to Thomas Hutchinson, the *Liberty* Riot in Boston in 1768 may have been as much against impressment as against the seizure of Hancock's sloop: *Romney* had pressed before June 10, and on that day three officers were forced by an angry crowd "arm'd with Stones" to release a man newly pressed from the Boston packet. *Romney* pressed another man, and on June 14, after warding off "many wild and violent proposals," the town meeting petitioned the governor against both the seizure and impressment; the instructions to their representatives (written by John Adams) quoted the Sixth of Anne at length. On June 18 two councillors pleaded with the governor to procure the release of a man pressed by *Romney* "as the peace of the Town seems in a great measure to depend upon it."

There were other impressment riots at New York in July of 1764 and July of 1765; at Newport in July of 1764; at Casco Bay, Maine, in December 1764. Incidents continued during the decade following, and impressment flowered on the very eve of the Revolution. Early in 1775 the practice began to be used in a frankly vindictive and political way— because a town had inconvenienced an admiral, or because a town supported the Continental Congress. Impresses were ordered and took place from Maine to Virginia. In September a bundle of press warrants arrived from the Admiralty, along with word of the repeal of the Sixth of Anne. What had been dubious was now legal. Up and down the coast, officers rejoiced and went to work.

Long before 1765 Americans had developed beliefs about impressment, and they had expressed those beliefs in words and deeds. Impressment was bad for trade and it was illegal. As such, it was, in the words of the Massachusetts House in 1720, "a great Breach on the Rights of His Majesties Subjects." In 1747 it was a violation of "the common Liberty of the Subject," and in 1754 "inconsistent with Civil Liberty, and the Natural Rights of Mankind." Some felt in 1757 that it was even "abhorrent to the English Constitution." In fact, the claim that impressment was unconstitutional was wrong. (Even *Magna Charta* was no protection. *Nullus liber homo capiatur* did not apply to seamen.) Instead impressment indicated to Benjamin Franklin "that the constitution is yet imperfect, since in so general a case it doth not secure liberty, but destroys it." "If impressing seamen is of right by common law in Britain," he also remarked, "slavery is then of right by common law there; there being no slavery worse than that sailors are subjected to."

For Franklin, impressment was a symptom of injustice built into the British Constitution. In *Common Sense* Tom Paine saw in impressment a reason for rejecting monarchy. In the Declaration of Independence

Thomas Jefferson included impressment among the "Oppressions" of George III; later he likened the practice to the capture of Africans for slavery. Both "reduced [the victim] to . . . bondage by force, in flagrant violation of his own consent, and of his natural right in his own person."

Despite all this, and all that went before, we have thought little of impressment as an element in explaining the conduct of the common man in the American Revolution. Contemporaries knew better. John Adams felt that a tactical mistake by Thomas Hutchinson on the question of impressment in 1769 would have "accelerated revolution. . . . It would have spread a wider flame than Otis's ever did, or could have done." Ten years later American seamen were being impressed by *American* officers. The United States Navy had no better solution for "public Neccessities" than had the Royal Navy. Joseph Reed, President of Pennsylvania, complained to Congress of "Oppressions" and in so doing offered testimony to the role of *British* impressment in bringing on revolution. "We cannot help observing how similar this Conduct is to that of the British Officers during our Subjection to Great Britain and are persuaded it will have the same unhappy effects viz., an estrangement of the Affections of the People from the Authority under which they act which by an easy Progression will proceed to open Opposition to the immediate Actors and Bloodshed." Impressment had played a role in the estrangement of the American people from the British government. It had produced "Odium" against the navy, and even six-year-olds had not been too young to have learned to detest it. The anger of thousands of victims did not vanish. Almost four decades after the Declaration of Independence an orator could still arouse his audience by tapping a folk-memory of impressment by the same "haughty, cruel, and gasconading nation" which was once again trying to enslave free Americans.

III

The seamen's conduct in the 1760's and 1770's makes more sense in the light of previous and continued impressment. What may have seemed irrational violence can now be seen as purposeful and radical. The pattern of rioting as political expression, established as a response to impressment, was now adapted and broadened as a response to the Stamp Act. In New York General Gage described the "insurrection" of October 31, 1765, and following as "composed of great numbers of Sailors." The seamen, he said, were "the only People who may be properly Stiled Mob," and estimates indicate that between a fifth and a fourth of New York's rioters were seamen. The disturbances began among the seamen—especially former privateersmen—on October 31. On November 1 they had marched, led primarily by their former captains; later they rioted, led by no one but themselves. Why? Because they had been duped by merchants, or, if not by merchants, then certainly by lawyers. So British officials believed—aroused by these men who meant to use them, the seamen themselves had nothing more than plunder on their minds. In fact, at the point in New York's rioting when the leaders lost control, the seamen, who were then in the center of town, in an area rich for plunder, chose instead to march in an orderly and disciplined way clear across town to do violence to the home and possessions of an English major whose provocative conduct had made him the obvious political enemy. Thus the "rioting" was actually very discriminating.

Seamen and non-seamen alike joined to oppose the Stamp Act for many reasons, but the seamen had two special grievances: impressment and the effect of England's new attitude toward colonial trade. To those discharged by the navy at the end of the war and others thrown out of work by the death of privateering were added perhaps twenty thousand more seamen and fishermen who were thought to be the direct victims of the post-1763 trade regulations. This problem came to the fore in the weeks following November 1, 1765, when the Stamp Act went into effect. The strategy of opposition chosen by the colonial leadership was to cease all activities which required the use of stamps. Thus maritime trade came to a halt in the cities. Some said that this was a cowardly strategy. If the Americans opposed the Stamp Act, let them go on with business as usual, refusing outright to use the stamps. The leaders' strategy was especially harmful to the seamen, and the latter took the more radical position—otherwise the ships would not sail. And this time the seamen's radicalism triumphed over both colonial leadership and British officials. Within little more than a month the act had been largely nullified. Customs officers were allowing ships to sail without stamps, offering as the reason the fear that the seamen, "who are the people that are most dangerous on these occasions, as their whole dependance for a subsistence is upon Trade," would certainly "commit some terrible Mischief." Philadelphia's customs officers feared that the seamen would soon "compel" them to let ships pass without stamps. Customs officers at New York yielded when they heard that the seamen were about to have a meeting.

Customs officers had worse luck on other days. Seamen battled them throughout the 1760's and 1770's. In October 1769 a Philadelphia customs officer was attacked by a mob of seamen who also tarred, feathered, and nearly drowned a man who had furnished him with information about illegally imported goods. A year later a New Jersey customs officer who approached an incoming vessel in Delaware Bay had *his* boat boarded by armed seamen who threatened to murder him and came close to doing so. When the officer's son came to Philadelphia, he was similarly treated by a mob of seamen; there were one thousand seamen in Philadelphia at the time, and according to the customs collector there, they were "always ready" to do such "mischief." This old antagonism had been further politicized in 1768 when, under the American Board of Customs Commissioners, searchers began to break into sea chests and confiscate those items not covered by cockets, thus breaking an old custom of the sea which allowed seamen to import small items for their own profit. Oliver M. Dickerson has described this new "Invasion of Seamen's Rights" as a part of "customs racketeering" and a cause of animosity between seamen and customs officers.

Many of these animosities flared in the Boston Massacre. What John Adams described as "a motley rabble of saucy boys, negroes and molattoes, Irish teagues and out landish jack tarrs," including twenty or thirty of the latter, armed with clubs and sticks, did battle with the soldier. Their leader was Crispus Attucks, a mulatto seaman; he was shot to death in front of the Custom House. One of the seamen's reasons for being there has been too little explored. The Massacre grew out of a fight between workers and off-duty soldiers at a ropewalk two days before. That fight, in turn, grew out of the long-standing practice in the British army of allowing off-duty soldiers to take civilian employment. They did so, in Boston, and elsewhere, often at wages which undercut those offered to Americans—including unemployed seamen who sought work ashore—by as much as 50 per cent. In hard times this led to intense competition for work, and the Boston Massacre was in part a product of this competition. Less well known is the Battle of Golden Hill, which arose from similar causes and took place in New York six weeks before. In January 1770 a gang of seamen went from house to house and from dock to dock, using clubs to drive away the soldiers employed there and threatening anyone who might rehire them. In the days of rioting which followed and which came to be called the Battle of Golden Hill, the only fatality was a seaman, although many other seamen were wounded in the attempt to take vengeance for the killing. The antipathy between soldiers and seamen was so great, said John Adams, "that they fight as naturally when they meet, as the elephant and Rhinoceros."

IV

To wealthy Loyalist Judge Peter Oliver of Massachusetts, the common people were only "Rabble"—like the "Mobility of all Countries, perfect Machines, wound up by any Hand who might first take the Winch." The people were "duped," "deceived," and "deluded" by cynical leaders who could "turn the Minds of the great Vulgar." Had they been less ignorant, Americans would have spurned their leaders, and there would have been no Revolution. I have tested this generalization and found it unacceptable, at least in its application to colonial seamen. Obviously the seamen did not cause the American Revolution. But neither were they simply irrational fellows who moved only when others manipulated them. I have attempted to show that the seaman had a mind of his own and genuine reasons to act, and that he did act—purposefully. The final test of this purposefulness must be the Revolution itself. Here we find situations in which the seamen are separated from those who might manipulate them and thrown into great physical danger; if they were manipulated or duped into rebellion, on their own we might expect them to show little understanding of or enthusiasm for the war.

To a surprising extent American seamen remained Americans during the Revolution. Beaumarchais heard from an American in 1775 that seamen, fishermen, and harbor workers had become an "army of furious men, whose actions are all animated by a spirit of vengeance and hatred" against the English, who had destroyed their livelihood "and the liberty of their country." The recent study of loyalist claimants by Wallace Brown confirms Oliver Dickerson's earlier contention that "the volumes dealing with loyalists and their claims discloses an amazing absence of names" of seamen. From a total of 2786 loyalist claimants whose occupations are known Brown found only 39, 1.4 per cent, who were seamen (or pilots). (It is possible to exclude fishermen and masters but not pilots from his figures.) In contrast, farmers numbered 49.1 per cent, artisans 9.8 per cent, merchants and shopkeepers 18.6 per cent, professionals 9.1 per cent, and officeholders 10.1 per cent. Although as Brown states, the poor may be underrepresented among the claimants, "the large number of claims by poor people, and even Negroes, suggests that this is not necessarily true."

An especially revealing way of examining the seamen's loyalties under pressure is to follow them into British prisons. Thousands of them were imprisoned in such places as the ship *Jersey*, anchored in New York harbor, and Mill and Forton prisons in England. Conditions were abominable. Administration was corrupt, and in America disease was rife and thousands died. If physical discomfort was less in the English prisons than in *Jersey*, the totality of misery may have been as great, with prisoners more distant from the war and worse informed about the progress of the American cause. Lost in a no-man's land between British refusal to consider them prisoners of war and Washington's unwillingness in America to trade trained soldiers for captured seamen, these men had limited opportunities for exchange. Trapped in this very desperate situation, the men were offered a choice: they could defect and join the Royal Navy. To a striking extent the prisoners remained patriots, and very self-consciously so. "Like brave men, they resisted, and swore that they would never lift a hand to do any thing on board of King George's ships." The many who stayed understood the political significance of their choice as well as the few who went. "What business had he to sell his Country, and go to the worst of Enemies?" Instead of defecting they engaged in an active resistance movement. Although inexperienced in self-government and segragated from their captains, on their own these men experienced no great difficulties in organizing themselves into disciplined groups. "Notwithstanding they were located within the absolute dominions of his Britanic majesty," commented one, the men "adventured to form themselves into a republic, framed a constitution and enacted wholesome laws, with suitable penalties." Organized, they resisted, celebrating the Fourth of July under British bayonets, burning their prisons, and escaping. Under these intolerable conditions, seamen from all over the colonies discovered that they shared a common conception of the cause for which they fought.

At the Constitutional Convention Benjamin Franklin spoke for the seamen:

> It is of great consequence that we shd. not depress the virtue and public spirit of our common people; of which they displayed a great deal during the war, and which contributed principally to the favorable issue of it. He related the honorable refusal of the American seamen who were carried in great numbers into the British prisons during the war, to redeem themselves from misery or to seek their fortunes, by entering on board of the Ships of the Enemies to their Country; contrasting their patriotism with a contemporary instance in which the British seamen made prisoners by the Americans, readily entered on the ships of the latter on being promised a share of the prizes that might be made out of their own Country.

Franklin spoke *against limiting* the franchise, not *for broadening* it: he praised the seamen, but with a hint of condescension, suggesting that it would be prudent to grant them a few privileges. A decade later a French traveller noticed that "except the laborer in ports, and the common sailor, everyone calls himself, and is called by others, a *gentleman.*" Government was still gentleman's government: more people were defined as gentlemen, but Jack Tar was not yet among them.

V

Bernard Bailyn has recently added illumination to our understanding of pre-Revolutionary crowd action. Bailyn has disagreed with Peter Oliver and with modern historians who have concurred in describing pre-Revolutionary rioters as mindless, passive, and manipulated: "far from being empty vessels," rioters in the decade before the outbreak of fighting were "politically effective" and "shared actively the attitudes and fears" of their leaders; theirs was a " 'fully-fledged political movement'." Thus it would seem that Bailyn has freed himself from the influential grasp of Gustave Le Bon. But Bailyn stopped short of total rejection. Only in 1765, he says, was the colonial crowd "transformed" into a political phenomenon. Before then it was "conservative"—like crowds in seventeenth- and eighteenth-century England, aiming neither at social revolution nor at social reform, but only at immediate revenge. Impressment riots and other "demonstrations by transient sailors and dock workers," Bailyn says, expressed no "deep-lying social distress" but only a "diffuse and indeliberate antiauthoritarianism"; they were "ideologically inert."

Other historians have seen the colonial seamen—and the rest of the lower class—as mindless and manipulated, both before and after 1765. The seeming implication behind this is that the seamen who demonstrated in colonial streets did so as much out of simple vindictiveness or undisciplined violence as out of love of liberty. Certainly such motivation would blend well with the traditional picture of the seamen as rough and ready. For along with the stereotype of Jolly Jack—and in part belying that stereotype—is bold and reckless Jack, the exotic and violent. Jack *was* violent; the conditions of his existence were violent. Was his violence non-political? Sometimes. The mob of seventy to eighty yelling, club-swinging, out-of-town seamen who tried to break up a Philadelphia election in 1742 had no interest in the election; they had been bought off with money and liquor.

Other violence is not so clear-cut. Edward Thompson has seen the fighting out of significant social conflict in eighteenth-century England "in terms of Tyburn, the hulks and the Bridewells on the one hand; and crime, riot, and mob action on the other." Crime and violence among eighteenth-century American seamen needs reexamination from such a perspective. Does "mutiny" adequately describe the act of the crew which seized *Black Prince,* re-named it *Liberty,* and chose their course and a new captain by voting? What shall we call the conduct of 150 seamen who demanded higher wages by marching along the streets of Philadelphia with clubs, unrigging vessels, and forcing workmen ashore? If "mutiny" is often the captain's name for what we have come to call a "strike," perhaps we might also detect some significance broader than mere criminality in the seamen's frequent assaults on captains and thefts from them. Is it not in some sense a political act for a seaman to tear off the mast a copy of a law which says that disobedient seamen will be punished as "seditious"?

Impressment meant the loss of freedom, both personal and economic, and, sometimes, the loss of life itself. The seaman who defended himself against impressment felt that he was fighting to defend his "liberty," and he justified his resistance on the grounds of "right." It is in the concern for liberty and right that the seaman rises from vindictiveness to a somewhat more complex awareness that certain values larger than himself exist and that he is the victim not only of cruelty and hardship but also, in the light of those values, of injustice. The riots ashore, whether they be against impressment, the Stamp Act, or competition for work express that same sense of injustice. And here, thousands of men took positive and effective steps to demonstrate their opposition to both acts and policies.

Two of England's most exciting historians have immensely broadened our knowledge of past and present by examining phenomena strikingly like the conduct and thought of the seamen in America. These historians have described such manifestations as "sub-political" or "prepolitical," and one of them has urged that such movements be "seriously considered not simply as an unconnected series of individual curiosities, as footnotes to history, but as a phenomenon of general importance and considerable weight in modern history." When Jack Tar went to sea in the American Revolution, he fought, as he had for many years before, quite literally, to protect his life, liberty, and property. It might be extravagant to call the seamen's conduct and the sense of injustice which underlay it in any fully developed sense ideological or political; on the other hand, it makes little sense to describe their ideological content as zero. There are many worlds and much of human history in that vast area between ideology and inertness.

Suggestions for Further Reading

Gary Nash provides an excellent introduction to the various cultures in the colonies in *Red, White and Black: The Peoples of Early America** (Prentice-Hall, 1974). Two additional works by James Axtell are *The Invasion Within: The Contest of Cultures in Colonial North America* (Oxford University Press, 1985) and *The European and the Indian: Essays in the Ethnohistory of Colonial North America* (Oxford University Press, 1981). See also Francis Jennings, *The Invasion of America: Indians, Colonialism, and the Cant of Conquest** (University of North Carolina Press, 1975). Other recent works of interest are Henry F. Dobyns, *Their Number Became Thinned: Native American Population Dynamics in Eastern North America** (University of Tennessee Press, 1983), Henry Warner Bowden, *American Indians and Christian Missions** (University of Chicago Press, 1981), and Bernard Sheehan, *Savagism and Civility: Indians and Englishmen in Colonial Virginia** (Cambridge University Press, 1980). An important and fascinating study of the ecology of early America can be found in John R. Stilgoe, *Common Landscape of America, 1580–1845** (Yale University Press, 1982).

Works that provide an overview of the history of women in America are Nancy Woloch, *Women and the American Experience** (Knopf, 1984), and Carol Ruth Berkin and Mary Beth Norton (eds.), *The Women of America: Original Essays and Documents** (Houghton-Mifflin, 1978). For the early period, see Laurel Thatcher Ulrich, *Good Wives: Images and Reality in the Lives of Women in Northern New England** (Knopf, 1983), and Lyle Koehler, *A Search for Power: The "Weaker Sex" in Seventeenth-Century New England* (University of Illinois Press, 1980).

A recent book on indentured servants is David Galenson, *White Servitude in Colonial America: An Economic Analysis** (Cambridge University Press, 1984).

American slavery is placed in the context of world history in David B. Davis' works, *The Problem of Slavery in Western Culture** (Cornell University Press, 1966) and *The Problem of Slavery in the Age of Revolution, 1770–1823** (Cornell University Press, 1975). On the origin of slavery in the United States, see Winthrop D. Jordan, *White over Black: American Attitudes Toward the Negro, 1550–1812** (University of North Carolina Press, 1968), and Edmund S. Morgan, *American Slavery, American Freedom: The Ordeal of Colonial Virginia** (Norton, 1975). Philip D. Curtin's book *The Atlantic Slave Trade: A Census** (University of Wisconsin Press, 1969) is a provocative study of the numbers of slaves imported to the New World. On slavery in the individual colonies, see Lorenzo

*Available in paperback edition.

Greene, *The Negro in Colonial New England* * (Colonial University Press, 1942); Thaddeus Tate, Jr., *The Negro in Eighteenth-Century Williamsburg* * (University Press of Virginia, 1965); and Peter H. Wood, *Black Majority: Negroes in Colonial South Carolina from 1670 Through the Stono Rebellion* * (Knopf, 1974). Two interesting studies of the Chesapeake area are T. H. Breen and Stephen Innes, *"Myne Owne Ground": Race and Freedom on Virginia's Eastern Shore, 1640–1676* (Oxford University Press, 1980), and Barbara Jeanne Fields, *Slavery and Freedom on the Middle Ground: Maryland During the Nineteenth Century* (Yale university Press, 1985).

For studies of the role of the common people during the revolutionary era, see Alfred F. Young (ed.), *The American Revolution: Explorations in the History of American Radicalism* * (Northern Illinois University Press, 1976), and Edward Countryman, *A People in Revolution: The American Revolution and Political Society in New York, 1760–1790* (Johns Hopkins University Press, 1981).

2

THE NEW
NATION

Artisan Republicanism

SEAN WILENTZ

The new nation sought to embody an old but rarely realized political philosophy—republicanism, a form of government in which the people would rule. Republicanism in theory, however, has never been republicanism in practice. The issue was then, and still is today, how near to the theory can the reality draw?

In his book on the American working class in the early nineteenth century, Sean Wilentz (Princeton University) suggests that the idea of republicanism contains five elements. The first four, drawn from the work of J. G. A. Pocock, are (1) an attempt should be made to establish the public good; (2) citizens should exercise virtue—that is, place the common good above their own needs; (3) in order to exercise virtue, citizens have to be truly free, not dominated by others; and (4) citizens have to participate actively in political affairs. Wilentz has added a fifth element that is particularly relevant to his study: citizens should be equal and should possess civil and political rights in a democratic system of government.

From the foregoing, we can easily see how elusive genuine republicanism, however well-intentioned, would be in any actual society. What interests Wilentz, in the chapter from his book reprinted here, is the way in which the artisans in New York City at the turn of the century sought to embody those republican ideals in their public and private lives. To some extent, the very structure of the craft system worked against them. The three-tiered system of masters (those who ran the shops and paid the workers), journeymen (those who were equipped to exercise their craft but worked for wages), and apprentices (those who were in training, learning the skills that would allow them to become journeymen) had a built-in notion of inequality that was at odds with the egalitarian ideal.

As the artisans struggled with this issue in the work place, certain changes taking place in the broader society would make it even more difficult for working people, skilled and unskilled, to exercise their republican ideals. The developing bourgeois capitalism would further divide those who owned the means of production from those who worked for wages. In addition, the gradual "deskilling" of production workers would lead increasing numbers of employees into patterns of dependency that would erode their sense of independence and autonomy, the qualities that figured so largely in the period described by Wilentz. By the time the factory system was in place in the second half of the nineteenth century, it became increasingly difficult to find the aforementioned republican ideals widely practiced in any economic sector of American society.

I n the early nineteenth century, to be an American citizen was by definition to be a republican, the inheritor of a revolutionary legacy in a world ruled by aristocrats and kings. What it meant to be an American republican, though, was by no means self-evident. As early as 1788, James Madison observed that political writers had used so many definitions of the term that "no satisfactory one would ever be found" by recourse to texts alone; more democratic-minded New Yorkers agreed. With the social and political transformations of the next half-century, the versions of American republicanism multiplied, as men of different backgrounds and conflicting social views— eastern bankers and western yeomen, slaveholders and abolitionists, evangelicals and infidels—came to judge themselves and each other by their adduced adherence to republican principles. A singular political language bound Americans together, an extraordinary manifestation of apparent unity when set against the continental and British experience of the age of revolution. Beneath this superficial consensus, Americans fought passionately over the fundamentals of their own Revolution, in a nation gripped by profound (if fitful) changes in economic and social life.

New York's artisans, masters and journeymen, had their own sense of what it was to be a republican, as the English writer James Boardman discovered during a visit in the late 1820s. Like some of his more celebrated countrymen, Boardman was fascinated by America and its com-

ARTISAN REPUBLICANISM   From "*Chants Democratic*": *New York City and the Rise of the American Working Class, 1788–1850* by Sean Wilentz (New York: Oxford University Press, 1984), pp. 61–103.

mercial capital, but he refused to restrict himself to the urbane literary drawing rooms that misled many visitors into describing New York as a genteel haven from the barbarism of the backwoods. Boardman was after the lowly shopkeepers, the poor mechanics who he hoped would enlighten him about ordinary Americans. One afternoon, he interviewed a local jeweler, who summarized the artisans' political beliefs with an anecdote. It seemed that earlier that day the jeweler had sold an ornate brooch, "executed in garnets and of French workmanship," to a fortunate young mechanic. The youth, it turned out, could not distinguish an emblem of royalty from other designs, and when a friend later told him that his new prize was in fact the Bourbon device, he blanched. "His republican feelings would not permit him to wear the badge of tyranny for a moment," Boardman later recalled, "and with breathless haste he hurried back to the jeweller for something more congenial to democratic feelings."

Some months later, an immigrant workman named John Petheram learned that the artisans' "republican feelings" were sufficiently strong to help dictate the organization of the workshop. Petheram, the articulate son of a family of textile workers, fled to New York to seek his fortune in 1830, as rick burning and loom smashing spread across the English countryside. Trying his hand in several shops and stores, the young man was amazed at the apparent backwardness of the city's employers. He later remembered one, the drug maker John Morrison, as typical. "I tried to make the old fool Morrison believe," Petheram related, "that by dividing the labour, which was not done there as it [is] in England, more work could be done." The benighted man, it seemed, "had never read Adam Smith," nor had he considered "the volume of experience which is open to every man but which ignorance, bigotry, or prejudice prevents so many from ever looking into." "This, sir, is a free country," the offended Morrison shot back. "We want no one person over another which would be the case if you divided the labour." Morrison, it turned out, was not alone in his "prejudice." "They were all alike," Petheram lamented of the small master employers, "I have heard this over again, with the addition of 'Tories may be very well in England but we want none here.' "

Reading these stories today brings a jolt: here is an America that confounds our expectations, one that does not entirely square with the impressions of the most thoughtful traveler of the age, Alexis de Tocqueville. As Boardman found out, conformity to the egalitarian ideal, far from a pretext for money grubbing, still had visceral political meanings for ordinary mechanics; Petheram, apart from suffering the irony of having to tell his bosses how to be better capitalists, discovered that acquisitive individualism, the pursuit of profit, was not necessarily the summum bonum of the American republican character, at least when it came to division of labor in the workshops. Both men, in their search for America, stumbled upon what remained of a distinctive system of meanings, one that associated the emblems, language, and politics of the Republic with the labor system, the social traditions, the very products of the crafts.

First evident in the pre-Revolutionary crisis, this artisan republicanism hardened in the 1790s, as the craftsmen came to terms with what the Revolution meant to them; through the late 1820s, it helped mold them as a social group and offered some real basis of solidarity between masters, small masters, and journeymen. At the same time, however, the craftsmen re-examined the meanings of both craftsmanship and republicanism, in view of the ongoing changes in the social relations of the trades. As late as 1825, artisans of all ranks could still join together, much as in 1815, in mass proclamations of artisan republican unity; simultaneously, a complex process was underway, in which masters and journeymen in the dividing crafts began to invent opposing interpretations of the artisan republican legacy. From this ideological counterpoint, between continuity and change, consensus and conflict, came evidence of both the lingering power of old patterns of thought and the emerging shape of class consciousness. Its origins lay in politics and in the artisans' fight against political subordination in the mercantile city.

REDEEMING THE REVOLUTION

For the leading citizens of eighteenth- and early-nineteenth-century New York, society was meant to be a network of lower-class loyalty and elite influence. Social distinctions derived from a combination of occupation, wealth, religion, ethnicity, and family ties; the artisans, even the wealthiest among them, were generally held at arm's length by the mercantile elite, scorned as "mere mechanicks," men of the lower or middling sort. When applied to New York's shifting array of competing family interests, this social code helped foster a fractious political system of patrician control and popular participation. Independent artisans did have an important place in electoral affairs as early as the seventeenth century, both as candidates and as voters; far more than their counterparts in Boston and Philadelphia, New York's contending gentry and merchants actively (if with detectable condescension) sought the craftsmen's support. Participation in politics did not, however, guarantee the artisans power or unity. Caught as they were in webs of patronage, restricted by the scrutiny of viva voce polling and divided to a degree by the competing religious claims of Anglicans and Presbyterians, the artisans remained politically fragmented and beholden to their social superiors until the eve of the Revolution. The popular movements of the 1760s and 1770s widened some cracks in this establishment and permanently altered the way in which mechanics and other urban plebes took part in New York City politics. But as the elitist political persuasion revived after the Revolution and persisted after 1800, the artisans once again had to find their political voice and fight for a share of local power. Over the next two decades, in alliance with non-artisan politicians, they consolidated their position as a vital political interest and affirmed, in the reflection of the Revolution, an egalitarian political tradition all their own.

To understand fully the passions and traditions behind these developments, we must retrace our steps back to the streets and committee rooms of the 1760s and 1770s. Historians have long puzzled over the social significance of the Revolution for the urban mechanics; most recent work agrees that a democratic artisan-based popular movement evolved in New York from the Stamp Act crisis to the coming of the Revolution (culminating between 1774 and 1776), one allied with and for a time led by West Indies–trade merchants and shippers but one with its own awakening political consciousness. The movement arose only gradually and on several fronts. Mobbing and ritualized street demonstrations, the chief forms of collective protest for urban plebes in the Old World, were quite familiar to late-eighteenth-century New Yorkers, accepted as normal (if, to some, undesirable) manifestations of lower-class displeasure and high spirits. As in Hanoverian London, the causes of these disturbances ranged from the mundane to the seemingly bizarre, from competition for work and suspected price fixing to alleged grave robbing by cadaver-hungry medical students from Columbia College. So, too, the New York crowds generally stuck to the Anglo-American norms of highly symbolic actions (burning of effigies, wearing of costumes) interspersed with limited and discriminate violence to property. During the Stamp Act crisis, the mobs also assumed a distinctly political and oppositional character, as crowds of Liberty Boys, led by small merchants and privateersmen, sacked the home of one British officer, forced the resignation of the local stamp distributor, burned effigies, destroyed the governor's coach, and posted placards, signed "Vox Populi," that threatened any printer who used stamped paper. Political crowds reappeared to defend the liberty pole against royal soldiers in 1766, to cheer a jailed leader of the Sons of Liberty in 1769, to engage the garrison in bloody street fights in 1770, to dump a small consignment of tea into the harbor in 1774, and to seize the local armory after news arrived of the Lexington battle. In June 1776, crowds stripped professed Tories of their clothes, rode them through the streets on rails, and threw them in jail. Political ideals and more everyday social resentments mingled in these outbursts: anger at impressment and at moonlighting troops, for example, was indistinguishable from broader issues of American liberty in the confrontations of 1766 and 1770. By taking to the streets, however, and by exerting their will—sometimes beyond the intentions of their leaders—the crowds also challenged the course and prerogatives of New York's loyalists and more conservative Whigs, in ways far more threatening to established political standards

than those of earlier crowds—or so it seemed to their opponents, one
of whom wrote in 1774 of the need to halt the activities of *"Cobblers
and Tailors* so long as they take upon their everlasting and immeasurable
shoulders the power of directing the loyal and sensible inhabitants of
the city."

While the mobs established a ritualized, boisterous artisan political
presence, regularly organized groups created a new framework for popular patriot politics and in time elaborated a coherent set of democratic
political ideals. The first semiformal associations arose alongside the
mobs, as radical mechanics helped lead the anti-British agitation by
adapting established campaign techniques. Open-air meetings and door-
to-door canvassing, coordinated by the Sons of Liberty, galvanized opposition to the Quartering Acts and support for nonimportation. Similar activities followed the imposition of the Intolerable Acts. The
formation of an independent Mechanics' Committee to replace the Sons
of Liberty in 1774 revealed a maturing artisan self-confidence in political affairs, as well as a deep distrust for the city's more moderate Whigs.
It also insured the survival of what Alfred Young has described as the
city's militantly anti-British, increasingly democratic brand of popular
Whiggery. Plenary sessions met in the committee's new Mechanic Hall,
sometimes as often as once a week, to debate the intensifying crisis and
coordinate radical actions. In 1776, as war became inevitable and Loyalists temporarily fled the city, the committee exercised a growing measure of power, issuing a string of declarations on American independence
and demands for political reforms, including universal manhood suffrage. For one heady spring and summer, the city fell under the sway of
an extraordinary popular political debate, heavily influenced by Paine's
electrifying *Common Sense* (published the preceding January). The
groundswell at once coalesced anti-British opinion and opened discussion about what an independent American would look like. Gouver-
neur Morris, that shrewd conservative, had seen what was coming two
years earlier: the "mob" had, indeed, begun to think and reason.

A new political world took shape in these efforts; although the
British military occupation in 1776 halted popular politics in New
York, the artisans resumed political action as soon as the redcoats departed. Mobbing and street demonstrations reappeared as instruments
of the popular will, when reactions to the French Revolution, the panic
of 1792, the announcement of the Jay Treaty in 1794, and several more
minor disputes prompted the usual parades and destruction. The spectacular William Keteltas affair of 1796 repeated the pattern, with all
the bravura of the London Wilkesite disturbances and the Sons of Liberty campaigns of thirty years earlier. The fracas began when two Irish
ferryboat men were convicted and sentenced—one to a public whipping—for having cursed a local alderman and refused to depart from
their schedule to carry him across the East River. Keteltas, a young,
struggling Democratic-Republican lawyer, took up the ferrymen's case,

calling the court's decision an abomination and the state legislature's failure to intercede "the most flagrant abuse of rights . . . since the Revolution." Keteltas's persistence earned him a jail sentence as well, for contempt of the authority of the assembly—but not before Keteltas and his Republican friends had mobilized the political nation out-of-doors, to accompany the lawyer to his final showdown with the legislators. The passions were genuine, but the proceedings could have been prepared as a script, as Keteltas (the assembly chamber hushed, its galleries packed to overflowing) delivered his final defiant refusal to recant, only to be lifted on a chair and carried through the streets to the jailhouse while thousands chanted, "The Spirit of '76." Two months later, when Keteltas was released, he was met by another crowd that once again carried him in parade, this time on a phaeton bedecked with American and French flags, a phrygian cap, and the inscription "What, you rascal, insult your superiors."

All of this would have been familiar to anyone who had lived through the 1770s. The difference, betrayed in the almost comic tone of some of the press reports on the Keteltas affair, was that the dramaturgy of the crowd was of decidedly secondary importance in the 1790s, displaced by the more regular forms of participation begun by the artisan committees. In 1783, the mechanics' votes elected a popular Whig ticket to the assembly; in 1784 and 1785, a new committee of mechanics nominated its own slates; committee petitions pressed the legislature and the Congress for protective tariffs, payment of state debts, free public education, and restrictions on the political rights of former loyalists. Over the next two years, the mechanics' links with politicians soon to be identified with the city's Federalists also strengthened, as concerns over the tarriff—and approval of a national Constitution strong enough to enact one—led them directly to Alexander Hamilton and the city's conservative nationalists. The conservatives, for their part, courted the trades, with hopes of gaining a popular base to break the radical ascendancy in state politics. When George Washington was inaugurated president in 1789, no group in the country was more fervently pro-Federalist than the New York artisans.

The Federalist liaison, convenient for a time, was far too rife with contradictions to last long. From the start, the conservatives' political assumptions flew in the face of the legacy of democratic action left to the artisans after the Revolution. Although Hamilton learned to suppress his elitism and politic among the mechanics, he never quite abandoned his faith that the artisans regarded the elite as their natural superiors—that "Mechanics and Manufacturers will always be inclined with a few exceptions to give their voices to merchants in preference to persons of their own professions and trades." Any chances for a more permanent Federalist-artisan alliance eroded in the early 1790s, amid numerous local controversies—above all over the chartering of the mercantile bank and the legislature's failure to charter the Mechanics'

Committee—all exacerbated by the Washington administration's Anglophilic foreign policy and backtracking on the tariff. By 1794, some of the city's most politically active artisans had grown so disgruntled that they allied with like-minded men from outside the trades to form the Democratic Society of New York.

"[B]utchers, tinkers, broken hucksters, and trans-Atlantic traitors"—thus the temporary exile William Cobbett (still the Cobbett of "Peter Porcupine," not yet the Radical Cobbett of the *Political Register*) on the Democratic-Republicans. The New York society came, in time, to turn such descriptions to its advantage; some members even took a measure of pride in the titles attributed to them. All such descriptions misled: the Democratic Society was far from wholly plebeian; in the American context, it bore only fleeting resemblance to the French Jacobin clubs, and still less to the sansculotte sections of revolutionary Paris or the "Jacobin" artisan corresponding societies of London and the English provincial cities. Its officers were merchants and professionals of wealth like the redoubtable rentier Henry Rutgers; only in the ranks of the secondary leadership did craftsmen begin to show up in any numbers, along with young lawyers and teachers. The membership was small, probably numbering no more than two hundred. Although fiercely antiaristocratic, its circulars and protests displayed none of the root-and-branch democracy, none of the belief in "Members Unlimited" and universal suffrage that propelled the British and French artisan societies. Its public stance cannot be understood as "radical," let alone "revolutionary"; in the truest test of its faith, during the Whiskey Rebellion, the society condemned government repression and the excise tax system but also stoutly disapproved of the rebels' armed resistance to "the execution of constitutional law." In its structure, temperament, and intent, the Democratic Society was more an embryonic political party–cum–vigilance committee than a revolutionary club or a mass movement. Although decidedly more egalitarian and outspoken than the mainstream of the emerging Republican opposition, it was destined to remain within the boundaries of what one historian has called New York's post-Revolutionary "partisan culture."

To stop there, however, would be to miss the importance of all that prompted Cobbett's denunciation and the society men's ripostes— and hence of the Democratic Society itself. While led by the familiar radical elite—the well-to-do libertarian dissenters, young lawyers, and shopkeepers who frequented the coffee houses and taverns off Liberty Street and Wall Street—the society also stretched into the artisan wards. How far is not clear. We know that the society held its meetings after dark because, it claimed, "[w]orkingmen must meet in the evening"; Alfred Young reckons that the vast majority of the rank and file were men of the "middling" and "lower" sort. Certainly the society reached the downtown printing shops and the tanneries and workshops in and around "the Swamp." More important, it built its primary alliances with the Mechanics' Committee (finally incorporated in 1792 as the General Society), the individual craft groups, and the militia—the updated versions of what had been the hard center of the popular democratic movement of the mid-1770s.

Furthermore, it is important to recall the political context of the mid-1790s—the *tone* of politics as conservatives dropped their conciliatory rhetoric for an undisguised contempt for democracy, the French Revolution, and (in some cases) the lower classes in general. Cobbett's rantings and the ham-fisted elitism surrounding the Keteltas affair were only examples of a pattern of antidemocratic alarmism in the eastern cities, a pattern less virulent in New York than in New England or Pennsylvania but just as ominously unctious in temperament. Charges that opposition to the administration was promoting demagogic factionalism soon passed into the pseudonymous slurs of one "Acquiline Nimble Chops, Democrat," who saw fit, in one of his milder passages, to dismiss the dissenting mechanics as "the greasy caps," the mindless multitude. A New York cartoonist's lampoons of the Democratic-Republicans made sure to include a tailor along with a pirate as part of the ignorant democratical crowd. Federalists were not being complimentary when they claimed that the Democratic Society had managed to attract "the lowest order of mechanics, laborers, and draymen." "Rabble," "a monster," "an incoherent mass of people"—all this (and there was more) might have been excused as the hyperbolic paranoia of procrustean conservatives, had it not been delivered by the very men, and the friends of those men, who now governed in the name of the Republic, men who denounced republican France and supported the Jay Treaty and who took heart at the admonition that one high-minded Federalist directed to the upstart mechanics:

> No tinker bold with brazen pate
> Should set himself to patch the state
> No cobbler leave, at Faction's call
> His *last,* and thereby lose his *all.*

It all at least sounded like 1774.

Against these outbursts and against Washington's excoriation of all "self-created societies," the Democratic Society raised the banner of Paine's *Rights of Man,* a defense of the French republican regicides and an egalitarian interpretation of the American Revolution, based on "sentiments of Democracy, founded upon the Equal Rights of Mankind." In strictly institutional terms, its efforts were most important in helping bring individual, and sometimes lowly, craftsmen and craft groups (including a portion of the fraternal, artisan-dominated Tammany Society) into what was becoming a disciplined local political opposition in Manhattan. In ideological terms, it captured the democratic thrust lost amid the Constitution debates and the consolidation of power by

New York's conservative nationalists, in effect making democracy a sine qua non of republicanism. "Painite" describes the society's politics best, with its hatred of all deferential forms, its distrust of the past and mere tradition, and its admiration for the man himself (who, ironically enough, spent most of 1794 languishing in a Jacobin prison, a victim of Robespierrist virtue):

> To conclude—Here's success to honest TOM PAINE:
> May he live to enjoy what he does well explain.
> The just Rights of Man we never forget
> For they'll save Britain's friends from the BOTTOMLESS PITT.

In time, such pronouncements, delivered at a Democratic-artisan Fourth of July festival in 1795, acquired something of a social coloration as well, as the society and its allies moved beyond defense of their right to associate, to ponder issues like the Hamiltonian finance program. Without coming close to questioning private property or raising the rights of the dependent poor, Democratic-Republicans did turn the classical republican fears of centralized financial power into suggestions that those who accumulated property without following a productive trade (that is, bankers, merchants, speculators) were politically suspect—suggestions that had arisen at the time of the nonimportation struggles, but never with such clarity and force. "Less respect to the consuming speculator, who wallows in luxury, than to the productive mechanic, who struggles with indigence," ran one toast of the New York Juvenile Republican Society in 1795. Such ideas, far from those of potential social revolutionaries, would be most effective in bringing the artisans into a developing party system. They also established in New York at the dawn of the industrial revolution the rough equation, elaborated for the British context in the second part of *The Rights of Man*, between political virtue and what would later be called the producing classes. For decades to come, such references to the spirit of '76 and the nobility of the productive mechanics would be the warp and woof of artisan political rhetoric.

It was, then, as a way-station, between revolution and egalitarian party politics, that the Democratic Society made its mark; although the group began to fade in 1797, the artisans it helped galvanize were already well on the way to forming more enduring coalitions to beat back the threat of "aristocratic" supremacy. By 1800, a clear mechanics' interest had developed, in league with Republican politicians, fed by pro-tariff sentiments in the trades, and fully integrated as a pressure group in the city's politics. (Mobbing, of course, continued in early-nineteenth-century New York, with, if anything, greater frequency than before, but through the mid-1820s, New York crowds arose more from ethnic and racial conflicts and the punch-ups of the gangs than from political controversy. In politics, the artisans and others concentrated on party campaigns—with a street theater of their own—and on battles for local power.) Although they never challenged the mercantile elite's hold on most elective offices, craftsmen and former craftsmen, working mainly but not solely with the Jeffersonians, won a significant share of nominations between 1800 and 1815, especially to the state assembly and municipal posts. The selection of the sailmaker Stephen Allen as mayor in 1821 and the continued presence of craftsmen on party tickets until 1825 confirmed their political presence through the Era of Good Feelings. Throughout, the city's most prominent mechanics, particularly those in the General Society, used their good offices and political clout to win concessions, on restricting state prison labor, rejecting municipal workshop plans, widening the suffrage, and furthering endless more private concerns.

Plying the machinery of the early party system, the mechanics' interest assumed a political style that later generations of New Yorkers would come to associate with the New York Democracy. Unbending elitists like the young Washington Irving looked on aghast while "old cartmen, cobblers, and tailors" clambered onto the hustings, as if a set of demotic lunatics had been turned loose to arouse "that awful despot, the people." In fact, they were witnessing the emergence of a new social type, the enterprising artisan party politician. Stephen Allen was the exemplar; indeed, his political career, like his rise in business, read like a parable of the transitions from the 1770s to the Jeffersonian era. As a boy, Allen had thrilled to the activities of the popular pre-Revolutionary movement and pored over the popular Whig and radical republican texts, above all *The Crisis:* reading Paine aloud to his uncle, he later recalled, inspired "a feeling of reverence" and drew the youngster into "the enthusiasm of the people of this city in favor of liberty." This informal political education—reinforced by the frustrations of living in a patriot household during the British occupation of the city—set Allen's democratic views, and in the 1790s he joined the Democratic-Republican opposition. Soon thereafter, Allen's rising stature in the trades, capped by his election to the presidency of the General Society in 1802, attracted Jeffersonian politicans to him. In 1812, he was elected to the Common Council, where he remained for nearly a decade to devote special attention to reordering the city's finances and minor democratic reforms. His success and undisputed popularity among the mechanic voters won him three terms as mayor from 1821 to 1824.

Another side of artisan politics appeared in the person of the Tammany brave, Matthew Livingston Davis. Davis, a printer, was like Allen an officer in the General Society and, at least initially, a genuinely dedicated Democratic-Republican partisan. In the 1790s, Davis and his partner, the journalist-poet Philip Freneau, led the counterattack in defense of the "self-created" societies; in 1800, having joined the Tammany Society, he actively supported Thomas Jefferson. Casting his lot with the friends of Aaron Burr, Davis became, over the next quarter of a century, one of the most accomplished wire-pullers and political agents in the city, pioneering the art of painting his opponents (whatever their creed) as aristocrats, while he appropriated the rhetoric of the humble artisan. In 1803, he tried to lead the mechanics' interest into a Burrite schism, playing upon artisan dissatisfaction with Mayor Edward Livingston over the mayor's proposal for a municipal workshop for criminals and the poor; Davis's speeches rang with charges that Livingston's humanitarianism disguised aristocratic plans to build a state monopoly with convict labor and "reduce the mechanics of this city to the degraded state of those of England." Five years later, unperturbed by the failure of his scheme, Davis outlined a precocious vision of organized party politics, in which party regularity and loyalty—staying "in unison with the wishes and expectations of the party"—would be the main standard of political virtue. Davis's personal power fluctuated through the 1820s, but his achievements helped pave the way for a kind of thoroughly professional democratic party politics that would come into its own during the ascendancy of Martin Van Buren.

These artisan Jeffersonians were effective. The tallies for the state-assembly and city-council elections, in which virtually all masters and journeymen were eligible to vote, leave little question that the mechanics' interest and the artisan vote usually remained loyal to the Jeffersonians. This did not, of course, imply absolute political unanimity in the trades. Even as the crises of the 1790s shook artisan allegiances, some craftsmen—above all those not in need of tariff protection, poorer mechanics caught in clientage networks, some more substantial masters, and the relatively few ex-Loyalist artisans—remained in the Federalist fold. After 1800, the Federalists could count on winning at least one-third of the vote in the central and outer wards, and they never failed to field tickets on which at least one of the four candidates was from the crafts. Some of the city's most renowned master artisans, including Duncan Phyfe and the tanner Jacob Lorrilard, were active Federalists. Other artisans, disgusted at the rise of the new parties, condemned Republican and Federalist alike, as fixers who would make "abject slaves" of independent republicans. Joseph Harmer, for one, emphasized that the title of his newspaper, *The Independent Mechanic*, should be taken literally with respect to party politics, those "filthy sloughs of party declamation, those seas of error which have neither bottom nor shore." By one estimate, upward of one-third of the eligible "lower-class" voters (including artisans, carters, and laborers) failed to vote in any given election, a low figure by today's standards, but a mark of some apathy and early "anti-party" disenchantment among the trades. Nonetheless, apart from the years of the embargo, when Federalist candidates made inroads into the normally Republican districts, the Jeffersonians consistently carried the central and outer wards, with total significantly higher than those they received from the city as a whole. For most of the active artisans, masters and journeymen, politics meant supporting the mechanics' interest and voting the Jeffersonian ticket.

The political and ideological ramifications of these developments were profound. As in the debates of the 1790s, the early Jeffersonian campaigns, whether led by apparently sincere men like Stephen Allen or by more opportunistic polls like Davis, connected the fate of American equality to the political well-being of the middling producers—and of the Jeffersonians. Their messages were less "democratic" than those of the Democratic Society and its allies; the society, for example, had, in good Painite fashion, included several abolitionists in its ranks, while both the General Society and the Sailmakers' Society called for the end of slavery; the Jeffersonians, partners in an increasingly Negrophobic national political coalition, left the city's small black vote to the Federalists. Paine himself, his outspoken deism a political liability after his return to New York in 1803, was forsaken by the Republican politicians; he died nearly forgotten, in 1809. Within the limits of partisan politics, however, the Jeffersonians did their best to turn contests for the most minor of city posts into reprises of the 1790s—and, they implied, of the Revolution itself. Until 1807, the rhetoric changed little, as New York's slow-learning Federalists made no pretense about their belief that the Revolution had been fought for limited political goals, or about their Burkian fears that "Jacobin" Jeffersonians would excite "irreconcilable enmity between the rich and the poor" by stirring the swinish multitude. The Republicans—no Jacobins—gleefully attacked such notions as the musings of "Federal lords," the well-born nabobs and aristocrats whose goal was to "rob the mechanics and laborers of their independence of mind," and (as the Republican "Mechanic" told the trades in 1805) to "wantonly and basely take away your rights." After 1807, when the embargo and the war finally handed New York City's Federalists some popular issues, they altered their tone, and reached for popular support with their own "club," the Washington Benevolent Society—but they could do no better than to appropriate the artisan as hero and condemn their foes as "pampered sons of luxury" out of touch with the suffering workingmen. Even then, the Federalists retained some of their Anglophilic anti-Jacobinism of the 1790s, so much so that they reprinted pieces like Robert Southey's well-known philippic "The Friend of Humanity" in their party newspaper. The Republicans, for their part, denounced the Federalists as secret allies of the British war effort, fomenters of American disunity and therefore enemies of popular rights and independence. The links between the crafts and the vindication of political equality remained about the same as when they had first been forged during the Revolution. They lasted through the "one-party" politics of the 1820s.

The importance of this discourse, apart from its evocation of 1776 and the 1790s, was its social imagery: just as the largest of the city's trades were beginning to divide along new lines, the artisans remained, in politics, the "noble mechanics," graced with an assumed unity of purpose and interest against aristocratic foes that belied all evidence of strife in the shops. In fact, the mechanics' interest, the purported political voice of all tradesmen, was decidedly controlled by the city's leading masters. Nothing assured an artisan's success in politics more than election as an officer of the General Society. All but three of the twenty-eight society presidents who served between 1785 and 1815 were eventually nominated for either the Common Council or the assembly, and of those nominated nineteen were elected. None of the artisans who ran for the senate or assembly was a journeyman at the time of his nomination. While the issues raised by mechanic politicians—convict labor, the tariff, Livingston's workshop scheme—touched the lives of lesser artisans and journeymen, they were of utmost direct import to independent artisans. The journeymen's protests provoked very different responses. The organized cordwainers tried for conspiracy in 1809 received virtually no political support, apart from that of their two Republican lawyers. Strikes, when reported in the party press, were treated gingerly, usually with a simple statement of the facts. One of the few exceptions, a commentary on the carpenters' turnout in 1810 by the English Jacobin emigré and Republican editor James Cheetham—himself a former journeyman hatter—denounced the strikers for raising "unreasonable" demands and threatening commerce. In a rare instance when one of the parties addressed the journeymen, it was a Federalist apologist, "Brutus," who attacked certain Republican tanners and master shoemakers for alleged meanness to their employees; "Brutus"'s sincerity, though, was suspect from the beginning, suspicions borne out when he dropped all references to the journeymen after the autumn election. By otherwise sidestepping emerging class divisions within the trades, the mechanics' interest and its allies at once revealed the limits of their concerns and insulated politics from possibly fractious disputes; attacks on alleged "aristocrats" tapped an older set of anti-aristocratic, anti-elitist social resentments to provide all artisans with a common ground.

Thus, the Revolutionary legacy left artisan political life with a potentially powerful set of contradictions between the rhetoric of collective equality and the actual conditions in the trades, between the street cries of party democracy and the realities of who, in fact, held political power. In time, the underlying social divisions in the crafts and the political alienation shared by some artisans would replace the mechanics' interest and the Republican alliance with very different kinds of commitments and coalitions—but only after the Republican coalition itself collapsed in the late 1820s, the victim of its own internecine strife. In the aftermath of the 1790s, and for a quarter of a century thereafter, New York's masters and journeymen retained and responded to the ideals of the late eighteenth century, for the protection and expansion of their collective political rights against the static, deferential harmony of unquestioned elite supremacy—or, more loosely, for "equality" against "aristocracy." Even as they came to blows in the workshops and the courts, they were as one in politics—the "sinews and muscles of our country," as one Jeffersonian put it—ever prepared to redeem *their* Revolution against any who would trample on their political liberties, against any who would inject "corruption . . . through the veins of the body politic."

REPUBLICAN RELIGION

While politics offered the artisans some unifying continuities with the Revolution, the city's religious life reinforced their egalitarianism and widened their cultural distance from the mercantile elite. Colonial New York had been the most Anglican of American cities; through the early 1790s the Episcopalians (especially) and the Presbyterians, along with the remnants of the Old Dutch Reform establishment, were the city's reigning denominations. Apart from those dissenting Presbyterians who had been caught up in the millennial fevor of the Great Awakening or been pushed to the borders of Unitarianism, New Yorkers worshiped their fathers' faiths, with a dogma and sense of social exclusiveness—symbolized by the church pew rents—that enhanced the prestige of the city's leading families. Trinity Church, that former bastion of elite Anglican respectability, was formally disestablished in 1784 but retained the immense tracts of land that made it the wealthiest institution in Manhattan. So the smaller churches continued to give New York high society much of its prestige. Timothy Dwight, during his famous visit, noted with satisfaction that the city was an eminently religious one, where "few, even of the licentious, think it proper to behave disrespectfully toward persons or things to which a religious character is attached."

No one body of doctrine prevailed among New York's artisans during these years. A minority belonged to the more respectable Episcopalian and Presbyterian congregations; a disproportionate number of artisan Democratic-Republicans seem to have adhered to Presbyterianism, with its strong connections to American Whiggery and the patriot cause. The remainder included infidels, Methodists, Baptists, and an unchurched majority. Religion certainly played a part in the collective life of the trades: the craft societies' annual Fourth of July exercises, for example, invariably ended in a church, usually Presbyterian or Dutch Reform, and often included a sermon from a local clergyman. Even in church, however, the artisans warned of the evils of ecclesiastical authority and of the lurking dangers of a resurgent, corrupt, European-style clericalism. In their diversity, they shared common ideals about the place of religion in a secular republic.

The deist movement of the late 1790s contributed, if only in a minor way, to the stock of artisan religious views. To the shock of Federalist leaders and orthodox clerics, Elihu Palmer, a blind itinerant preacher, managed to turn his newspaper, the *Temple of Reason,* into the leading exponent of early national American freethought. Lambasting Christianity as an instrument of despotism, Palmer (in time, with the help of Thomas Paine) blended humanist ethics and the natural religion of Paine's *Age of Reason* in a celebration of science and republican equality: "Poverty and riches, misery and happiness, are generally the results and consequences of good or bad governments—of wise or unwise laws—of the influence of virtue, or the prevalence of vice; and all the *natural* offsprings of human actions, not the *partial* operations of an all-just and all-wise Being." Drawn both from the French and from the rich body of English Dissenting skepticism, Palmer's American deism attracted a mixture of homegrown merchant philosophes, liberal professionals, and artisans (with their own backgrounds in workshop science and democratic politics). Their numbers were hardly overwhelming. Even in the libertarian milieu of the Democratic Society (of which Palmer was a member) at best a handful of activists joined the deists. The milder Unitarianism of Joseph Priestley (welcomed by the Democratic-Republicans upon his arrival in New York as an exile in 1795) was better suited to New York's unorthodox democrats; when the Republican Patriotic Junior Association toasted Thomas Paine in 1797, it celebrated *The Rights of Man* but condemned *The Age of Reason.* The deists' real impact reached beyond their followers to reinforce more widespread and nebulous anticlerical suspicions. Thus the Democratic Society, in a circular letter issued in 1794, noted that "SUPERSTITION in a religious creed, and DESPOTISM in civil institutions, bear a relation to each other similar to that which exists between the children of common parents." For a time, it was enough to convince even levelheaded Episcopalian conservatives like the Reverend Clement Clarke Moore that the de-Christianizing Jacobin uprising had begun, led by the Democratic-Republican followers of "those imps who have inspired all the wickedness with which the world has of late been infested."

Nothing of the kind was in the offing: organized deism declined rapidly between 1804 and 1810, caught between the Second Great Awakening and Republican confidence that the re-election of the freethinker Jefferson had vindicated the separation of church and state. But its traces—and the traces of a rowdier popular impiety joined to democratic politics—lingered. A few small Universalist sects like the Society of United Christian Friends struggled and survived, kindling among the craftsmen ideas on universal salvation not entirely unlike those of Paine and Palmer. Cruder activities brought legal consequences for a few men hauled before the Court of General Sessions to answer charges that they had scandalized Christianity. Anti-Federalist politics sometimes mixed with irreverence, as they had in the 1790s: in 1821, the printer Jared Bell was arrested for allegedly entering a store, cursing and swearing and using profane language saying " 'God Almighty was a *dam fool*' for creating such men as composed the Hartford Convention and that if it was in his power he would send them and the whole

British nation to Hell together. . . ." More forthrightly blasphemous was the reported crime of one John Danforth—a shout in the street that "Jesus Christ is a bastard, his mother a whore, and God a damned old whore master." Even angrier spirits attacked clerics with chamber pots, menaced would-be missionaries, and destroyed church property.

The passions of revivalist religion, quite unlike the intensely cerebral democracy of the deists or the impiety of the rowdies, also distanced its adherents from orthodox devotions. Compared with other eastern cities, particularly Boston, New York had shown little interest in the great religious upheavals of the eighteenth century, but the Second Great Awakening brought a sharp rise in church membership between 1800 and 1825. Encouraged by itinerant veterans of the British and rural American circuits, a series of increasingly intense waves of revivals hit Manhattan after 1805, on a scale that surprised even seasoned clergymen. The Methodists, a persecuted sect in colonial New York, made the greatest progress. Due largely to the efforts of Methodist missionaries in the city's central and outer wards, what had been a handful of congregations in 1800 became, in twenty-five years, one of the three leading centers of Methodist worship in the United States.

Methodism, like the other evangelizing faiths, carried with it a gamut of impulses to New York—all tied to the tensions between submissiveness and egalitarianism that lay at Methodism's core. None of the Methodist congregations, not even the most "popular," preached a faith comparable to the deists' and liberal Presbyterians'; as Sydney Ahlstrom reminds us, early-nineteenth-century Methodism derived neither from an optimistic view of human nature nor from American democracy, "but from John Wesley—a different source indeed." More orthodox, authoritarian Wesleyans like the Reverend Nathan Bangs deplored the "extravagant excitements," the "clapping of hands, screaming, and even jumping" reported in congregations that kept to the looser ways common in eighteenth-century popular churches. Eventually, Methodist leaders, headed by Bangs and allied with the city's New School Presbyterians, would be more closely identified with efforts to enforce an industrious morality of self-discipline. But this took time to achieve: in post-Revolutionary and early national New York, Methodism was preeminently a religion of and for the middling and the poor, its Arminian doctrines on grace slicing through the social exclusivity of conventional Episcopalians and orthodox Calvinists. Preachers from humble backgrounds themselves—Bangs was the son of a Connecticut blacksmith—pointed out that in their churches, seats were free and open to all. Here, even journeymen and lowly day laborers could know the Redeemer, He who, in Bangs's words, "hath died for all men, and thereby opened the door of mercy for all to return and find peace and pardon." It was a message that families of the middle and outer wards had never heard; the overwhelming majority of those who heeded it were small shopkeepers, artisans, and laborers.

The more democratic aspects of evangelical religion permeated all sorts of popular devotions. Thurlow Weed noticed the difference when he visited the Methodist congregation of the immensely popular John Summerfield after having spent his first Sundays in New York at more staid Presbyterian and Episcopalian churches. What struck Weed most was the near charismatic rapport between the preacher and his audience:

> He was followed from church to church by great numbers, cheering and chastening all ears and all hearts. If any went to scoff, they immediately "remained to pray." . . . [H]e was himself a simple, unostentatious, "meek and holy" believer and follower of that Saviour to whom, in person and character, he bore such striking resemblance.

More idiosyncratic—and still more democratic in faith and style—were the sectarian preachers, the "religious enthusiasts of every belief" who David Bruce recalled could be seen along New York's thoroughfares at almost any time of day. These included some well-known locals and visitors—Lorenzo Dow, the Methodist apostle of love who used New York as a rest stop during his eastern travels; Domanic Van Velsor, the so-called stove-fence preacher; and Amos Broad, the much-persecuted upholsterer and evangelist of Rose Street—but none attracted more attention than Johnny Edwards, the Welsh immigrant small master scale-beam maker of the Ninth Ward. Edwards (it appears to have been his real name) arrived in New York in 1801 and swiftly passed through a series of religious affiliations, from Anglican to Methodist and Baptist and Quaker, before he founded his own Church of Christ, in Greene Street in about 1808. As much showman as evangelist, Edwards would drive his scale-beam wagon to the most crowded parts of the city to regale the sinful passerby. His thoroughgoing vision of earthly corruption (according to Bruce, he would always balance his beams in his cellar because he insisted that "there is no virtue on the surface of the earth"), his devotion to the poor, and his defiance of the rich all marked him as a "mechanick preacher," in a tradition that stretched back to the English radicals of the Commonwealth. In 1810, when Edwards joined with one Dorothy Ripley to attempt a revival, he took to appearing in Wall Street, where he shouted through a three-foot-long tin trumpet for the moneylenders to repent. Undaunted by the failure of his prediction that the world would end on June 10, 1810, he remained active; more than a dozen years later, he scoffed at efforts by city fathers to subsidize missionary efforts by more reputable clergymen: "I firmly believe it would be far more acceptable to God and all good and wise men," he wrote in one petition to the Common Council, "had you laid out 300 dollars in fat geese and turkeys and given them to the poor who have seen better days and they would prefer it any time to 300 dollars worth of wind." Other lay preachers expounded more directly political beliefs. One, a gardener named David Whitehead, delivered a mock Fourth of July sermon at Potters Field in 1826, calling down wrath upon New York's "pretty set" who dressed in rich attire and lived in luxury and abundance. "They have established robbery by law and a law for the protection of robbers," Whitehead exclaimed; all they cared for was wrestling property from workingmen and propping up their privileges with "threats of sedition and blasphemy" borrowed from "King John the First"—John Adams.

Politics and religion also commingled in the artisan neighborhoods as matters for intense debate and discovery. They dominated the discussions of one group of artisans who met regularly in "Saturday night sessions" at the shop of Cox the Cooper, near Corlears Hook, about 1820. Celebrations of republican heroes and attacks on supposed Tory villains dominated the conversations; military relics from the Revolution and the War of 1812 were occasionally passed around for appropriate veneration. Several participants also had "brimstone on their shoulders," and endless arguments pitted a few Calvinists and Presbyterians against an array of Methodists, Close Communion Baptists, Universalists, and a man who arrived one evening to declare that he had "renounced the iron-clad mysteries of the Presbyterian Westminster Oath." The most heterodox views received a hearing, if not always a friendly one: at least one of Cox's friends reported he had been swayed by the sea-captain disciple of a Universalist minister "who had invented a new religion that left Hell out altogether." "Soon as I get time," the curious blacksmith Joe Holden wrote to his mother, "I intend to study the matter for myself and see what there is in it. Like as not his doctrine may not be so bad after all."

Yet in the end, while impiety and popular enthusiasm exerted their influences, most artisans held to a profound and shameless indifference toward any kind of organized devotion. The extent of apathy became clear just after the War of 1812, when groups of younger, affluent Presbyterians, mindful of the evangelicals' success, tried to bridge the social gap by sponsoring interdenominational missions, Sunday schools, and Bible groups in the central and outer wards. On ordinary Sundays, the tract missionary Ward Stafford found in 1817, fewer than one in four New Yorkers—and far fewer in the poorer areas of the city—attended church. Emblems with a magical (and, to Stafford, pagan) significance—horseshoes and other talismans—were more in evidence in lower-class homes than were Bibles. "We have found the people deplorably ignorant as it respects the subject of religion," Stafford lamented.

It would be foolish to try to impose unity upon such diverse currents of artisan piety, irreligion, and apathy; most of the time, these tendencies were at war. Even so, the most contradictory forms of artisan devotion had some things in common. Among those of some faith, Christian and non-Christian, doctrines of spiritual equality and objections to unquestioned deference recurred in various contexts, implying a cultural independence and mistrust of the city's gentlemen and their clerics. The deists and Universalists were explicit on this: "It is a point of policy in the hierarchy," Palmer held, "to cherish [a] submissive temperament, and cultivate in the soul of man the divine virtue of humility." More pious declarations stressed that possession of earthy riches and power did not signify grace—indeed, to some, the accumulation of great personal wealth raised suspicions of sinfulness. The Methodists' appeal to the lower classes, despite the Wesleyan hierarchy, was quite direct here, as were the professions of spiritual equality published in the *Independent Mechanic*. The poem "Saturday Night," by "Journeyman Mechanic," was typical in its emphasis on the "blessed peace" that came with the Sabbath:

> Of rich and poor the difference what?—
> In working or in working not
> Why then on Sunday we're as great
> As those who own some vast estate.

From such statements, with all of their implied resignation to *earthly* inequality, it was a short distance to more forthright denunciations of the anxious pursuit of money and of all those who would imitate the ways of the mercantile elite, described by one mechanic as "the absurd and vicious positions of a gay, thoughtless, and licentious people," trapped in "a personal hell." And from here, it was a direct path to Johnny Edwards on Wall Street and David Whitehead at Potters' Field.

More straightforward was the artisans' overriding resentment at what craft spokesmen of all faiths described into the 1820s as unrepublican religious authority. Only in Old World aristocracies, they charged, would "presumptuous men" of "insolent morality" use God as an adjunct to political power and social prestige. Only enemies of the Republic would hold superstitious beliefs that elevated the clergy and some classes of men over others and that chained men's minds to a prescribed faith. As Thomas King, a Universalist shoemaker, told an Independence Day assembly of craftsmen in 1821, such "ecclesiastical depotism" had proven "the most cruel—the most unrelenting kind of despotism" that ever tormented man." Fortunately, religious reformation and republican revolution had shaped an America where such power was supposed to be illegitimate; all the same, in the wake of continuing clerical denunciations of the French Revolution and the "Jacobinical" Jefferson, the artisans and the politicans who sought their votes urged vigilance. The Republican George Eacker was direct in 1801 when he accused the Federalists of assuming a "garb of hypocritical sanctity," and warned the tradesmen to beware the combination of monied influence and ecclesiastical influence, "in the hands of faction . . . instruments more dreadful than the dart wielded by Death!" A generation later, speakers reminded the artisans that the Republic had been founded "on the broad basis of *rational* liberty," without any religious cast. For Thomas King, as for his fellow Universalists, such sentiments led to a celebration of rationalism and "the Sun of Science"; for the Methodists, it suggested pursuit of the millennium free from state interference; for most craftsmen, it meant that they should be left alone.

Only very late in the early national period did more portentous signs of religious strife begin to appear in artisan discourse. The most striking, anti-Catholicism, had always been implicit in artisan rhetoric and republican politics and religion. No "idolatrous invocation to saints" marred the artisans' public gatherings, Eacker told the crafts in 1801; on the contrary, their celebrations expressed only "abhorrence against such unblushing wickedness." In the streets, the maraudings of the gangs sometimes turned into full-fledged riots, pitting natives and Irish Protestants against Irish Catholics; there is evidence that a New York version of the Orange order gathered some underground support in the trades just after the War of 1812. But the Scarlet Whore of Babylon never quite turned up in artisan speeches in the early years of the century, and was unlikely to, given the relatively small numbers of Catholics in the city and their even smaller proportion in the crafts. If anything, Irish resistance to British and landlord rule prompted sympathy for the "persecuted catholick" and "poor peasant," whose talents, and intrepidity, Samuel Berrian pointed out in 1812, had won a "scanty and uncertain harvest." By the 1820s, however, antipapist expressions became more open, as Irish Catholics—carriers of what one printer's ode called "papal gloom"—figured more prominently in New York social and political life. In 1824, an Orange celebration of July 12, Battle of the Boyne Day, brought furious sectarian violence in and around the taverns of the Irish weavers' community in Greenwich Village. Nothing distinguished the men of Corlear's Hook more, one chronicler of the 1820s noted, than their "intense, ardent, and deep-seated" detestation of Catholicism. It would re-emerge, in more organized forms, in the 1830s and 1840s.

The continuing ferment of the Awakening and the changing relations in the workshops further altered the place of Protestantism in New York artisan life after about 1815. The tightening of Methodist discipline effected by Bangs had the dual effect of marginalizing some of the more enthusiastic preachers and congregations and binding evangelical religion ever closer to the creed of morality and self-repression. Simultaneously, the city's largely Presbyterian and missionary tract societies began to relax their more rigid Calvinist doctrines on conversion and grace. With their increased emphasis on actually winning poorer men to Christ, the tract societies and Sunday-school reformers stepped up their work, to make New York, by 1825, a leading center of what was soon to become an effective national evangelical united front. Their success at winning master craftsmen to the cause was evident in the Apprentices' School banner in the Erie Canal march; a broader evangelical insurgence lay behind the master stereotyper Adoniram Chandler's plea to his colleagues in 1816 to "suppress vice as well as encourage virtue," and behind the exhortation of a Presbyterian minister, delivered to the city's artisan-dominated fire companies nine years later, to take "a Bible in one hand and a sword in the other" in a popular crusade against deism, Socinianism, and other infidelities.

After 1825, artisan anti-Catholicism and the evolving strains of evangelical Protestantism would culminate in organized nativism and in abrasive clashes between infidels and believers, churched and un-churched. The point to stress, however, is that these later developments, with all of their divisiveness, should not be abstracted from their historical context. Although ethnic tensions were constant, only in the 1830s, when migration to New York from the most heavily Catholic peasant areas of Ireland accelerated, would antipapism become a potential political tool for organizing artisans and craft workers; only in the middle and late 1840s, when the famine wave hit New York and entered a far more fractured, industrializing craft economy, would economic nativism become a vital force in the crafts. Similarly, evangelicalism began to affect the shops directly only when the new workshop regime—and the social boundaries of class—that had begun to emerge in the Jeffersonian period matured. Until then, the artisans' disparate religious views provided a rough analogue to their democratic politics, opposed to all men of "insolent morality" who would ratify their presumed social superiority with the Word of God.

And so we return to democracy and egalitarianism, to the artisans' resistance to political and social deference, as a source of unanimity in the trades. Beyond this reverence of equality lay the deeper ideological connections, noted by Boardman and Petheram, that the artisans made between their ideals of the Republic and their ideals of craft. More than egalitarianism alone, it was the ways in which the craftsmen associated politics and craft production that distinguished them as artisan republicans in a city just entering the world of the nineteenth-century workshop and market. To understand what these connections were, we must look again, in more detail, at all of the artisans' regalia—for it was precisely in order to make the connections explicit that the trades maintained an extraordinary series of public ceremonies.

"ARTICELS EMBLEMATTICAL OF OUR TRADE"

On July 23, 1788, between five and six thousand craftsmen—virtually every artisan in New York City—turned out for a grand procession to support ratification of the Constitution. It was a well-organized political event (a similar parade had been held in Philadelphia two weeks earlier), "pleasing for every Federalist to see," one journalist observed—the first major street demonstration in the city since the Revolution and the emotional highpoint of the Federalist-artisan alliance. It also turned into a celebration of craft, as masters, journeymen, and apprentices marched together, each trade under its own banner, to affirm the artisans' contributions to the city and the benefits to be won with a protective tariff. The display of the blacksmiths, sailors, and ship joiners was typical, headed by a scaled-down model of a frigate (named, appropriately, *Alexander Hamilton*) and featuring a banner that proclaimed: "This federal ship will our commerce revive / And merchants and shipwrights and joiners shall thrive."

Nearly forty years later, and a decade after the celebration of the Treaty of Ghent, the craftsmen joined the procession to celebrate the opening of the Erie Canal. A great deal had changed—among other things, the hero on this day was Gov. DeWitt Clinton, the nephew of Hamilton's archrival in New York, George Clinton—but the crafts' regalia had not. Marching by trade (although a few journeymen's groups marched apart from their masters), the artisans once again honored their arts with ancient symbols and greeted the latest advance for American commerce as a boon to the commonwealth. Once more, nearly all employers and employees turned out, to carry banners (including some that had been used in 1788), to perform craft pageants in mock workshops, and otherwise to praise their arts. The printers' song extolled the typical themes:

> The Art, which enables her sons to aspire
> Beyond all wonders in story
> For an unshackled press is the pillar of fire
> Which lights them to freedom and glory.

As before, the artisans seized the opportunity to celebrate themselves.

So the trades trooped their colors continually in the early national years. In 1794, a grand parade of different crafts (now under Republican, not Federalist, leadership) marched with fife and drum to the Battery and then, by boat, to Governor's Island, to help reinforce the city's fortifications and demonstrate their displeasure at the Jay Treaty. Similar processions, complete with trade banners, traveled to Brooklyn in the summer of 1814 to work on the Brooklyn fortifications. Independence Day, initiated by craft groups and the Tammany Society in 1794, assembled masters, journeymen, and Republican politicians through the 1820s. On a less grandiose scale, the trades held exercises with the militia companies each November 25, to honor with "profuse and patriotic jollification" the day in 1783 when the British army evacuated Manhattan. Through the first decade of the nineteenth century, the General Society was almost as preoccupied with ceremony and with public displays of its crest as with its benevolent and financial projects. Journeymen's groups like the Society of Shipwrights and Caulkers spent most of the membership's dues on such items as "a skooner to be carried

in procession," "musick at celebration of the Grand Canal," certificates, badges, ceremonial caulking mallet, and other "articels emble-
mattical of our Trade." Special events—laying the cornerstone of the
Apprentice Library, dedicating the Mechanics' School—brought color-
ful exercises prepared by the General Society.

What are we to make of these demonstrations? Certainly they were
something new on the American scene: although the scrappy evidence
left by eighteenth-century mutual-aid societies suggests that American
artisans had at least some familiarity with older British trade iconogra-
phy, nothing that has so far been uncovered shows that the craftsmen
in New York or any other seaboard city held any craft processions or
ceremonies prior to the Revolution. Nor were the early national parades antiquarian curiosities, staged to honor a distant past: the largest
processions, after all, celebrated the artisans' support for economic expansion. Progress, innovation, and prosperity—these were the artisans'
themes, not static traditionalism or corporate deference.

With all of their innovations, however, festivities also linked the
artisans to long-standing craft ideals, to emblems and images that had
grown from the matrix of British guild regulations and that evoked what
one historian has called "the shadowy image of a benevolent corporate
state." In England many of the outward displays of craft pride—the
Lord Mayors' Shows, the banners, the craft pageants, the patron saints—
had long since faded or disappeared by the early nineteenth century,
victims of the dislocations of capitalist development—but they had not
died out completely. In New York, with the winning of independence
and the creation of a benevolent republic, the old emblems still seemed
appropriate enough to serve as proper representations of the crafts. A
full-scale retrieval of British craft ritual ensued. In 1785, when the Mechanics' Committee designed its seal, it borrowed the arm-and-hammer
sign used by several London trades as early as the fifteenth century and
appropriated the artful slogan of the London blacksmiths. The Constitution procession included several features of an old Lord Mayor's Show:
separate trades performed workshop pageants and carried banners that,
apart from their political allusions, would have been familiar to any
Elizabethan Londoner. The tailors' banner, like those in English
parades, depicted Adam and Eve and bore the legend "And They
Did Sew Fig Leaves Together." The cordwainers' flag included a view of
the good ship Crispin arriving in New York harbor. The ship model
carried by the joiners and shipwrights may have done Hamilton's heart
good; it was also a reprise of a motif dear to seventeenth-century
London shipbuilders.

The symbolism survived over the next four decades, to reappear in
even grander form in the Erie Canal parade. The journeymen tailors
returned to a pastoral image in 1825, with their banner of a "Native"
receiving a cloak, above the motto "Naked Was I and Ye Clothed Me."
The coopers carried the same banner they had used in 1788 and erected

a platform on which two men and a boy—the conventional trio of master, journeyman, and apprentice—built a large cask. The printers, as before, worked presses and turned out celebratory odes to the day. The master, journeymen, and apprentice combmakers featured a miniature workshop, in which seven men and boys "of the trade," using the latest in simple hand-powered machines, finished 600 combs. Seven other trades performed similar pageants in motion. The hatters carried a picture of their adopted patron with the words "St. Clement—Hats Invented in Paris in 1404." The Bakers' Benefit Society frankly copied its banner from the one presented by Edward II to the London Company of Bakers in 1307. Other insignias, guild heralds and incorporation dates appeared beside more predictable republican images, like the chairmakers' American eagle.

Between innovation and retrieval lay a set of connections between craft and politics spelled out in the banners, speeches, and street dramas. At one level, the ceremonies announced the artisans' determination to be part of the body politic—no longer "meer mechanicks," no longer part of the vague lower and middling sort of the revolutionary mobs, but proud craftsmen, appearing for all to see on important civic occasions, marching in orderly formation up and down lower Broadway with the regalia and tools of their crafts. Apart from their skills, this pride appeared lodged in the social solidarities evoked by the ideal craft communities of "the Trade." Marching together, the employers and employees in each craft formed a symbolic body of their own. To be sure, the independent masters took their rightful place at the head of the artisan order, a position emphasized in 1825, when highly respected masters from the different trades led their respective delegations; nonetheless, each trade stressed its collective harmony, cooperation, and self-respect. Even the most arcane icons contributed to the corporate trade ideal. The biblical allusions in the banners, for example, were no demonstrations of a secret baroque piety; rather, as in the earlier English artisan festivals, they offered each trade a collective identity, sometimes underscored in the banners' mottoes like the coopers' "Love As Brethren" and the cordwainers' "United We Stand."

Just as important were the marchers' contentions that their work was essential to the well-being of all, an integral component in the commonwealth of trade, agriculture, and industry. The tailors' banner, pointed out not only that their labors were as old as Eden or that they were unknown only to "Natives" but also that all God's children need tailors. At times, the artisans advanced what appear to have been residual "precapitalist" ideals about their relationships to their clients as well as about the relations of production: utility—the use value of the handicrafts, and not the luxury or special advantages of the artisans' goods—was their central claim for their products, voiced in the name of the trade as a whole rather than as a kind of boastful advertising ploy. As if to summarize their direct services to the city, some delegations to the

1825 march, most notably the printers and combmakers, handed out samples of their work to the throngs of spectators. Several trade banners, like the chairmakers' picture of a chair with the motto "Rest For the Weary," emphasized both pride in craftsmanship and a collective sense of public service. In all cases, a sense of worthiness prevailed, tied to an idealization of the artisan system of production and distribution quite unlike the entrepreneurial regime that had begun to emerge in the city's workshops. To drive the point home, craftsmen and Jeffersonian politicians at various celebrations noted that they had gathered to celebrate what one master called "the common bond and mutual sympathy," the "ties and attachments . . . interwoven with the strongest feelings of the heart," that supposedly governed the artisan community.

Linked to the commemorations of "the Trade" was the craftsmen's treatment of politics. Guild heraldry established the antiquity of the crafts but not the craftsmen's attitude toward monarchy; in place of the old holidays and saints' feasts observed in England, the artisans substituted suitably republican red-letter days. Independence Day and Evacuation Day were the most important annual celebrations; even in their occasional ceremonies, the trades tried to assemble on July 4 or November 25, when they would "swear eternal allegiance to the principles of Republicanism." In the processions of 1788 and 1825, patriotic banners billowed beside craft banners; on the Fourth, either an artisan or a Jeffersonian politican delivered an address on the blessings of republican government; through the 1820s, speeches rang with denunciations of Old World luxury and pomp and repeated the contention of an early spokesman that "the feelings expressed by a freeman on an occasion like this are unknown to the subjects of Kings." The craftsmen's grandest efforts celebrated a benevolent republican state—one that would enact tariffs and finance canal building—but also celebrated their own sovereignty over that state. The regalia had royal pedigrees; the artisans themselves were attached to "republican simplicity," "the genius of America" and "just notions of Liberty, founded upon the RIGHTS OF MAN."

These exhortations did not merely displace British loyalties with more patriotic, democratic sentiments; rather, they indicated how thoroughly the tradesmen understood the framework of republican political thought and how they associated the Republic with their conception of "the Trade." Most striking were the ways in which the speakers invoked the key concepts of eighteenth-century American republicanism—independence, virtue, equality, citizenship, and commonwealth (or community)—and explained their meaning for the crafts. Independence signified, in the first place, independence from Britain and the freedom of New Yorkers to ply their arts without foreign interference. "However great our natural advantage," the Reverend Samuel Miller claimed at one of the first artisan festivals, "they would have been in vain had the shackles of British power continued to bind and restrain us." Prior to the Revolution, the editor and General Society member M. M. Noah argued a quarter of a century later, "we saw and felt our dependent state," as "the native ingenuity of our Mechanics was checked"; only after the "legitimate owners of the soil" had reclaimed the city could mechanical genius flourish. Even more, independence connoted *personal* independence, or what John Irving called "independent equality"—the ability of each citizen to think and act free of the restraints of others and of the corrupt privilege so evident abroad. "Suffer no one to DICTATE imperiously what line of conduct you are to pursue," the sailmaker George Warner told the crafts in 1797, "but at the same time let no one be sacrificed on the altar of public opinion for a cordial and liberal expression of his sentiments." Later spokesmen picked up the argument and charted a course of personal independence through the preservation of "the rights of man," and resistance to all attempts to turn American mechanics into "vassals and slaves."

As they spoke of independence, the artisans also shied away from endorsing the pursuit of self-interest for its own sake: each citizen, spokesmen explained, had to be able to place the community's good before his own, exercising what they called, in classical republican style, virtue. Warner made it plain that those who sought personal gain alone, particularly in politics, were "distinct from the general interests of the community," unvirtuous men who would lead America, like the civilizations of old, "on an inalterable course towards despotism, where the dividing line between the rich and poor will be distinctly drawn and the *latter* will be found in a state of dependence on the former." "[L]et virtue be the foundation of distinction," George Eacker concurred a few years later. A proper republic, John Irving declared in 1809, sustained a polity where "those are exalted whose . . . superior virtue entitles them to confidence." Love for America's "splendid monument of political wisdom," Samuel Romaine remarked three years later, required recalling "that virtue is its basis."

These were ideas that came from the Painite tradition and broader currents of republican thought; accordingly, for the artisans, equality and citizenship did not imply a leveled society of absolute economic and social democracy. Not until the late 1820s did propertyless small masters and journeymen express any basic objection to what Mercein called society's "artificial distinctions" of wealth, or the inevitability that those would persist. Nor did the artisans, masters or journeymen, show any interest in promoting the fortunes of the poor, those dependent persons who could easily become the tools of tyrants, men Irving described as "that uniformed class . . . who, like dull weeds, sleep secure at the bottom of the stream." Equality instead connoted political equality, the right of all independent, virtuous citizens—including the artisans—to exercise their will without interference from a nobility of privilege, wealth, or title; citizenship, by extension, stood for men's obligations to exercise their natural political rights. It was in this sense, balancing libertarian ideas of political equality with social duties, that Warner berated those men of honest industry who "considered themselves of TOO LITTLE CONSEQUENCE to the body politic" as unintentional traitors; so, too, it was to equality and citizenship that Irving referred when he extolled the republican polity as one where leaders are "revered as legislators, obeyed as magistrates, but considered as equals."

These familiar republican concepts, on their own, linked the artisans with well-established patterns of American political thought and expression. What made their observations singular were the ways in which they blended American republicanism with the ideals of "the Trade." Even as they marched with other civic associations and celebrated the commonwealth, the artisans diverged from older assumptions that the trades were merely one of many important groups, a deferential estate within a larger social corporation. While they extolled commerce, they expressed misgivings about capital; without denying that prosperity demanded a proper balance between merchants, farmers, and mechanics, the artisans made quite clear that they considered the small shop as the very embodiment of republican values. Contrary to what some New Yorkers believed, Warner told the mechanics' societies, "the possession of riches is not necessarily accompanied by superior understanding or goodness of heart"; indeed, he remarked, "the experience of ages confirms that a state of mediocrity is more favorable to them both." Independence would be lost if men of great wealth ruled the Republic since, as the educator and Republican politician Samuel Mitchill (not a poor man himself) indicated, "it is soon discovered that *money* is *power*, that power gives the possessor of it *importance*, and that *importance begets respect.*" Men of relatively little means like the craftsmen were less likely to be seduced by "the studied refinements of luxury" or "the splendid follies of wealth," the mason John Rodman hinted in 1813; the domestic arts were, he thought, "more congenial with the nature of our government and conducive to the general happiness" than any other calling. In sum, an urban variation of the Jeffersonian social theme of the virtuous husbandman emerged, one that fused craft pride and resentment of deference and fear of dependence into a republican celebration of the trades. John Irving offered the image of the artisans as "the very axis of society," in whose hands "must the palladium of our liberty rest." Others stated flatly that the craftsmen's skilled labors facilitated republican politics and exposed aristocratic threats. The printers were especially eager to point out, as George Asbridge told his fellows in 1811, that their trade was "one of the most deadly engines of destruction that can possibly be arrayed against the encroachments of despotic power." Samuel Woodworth's odes to his trade made similar claims, with suggestions that Faust, the printer of legend, was the world's first republican.

The metaphorical association between the Republic and "the Trade" fortified the artisans' egalitarian republicanism. Like the Republic, the crafts themselves reputedly respected individual abilities but also stressed virtuous mutuality and cooperation. Each competent master appeared, in his workshop relations, as the quintessence of independence, free to exercise his virtue uncorrupted; the dependence of journeymen and apprentices—in principle a temporary condition—was tempered by their possession of a skill and graced with the affection and respect of their masters, in what Noah described as a web of "reciprocal obligation." The workshop, a site of collaborative labor, ideally turned out both handicrafts useful to the public and new independent craftsmen to replenish the ranks of the trades. The masters supposedly lived not solely by the labor of others but also, as in the mock workshops, by their skills and by the sweat of their brows; they along with the skilled employees were precisely the kinds of unselfish, productive men whom the Republic needed, for they neither exploited others nor were, in the words of one General Society speaker, "slavishly devoted" to anyone else. Moreover, the artisans' association between craft and politics was a dialectical one: just as the bonds of the craft supported and complemented the Republic, so republicanism, as the artisans interpreted it, enhanced the economic as well as the political position of the crafts. It did not surprise the New Yorkers that British and European craftsmen were "in subjection at the point of a bayonet." Only in republican America, they claimed, where workingmen were citizens, could the artisans hope to protect themselves from the whims of would-be aristocrats; only in a land where virtue and cooperation were prized would the arts be fostered and the connections between masters and employers endure. So corrupt were the Old World monarchies, Eacker noted, that "even with their masters, manly dignity degenerates into haughtiness and sullen pride." It was, by contrast, "in consequence of our Republican form of government," Samuel Berrian intoned in 1815, that "our whole experience has been a series of brilliant improvements and expanding prosperity."

Here, all the strands of artisan political egalitarianism, craft pride, and social commonwealth pulled together. Like other social groups, the artisans sustained a classical republican political language long after what Gordon Wood has described as the death of "classical politics" in America. With that language, the artisans blended the cooperative ethos of "the Trade" with the democratic, libertarian sentiments characteristic of Paine, the artisan committees of the Revolution, and the Democratic Society—all to the point where each was indistinguishable from the other. Adaptation of those long-established ideals did not signal a mass yearning for a static past; repeatedly, the artisans railed against their former economic and political dependence and looked with optimism to a prosperous future. Their vision was egalitarian and suffused with the ethic of the small producer—but not "liberal" or "petit-bourgeois," as the twentieth century understands the terms. It was a vision of a democratic society that balanced individual rights with communal responsibilities—of independent, competent citizens and men who would soon win their competence, whose industry in the pursuit of happiness, as in politics, was undertaken not for personal gain alone but for the public good.

Obviously, the longer the artisans repeated these idealizations, the more they diverged from actual conditions in the shops. At times, the artisans appeared to take account of these disparities by altering their rituals and speeches accordingly, attaching new meanings to the old language. On at least three occasions (and probably more often), individual journeymen's societies held their own Fourth of July ceremonies independent of their masters, to toast themselves, as the shoemakers did in 1811, as "a useful and intelligent class in society." In the Erie Canal march, five journeymen's groups assembled under their own banners. For their part, the master craftsmen, from about 1815 on, began adding exhortations to entrepreneurship to their glorification of rights and virtue, transforming the very definitions of the familiar terms. "Equality," for M. M. Noah in his 1822 address to the mechanics, also stood for equality of opportunity for men to rise in the world by dint of their own ambitions, talents, and merits. "In large cities," Thomas Mercein told the celebration to honor the Apprentice School in 1820, "employment and intercourse with the rest of the community are extensive and multifarious, and contracts and responsibilities are constantly entered into"; thus, each artisan had to learn the ways of the counting-house, to avoid dissipation and follow "the paths of industry and virtue, morality and religion" in order to enlarge his "capacity and knowledge to understand rights and detect errors" in his contractual dealings. Even with these adjustments, however, the festivities preserved at least a semblance of their original purport. Journeymen, even those who celebrated on their own, usually stuck to honoring the Republic, their arts, and the trades. In the Erie Canal parade, at least two of the journeymen's societies saw fit to march side by side with their masters, in joint contingents of "the Trade"; the vast majority of journeymen, including the shoemakers and hatters, performed in the time-honored fashion. The masters still spoke of their obligations to the crafts, still performed in the pageants of 1825, still retained the forms of the republican trades.

In the 1830s, even such ceremonial camaraderie could not be reconstructed; celebrations and symbols reappeared, but to define the rifts of class between masters and journeymen, not to celebrate the harmony of craft. As E. P. Thompson has remarked about similar changes in English craft ritual, this passage from the corporate identity of "the Trade" to the duality of employers' groups and journeymen's unions "takes us into the central experience of the Industrial Revolution." For the moment, however, it is essential to note the power and persistence of craft themes of mutuality and cooperation in early national New York. Despite all that was dissolving the customary social connections, the artisans' egalitarianism remained inseparable from their small producers' ethic. At the dawn of the nineteenth century, with the American Revolution still a fresh memory—to be rehearsed and refought in elections—and with New York's variant of the industrial revolution barely underway, this set of associations produced the most clearcut definitions of artisan pride and social identity. They remained strong enough to unify the republican trades through the early 1820s, if only for a few days a year.

REPUBLICANISM AND CONFLICT

What, then, became of artisan republicanism during those episodes when the harmony celebrated in the mock workshops dissolved into strikes and protests? Evidence about the ideological dimension of these events is scanty, amounting to little more than a few brief newspaper dispatches, some letters, and some courtroom speeches and testimony, only a fraction of it by the artisans themselves. What remains reveals craftsmen struggling to match their artisan republican idealism with their recognition that the trades were changing and, in some cases, had begun to disintegrate. Neither republicanism nor its artisan variant could on its own fully explain or solve the issues raised; even so, artisan republicanism, though tested and at times revised, was not obliterated. This struggle to fit old ideals to new conflicts was most clearly displayed at the trial of the journeymen cordwainers in 1809.

The trial followed one of the many attempts by journeymen in the consumer finishing trades to regulate the composition of the work force. In 1808, members of the Journeymen's Cordwainers' Society, the best-organized in the city, accused the partners James Corwin and Charles Aimes of hiring an elderly nonsociety journeyman and an illegal apprentice, contrary to society regulations. Corwin and Aimes begrudgingly fired the objectionable journeyman but refused to release the boy, and their men walked out. When, soon afterward, other masters agreed to take on Corwin and Aimes's orders, the society called a general strike of the trade and demanded both an end to the masters' collusion and an increase in piece rates. Some twenty master shoemakers, including the city's largest shoe employers, then swore out a complaint against two dozen union leaders, charging them with raising a conspiracy to interfere with trade and deprive the journeyman fired by Corwin and Aimes of his livelihood. By requesting a conspiracy prosecution, the masters hoped to sustain a judgment brought in a similar case in Philadelphia in 1806; at the least, the masters might break the union; at most, they might obtain a de facto legal ban on trade unionism. For their defense, the journeymen managed to acquire the services of the exiled Irish Jacobin and Jeffersonian William Sampson; the prosecution was handled by another Irish Jeffersonian with equally impressive Jacobin credentials, Thomas Addis Emmet, Robert Emmet's brother. Although the prosecution would resort to arguments about the applicability of the common law that were then popular in Federalist circles, there is no evidence that the trial was a surrogate battle between antilabor Federalists and prolabor Jeffersonians, as historians once supposed; Sampson and his assistants were the only Jeffersonians to come to the journeymen's aid. New social problems, far more perplexing than the ins and outs of party philosophy and politics, prompted the legal debate.

Emmet opened up an attack on the journeymen for violations of both political and economic equality. How, he asked, could the unionists' attempts to coerce their masters and their impositions on the nonsociety journeymen and the shoeless customers be deemed "the mere exercise of individual rights?" More directly, how could the right to strike be considered "sound political economy"? Individual rights, Emmet insisted, were secured by allowing "every man, according to his own will, follow his own pursuits"; by making a combination for their own private benefit, the journeymen had perpetrated the most tyrannical violations of private right. Sampson, lacking any coherent theory of trade unionism but well-schooled in the ambiguities of political economy, tried to demolish the prosecution with the arguments of "the profound and perspicacious Adam Smith." As the defense interpreted him, Smith had proven that master tradesmen were in permanent conspiracy against their workmen, "so much so," Sampson observed, "that it passes unobservable as the natural course of things, which challenges no attention." It was this prior "sordid combination" to oppress the journeymen that led the unionists to organize; their right to do so was questioned, in Sampson's view, only by those smitten by the "superstitious idolatry" of the common law.

Such arguments could not have demonstrated more forcefully that conceptions of labor as a commodity, free and unrestricted in the market, had badly eroded older artisan notions of workshop justice and mutuality, at least among the master shoemakers. The trial's significance, however, rests less in the differences between master and journeyman than in how both sides tried to adapt egalitarian republican politics to a still unfamiliar confrontation: above all, it is the *plasticity* of ideals about individual rights that stands out. Compared with the adversaries of the 1830s, the parties of 1809 appear oddly awkward, unsure of where their arguments might lead; it was as if they were improvising for the first time, in the closeness of a New York courtroom, the accusations and appeals that would arouse thousands in the future. Even more, artisan republican standards of commonwealth and independence remained at the heart of the matter. As Emmet explained it, the selfish journeymen had violated not only the masters' market rights but their own duty to the commonwealth, that "tacit compact which all classes reciprocally enter into, that when they have partitioned and distributed among the different occupations . . . they will pursue those occupations so as to contribute to the general happiness." Having been seduced by private interest, they had declared war on public policy and tried to constrain the independence of others, exerting what one prosecution lawyer labelled an "aristocratic and tyrannical control." The journeymen's defense in turn admonished the employers for their hypocrisy and their own unrepublican tyranny. Paradoxically, by his own use of Smith, Sampson tried to undercut the idea that the masters were simply individuals pursuing their rights; as much as ever, he proclaimed, they had collective interests—interests invisible to a casual observer. The problem, Sampson insisted, was that the "rapacity of the masters" had led them to switch their allegiances from the trade to themselves, to violate accepted workshop practices and deny their obligations, in Sampson's phrase, to "do justice by" their apprentices. Even worse, the masters, with the aid of the prosecution, tried to reinforce their position by smuggling aristocratic, unequal laws to America. "[I]s this not repugnant to the rights of man?" Sampson queried. "If it be, is it not repugnant to our constitution? If it be repugnant to our constitution, is it law?"

The trial ended in something of a draw. A guilty verdict was almost assured once the court had rejected defense motions to quash the indictment on the common-law question. In passing sentence, however, Mayor Jacob Radcliff equivocated, claiming that the journeymen's equal rights included "the right to meet and regulate their concerns and to ask for wages, and to work or refuse," but not to deprive their fellow citizens of their rights. He then imposed the light fine of one dollar plus court costs. It was hardly a judgment immediately to squelch journeymen's unions; within six months, the journeymen carpenters had commenced a long and bitter strike for higher wages; in 1811, the cordwainers' society—led by the very men indicted earlier—won a raise in pay with another general strike.

As the tensions in the crafts remained, the artisans in the city's fastest-changing trades continued to adjust their outlooks and their language. The masters, on several occasions, condemned the selfishness and unreasonableness of journeymen's demands and mixed a liberal interpretation of their market rights with professions of their supposed benevolence and superior knowledge of the conditions in the trades—those ideas proclaimed, in different contexts, by the General Society and the *Mechanics' Gazette*. By 1825, they were on the verge of making Smithian ideas irrevocably their own. Haltingly, meanwhile, the organized journeymen tried to construct a consistent justification for their actions. The union printers' declaration of 1816 on the inevitably opposing interests of masters and journeymen suggested a temporary hardening of distinctions; by the early 1820s, some journeymen had begun to examine the deeper social and economic matrix of their plight. Throughout, however, artisan republicanism provided the journeymen a kind of moral ledger with which to judge their masters and defend themselves. Their new understanding of artisan republicanism surfaced with peculiar force during the carpenters' strike of 1810. The masters, joined by the city's architects and surveyors, adamantly refused to concede their privileges in the face of the "increasing evils and distressing tendency" of the journeymen's militancy; least of all would they grant a standard rate of wages, by which they could no longer decide what to pay journeymen "according to their several abilities and industry." The journeymen replied that they had struck because their "haughty, overbearing" masters—including some "master builders in name only"—had misinterpreted their own interests and those of all carpenters by hiring men below accepted wage rates and by depressing the earnings of all, so that the journeymen could not expect to become masters. Even those employers whose abilities as workmen still held respect had forfeited all allegiance, by riding about in their carriages, building themselves brick homes, and assuming a demeanor that "better fits them to give laws to slaves" than to be master mechanics. The masters had denied both their fellow tradesmen and the Republic and had become paragons of acquisitive corruption; the journeymen struck as free men for republican justice. "Among the inalienable rights of man are life, liberty, and the pursuit of happiness," the journeymen declared:

> By the social contract every class in society ought to be entitled to benefit in proportion to its qualifications. . . . Among the duties which society owes individuals is to grant them just compensation not only for current expenses of livelihood, but to the formation of a fund for the support of that time when nature requires a cessation of work.

After 1825, such thoughts on class, natural rights, just wages, and the proper expectations of "journeymen through life" would help lead organized wage earners to draw even more audacious conclusions—conclusions which stressed individual liberty and moral benevolence but which also took a step beyond the perspicacious Adam Smith.

ARTISAN REPUBLICANISM AND THE LIMITS OF BOURGEOIS INDIVIDUALISM

It has long been a fashion among historians of disparate viewpoints to describe American northern society as "bourgeois"—"middle-class," "profit-oriented," and "modern" are other common terms—virtually from the seventeenth century on. Apart, perhaps, from the would-be demesnes of the Hudson Valley landlords and patroons, no real vestiges of feudalism ever developed in this country. With its abundance of land, its great need for initiative, and a population that had fled the authoritarian monarchies of the Old World (so the argument goes), America escaped the social tensions and political economy of Europe. Capitalism arrived with the first shiploads of white men: within the fluctuating limits imposed by London, the yeoman farmers, city merchants, and industrious artisans of the colonies eagerly competed in local and, in some cases, regional markets, exemplars of a competitive and democratic individualism, neither aristocratic landlords nor downtrodden cottiers. Richard Hofstadter, who caught the emptiness as well as the opportunities of this culture, most cogently stated as a "profound truth" that in order to understand early America, one had to envisage a "middle-class world." Early-nineteenth-century economic growth required no great ideological or social changes, but only those "revolutions" in transportation and communication necessary to unleash a pre-existing capitalist spirit, what Hezekiah Niles of *Niles' Review* called, in 1815, "the almost universal ambition to get forward."

In some respects, the artisans of early national New York conformed to these descriptions. Producing for a widening and increasingly competitive market, they could be clever entrepreneurs. The masters, or at least the leading craft entrepreneurs, had proven alive to (if not always adept at) capitalist business practices. Any doubts about the artisans' acquisitiveness would be overturned by the oratory of the General Society or the sign of the cornucopia of dollars that illuminated the peace celebrations of 1815. If any visitors questioned their abilities as businessmen, they had only to drop by Duncan Phyfe's workshop or to observe masters arranging for export of their goods to other cities. If any suspected that the masters and journeymen lacked appreciation of the benefits of commercial expansion, they had only to view the parade in celebration of the Erie Canal.

The "middling" republican politics of the mechanics—with their distrust of the power and culture of New York's nabobs and their lack of sympathy for the dependent poor—also called to mind what C. B. Macpherson has described as the more radical variants of bourgeois possessive individualism. The artisans' praise of their crafts, their resentment of the unskilled, and their attacks on merchant aristocrats and overbearing clergymen, all tempered by a respect for private property, exemplified a belief that independent men of relatively small means were both entitled to full citizenship and best equipped to exercise it. Their democratic assaults on political and religious deference, their professed respect for individual initiative, and their efforts in support of the economic interests of the trades all made them appear champions of those Franklinesque virtues that have long been interpreted as the germ of bourgeois propriety.

Yet the mechanics, with their artisan republicanism, also stood for much more. With a rhetoric rich in the republican language of corruption, equality, and independence, they remained committed to a benevolent hierarchy of skill and the cooperative workshop. Artisan independence conjured up, not a vision of ceaseless, self-interested industry, but a moral order in which all craftsmen would eventually become self-governing, independent, competent masters—an order to match the stonemasons' ditty that they would "steal from no man." Men's energies would be devoted, not to personal ambition or profit alone, but to the commonwealth; in the workshop, mutual obligation and respect—"the strongest ties of the heart"—would prevail; in more public spheres, the craftsmen would insist on their equal rights and exercise their citizenship with a view to preserving the rule of virtue as well as to protecting their collective interests against an eminently corruptible mercantile and financial elite. This fusion of independent liberties and personal sovereignty with social and corporate responsibilities—very akin to what others have called "collective individualism," the core of early American political thought—remained in uneasy and increasingly contradictory relation to the bourgeois tendencies of artisan thinking and to the inescapable fact that with the expansion of the craft economy and the transformation of labor relations, some craftsmen would never escape dependence on their masters and on the wage. Certainly, by 1825, much of what vitiated artisan republicanism had at some point been re-examined, interpreted by some masters as a justification for their own economic well-being and their innovations in the shops, and by the organized journeymen as a defense of their societies and strikes. Yet even then, the trades had to travel some social and ideological distance and to endure more momentous changes in the crafts before they would be governed by the kind of individualism that Tocqueville observed in the 1830s. And as the journeymen shoemakers' and other early strikes portended, this transit would be resisted.

Women, Revival, and Reform

MARY P. RYAN

When historians discuss the religious history of the American colonies and new nation, they tend to stress two related elements: Puritanism and the Great Awakening of the mid-eighteenth century. Puritans and their successors who led the Great Awakening left voluminous written records of themselves, and these records tend to overshadow accounts of the influence of other religious movements in our culture. In addition, historians often mention in passing the development of theories and practical methods for working out a separation of church and state, a unique phenomenon in Western civilization. In this connection, Roger Williams' halting efforts at promoting religious toleration in Rhode Island and the intellectual impact of the Enlightenment on certain of the Founding Fathers are prominent.

By 1800, however, the Puritan tradition began to give way. New England Congregationalism went through the throes of the Unitarian schism, and Calvininst theology was fast being replaced by the more humane doctrines of Arminianism, seen primarily in the work of the Methodists. It now seems clear that the most critical period of American religious development, and the one which has had the most lasting impact on the lives of religious Americans, was not the colonial era of Puritanism but the period known as the Second Great Awakening.

This movement is best known for its religious camp meetings that took place on the southern and western frontier at the turn of the nineteenth century. The Old World churches had brought to the New World certain traditions that were inappropriate in the rapidly spreading new nation. The tradition of high culture, with an emphasis on education and public decorum, did find a narrow foothold on the eastern seaboard, but it languished even there. As settlers moved to the interior, high culture did not follow. In the pioneers' lonely and risky lives, tradition was not as important as sociability and eternal security. The camp meetings provided the former need, and the Arminian theology, with its stress on the availability of salvation to all, served the latter.

The northern counterpart to the Second Great Awakening in the South was equally enthusiastic, although it did not have the peculiarly denominational character of the southern revivals. In the early nineteenth century, western New York State was so swept by religious fervor that it became known as the "burned-over" district. In her book *Cradle of the Middle Class*, Mary P. Ryan (University of California at Irvine) discusses the growth of the middle-class family in the heart of the northeastern revival area. In the chapter reprinted here, Ryan describes the impact of the Second Great Awakening on the family structure. She found that the traditional patriarchal family, already strained by social changes taking place was challenged by the patterns of conversion and organizational development that followed the revivals. A separate sphere of female activities developed both in the religious life of each community and in the life of the denominations most affected by the awakening. Women were provided with a realm of behavioral possibilities relatively free from traditional male dominance. The reform movements of the period owed much to this development, as the churchwomen sought outlets for their newly minted activism.

T he farmlands of Oneida County are still dotted with a few Greek Revival houses, most of them larger and more ornate than that depicted in the sketch of the Utica Building Association in 1820. They survive to testify that at least a few families resolved the contradictions of the New York frontier and managed to sustain a lineage of small farmers for generations into the future. By the fourth decade of the nineteenth century the men and women of Whitestown had made the necessary accommodations with the advances of commerce and rapid population growth, but not without a struggle. The sleepy villages of western New York did not retreat from history without one last burst of remarkable energy and creativity. A sequence of religious revivals and reform movements identified rural backwaters like Whitestown as the heartland of the Burned-Over District. Whitestown itself was crucially implicated in those epochal historical events. It was one of the first townships to be set ablaze during Charles Finney's tour in 1825. Ten years earlier Finney's future wife,

WOMEN, REVIVAL, AND REFORM   From *Cradle of the Middle Class: The Family in Oneida County, New York, 1790–1865* by Mary P. Ryan (New York: Cambridge University Press, 1981), pp. 60–104. Material copyrighted and reprinted by permission of Cambridge University Press.

Lydia Andrews, had confessed her faith in the religious center of the township, the First Presbyterian Society. The same congregation also enrolled the founders of the Oneida Female Missionary Society, which in 1824 allocated $192 to support Finney's first evangelical ministry.

The Female Missionary Society was the favorite project of a group of women who resided with their lawyer- and merchant-husbands around the port on the Mohawk River in the village of Utica, within the township of Whitestown. Itself an offshoot of the Whitestown Charitable Society, the Missionary Society adopted its evangelical focus in 1814 and promptly began to set up auxiliaries throughout the evangelical route that Finney would follow during the Second Great Awakening. These matrons of Utica commandeered a key social position at the foundation and within the infrastructure of the subsequent revivals. It would take more than thirty years for the cycle of conversions to run its course. The history of evangelism proceeded in the rhythms of family time, spanning the years between 1814 and 1838, when many of the first converts saw their lastborn reach early adulthood and join the church. Throughout the entire period Utica's coterie of evangelical females also nurtured strong ties to some fictive kin, to their "beloved sisters," assembled in churches throughout Oneida County and western New York State. This chapter will recount how and why Utica's women became the central nervous system of this evangelical network, which extended far into the surrounding agricultural districts. The Female Missionary Society and similar evangelican institutions were keenly sensitive to the family tension that sparked through town and country in the early nineteenth century. We shall see how, in converting these inchoate impulses and half-conscious concerns into revival enthusiasm, these evangelicals came to terms with some more terrestrial problems as well, not the least of which was the progressive erosion of the corporate family economy.

It is no coincidence that the course of the revivals paralleled the trade routes through Oneida County. The structure of communication, the divisions of labor, and the underlying causes of evangelism all followed the contours of a regional economic network. A market in goods as well as converts had its organizational nucleus in Utica. More than 40% of Oneida County's retail establishments were located in Utica, where the professional and financial services subsidiary to commerce, chiefly law offices and banks, were also centered. The first village directory, compiled in 1817, revealed that Utica was top-heavy with ambitious merchandisers. No less than 17% of the entries in the directory boldly put forth the business cards of "merchants," often prefixed with such terms as *commission, auction,* and *wholesale,* which announced the voluminous scale of these enterprises. The largest wholesalers among them dealt in agricultural commodities such as flour or leather. By the close of the revival cycle, the forces of commerce had penetrated into every corner of Oneida County to collect and distribute agicultural products. The fields of Whitestown were soon yielding tens of thousands of bushels of wheat, corn, and potatoes annually, and its dairies produced more than three million pounds each of butter and cheese. Marketing this surplus drew the farm families of Whitestown ever more closely into a commercial network whose traffic in cash, credit, and wages introduced some potentially divisive monetary interests into corporate farm families.

The families situated within Utica proper experienced the most explosive commercial fission. The demographic conditions of Utica during the canal era rivaled frontier Whitestown in their volatility. The town's population more than doubled between 1820 and 1830 and had quadrupled by 1840. Instant cities like Utica were no more hospitable to family formation than was a raw frontier. Few of Utica's newcomers, furthermore, seemed to share the strong family loyalties of pioneers like Hugh White. Most arrived in the busy marketplace alone, young, and unmarried. In 1820 more than one-fifth of Utica's population was between the ages of sixteen and twenty-six, whereas the supposedly more staid and rooted age group of over forty-five accounted for only 7.2% of the city's residents. Males and females were so mismatched in numbers and in ages as to discourage or postpone the formation of families. After the years of childhood, when boys were in the majority, females either arrived or remained in Utica in excess of their male peers and consequently dominated every age group. The pattern of sex and age stabilized in 1840 but with permanently unbalanced ratios. Women outnumbered men in Utica for the remainder of the antebellum period. Uticans employed a novel form of household organization and a new terminology of residence to identify this young, single population. In 1828 the city directory began to employ the term *boarder*, which in that year described the family status of no less than 28% of the employed males of Utica.

When families did form within the commercial entrepôt of Utica, they were rarely bound together in the manner of Whitestown's original corporate household economies. Wills probated in Utica, even before 1825, seldom paid homage to the stem family or to the generational continuity of the household unit of production. The fathers of Utica were four times more likely than their counterparts in Whitestown to provide for their children on the basis of simple equality and outright cash grants. Uticans also preferred to regard their widows as free economic agents; only 1 in 7 wills referred to the practice of dower. After 1825 the vestiges of the older patterns of inheritance all but disappeared in Utica. Discrimination on the basis of age and sex was rarely detectable in the will books. Conversely, the majority of the wills used the phrase "share and share alike" to underscore the simple egalitarian basis of children's bequests. The terms *free* and *simple* denoted a similar transformation in the inheritance of wives, the majority of whom were given absolute control of their husband's full estate after 1845. Thus, from an early date, the families of commercial Utica had revised the agricultural pattern of inheritance and seemed thereby to undermine the corporate, intergenerational dimension of the family.

This reformulation of the principles and practice of inheritance is rooted in the shrinking size of the material base of the corporate family economy, productive property. By 1835 less than half the household heads in Utica owned as much as the $100 in property that would subject them to taxation. Most of the citizens whose names appeared on the tax list, furthermore, owned merely a place of residence, a dwelling house rather than a place of business. Even before 1825 only one of the twelve wills probated in Utica transferred a productive enterprise, a farm, shop, or store, directly to the second generation. After that date the proportion fell to less than 2%. Most residents of Utica, including the majority of those who never bothered to write a will, probably owned too little to justify a complex pattern of inheritance. Abraham Miller's short will, which was probated in 1837, made this reasoning explicit. Miller prefaced his will with a reference to "my little property" and then proceeded to grant his entire estate to his wife. If any property remained after Mrs. Miller's death it was to descend in equal portions to their four children. Fathers like Miller simply did not possess the extent of productive resources that required the elaborate procedures for generational transfer once employed by the farmers of Whitestown. In this Miller was typical of the town's household heads, the majority of whom were employed in retailing, professional services, or casual labor, that is, bereft of any integral productive enterprises that could engage and unite the members of their families. Only Utica's artisans, with their family workshops, domestic division of labor, and productive resources, had the wherewithal to duplicate Whitestown's traditions of the corporate family economy.

As long as Whitestown's fathers retained their farmsteads, the corporate household economy was protected from the utter ravages of commerce. Thus in the 1820s and 1830s Whitestown still maintained allegiance to such corporate customers as dower and the stem family. At the same time, and again in opposition to the pattern in Utica, the incidence of simple equality in bequests to children declined dramatically in Whitestown. The majority of wills probated in Whitestown between 1825 and 1845 were so intricate that no clear overall pattern to the discrimination among children is discernible. This would suggest that it was becoming increasingly difficult and costly to preserve the family farm. As the supply of unimproved land dwindled and the cost of farm real estate rose, many small farmers were forced to distribute their agricultural property in an arbitary and unequal fashion, perhaps even excluding some offspring from the family patrimony. Alternatively, the profits reaped in commercial agriculture may have allowed more prosperous farmers to educate their sons or set them up in some nonagricultural business. In still other cases. Whitestown's sons and daughters might have responded directly to the enticements of market capitalism by breaking their own trails out of the agricultural family economy. Even in Whitestown, then, commerce had introduced a divisive wedge into the corporate family and opened up independent economic paths, especially for the second generation.

Similar changes were also under way in the growing industrial segment of the local economy. When Benamin Walcott, Jr., put his new textile mill into operation in 1827, less than one-fourth of his workers were employed in family groups. The bulk were listed on the payroll by individual names and issued independent cash wages. By the end of the next decade, when New York Mills had become one of the top ten cotton manufacturers in the United States, the family system of accounting was no longer in use at all. The labor force was composed entirely of independent workers, most of them young and female. Thus the increasing differentiation of the economic network had installed, in the very center of the township of Whitestown, a system of production that seemed to repudiate the family order. One of Walcott's mills employed 250 females, 100 boys under sixteen (30 of them under twelve), and a mere 6 adult males.

The increasing regional specialization of production had a decided effect on the division of household labor. Most directly, the advance of textile manufacturing coincided with a diminished domestic production of cloth. The home manufacture of textiles declined to one-fourth of its former volume between 1820 and 1835. Other aspects of domestic production were surrendered to the artisan shops of Utica, which by the 1830s were producing and selling such domestic staples as soap, candles, and medicines. The diversification of the regional economy was accomplished by the transfer of expendable labor, especially that of children, from family farms to shops and factories. Most migrants into both the factory village of New York Mills and into commercial Utica were young natives of New York State. Many of them were born in Oneida County. In other words, they were probably the sons of daughters of the first generation of farmers, the stepchildren of the family economy, whose roles in the farm household had been transferred to other segments of an increasingly complicated regional economy.

Throughout the regional marketplace the corporate character of family economics was either tattered or torn asunder. Be it in Utica, Whitestown, or New York Mills, it was the generational ties of the home economy that seemed most fragile, most vulnerable to the corrosive power of commerce. The men and women of Oneida County were not unaware of this fact. They did not express their family concerns in economistic terms, however, but rather in the language and central ideological structure of their time, that is, in an essentially religious mode of thought.

RELIGION IN DEFENSE OF PATRIARCHY

The increasing fragility of generational bonds was greeted with particular alarm by the guardian of the old family order, the Presbyterian Church. The Presbyterians had attempted from the first to shore up the patriarchal household and had defended its bulwarks with special diligence in the 1820s against the "restless and wandering activity of youth." Their church trials and those of Baptists and Methodists could keep the families of loyal church members in line but were helpless before the turbulent multitude, the "mixed mass" of the bustling canal town. By 1820 Utica supported Episcopalian, Roman Catholic, and Universalist congregations and harbored growing numbers of the unchurched and unbelieving as well. Pious Calvinists might well despair of conferring a heritage of salvation upon the sons and daughters who inhabited this heterogeneous and secular town. Their attempts to find new methods of securing these familial ties generated the liveliest era in the social and religious history of Utica and Whitestown.

The church and the family found a principal ally in this work in the local press. The early printers of Oneida County were Presbyterians almost to a man and acted as a commercial arm of the clerical establishment. They were also among the foremost exemplars of the old family order. Merrill and Camp, Book Publishers, whose own extended family economy has already been described, issued countless sermons and several periodicals, among them the *Utica Christian Magazine*, which was a major source of evangelical communication beginning in 1813. The Merrills took a new partner, Thomas Hastings, in 1824 when they began to publish a second organ of revivalism, the *Western Recorder*. Evangelism was also reported and orchestrated in a third magazine, the *Utica Christian Repository;* this too was published by founding families of the First Presbyterian Church, those of William Williams and Asahel Seward. These printers enacted the same artisan version of the family economy exemplified by Merrill and Camp. William Williams was first apprenticed to his brother-in-law, Oneida County's first printer, William McClean, and next formed a partnership with Asahel Seward. Kinship cemented this last business alliance when William's sister Martha married his new partner. The body of religious literature issued by this band of Presbyterian printers supplies the earliest source of literary evidence for a major transition in the family order. From his base in Utica, the Presbyterian printer spoke to and for a population that was scattered all across western New York, as far as the turnpikes and canals could carry his little tracts and magazines.

From the first, these printers were embroiled in religious controversies that bespoke family concerns. The sectarian argument that inaugurated the lively religious history of Utica and Whitestown, the debate about infant baptism, was addressed explicitly to the generational and familial continuity of religion. The first skirmish between Baptists and

Presbyterians began in a small rural village within the township of Whitestown. It was reported in a pamphlet subtitled "The Rise and Progress of a Dispute Carried on Between Certain Members of the Congregational and Baptist Churches in Sangerfield." The short piece recounted a series of discussions that took place every Wednesday night for more than six months, involving clergy and laymen from both denominations. The lively debate, conducted in local farmhouses, was described as "promiscuous discourse" and merged private and public, along with persons of both sexes and all ages, in one informal community. Much of the discussion involved arid theological matters—searches through scripture for references to baptism, the source of grace, and the moral nature of infants. But just beneath the surface lay the more earthly concerns of this excited band of farmers. The Baptist controversy posed in religious terms a question of great practical concern to parents and children, the opposition between inherited and achieved status.

The Calvinist defense of infant baptism began: "Our children are part of ourselves—God has constituted the parent the head of the family, and so it is so in nature. Would it not be inconsistent to take in the head and leave out the body. Households are saved on account of the head, whether they be infant or not, that is they are reputed and treated so." The last sentence displayed considerable carelessness about the fine points of Calvinism and the basic doctrine of predestination. The first, however, displayed an adamant commitment to an organic family and the generational extension of the Christian covenant, even on to "a thousand generations." The Presbyterian party to the debate repeatedly asserted one defense of infant baptism, the doctrine of the Abrahamic covenant: "God does connect parents and children together in dispensing his favors; and . . . he does so in a covenant, in fulfillment of his promise to bless the seed of the righteous." The defense of this family bond generated virulent debate among the simple farmers of Sangerfield in 1803. It would still be exercising Oneida County in 1820 when another sermon printed by William Williams noted that "the bitterest spirit of party" still reigned on this issue.

The source of all this excitement can be gleaned from the arguments of the Presbyterians' opponents. The exponents of the Baptist position in Sangerfield were capable of arguments like this: "I was once a Pedo-Baptist. My parents taught me that way and I received it upon their instruction. While I was a Pedo-Baptist I put forced construction on scripture." A later writer presented this filial rebellion more openly: "How small a number of those who at this day belong to the Baptist Churches, can say that their present view of the subject was early impressed upon their expanding minds by the kind instruction of a pious father; or the still more enduring solicitude of a tender mother. You will find by far the greater will say . . . they were compelled to forsake father and mother, brother, and sister, and in the face of a sneering world, were enabled to take up the cross." In short, the Baptists expounded, at least for the sake of argument, a doctrine of independence for the patriarchal household. They were apparently joined in this opinion by the local Methodists. In a pamphlet dated 1812 the Reverend Elijah Norton deemed Methodism a direct threat to patriarchy. This Oneida County Presbyterian accounted a host of impudent children among the consequences of Methodism: "Some children and youth among them (as we have seen) behave themselves proudly against the ancient, and treat old men, even ministers, and parents with great contempt who hold the doctrine of election. This I have seen and experienced in a family and a public assembly also." In his paranoia about the maintenance of family authority the Reverend Mr. Norton reached the heights of hyperbole. He saw the Methodists "swarming out like the locusts, out of the pit, and like grievous wolves and roaring lions, with deadly poison among our lambs render our families, societies, and churches in pieces." As if this menagerie of mixed metaphors were not enough, Norton invoked the most extreme image of family disorder. The Methodist doctrine, he said, "has a direct tendency to kill and murder fathers and mothers."

Sermons like this bespoke high-pitched anxiety among the first generation of the New York frontier about their bonds to their children. The direct descendants of the Puritans, most of whom had under the Plan of Union formed Presbyterian rather than Congregationalist parishes, perceived this threat as an assault from their sectarian rivals, Baptists and Methodists. The intensity of their reaction, however, was churned by palpable and immediate problems: the closing of the agrarian frontier, the imminent passage of the corporate family economy and covenanted community, and the portended dissolution of generational ties. In these circumstances the simple invocation of doctrine, be it the Abrahamic covenant or adult baptism, was an ineffectual and ultimately unsatisfying recourse for all the New England denominations.

Therefore, Presbyterians, Baptists, and Methodists alike began to devise more concrete methods of reinforcing parental ties to their children. In 1808 Joshua Leonard rose before the Presbyterian congregation to remind his parishioners that the lineage of grace was sealed by a covenant, an agreement with the Almighty that obliged parents to abide by their side of the bargain. Parents were sworn by the covenant to fulfill an "awesome responsibility" to train, instruct, and admonish their children in the ways of God and grace. It was not mere coincidence that ministers throughout Oneida County frequently chose this theme as the text of their Sunday sermons. One of the first recommendations of the Oneida Presbytery, founded in 1808, was an annual sermon on "the privileges and obligations of the Abrahamic covenant, presenting distinctly the duty of pious parents to dedicate their infant children to God in baptism, their responsibilities in connection with their religious training and the precious grounds of expectation and confidence that if found faithful, 'saving blessing,' would follow." Not the doctrine of grace stemming from an arbitrary God but the duty of parents to educate and sanctify their children had become the crux of the pastoral message.

Accordingly, infant baptism itself had primarily symbolic and monitory value. It was a rite in which parents publicly assumed and resolved to fulfill their religious responsibility to their sons and daughters. Without such a ritual, the Reverend Jabez Chadwick feared that parents would feel free to deny the Sabbath, distort scripture, and neglect family prayer. In fact, he already saw the dire consequences of parental complacency all around him on the New York frontier. He observed that many parents were "awfully insensible of the truth of this subject, and neglectful of their duty to their children." "If they did not reform," he warned, "parents themselves would bring a curse upon their posterity, instead of a blessing." By underscoring the fine print in the Abrahamic covenant, the clerical leadership of Onedia had arrived at a point of agreement with their denominational rivals. The Baptists, their rhetoric of independence aside, also held parents practically responsible for the souls of their children. One of their pamphlets ended on a familiar note: "What an awful judgment will those unnatural parents draw upon their heads who neglect to bring up their children in the nurture and admonitions of the Lord." The same refrain could be heard in Methodist quarters. *The Methodist Magazine*, briefly published in Utica, harbored its own essays on "Parental Duty and Responsibility." Indeed, the religious press of all denominations was littered with essays on "Parental Duties" and "The Christian Education of Children."

The actual working out of the dictums of Christian education was fraught with difficulties, especially for the descendants of Calvinists. Early writers like David Harrowar (published by Merrill and Camp in 1815) were bold enough to invoke undiluted Calvinism in sermons with such uninviting titles as "On the Total Depravity of Infants." Baptism was not equivalent to salvation according to Harrowar, who was coldly unsentimental in his Calvinist purity: "If the infants of pious people die without its attainment they must be consigned to eternal ruin." Within the next decade some Presbyterians began slowly to work their way toward a new, less callous child psychology. In 1813 Merrill and Camp printed this novel definition of the child's nature: "Infants are *moral agents* and possess *moral characters.*" This moral capacity appeared even before a child was capable of the most rudimentary acts of reasons and the most fundamental knowledge of Christian doctrine: It was a faculty of the heart rather than of the mind. The precise nature of the moral agency of infants was very vaguely illuminated. The anonymous author spoke of "impressions on their minds, . . . accompanied with feelings or exercises which partake of a moral quality"; he resorted to emotional rather than cognitive terms, to feelings, affections, the heart.

However cloudy the concept and insubstantial the logic, the notion of the moral agency of childhood opened a wedge into Calvinism, through which parents could actively enter into the salvation of their children.

Armed with this doctrine, parents and parsons could begin, and begin early, to secure the promises of the Abrahamic covenant. The Reverend Joshua Leonard offered the parents of Oneida County a model of the new Christian socialization in his sermon to children published in 1808. Leonard assured his young listeners that "there are numberless pleasing instances, of children and youth of the church, whose hearts, under the pious instructions, and in answer to the effectual prayers of faithful parents, have been quickly ripened for heaven; and made thoroughly to confide in their Father's will; resigning the world not with submission only, but with pleasure." Fifteen years later, in 1823, the *Utica Christian Repository* printed a sermon that translated Leonard's ad hoc strategies for converting children into a new formulation of the relationship between the child and the church. The anonymous author offered children a secure and comfortable, indeed, almost an honored and superior, place in the Christian community. "The truths of religion which are necessary to be known to enable the soul to fix its affection on God, are so simple, so evident and so impressive, that we cannot deem them above the capacity of childhood; and there is on the contrary a less perverted state of the feelings to obstruct the acquirement of this necessary elementary knowledge in childhood than in maturer years." As the author approached close to the doctrine of infant innocence, he glimpsed the possibility of infant salvation. Ever so cautiously, he questioned the belief that "the conversion and piety of children except in very extraordinary cases was not to be expected until they arrived at the years of discretion."

The Oneida County theologians had arrived at an auspicious point in the history of religion and of child psychology. They now entertained optimism about the salvation of the second generation, happy prospects that grew from the wholesome feelings of the young, rather than from the will of the Almighty. The ministry and the publishing arm of the First Presbyterian Society of Whitestown had found a means of concertedly and swiftly linking their children to their own church and the lineage of Abraham.

The religious press was more conservative about the secular aspects of childrearing, the practical matters of parental discipline, moral education, and character formation. The *Utica Christian Magazine* reprinted a Connecticut treatise, for example, which excoriated "the fashion of the times to be lenient, loose, licentious . . . out of mere *parental affection.*" This writer preferred the traditions of the seventeenth century. He reminded the Christian father that "*his* offspring, *his* darlings, are naturally perverse; that they are by nature just as bad as the children of other people; that they are possessed of the same natural temper, have the same malignant passions." With such a vision of the child's nature, parents had no recourse other than the method of discipline employed by their ancestors: "Let every parent make it his inflexible determination that he will be obeyed—*invariably* obeyed." This was little more than a reiteration of that childrearing method favored in seventeenth-century Plymouth Colony, will-breaking. This ancient childrearing regimen was still recommended to the readers of the *Western Recorder* in 1824. In an essay originating in England, lifted from a Massachusetts publication and sent into the Western District of New York by Merrill and Seward, a pious couple described the ideal method of managing children as follows: "Our will, when once announced, was the law of the house. . . . We demanded an entire acquiescence in our determination whether he saw its reasonableness or not." As in the seventeenth century, this test of wills occurred at age two and left the parents victorious. This doctrine was modulated by only the most cautious praise for the use of reason and restraint of the rod. In the secular relations of parents and child, authority rather than affection still reigned supreme. Those relations were still perceived, furthermore, as elements of a patriarchal family order. In the pages of the Presbyterian, Methodist, and Baptist press, it was fathers rather than mothers who exercised supreme authority and responsibility in the education of children.

Local publishers upheld this traditional hierarchy of the sexes in every aspect of family and public life. On the New York frontier, however, there were some temptations for women, like youth, to step out of their assigned place in the patriarchal order. The first minister of the Whitestown Society sounded the alert on this issue in 1808. The Reverend James Carnahan trumpeted his ire at the approach of a woman named Martha Howell, an itinerant Baptist, who had been testifying to her sect's doctrines throughout the Western District. According to Carnahan, certain churches in the neighborhood of Whitestown had even allowed her to mount the pulpit to discourse on the subject of baptism. Carnahan invoked the standard scriptural condemnation of such behavior: "She contradicts the apostle Paul who says: I suffer not a woman to teacher; but to be silent." James Carnahan unleashed the most belligerent rhetoric against the denominational rivals who sponsored this offense. "The leaders of this party are those who go bawling through our streets—baptism! baptism! baptism! in our way, or no salvation!" Carnahan's charge against the Baptists was spiced with images of sexual license: "They suffer that woman Jezebel which called herself a prophetess, to teach and to seduce the servants of the Lord." From the alarmed perspective of the leader of the Presbyterian flock in Whitestown, the Baptists were unleashing the unsavory powers of Eve and sponsoring independence among women as well as children.

The details of Martha Howell's travels through Whitestown have been lost to history, but other fragments of evidence testify to such aggressive female religiosity. A short, crudely printed pamphlet entitled "A Scriptural Vindication of Female Preaching, Prophesying and Exhortation" dates from this period. The author announced herself as "Deborah Pierce of Paris, Oneida County, New York," a village just south and west of Whitestown. Deborah Pierce called upon the members of her sex to publicize their religious beliefs in no uncertain terms: "Rise up ye careless daughters, for many, many days shall ye be troubled, for ye have not harkened to the voice of God yourself." It would appear the openness of the frontier combined with the democratic tendencies of the Baptist faith had threatened to sunder the sexual hierarchy of the convenanted community. Not only did local Baptists follow female preaching, according to Carnahan, they also permitted women to participate in the church discipline, to usurp the role of the household head in the public jurisdiction of church government.

Once again a nervous Presbyterian imagination had exaggerated the extent of this subversion of the patriarchal system. The Baptists denied Carnahan's charges in the case of Martha Howell. In their estimation she had only spoken of her own personal religious experience, testifying to her own faith, "presuming neither to preach nor to teach." "Were she to attempt to teach in public," they went on, "we should immediately interpose; she has, however, no inclination for any such thing." Likewise, on the score of women's participation in church discipline, the Reverend Elias Lee described Baptist policy as "a majority of the brethren present shall perform the business and the sisters are consulted only to avoid grieving them immeasurably." A partial admission of special deference to women is imbedded in this statement, but neither were the Presbyterians immune to such charges. The Baptist rebuttal to the attack on Martha Howell threw Carnahan's charges back on his own congregation: "What is the propriety of your complaining of us, for admitting her into Christian pulpits, to relate the dealing of God with her, as above mentioned; when but a few months ago, a woman, a professed teacher of divinity, was admitted into your meeting houses, for the express purpose of fulfilling her mission." Carnahan's rejoinder was merely to say that this anonymous woman spoke from the body of the church rather than the pulpit, a technicality that did not impress the Baptists. Still, both sects wished to dispel the impression that they in any way condoned female usurpation of male religious authority.

Closer examination of the exhortation of Deborah Pierce reveals the limits of her subversion, as well. She addressed herself to the male heads of households in an assertive but deferential manner, arguing that the blanket prohibition of female preaching would only lead to the weakening of male authority. On the other hand, Pierce advised the local ministry, "if you would follow the Lord yourself, and charge your family to follow you as you follow Christ, and fear God more than man, you would be more united in serving God, and the woman would more willingly obey, love, and fear you; and you would live together as the hiers of the grace of life." In the promise of wifely obedience, of fear as well as love for the head of the household, Deborah Pierce subscribed to the sexual hierarchy of a little commonwealth. In the hope of "living together as heirs of grace" she endorsed the spiritual equivalent of a generational and corporate family. Once again the Baptists hesitated to translate their religious radicalism into familial and social terms. The Methodists also kept within the bounds of the patriarchal household: Their publications consistently downplayed and apologized for the heritage of assertive women that could be found in the English Wesleyan tradition and in the history of the sect in America.

Nonetheless, cracks in the foundation of religious patriarchy were clearly visible and particularly alarming to the Presbyterian church fathers. Accordingly, some elaboration or modification of the pastoral position on the relations of the sexes was in order. Hence, a few minor adjustments in the doctrine of patriarchy were recognized in a pamphlet issued by the Utica Tract Society (largely a Presbyterian operation) in 1823. Entitled "Female Influence," this tract articulated what would become a central ideological tenet of nineteenth-century womanhood. Although the author fortified the public sphere against the intrusion of females and denied women the right even to "lead the devotions of the church," he at the same time invited the second sex to play an expansive social role. "That females are capable of exerting great and happy influences in the world cannot be doubted by any. And all who have a favorable view of the sex must see the influence preserved from diminution, and directed in its proper channels." The language here was precise and apt. Female influence operated not in a circumscribed sphere but as a network of "channels" through the local community. Woman's domain was not exclusively her own fireside but extended to all "familiar conversation" and along the many informal social avenues that lined the borders of the public sphere. A woman had the right to "unrestrained intercourse with Christian friends in both circles," that is, in both the household and the church community. At the same time she was permitted to teach her children and domestics, instruct her own sex in private, and collect alms in the wider private circles. To lead prayer in promiscuous circles outside her own home was, however, still strictly forbidden a female member of the Presbyterian Church.

In itself, this codification of woman's place was not particularly novel. Rather, it was the heightened degree of influence attributed to women within it that is significant. As long as they acted through persuasion rather than authority, women were promised extensive power, particularly over children, and even over patriarchs. "And who can so successfully wield the instrument of influence than women. By force of persuasion, how often has woman prevailed, especially when accompanied by submission and entreaty, where strength and courage and boldness would have accomplished nothing. . . . A sensible woman who keeps her proper place, and knows how to avail herself of her own powers, may exert, in her own sphere, almost any degree of influence that she pleases." The Presbyterian faction had been moved to recognize some legitimate expansion of women's power but only outside the public sphere and even then in an almost covert and wily fashion. This prescient statement of the concept of female influence, like the interest in the Christian education of children, was the subject of essays in the press of each major Protestant denomination, Presbyterian, Methodist, and Baptist alike.

When these sects finally made their peace, however, it would be on a battteground strewn with such doctrinal casualties as the Abrahamic covenant, will-breaking, and patriarchal authority. The mild concessions to Christian education and female influence would not be sufficient to calm the troubled churches and households of Oneida County. The theological controversies of the second and third decades of the nineteenth century derived their special virulence from the social and familial dislocations that accompanied the closing of the frontier and the encroachment of market capitalism. It would take major ideological changes and a full-scale social movement to resolve them. This societal transformation is written into the historical record as the Second Great Awakening.

THE DEMOGRAPHY OF THE SECOND GREAT AWAKENING

A glance through the membership lists of the evangelical churches of Oneida County reveals that this epochal upsurge in religious conversions began in the winter of 1813–14. It was at about the same time that the Reverend John Frost toured the vicinity of Whitestown and Utica inquiring about the state of local souls. His report provides a graphic portrait, a kind of spiritual demography, of the popular concerns that gave rise to the Second Great Awakening. When Frost made his pastoral rounds between 1813 and 1816, Presbyterians maintained a religious plurality over large numbers of Baptists, a few Methodists, and an occasional Quaker, Universalist, or infidel. Most striking of all, however, was the number of lapsed Christians, baptized members of any denomination, who were not in the habit of either attending church or practicing religion at home. Almost half the households did not contain a single practicing member of a local church. Of the remainder, only 46% enrolled the entire family, husband and wife and children, in some local demonination. The bulk of the remainder, 47% of the families of church members, were headed by women, who joined the congregation and often baptized their children without the sponsorship of the male head of the household.

The Reverend John Frost's census of souls also revealed that this conspicuous absence of men in the churches of Oneida County was more than a matter of absentmindedness. It was accompanied by some genuine disenchantment with religious doctrines. The men Frost queried repeatedly gave vent to serious doubts about religious subjects and evinced a notable lack of deference to the pastor. A Mr. Kent, for example, made it known that "I have not settled my mind on religious subjects, not even on the immortality of the soul." Theodore Still had the most difficulty with the doctrine of original sin, which he could not "reconcile with our most common ideas of justice." His neighbor Mr. William Tracy expressed doubt on the subject of "atonement and free agency." Then he had the temerity to tell the minister, "I do not think it my duty to perform family prayer." The Reverend Mr. Frost's transcription of such dilute religious beliefs introduces a new dimension of local culture, one that is conspicuously absent in the publications of the local religious press. It would indicate that the Enlightenment had intercepted the passage of the New England way into New York State. Rationality, skepticism, a secular perspective, all projected a mentality that would subvert the Christian corporate community. It certainly did not seem conducive to a religious awakening.

An analysis of the response of women to Frost's interrogation reveals a completely different picture, however, and another prognostication. Mr. Kent's wife hardly shared his skepticism. She, like the majority of women, responded to the pastoral inquiries with a contrite and humble account of the state of her own soul and her prospects for salvation. "I have entertained some hope of several years; but my doubts are distressing." Similarly, the wife of the heretical Theodore Sill expressed "much anxiety on the subject and at times am very unhappy." Mrs. Tracy put it this way, again in direct contrast to her husband's response: "I am a poor creature. I have an increasing sense of the excellence of God's character." The women in the vicinity of the Whitestown Presbyterian Society not only accepted the terms of Frost's questions, and showed respect for his office, but also took the state of their own souls painfully seriously. The combination of humility, seriousness, and anxiety was taken to its extreme by a Miss Fowler who lived with a married sister and her family. "I am dead to the world, I have a long time felt that it cannot give me happiness. I have no object in view on Earth. I do not pray, I am good by selfishness, and I know that my prayers are not heard. I cannot go to meeting because that it will increase my condemnation. I would do anything I could to obtain salvation." The timidity and self-deprecation of other women was transcribed by Frost as "vile sinner," "poor guilty sinner," "afraid to hope."

These same women often expressed a sense of social isolation, the counterpart and contrast to the absorption with worldly concerns noted by their mates. Four women acknowledged that they were unable to attend meetings because they had young children to care for. Others lacked the clothes, shoes, or transportation to get them to church. Mrs. Hunston's neglect of public worship was excused simply enough: "She has not clothes decent to wear. She has no bonnet." Other women felt chilling isolation in the private relations: One noted pathetically, "Nobody visits me here"; another, "Nobody talks to me at meeting." At other times the religious anxieties of Frost's female respondents festered in the most desolate privacy. Sally Edmond confessed, "I do not go to meeting. I try to worship God in secret," and Widow Slater humbly acknowledged, "I entertain some hope. I cannot read. I am unworthy. I am most of the time in the cellar. I endeavor to bring my children for the Lord. My children read to me." In other cases this isolation and self-abasement was exacerbated by subjection to tyrannical patriarchs. Mrs. Rebecca Leach, a baptized Presbyterian who retained "some hope" of salvation, went infrequently to meeting. Her husband, she said, was "unwilling . . . I shall unite with a church. I maintain secret prayer."

It was these timid and isolated women who formed the fragile backbone of the Whitestown Presbyterian Society. Prior to 1814, 70% of those admitted to full communion in the society were females. Male ministers might sermonize about family prayer and the Abrahamic covenant; male elders might sit at the church trials in stern judgement over family abuses; and male printers and publishers might address their pamphlets and magazines to patriarchs; but it was women who flocked into the local churches. It was women, furthermore, who most often forged the feeble generational links in the church corporation. According to Frost's church census, twenty solitary women, as opposed to only one man unaccompanied by his wife, brought their children before the church for baptism. In sum, on the eve of the revival cycle in Whitestown, it was women who were most receptive to the admonitions of the evangelical clergy, who were most eagerly awaiting salvation, and who were most concerned with the Christian education of their young offspring.

Contemporary observers of the revivals all concurred in the estimation that women and youth, and not household heads, constituted the majority of converts. There was considerable debate, however, over the nature, relationship, and legitimacy of their awakening to grace. Young men or women could enter a revival church as the grateful beneficiaries of the Abrahamic covenant, humbly taking up the religious standard bequeathed to them by their fathers, or they could be entering the church in audacious willfulness, inspired with a pious superiority to their own parents. Women, for their part, could be either obeisant and submissive recipients of Almighty grace or inspired to the aggressive religiosity of a Deborah Pierce. Children could rebel against patriarchy or succumb to women's influence, obey their fathers or desert their mothers, all in the same act of conversion. They could mount the anxious bench independently of family ties entirely. Every one of these interpretations found adherents among Oneida County observers.

The Presbyterian Church, the center of the Oneida County revivals for all denominations, was itself divided on the question, particularly after Finney's appearance. In 1826 the Reverend John Frost co-authored "A Narrative of the Revival of the Religion in the County of Oneida," which put the most sanguine construction on the sex and age characteristics of the converts. According to Frost's calculations, Utica and Whitestown converts included a goodly sum of household heads, but the majority of the subjects were "among the younger class of society." In Frost's estimation these young converts behaved in an orderly and submissive manner. He observed that many had been the beneficiaries of baptism in their youth and that the parents of others had renewed their vows to catechize children and exercise family prayer. Frost also acknowledged some shift in the pattern of relations by age and sex during the course of the revival, namely, the formation of segregated circles of youth and women for the purpose of private prayer and education. These bodies were, in Frost's opinion, entirely decorous and legitimate. He even sponsored a resolution before the Oneida Presbytery allowing women to speak their conversion in public meetings.

Other segments of the community were not as hospitable to these new methods. A pastoral letter was issued in 1827 by the Oneida Association, a group of Presbyterian ministers vehemently hostile to revivals and fearful of their familial consequences. Where Frost saw an orderly increment in the church membership, these ministers observed "disregard of the distinctions of age or station." They were appalled by the practice of "allowing anybody and everybody to speak and pray in promiscuous meetings as they felt disposed." The Oneida Association assembled evidence for each charge. They found "such language as this in the mouths of young men and boys, 'you old grey headed sinner, you deserved to have been in hell long ago,'—'This old hypocrite'—'That old apostate'—'that grey headed sinner, who is leading souls to hell'—'That old veteran servant of the devil'—and the like." Apparently adult female converts were not quite so impudent in their language, but after all women were not expected to utter a word in church and had to be reminded that "God has not made it their duty to lead, but to be in silence." Criticism like this came from the more conservative members of Baptist, Presbyterian, and Methodist churches.

The revivals were also the object of criticism in more liberal quarters. Utica supported a small Universalist congregation, which boasted its own periodical published by one Dolphus Skinner. Skinner issued his first publication, *Utica Magazine,* in 1827 in direct response to Finney's tour of Oneida County. This publication and its immediate successor, the *Evangelical Magazine and Gospel Advocate,* conducted a systematic campaign to expose the Presbyterian faction, condemn revivalism, and propagate the opposing principles of "Free Inquiry, Religious Liberty and Intelligence." Skinner's accounts of the revivals were also laden with references to the age and sex of the converts. He described an "animal excitement" that engaged "some men but many more women and children." A few years later Skinner reviled the converts in the awakening at the Reverend Mr. Lansing's Presbyterian Church as "a few weakminded and ignorant females." He characterized the Methodist Camp meeting of 1831 in a similar fashion. Although he did not observe a single adult male in the throes of a conversion, he noted that the females often approached the anxious seat with their children in tow. This procession followed upon the evangelist's exhortation: "Here comes mother; children your mother has come to seek religion. Now is the time to come along with your mother." According to the *Evangelical Magazine and Gospel Advocate*, the revivalists were manipulating ignorant women and children for sectarian purposes. Skinner had introduced a new interpretation of the lineage of conversions: Rather than destroying family ties, revivals wielded them in a novel and wily fashion, trapping large numbers of converts in a net of associations between women and children.

In order to judge the accuracy of any one of these conflicting interpretations of the revivals, one needs to identify the actual membership of evangelical churches. Four church registries, three Presbyterian and one Baptist, survive to provide bits and pieces of empirical evidence about the convert population of Utica and Whitestown. All four concur, first of all, in charting an extended chronology of revivalism. New admissions to all the churches clustered in similar lengthy pattern, which peaked in the years 1814, 1819, 1830–32, and 1838. Revivalism should be examined, then, not as the spontaneous outburst associated with Finney's arrival in the mid-1820s but as part of this undulating wave of evangelical fervor.

A cursory analysis of these church records confirms the observation that revivalism was particularly popular among women. The distribution of Christian names within this population indicates that women were the simple majority during each revival and at every church. The proportion of female converts ranged from a low of approximately 52% in the Whitestown Baptist revival of 1814 to a high of almost 72% in that church's Awakening of 1838. Although the proportion of females in the revivals was in excess of their presence in the population of the township, it was slightly lower than their proportion of overall church membership. The preponderance of women also varied slightly over time, tending to decline in the middle of the revival cycle. Slowly, and at a rather minuscule rate, the sequence of revivals actually increased the representation of men in the church.

The male converts were rarely, however, heads of households. Although household heads and employed men above the age of seventeen were listed in the *Utica City Directory*, less than one-quarter of the male converts could be located in volumes of the directory issued within two years of each revival. Those converts who could be identified, furthermore, seldom headed their own households. Boarders constituted 65% of the male converts who could be located in the directly at all. The title "boarder" suggests youth, singleness, and deracination from the parental family. The majority of female converts probably resembled the males in age and marital status. Of the female converts at the Utica Presbyterian Church, 60% appeared in neither the marriage records nor as parents of newly baptized children. A substantial proportion of the converts of both sexes were young and mobile as well, according to the church records. Of the new church members, 30% requested official letters of dismissal within five years of their conversion. Countless others must have left the church more hastily and without this formality. Many of those who exuberantly confessed their faith during the revivals probably left for parts unknown even before their names could be inscribed on church ledgers. Women registered their intention of leaving the church less frequently than men, yet one-quarter of the female converts also requested letters of dismissal within five years. It is safe to make this single conclusion about the silent majority of converts: They were largely young and, in the short term at least, a peripatetic lot with fragile roots in church and community. This far it would seem that the Second Great Awakening expressed the waxing religious enthusiasm of a second generation, recently uprooted from their frontier families.

This is not to say, however, that these young, mobile converts acted alone and independently of parents and kin. Common surnames are, in fact, laced throughout the records of Oneida County revivals. Depending on which church or which revival year is considered, from 17% to 54% of the converts apparently professed their faith in the company of relatives. There is also reason to believe that females played a leading role in the kinship organization of revivals. The records of the Whitestown Presbyterian Society, for example, reveal that almost 30% of all converts had been preceded into the church by relatives, most of whom were females. Of these converts, 61% were preceded into the church by a solitary woman, 24% by relatives of both sexes, and only 15% by solitary men. In sum, the disproportionate tendency of men to enter the church accompanied, or preceded, by females might mean that Dolphus Skinner was onto something: That women cajoled, manipulated, or simply led their children into the evangelical sects.

Only precise evidence of kinship, confirmed by vital records, can provide a valid test of this hypothesis. Such records are very hard to find in Whitestown and Utica. The only religious body that recorded demographic events in sufficient detail and completeness was the First Presbyterian Church of Utica. Yet even here, within one of the most stable institutions of the community, only a minority of church members ever registered a birth, marriage, or death. Only 1 in 3 revival converts left any vital records, and these most often document a single event in the life cycle, a lone marriage, a baptism, or a child's christening. These records provide only a faint, suggestive track through the history of family and religion. Nonetheless, this documented minority commands attention, both as the historian's last resort and because of its more durable ties to the church and consequent capacity to affect the course of evangelism itself.

This narrower, but more detailed and accurate, analysis of the kin ties that surrounded conversion reveals a pattern not unlike the stages of the individual family cycle. The revival of 1813, for example, coincided with Sophia Clarke's entry into Utica's newly founded First Presbyterian Church. At the end of the revival cycle in 1838 her youngest child, then approaching adulthood, joined the same religious community. During the same period Sophia Clarke saw the village of Utica and the benevolent organizations she founded grow ever more dense and complicated as they expanded to occupy a whole regional marketplace. The minute examination of evangelism within Sophia Clarke's congregation exposes the structures of family, economy, and society that intersected at this religious nucleus of the region and gave a multifaceted meaning to the Second Great Awakening.

The revival cycle began in Utica with the conversion of the parents of young children. Although less than half of those men and women who professed their faith during the 1814 revival left any trace in the vital records, 65% of these (or 43% of all converts) were married. Almost 1 in 4 of them baptized an infant child within a year of their conversion. In addition, more than a dozen older children were promptly brought forward to be christened by a newly converted parent. The revival of 1814 offered direct testimony to a strong commitment to the Abrahamic convenant on the part of Utica's first generation. Coinciding with the highest birth and marriage rates in the history of the First Presbyterian Church, it planted the religious roots of many young families along the banks of the Mohawk.

The first revival also exhibited a relatively high degree of patriarchal sanction. Twelve of the sixty-four converts were accompanied into the state of grace by their spouses. The ministers were proud of pointing to the relatively large number of male household heads who assumed full church membership during this revival. The names of at least nine married men were inscribed on the church records in that revival season. Some of them represented the pinnacle of the societal as well as the familial hierarchy. Almost half the converts who could be identified in the *City Directory* were members of elite commercial families. The first revival witnessed the wholesale conversion of the Van Rensselaer family, scions of the colonial New York aristocracy. The prominent export merchants James and Jeremiah Van Rensselaer entered the church in 1814 along with their wives, Susan and Adeline, and sister Cornelia. Phoebe Stocking, the wife of a wealthy hat merchant and manufacturer, joined the church at the same time, as did Harriet Dana, consort of another substantial Genesee Street merchant. Lawyers and their wives and daughters were also conspicuously present in the front ranks of the revival cycle, constituting 16% of the converts and including members of prominent Federalist families, the Breeses, Ostrums, and Walkers. The publishing arm of the Presbyterian faction also pledged allegiance to evangelism in 1814. Horace Camp and Asahel Seward experienced saving grace at that time, and the Merrill family was represented among the converts by Bildad, Jr., and his mother, Nancy Camp Merrill. A fourth Presbyterian printer, Charles Hastings, would be converted in the revival of 1819.

It was in the later revival that the less prestigious and wealthy, but nonetheless respectable, families were gathered into the evangelical fold. In that year Utica's sturdy artisans and smaller shopkeepers advanced to salvation en masse. Only a handful of common laborers, however, are known to have joined the ranks of the converts in either revival season. The lower orders might have been more likely to join the Methodist and Baptist denominations. Yet these sects were not notably active during the early stages of the revival cycle. In sum, the revivals of the 1810s, the first decade in the history of Utica's Presbyterian Church, were conducted in conformity with the hierarchical social and family order; they enrolled the best families, often in corporate kin groups and accompanied by the head of the household. The only disappointment an old-light divine might have with these early revivals was the still meager, but growing, participation of male heads of households.

It was more often mothers than patriarchs who took the initiative in planting familial roots in the frontier church. Women certainly played a uniquely maternal role in the first revival: 12% of them were pregnant when they professed their faith. Mothers unaccompanied by their mates also accounted for the majority of the baptisms that followed in the wake of revivals in 1814 and 1819. A woman named Nancy Lynde exemplified this maternal fervor. Within two years of her own conversion in the 1814 revival, she had given six children to the Lord in baptism. The church records referred to the children's father, who was not a member of the congregation, by the truncated title Mr. Lynde. No family by that name appeared in the village directory of 1817. Yet in some later revival, perhaps somewhere to the west, the children whom Nancy Lynde baptized in Utica's first awakening may have fulfilled the Abrahamic covenant and entered another evangelical church.

THE WOMEN BEHIND THE REVIVAL

The role of women in the inauguration of the revival cycle was actually more extensive than the roster of church members, contemporary observers, or historians have acknowledged. It was in the midst of the first revival that the Whitestown Female Charitable Society changed its name to the Oneida Female Missionary Society and began to sponsor the frontier ministry. More than half the female converts of 1814 would ultimately be found on the membership lists of this earliest evangelical organization. Another thirteen members converted five years later. These women were something more than passive converts, emissaries of their pastors, or private guardians of the Abrahamic covenant. They had created the organizational underpinning of the revivals that would follow. By 1817 they reported a success in the expansion of the frontier missions that "exceeds the highest expectations." By 1824 their reach extended beyond Oneida County. Renamed again as the Female Missionary Society of the Western District, they spawned seventy auxiliaries and contributed more than $1,000 annually to support dozens of missionaries. These women orchestrated the revival and devised a sphere for women that had not been anticipated, either by the partisans of female influence or the castigators of female preaching.

The organizational and financial sophistication of this women's group invites comparison with the trading networks and political parties of Utica's merchant capitalists. Throughout their history the members of the Female Missionary Society elected presidents, vice-presidents, and trustees, met in informal annual meetings, and kept meticulous accounts, much in the manner of astute and conservative businessmen. The ties between Female Missionary Society members and male merchants were actually far more substantial than mere analogies between their modes of organizing. In fact, 31% of the members were married to substantial merchants like the Van Rensselaers, the Stockings, the Danas, and the Doolittles, who conducted a regionwide trade in agricultural commodities. The officers of the society had mates in the city corporation, on the boards of directors of banks and cotton factories, and at the helm of the Federalist party. Attorneys' wives made up 33% of the membership of the Female Missionary Society, and the perennial officers drawn from their ranks, Ann Breese and Sophia Clarke, continued their reigns long into widowhood. By contrast, smaller numbers of the wives of petty artisans and shopkeepers, majority occupations in Utica at that time, enrolled in the Female Missionary Society. It would appear that involvement in the organization of the missionary enterprise was characteristic of the sexual division of labor within Utica's more prominent merchant and professional families. By joining the Female Missionary Society women of the upper class publicly assumed the moral and religious responsibilities of their mercantile households and a major role in social reproduction. By efficiently and successfully fulfilling such social obligations, these women undoubtedly enhanced the elite status of their mates and added cultural and religious reinforcement to the male links in the local trade networks.

At the same time, these women's groups engineered a considerable expansion of woman's social role in a sphere that was organizationally independent of the male head of the household. Although not within the established centers of public power, their self-created societies and offices commanded considerable notice in the press and the community. Their formative contributions to revivalism and their innovative participation in the reorganization of sex roles raises some perplexing historical questions.

One social characteristic of these women, in addition to their position in the Utica class structure, offers an especially important clue to the social-historical origins of their activities. Analysis of the *City Di-*

rectory reveals that almost 80% of the identifiable members of the Female Missionary Society were married to men who maintained a business address that was detached from their place of residence. The comparable figure was 69% for merchants in general and only 13% for the population at large. In other words, the members of the Female Missionary Society had been physically removed from the corporate family economy well in advance of the mass of the local population. These women were relieved from assisting in the farming, artisan production, or sales that once took place within the household workplace. Many of them were wealthy enough to purchase household supplies in the shops on Genesee Street and to employ servants to meet the domestic needs of husbands and children. It would follow that involvement in the benevolent activities filled a vacuum recently opened in the everyday lives of urban upper-class women as the work of men was removed to the shops, stores, and offices of Genesee Street. Or, to put it another way, missionary societies might constitute one mode of exercising that modicum of freedom that fell to women upon the disintegration of the patriarchal home economy. The relative openness of the newly settled community enhanced these opportunities to experiment with such new roles, free from the scrutiny of entrenched authorities and without competition from long-established institutions.

The alternative roles that members of the Female Missionary Society designed for themselves were more social than domestic. The primary interest was the financial and institutional support of missionaries; collecting and dispensing money, organizing auxiliaries, issuing pamphlets, electing officers, were their forte. They set out on an evangelical mission through the Western District and through Utica's social ranks, not just within their own families. This relatively impersonal approach to benevolence was typical of the class, the period, the first stage of the revival cycle. The revival of 1814 also gave birth to the first Sunday schools founded by the teen-age daughters of the same mercantile and professional elite. This junior partner of the Female Missionary Society also set out to educate the children of the poor and the outcasts, rather than their own brothers and sisters. Another recent convert, Eunice Camp, founded a school for the lowest rank of Uticans, black children. The founder of another school for the poor, Sophia Williams, incubated her benevolent enterprise in actual violation of maternal and domestic precepts. She came upon the humble objects of her charity while visiting a village outside Utica where she had placed her own infant with a wet-nurse. All these by-products of the first revival tended to subordinate such personal interests to wider-ranging goals and a more highly rationalized and hierarchical mode of social organization.

The Female Missionary Society was at the same time very much atuned to the domestic concerns of the women of the Western District. When they petitioned for support in 1819 they used this rhetorical device as an entrée into the homes of Oneida County members: "Let us imagine a pious mother surrounded with a numerous family—none of them give evidence of possessing an interest in Christ. Without a public place of worship, and surrounded by vain amusements and unholy neighbors, the rural mother despairs of saving the souls of her children. When the itinerant minister is introduced into this sad picture by the Female Missionary Society, the mother's joy is too big for utterance; she manifests it by her tears. This is no picture of fancy. Our missionaries often witness such affecting scenes." The circulars of the Female Missionary society maintained regular communication with women in the more isolated frontier settlements. They were forever appealing to maternal anxiety about the salvation of children. The 1816 circular addressed the predicament of the pious frontier mother this way: "And when they sleep in dust, shall their children, who might become pillars in the temple of God, be abandoned to all the vices of the new settlement and *entail their examples to unborn generations*" (emphasis mine). Such an oratorical ploy was calculated to strike a sensitive chord in the hearts of rural parents. It combined the ever-effective image of a dead mother with metaphorical allusions to generational ties and the process of land inheritance, hardly innocuous themes in the 1810s and 1820s.

Mothers enrolled in the auxiliaries of the Female Missionary Society sent back heartfelt messages of gratitude to the women of Utica: "We mutually look up to you as our parent society, both for information and direction." All along the network of the Female Missionary Society came "heartfelt communications, of hope, joy, and gratitude," always addressed to "beloved sisters." The society cherished the fact that a web of "mutual dependency exists between the units full force." This highly emotional interchange between the leadership of the Female Missionary Society and their auxiliary members called forth a novel sequence of female responses and anxieties. It played upon a sense of religious intensity, maternal concern, and social isolation among rural women, a state of mind such as John Frost found on his tour of Whitestown's more isolated households. The Female Missionary Society harnessed these concerns and this energy to an evangelical purpose and plowed a route of societies, churches, and conversions through the Western District. Hundreds of women banded together in what they considered "the greatest work in which mortals are permitted to engage, the salvation of immortal souls."

From this and other sources came veiled instructions on how these women might use their private powers to stir up saving graces in the souls of kinsmen. These covert instructions are found in the memoirs of the pious, which were a regular feature in the evangelical magazines published in Utica. In this religious sphere women outnumbered laymen and challenged clergymen for numerical domination. One plot line recurs over and over again in these memoirs, almost as if the lives of women complied with a sentimental formula. The subject's heedless and happy youth was curtailed by a wrenching conversion experience, the premonition of death, and a swift decline in health. Yet the young woman's influence grew apace with her final illness. Her deathbed became the center of community and family attention, a kind of makeshift pulpit. One of the earliest examples of this literature was published by Seward and Williams in 1814. The subject was Miss Huldah Baldwin, an Episcopalian. At the time of her confirmation early in her teens Huldah Baldwin forsook the secular delights of her youthful social circle for the contemplation of the state of her soul. Her illness and death followed quickly, almost as if it were a willful act of repentence. At every turn in her frail health she gathered family and friends to her bedside and ministered to their souls. The coup de grace came on her deathbed with the following speech: "Oh beloved parent, my tender brothers, my affectionate sisters, my dear friends, do you know how rending the thought that I may be separated from you through all eternity! O live not to the world but to God. O live, O live for him that we may meet hereafter and enjoy a blessed eternity together. If you have loved me; if you have loved my company and still love it, live that you may enjoy it in Heaven."

Soon every denomination was publishing memoirs of this sort, written either by a relative or the pastor of a pious young woman and often containing a few words or letter fragments from the deceased herself. *The Methodist Magazine* reached back into English history for the pious example of Mrs. Ursula Millward, whose deathbed oratory was prefaced by an invitation to "all the people in the town" to "come and see how a Christian can die." As the townspeople crowded around her bedside she admonished, "I fear you are on the way to destruction; you cannot be offended with me now, for I am dying." From closer to Utica, in the town of Norwich, comes the account of Eliza M. Hyde, who, being too feeble to attend church, gathered the "people of God to meet at her father's house" where, at age nineteen, she delivered similar caveats to endangered Christians. Other young women acquired a ghostly deathbed right to preach in the church itself by composing their own funeral sermons. Such death was no stranger to fiction: Emily Chubbuck drew on a stock of such personal experiences both during her conversion and in the course of her literary career. Her own sister Lavinia died according to the religious-sentimental formula to which Emily Chubbuck added one particularly maudlin garnish: She portrayed the dying Lavinia pathetically sewing funeral clothes for her young sisters. By 1825 the religious press was beginning to articulate the moral of these stories and to recommend it as a device to foster conversion. In that year the *Western Recorder* gratuitously reported the case of a mother whose saintly death led to the salvation of seven children. This extraordinary measure would hardly become a popular conversion technique; few women chose to die in order to convert their kinsmen and neighbors. These deathbed scenes were, however, hyperbolic symbols of a new species of women's influence, the right to hold forth on religious

subjects from a position of apparent weakness and to wield the emotional persuasiveness that accompanied these pathetic scenes.

Early in the 1820s all these variations on the relationships between
women and youth, mothers and children, began to percolate very close
to the surface of religious history. They began to assume an organized,
pseudopublic form. The session records of the Presbyterian Church for
1822 reported that meetings were underway among "pious females for
prayer and religious conversation" and young men met "for religious
conference and exercise and improvement." A few weeks later they
noted: "An awakening is evidently going on among the female members of our church." In 1824 the Female Missionary Society observed
that "it is true that no very general and extensive revivals are stated to
have taken place . . . , but the still, small voice has gone forth, and
in the ears of many, in different places we have reasons to hope, been
heard and regarded." As Finney's tour was imminent, the Presbyterian
pastor reported: "Christian mothers meet accompanied by their little
children that they might in united prayer commend them to God and
implore for their regenerating grace." This last instance of evangelical
organization was not as vague and casual as the pastoral observer implied. The minister of Utica's First Presbyterian Church was referring
to tightly organized bodies of women who called themselves maternal
associations and met bimonthly in compliance with the dictates of a
formal constitution. Maternal associations, founded at the First Presbyterian Church in Utica in 1824 and in the Baptist congregation shortly
thereafter, were the final fruition of a decade of cogitation about the
religious bonds between mothers and children.

Again this organization had its New England precursor. The first
maternal association, established in Portland, Maine, in 1815, was,
however, almost stillborn on the New England frontier. When the Utica
organizations were formed they were the first outside New England and
arose almost simultaneously with the inaugural associations of Massachusetts and Connecticut. The constitution of the Presbyterian Maternal Association, adopted on June 30, 1824, had the following prologue:
"Deeply impressed with the great importance of bringing up our children in the nurture and admonition of the Lord, we the subscribers
agree to associate for the purpose of devising and adopting such measures as may seem best calculated to assist us in the right performance
of these duties." From this premise the assembled women undertook an
intensive campaign to save the souls of their children. The articles of
the Maternal Association's constitution pledged each member to perform an elaborate set of religious and parental duties. These included:
praying for each child daily, attending meetings semimonthly, renewing
each child's baptismal covenant regularly, reading systematically through
the literature on the Christian education of children, setting a pious
example to children at all times, and spending each child's birthday in
prayer and fasting. These women, unlike the Female Missionary Soci-

ety, assiduously focused on the salvation of their own progeny. Their annual reports featured an exact accounting of the number of conversions among the children of members.

The tenor of organization within the Maternal Association contrasted decidedly with that of the Female Missionary Society. Rather than a complicated system of officers and a wide network of influence, the assembled mothers practiced the cooperative interchange espoused in article six of the association's charter. It simply stipulated that each mother should "suggest to her sister members such hints as her own experience may furnish, or circumstances seem to render necessary." The personal bonds among members were a prime concern, a major solace. The Maternal Association reports tearfully announced deaths among the members or jubilantly exclaimed that their loving band remained intact for another year. They pledged themselves to rear the children of any deceased sister. In sum, the Maternal Association was a neighborly grouping of peers, which operated snugly within women's private but social channels. It resembled a frontier auxiliary of the Female Missionary Society more than the parent organization located in Utica.

These two organizations, the Female Missionary Society and the Maternal Association, recruited members from two distinct populations of women. Only six women belonged to both groups and thus spanned the two short generations of women's religious benevolence. These six were all representatives of the pioneer generation in Utica, converted before 1820, and members of lawyer families. At their center was the ubiquitous Sophia Clarke. Professional families were, however, poorly represented in the general membership of the association. In fact, they were outnumbered more than two to one by the wives of artisans, who assumed the dominant position maintained by merchants' wives in the Missionary Society. The class composition of the Maternal Association better reflected the actual social structure of Utica as of 1825, when more small manufacturers and shopkeepers joined the large wholesale merchants who had originally settled along the commercial artery of Genesee Street. It was in the Maternal Association, furthermore, that the wives of the artisan aristocrats, the printer-publishers, congregated. The Presbyterian Maternal Association was full of printers' wives. The Mmes. Thomas and Charles Hastings were founders. No less than four Merrills as well as Martha Seward were also found in the ranks of the organization. Wives of clockmakers, shoemakers, bakers, and blacksmiths joined the congregation of mothers, making it an institutional expression of the old middle class. Most of these skilled mechanics operated their own small units of production and exchange, which employed only a few apprentices and kinsmen.

The family tensions endemic to this class have already been illustrated in the case of the Merrills. Julia Merrill, but not her quarrelsome mother-in-law, was a member of the Maternal Association. Julia had found that the difficulties of maintaining a three-generation artisan household could interfere with the Christian care of her progeny. During the church trial of her mother-in-law, Julia Merrill lamented that "my little children have often asked why Gramma talks to me so and asked why mama cried so." Such a difficult atmosphere was not the recommended environment for the Christian education of children. It might, however, have been quite commonplace among the mistresses of artisan households, so many of whom lived in or near their husbands' workshops. The members of the Maternal Association were far more likely to be conducting their household tasks in the company of workingmen, husbands, sons, apprentices, than were the members of the Female Missionary Society. Only 35% of them (as opposed to 80% of the members of the earlier women's organization) had husbands who listed a separate business address. Their maternal roles were still performed amid the bustle, crowding, and din of the home economy. These were not the best conditions in which to maintain vigilant, undistracted watch over a child's soul. The literature of the Maternal Association repeatedly lamented the difficulty of fulfilling maternal duties along with all the "arduous responsibilities" of ordering the household. Understandably, the busy mistresses of artisan households craved the more cooperative, mutually helpful style of organization that was the Maternal Association. They had little time to promote the salvation of souls in the remote regions of the Western District.

Despite such obstacles, however, it was largely these women of the middling sort who converted the relationships between mothers and children into the building blocks of evangelism. It was these women who knit together the sermons of the Abrahamic covenant, the essays on Christian education, and the suggestions of female memoirs into a practical regimen for converting children. Their collective construction of this bridge between the history of women, the family, and religion was accomplished under the extraordinary conditions of Utica, New York, in the 1820s. The Maternal Association was founded just as the construction of the Erie Canal was completed in Utica and continued on to Rochester, doubling the city's population and proliferating grog shops, boarding houses, and brothels in the process. The cracks in the family economy and fissures in the lineage of grace were particularly threatening to those artisans and small shopkeepers who still attempted to practice the techniques of a generationally extended family amid all the individualizing forces of a rowdy commercial city. The steady influx of youth and the appearance of boarding as a prevalent style of residence must have generated special anxiety about adolescent sons and daughters. The wills of the period evidenced the shaky prospects of providing for the second generation of artisans. Artisan printers were capable of expressing these concerns through their presses. Their wives turned to the only power base they commanded: the personal and moral surveillance of their children during the early years of life before they were surrendered to their father's shop, the boarding house, or the new frontier. From their position as mothers they attempted valiantly to shore up the Abrahamic covenant and coincidentally set the stage for Charles Finney's arrival in Oneida County.

Financed by the Female Missionary Society, Finney had been generating modest revivals in the northern regions of Oneida County when he traveled on to Utica in the winter of 1825–26. His initial stop was the First Presbyterian Church where he inquired about the local religious atmosphere. The Reverend Samuel Aiken, the shepherd of a flock that included the Merrills, Clarkes, and the Hastings, recounted this telling incident to Finney: "One of his principal women had been so deeply exercised in her soul about the state of the church and of the ungodly in that city that she had prayed for two days and nights almost incessantly . . . when her strength was exhausted she could not endure the burden of her mind unless somebody was engaged in prayer with her, upon whose prayer she could lean." Finney put it aptly in his memoirs: "The work had already begun in her heart." From this inspired act of woman's influence, the revival took hold and proceeded to capture the heart of the commercial town. It proceeded out of the church and onto Genesee Street. Finney told of men who stopped for the night and stayed to be sanctified. Visitors to the city complained that one "could not go into a store but religion was intruded upon him and he could do no business." Even Bagg's Hotel, the center of the regional commercial network, was infested with religion, which enveloped the most stonehearted travelers and tradesmen.

When Finney moved on to Whitestown, the birthplace of his wife, of the Female Missionary Society, and of the Presbyterian establishment of Oneida County, he catalyzed a revival of the industrial hub of the village. Again, it was a woman who lighted the first sparks. "As he entered the factory [Finney] looked solemnly at her and quite overcome she sunk down in tears. The impression caught on almost like powder, and in a few moments nearly all in the room were in tears. This feeling spread through the factory." When the Methodist evangelist the Reverend Mr. Giles arrived at New York Mills he met a similar reception. "Some of the younger class [were] grouped together in small companies, conversing and weeping in great distress of mind, being too much excited to perform their regular work." Benjamin Walcott stopped the machines to allow the revival to proceed among his young workers, most of whom were female.

If these accounts are taken singly, it would seem that the outbreak of revivalism in 1825 occurred among the young of both sexes and was characterized by a sudden and intense emotional outburst to which women were particularly susceptible. The prior history of religion in Utica and Whitestown would suggest, however, that the contagion was not so spontaneous, that young converts were not as alone and deracinated as they seemed at first glance. It is just as reasonable to hypothesize that these young converts were the offspring of the first generation of church members, especially of mothers who had professed their own faith earlier in the revival cycle. Other converts might be sons or daughters of the rural members of the Female Missionary Society, recently displaced from the home economy by the waning of the frontier, who had migrated to the city or the mill town in search of employment. This uprooting and the uncertainty of a new environment might well foster the excited responses to Finney's exhortations. Nonetheless, the prayers, affections, and Christian rearing of evangelical mothers might well have accompanied many young men and women into the revival churches.

Unfortunately, the maternal links in the revival chain are rarely recorded in the fragmentary and far-flung records of the Second Great Awakening. But for Utica's First Presbyterian Church, at least, there is convincing evidence of a relationship between the family cycle and the revival seasons. Despite an increase in the proportion of mobile and migratory converts during and after the revival of 1825, more than 20% of the new communicants can be identified as the children of church members. Some of these very children had been presented for baptism in the full flush of their parents' conversions in 1814 or 1819. The revival of the 1820s and 1830s can be attributed, in part, to the echo effect of the high birth and baptism rates of the early nineteenth century. The children of the prolific first generation had come of age, grown in grace, and professed their faith in the church of their parent. To some extent, then, the family pattern of revivals was a reflection of the demographic history of the First Presbyterian Church.

Still, the family cycle is not a *sufficient* explanation for either revivalism or the conversion of the second generation. A long history of pastoral reminders of parental responsibility had preceded the entrance of the second generation into the church. These clerical directives were addressed specifically to male heads of households, however, and seem to have been unheeded. More than 68% of the converts affirmed the faith of their mothers but not their fathers. The later revivals brought some of Utica's mothers a pious sense of achievement when, after years of prayer and instruction, their children pledged their souls to Christ. Harriet Dana must have felt this satisfaction when her son John joined the ranks of the saved in 1826 and again in 1838 with the belated conversion of her son James Dwight (the famed natural scientist of Yale University). Mrs. Dana's own conversion had occurred in July 1814, at the zenith of Utica's first revival. She was most likely pregnant at the time; her son James was baptized the following September, his brother John two years thereafter. The religious biographies of eight more of Harriet Dana's children lie outside the purview of Utica's church records and beyond the time span of the revival cycle.

Another episode in the private revival of Harriet Dana, however, is worthy of note. In 1826 James Dana, Sr., officially joined the church of which his wife had been a member for a dozen years. This conjugal rendition of the kinship of conversion was not unusual. In the revival occasioned by Finney's appearance in Utica, for example, seven husbands took up full church membership several years after the conversion of their wives. This trend continued in the revivals that followed, much to the delight of the local ministry, ever eager to snare a head of household. One church history, written forty years after the event, recalled with special pride the conversion in 1838 of John H. Ostrom, lawyer, bank officer, and prominent Utica politician. The author failed to mention that Ostrom's wife, then the young Mary Walker and later "a principal woman" of the church and community, had converted in a revival that occurred almost a quarter of a century earlier.

Another example will illustrate the matrilineage that runs through the entire history of revivalism in the Utica Presbyterian Church. This story of domestic evangelism begins in 1814 with the conversion of Mrs. Sophia Bagg, who professed her faith on July 7, 1814, and helped to found the Oneida Female Missionary Society in the same year. Her daughter Emma was baptized the following September; the baptismal convenant was recited for her son Michael fourteen months later, and two more sons were christened before 1820. When Finney arrived in Utica, Sophia's daughter Emma, who was at least eleven years old, promptly entered the church. A Mary Ann Bagg who was examined for admission to the church at about the same time, whose baptism had not been recorded in the church records, may have been another of Sophia's daughters. At any rate, the family of Sophia Bagg figured prominently in the revival of 1826, for it was in that year that Moses Bagg, the hotelkeeper, a wealthy and respected son of one of Utica's very first entrepreneurs, joined his wife and children in full church membership. Moses Bagg was one of those "gentlemen of property and standing" who helped to organize Utica's anti-abolitionist riot in 1835. Even amid the uproar of the 1830s, however, the Bagg family continued quietly to play out the family cycle of revivals. Moses, Jr., ranked among the converts of 1831, and his brother Egbert enrolled in the church in 1838. The family of Sophia Bagg may be atypical only in social stability, public prominence, and consequent wealth of historical documentation. Perhaps countless anonymous women left a similar legacy of conversions across the frontier or in the poorly documented evangelical denominations, the Baptist and the Methodist.

Neither do the church records reveal the more extended kinship ties that underpinned the revival. Utica supplies one anecdote that illustrates this wider network of revivalism and at the same time suggests the modes of evangelism peculiar to women. The central female character in this religious homily generally appears in nineteenth-century church history under the name of "Aunt C." During the revival of 1825 and 1826 "Mrs. C." was visited by a nephew, a student at nearby Hamilton College. The nephew in question came from conservative Calvinist stock and looked with disdain upon the vulgar evangelist Charles Finney, a friend and temporary neighbor of his aunt. Thus "Mrs. C." resorted to a pious deception to entice her young kinsman to a revival meeting at the Utica Presbyterian Church. She convinced him to attend a morning service on the pretense that Finney would not be preaching until later in the day. Once in the church and in the presence of the despised preacher, the young man realized that he had been caught in a female trap. He recalled it this way: "When we came to the pew door [Aunt 'C.'] motioned me to go in and followed with several ladies and shut me in." When he attempted a second escape, the pious but wily aunt whispered in his ear, "You'll break my heart if you go!" Woman's role in the conversion that ensued would have remained forever unrecorded were it not that the convert in question was none other than Theodore Dwight Weld. The famed abolitionist's aunt turns out to be Sophia Clarke, whose many unheralded accomplishments included a founding membership in both the Female Missionary Society and the Maternal Association and the enrollment of at least three children among the revival converts.

Women's role in the revivals was not confined to private, individual efforts like these. Rather, it was often conducted openly, in the quasi-public forums of the Female Missionary society and the Maternal Association. Despite the fragmentary records of these institutions, fully one-third of the converts, or their mothers, can be traced to one or the other organization. Harriet Dana, Mary Walker Ostrom, and Sophia Clarke, for example, were all members of the Female Missionary Society. Although the early awakenings enrolled the actual members of these organizations, the later stages of the revival cycle brought their children into the church. Eighteen of the converts of 1826 can be identified as children of the members of the Female Missionary Society and account for 15% of the conversions. The same revival brought saving grace to sixteen children (13% of all converts) whose mothers belonged to the newly formed Maternal Association. In the subsequent revivals, 1830 and 1838, the imprint of the older organization disappeared but the Maternal Association continued to exercise power behind the pulpit. All in all, known members of the Maternal Association brought at least fifty-five children into the revival ranks. Within these organizations, women consciously wove the social and familial ties that laced through the revival cycle.

In the aftermath of Finney's tour, Utica's male elite took greater interest in revivalism, now clearly a cause to be reckoned with. They quickly established several missionary societies of their own. The membership lists of the Western Domestic Missionary Society, founded in 1826, reiterated the same surnames that stocked the earlier female organization: Bagg, Hastings, Stocking, Doolittle, and Van Rensselaer, to name a few. From the date of its founding, the Western Domestic

Missionary Society courted the cooperation of women and within a year invited the female organization to become a formal auxiliary. The Utica-based leadership of the Female Missionary Society of the Western District voted to accept this invitation. Soon they were absorbed into the male association and women's identity as an independent force for revivalism was erased from the public ledgers. The names of these women no longer appeared in addresses, circulars, and religious periodicals; they were reincorporated into the household order of the male elite. Women ultimately proved to be poor competitors for public stature, at least among the elite of the commercial town.

Off in the rural areas, however, the female organization of evangelism died a slower death and, in fact, experienced a brief renascence. The auxiliaries regarded the decision to consolidate with the Domestic Missionary Society as only tentative, and in 1829 they came back into operation. Even if the evangelical goals could be achieved without the Female Missionary Society, these women argued, "we should ourselves at any rate loose an important benefit. That pleasing interchange of views and feelings on the grand objections of our association—those heartfelt communications of hope, joy and gratitude, to which our connection gives rise, would nearly, if not entirely be lost. The deep interest produced by the work would give way to lassitude, and the living animation which they inspire be succeeded, we have reason to fear, by a chilling indifference." Significantly, neither Utica nor Whitestown appointed trustees to the revised association. In the absence of their sponsorship, the society collected only $365, sponsored one missionary, and disappeared within two years. With the disappearance of the Female Missionary Society, the more expansive and broadly social wave of women's evangelism subsided.

It had served its purpose, however, and created a powerful successor in the Maternal Association. At the conclusion of the revival cycle, members of the Maternal Association accounted for more than one-third of the converts in the First Presbyterian Church. By this date, furthermore, the Maternal Association had acquired its own machinery for reaching out to women dispersed in their isolated homes. In 1833 the First Presbyterian Society commissioned one of its own members to edit a periodical on the subject of their mutual interest. *Mother's Magazine* was followed in but a few years by a Baptist equivalent, *Mother's Monthly Journal.* Other female organizations also continued to share in the exercise of women's converting power. The Sunday schools founded in 1815 flourished, expanded, and enrolled a broader spectrum of the population in the later stages of the revival cycle. The Sunday-school journal published by Merrill and Colwell regularly reported that scores of their students were converted during each revival season. Female academies were yet another organizational setting for revivals. A revival at the Select Female School of New Hartford, a Utica suburb, was engineered almost single-handedly by a female teacher in 1831.

THE DOMESTICATION OF RELIGION

Such feminine methods of evangelism had become institutionalized and were almost routine by the close of the revival cycle. In the end it seemed that the women of Oneida County could do without the assistance of Charles Finney or any other minister. The accounts in the mother's magazines seldom recognized ministerial interference in the conversion of children. In 1833 the editor of *Mother's Magazine* put it directly: "The church has had her seasons of refreshing and her turn of decay; but here in the circle of mothers, it is felt that the Holy Spirit condescends to *dwell*. It seems his blessed rest." Indeed, the last revivals were very domesticated operations. In 1838, 42% of all converts at Utica's First Presbyterian Church could be identified as children of church members.

The soberer nature of the later revivals was also attributable to their class composition. Merchant families recaptured the prominent position they had held in the first revivals. They were joined, however, by growing numbers of professionals and clerks. No laborers appeared in the ranks of the converts, and artisan families occupied only 6.3% of the places among the saved. If only the male converts are considered, the class nature of the 1838 revival seems even more homogeneous. The majority of the male converts of 1838 could be located in the *City Directory* where, in almost equal proportions, they could be identified as merchants, professionals, and clerks. The converts who joined the revivals of the First Presbyterian Church in the 1830s were largely white-collar workers whose social status conforms to contemporary notions of the middle and upper-middle class. The high incident of clerks is particularly interesting. More than 15% of the converts had entered the most rapidly growing occupational sector within the commercial city. Thus the revival cycle ended on a quietly portentous note, with suggestions that the waves of evangelical enthusiasm may have had a transforming effect on class as well as family structure.

After 1838 church enrollments in Utica and Whitestown occurred at a slow and even pace. In the quiet after the evangelical fire storm, the men and women of the Burned-Over District took stock of a transformed religious and social landscape. They lost little time, first of all, in confirming a fundamental alteration in the relationship between age, parentage, and salvation. At the end of the revival cycle, the doctrine of infant depravity, long maligned by the Universalists, was dealt its final blow. The bluntest assault came from the Reverend Beriah Green, the controversial pastor of Whitestown's Congregational Church.

Writing in 1836, Green was prepared to be more explicit about the "moral agency" of childhood than were theologians a generation earlier. It was the peculiar dependency and vulnerability of infants and children, in Green's opinion, that made them susceptible to Christian education and open to the reception of grace. "Unembarrassed by any pretension to self-sufficiency [children] readily and affectionately receive from a supervisor whatever necessities may require. Their sense of dependence is as natural as their breath." Whoever provided those necessities, it would follow, could wield considerable power over the formation of the child's character. Thus, in the privacy of the home, parents formed the cradle of both conversion and character formation. According to Green, the young home-bound child was nestled "amid circumstances and relations which naturally lead to such exercises of mind and of heart, as give his parents high advantages for instructing and impressing him respecting his relations, duties, and prospects, as a creature of God. Now is the time to conduct him to the bosom of the saviour." Green had traversed considerable theological and psychological territory in his brief essay. His depiction of a youth's route to salvation disarmed the concept of infant depravity, revised the theory of infant nature, and proposed a new method of rearing children to Christian standards of behavior.

His typology also reordered the timing and changed the administration of childhood socialization. Brutal will-breaking at age two gave way to a more tender and gradual procedure. The brief and definitive interference of the patriarchal authority was supplanted by constant, monitory, and affectionate parental guidance from infancy through childhood. Both the touted affections of mothers and their superintendence of infancy and early childhood recommended them for this task. To the hallowed role of bringing souls to Christ, wrote, Green, "none have higher claims than mothers." Green reserved his fondest praise for the mother who administered Christian instruction along with the tender and faithful care of her baby. "Wise and happy mother! A better method to raise the hearts of her little one to heaven she could not have adopted." The entire transformation of the process of conversion is compactly compressed into the Reverend Mr. Green's accolade: Children had become innocent "little ones," whose "hearts" (not minds or wills) would be led to God by the care of the mother (not the authority and responsibility of the father). This renovation of the relationship between children and the Calvinist church was articulated in Oneida County, New York, more than a decade before its usual dating, the publication of Horace Bushnell's *On Christian Nurture* in 1848.

In point of fact, the transformation, was under way even before Green's tract appeared. Perhaps the first institution to employ this affectionate, maternal, and gradual method of courting children's souls was the Presbyterian Sunday School founded by five young women in 1815. In an address to the Utica Sunday School Union in 1824 a local pastor exclaimed, "Behold our beloved teachers—whose care for us is like a mother's for her infant child—whose kind instructions drop like honey from her lips." The pages of the *Sabbath School Visitant* supplied teachers with parabolic instructions for employing this technique. The successful practice was illustrated by this speech to two unruly boys: "I forgive you both," began the teacher, "and if you are sorry, and do so no more, may God forgive you, and your mother and I will be so happy." Gentle nurture reigned triumphant: "The children burst into tears. It was a triumph of kind and temperate discipline." The Sunday-school teacher was the first to be exempted from the suspicion of excessive affection heretofore negatively associated with doting and indulgent mothers.

Maternal associations had been moving cautiously but surely toward this new method of child treatment since the early 1820s. The first pronouncements of the Utica Maternal Association conveyed a sense of urgency based on the traditional timing of the mother's role. "The time for your exertion is very short. Soon your children will arrive at the period of life when a mother's influence will be very feebly felt unless it is early exerted." Even before the children passed into the sterner jurisdiction of patriarchs and employers, however, these mothers aimed to keep parental affections under tight rein. A circular of the original Portland Maine Association, reprinted in Oneida County, included the admonition to avoid "that false tenderness and those ruinous indulgences, which, by forfeiting appetites and passions of your children, prepare them for a useless, wretched life, a still more miserable death, and a despairing eternity." Utica's Baptist Maternal Association chimed in: "The young passions and propensities of depraved nature gain strength by indulgence, and become inveterate by the force of habit." The members of the Maternal Association came to their responsibilities from a uniquely female, but nonetheless traditional, perspective: They were painfully aware of the brief tenure of their parental role and at the same time suspicious of emotionally intense bonds between parents and children. This state of mind was symbolized in the popular image of the pious woman who prayed that she might not "nurse a child for the devil."

Maternal associations had, however, put in motion the forces that would lead almost inevitably to the new childrearing. As mothers, the members had assumed responsibility not only for the physical care of infants but also their salvation and the formation of character. They set out to investigate and implement the best methods to achieve that end at a time when patriarchs had become preoccupied with secular and economic concerns outside the household and in the marketplace. It is tempting to assert that all along women had been orchestrating changes in the theology of childhood from behind the scenes. After all, many printers' wives were deeply involved in the Utica Maternal Association, and when Beriah Green wrote his treatise on childhood he had an overwhelmingly female flock. The more likely process, however, was a transfer of functions from male to female as mothers' concern for child care expanded into a vacuum left by the indifference of fathers. This is illustrated by the history of the religious press. Most evangelical periodicals suspended publication after the 1830s, at which time the mother's magazines quickly took over the function of translating the morphology of conversion into a method of childhood socialization.

Mother's Magazine, nominally a Presbyterian publication, assumed from the first that children were sweet innocents, susceptible to affectionate rearing. The editors of the Baptists' *Journal* spoke out definitively in 1837 when they opined that God in his justice wouldn't do such a nasty thing as send a little child to Hell. The mother's magazines were also quite explicit about the changes in sex roles their publication protended. In 1836 *Mother's Monthly Journal* put it this way. "Not that I would derogate from the prerogative of the father, or depreciate the influence which he is capable of exerting upon the character of his family; but the mother's appropriate sphere and pursuits give her a decided advantage in the great work of laying the foundation of future character; inculcating those principles and sentiments [which] are to control the destiny of her children in all future time." The means to this ponderous maternal goal—"to control the destiny of her children in all future time"—would be worked out in detail in the pages of the mother's magazines. They would pose a resolution to the problem first articulated as the fragility of the Abrahamic covenant. They were designed to bring the generations together on new terms, terms appropriate to a new age.

The revival cycle ended as it had begun, at a knarry juncture between family, society, and religion. Under its auspices, the relations of the ages and sexes had undergone a complex sequence of changes, which can be summarized only with difficulty and oversimplification. The transition from patriarchal authority to maternal affection as the focal point of childhood socializing was the linchpin of this transformation. But the historical process was far more convoluted and hesitant than a direct transfer of sex roles and a simple shift in childrearing techniques. This transformation passed through a period of particular flux and uncertainty in the 1820s. The most frenetic stage of revivalism centered around Finney's 1825 tour of Utica and Whitestown and coincided with the stagnation of population growth on the agrarian frontier and the completion of the Erie Canal. These economic changes entailed the migration of young men and women to the factories of Whitestown and the commercial shops of Utica. All along this regional economic network young men and women responded to the novelty and uncertainty of their positions with anxious, enthusiastic, and intense religious experiences. They seemed to announce their entrance into the busy commercial world of the canal era with an exuberant and independent mode of religiosity.

Yet the process of history and the lives of families are far more continuous than this, changing and stabilizing, breaking down and building anew, in one seamless process. The continuous and conservative element in the history of revivals was woven around the family cycle. A large minority of the young converts, particularly after 1825, could be definitely linked to parents who had long been members of the church. It cannot be denied, however, that their ties to the religion of their parents were forged in the fires of the Burned-Over District and in a new and ebullient fashion. The greatest innovations in the methods of conversion, furthermore, came from an unprecedented source, from women organized at the borders of the public sphere. Women's role in revivalism took two forms, diverging according to class and time. First, the wives of merchants founded a network of societies that built the infrastructure and financed the operations of the revival ministry. The less affluent, largely rural women of the 1820s seemed particularly responsive to the Female Missionary Society and acutely concerned about the salvation of their own children. Meanwhile, the middling ranks of the urban social structure, in particular the wives of Utica's artisans, were expressing their own anxieties about the souls of their progeny. It was out of this charged atmosphere that the material methods of conversion and child care emerged. The second mode of women's organization, the maternal association, contained conversion within the relationship of mothers and children and, in the process, did much to tame the righteous furor of the Second Great Awakening.

The revivals occasioned some fundamental shifts in the relations of class as well as gender. At first glance it may seem, as historians such as Paul Johnson and Anthony Wallace have argued, that evangelism was a weapon of class domination employed by local elites to bring their workers into compliance with the exigencies of capitalist development. Certainly the merchant leaders of Utica, many of whom sat on the boards of directors of local banks and nearby factories, played a prominent role in such revival organizations as the Domestic Missionary Society of the Western District. Their wives furthermore had played the key role in organizing the first revivals. The regional economy of Oneida County during the canal era did not, however, pit capitalists against proletarians. Rather, it linked large merchants to small producers, both farmers and artisans. The Female Missionary Society, accordingly, extended its influence horizontally as well as vertically, out through the agricultural hinterland and down through the middle ranks of the urban population. Both these directions led through the essential links of the regional marketplace where the husbands of female missionaries made their fortunes.

The fact that the top of the social structure exerted a powerful influence on religious and social change does not overrule the possibility that other ranks of society maneuvered successfully for their own measure of power. In Utica, New York, in the 1820s, at any rate, some robust and creative social influences percolated up from the middle ranks of the population. While the elite women of Utica were working out new religious relationships with members of other social strata, the wives of artisans, professionals, and shopkeepers devised major alterations in the internal family order. It was the Maternal Association with its strong constituency of artisan wives that did most to recast the lineage of grace in the prescient form of gentle motherly nurture. Finally, these families of the middling sort and the voluntary associations they formed seemed to serve as crucibles of further social changes. When the evangelical mothers brought their progeny into the church in the 1830s, a significant number of their sons had also secured clerical occupations and were on the path to white-collar careers. The suggestions of a relationship between the association of evangelical women and the development of the new middle class will be examined in subsequent chapters. For the time being, suffice it to say that during the Second Great Awakening the lines of gender and class crisscrossed one another in multiple and dialectical ways, giving play to creative social change among large segments of Oneida County's diverse and volatile population.

Finally, a moment's glance back over the history of revivals in Oneida County will spotlight a new pattern in the whole fabric of society. At the close of the Second Great Awakening, Oneida County could no longer be characterized as a community whose central constituting element was the patriarchal household. The most obvious alteration of the old New England way was the splintering of the Christian community into an assortment of religious sects whose members were recruited on the basis not of inheritance but of voluntary association. At the same time, the authority of those churches had been challenged by the aggressive involvement of families and voluntary associations in the religious socialism of the next generation. Within families, furthermore, it was mothers rather than patriarchs who exerted increasing control over the religious allegiances of the young. In other words, a more decidedly privatized and feminized form of religious and social reproduction was beginning to take shape around the relationship between evangelical mothers and converted children. This was perhaps the most significant social change that germinated on the charred landscape of the Burned-Over District.

Indian Removal

MICHAEL PAUL ROGIN

Much has been written about the removal of the Cherokee Indian nation from Georgia, partly because this episode furnishes a dramatic illustration of conflict between the executive and judicial branches of the government, represented by President Andrew Jackson and Chief Justice John Marshall. But the attempts to remove the Creeks, Choctaws, Chickasaws, and Seminoles from the South have been less widely noted, although they offer valuable insights into conflicts between red and white culture in the United States, as well as into the government's method of handling Indian affairs.

What makes the removal of the Five Civilized Tribes of the South particularly ironic is that, more than most other Indian nations, they sought to accommodate themselves to the culture of the white man. By tradition, these Indians were village agriculturalists rather than hunting nomads, so it was relatively easy for them to adjust to white ways. Many of them embraced while culture completely, drawing up constitutions, accepting the white man's religion and style of dress, and even owning Afro-American slaves. Only the Seminoles maintained a warrior tradition; the other nations settled down to farm their rich lands, feeling secure under the eighteenth-century treaties. By denying their own cultural traditions, the Indians eliminated much of the ostensible basis for white antipathy. Yet because they stood in the way of the advancing white frontier, methods of removing them were found. The "legal" basis for their ultimate dispossession was a result of a cultural difference that remained between them and the European settlers—a difference in the idea of land ownership.

When the English colonists first arrived in the New World, they brought with them the recently developed Anglo-Saxon notion of private land ownership. Many of the white settlers had themselves been driven off land in the Old World during the eighteenth century as a result of the consolidation of communally held lands into large, single-owner estates. But they still believed in the notion of permanent and exclusive ownership of land by individuals. In contrast, the Indians understood possession of the land as a matter of use rather than ownership. Since the New World seemed to contain plenty of land for all, the Indians originally greeted the white settlers hospitably. Yet as the years passed and white settlers occupied more and more land, barring the Indians from their claims, the implications of exclusive ownership became clear, and hostilities followed.

In the nineteenth century, the federal and state governments cooperated to convince Indian nations in the Southeast to divide communally owned lands among individual Indians, who were then persuaded sometimes fraudulently, to sell their property to speculators. The growth of large-scale cotton culture in the Deep South was a major factor in the ultimate removal of the Indians from their home ground.

When this method failed to eliminate many of the southeastern Indians, the federal government took more direct action. According to Michael Paul Rogin (University of California at Berkley), the author of the selection reprinted here, the dominant rationale for the government's policy was paternalistic. The federal government, with the president as "Great White Father," had to act in ways that would be beneficial to its red children (the Indians). Therefore, acting in the children's best interests, the fatherly authorities forceably removed them from danger. While Rogin's thesis has been criticized, his description of the removal process and the resistance some Indians offered to this strategy graphically portrays the genocidal results of the government's actions.

Of the five southern Indians tribes, only the Seminoles made a determined physical resistance to removal. In part, these several thousand Florida Indians shared grievances with other tribes that did not go to war. Their removal treaties, for example, were probably fraudulent. The first, signed in 1832 under dubious conditions, provided that several Seminole chiefs examine the proposed western country before removal was confirmed. It was not clear whether the chiefs alone or the tribe as a whole had the power to agree to removal. J. F. Schermerhorn, shortly to negotiate the Cherokee treaty of New Echota, accompanied the chiefs west; there they signed a removal treaty. Seminole bands in Florida protested against this treaty; Jackson and

INDIAN REMOVAL   *From Fathers and Children: Andrew Jackson and the Subjugation of the American Indian* by Michael Paul Rogin (New York: Knopf, 1975), pp. 236–48. Reprinted by permission of Random House, Inc.

other government officials in Florida threatened to remove them forcibly if they did not abide by it. Florida Indian agent Wiley Thompson "rebuke[d] the Indian chiefs as if they were wrong-headed schoolboys" and stripped those who opposed removal of their titles. He placed the influential warrior Osceola in irons for opposing removal, and released him only after Osceola and his followers signed an agreement to move west. "These children of the forest," General Clinch explained to Cass, "are from peculiar circumstances and long habits suspicious of the white man." But, continued Clinch, "the manly and straightforward course pursued toward them by Genl. Thompson appears to have gained their confidence." Thompson's intimate relationship with Osceola, alternating between protectiveness and punitiveness, typified relations which often developed between Indians and government agents. Osceola killed Thompson at the outbreak of the war.

Like members of other southern tribes, hungry Seminoles committed depredations in the 1830s. There was factional conflict among bands opposing and favoring removal, as well as conflict between Indians and whites. Late in 1835, after Osceola's band killed a chief who favored removal, federal troops marched against the tribe. The Seminoles ambushed a boat coming up the Apalachicola River, killing soldiers and their families, and the Second Seminole War had begun.

Fraudulent treaties, government attacks on the tribal structure, and interracial and intratribal conflict were not peculiar to the Seminoles, and cannot by themselves account for the war. Two factors were unique to the tribe. The first was a history of hostility to and independence of American authority. Tribal villages had long enjoyed freedom under weak Spanish rule. Jackson invaded Seminole country in 1814 and 1818, and the tribe was augmented by the migrations of hostile Creeks to Florida at the end of the First Creek War. The Seminoles were moved to south central Florida in the 1820s. Then Jackson insisted, over the bitter protests of the tribe, that it would have to live under the authority of the Creeks in the west. Seminole independence always angered Jackson. He justified his Florida invasions in part on the grounds that the Seminoles were merely a division of the Creeks. He urged in 1821 that the Seminoles be sent back to the Creeks. They ought now to join, in Benton's words, "the mother tribe, in the west."

Actually there was severe conflict between the two tribes, particularly once the Seminoles were joined by red sticks who had fought on the losing side of the Creek civil war. Creeks fought with Jackson against the Seminoles in 1818. Jackson's removal plan was thus part of his continuing vendetta against the tribe. By August 1835 the Seminoles were reconciled to removal if they could retain tribal independence in the west; the administration refused.

The Seminoles had an additional reason to resist amalgamation with the Creeks. They feared the Creeks would appropriate the escaped slaves, free blacks, and Indian slaves who lived freely as part of the Seminole tribe. The Creeks demanded Seminole Negroes to obtain their share of $250,000 appropriated by Congress under an 1821 Creek treaty. This sum was to pay Georgia's claim for slaves stolen by the Creeks prior to 1802 and taken to Florida, and whatever offspring such slaves had produced. The War Department was sympathetic to the Creek claim, which was being pushed by the small group of western Creeks friendly to Georgia who had illegally ceded tribal land in Georgia and moved west. The removed Seminoles were to be placed under the authority of this Creek faction. The western Creeks sent a white lawyer into Seminole country to appropriate Negroes. He was to receive a share of the profits from his undertaking and sell slaves to white claimants and traders.

The presence of these Seminole Negroes was the most important distinguishing feature of the tribe. Seminole Negroes had the greatest reason to fear removal. They were not only in danger from the Creeks; they also made the tribe a target of white slaveholders. The blacks feared, with good reason, that they would be seized by slave-catchers when the Seminoles gathered for removal. Southern speculators and Florida planters wanted to appropriate the Negroes before the tribe went west. Raiders had already attacked Indian reserves along the Apalachicola River and stolen Negroes belonging to Indian planters. Apalachicola Indians attempting to move west with their slaves were pursued by white claimants and stripped of property and Negroes.

Jackson's protégé Richard Keith Call, a leading Florida politician and speculator, urged Jackson to grant permission to a group of speculators to purchase Negroes in Seminole country. Call explained, "If the Indians are permitted to convert them into specie, one great obstacle in the way of removal may be overcome." Jackson agreed, "directing the agent to see they obtain a fair price for them." Commissioner Harris explained to objecting Florida Indian agent Wiley Thompson that "their resources will be augmented, and they will not, upon their arrival west, have in their possession a species of property which . . . would excite the cupidity of the Creeks, and be wrested from them by their superior numbers and strength." True, the Negroes would be enslaved, wrote Harris, but "it is not to be presumed the condition of these slaves will be worse then that of others in the same section of the country." Thompson, however, objected that the change in the Negroes' condition would be "oppressively great," that no Indians wanted to sell Negroes, that speculators would use improper means to obtain them, and that the entrance of white slave-dealers would retard rather than further removal. Jackson retracted his permission, but it was too late to reassure the blacks.

Seminole Negroes, their freedom endangered, prepared to resist removal. They received covert support from Florida free blacks and slaves, who helped supply ammunition for the tribe. Seminoles attacked Florida plantations at the outset of the war, and threatened St. Augustine in south central Florida. Some field slaves joined the uprising. General

Philip Jesup, assuming command of the American troops, wrote the Secretary of War, "This, you may be assured, is a negro, not an Indian war; and if it be not speedily put down, the south will feel the effects of it on their slave population." Benton, obliquely recognizing the importance of slavery, blamed the war on the abolitionists.

The administration, meeting the wishes of Florida planters, insisted it would not end the war on terms permitting Seminole Negroes to go west. Cass ordered General Winfield Scott at the outbreak of the war to "allow no terms to the Indians until every living slave in their possession, belonging to a white man, is given up." Decades-old white claims were recognized, including title to the then unborn children of escaped or captured slaves. Indians, moreover, rarely had proof they owned slaves they had actually purchased. Cass' order thus endangered the freedom of most Seminole Negroes, not merely of slaves who had escaped once the war began. To underline its interest in the Negroes, the War Department enlisted Creek warriors against the Seminoles, promising them that a bounty for captured Negroes would be paid from the Seminole annuity.

General Jesup negotiated an end to the war in March 1837 which permitted Seminole Negroes to go west. Under Florida pressure, he reneged. He signed a secret agreement with some Seminole chiefs in which they agreed to turn Negroes over to white claimants. He reserved an order prohibiting slave-catchers from entering Seminole country and appropriating blacks who had gathered in camps to await removal. Negroes and Indians fled these camps, and the war continued.

Many Seminole Negroes and slaves who had joined the war were dead or captured by 1837. Most of the rest responded to Jesup's renewed promise they could go west in safety. But the lawyer for the Creeks and other slave-traders tried, with administration support, to capture and sell these Negroes. Secretary of War Joel Poinsett and Commissioner of Indian Affairs C. A. Harris sought to obtain the Negroes for speculators in Creek lands. James C. Watson, a leading participant in the Creek land frauds, took Poinsett's advice and made large purchases of claims on the Seminole Negroes. Watson's brother-in-law followed the Negroes west, but the army, to Harris' dismay, thwarted his efforts to appropriate them. Finally, in 1841, the new administration determined that the 1832 Seminole treaty settled all white claims on Seminole Negroes originating prior to 1832.

The august *Niles' Register* hoped, at the outbreak of the Second Seminole War, "that the miserable creatures will be speedily swept from the face of the earth." But the tribe scored early victories over American troops and forced whites to abandon most of the territory south of St. Augustine. The American army was plagued throughout 1836 by disease, insufficient numbers, rivalry among its commanders, difficulties in supplying troops in the Florida interior, and a tropical terrain uniquely suited to Indian guerrilla warfare. Jackson had faced all these problems but the last in the Creek War and overcome them. Now he gave Call, whom he looked upon as a son, an opportunity to do the same. Call had no more luck than his predecessors. He ran out of supplies, was forced to retreat, and was then incapacitated by ill health. Jackson had triumphed over these adversities; Call was dismissed in an angry letter.

There were enough troops in Florida, Jackson insisted, "as might eat Powell [Osceola] and his few." Army failures made the conflict "a disgraceful war to the american character," Jackson wrote after he left office. As the war dragged on, he resorted to the language and proposals of his own earlier Florida campaigns. He complained that General Scott's "combined operations, without knowing where the Indian women were, was like a combined operation to encompass a wolf in the hamocks without knowing first where her den and whelps were." To the Secretary of War he suggested search-and-destroy missions against hidden Indian villages. American commanders should have found "where their women are" and "captured or destroyed them."

Seminole resistance did not merely provoke such proposals from Jackson. It led General Jesup and his successors to violate flags of truce, capture Indians invited to negotiate, hold them as hostages, threaten them with execution if they did not bring in their followers, employ bloodhounds against the tribe, and kill cattle that American troops did not need in order to deprive the Indians of food. The barbarous treachery of the Seminoles justified these measures, Jackson and Benton insisted. In Benton's words, "A bit of white linen, striped, perhaps, from the body of a murdered child, or its murdered mother, was no longer to cover the insidious visits of spies and enemies. A firm and manly course was taken."

Jesup captured the majority of the tribe by 1838; the remaining Indians fought bitterly for four more years. They raided white settlements for food and supplies, but promised to stop fighting if they could stay in Florida. In 1842, their ranks further reduced by death and capture, the few hundred remaining Seminoles were permitted to do so.

Violent rage marked Jackson's pre-presidential Indian relations; it surfaced again among Jacksonians during the Indian wars of the 1830s. War and primitive verbal violence were not typical, however, of Jackson's presidential Indian policy. The vast majority of Indians were removed without war. The administration met their intensified, prolonged suffering with a steady impoverishment of affect.

The southern tribes experienced intense hardships in their original homes after 1828, but the long journeys were worst of all. Tens of thousands were clothed inadequately and marched through freezing southwestern winters. Those who made the trip in the summer suffered from extreme heat and drought. Indians were fed inadequate and contaminated rations, including rancid meat, spoiled flour, and bad drinking water. In some cases food offered them was years old and had already been declared unfit to eat. They were crowded together on old, unseaworthy boats—the worst single accident killed 311 Creeks—and separated from their remaining possessions by emigrating agents, local citizens, and sheriffs prosecuting alleged debt claims. They traveled through areas in which cholera was raging. Weakened by the exhausting journey and bad food, tens of thousands caught fevers, measles, and cholera; thousands died from disease and exposure on the removal journeys alone. War, disease, accident, starvation, depredations, murder, whiskey, and other causes of death from the extension of state laws through removal and resettlement had killed by 1844 one-quarter to one-third of the southern Indians.

The insistence on removal and the deadlines enforced on the tribes insured much of this suffering. Government methods also made matters worse. Contractors hired to provision Indians made money at their expense. They increased their profits by supplying bad food and unsafe boats. Jackson assigned the entire responsibility for Creek removal to contractors. In Cass' words, "The President, on full consideration, has determined to make an experiment to remove the Creek Indians by contract." The contractors would be paid $20 per head for the number of Indians they emigrated. Cass hired the very speculators who had defrauded the Creeks, and who now saw an opportunity to make more money off the tribe. These men desired removal, Cass apparently reasoned, and they would have the incentive to accomplish it.

The Creeks objected from the outset to removal by the speculators. Cass told Hogan not to "yield to the idle whims of the Indians, and indulge them in unnecessary preferences, which amount in fact merely to a wish that certain individuals, rather than others, should be concerned in their removal." Jackson had once sworn that "a pure government" would "make no concession" to "such men," but a contractual relationship was not a concession. Contracts, in a liberal society, created reciprocal obligations. Contractors had been paid to take responsibility for removal off the shoulders of the government.

The army also played a role in removal. The contractors were retained after the Second Creek War broke out, but they were joined by the army. It identified 2,500 Creeks as hostile, and removed the warriors among them in chains. Soldiers scouted Cherokee country to round up Creeks who had fled there during the war; they also collected long-time Creek residents among the Cherokees, married or otherwise connected to that tribe.

Two years later, in the spring of 1838, the army rounded up 15,000 Cherokees who had refused to remove in the time allotted under the New Echota treaty. They were seized as they worked in their farms and fields, separated from their possessions, and taken to military detention camps. They remained in captivity for months while hundreds died from inadequate and unaccustomed rations. The debilitation of others contributed to deaths during the removal march.

Eaton had promised during the debates on the Indian-removal bill,

"Nothing of a compulsory nature to effect the removal of this unfortunate race of people has ever been thought of by the President, although it has been so asserted." The treaty of New Echota, the government now claimed, had committed the tribe; if Indians were not mature enough to fulfill their promises, the government would have to force them.

Creek removal combined military with market pressures. Emigration was stalled after the Creek War; county officials arrested many principal men of the tribe for alleged debts, in an effort to strip the Creeks of their remaining possessions. The Creeks asked the government for an advance payment of their 1837 annuity to pay these debts. General Jesup, who had put down the Creek uprising and was on his way to Florida, insisted that to obtain the annuity several hundred Creek warriors would have to fight the Seminoles. Their families, sent west without them, were deprived of their help during removal and resettlement.

Another group of several hundred Creek warriors was recruited to fight voluntarily in Florida. The government wished to avoid "sacrificing our own troops to the unhealthful climate in the sickly season of the year." It detained the warriors' families in Alabama camps and promised to feed and protect them. General Jesup kept these Creek warriors, over their objections, several months past the expiration of their terms of enlistment. He explained that he would otherwise have incurred the expense of hiring militia. But Georgia and Alabama wanted the Indians out of the south. Companies of county militia invaded the Indian camps, stole stock and possessions, raped women, manhandled and mistreated the Indians in other ways, and insisted they be removed from Alabama. Commissioner Harris responded to reports of these events by initiating the removal of the Indians. The government, "guardian and protector" of the Indians, was required by "the change in the state of things" to transport them west immediately. The Creek warriors were finally permitted to leave Florida, discharged, as Secretary of War Poinsett explained to Congress, because of the expense of maintaining their families.

The War Department, violating its original agreement with the Creeks, did not wait for the warriors' return before removing their families. It gathered them at Pass Christian, near Mobile, where disease, exposure, and starvation claimed 177 deaths in the party of 3,500 between March 7 and July 31, 1837. Harris regretted this suffering "as sincerely as any man can," but doubted that "anything further can be done by this office." In fact that same day he did do something further. He was concerned that the contractors would demand more money to transport Creek possessions. Creeks "had collected a much larger amount of baggage than the company, by their contract, are bound to transport," he wrote, and "the Indians are unwilling to dispose of any part of it, or to leave any part behind." He ordered the emigrating officer not to transport any "evidently superfluous" possessions purchased from "whim or caprice," and to prevent any such purchases in the future.

The worse the Indian suffering and death, as Creek removal suggests, the more disassociated the reaction of Washington officials. Indian Office records reveal monumental concern for the details of organizing removal, and monumental indifference to the suffering and death it caused. Overriding all other matters was concern for the costs of removal. Reports of suffering and death were met with demands for economy.

The Choctaws were the first tribe to be removed; the disorganized, disease-ridden removal of the first group of Choctaws, with its share of deaths, foreshadowed the fate of the other southern Indians. The War Department, however, was most concerned because the costs of removal far exceeded government expectations. The government reorganized removal, fed the Indians more cheaply and with spoiled food, forced them to walk rather than ride, reduced its costs, and increased the number of Indian dead.

Creek removal caused the deaths of thousands of Indians, but that was not the government's concern. One of the Columbus speculators who had emigrated the Creeks wanted the contract to emigrate the Cherokees. Commissioner Harris listed the considerations which should govern the award, "1st, economy—2nd, the comfort, safety, and accommodation of the Emigrants, and 3rd the moral influence which the measure will probably have upon the Cherokees." Van Buren finally permitted "Ross and the others," "viewed in the light of contracters," to organize their own removal, although Jackson protested from the Hermitage that the "contract" was much too "extravagant." By the time the superintendent of Creek removal was ordered to close up Cherokee emigration, thousands of Creeks and Cherokees had died on the journey west. Commissioner Crawford's instructions made no references to these deaths. He insisted instead that the emigrating agent "avoid the loose and irregular manner of transacting business which occurred in the Creek removal." He sought to stop General Nathaniel Smith from feeding and clothing Cherokees who had escaped the military roundup and remained in the North Carolina mountains.

As Indians died, the government demanded "economy" and sought to correct "the loose and irregular manner of transacting business." It sought, in Call's words, "to convert them into specie." It offered money for homes, money for land, and money incentives for removal. When Hogan exposed the Creek frauds, specultors were sure it was only because they had not found his price. Georgia insisted that Ross refused to sign a removal treaty because the government would not bribe him. Whites consistently converted what Van Buren called the "debt we owe to this unhappy race" into money.

Dying Indians betrayed whites. They threatened to force them to encounter the consequences of their own policies and desires. To quote John Ross again, "the perpetrator of a wrong never forgives his victims." Whites responded to Indian deaths by deadening their own experience. Indians were turned into things—a small reserve remaining in Ohio after removal was a "blank spot," "a mote in the eye of the state"—and could be manipulated and rearranged at will. Money was the perfect representation of dead, interchangeable matter. It could not symbolize human suffering and human reproach. A money equivalent could be found for Indian attachments; they had no intrinsic, unexchangeable value. Indian love would give way to money; it could be bought. The "debt we owe to this unhappy race," converted into specie, could be paid.

Indians, children of nature, had an uncontrolled instinctual life. It caused them, in the white view, first to kill and then to die. Indians lived in a relationship of basic trust with nature, but that relationship did not help them survive. Indians dead and suffering were out of control; demands for economy expressed anxiety about the loss of control in an area in which administrators could more safely experience it. Money, the solid product of self-reliance, replaced unreliable nature. Bureaucratic removal offered an enclosed realm, divorced from the human, natural world. Interchangeable entries on bureaucratic ledgers, Indians were not particular, specific, humans whose suffering could be pitied. The government would not save Indians; it would try to save money.

Money, debt, and control were pervasive themes in Jacksonian democracy. . . . We turn now from defenses against death within the bureaucratic structure to return of death in the world. Death cast its shadow over the entire removal experience; it deeply affected perceptions of the westward journey itself.

Savagery, proponents of Indian removal claimed, could maintain itself only by fleeing westward. Providence decreed that "the hunting tribes must retreat before the advance of civilization, or perish under the shade of the white man's settlements." "Mature consideration," said Jackson in his Seventh Annual message, revealed that Indians "can not live in contract with a civilized community and prosper." White settlers would be excluded from the western lands; if the tribes chose to remain uncivilized, "they are upon the skirts of the great prairies" and could hunt the buffalo which roamed there. Entirely extruded from civilization, primitive experience could maintain itself. Alleged tribal willingness to go west had indicated to some writers that childhood would not resist maturity. "They are on the outside of us, and in a place which will ever remain on the outside," the Senate Committee on Indian Affairs declared as Indian removal came to an end.

But politicians who argued that isolating the savages would protect them also called for the march of civilization across the continent. Jefferson proposed the northern Louisiana territory as a home for the eastern tribes; at the same time he foresaw Indians retreating westward to the Pacific as the tide of white civilization advanced. "When we shall be full on this side [of the Mississippi]," he wrote, "we may lay off a range of States on the western bank from the head to the mouth and so, range after range, advancing compactly as we multiply." Cherokee agent R. J. Meigs, an early advocate of removal, explained,

> A disposition to migrate seems to pervade the whole eastern part of the United States; we invite that emigration here; obstacles ought to be removed. The tendency is as uniform as the law of gravitation. It can no more be restrained *until the shores of the Pacific Ocean make it impossible to go further.*

One Cherokee, said Meigs, suggested that land given the Indians not be bounded on the west. The Indians could then continue westward; they could flee, as the post Civil War chromolithograph *American Progress . . .* would picture it, before the advancing whites. Temporarily the west would place Indians "far beyond the reach of the oppression—and, I was about to say, the examples of the white man." Permanently, only death would. Savage integrity could ultimately maintain itself only in death.

Childhood experience could not be integrated into adult life; living it served as a reminder of what had been lost and rejected in the process of growing up. American nostalgia for childhood and the past reflected the failure of revered ideals actually to guide behavior, and the longing for what one's desires had killed. Like the dead twins in the frontier Tennessee poem, only dead Indians could safely be mourned. The white father was not merely helpless to prevent death; he identified with it, longed for it, and carried it out.

Indian removal carried out violence against symbolic childhood. The fantasies of its perpetrators also expressed longings for death itself. Americans wedded to competitive advancement in the world shared an arcadian dream life. The rural home would release them from worldly cares and return them to a state of primitive security. Such longings, however, did not protect whites from mobility "to better their condition," as Jackson put it, any more than they protected Indians. Jackson had longed to retire to his Hermitage refuge for thirty-five years. The heavenly father's eternal home offered the only permanent rest.

Removal promised the Indians, in Cass' words, "the probability of an adequate and final reward." It would transport them—the words are Jackson's on the death of John Coffee's mother—to "happier climes than these." Death was the western tribal utopia. Géza Róheim writes,

> [I]n the other world we have the land of wish fulfillment, the place where our infantile omnipotence of thoughts reigns supreme, and where we can be rid of all the pain and trouble that is inherent in the environment[.] The paradise once familiar to us all in our infancy, we have learned through bitter experience cannot exist in this world. Hence we use its shattered material to rebuild it at the

very moment when we stand in greatest need of consolation, at the moment of death.

Indians, the removal ideology asserted, were plagued by competitive forces which they and the government were powerless to resist. Removed Indians would benefit from "parental care and guardianship." Their land would be "forever secured and guaranteed to them." "If a paternal authority is exercised over the aboriginal colonies" west of the Mississippi, wrote Cass, "we may hope so see that improvement in their conditions for which we have so long and vainly labored."

A benevolent father would have total power in the west; he could free Indians from violent and competitive relations with their white brothers, and protect his red children. Jackson tried to convince the Creeks of this in the message he sent them three days after his inauguration. He told the tribe, "Your bad men have made my heart sicken, and bleed by the murder of one of my white children in Georgia. Our peaceful mother earth has been stained by the blood of the white man, and calls for the punishment of his murderers." In the west such conflicts would not arise. "Where you are now your white brothers have always claimed the land. The land beyond the Mississippi belongs to the President, and to none else; and he will give it to you forever. . . . You will be subject to your own laws, and the care of your father, the President." Jackson returned to the theme of refuge in his Farewell Address. "The philanthropist will rejoice," he said, "that the remnant of that ill fated race has at length been placed beyond the reach of injury and oppression, and that the paternal care of the General Government will hereafter watch over them and protect them."

The Creeks recognized the utopian character of these promises. As early as the 1820s whites west of the Mississippi had successfully demanded land promised the southern Indians. One Creek delegation pointed out to Jackson that Alabama had recently been a remote frontier territory inhabited, like the western land offered the tribe, by Indians protected by the United States. Now whites were not only crowding Alabama Indians; they were also moving into the western territory. Their great father Jackson, they said, might protect them for a time, but he was old and a successor might not be bound by his promises.

Jackson was old indeed. He suffered, as he said in his Farewell Address just before turning to the Indian question, from "advanced age and a broken frame." His promises of western utopia resembled his thoughts of death. Overton had gone beyond the reach of injury and oppression too, where his enemies could no longer hurt him. Emily Donelson also had an adequate and final reward; "she has changed a world of woe, for a world of eternal happiness." Elisabeth Coffee "has gone to the realms of bliss free from all the troubles of this wicked world." The old man, benignly surveying the destruction of the children of nature, was reconciling himself to death.

Indian deaths transcended individual will and merged with the providential movement of history. America had begun with a radical assertion of the power of men to control their fate. But the country progressed through the destruction of another set of men, and responsibility for that destruction could not be faced. "The extinction of the Indians," wrote Cass, "has taken place by the unavoidable operation of natural causes, and as the natural consequences of the vicinity of white settlements." White men were placed by "Providence" on the "skirts of a boundless forest." Subduing it by industry, they advanced and multiplied by providential decree. They had superiority in arts, arms, and intelligence. How, then, could whites be blamed for the Indian plight? "Their misfortunes have been the consequence of a state of things which could not be controlled by them or us." Cass drew practical lessons from his theory of history. If the Creeks chose to stay in Alabama and "finally melt away before our people and institutions, the result must be attributed to causes, which we can neither stay nor control."

As southern Indians actually began to die in large numbers, policymakers denied not simply responsibility but reality itself. The worse the events, the less they could be admitted into consciousness. During the last large-scale Indian removal, 4,500 Cherokees died. President Van Buren and Secretary of War Poinsett ignored the deaths. They congratulated themselves instead that removal was at an end, and that they had finally permitted Chief Ross to lead the bulk of his tribe west. As Poinsett described the process,

> The generous and enlightened policy . . . was ably and judiciously carried into effect by the General appointed. . . . The reluctance of the Indians to relinquish the land of their birth . . . was entirely overcome. . . . Humanity, no less than sound policy, dictated this course toward these children of the forest.

The Commissioner of Indian Affairs amplified:

> A retrospect of the last eight months, in reference to this numerous and more than ordinarily enlightened tribe, cannot fail to be refreshing to well-constituted minds. . . . A large mass of men have been conciliated, the hazard of an effusion of blood has been put by, good feeling has been preserved, and we have quietly and gently transported 18,000 friends to the west bank of the Mississippi.

In Van Buren's words, "The wise, humane, and undeviating policy of the government in this the most difficult of all our relations foreign or domestic, has at length been justified to the world in its near approach to a happy and certain consummation."

Instead of facing actual deaths, white policy-makers imagined Indian destruction as an abstracted and generalized process removed from human control and human reality. To face responsibility for specific killing might have led to efforts to stop it; avoiding individual deaths turned Indian removal into a theory of genocide. In Jackson's words,

> Humanity has often wept over the fate of the aborigines of this country, and Philanthropy has been busily engaged in devising means to avert it, but its progress has never for a moment been arrested, and one by one have many powerful tribes disappeared from the earth. To follow to the land the last of his race and to tread on the graves of extinct nations excites melancholy reflections. But true philanthropy reconciles the mind to these vicissitudes, as it does to the extinction of one generation to make room for another.

Weeping over Indian deaths was immature. History rescued a man from melancholy; he could tread on Indian graves in peace. "Independance of mind and action," to recall Jackson's advice to his nephew, could not be borne. Instead a man like Jackson had to justify himself as a "real tool in the hands of" "his creator," "wielded, like a mere attamaton, sometimes, without knowing it, to the worst of purposes." To be a man meant to participate, separated from the actual experience, in a genocide.

Learning to Be Americans:
Schooling and Political Culture

JEAN H. BAKER

Education has been an intermittent but continuing concern of American government. From the Founding Fathers' unrealized determination to establish a national system of schooling and a national university to the present administration's desire to reform primary and secondary education through what it refers to as a strengthening of basic skills, political leaders have shown an interest in what takes place in the American schoolroom.

In the early nineteenth century, the developing political culture was seen as needing reinforcement to continue the republican spirit established in the new nation. Those interested in keeping the democratic spirit alive and growing felt that an important way to achieve this was through a system of public schools that would instill the appropriate values in America's young. The educational process would reflect and pass along those values that had led to the establishment of the nation. Clearly, this idea of education created some difficulties for the instructors in the schools. If democracy required a sense of equality and participation, then the process of schooling should reflect these values. On the other hand, effective schooling called for imposing some hierarchy on knowledge. This conflict between the democratic classroom and the structure of knowledge has remained an issue in American education.

Given the difficulty of training for democracy in the classroom, educators began to stress the importance of certain subject matter in developing a devout citizenry. The study of American history was seen as the primary means of eliciting national loyalty in students. The history that they learned dealt primarily with military exploits, particularly American victories, and the sacrifices of those who had brought about independence and nationhood. The lesson to be learned from this material was that a citizen's proper responsibility was to heed the call of the nation in time of crisis.

In the selection that follows, Jean H. Baker (Goucher College) describes the attempts to establish a democratic system of education in the first half of the nineteenth century. In doing this, she discusses the early unsuccessful efforts of political leaders to establish a national system and goes on to look at the way schools were set up and operated. She points out the difficulty of employing and keeping teachers and explores the restlessness and rebelliousness of students in the period. Many of the problems she deals with remain with us today and continue to remind us of the difficulties of providing effective political education in a democratic society.

The easiest way of becoming acquainted with the modes of thinking, the rules of conduct, and the prevailing manners of any people is to examine what sort of education they give their children.
—Hector St. John Crèvecoeur

While nineteenth-century families shaped their sons' partisan course, schools trained young white males in their public roles of delegating power, rotating leadership, limiting power, and supporting the government. In time, these behaviors were also enacted within the nation's political parties, which, while imitating the general political culture, came to constitute and construct the very thing they imitated. Contemporary studies of political culture suggest that the family has never been the prime agency in this process of inculcating national values; thus, although sons usually took their party choice from their fathers, their attitudes toward authority, understandings of participation and efficacy, and evaluations of government were defined by schools. The reason for this was simple: families were not public environments; Americans learned at home how to be mothers and fathers, and at school how to behave as jurors, magistrates, and voters. Sensing this, the nation's early leaders linked formal schooling and political culture, and the schoolroom became the essential mechanism for training Americans. The challenge was to produce an active

LEARNING TO BE AMERICANS: SCHOOLING AND POLITICAL CULTURE   From *Affairs of Party: The Political Culture of Northern Democrats in the Mid-Nineteenth Century* by Jean H. Baker (Ithaca: Cornell University Press, 1983) pp. 71–107. Copyright © 1983 by Cornell University Press. Used by permission of the publisher.

citizenry who attended public affairs (thereby preventing tyranny), who accepted a new system of government (thereby installing federalism), and who exchanged positions of leadership without violence (thereby assuring a representative government). Convinced that schools should do more than convey moral and academic instruction, early opinion-makers offered extensive plans for a national system of education.

SCHOOLING AS CIVIC TRAINING: THEORY

Even before the revolution, Benjamin Franklin and James Otis had cited schooling as the taproot of public culture. In their view, not only did elected officials require training, but the people—at least those possessing citizenship—must vote, run for office, serve as sheriffs, and participate in local affairs. By the late eighteenth century the colonists had become adept in these roles. They operated a political system that required participation, and from this experience many future Americans learned how to behave in a democracy. Even before their own opposition to England had crystallized, Otis and Franklin connected schooling and politics in recognition of the need for colonists to have specific information that formerly only king and court had required.

The revolution reinforced this felt need for formal agencies of political learning. The process of building a nation, even in its comparatively placid American version, had alerted a generation of venturesome conservatives to centrifugal tendencies within their society. Having overthrown king and parliament, political notables worried that disorder and confusion would continue to afflict their communities. Intellectuals as well as politicians expressed these fears; Noah Webster was concerned that "these states will always be exposed to anarchy and faction because these evils approach under the delusive but specious guise of patriotism." Because his nation had none of the institutional mucilage of other societies—no standing army, no national past, no state religion, not even a nearby foreign enemy—Webster considered schooling an essential glue and called for an association of patriots to develop a uniform national character. Benjamin Rush agreed and hoped education would install a stable political culture: "We have changed our forms of government, but it remains yet to effect a revolution in principles, opinions, and manners so as to accommodate them to the forms of government we have adopted." Jefferson might preach the need for revolution every generation, but by the last decade of the eighteenth century Americans believed theirs complete. Now they must preserve a fledgling political culture and create, through formal agencies of learning, a homogeneous public mind.

In a representative version of such prescriptions, George Washington argued that schooling alone could free youth from "those prejudices" and "unreasonable fallacies which would end in diversity" and destroy the newly established union. Local institutions, however respectable and useful, could never develop American values, and like most of the founding fathers, Washington sought to neutralize variations. "The more homogeneous our citizens can be made," he concluded in his final message to Congress, "the greater our prospects of permanent union." Washington's fear of diversity included the economic sphere. For it was not only the republic's regional, racial, and ethnic heterogeneity that alarmed this generation; its variations in wealth did, too. Schooling emerged as a potential solvent, responsible for mixing the able poor in with the middle ranks while simultaneously dispelling any dangerous social ideas of the radical and dispossessed. As Ralph Waldo Emerson later explained: "The cause of education is urged in this country . . . on what ground?—Why on this, that the people have the power, and if they are not instructed to sympathize with the intelligent, reading, trading, and governing class; inspired with a taste for the same competitions and prizes, they will upset the fair pageant of Judicature and perhaps lay a hand on the sacred muniments of wealth itself and new distribute the land." The English traveler George Combe agreed: "The ignorance of the masses," he wrote in 1840, "is filling the wealthy with terror for their own safety so that they are ardently anxious to educate the people." From this perspective schooling served the ultimate political function—it preserved the system and kept, as Emerson acknowledged, "The people from our throats."

From the beginning of their national existence, Americans believed their society could not depend on haphazard socialization by family, church or apprenticeship, and this widely held attitude sparked a durable commitment to education as an adjunct of politics. First, American schools were expected to cement the young to the regime and instill national values amid the temptations of provincialism; second, by supplying large doses of republicanism and patriotism, they were expected to inoculate citizens from subversive beliefs, whether those of Roman Catholic, monarchist, socialist, demagogue, or Native American. For people with this viewpoint, formal education emerged as more than a cognitive process involving skills in reading, writing, and numbers; and although the development of good moral habits among the young was a continuing expectation, there was little sense of schooling for scholarship, for personal satisfaction, and for intellectual liberation. Instead, the children of the republic must become Americans and never know themselves as anything else.

Once established, schools would serve, along with the republic's other institutions, as models for imitation. Because Americans could not be free and ignorant at the same time, they would be the best informed and therefore the freest. According to Madison, "a well-instructed people alone can be permanently free," and a national school system constructed to protect liberty would "adorn our free and happy system of government." To Joel Barlow, who besides his well-known epic "The "Columbiad" wrote *A Prospectus for a National Institution,* this meant that "mankind have a right to expect this example [of superior schools] from us." Linking patriotism and professionalism, Barlow believed a national system of education would furnish experts—engineers, roadbuilders, and surveyors—whose superior technology would further unite citizens in a collective pride of achievement. To William Manning, a Massachusetts farmer, education was necessary for an understanding of government laws, and constitution. "Learning and Knowledge," wrote Manning, "is essential to the preservation of Libberty and unless we have more of it amongue us we cannot seporte our Libbertyes long." State charters made the connection explicit. The Massachusetts constitution of 1780, for example, enjoined its elected officials "to cherish the interests of literature and the sciences and all seminaries of them," and in 1789 the state legislature continued the prerevolutionary practice of requiring towns of a certain size to maintain schools. Four years earlier, the Northwest Land Ordinance had introduced the principle of reserving land in the territories for "public school," and even the crowded agenda of the constitutional Convention included hot debate on James Madison's proposal for a national university. What was surprising about the latter was not that the proposal lost, but that supporters appeared at all and that Madison—usually so apprehensive of any concentration of power—contended that Congress had the authority to organize a federal university.

By 1820, presidential comments on education had become a staple both in inaugural addresses and in annual messages to Congress. Every president from Washington to Jackson encouraged the formation of a national university, the public funding of local schools, and the necessity of "diffusing knowledge" throughout the republic. The parsimonious Washington felt so strongly that he willed fifty shares of stock to establish what he invariably capitalized as a NATIONAL UNIVERSITY. Even Jefferson and Madison, who flinched at the creation of a United States Bank, lobbied for a publicly financed and administered educational system. Jefferson's usually felicitous prose departed in his tortured pleas for public schools. "Education," he said in his 1806 message to Congress,

> is here placed among the articles of public care, not that it would be proposed to take its ordinary branches out of the hands of private enterprise, which manages so much better all the concerns to which it is equal, but a public institution can alone supply those sciences which though rarely called for are yet necessary to complete the circle, all the parts of which contribute to the improvement of the country and some of them to its preservation.

Armed with his protean constitutionalism, Jefferson transformed schooling into an internal improvement and was thereby able to dissociate it from the great watchword of the time—a specific constitutional provision giving Congress jurisdiction. Meanwhile his colleague Madison supported an amendment giving Congress special power over education. Encouraged by pleas to deliberate on educational matters, Congress organized ad hoc committees, and in 1796 one recommended that "a national university be established to help preserve the morals and principles of youth, reduce local prejudices, attract the youth of other countries to the United States, and save American youth the expense of going abroad for higher education."

Despite such widely held convictions, a national university was never organized, and as the republic aged, the importance of political indoctrination lessened. Presidents after Jackson were less concerned with a national school system or university, and by the 1830s the standard presidential paragraph on diffusing public knowledge was omitted from executive messages.

Disregarding the topic's disappearance from national politics, intellectuals continued to provide explicit plans to place schools in the federal service. Benjamin Rush, anxious to lay "the foundations for nurseries of good Americans," proposed the early inculcation of "republican duties." The Philadelphian wished to adopt "our modes of teaching to our peculiar form of government." In 1786 Rush wrote:

> The principle of patriotism stands in need of the reinforcement of prejudice, and it is well known that our strongest prejudices in favour of our country are formed in the first one and twenty years of our lives. . . . Our schools of learning, by producing one general and uniform system of education, will render the mass of people more homogeneous and thereby fit them more easily for uniform and peaceable government.

In Rush's view, only formal schooling could teach Americans that they "do not belong to themselves" but rather are "public property," and he insisted that the purpose of schooling was to make "republican machines." (The pervasiveness of this idea was evident years later, when, in nearly the same language, an Illinois law passed in 1825 held that "the mind of every citizen of a republic is the common property of society.") At the top of Rush's educational hierarchy stood a federal university where the youth of all states would be joined "into one mass of citizens after they have acquired the first principles of knowledge in the colleges of their respective states." Here they would learn "the law of nature and nations, the common law of our country, the different systems of government, history and everything else connected with the advancement of knowledge and principles." Only graduates of such a national university would be eligible for power and office. Depending on schooling to ensure similar perspectives and public behaviors, Rush proposed to incorporate his plan into the Constitution by an amendment.

Like Rush, Noah Webster linked political culture and schooling, and the author of the popular blue-backed spellers spun a series of elegant phrases to bolster his points. Not only must schools create a "political bigotry out of which real allegiance springs"; they must also teach the young to "rehearse the history of their country," even to the point of speaking Washington's name as their first "public word." To accomplish this was the "first article in the code of political regulations." Webster grounded his pedagogical system in John Locke's state of nature—a concept well known to Americans of this generation—in which man's ungovernable instincts had necessitated the institution of government. Like Locke, who compared young minds to "water, easily turned this way or that," Webster likened children to "tender shrubs or seedlings in fertile soil," whose political growth required formal pedagogical attention. Without such instruction young republicans would retain their unruly behavior and would lack the personal self-control that sustained their community's self-government.

That children learned political habits at an early age seemed obvious to these nineteenth-century Americans, who frequently referred to the "season of youth" as the time best suited to such learning. Samuel Knox, a Presbyterian minister and principal of Baltimore College, based his prizewinning plan for a national educational system on the need for early political training. His structure of publicly financed parish schools, country academies, and state colleges began with compulsory attendance for all children and ended with a national university attended by the best students, who, in a process Jefferson once described as "raking a few geniuses from the rubbish," would continue their education at public expense. Fearful of his nation's "diversity," Knox intended to "harmonize" schooling by placing it under a federal board of control; such centralization appealed to the American Philosophical Society, which awarded him $100. He shared his prize with Harrison Smith, whose educational system also aimed at homogeneity. Smith argued in his award-winning prospectus that children "belonged" to the state, and that it was the duty of the nation to superintend and even coerce the public attitudes of the young. In both plans, only a few children needed advanced study. It was enough to give the exceptional students access to a federal university, where, in Knox's system as in Jefferson's and Rush's, they learned "the science of government."

In theory, then, many nineteenth-century Americans agreed that young white males must go to school—there to be political as much as grammatical abecedarians. Although statements to that effect often glossed over the issue of who should pay, the decline in deferential politics and the expansion of voting and officeholding provided further impetus to the notion that the republic depended on education. By the 1830s new interest groups espoused the common school cause: businessmen, as Michael Katz has demonstrated, saw it as a capitalist adjuvant delivering properly disciplined workers to the factory. Workingmen's groups viewed education as a passport to the middle class—or at least a protection from any downward slide in social and economic status. Like all prescriptions, such appeals should not be confused with actual conditions. Nevertheless the persistent commitment to education reveals the widespread expectation that schools (more so than any other institution) would provide training in political deportment.

SCHOOLING AS CIVIC TRAINING: PRACTICE

Amid such conscious efforts to link school and society, American history emerged as essential subject matter. "Not teaching U.S. history," explained the editor of the *American Annals of Education and Instruction* in 1832, "is a little like going into a foreign market with a curious collection of ancient coins, but without any circulating currency of the country." Although educators increasingly complained about the amount of attention given the classics—such studies supposedly squandered time better spent on the United States—they nonetheless found in ancient Rome a society that appreciated the didactic importance of history.

Early views of pedagogy reinforced the importance of history to the nation's political culture. Most nineteenth-century Americans believed that children's cognitive development depended on the exercise of memory, which, like a muscle, strengthened with use. Later the influence of object teaching challenged this conception of learning as a mnemonic process. Certainly Jean Piaget did so in the twentieth century. But in the first part of the nineteenth century most Americans held the recall of data to be the proper way to teach children, and with only a few exceptions such as Joseph Neef's Philadelphia school, this approach was universally applied. No better subject existed for such purposes than history, which, by furnishing a never-ending source of facts to be remembered, provided material for recitations. "History," a disgruntled American follower of the Swiss educator Pestalozzi complained, "is a mere thread to string dates and events on"—a judgment with which nineteenth-century children would probably have agreed. A typical catechism on the American Revolution proceeded with the following questions and answers:

Q. What victory soon followed that at Trenton?
A. The battle of Princeton [3 January].
Q. Who commanded the Americans at Princeton?
A. Washington.
Q. Where did Washington pass the winter, in the beginning of 1777?
A. At Morristown, New Jersey.

Q. Where was the Battle of Brandywine fought?
A. At Chad's Ford on Brandywine Creek in the southeastern part of Pennsylvania.

History was also admired for its didactic qualities: its heroic homiletics could inspire the young with examples of duty and service to country; it could present for emulation the lives of national leaders—particularly that of George Washington—and with proper handling its chronologies could display the progress of the nation. Most important, it could teach future citizens "the price of liberty"—the cost in personal suffering and sacrifice necessary to create—and, by implication, maintain—the republic. Typically, notions of national uniqueness pervaded such thinking. Not only did early Americans believe they had created a new era whose origins needed telling, but because they knew their beginnings (unlike other societies, in which, according to Madison, "the infant periods are buried in silence and veiled in fable"), they must explain their past for the edification of others. As an example of their exceptionality, "the origin and outset of the American Republic contains lessons of which posterity ought not to be deprived."

Throughout these educational prescriptions ran the theme that American history must be made interesting. Although it did not matter how pupils felt about geometric theorems or the rivers of India, it was essential that they love their country and that its study inspire affection. To accomplish this, most authors of early history books included anecdotal, biographical, and local materials chosen to foster such sentiments. In 1856, John Jay wrote to Horatio Seymour: "There is nothing like commencing with the foundation. The school is the place for implanting correct knowledge and true principles and our children will take kindly to a volume [of New York history] containing so much to kindle their patriotic pride and affection for our noble state and by association to strengthen their attachment to the soil." Seymour responded with *A Lecture on the Topography and History of New York;* similarly dedicated authors wrote "vivacious" histories full of biography and local color. Samuel Goodrich was especially adroit at this; his 170 separate titles—which included the Peter Parley Series—sold 22 million copies, and an admiring President Fillmore concluded that Goodrich had done more than any other American "to infuse information."

Gradually schools included American history in their curriculums. By 1813 Phillips Academy offered American history in its literature department, as did the famous Boston Latin School. But generally the acceptance of a new subject—unfamiliar to teachers, unknown in English schools, and unaccompanied by the texts necessary for recitation—was slow. In 1810 most schoolboys in prestigious northern academies still read Hume and Goldsmith, and even after the War of 1812 American history was taught from English texts. In the nation's few colleges, American history remained an afterthought, relegated, as at Harvard, to Saturday afternoons.

Not until the 1830s did the increased school population, an expansive nationalism, and the installation of history in state systems inspire a profitable enterprise—the writing, publishing, and selling of textbooks, accompanied by that uniquely American feature, the teacher's manual. Popularizers who lacked Richard Hildreth's grasp of events or George Bancroft's ability to procure documents from European archives rewrote these secondary sources into their own versions of the past. Plagiarism was common, and because this generation lacked any sense of historical relativity, it anticipated a uniform version of the past. Hence to copy from another author was not stealing, but was considered "parallelism" and "imitation." John Marshall cribbed from William Gordon; Marcius Willson (who pleaded similar sources and "stereotyped instances") plagiarized Emma Williard; and everyone appropriated Bancroft—who was himself dependent on Edmund Burke's *Annual Register.*

As a result a standard version of national history emerged by the 1840s, and the different books that children brought from home were interchangeable. Influenced in a narrow sense by Bancroft's *History of the United States from the Discovery of the Continent* but more generally by the political environment of which they were a part, authors focused on the revolution. It became the centerpiece of a story taught thousands of northern school children. Even when authors charted American chronology, they routinely gave disproportionate emphasis to the years 1770–1783. Emma Willard used 124 of 364 pages to cover the revolution, and most of these were devoted to battles. Like Bancroft, who acknowledged that his preoccupation with "the struggle for liberty had destroyed the proper symmetry of his volumes," Marcius Willson and S. R. Hall also concentrated on the revolution. They included in their catechisms the hardships of the Americans, hoping thereby "to enhance the affection" of future generations for the government that warranted such suffering. On the assumption that tales of easy victory would never inspire lives of hard devotion, most textbooks gloried in the "suffering and death of our martyred spirited forefathers—the blood and treasure they sacrificed." To the question what was the climate of 1776, children recited from William Grimshaw's *History of the United States,* "a gloomy season of adversity." In such accounts, the English were so often cast as villains that British visitors complained about their mistreatment in American history. Wrote James Burn:

> Many of our worst Kings and nobles are exhibited in the darkest phases of their characters, and held up as types of their class. If the American instructors of youth in their desire to furnish useful historical lessons had used the same freedom with Bible history as they have done with that of Great Britain, I think they would have found very few whose lives could be held up as examples of young Americans to follow.

The reason for such criticism went beyond anglophobia or even the unity achieved by hating a common enemy. Intent on producing a serviceable past, writers created polarized images in which free religion in the United States was contrasted with state churches in Europe; republican vigor in the New World with autocratic decay in the Old; monarchy in England with democracy in America. Given the public reasons for learning history, objectivity only cluttered themes best transmitted to the young in sharp, pictorial terms, as occurred in the period's most frequently reproduced line drawing, that of a noble George Washington and a treacherous Benedict Arnold. Without official direction a homogeneous version of national history spontaneously emerged, and this one-sided treatment of past events furnished pre–Civil War schoolboys with a model of proper civic conduct.

George Washington was the central figure in this national history, and both anthologies of oratory and readers included his Farewell Address. Many also provided a biographical section in which the first president emerged as dutiful son, loyal husband, lovable father to his country, and reluctant but effective commander of its revolutionary forces. Thus nineteenth-century children first encountered their government through a personable leader who exemplified correct civic behavior. Parson Weems's legend of the cherry tree was only one of several anecdotes conveying the importance of integrity and self-discipline. As portrayed by textbook writers, Washington displayed the restraint required in a self-governing society, and the emphasis on his sacrifice of private interest, his perseverance amid hardship at Valley Forge, and his lifelong ability to subdue his own passions and "hold them in subjection to reason" provided a forceful model of the ideal American citizen.

Preoccupied with military history and the life of Washington, schoolbooks avoided other periods and topics. Some of this neglect reflected a fear of distorting events by being too close to them. In 1826 the *North American Review* speculated whether "enough time had passed" to write modern history, "to bring facts to light and to soften down the rough aspects of events and divest them of passion and partiality." As late as the 1850s, schoolbooks shunned the postrevolutionary period; James Monteith's catechism, for example, devoted over a hundred questions to the revolution but dispatched the administrations of Madison, Monroe, Jackson, and Van Buren with four. Abridged versions of William Grimshaw's popular history never mentioned Monroe, Adams, and Van Buren. Such historical astigmatism served two ends: it permitted more attention to be given to the military events considered inspirational for young children, and it solved a difficult interpretative problem. If U.S. history was a providentially directed progression toward liberty and freedom, and if the revolution had already instilled these ideals through its model government, then later events were superfluous. Accordingly, disputes among nineteenth-century Americans might signal and decline in republican virtue, but such pessimism was hardly appropriate for schoolboys, who needed to be instructed in public excellence—what Willard called "the mental sublime of the character of their fathers." Hence the typical pre–Civil War history concentrated on the nation's progress from discovery to the writing of the Constitution.

Those writers who did extend their histories into the nineteenth century replaced domestic history with accounts of the nation's wars, when, united against an enemy, Americans retrieved their patriotism. Careful studies of early textbooks disclose the extent of this preoccupation with military history. According to Chauncey Jacobs, nearly half of the texts published from 1795 to 1860 were devoted to war, with the most bellicose author, the Reverend T. F. Gordon, lavishing 6 of every 10 pages on battles. For the postrevolutionary years, the percentages are higher. Emma Willard allotted 77 of 124 pages covering the period 1800–1848 to American military adventures with the Indians, the English, the deys of North Africa, and the Mexicans. John Frost devoted 3 pages to the internal affairs of Madison's administration and 40 to the War of 1812. Nor was war portrayed as hell; in these early textbooks, its hardship and sacrifice were redeemed through glory and service to the nation.

Skewed as to time and subject, textbooks neglected domestic controversies. Less harmonious moments from the nation's past—such as the Whisky and Shay's rebellions—were included by some authors as examples of bad conduct. Like the Hessian troops whom Bancroft's God punished for fighting against the Americans during the revolution, these "mobs of insurgents and malcontents" were benevolently dealt with by a just government. Such incidents, according to Willard, must be brought to the attention of "youthful hearts," but unlike good deeds, which "kindled into desires of imitation," they should be only briefly mentioned—the result given, not the details.

Political parties, if mentioned at all in early schoolbooks, were described as vehicles of passion and intemperance; with only their results discussed, presidential elections emerged as a spontaneous expression of the people's will—a republican parthenogenesis unattended by contentious parties. It was the peaceful transfer of power that textbooks emphasized. "The people," explained John Frost of Jefferson's and Jackson's victories, "regarded the change in their executive with very little solicitude." Some authors specifically condemned political parties, thus transmitting antipartyism. According to Emma Willard, "Congress showed how little party spirit cares for the public good." But William Grimshaw was more typical; he avoided party politics by arranging his text around the decadal census rather than presidential administrations, explaining his omission as a "willing exclusion."

In time, authors included information about federal and state governments as well as catechisms based on the U.S. Constitution. Marcius Willson sought to introduce young boys "to the principles and practical operation of our republican institutions," but, like William Sullivan, the author of *The Political Class Book*, he spent more time proclaiming "the moral dignity of our federal representative system" than explaining it. As with American history, imitation—in this case of Francis Wayland's 1837 *Elements of Political Economy*—expedited the creation of a standard interpretation of "the science of politics." And because they were traversing uncertain territory, authors self-consciously claimed impartiality. "On the subjects of party controversy," wrote Andrew Young, "[I] have withheld the expression of [my] opinions, deeming it best to leave the unconfirmed politician to the exercise of his own unbiased judgment in forming his conclusions." Such an approach guaranteed that children would learn the virtues of America, but it also assured little understanding of its weaknesses or of the ways in which public differences were resolved.

Typical of the readings for younger children were Noah Webster's widely used spellers and geographies. They contained a "federal catechism," in which teacher queried student on the principles of government. Thousands of young Americans were indoctrinated in the merits of their political system by chanting Webster's litany:

> Question: What are the peculiar advantages of representative governments?
>
> Answer: . . . the great security of such a government is that the men who make laws are to be governed by them; so that they are not apt to do wrong wilfully. When men make laws for themselves, as well as for their neighbors, they are led by their own interest to make good laws.

By the 1860s, generations of northern schoolboys had absorbed a standard view of American history and government, and their cognitive perceptions in turn framed public values, attitudes, and behavior. There were variations in this information. Not only did Americans differ in their levels of training, but also in regional, religious, and ethnic emphases. A few had read Joseph Story's *Commentaries on the Constitution* and Bancroft's *History;* others had not gone beyond the first Peter Parley readers. Naturalized citizens often did not attend American schools at all, and in some frontier communities only one of every three school-age boys in the 1850s was enrolled in school. In any case the amount of factual material retained from memorized recitations is unknown, and if school reformers of the 1840s were correct, little endured from a process in which imagination and inquiry were discouraged. But regardless of the depth and length of students' exposure or the deficiencies of pedagogical technique, American images, values, and symbols were uniform. A homogeneous message—simultaneously the product and fabricator of nineteenth-century political culture—conveyed the sense of a martial nation susceptible to military engagements fought by citizens, not by professionals. America's most heroic times had occurred on the battlefield, although the personalized image of Washington linked the young to a benign government. Finally, because liberty, union, and Constitution had been accomplished at great sacrifice, the "world's best government" merited keeping.

HIDDEN AGENDAS

Schoolbooks and recitation were not the only ways in which young boys learned how to be Americans. Also imbedded in classroom activities—in a student's expected conduct toward a teacher, in the community's attitude toward schools, in the relation of students to one another, and even in the spatial details of the classroom—were various arrangements that conveyed political culture; and, just as didactic literature gave formal expression to the requisite values of democratic citizens, so this hidden curriculum transmitted public habits. Recently historians have focused on the ways in which schooling trained nineteenth-century Americans to become industrial workers, but this influence was not restricted to economic behavior. Latent school agendas also taught young Northerners how to be Americans.

Some schoolmasters were aware of this hidden curriculum and went beyond the formal substance of political learning to explore its effects on their students. The most perceptive was Enoch C. Wines, whose numerous pamphlets on education were the pedagogical counterparts of William Alcott's behavior manuals. Convinced that learning was more than the transmission of facts or the memorization of details, Wines defined education as everything from marble games and ballroom dancing to the internal dynamics of the schoolroom. "I understand by education," wrote the New Jersey schoolmaster in 1838, "contact with each other, by business, by newspapers, and circulating libraries, lyceums, public meetings, and conventions, speeches in Congress, in state legislatures—in churches, halls of education, popular assemblies, theatres, race courses, barrooms, the very streets of our cities." Later, Wines linked schooling, culture, and national character: "The mysticism of Egypt, the courage of Sparta, the disputatious subtlety of Attica, the high honour and commanding influence of the early Persians and the military spirit of the Romans may be traced to the schools of these several nations, as of controlling influence in producing the predominant traits of their respective national characters."

The point was clear: the United States must replicate its government within its schools, for, sufficiently developed, the latter would define its political culture. According to Wines, teachers, like political leaders, must establish an authority based on a combination of moral influence and physical force, to which schoolchildren would submit in exactly the same way and for the same reasons that citizens of the republic did. In a directive that might have served constitutional conventions, Wines advised teachers to "avoid the multiplication of trifling rules, seize upon principles as comprehensive as possible. Establish your authority upon a firm basis and require invariable obedience." Pupils, like adult Americans, would "freely submit to a government founded in reason and administered with firmness, consistency and perfect impartiality." In his own classroom, Wines introduced such "reasonability" by means of contracts, negotiation, and even student petitions. But the prerogatives of self-government did not extend to unrestricted majority rule any more than the Constitution did. Unlike Joseph Neef, the Alsatian-born follower of Pestalozzi, Wines did not permit students to have a veto power, and although he did not hesitate to flog "rebellious" students who had committed "treason," he nevertheless delegated considerable responsibility.

Using political images, Wines concluded that the power of the teacher must be absolute, like a sovereign's, and he compared his authority to that of the federal government with its muskets at Springfield and Harper's Ferry:

> The United States employs its hundred of workmen at Springfield and at Harper's Ferry in the manufacture of muskets. A hundred thousand of these deadly instruments form a violence of slumbering power which has never been awakened. The government never makes use of them. One of its agents, a Custom House officer, waits upon a merchant for the payment of a bond. He brings no musket. He keeps no troops. He comes with the gentleness and civility of a social visit. But the merchant knows that if compliance with the just demand of his government is refused and resistance to it is sustained, force after force would be brought to bear upon him till the whole hundred thousand muskets should speak with their united and tremendous energy. The government of these United States is thus a tremendous engine, working with immense momentum; but the parts which bear upon the citizens conceal their power by the elegance of their workmanship and by the slowness and apparent gentleness of their motion. If you yield to it, it glides smoothly and pleasantly by; if you resist it, it crushes you to atoms.

Other nineteenth-century educators lined the political behavior of the adult world and the hidden curriculum of classrooms, though few as fulsomely as the schoolmaster of Edgehill. Like Wines, most recognized that the internal environment of the nation's schools inculcated public behaviors along with supplying factual information about the political system. Their metaphorical language was suggestive: schools were governments, with teachers granted authority. But power must be reasonably applied in the classroom, and, as with government, the fewer the rules and the less capricious their application, the happier the classroom. To apply sanctions in a tyrannical fashion was to risk a subservient class, unable to make independent judgments and therefore unfit for the administration of government. America was not Turkey or Prussia, where the young might be subjected to brute force without political effect; to coerce unreasonably in a free society was no way to raise citizens. As a midwestern journal suggested, "If you will have republican men, you must have republican education." But the other extreme was equally dangerous; a permissive classroom with no respect for authority encouraged tumult, anarchy, and a rebellious citizenry. Teachers who were too permissive often lost their pupils; in fact some of Joseph Neef's students were uncomfortable with his egalitarian notions of teachers as "playfellows and messmates." Wrote one: "There existed between Neef and his pupils a freedom so great as to be sometimes, I fear, slightly inconsistent with good breeding or the deference due from pupil to teacher." As in government, ideal management involved using moral influence to inspire a sense of spontaneous allegiance. "The schoolroom," wrote a New York teacher, "is a peculiarly appropriate place to teach respect for the rights of others. The little community here assembled contains all of the great community without."

Throughout these earnest prescriptions ran a common theme: misused authority was a failure of self-government by the schoolmaster and a dangerous example for schoolboys learning to subdue their passions and instincts. Ideal behavior for politician, teacher, citizen, and schoolboy required mastery over self—a control based on individual restraint and a denial of selfish passion. "Those whose feelings are properly trained," explained a New York educator, "are always good citizens. We have enough of laws; now let us train some men for the laws." "Passions are to be regulated into proper discipline for self-command, social order, and regular subjections," wrote William Woodridge of the educational ideals that inspired his prizewinning schoolhouse design. The best schools, agreed Hiram Orcutt, were those in which power was "not visible" and in which teachers could leave the room without the class's lapsing into disorder. In such schools pupils had learned the self-government necessary for "miniature men soon to control the affairs of state." They had gone beyond the "commands and prohibitions regarding what they may or may not do . . . and had been taught that, as ere long as it is theirs to determine in reference to their conduct in life with no parents' and teacher's watchful eye or warning voice to approve or encourage them in the right or deter them from the wrong, then they should accustom themselves to consider what is right and proper under the circumstances."

Teachers who had not conquered their own impulses were the ones who hurled ferules and precipitated either disorder or, at the other extreme, the silent classroom in which brute tyranny had won the day. But government by moral persuasion was not always easy. "I feared," wrote one anguished young teacher, "that if I conquered [a rebellious student] I would be the conquered party."

INSIDE THE CLASSROOM

It was a long way from this advice literature to the northern classrooms of the early nineteenth century. Although many observers acknowledged schools as an entity shaping public life, the institutions themselves were neither universal nor homogeneous. They ranged, by the 1840s, from the nearly extinct dame schools organized by impecunious widows and unmarried women to the prestigious Latin schools where sons of wealthy city merchants studied the classical curriculum necessary for admission to America's handful of colleges. Over the years community-funded systems had superseded informal arrangements, and by the Civil War the private schoolmaster who recruited students had disappeared, replaced by a trustee-approved instructor. Moreover, there were substantial differences between district schools of fifty pupils and Lancastrian schools of nearly a thousand. Some Northern institutions were coeducational; others were single-sex; some were supported by local property taxes, others by private fees, and a few by rates based on parents' income. In the newer states of the West, many children went to a neighbor's home, others to a log house. Some states had constitutional provisions establishing public systems. Others depended on county and township laws to which, in many cases, officials paid little attention. Schools themselves often varied according to the season. What might be in summer a relaxed custodial center supervised by a kindly young woman often became, in winter, a formal institution presided over by a punctilious male disciplinarian. Nor did all Americans attend school; some, like Ohioan Alfred Holbrook, studied at home; a greater number spent their days in apprenticeships, their evenings in night schools, and their Saturdays in so-called half-schools.

Gradually, however, a standard version of Northern schooling developed until, according to one optimistic education manual, every Northern state had a creditable school system based on the district school. In 1840 a majority of Northern children from ages five to nineteen were enrolled in either private or public schools, and in many communities the figures ran as high as 75 percent, with males—the essential group in supervising the nation's political culture—outnumbering females in the early grades. Not only did the length of the school year increase (by mid-century rural schools were open five months of the year, urban schools eight); the average student's daily attendance also improved. By the time of the Civil War, primary schools had thus become the essential institution in teaching children to be Americans.

Whether Lancastrian or Pestalozzian, common or secondary, district or academy, English or Latin, Presbyterian or Methodist, rate, free, or charity, Northern schools had similar internal arrangements for instructing young boys in American values. In their preoccupation with external variations, historians have sometimes neglected these internal similarities, such as the use of student assistants and monitors, the lack of age-grading, the inconsistent postures toward authority, and the physical environment of the classroom. Such mechanisms inducted young Americans into their national political culture, and although the expectations of educational theorists like Rush, Knox, and Washington for a uniform system were not achieved, their aim was served by this universally applied hidden curriculum. Like moons, American schools reflected community goals, but like the sun, they diffused political culture by educating future citizens in their civic roles. And if uniformity within the classroom was any test, there was broad agreement on the matter of training future citizens.

For the observer of political culture, the most significant mechanism was the use of students in positions of authority. Primarily associated with Lancastrian schools, monitors—students who served in an official capacity—were to be found in nearly all northern schools. Joseph Lancaster gave the most explicit statement of their duties:

> To promote emulation, and facilitate learning, the whole school is arranged into classes, and a monitor appointed to each class. A class consists of any number of boys whose proficiency is on a par. These may all be classed and taught together. If the class is small, one monitor may teach it; if large it may still continue the same class, but with more or less assistant monitors, who under the direction of the principal monitor are to teach subdivisions of the class. . . . In teaching the boys to print the alphabet, the monitor first makes a letter on the sand, before any who knows nothing about it; the boy is then required to retrace over the same letter which the monitor has made for him with his fingers.

Armed with an extensive patronage system of money, toys, and food, monitors not only heard recitations but also gave out rewards, assisted in discipline, helped younger children with their handwriting, stoked the fire, made and repaired quill pens, supervised from prominently arranged desks, and conveyed student problems to the teacher. Their term of office was at the pleasure of the schoolmaster who had picked them; sometimes an automatic rotation took place within a specific group. As Lancaster explained, "Though he [a monitor] may be one minute a commander, yet he feels no hesitation in yielding the most prompt and decided obedience to another. When he retires to his seat as a private member of his class, he is succeeded by another." Despite the transience of power, boys (girls were never monitors in coeducational schools) aspired to such prestigious posts, where they were distinguished by the special badges, chains, and stars they wore as well as by the power they wielded.

Most teachers in a system lacking sufficient personnel found the mechanism useful. In one Boston school during the 1830s three schoolmasters presided over 1,547 students, and in the 1850s the city's 164 primary school teachers supervised 11,000 pupils. Even in rural schools with smaller numbers of students, the diversity of tasks and range of ages made monitors a welcomed addition. Because teachers "kept" schools before 1840, neither interpreting nor explaining material, proficient young males filled roles of authority and prestige with ease.

One reason for Lancaster's instant success in the early nineteenth century was that many American schools already used his techniques. His appeals for cheap mass education on a nonsectarian basis meshed with the needs of a growing nation, and an early poll of Massachusetts schoolteachers revealed that most were familiar with his system in practice, if not theory. In some schools, monitors were called preceptors, in others tutors or assistants. But as Edward Everett reported, even in rural schools "special" boys held official responsibilities such as procuring wood, tending the all-important fire, making pens, as well as teaching. The pervasiveness of mutual instruction was illustrated in one. Sent "to spell" another student who was cutting firewood, a New Hampshire boy promptly took on a monitor's role and, instead of replacing his toiling classmate, heard his spelling lesson.

For the student of political culture, the significance of monitors rests with the delegation of powers to pupils who performed official functions, who wielded authority based on coercion as well as persuasion, and who competed for their position. Chosen from the student body because of their achievement and obedience as well as their skill at ingratiation, monitors served as models for their fellows, who could simultaneously aspire to such honorific posts and observe authority exerted by an equal. Even the rewards monitors dispensed were reminiscent of political patronage; certainly the system acquainted young Americans with the repertoire of roles they would meet as citizens, including shared officeholding, rotation in office, and representation by untrained officials. After 1860, reformers, intent on training teachers who could interpret and explain subject matter, sought to replace monitors with professionals. But the use of student assistants survived beyond the Civil War, and this unique arrangement introduced thousands of Northerners to the structure of leadership in a republican society.

Northern schools also had similar internal environments. Externally there was wide variation: an "unpainted drab leaky edifice" in New Hampshire; a substantial brick building with a "commodious garden" in Massachusetts; a basement in a New York church; and a log cabin with an earth floor and no windows in Franklin County, Indiana. But whatever the exterior of their building, children learned their lessons in one large common room that varied in size from the typical 15-by-20-foot district school to the huge 150-by-75-foot schoolrooms in larger towns and cities. Only in the 1840s did the idea of separate places for recitation develop, and even then children still spent most of their time in the same room. As late as 1830 William Alcott, anxious to improve schools by providing better air circulation, retained the traditional common room in his prizewinning design. Typically, this was one rectangular space with two doors, a chimney at one end, and small raised windows—usually shuttered or covered with broken glass or paper. In any case it was against the rules to look outside. School-children, arranged on long hickory, walnut, and pine benches or seated at separate (though connected) desks, turned inward. What they saw, heard, touched—and doubtless smelled—in their allotted five or six square feet of space was their neighbor. There was little privacy amid the constant activity of such surroundings. But these serried ranks were often broken, when groups of children took their places in semicircles for recitation where they read, spelled, and summed aloud; as a result of proficiency in such exercises, pupils either gained or lost rank before the entire student body.

Although Lancastrian schools were renowned for the activity of their students, all schools fostered busyness, with a daily program based on participation. Punishments were community affairs, with work suspended for a public viewing of some fellow pupil's humiliation. In Stratham, New Hampshire, the names of those who had broken rules were entered in a "Black List or Book of Disgrace" and reported not only to parents but also to the school committee and selectmen. Even when individual recitation in a separate room was possible, schooling was an open process, and the so-called loud schools, where collective recitations could be heard for miles, though not typical were symbolic of this collective arrangement. Many pupils recognized the communal aspect of their education and spoke, as did one New York boy, of a "common purpose and unity" in the classroom. Another felt as if he were part of a sea. Given the communal atmosphere, it was natural to invite parents and local officials to recitations—a practice also employed in colleges. As the organizer of his local district school, Henry Van der Luyn soon found that his appearances at recitations took most of his free time, and after listening to endless school exercises, he reported that he knew the names of New York's sixty counties.

Within this community there was no age-grading, and although students were arranged according to their individual proficiencies, such groups varied widely. In one Vermont school, a seventeen-year-old teacher instructed pupils from ages four to twenty-five. Even when classified according to ability, a reading group often included, as did John Badger's third class in a Vermont school, one five-, three six-, two seven-, one eleven-, and one twelve-, and one fourteen-year-old. Respecting such diversity, early American textbooks made no effort to classify their materials into age grades.

Later, Americans would separate pupils spatially and chronologically, but before they did, the pedagogical universe was a little community, its inhabitants what David Tyack has called "a tribe," and what a contemporary described as a "moral community with conforming sentiments." This is not to say that all classes, races, or even sexes attended the same schools. Neither equality of opportunity nor of condition characterized early classrooms. Girls, blacks, the very rich, and the very poor rarely sat side by side on the hardwood benches learning about each other. Nor were students encouraged to work together in groups. Instead, cheating—from the beginning of formal schooling the most heinous of academic sins—restricted collective learning and compelled individual attention to lessons. Moreover, as the diaries of nineteenth-century schoolchildren indicate, there was considerable individual competition to be the best speller.

But the one-room environment did promote a sense of community, for, as Benjamin Rush explained, "young men who have trodden the paths of science together or have joined in the same sports . . . generally feel, thro' life, such ties to each other as add greatly to the obligations of mutual benevolence." Even private academies were neighborhood ventures dependent upon the involvement of leading citizens and officials. Moreover, the competition between towns for pupils transformed these academies into something more than isolated private institutions. In the case of district schools, elected committees hired and fired teachers, set rules, and supervised financial affairs in a manner that linked public and private worlds. Later, a man's town, district, or county would become a larger likeness of the neighborhood he first experienced in the one-room schoolhouse.

Like all institutions, schools developed rituals that by the 1840s were so universal as to demonstrate the homogeneity of American education. At the end of each year parents and the district committee visited the classroom for a day of patriotic oratory. In most districts these celebrations extended beyond the schoolhouse. In Seneca Falls, New York, for instance, children annually paraded on "School Day," carrying banners emblazoned, in the 1850s, with "We believe in Progress" and "Russia depends on her bayonets, America on her common schools." Encouraged by officials seeking community support, such festivals linked pupils to their neighborhoods and began the process of layered affections whereby primary groups connect citizen to nation in a spiral that, according to Morton Grodzins, "energizes and expresses" national loyalty. A nineteenth-century teacher expressed this idea in stronger language. "Schools," he wrote, "grind children into the vortex of human society, for our government depends on such sentiment."

Even the ritualized spelling bee in which schools as well as individuals competed had public overtones; it began with the singing of "America," "Columbia," and "I Love My Native Land Best." In such affairs a series of national values was enacted: the sense of competition, or, as nineteenth-century Americans preferred to call it, "emulation"; the spirit of differential achievement based on individual merit (there was no group consultation for a correct spelling); and the merging of individual success with that of the school.

Within their educational communities, however, schoolchildren faced inconsistent patterns of authority. On the one hand, teachers held absolute power, like old-fashioned despots. In theory, few disputed the control of the male schoolmasters who presided over most pre–Civil War classrooms, although by the 1840s some reformers spoke out for disciplinary practices based on moral persuasion rather than on physical coercion. Most Northerners accepted the convention that the internal government of schools must be complete and arbitrary, for only in this way could future citizens learn submission to distasteful laws. "Order in school," concluded the Boxford, Massachusetts, school commissioners, "is of the first and of the greatest importance. Here are the materials that will soon form an active and influential part of the community. . . . If the members of the schools are well trained, they will likely to be in after life, the promoters, supporters and defenders of good order in the community and in the country." Just as society required subordination to legitimate authority, so pupils must not dispute the teacher's word. Certainly few parents did, and the rare suits brought against teachers for physically abusing children and their summary dismissal by judges who nearly always ruled in the teacher's favor reflected the general acceptance of the schoolmaster's jurisdiction. Of ten cases whose verdicts have been studied, only one teacher was found guilty and fined. The case of Jonah Parker, a twelve-year-old Connecticut student, was typical. His parents swore out an assault warrant against his teacher, Nancy Morgan, but despite his broken arm and lacerations, she was acquitted on the grounds that her efforts to keep order did not constitute criminal force. The raised podium and elevated schoolmaster's desk symbolized the prescribed relation of pupil to teacher, as did regulations requiring boys to bow and girls to curtsy to their teachers. A schoolmaster who could not keep order with such prerogatives usually found himself out of a job.

Most teachers used a variety of coercive techniques to prevent such humiliation. Punishment in a New Hampshire school was typical. According to Warren Burton: "Some were feruled on the hand; some were whipped with a rod on the back. Some were compelled to hold out, at arms length, the largest book which could be found on a great leaden inkstand, till muscle and nerve, bone and marrow, were tortured with the continued exertion." Other teachers used shaming techniques, publicly humiliating students with dunce caps and lazy-boy stools, and forcing disobedient pupils to stand with noses wedged into circles drawn on walls.

Teachers gained added power from the didactic practices of the day. Serving as drill sergeants and overseers, schoolmasters before the Civil War neither interpreted nor discussed materials. Instead they relied on recitation and rarely engaged students in the more egalitarian process of discussion. Barbara Finkelstein has found only three instances of the latter in a sample of a thousand cases, and even at an innovative school like that in Round Hill, Massachusetts, there was little self-directed study or debate. Nor was there any sense of pedagogy as a means of increasing creativity. Instead the schoolbook (properly called the text) provided a litany and became the final word—an educator's Constitution and Bible—with pupils memorizing the catechism according to Webster, Bingham, and Parley. "Why do we bring down that number?" inquired one student perplexed by an addition problem. "Because," snapped the teacher, "the book tells us to."

By the 1850s, critics complained that such techniques made pupils into "passive receptacles" burdened, according to one New England reformer, "like Roman maids crushed under the weight of golden bracelets." It was possible, as visiting committees discovered, for students to know the name of every Turkish city but not know where Turkey was, and it was possible to memorize Webster's *Speller* but not know how to read. Whatever its pedagogical deficiencies, this catechistic process increased the authority of schoolmasters, who asked the questions and controlled the responses. According to Finkelstein, "teachers sought to exercise near-total control over the intellectual progress of their students. . . . [They organized] classroom activities in such a way as to force each student systematically to practice skills and acquire knowledge from carefully defined, skillfully blocked-out, predetermined courses of instruction." Imagination was actively discouraged, for it might result in spontaneous, unprescribed answers. That such procedures made students intellectually submissive was clear to one New Yorker who described his classroom experience of the 1840s: "The dictator paces to the next class and continues. Second of the class: May: M-a-y- first enunciating the word, then spelling it and turning the wooden block. Hands instantly unlock themselves from behind, grasp pencils and write down the word quickly on ruled slates. At the next word of command hands again revert to their places and the dictation thus proceeds from class to class. . . ."

District schools replicated these arrangements, with pupils using slates for their dictation. Writing classes repetitively traced copy such as "Our nation rules the best" and "Education forms the common mind" from a model set in the teacher's elegant hand. Compositions based on independent thought were unknown in early nineteenth-century schools. "Frequent repetition of the same subject," explained the trustee of a private academy in New York, "is necessary to fix it indelibly on a young man's mind and unless this is done, it passes through their memories." Even advanced classes memorized history and geography texts, giving rote replies to the teacher's questions or writing countless imitations of set letters. Such instructional methods added intellectual weight to the physical force already granted the schoolmaster.

Rarely encouraged to challenge or investigate the givens of their texts, students parroted the "right" answer under threat of a tweaking on the nose, rapping on the knuckle, or wearing of the dunce's cap. Because most nineteenth-century Northerners believed the failure to learn to be an aberration of will—and therefore a form of misbehavior—the schoolmaster's physical and intellectual authority converged.

As New York's Governor De Witt Clinton explained: "The beauty of the system is that nothing is trusted to the boy. He does not only repeat the lesson before a superior but he learns before a superior." This repetition without understanding, challenge, or choice conditioned future citizens to accept givens—whether of geography or government—and in this way the hidden curriculum of the mid-nineteenth century taught Americans the basic lessons of political compliance.

Yet, despite the teacher's supremacy in this repressive mode of pedagogy, schoolboys dissented, protested, and disobeyed. Just as America's revolutionary traditions, heterogeneous population, and frontier settlements guaranteed ambivalent attitudes toward established sources of authority and inspired continual fears among traditionalists that the nation's political center might fall apart, so schools sanctioned equally inconsistent behavior. Early nineteenth-century education taught obedience to the government at the same time that it developed three other characteristics—an instinct of participation, a sensitivity to tyranny, and an understanding of the difference between an office and its holder. Occasionally (although this became more common in the late nineteenth century) self-government was consciously encouraged. At Enoch Wines's Edgehill, according to one observer, "the boys have a lot of power over each other." Some district schoolteachers even permitted voting for special offices, although they limited the areas of decision and reserved final authority for themselves.

But even in schools without self-government there was student resistance. Certainly some mischief was to be expected—boys will be boys—but young Americans went beyond personal rebelliousness to organize collective acts of disobedience. Contemporary accounts distinguished between rowdies who misbehaved as individuals and classroom-supported challenges to a teacher's domination. According to one Nebraska schoolgirl, when "the teacher went beyond his authority the whole school community seized his arm, wrested his ruler," and throwing this symbol of command into the stove, "rolled him down the hill and admonished him." In Manchester, New Hampshire, according to one pupil, "After due deliberation, the larger boys all agreed in not liking the Master and then one of them climbed on top of the house and stopped up the chimney and smoked him out." Alfred Holbrook remembered an incident from his schooldays in which "bad governance" in the form of capricious punishment produced "indignation beyond control" and led eventually to the closing of the school." This unified resistance was quite different from an Indiana schoolboy's personal battle with his teacher. John Caton resolved "not to quietly submit to her government," and later as a teacher himself he distinguished between personal rebelliousness and classroom mutiny. Confronted with challenges to his public power, not to his private self-restraint, Caton felt that his class must submit to his authority or he must "abdicate."

Nineteenth-century schools provide numerous examples of ungovernable classrooms driving out schoolmasters and committing what teachers called treason. Each term the contest was renewed, and according to Geraldine Clifford, "The teacher who lost the battle lost community support." Most districts dismissed those who could not control these rebellions, making clear their disapproval by hiring a replacement or in some instances refusing to supply wood to heat the school. Apparently parents, trustees, and district commissioners approved the punishment of fractious individuals, but communities withheld support from inept teachers who could not control their classrooms. The well-known aphorism "Cuff 'em, thrash 'em, Anyway to learn 'em / But whatever you do / Don't let 'em thrash you" was fair warning.

One practice that occurred so frequently as to become a ritual by the 1830s was that of "barring out" the schoolmaster, who then negotiated with student leaders before being readmitted to the classroom. One New Hampshire district school reversed the process by carrying its teacher, kicking and swearing, out of doors. "To the side-hill, to the side-hill, cried Mark. . . . To this pitch, then, [the teacher] was borne, and in all the haste that his violent struggles would permit. Over he was thrust, as if he were a log; and down he went. . . ." Later, student leaders agreed to the return of this particular schoolmaster but warned, "The ship is no longer yours so look out, for we are our own men now." The teacher refused their conditions, muttering in the political language typical of these encounters: "But there is another law besides club law, and that you have to take." In Ohio, future congressman Alexander Long and his classmates triumphantly locked out the teacher and before entering into negotiations renamed their log-cabin schoolhouse Fort Defiance. The best-known description of barring out occurred in Edward Eggleston's fictional account of an inexperienced Indiana schoolmaster who was warned that "the boys in Flat Crick doestrict have driv' off the last two [schoolmasters] and licked the one before them like blazes. . . . They'd pitch you out of doors, sonny, neck, and heels, afore Christmas."

European travelers were continually surprised by the extent of organized dissent within American classrooms. Austrian-born Francis Grund described northern schools as "a congregation of young republicans" who would not give obedience "to the uncontrolled will of their masters" any more than their fathers "would submit to the mandates of kings. The Swedish educator Per Adam Siljestrom detected a similar ambivalence toward authority in the northern classrooms of the 1840s. According to Siljestrom, in theory Americans accepted the supremacy of the schoolmaster, but in practice they challenged his power. Siljestrom's travels introduced him to a few peaceful, "well-regulated" American schools, but more often he encountered collective insubordination "unheard of in our country," including the barring out ritual practiced in district schools.

It is clear that the youth and inexperience of schoolteachers undermined authority and encouraged efforts to impeach officials. A recent study of schoolteachers in pre–Civil War Massachusetts reveals that 70 percent of those hired in a typical rural district taught only one term, and the longest tenure was four consecutive terms. The same rate of turnover existed in Baltimore, and in Illinois fourteen-year-old Esther Hornaker was surprised when "the directors thought I might have trouble with my former schoolmates," many of whom were older than she. Most teachers boarded with local families, and it was hard to be an effective disciplinarian after carrying out the slops or receiving a tonguelashing from parents. Hiram Orcutt, a well-known nineteenth-century schoolmaster, attempted to separate his position in the classroom from his offduty associations with pupils but finally admitted that the boarding-out system lacked propriety and threatened his discipline. Alfred Holbrook agreed and concluded that, besides disrupting his family life, the informal contact with pupils diminished his authority. Women constantly discovered that their presumptive power was eroded by sexual politics. A teacher at New York's Oxford Academy found it more difficult to control her classroom after rumors spread about her boarding with a "dissolute" local family, and Frances Meritt, a young Masachusetts schoolteacher, nervously declined a party. "I feel," she wrote in her diary, "that I ought to go on account of my being teacher in the district. Yet I have doubts whether it is right for me to give countenance by my attendance to anything of that kind."

No more than king to valet could schoolteacher be hero to local schoolboy. In sociological terms there was little distance between nineteenth-century pupil and teacher, and the necessity of reappointment by a committee that often included the fathers of rebellious pupils further limited power. Nor was schoolteaching an admired occupation. The contempt that led one Baltimore merchant to discourage his daughter's romance with a schoolteacher by singing "ABC. ABC. . . . That's a hell of a way to make a living" was widely shared. Moreover, by increasingly accepting women—the very symbols of public powerlessness—as schoolteachers, nineteenth-century Americans muted classroom authority and demonstrated that whereas they expected obedience to the law, the dispensers of that law were not the source of its sanction. Finally, by delegating both community and family control to others, district committees and parents modeled the shared decision-making and derived authority of their government. The resulting prerogatives were limited, not overwhelming; episodic, not continuous; subject to contest, not irresistible.

For a few Northerners—about six thousand in the 1840s—the influence of the hidden curriculum did not end in primary school or an academy but continued during college. Despite differences in curriculum and living arrangements, the classrooms of northern colleges were remarkably similar to those of schools. This was partly because so many academies had been upgraded to colleges. Yet even at older institutions like Harvard, Yale, and Brown, college men found that their classrooms duplicated those of their school years. The process of transmitting information was the same—endless recitation, memorization, and public examination. Nor had the trappings of authority changed. At Brown, for example, students had to stand when officers of the college entered a room. But in college the barrings out of schooldays became organized student "rebellions," so large and frequent that they merited special names. Graduates of Harvard remembered the Great Rebellion of 1832 (to distinguish it from the earlier Uprising of the Rotten Cabbage); those at Yale spoke of the Bread and Butter Riot and the Conic Revolt—the latter one of the rare confrontations involving an intellectual issue, in this case the interpretation of a geometric theorem. Few colleges managed to avoid collective disobedience, which usually erupted over public issues—food, a change in the rules or an alleged misuse of power.

Recently Burton Bledstein has interpreted these nineteenth-century challenges to college administrations as efforts by students to achieve more systematic professional training—and thereby to assure themselves the benefits of a career in an established discipline. Another explanation is possible. Nineteenth-century students were protesting the insufficient self-government that left them, as one recognized, "disenfranchised." Ready for public life, men cloistered in college residence halls resented treatment that made them political children without rights and privileges. In this sense episodic rebellions acted out the republican instincts of future citizens shut off from politics by institutions that disdained partisan issues and social involvement. "We have no political parties here," wrote Yale's president Timothy Dwight in a representative judgment. "We ask what kind of a scholar is he—not to what party does he belong." But Dwight's students, restless in their apolitical setting, sought, through their protests against college authorities, "to stand with the Founders." Their arson, shuffling in chapel, boycotts, and destruction of property were aspects of learning in a political culture created by revolutionary dissent and maintained by participatory democracy. Both administrators and students recognized the parapolitical nature of the student revolt. Brown's president Jonathan Maxcy was typical. After a long confrontation with students, he negotiated what both sides called a "Treaty of Amity and Intercourse between the President of Rhode Island College and the Party of the Rebellious." According to its terms, if students returned to the commons, the faculty would grant amnesty and review the boarding charges likened by undergraduates to England's oppressive taxation of the colonies.

Similar student needs fostered the vibrant extracurricular life on pre–Civil War college campuses. Life outside the classroom was often the most memorable of the college years for the very reason that it focused on politics. Students organized their own literary societies, wrote constitutions for their debating clubs, elected officers of their associations, and held debates. Only in such associations did they act as public men; accordingly, these were the activities alumni recalled with satisfaction when they reviewed their college years.

Learning to be Americans through the formal and informal curricula of antebellum schools and colleges was not restricted to future Democrats, but it was limited to Northerners once Southerners developed a qualitatively different educational system. One way of assuring national consensus within a competitive party system was to provide standard training inside the classroom. Thus, as a means of conveying the nation's political culture, northern schoolrooms became miniature theaters where those who might later disagree over tactical matters of partisan policy learned to agree about public strategies of authority, decisionmaking, allegiance, and leadership. Inside the disparate exteriors of northern schools, the national system of education envisaged by the founding generation emerged, for it was here that future citizens first became members of a community at the same time that they maintained their individuality as competitors. Through the classroom's environment as much as through its transmission of subject matter, schoolboys from Maine to Oregon learned how to delegate and then rotate authority among equals, how to separate the powers of the office from its holder, how to impeach those in power, and, finally, how to participate in public events. This form of political schooling provided important instruction in maintaining a system sufficiently new to be considered an experiment for its first century. Schools did not introduce their students to public issues or political parties, as twentieth-century civics courses would. Instead, they taught future Democrats and Republicans to conform to the American way—in Noah Webster's provocative image, "to lisp the praise of liberty and become political bigots for their nation." Having absorbed the lessons of compliance, collective support, and individual participation, young Northerners whose fathers had already shaped their selection of the Democracy brought these lessons to their party.

Suggestions for Further Reading

The development of working-class life in American cities is described in Gary B. Nash, *The Urban Crucible: Social Change, Political Consciousness, and the Origins of the American Revolution** (Harvard University Press, 1979). Changing work conditions are charted in W. J. Rorabaugh, *The Craft Apprentice: From Franklin to the Machine Age* (Oxford University Press, 1986); Jonathan Prude, *The Coming of Industrial Order: Town and Factory Life in Rural Massachusetts, 1810–1860** (Cambridge University Press, 1985); Paul G. Faler, *Mechanics and Manufacturers in the Early Industrial Revolution: Lynn, Massachusetts, 1780–1860** (State University of New York Press, 1981); and David A. Hounshell, *From the American System to Mass Production, 1800–1932** (Johns Hopkins University Press, 1985).

Revivalism in American life is analyzed by William G. McLoughlin in *Revivals, Awakenings, and Reform: An Essay on Religion and Social Change in America** (University of Chicago Press 1978). An important older study of the Northern revival is Timothy Smith's *Revivalism and Social Reform** (Harper & Row, 1957). The basic study of revivals in New York State is Whitney R. Cross, *The Burned-over District: The Social and Intellectual History of Enthusiastic Religion in Western New York, 1800–1850** (Cornell University Press, 1982). An excellent recent book is Paul E. Johnson, *A Shopkeeper's Millennium: Society and Revivals in Rochester, New York, 1815–1837** (Hill & Wang, 1978). On the subject of women in the nineteenth century, see Catherine Clinton, *The Other Civil War: American Women in the Nineteenth Century** (Hill & Wang, 1984), and for nineteenth-century reform in general, see Ronald G. Walters, *American Reformers, 1815–1860** (Hill & Wang, 1978).

For the Indian policy of the federal government in the early years of the new nation, see Francis Paul Prucha, *American Indian Policy in the Formative Years** (Harvard University Press, 1962). The southern Indians are dealt with in J. Leitch Wright, Jr., *The Only Land They Knew: The Tragic Story of the American Indians in the Old South** (Macmillan, 1985). Attempts at acculturation are described in Robert F. Berkhofer, Jr., *Salvation and the Savage: An Analysis of Protestant Missions and the American Indian Response, 1787–1862** (Atheneum, 1972).

A study of the emergence of public schools in the new nation can be found in Carl Kaestle, *Pillars of the Republic: Common Schools and American Society, 1780–1860** (Hill & Wang, 1983). The role of the schools in society is analyzed in Michael B. Katz, *The Irony of Early School Reform: Educational Innovation in Mid-Nineteenth*

*Available in paperback edition.

Century Massachusetts (Harvard University Press, 1968), and Carl Kaestle and Maris A. Vinovskis, *Education and Social Change in Nineteenth-Century Massachusetts* (Cambridge University Press, 1980). An older but still valuable study is Rush Welter's *Popular Education and Democratic Thought in America* (Columbia University Press, 1962).

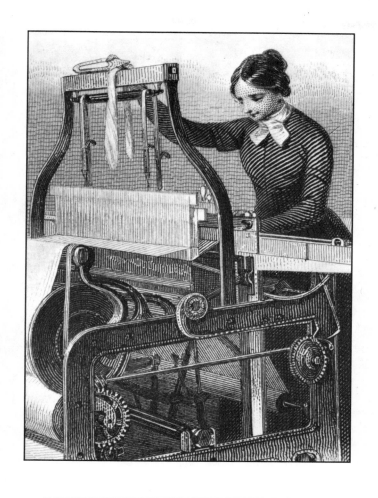

3

THE
ANTE-BELLUM
NORTH AND SOUTH

Natives and Newcomers: Confrontation

THOMAS J. ARCHDEACON

Nativism, or anti-foreign sentiment, has been a persistent force in American history. Between the 1840s and the 1920s, this feeling reached a peak of virulence, but intimations of it were present much earlier. The Alien and Sedition Acts, for instance, passed in 1798 by the Federalist-dominated Congress, provide an example of nativism, as well as of early attempts to suppress political dissent.

In the first half of the nineteenth century, conflict was common as the pluralistic new nation struggled to establish an identity for itself. Unfortunately for the existing minorities, the Anglo-American elite and its followers felt that the nation should mold itself in the white-English-Protestant pattern. All who deviated from that norm were looked upon as inferior and were suppressed to the full extent of the dominant group's ability. Not surprisingly, this conflict involved Indians, blacks, and Mexican-Americans—groups whose history and background deviated sharply from Anglo-American culture.

Religion was another area of conflict that had been present since the beginning of American life. One of the most vicious outbreaks of religious prejudice occurred in the 1840s and '50s, when tens of thousands of Irish Catholic immigrants arrived on the eastern seaboard. Fleeing the horrors of famine in Ireland, many came to America destitute and deeply antagonistic toward all things English, including the Protestant religion. Irish immigrants had come to America before. They were those deported in the civil wars of the seventeenth century and the United Irishmen refugees from the attempted republican rebellion of 1798. But never before had the Irish come in such numbers, and never had America been so ill-prepared to receive them.

Many German Catholics also immigrated to America in those years, but most avoided religious conflict by moving to the West, where they formed homogeneous farming communities or settled in such cities as St. Louis and Milwaukee. The Irish, in contrast, tended to gather in the older cities and in the new factory towns of the East. There they competed with the established residents for unskilled and industrial labor, thus intensifying the negative feelings toward them. The United States economy had just begun to recover from the depression of 1837, which had closed thousands of businesses and manufacturing plants and caused widespread unemployment. Then suddenly there was a great flood of cheap labor, creating the first real labor surplus in American history. Industrialists responded by cutting wages drastically in the mills and other eastern manufacturing enterprises. The labor classes tended to blame the Irish for the worsening economic conditions. Religious bigotry and nativism added to the discontent, and violence of major proportions erupted in several eastern cities.

In his history of immigration and ethnicity, Thomas J. Archdeacon (University of Wisconsin at Madison) has included a chapter, reprinted here, on the confrontation between the Anglo-Americans and those they considered a threat to their dominance. Many of the areas of conflict explored here still beset American life, as a genuine pluralism struggles to become a reality.

W hen the delegates to the Constitutional Convention gathered in Philadelphia in May 1787, the Declaration of Independence was barely a decade old. The former colonies had yet to establish a unique national and cultural identity, and the new nation's attitude toward immigration was an amalgam of experience, idealistic theory, and insecurity. In 1776 the Continental Congress had considered including symbols of the population's six major European sources—England, Scotland, Ireland, France, Germany, and Holland—in the Great Seal of the United States. Indeed, the members associated the motto E Pluribus Unum as much with the joining of different peoples as with the alliance of formerly separate colonies. A few years later, the Founding Fathers no longer thought it appropriate to emphasize America's ethnic diversity, but they still saw no reason to restrict the familiar influx of Europeans, whose presence contributed to the prosperity of the nation. Some leaders, like Alexander Hamilton, were willing even to offer inducements to prospective settlers with needed skills. Thomas Jefferson at times wondered whether the small increment

NATIVES AND NEWCOMERS: CONFRONTATION   From *Becoming American: An Ethnic History* (New York, Free Press, 1983) pp. 57–84. Reprinted with permission of The Free Press, a Division of Macmillan, Inc. Copyright © 1983 by The Free Press.

to growth provided by newcomers was worth the risk of social disruption inherent in a heterogeneous population, but most American politicians did not envision the dramatic changes that were to occur in the volume and character of the European immigration. Their lack of concern was reflected in the Constitution, which devoted only one paragraph to the subject of immigration. The vaguely worded ninth section of Article I was obviously a compromise between proponents and opponents of the slave trade and was probably also a warning against the dumping of British convicts in the United States. It forbade Congress to stop before 1808 the migration or importation of persons currently being accepted by any of the thirteen states. Commentators expected that Congress would halt the slave trade when the period of grace expired, and in the meantime federal authorities had the power to impose a $10 levy on each imported person.

Attitudes toward the political position of the immigrants were ambivalent. The Founding Fathers, from their experience with foreign volunteers during the War of Independence, knew that the United States was vulnerable to invasion by Europeans of high ambitions and varying abilities who believed their continental background and training entitled them to immediate preferment. American leaders also worried that popular foreign newcomers might lead the people down paths alien to republican goals. Some were even concerned that advocates of reunification with England might infiltrate the country. These fears surfaced in the framers' adoption of constitutional provisions limiting the access of foreign-born Americans to elected federal offices. Article I stipulated that would-be U.S. representatives and senators had to be citizens for at least seven and nine years, respectively, prior to taking office, and Article II decreed that no immigrant naturalized after the adoption of the Constitution could become president or vice-president.

Within these limits, the framers generally were sympathetic to extending political rights to the foreign born. They were especially lenient in regard to criteria for naturalization, the sine qua non of the franchise and eligibility for office. The Naturalization Act of 1790, which was based on colonial practices, made immigrants eligible for citizenship after only two years' residence in the United States. The Founding Fathers had moved far toward accepting the idea that citizenship was a voluntary contract, rather than a perpetual and immutable relationship between subject and king that was based on the laws of nature. After all, they had justified the Revolution in terms of a contract theory of government. The argument implied the wisdom of acting quickly both to integrate willing newcomers into the political community and to make formal their allegiance to their new country. Moreover, the Americans readily accepted the image, which European liberals were busily promoting, of their nation as a land of liberty and political refuge.

From almost noncontroversial beginnings, immigration and naturalization became hotly debated matters by the end of the 1790s. Frenchmen and Irishmen, the most notable newcomers of the decade, were neither so numerous as to inundate the communities they entered nor so poor as to become an unbearable burden. As persons whose migration was directly or indirectly the consequence of the French Revolution, however, they were a center of political controversy. Many Americans saw them as a threat to extend to the New World the turmoil of the Old and as advocates of unnecessary involvement by the United States in the affairs of Europe. This fear was not without foundation. Edmund Genêt was initially an envoy of the French government, rather than an immigrant, but his appeals over the head of the U.S. government for popular support against the English underscored the dangers aliens in America posed to neutrality. Genêt's French compatriots were, by and large, reserved in their behavior, but Irish refugees carried their struggle to American soil. Rebels like Napper Tandy and Wolfe Tone planned for the moment of their return to the Emerald Isle, while other Irishmen were, for example, in the forefront of the opponents of Jay's treaty, the Washington administration's major diplomatic initiative to achieve rapprochement with England.

The partisan activities of the French and Irish exiles coincided with the crystallization of the first American political parties and were a matter of concern to the leaders of the opposing organizations. The Democratic Republicans, forming around Thomas Jefferson and James Madison, most often came from areas dominated by agriculture and from rapidly growing states with populations of varied ethnic backgrounds. They accepted the democratization of politics accompanying the Revolution, looked upon events in France as at least a partial replication of their own earlier struggle, and gratefully remembered French support during the War of Independence. The Republicans were aghast at the thought of aristocratic emigrés using the United States as a refuge and a base of operation. The Federalists, aligning behind the administrations of George Washington and John Adams, were strongest in districts heavily involved in commerce and settled largely by people of English origin living in stable communities. This party was uncomfortable with the erosion of the political influence of the social and economic upper class in the wake of the Revolution, looked upon the aims of the French insurgents as much more radical than the goal of national independence they had pursued, and saw the fate of the United States as inextricably interwoven with the success of the English mercantile network. The Federalists were alarmed by those who threatened to thwart Anglo-American rapprochement and to promote political and social leveling. Mutually fearful of foreign agitators, though for almost contradictory reasons, the Republicans and the Federalists by 1795 were willing to accept a new naturalization act that required aliens to reside in the United States for five years before gaining eligibility for citizenship.

After 1795, the Republicans became less worried about outside influences operating in the United States. The inauguration of the First Directory led to the voluntary repatriation of many conservative French exiles. The Federalists, however, found no comfort. France's move to the right did not silence the revolution's supporters in the United States, and the suppression of the uprising of the United Irishmen in 1797–1798 intensified the emigration from Ireland. Indeed, Rufus King, the American minister to Great Britain, had to convince the English not to use the United States as a place of banishment for Irish political prisoners. Federalists, especially those from New England, which had never welcomed Irishmen, found Celtic immigrants obnoxious, democratic, and generally supportive of the well-organized Jeffersonian critics of Adam's administration. The existence of a political party composed of opponents to the elected government was novel and to many Federalists this situation smacked of conspiracy; the adherence of the Irish to the Republican camp only served to make the situation appear more sinister. The Federalists found the opportunity to strike back at their enemies—France, that nation's American friends, alien radicals, and the Democratic Republicans—in the furor caused by the XYZ Affair. The demand by three French diplomats that the United States offer a loan to their nation and a bribe as the price for commencing negotiations on outstanding differences offended all Americans. That incident brought the nation to the verge of war and embarrassed the Republican party.

Striking while the iron was hot, the Federalists in 1798 pushed through four pieces of legislation that limited the political impact that immigrants could have on American politics and at least temporarily deprived their Republican opponents of a potentially important base of supporters. The Naturalization Act included a provision, passed by the narrow vote of forty-one to forty in the House of Representatives, that raised to fourteen years the residence requirement imposed on immigrants who sought American citizenship. The law also demanded that aliens declare their intention to seek naturalization five years before obtaining it and spend five years in the state or territory in which they were to reside as citizens. The law's only concession was to allow foreigners resident in the United States before 1795 to take advantage of the more liberal provisions of the naturalization act passed in that year. The Alien Enemies Act authorized, in time of war, invasion, or attack, the arrest, imprisonment, and deportation of immigrant males from enemy nations who had passed their fourteenth birthday without taking up U.S. citizenship. The Federalists wanted to give the president almost the entire responsibility for implementing the law, but the Republicans managed to put the courts and other agencies in charge of enforcement. A temporary Aliens Act strengthened the president's hand in the immediate crisis by empowering him to order out of the United States any alien suspected of being dangerous to the nation's peace and safety. The Republicans argued in vain that Article I, section 9, of the

Constitution expressly forbade congressional action against immigration before 1808 and that in any circumstance the law was so arbitrary as to be invalid. The Federalists proclaimed that the needs of national defense had to be the prime consideration and that aliens were not protected by the Constitution. Finally, the Sedition Act prohibited, among other deeds, the publication of any false, scandalous, or malicious writing against the government. The Federalists used the act, which expired on March 3, 1801, to try to silence several Republican newspaper editors, including immigrants like James Thomas Callender from Scotland, Thomas Cooper from England, and Matthew Lyon from Ireland.

The four Alien and Sedition acts are important in American history less as effective laws than as omens. The two most punitive measures expired within a few years, and the possibility of harassment would not have been enough to discourage potential immigrants had countervailing social and economic forces been at work. But the laws showed how, in a society in which political allegiance is as much a voluntary commitment as an accident of birth, it is easy to doubt the loyalty of the different and the dissident. And they did reveal a tendency common among Americans, but not exclusive to them, to blame domestic turmoil on the intrigues of minority or alien elements in the population rather than to see internal problems as by-products of conflicting values or social inequities. Fortunately, the United States was spared from a recurrence of this phenomenon for the next generation, a period of great importance in the nation's development.

A low level of immigration between 1800 and 1830 allowed the components of the U.S. population to homogenize and this process, in turn, combined with the political maturation of the country to produce a clearer sense of an American nationality. In the years before 1830 the integrity of the non-British cultures present in the United States eroded. The low volume of immigration in the first decades of the nineteenth century deprived the descendants of persons who had come from continental Europe during the eighteenth century, most notably Germans, of the reinforcements that might have allowed them to maintain their ethnic identities in the midst of the dominant Anglo-American society. Technological change, commercial development, and the geographic expansion of the United States also hastened the acculturation of the foreign born. Improvements in transportation and an increasingly broad network of business connections naturally brought people into contact and reduced the isolation that kept ethnic feelings intense. The westward migration that attracted so many Americans of all backgrounds separated people from their national enclaves and recombined them in more mixed communities. The intermarriages that inevitably took place also weakened ethic ties, though the extent of this amalgamation is in doubt. Marriages between persons of different nationalities seem to have been common among the upper classes. They also occurred frequently enough among ordinary folk, at least on the frontier in the late eighteenth century, to worry ethnic loyalists like the German minister Arnold Roschen of North Carolina. On the other hand, many communities retained a reputation for ethnic homogeneity in the early nineteenth century, and generalizations about the frequency of intermarriage rest more on speculation than on evidence.

Though the new American, whom the French writer J. Hector St. John de Crèvecoeur described as an amalgam of the peoples of Europe, may have been an idealized image, the growing dominance of an Anglo-American culture was real. By the middle of the eighteenth century, colonists of Dutch and Swedish extraction had already begun to succumb to this force. In 1748 Peter Kalm, the Swedish botanist, noted during a visit to New Jersey that Swedish settlers were incorporating English words into their speech. Swedish children were not properly learning their ancestral tongue or hid their knowledge of it for fear of being thought inferior to their English peers. The larger Dutch population in rural New Jersey, and especially in the Hudson Valley of New York, kept their language alive longer but, without enrichment from abroad, the Dutch spoken in America degenerated into a dialect unaffected by the linguistic changes that took place in the Netherlands after 1664. Even German, the most widespread and recently introduced of the non-English languages, withered in most areas. The tongues of the ethnic minorities survived for many decades among older people and in informal conversation, especially in rural areas, but the abandonment of the vernacular by the churches of the various groups was the surest sign of the Anglicization of speech.

America's European sponsored churches were under a dual pressure. As time passed, fewer people understood the languages used in non-English services, and clergymen admitted that they had to make concessions in order to keep the allegiance of their followers. English became the standard language in the services of New York City's Dutch Reformed churches by the 1760s and won even wider acceptance after the Revolution. In 1790 the Dutch Reformed Synod adopted English as the official language of worship in all its churches. Among Lutherans, English replaced German as the language for sermons in Philadelphia in 1806, in New York City in 1807, in Albany in 1808, and in Harrisburg in 1812. German remained alive in the form of Pennsylvania Dutch in some areas of that state, but this language faded in most others and lost out completely to English in North Carolina after 1825. Independence and American national pride also took their toll, and the Protestant churches that had institutional ties to European states cut them: the Dutch Reformed church declared its independence from the Netherlands; the Anglican church became the Episcopal; and by 1800 the Swedish Lutheran churches of New Jersey affiliated with the latter, at the same time informing Swedish ecclesiastical authorities that missionaries were no longer needed.

The relatively rapid decline of non-British white cultures in the

United States during the opening decades of the nineteenth century was of fundamental importance for the future of the nation. This process, for example, helped put the country on a different course of ethnic development from that which eventually emerged in Canada. The British residents of His Majesty's remaining North American colonies expected, like their cousins in the independent United States, to impose a more or less English culture on their corner of the New World. But the British formed such a small minority of the population north of the St. Lawrence that they had to rely on politics, rather than gradual demographic change, to achieve their goal. The Constitution of 1791, which divided old Quebec into Upper and Lower Canada, was seen as the first step on the path to complete British supremacy. That measure not only gave the conquerors control in the former district, in which they were more numerous, but also allotted them majorities in the upper house and executive council of the latter, where the French made up over 90 percent of the population. The British conceded the equality of French for use in legislative debates but made English the language in which laws were officially promulgated. Moreover, they subsequently diverted money generated by the properties of the banned Jesuit religious order—funds that the French had used to underwrite parochial education—to the support of a state sponsored, Anglicized school system.

Despite such measures, French influence refused to fade in Canada, and the British resorted to harsher political pressures. During the Napoleonic era, Governor Sir James Craig, who failed to recognize that the generally conservative French Canadians lacked sympathy for revolutionary France, conducted a repressive campaign against the allegedly subversive French population. Even after the French Canadians proved their loyalty in the War of 1812, proposals to diminish their status continued to surface. The nadir for the French came after French Canadian radicals, known as *patriotes,* joined like-minded English Canadians in an unsuccessful effort in 1837–1838 to extract from the English Parliament more autonomy for the North American settlements. The zeal with which British regular soldiers and English Canadian volunteers put down the uprising left a legacy of bitterness, especially in Quebec, and the report on the crisis made for Parliament in 1839 by the Earl of Durham aggravated the situation. Durham, who was a liberal in the context of English politics, urged England to give Canada greater self-government, but he saw at the root of the problem a conflict of races rather than of political principles. For the earl the best hope for a complete resolution of Canada's difficulties lay in the creation of a Canadian nationality. He assumed, however, that such a development could be achieved only through the extinction of French Canadian culture, which he deemed inferior to English culture and incompatible with freedom and intelligence.

While the peoples of British North America were struggling in the early nineteenth century to create a Canadian identity, the increasingly homogeneous population of the independent United States was able to discover a set of values and attitudes that would distinguish the American character from the English and all others. It was an era of nationalistic fervor in the republic. Authors like Washington Irving and James Fenimore Cooper created a distinctly American genre and the lexicographer Noah Webster helped distinguish the American variety of the English language from the parent tongue. In politics and diplomacy the public managed to forget the young nation's narrow escape in the War of 1812 by turning General Andrew Jackson's victory over the British at New Orleans into a legend proving the superiority of America's frontier virtue and raw vigor over European wealth and might. Americans also directed their energies to a quest for their so-called Manifest Destiny, in the words of John L. O'Sullivan, editor of *The United States Magazine and Democratic Review.* At face value, the term referred to the apparently inevitable territorial expansion of the United States. Most Americans assumed that the nation would naturally expand to the Pacific coast, and some dreamt of absorbing Canada, Mexico, and even the remainder of the Western Hemisphere. But Manifest Destiny also touched on a long-standing belief that the United States had a providential mission.

From the time of the Puritans, Americans had seen the settlement of the New World as a climactic moment in the history of religion, and by the middle of the eighteenth century they had added an important secular dimension to their understanding. The development of America became, in their minds, the first step toward the establishment of the millennium, a time in which holiness would prevail and Christ would reign on earth. The Revolution, with its strong tones of regeneration, reaffirmed this message, and independence became the political and social complement of the spiritual redemption. In this context, the history of the United States became the unfolding of God's kingdom on earth, and the conquest of the continent loomed as the fundamental assignment in the creation of a new world order.

The goal of American expansion was to create an empire of political liberty, economic opportunity, and, most important, Christian civilization. During the first half of the nineteenth century, the rhetoric of the millennium was common in American churches, especially in the revivalist ones that became the dynamic element of Protestantism. The churches were convinced that they had not only to spread the Gospel to individual souls but also to take part in the salvation of society. Religiously minded Americans were in the forefront of the reform movements of the era. They sought to establish perfect communities and to find the key to rehabilitating the criminal, the mentally ill, and the poor. In the North they led the fight against slavery. Church activists were convinced that an ecclesiastically sanctioned civic morality was necessary to keep the nation true to its mission. Despite the constitutional separation of church and state, they conceived of the United States as a nation whose laws and policies ought to reflect the country's essentially Christian character. Ministers and their supporters deemed it proper that public institutions, including schools, have a specifically Protestant outlook. They also expected that the government would endorse and enforce a broadly shared set of moral standards. These could touch every human endeavor but in the pre–Civil War years the churches focused on the two contemporary abuses whose prevalence symbolized the dangers to America's mission. They stressed the importance of keeping the Sabbath free from profanation, so that the people might turn their minds to God, and they argued forcibly for the prohibition of alcohol, that fundamental threat to spirituality and responsible citizenship.

Cultural homogeneity, national pride, and millennial expectations combined to create the history of ethnic and racial relations in America during the decades before the Civil War. For the most part, these forces set a tone of confrontation. As the diversity of the population lessened before 1830, the majority of white Americans, and especially those of Protestant background, became less tolerant of differences. Paradoxically, at the very time the institution of slavery came under sustained attack, the position of blacks in American society reached new depths of isolation and vulnerability. As the sense of providential concern for the United States and of its special mission in the world became fully articulated, the nation willingly overwhelmed any peoples it encountered on the way west. The Indians, who had symbolized America, were denied a place in the country's future, and the Mexican inhabitants of the West were subjugated in the name of liberty. As the opportunities to achieve an unprecedentedly high level of public and private morality and to establish an almost ideal community seemed to come within reach, even the most generous and optimistic bristled against any threats to reaching these goals. In this regard, the European immigrants, whose arrival signaled their acceptance of the promise of America, felt the sting of those who declared them unworthy of it.

African peoples living in the United States in the early nineteenth century shared an experience superficially similar to that of the descendants of non-English Europeans but in fact profoundly different from it. Congressional action banned the importation of slaves into the United States after December 31, 1807. Though smugglers thereafter managed to slip an estimated 10,000 slaves into the country during each decade before the Civil War, effective African reinforcement of black culture in the United States became an impossibility. Had race and the stigma of slavery not been more serious distinguishing marks than nationality, persons of African blood, like those of European origins, would have been absorbed at least in part into the dominant society. White Americans, however, thought of blacks as either innately inferior or, in the opinion of the most sympathetic observers, irretrievably damaged by the environment of limited opportunity and apparently insurmountable discrimination in which they lived. Whites also viewed blacks as dangerous, particularly in the wake of various slave rebellions in the late eighteenth and early nineteenth centuries.

Both in the North, where slavery was dying, and in the South, where it held sway, the position of blacks deteriorated. Slave codes became more restrictive, and free blacks had their rights curtailed. By 1840 Rhode Island, Connecticut, New York, Pennsylvania, North Carolina, and Tennessee had eliminated or limited the right of free blacks to vote. Signs of segregation appeared in hospitals, prisons, and other institutions, and America's churches began to cleave along racial lines. Even to foes of slavery, the prospects of Africans in the United States appeared bleak. The common wisdom called for the repatriation of American blacks to Africa, where they would be free and could help civilize the continent. To this purpose, the Reverend Robert Finley; his brother-in-law Elias Boudinot Caldwell who was clerk of the U.S. Supreme Court; and Francis Scott Key, a lawyer, as well as the composer of the "Star-Spangled Banner," laid the groundwork for the formation late in 1816 of the American Society for Colonizing the Free People of Color in the United States. The colonization movement helped establish the independent republic of Liberia in Africa in 1822 and transported 12,000 blacks there by 1860, but this effort lost its popularity as the financial and practical problems of repatriating millions of former slaves became clear.

Throughout the pre–Civil War era, whites continued to emphasize the differences between themselves and blacks. Leading scientists offered the theory of polygenesis to explain the apparent mental and physical divergences between the races. The thesis, which won the support of Louis Agassiz, the famous French botanist and Harvard professor, proposed the existence of acts of creation in addition to that which made Adam and Eve. According to the theory's adherents, blacks were literally created separate and unequal. Abolitionists, on the other hand, were willing to recognize the equality of the Africans' humanity with their own, but they separated the races in regard to moral characteristics. As can be seen in Harriet Beecher Stowe's novel *Uncle Tom's Cabin,* blacks became for the abolitionists the preeminent possessors of the Christian virtues of childlike simplicity, docility, and unselfishness. Whites, on the other hand, were intellectual, aggressive, and efficient. The contrasting images favored the blacks but suggested that they were at a competitive disadvantage in the white man's world. Ordinary Americans probably rejected polygenesis as inconsistent with the Bible and dismissed the more benign aspects of the abolitionists' description as sentimentality. For them, the superiority of whites was self-evident, as was the future of the United States as a white man's country once the institution of slavery disappeared. Most people believed that once freed the mass of blacks would have to separate themselves from the white population by concentrating in sections of the South or by migrating to the Caribbean islands or to Latin America or back to Africa. If the blacks insisted on staying among the whites, they would fail in the competitive struggle and their race would gradually die out.

The persistent refusal of white Americans to accept blacks as partners in the New World was less striking than their increasing despair in the early nineteenth century over the possibility of absorbing the Indian population of the continent into Western culture. Africans had been consistently a source of fear and an object of derision in America, but Indians had an ambiguous status in the white imagination. Colonists and frontier dwellers encountered the Indians at their most fearsome and recalcitrant, savagely wielding tomahawks and firebrands to prevent the loss of familiar lands and ways of life. When such incidents became a less frequent part of the white population's experience, however, other components of the Indians' situation gained significance. As the original inhabitants of North America, the Indians were inextricably part of the story of the nation. They could not be seen as an extraneous element, fit, like the blacks, to be returned to their homeland. The worthy foes who managed to escape enslavement and to operate successfully on the periphery of the white man's world seemed superior to the blacks. The standard racial hierarchy placed America's tribal peoples between whites and blacks, and Americans were not particularly disturbed by copper-colored skin. Indeed, intermarriage between Caucasian men and Indian women did not excite strong aversion and sometimes was looked upon favorably by the authorities. White Americans of the early nineteenth century were willing to judge the Indians as having achieved a level of civilization to the environment in which they lived, and the romantic among them envisioned the natives as noble savages in communion with an idyllic natural world. Reasonable people like Thomas Jefferson assumed that the Indians would soon absorb the benefits of white civilization.

Missionary schools, established with the support of the government by several Protestant denominations, became the primary means of disseminating white culture among the Indian tribes. By concentrating their efforts on the young, on women, and on the offspring of white and native unions, the missionaries were able to make some progress. A number of Indians became nominally Christian, learned English, and abandoned part-time hunting and fishing in favor of full-time agriculture. The expected total absorption of the whole of the whites' ways, however, did not take place. The Indians proved exasperatingly able to adopt bits and pieces of white culture and to use those elements for the ultimate preservation of their own ways. The Cherokee chief Sequoya devised an alphabet that allowed his people's tongue to compete with English as a written language. His tribe also used its knowledge of American laws and institutions to develop a constitution that attempted to make the Cherokee a political entity separate from the federal and state governments. Unfortunately for the Indians, they were not always discriminating in what white cultural elements they chose. Their affection for the wares of Euro-American civilization, including clothes, guns, and sundry implements, made them dependent on that culture without making them fully part of it and went far toward undermining their own skills. Worst of all, the Indians took on the vices, as well as the virtues, of white society; alcohol, in particular, had horribly debilitating effects on the native peoples. By the 1830s the stubborn vitality of some aspects of aboriginal life and the simultaneous deterioration of others, without the substitution of approved new forms of behavior, reflected contrasting aspects of the impact of white culture. But both tendencies pointed to the conclusion that the Indian was not ready to be absorbed into mainstream society.

Once the Indians were judged unready for incorporation in white culture, removing them from their homelands to points beyond the fringe of American settlement seemed the obvious course of action. The policy promised the avaricious quick access to the desirable lands of troublesome neighbors. At the same time, persons sympathetic with the Indians could believe that this policy would allow the tribes more time to achieve civilization. A number of treaties negotiated after 1815 provided for the voluntary surrender of tribal lands east of the Mississippi, and the Removal Act, passed by Congress in 1830, set up a program for sending tribes across that river. The removals were often carried out under dishonorable circumstances. In December 1828, the state of Georgia unilaterally abolished the government of the Cherokee nation, and the tribe's situation became worse in 1829, when gold was discovered on Cherokee land. With President Andrew Jackson supporting Georgia, not even the United States Supreme Court, which denied the state's jurisdiction over the Cherokee, could help the tribe. Some Cherokees agreed by the Treaty of New Echota in 1835 to cede their lands to the federal government, but about three-quarters of the tribe refused to cooperate. The government then removed the recalcitrant in a forced migration that cost over 4,000 lives.

Violence accompanied other removals. The Black Hawk War erupted in 1832, when the Sauk and the Fox refused to honor an agreement made in 1804 to leave the Illinois Territory. The Second Seminole War broke out in 1835, when this tribe would not leave Florida. In 1830 federal troops drove the Creek from Alabama after they attacked whites out of frustration at incursions on the small homesteads left to them as compensation for a major land cession. Soldiers were also used to hurry the Winnebago tribe of the Wisconsin River area across the Mississippi in 1840.

White thoughts of the trans-Mississippi West as a place of protected isolation for the Indians faded in the 1840s and 1850s before dreams of reaching the shores of the Pacific as soon as possible. Explorers and settlers entered the region in large numbers, and the earlier pattern of Indian–white contact was repeated. Epidemic diseases quickly spread among the tribes with disastrous consequences. In the northern Plains smallpox virtually wiped out the Mandan in 1837–1838, and recurring episodes of the disease took a heavy toll among the Blackfoot before the Civil War. Asiatic cholera, which swept the nation in 1849, may have reduced the Comanche population of the southern Plains by more than half and affected other tribes as severely. Treaties negotiated with the U.S. government in the 1850s cost the Indian nations of Kansas more than 90 percent of their land and drove them toward agricultural pursuits, to which they were culturally unsuited. American migrants simply overwhelmed or bypassed the smaller tribes of the arid western regions and drove the Indians of the northern Pacific coast onto reservations. Whenever necessary, force became the ultimate argument against the defiant. In 1849 the army established garrisons at Forts Laramie and Kearney to protect persons traveling the Platte River route to the gold fields of California, and the introduction of expensively maintained cavalry units gave the whites the final edge over the strong tribes of the Great Plains.

The expansion of the United States brought cultural subordination not only to the Indian tribes of the Plains and beyond. As the nation's western frontier touched Mexico's northern, Americans came into contact with a final group to be added to their list of peoples fated for demise. The Spanish-speaking inhabitants of the region from Texas through southern California fell short of American standards in several respects. They bore the political and religious heritage of Spain, a nation excoriated by Americans since the days of English colonization as a bastion of despotism and superstition. Worse, their Spanish blood had been mixed with Indian and black, creating a breed thought by most Americans to be clearly inferior. Visitors to the Southwest in the early nineteenth century forecast that the Mexicans would not be able to hold the area indefinitely, and their prophecy was fulfilled. Migrants from the United States entered Texas in the 1820s and by 1836 were numerous and strong enough to declare their independence from Mexico. Congressional action in 1845 to admit the Republic of Texas to the Union led to a war with Mexico that cost the losers dearly. The Treaty of Guadalupe Hidalgo, signed in 1848, ceded to the United States the lands known today as Arizona, New Mexico, Colorado, Nevada, and Utah, as well as the major prize of California, which had received many American settlers in the 1840s. Time reduced the Mexican proportion of the population to 10 percent in Texas by 1860 and to 25 percent in southern California twenty years later. The Mexicans, moreover, were swiftly relegated to the periphery of the society and the economy, with their Spanish land titles brought into question and their right to participate in America's growth limited by discrimination.

Compared with the blacks, Indians, and Mexicans, the European immigrants of the mid-nineteenth century were in an ambiguous position. As whites they were safe from being categorized as hopelessly inferior and as refugees from the political and economic darkness of the Old World they were evidence that mankind recognized America's mission. But the immigrants were, at the same time, a serious challenge to the establishment of a Christian utopia in the United States. The newcomers became strongly identified with the industrialization and urbanization that was changing the nation in ways disfavored by many socially conscious and concerned people. Foreigners provided the manpower for the growth of the American economy, but their presence also helped make the nation's new factories distressingly similar to those of Europe and their low status belied the magic of the United States as a society of open-ended economic mobility. The arrival of the first wave of European immigrants in an era that saw patterns of familiar communal life waning hastened the decline of these arrangements and stimulated the Americans' fears that the social order was crumbling. Because of the desperate circumstances in which they came, the Europeans were the agents and victims of crime, disease, and disorder with a frequency that far exceeded their proportion of the population. Perhaps worst of all, large numbers of the immigrants flouted Protestant America's version of civic morality and rejected the use of public institutions to propagate this view. Too many immigrants landed on the wrong side of the various reform movements of the era. That the most numerous and troublesome of the early arrivals came from Catholic Ireland, whose people and religion had been hated and distrusted in America since colonial times, only aggravated the multiple problems. Conflict was unavoidable in such an atmosphere, and bitter clashes between natives and immigrants colored American history throughout the pre–Civil War era.

Europeans came to the United States in large part because of America's labor shortage, and their muscles helped propel the nation into the industrial age. But native-stock workers tended to see the immigrants' role in the work force in terms of individual profit and loss rather than of half-understood concepts of societal progress. Those who employed the abundant unskilled labor or rose to advanced positions in new industries dependent on this sector could feel superior to lowly foreign toilers. Those who lost ground had reason for bitterness. The unskilled faced the worst competition from the newcomers, but skilled workers also blamed the immigrants of the 1840s for keeping down wage rates, which had tumbled after the Panic of 1837.

The truth about the newcomers' economic impact is complex. Some jobs taken by them, such as railroad construction labor, had barely existed before their coming. Even in many traditional lines of work the immigrants' effect was mixed. No doubt their presence limited wages, but that curb in turn created employment by coaxing into the marketplace persons who would have been unwilling to hire had higher rates prevailed. The immigrants' coming was most disastrous for native-stock workers in trades that technological and entrepreneurial innovation had already undermined. Mechanization and the division of production tasks reduced the need for skill in endeavors like weaving and vitiated the apprenticeship systems that had controlled the flow of trained crafts workers. Artisans in doomed specialties found it easier to blame their plight on the immigrants who took over their tasks than on the larger revolution that enabled unskilled hands to replace them. The foreigners were a concrete object for the wrath of those who could reason that, had the newcomers been unavailable, labor-replacing technology would have made no headway against their occupations.

The same forces creating the jobs that invited the immigrants to America were simultaneously changing the face of the nation to which they came. This was particularly true in the older cities, where so many of the foreign born were concentrated. The technological revolution of the nineteenth century brought an end to the "walking city," which the absence of public transportation, the rarity of privately owned coaches, and the poor condition of roads had created in the colonial era. Families no longer had to operate their businesses at or near home. The rich no longer had to build their homes at the commercial centers of the cities, as in colonial New York, where the most elegant houses lay adjacent to the docks. The periphery of the town was no longer the preserve of the poorer sort. The introduction of the steam railroad in the 1840s allowed the affluent to commute from as far away as ten miles, and the appearance of streetcars pulled by horses over iron tracks made it possible for middle-class persons to relocate several miles away from downtown. Those willing and financially able to travel daily were the first suburbanites; they enjoyed access to fresher air and more space and escaped the aesthetically displeasing changes associated with the major expansion of wharving and warehousing facilities in the business districts.

America's immigrants inherited the urban void created by the birth of the suburbs. European newcomers were usually trapped near the downtown or in undesirable commercial areas. Several family members usually had to work, and their places of employment changed frequently as they searched for temporary, unskilled jobs. They could afford neither carfare nor travel time added to their long day, and even those with some money could not depend on lines that did not offer cross-town transportation. Immigrants filled the houses left behind in the exodus from the city. The owners subdivided their dwellings and rented them or they leased their buildings to persons who in turn sublet the units. In general, the owners allowed the property to deteriorate with the expectation of selling it at a handsome price as the business district sought space for expansion. The immigrants also crowded into unwholesome areas on the periphery of the downtown; in New York, for example, Irishmen and blacks congregated in the notorious Five Points district. Such changes only hastened the abandonment of the affected districts by the native citizens and transformed them into immigrant slums. In turn, these geographic expressions of the social and economic divisions developing in urban life demonstrated the connection between immigration and the maladies of America at mid-century.

Increases in disease accompanied the deterioration of the old city districts. The expanded commerce of the first half of the nineteenth century made it inevitable that the maladies of Europe would quickly cross the Atlantic to American ports. In the absence of advanced medical knowledge, public health regulations, proper sanitation, and even clean water, virulent epidemics were common. The immigrants, weakened by hardship and unfamiliar with the hygiene demanded by urban life, naturally became prime carriers and victims of such illnesses. Irish residents were the first laid low in the cholera epidemics of 1832 and 1849 in New York City; these outbreaks took a disproportionately large toll among their compatriots and other poor people across the nation.

Crime also flourished in the bowels of the city, where the new wealth and impersonality of life sorely tempted impoverished and marginal people toward wrongdoing. Immigrants received much of the blame for the perceived increase in disorder. Modern experience suggests that the accusations were exaggerated. Discriminatory law enforcement and the glut of young people in the foreign population undoubtedly contributed to the disturbing frequency of immigrants' names on the arrest rolls. Moreover, the vast majority of foreigners in trouble with the law were accused only of minor offenses that a society less concerned with the need for order would have regarded as inconsequential. But crime obviously did play an important role in some immigrants' efforts to adjust to their new surroundings. Theft and prostitution offered desperate people the means to survive, and many young immigrants found acceptance only on the streets among their own kind. Organized in gangs, such as the fancifully named Bowery B'hoys, Dead Rabbits, and Plug Uglies of New York City, Irish males took part in the shenanigans of rival volunteer fire units in the prewar era and provided Election Day muscle for ward politicians. On the slightest pretext, such as the appearance in 1849 of an unpopular English actor at the Astor Place Opera House, they turned the troubles of Ireland into American melees. Most of all, they expressed in battles against each other and equally violent native gangs the anger, frustration, and thirst for adventure endemic among slum dwellers.

The reputed association between immigration, on the one hand, and disease and crime, on the other, hastened the depersonalization of the poor and deviant, a process that had begun in the late eighteenth century with increased rates of internal migration and the rapid growth of cities relative to the countryside. The poor and problem-racked were no longer individual men and women whose problems were handled in the context of small communities or families. They were collectivities of strangers inhabiting social netherworlds. Americans came to see the unfortunate and unpleasant people of the nation less as the victims of luck or societal malfunctions and more as the perpetrators of their own problems. Lawbreakers had never been objects of sympathy, but poverty once had been identified as primarily the lot of the widowed, the orphaned, and the infirm. By the middle decades of the century, however, Americans were inclined to define poverty as a badge of intemperance and shiftlessness rather than as a by-product of the progress that was making so many U.S. citizens prosperous. In the scientific ignorance of the era, even the sick became objects of contempt. During the cholera epidemic of 1832, pastors assured their flocks that the disease was God's scourge against those whose depravity had robbed their bodies of the power of resistance; the virulence of the malady in the darker corners of the cities seemed to confirm this judgment.

Some Protestant ministers, in the millennial flush of the 1820s and 1830s, retained hopes of redeeming the sinners of the slums. Members of the New York City Tract Society, for example, spent much of their time distributing Bibles and religious literature among the poor. They hoped to bring these people an understanding of Christ's work of salvation and assumed that an amelioration in the living conditions of the converts would naturally follow their adoption of high moral standards. Reformers were confident that even those who had already run afoul of the law or proved unproductive might be rehabilitated. They believed that new institutions, like penitentiaries, and revitalized ones, like workhouses, might provide the moral training and exposure to good habits that seemed to have been uniformly absent in the personal histories of their inmates. Such optimism faded in the 1840s and 1850s. The great migration of these decades made the magnitude of the problem seem overwhelming, especially because the newcomers, so many of whom were Roman Catholics, proved as unreceptive as the Indians were to the missionaries' message. In despair, many reformers concluded that the nation's poor were incorrigible. Ministers lost hope in a mass conversion of slum dwellers, and the operators of the society's penal institutions, whose cells were increasingly filled with foreigners, gradually deemphasized rehabilitative aspirations in favor of the custodial responsibility of isolating miscreants from the general population.

The Roman Catholic religious affiliation of many of the residents of the worst districts of the eastern cities was especially galling to American Protestants. Catholicism not only explained the moral recalcitrance of the immigrant poor but also signaled a profound change in the ecclesiastical makeup of the United States. At the time of the first federal census, Roman Catholics constituted less than 1 percent of the American population; 16,000 of the faith's 25,000 adherents lived in one state, Maryland, and the church may have been failing in its efforts to hold the loyalty of Catholic immigrants, particularly Irish servants, settled in strongly Protestant areas. A weak institution, the Roman church hardly seemed a threat; in fact, some Americans found it attractive. Dominated by French clergymen who were refugees from the revolution, the Catholic church had a somewhat aristocratic quality and offered a conservative alternative to Protestants offended by the increasingly evangelical character of their denominations. The influx of immigrants, however, destroyed this equilibrium. By 1850, Roman Catholicism was the largest Christian denomination in the United States, calling 7.5 percent of the population of some 23 million its own. It was a truly national church, with six metropolitan and twenty-seven suffragan bishops in 1852, the year of the First Plenary Council in America. Catholicism was becoming the religion of the great cities, and though many German immigrants also filled the church's ranks, the long despised Irish were quickly taking over its leadership and membership.

For Protestant Americans, particularly those under evangelical influence, the Roman Catholic church remained the fabled Whore of Babylon. Protestant spokesmen used their pulpits and the numerous religious periodicals available to them to rekindle hatreds dating back to the Reformation and the Counter-Reformation. They lashed out at favorite targets, including the primacy of the pope; the doctrine of Transubstantiation; the veneration of the Virgin; vestments; rituals; and miracles. But the central complaints were timely, as well as traditional, and revealed less about Catholicism than about the values and concerns of mid-nineteenth-century America. The supposed subservience of Catholics to the pope caused problems in an age of awakening American nationalism. Commentators frequently expressed doubt that Catholics could be completely loyal to the United States when their spiritual leader was also a temporal prince in the Italian boot. They suggested that the hierarchical structure of the Roman church and its emphasis on obedience, which offended Protestant America's affinity for decentralization, made Catholicism inimical to democracy and liberty. To extremists, the presence of Catholics in the United States was part of the reactionary plot to stymie the fulfillment of America's providential mission. Samuel F. B. Morse—author, artist, and inventor—pointed out the connection between immigration and these machinations. His *Imminent Dangers to the Free Institutions of the United States through Foreign Immigration,* which appeared in 1835, argued that the Jesuits were in control of the transatlantic movement of Catholics and were directing the newcomers to strategic points in the nation in preparation for an attempt to overthrow the government. The next year, Samuel B. Smith, editor of the anti-Catholic newspaper *The Downfall of Babylon,* outlined in a book, *The Flight of Popery from Rome to the West,* the role immigrants would play in a papal military invasion of the United States.

Concerned about Rome's political and ideological threat to the nation, American Protestants also were peculiarly interested in the private morals of Catholic priests and nuns. Criticism of celibacy as unnatural and wasteful was common among Protestants and easy to understand in a youthful, half-empty country. But popular interest went beyond the utilitarian disapproval of abstinence to a lurid fascination with tales of sexual indulgence. Most likely, this obsession was a by-product of the repressive attitude toward sexuality that took hold in the United States in the middle of the nineteenth century. In such an atmosphere, the attribution of immorality to an enemy allowed Protestants to express their misgivings over their own secret desires, and the supposed need to educate the innocent about the danger of Catholicism served as an outlet for their fantasies. As the historian Richard Hofstadter once explained, anti-Catholicism became the pornography of the Puritans. Whatever the underlying cause, literature describing, in almost salacious terms, the depravity practiced by the men and women of the Roman church became enormously popular. The themes were consistent. Priests were seducers who used the confessional to gain control over virtuous young women and to put in their minds suggestions of impurity that would eventually lead to assignations. Convents were brothels, where nuns catered to the pleasures of the priests. When their unions produced offspring, the infants were baptized, murdered, and buried secretly on the convent grounds.

The history of Maria Monk's *Awful Disclosures of the Hotel Dieu Nunnery of Montreal* reveals the pervasive impact of prurient anti-Catholic propaganda on American society before the Civil War. The most notorious of the exposés of convent life, this book purported to recount the experiences of its author before her escape. In fact, Maria Monk had never been a nun, though she had spent time as an inmate of a Catholic asylum in Montreal. Brain damaged as a child, Monk was incapable herself of writing the book, which had been germinated in the minds of several New York City ministers. Harper's, which printed the book through a dummy firm, was the preeminent American publishing house. Responsible critics, including Colonel William L. Stone, the Protestant editor of the *New York Commercial Advertiser,* soon proved the story a sham, and Monk, cut out of the profits by her manipulators, ended her days as a prostitute and pickpocket. The shame surrounding the book, however, failed to hurt its popularity among a good percentage of America's reading public. With 300,000 copies sold between its appearance in 1836 and 1860, *Awful Disclosures* was, next to *Uncle Tom's Cabin,* the best-selling piece of American literature in the pre–Civil War era.

Conflicts emanating from the immigrants' rejection of a package of reforms that were the substance of the program to Christianize America overlapped with and aggravated worries caused by the hold of Roman Catholicism on the mass of arrivals. Protestant efforts to curtail secular activities, including mail delivery, on Sundays and to discourage or prohibit the consumption of alcohol caused much irritation. The Sabbatarian and temperance movements had multiple, related sources of strength. These efforts responded to highly visible and symbolically important affronts to American Protestant morality and, at least in the case of temperance, to a real social problem. Popular neglect of the Sabbath underlined the decline both of religious enthusiasm and of the churches' coercive abilities following the loss of governmental support after the Revolution. Drinking suggested not only worldly pleasures but also alcoholism. The latter equation was not beyond reason: native-stock American drinkers favored hard liquor almost to the exclusion of beer and wine, and such a pattern of consumption is often associated with alcohol abuse. Sabbatarianism and temperance had their initial appeal among conservatives, who used these movements to attack real problems and to reassert the superiority of their values over the looser democratic mores of the early nineteenth century. Congregational and Presbyterian ministers from older Federalist communities, for example, founded the American Temperance Society, which in 1826 became the first national organization devoted to the issue. But Sabbatarianism and temperance quickly grew into broad-based movements. The revivalist ministers of the Second Great Awakening adopted these reforms and even extended temperance from a call to avoid hard liquor to a demand to abstain from all alcoholic beverages. And the advocates of reform adeptly enhanced the attractiveness of their message by arguing that high morals were more than their own reward; they were also the surest guarantee of worldly success.

With the coming of the immigrants, Sabbatarianism and temperance took on new dimensions. The most numerous foreign groups in the United States did not see these movements as reforms. Germans, whether Catholic or Protestant, looked upon Sunday as a time for social, as well as religious, functions, and they had no reservations about the moderate consumption of spirits. They, of course, brought with them skills that substantially advanced the art of brewing in America. Drinking was also well established in Gaelic culture, and in the desperate conditions of life on both sides of the Atlantic alcoholism had become a serious enough problem to bring forth an Irish temperance crusade led by the renowned Father Theobald Mathew. Thus, native-stock Americans viewed the immigrant cultures as alien to their own values and, most notably, as inimical to the American vision of Christian civilization.

By their adherence to Sabbatarianism and temperance, native-stock Protestants convinced themselves of their superiority to foreigners and they turned these movements into weapons to reinforce their dominant position. The native stock found in the Catholic identity of the Irish, the foreign group most reviled for its drinking habits, confirmation of the subversive role of the Roman church, but they also criticized Protestant immigrants for their behavior. Resorting to legislative action, as well as moral suasion, to convince the entire society to adopt their norms, the native-stock Protestants attempted to assert their political advantage over the newcomers. More important, the native Protestants, especially ones in marginal or economically declining positions, traded on their avowed morality in convincing employers to hire and promote them ahead of their numerous immigrant competitors.

No portion of the program to Christianize America caused more bitterness between the native stock and the immigrant than the public school movement. The common schools, as they were called, were perhaps the most noble and practical reform experiment of the first half of the nineteenth century. Their advocates expected to improve American democracy by bringing to the masses of people unable to afford private schooling the knowledge necessary for economic success and responsible political participation. Public school proponents also hoped to curb some of the disorder of American society by bringing discipline to those at the bottom of the social ladder. The supporters of public education were agreed that moral training should be a fundamental part of schooling, but they recognized that the multiplicity of religious allegiances found in the population doomed any effort to foster the beliefs of a single denomination. Therefore, they ordained that the schools attempt to inculcate only generally accepted moral standards and Christian tenets. Within the context of the basically homogeneous American society that the reformers had known since childhood and wanted to preserve, this arrangement was a liberal and advanced compromise. Within the framework of a nation experiencing rapid immigration, this approach became a weapon against the culture of the newcomers.

Catholic leaders, especially clergy, recognized that the public schools were not nondenominationally Christian but nondenominationally Protestant. All parts of the common school regimen were a point of controversy because they reflected the dominant Protestant milieu of the host community. Textbooks routinely presented history from a perspective that lauded Protestantism and defamed the Roman church. That difficulty might have been overcome. In New York City, the private corporation that administered the publicly supported schools offered to cooperate with Catholics to revise or remove offensive literature. Unfortunately, trust was at a minimum and the offer was minimal. The Catholic hierarchy wondered why the school leaders could not act unilaterally, expected that Protestants would soon reinsert new derogatory material, and feared implicitly endorsing whatever items they did not request deleted. Catholics also knew that removing objectionable books would not silence teachers who shared the disdain of average citizens for immigrants and routinely belittled the ethnic and religious heritages of their foreign pupils. Most important, the Catholics were aware that they had no hope of ending what they believed to be the worst abuse. Protestants considered Bible reading the linchpin of moral training in the schools, but Catholics saw this practice as a double threat. The schools' consistent use of the Protestant, King James Bible rejected the Roman church's position that the Douai translation was the only authoritative version. And the teachers' practice of reading Bible passages without comment, a tactic adopted as a means of avoiding sectarianism, endorsed Protestant doctrine in favor of private interpretation of Holy Writ and denied the Catholic church's claim to be the sole interpreter of the Scriptures. This latter point, of course, had been a central issue in the Reformation.

The Protestant-Catholic split over the public schools concerned policy more than philosophy. Neither party wanted a truly secular system; their differences revolved around the possibility of separating Christian moral training from sectarian indoctrination. The Protestant leaders of the common school movement believed that they had made the distinction; their critics disagreed. Most Catholic spokesmen, indeed, argued that separating morality and sectarian teaching was impossible without resorting to an unacceptable deistic rationalism. The only solution they saw was public support of schools whose outlook corresponded to the beliefs and values of the specific communities being served.

The lines of contention became clearest in a New York City struggle. In 1840 New York's Catholic bishop, John Hughes, asked the common council to allow parochial schools a share of the education funds, which were then given exclusively to the Public School Society, a private corporation led by Protestant philanthropists. Hughes claimed that the church institutions would be as nonsectarian as the common schools; they would employ Catholic teachers approved by the authorities to teach academic subjects in a manner inoffensive to Catholic sensitivities, but they would avoid religious instruction during regular hours. The Public School Society and Protestant spokesmen disagreed with the bishop, and the common council dismissed his petition. Hughes, however, had the support of Governor William Seward. Though a Whig, Seward did not share his party's aversion for immigrants and was sympathetic with the plight of the Irish. He hoped that the immigrants would fully share in American blessings and recognized that clerical disapproval of the common schools was keeping countless young Catholics from receiving an education. The governor urged the legislature to aid the parochial schools. The bishop, in turn, impressed city Democrats with the importance of the Catholic vote; ten Tammany candidates with his endorsement won election to the assembly in 1841; three without his support lost. In 1842 the assembly passed a bill that divided New York City's political wards into separate school districts with locally elected boards. The measure would have given Catholics control of schools in their neighborhoods, but the senate amended the law to prohibit explicitly sectarian instruction in the schools and to establish a central board of education to supervise the local districts. In the end, Hughes's victory was small. His old foes in the Public School Society lost their monopoly of education, but the newly formed elected board of education fell under control of Protestants who continued the old sectarian practices. The alienation of Catholics from the common schools intensified.

The tragic culmination of the immigrants' confrontation with the American reform movement came over the issue of slavery. Despite their disagreements with native-stock citizens on a host of issues, foreign Americans of the antebellum era shared certain fundamental attitudes with their hosts. The most notable of these involved slavery and race. Like the great majority of Americans resident in the northern states, the newcomers disliked slavery and opposed its expansion into the free western territories. They also were unwilling to risk the future of the Union in order to eradicate the institution in Dixie. Only a leaven of articulate, liberal political refugees, particularly among the small band of German Forty-eighters, endorsed abolition. Immigrants, like other white Americans, assumed that the Africans were inferior, and as the group most directly in competition with free black labor they grasped this belief all the more tightly. The foreign born shared the fetid urban living quarters of the blacks, vied with them for the unskilled jobs available in the eastern cities, and took advantage of their own light skins to oust Afro-Americans gradually from domestic and personal service occupations. Ironically, in asserting cultural and moral superiority over their competitors, the immigrants did unto the blacks what they were suffering themselves at the hands of the natives. The Irish, the most marginal of the newcomers, were probably the worst offenders. But immigrants of other nationalities who were in frequent contact with blacks also showed bias; indeed, members of the large German population in Texas went so far as to own slaves.

Immigrants fed their hostility to abolition on the awareness that it and nativism overlapped. It was only partly fortuitous that Harriet Beecher Stowe, the author of *Uncle Tom's Cabin*, was the daughter of the Reverend Lyman Beecher, whose sermons had helped incite a mob to burn the convent of the Ursuline nuns in Charlestown, Massachusetts, in August 1834. And, though regrettable, the Reverend Arthur Tappan's involvement with the production of Monk's *Awful Disclosures* was not entirely inconsistent with his role as a founder of the American and Foreign Antislavery Society. Abolition and the anti-Catholic agitation that polluted the natives' reception of the foreign born were integral parts of the general Protestant reform movement that distinguished the second third of the nineteenth century. The sense of civic responsibility and Christian perfectionism and the desire to reestablish social preeminence that combined in the Sabbatarian, temperance, and antipopery movements also infused abolitionism. Morally conscious Americans reasonably felt guilty for the existence of slavery, and the coming of the immigrants inflamed their sensibilities. The nation's willingness to accept benighted foreigners as voting citizens while denying American blacks, free as well as bound, basic rights highlighted the country's racism, and the newcomers' bestowal of their allegiance on the prosouthern Democratic party limited the prospect of ending slavery. The mutual antipathy of abolitionists and major foreign-born groups had unfortunate longlasting results. This situation shut off the possibility of the newcomers' receiving substantial assistance from the most progressive groups in the United States and helped create an attitudinal gulf that has constantly divided America's ethnic groups, particularly the urban Catholic ones, from the Protestant, middle-class reform tradition.

The antipathy between immigrant and native-stock Americans became one of the most disruptive forces in the United States in the 1840s and 1850s. In May 1844, three days of rioting in Kensington, an Irish, working-class suburb of Philadelphia, culminated in the burning of two churches, St. Michael's and St. Augustine's, and of other Catholic property. A network of cultural, economic, and social antagonisms underlay the clash of Irishmen and natives, but the immediate spark was the mistaken belief that Bishop Francis Kenrick was attempting to banish the Bible from the public schools. In fact, the bishop had simply sought and received permission for Catholic students to read their own version of the Scriptures in the classroom. When the threat of violence spread to New York, Bishop Hughes placed armed men around his churches and warned that the city would become a second Moscow if any of the edifices were attacked. Fortunately, cooler heads prevailed. Though undoubtedly the most dramatic, these were not the only instances of ethnic and religious violence in the era. The troubles reached another peak in the 1850s. An American tour in 1853 by a papal nuncio, Gaetano Bedini, who had been involved in the suppression of republican uprisings in Italy a few years earlier, inflamed the populace, and itinerant preachers like John S. Orr, "the Angel Gabriel," kept the fires of anti-Catholicism going. Of course, the problems associated with the massive influx of immigrants in these years immeasurably aggravated the situation. The result was the burning of a dozen Catholic churches, the desecration of many others, and physical attacks on priests and nuns.

Street battles were the most visible, but not the most important, part of the anti-immigrant struggle in antebellum America. Alone, such incidents were inchoate expressions of grievances. The heart of the movement, however, was political action that resembled older traditions of anti-immigrant maneuvering. Candidates from the nativist American Republican party won the municipal elections in New York City and Philadelphia in 1844; the highpoint of nativist political agitation came a decade later. By 1854 a well-organized American Republican party had emerged nationally from a coalition of local political groups in New York and other states. The Know-Nothings, as they were popularly called because of their refusal to divulge information about their ritualistic secret societies, won stunning victories that year and the next, sending seventy-five of their candidates to Congress and taking control of several state governments in the Northeast. The party also did well in the border states and even made inroads in the South. Know-Nothingism appealed to small businessmen and locally based professionals who considered themselves the cultural guardians of their communities. The movement attracted artisans and workers caught up in economic change and threatened by immigrant competitors. The

Know-Nothings, who presented themselves as foes of foreign influence, rather than as anti-Catholics, even won support among the old French settlers of Louisiana, whose position within the Roman church and the general society had been disturbed by the Irish influx. In short, the movement offered something to everyone shaken by the wave of recent immigration, and its appeal to an older, more stable America offered refuge to those dismayed by the other crises of the era.

As political leaders the Know-Nothings were failures. On the federal level they did not have the influence to enact their main programs. Had they been able, the Know-Nothings would have subjected future immigrants to a twenty-one-year waiting period before naturalization and barred them from political office. In state governments, they were an embarrassment. Know-Nothing legislators conducted unsuccessful searches for abominations in the convents of Massachusetts and then billed the public for the costs of their own roistering during the inspection tours. The American Republican party quickly faded, and in 1856 its candidate for the White House, former president Millard Fillmore, earned a paltry total of eight electoral votes. The decline of the Know-Nothings coincided with a steep drop in the volume of European immigration from a peak in 1854. The end of the Irish famine, the economic depression that began in the United States with the Panic of 1857, and the increasing political instability associated with American divisions over the issue of slavery made the Old World less desperate and the New less inviting. In 1861 only 81,000 Europeans reached American shores. The reduction alleviated the social strain in communities that had absorbed the brunt of the earlier influx and allowed the assimilation of the alien population to proceed without additional pressure.

As the fears and frustrations sparked by the preceding decade of mass immigration subsided, the even more serious issues of slavery and secession raced to the forefront of the public's consciousness. Regardless of their origins, the people of the United States were swept up in the Civil War. The available statistics on the composition of the opposing forces are incomplete and hard to evaluate, but they show clearly that the immigrants were overrepresented in the military forces of both the North and the South. The foreign born provided approximately 22 percent of the enlistments in the armies of the North, where they accounted for 18 percent of the population. They formed 5–10 percent of the forces in the South, where they constituted 4 percent of the white inhabitants. Overall, however, the Union, which was home to almost 95 percent of America's foreign born, has to be considered the prime beneficiary of the immigrants' military services.

In their individual decisions to join the military, the foreign born were responding to the same principles, emotions, community pressures, and interests that motivated their native-stock neighbors. The presence of sizable numbers of alien soldiers in the Confederate ranks vitiates specialized explanations that attribute Irish participation to hatred of England, which gave succor to the South, or that credit the Germans' involvement to a supposed detestation of slavery. For many aliens financial necessity was a powerful incentive to enlistment; the foreign born showed a strong inclination toward the military even before the opening salvos were fired at Fort Sumter. In the prewar era at least 50 percent and perhaps 60 percent of the enlisted men in the regular army were immigrants, usually from Ireland or Germany. For these soldiers, as for many marginal members of today's society, the military offered the guarantee of employment, food, lodging, and other care. The inducements expanded during the Civil War years. Union volunteers received bonuses and immigrants became naturalized immediately upon enlistment. After conscription began in the North in 1863, those who had not yet been called but who were willing to serve for a price could substitute for drafted men.

Perhaps the battlefield made brothers of newcomers and natives and won for the foreign born the respect of some of their erstwhile foes. But this idea can easily be exaggerated. Immigrants were among the most vociferous opponents of the war and some of their protests were so socially convulsive as to obliterate the goodwill generated by their countrymen's service. In New York the conscription into the Union army of several Irish members of the Black Joke Volunteer Fire Company sparked a series of riots that nearly tore the city apart in 1863. After learning that their names had been drawn on Saturday morning, July 11, the draftees plotted with friends to prevent the resumption of the process after the weekend and to destroy the records of their selection. On Monday morning a mob of men and women burned the draft office at Third Avenue and Forty-sixth Street and a half week of terror was under way. Rioters fought police and soldiers, invaded houses and stores, seized an armory, looted, and menaced both City Hall and Horace Greeley's *New York Tribune* building. Striking out at the war they disliked and at their traditional enemies, the participants saved their worst atrocities for the blacks whose slum neighborhoods they shared and whose competition for jobs they feared, especially in the wake of the Emancipation Proclamation. They drove 237 children from the Colored Orphan Asylum and burned the abolitionist sponsored institution to the ground, beat to death or lynched several adult blacks, and pummeled an undetermined number of other blacks. The disturbances subsided by Thursday night, but not until military units freshly returned from the battlefield at Gettysburg directed cannon fire at the crowd. Other places like Boston, Milwaukee, and the Pennsylvania coal mining district also experienced anticonscription insurrections, but New York's Draft Riots gained infamy as the bloodiest episode in American urban history. The official records directly tie 105 deaths to the affair, but this estimate remains conservative even with the addition of another score of related fatalities.

The Irish were flagrantly visible in the Draft Riots. Of the 184 persons of known nativity arrested, 117 were Irish. Their participation was more than enough to make the public forget that Irish policemen and soldiers had helped subdue the mob. For many this incident also outweighed the contributions of countless Irishmen serving in the Union army as members of primarily Irish regiments or of ethnically integrated units. Above all, the Draft Riots helped insure that although Know-Nothingism had died nativism would live on in American hearts.

Rioting in Its Jacksonian Setting

DAVID GRIMSTED

From the Stamp Act revolts of 1765 to the ghetto uprisings of the 1960s, mob violence has been a powerful influence in American history. Although the specific intent of the mobs has varied, the process by which they form has tended to be much the same, and the uprisings have generally had certain characteristics in common.

First, mobs rarely see the purpose of their action as illegal, although on occasion they see it as supralegal—that is, as carrying the enforcement of the law beyond its stated limits. A lynch mob, for example, may be unwilling to wait for or to trust the court system to reach what they consider a just verdict; thus, the mob may see itself as the executor of proper justice. Similarly, the vigilante groups that administered dubious justice in the old West joined together in posses allegedly to enforce the law.

Generally, mobs tend to rally around some real or imagined grievance that they believe the recognized authorities will not deal with properly. This is especially apt to be the situation when the ultimate authorities are far away or unsympathetic to local conditions, as in colonial America, the old West, or the pre–Civil War South; when authorities are nearby and repressive, as in urban ghettoes; or when local authorities side with citizen groups in opposition to higher authorities, as in colonial America or the South during the school desegregation crisis of the late 1950s and early 1960s.

Mob action is rarely directed against the idea of authority or order; rather, it is against some particular condition that the authority has either caused or allowed to exist. Studies of mob action in Europe in the eighteenth and nineteenth centuries, as well as studies of more recent riots in the United States, have shown that the targets of mob violence are limited and selective. This has been the case in the twentieth-century ghetto revolts in northern cities, for instance, in which attacks have been primarily on property and few deaths have occurred at the hands of the rioters.

In the article that follows, David Grimsted (University of Maryland) discusses rioting during the Jacksonian era, when democratic ideas were in ferment and the nation was struggling to find the proper balance between individual freedom and the requirements of social order. The riots studied here do not fit neatly into the paradigm just mentioned, because the government on all levels was testing the nature and limits of its authority and was reluctant to use excessive force against the citizens who were expressing their grievances, particularly when the victims of mobs were weak or unpopular.

A mericans have always been a beneviolent people." As the Romantics argued the kinship of madness and genius, so it is difficult clearly to segregate student inspiration from imbecility. And if not the student who wrote the comment in that eternal source of peculiar wisdom, last year's exam books, perhaps Providence acting through the student spoke suggestively, especially considering the root of the word: if *bene-volo* means to will good, "beneviolent" would suggest the willing of good in notably vigorous form. And here perhaps lies a clue to some of the paradoxes of both the origin and significance of social violence in its American contexts.

Social violence has obvious roots in both the psychology of its participants and their socioeconomic situation, and analysts of crowd behavior understandably have concentrated their examinations around such causes. Yet the extent, nature, and direction of mob violence depend equally on shared cultural assumptions about the nature of power and law, and the relation of the individual and the group to them. For the Jacksonian period, the diversity of type and circumstance of riot offers

RIOTING IN ITS JACKSONIAN SETTING   By David Grimsted, in *American Historical Review*, Volume 77 (April 1972), 361–97. Reprinted by permission of the author.
An earlier version of this paper was read at the joint session of the American Studies Association and the Southern Historical Association at the annual meeting of the Southern Historical Association, November 13, 1970, in Louisville. This study has been supported in part by fellowships from the National Endowment for the Humanities and the Charles Warren Center for Studies in American History and summer grants from the Social Science Research Council, the American Council of Learned Societies, and the University of Maryland.

presumptive evidence that social violence owed less to local and particular grievances than to widely held assumptions and attitudes about the relation of the individual to social control. Only a cause that was "general in its operation," wrote a Baltimore newspaper, could explain the variously directed outbursts of social violence in the mid-1830s.

Historians of eighteenth-century America have shown that mobs in that period functioned more as an accepted part of the political structure than an attack on it, largely because authorities unofficially recognized their legitimacy so long as they acted within certain bounds. This reflected in part English preference for granting the lower classes occasional informal sway to giving them any established influence on government and in part colonial willingness to use the mob to make imperial authorities heed local interests. With the achievement of independence both of these justifications of the mob were undercut. Power was no longer imperially centered, nor were there large groups of white males denied a measure of political influence through established channels. Royall Tyler's play, *The Contrast*, written partly as a Federalist political document in 1787, marked the change clearly. Tyler, who had been active in putting down Shays's Rebellion, has his likably naive American democrat, Jonathan, admit that he was talked out of siding with Shays only by the natural aristocrat, Colonel Manly, who explained to him, "It was a burning shame for the true blue Bunker Hill sons of liberty, who had fought Governor Hutchinson, Lord North, and the Devil to have any hand in kicking up a cursed dust against the government which we had, every mother's son of us, a hand in making." The strong though unvindictive action of the authorities toward Shays's and Fries's and the Whisky rebellions—even the fact that these incidents were labeled "rebellions"—made clear that the eighteenth-century role of the riotous crowd had ended.

The United States in the first quarter of the nineteenth century was relatively free of internal group violence, but in the 1830s riot once again became frequent. Between 1828 and 1833 there were some twenty incidents of riot, in 1834 at least sixteen riots took place, and in 1835 the number increased to thirty-seven, most of them concentrated in the summer and fall of that year. The Philadelphia *National Gazette* echoed the sentiments of many when it wrote in August 1835, "The horrible fact is staring us in the face, that, whenever the fury or the cupidity of the mob is excited, they can gratify their lawless appetites almost with impunity; and it is wonderful with all the evidence of the facts that have been furnished in such abundance, to behold the degree of supineness that exists." Never again in the antebellum period was rioting this concentrated, but it remained a regular social phenomenon to be accepted with a degree of "supineness." Some of these incidents were in result minor—for example, the anti-Garrison mob, which resulted in one torn coat and one broken sign—but property damage was often extensive, and numerous lives were lost. By 1835 at least 61 people had been killed in riot; by 1840 that figure goes above 125, and the worst destructiveness was yet to come. Certainly over one thousand people were killed in antebellum riots, and the draft riots of 1863 added probably another thousand to that roll. Even when the riots were comparatively undestructive, they revealed major tensions in the society; ethnic hatreds; religious animosities; class tensions; racial prejudice; economic grievances; moral fears over drinking, gaming, and prostitution; political struggles; the albatross of slavery.

That these incidents had been largely forgotten until the last few years tells us something, as current violence experts have said, about the way Americans have accentuated the positive in their past. More important, it reflects the way in which American democracy has been able to absorb quantities of violence in its structure without fundamentally shaking it. Historians have neglected the topic in large part because people so quickly forgot about the incidents. At times between 1834 and 1837 there was in some men's minds a sense of real possibility of social disintegration, but even during these years there was always a quick return to placidity after the outbreaks. And as resort to violence proved not a steadily spreading disease but a kind of periodic social virus, unpleasant perhaps but also unthreatening to the social organism, fearful responses became shorter and more ritualistic. For a day or two after a riot some papers explored the specific situation and the general problem; a week later, unless a trial or coroner's inquest reawoke interest, it would be publicly forgotten. Riot had regained its eighteenth-century status as a frequent and tacitly accepted if not approved mode of behavior.

Acquiescence in riot owed much to the fact that rioting was not basically an attack on the social system itself. Francis Grund, the Jacksonian publicist, wrote that lynch law, a term often used interchangeably with riot in these years, "is not properly speaking an opposition to the established laws of the country . . . , but rather . . . a supplement to them—as a species of *common law*." A working definition of riot would be those incidents where a number of people group together to enforce their will immediately, by threatening or perpetrating injury to people or property outside of legal procedures but without intending to challenge the general structure of society. Such a definition, in its psychological and social basis, distinguishes riot in a rough way from revolutionary violence, which aims at the destruction of the existing political structure; or insurrection, the uprising of people essentially excluded from political participation; or group criminality, where people act in defiance rather than alleged support of accepted communal standards; or acts of civil disobedience, which involve lawbreaking to dramatize a cause but without threatening injury or destruction; or acts of disruption or symbolic violence such as burning in effigy where no real threat is involved. Such a definition of riot would include some types of social violence—like lynchings or vigilance committees in areas where there were existing legal structures—often given other labels. Here, aside from some very quasi-judicial procedure, the main difference from riot was the unusual inactivity of the constituted power.

Defenders of specific riots in the period talked of the action not as revolution or even illegality but as an enforcement of justice within the bonds of society—an immediate redressing of moral wrongs or a removal of social dangers that for various reasons could not be handled by ordinary legal process. Justifications of riots and vigilance committees often invoked the precedents of 1776 in their defense, but such invocations invariably implied no intention to destroy society, suggesting instead that existing society entailed the right of popular correction of social abuses in instances when the legal system was unable or unwilling to act. In the United States the "right of revolution" justified not overthrowing the government but considerable group violence within its structure.

Observers realized that the traditional justifications of riot in colonial America or in Europe were absent, and they puzzled over explanations of why rioting re-established itself in the United States. In pondering the "disorganizing, anarchical spirit" of 1835, the editor of the Boston *Evening Journal* claimed, "There are strong reasons why the laws should be implicitly obeyed in this country for they are but the echo of public opinion. . . . Our laws are not made as in many countries abroad, by the few for the suppression of the many, but by the many for the advantage of the whole." Governor James F. Thomas of Maryland put the case most succinctly:

> In governments not formed in the principles of republicanism . . .
> these popular commotions may sometimes be palliated or excused.
> . . . But in a country like ours where the people are acknowledged
> to be supreme, and are in fact in the constant practical exercise of
> absolute sovereignty there can be no apology, there is no extenuation or excuse for such commotions, and their occurrence stains
> the character of the government and wounds deeply the cause of
> equal government.

The irony in these observations was that the reason for denying the old justification of riot—the institutionally clear power of the individual to influence the state—had become central to the new. The ideological tenets and political emotions of the age of Jackson, focusing on the centrality and sovereignty of the individual, both encouraged riotous response to certain situations and made it difficult to put riot down when it broke out. Jacksonian political notions were in no sense new, but the intensity, the immediacy, indeed the simplicity with which they were held gave them a fresh cast and social significance.

American political theory had long stressed the centrality in the social structure of the individual rather than the state: here the state was to have little power, no more than was needed to safeguard, or if broadly construed, to promote the individual's pursuit of happiness and search for fulfillment. Authority was subdivided among federal, state, and local groups; it was checked and balanced on each level and bound by constitutional, natural, and democratic controls to prevent tyranny over the individual. "In contrast to Europe, where society is everything and the individual nothing, and where society crushes without pity all who stand in its way," wrote one of the ablest defenders of early vigilante groups, "in America the individual is all and society nothing. There an admirable system of laws protects the feeble, the poor, the accused; there especially is the jury favorable to the defense; and finally, there all aspects of the law are subordinated to individual right, which is the basis and essence of the republic." Democratic government was not only to reflect the will of the people but also was not to interfere with the proper private will of the individual.

Historians have generally seen the Jacksonian period as marking the fruition of the nation's democracy—a notion upheld even as the evidence mounts that most of the legal changes toward democracy occurred earlier and that the major techniques of the second party system had been prefigured in the first. The answer may lie in seeing democracy less as a legal and technical system than as a psychological construct: Everyman's sense of his equality of right to participate and of his ability to decide. Democracy in this psychological sense reaffirms the importance of Jackson on the political scene: his lack of formal education, his intuitive strength, his belief that anyone had the ability to handle government jobs, his transformation of the presidency from that of guide for the people to a personalized representative of the Democracy, all helped create a sense of power justly residing in the hands of each man rather than in the state and a sense of the need for democratic citizens to pursue the right comparatively free from mere procedural trammels and from deference to their social and intellectual betters.

Andrew Jackson himself deplored the rioting that accelerated during his second administration. In at least three instances he sent federal troops to quell riots, and at the height of rioting in 1835 he wrote Amos Kendall, "This spirit of mob-law is becoming too common and must be checked or, ere long, it will become as great an evil as servile war, and the innocent will be much exposed." Yet in this same letter he showed his willingness to circumvent laws that he thought were protecting the guilty. He approved of Kendall's decision to let postmasters withhold abolitionist literature from the mail if they chose on the grounds that, in Kendall's words, citizens owed "an obligation to the laws but a higher one to the communities in which we live." Jackson thought Kendall had perhaps not gone far enough and suggested that postmasters be ordered to deliver abolitionist mail only at the receiver's request and that the names of all those accepting the material be published to "put them in coventry." Jackson's personality and actions rather than his ideas made him seem, more than any other American political figure, the anarchic hero, a man who when he decided something went ahead untouched by popular clamor in favor of the national bank, or judicial decisions supporting the Cherokees, or mere legal technicalities regarding bank deposits. The Whigs felt real fear at the implications of King Andrew's highhandedness, but their attempts to make political capital out of it foundered on popular acceptance of Jackson's own sense of his role: that he was the disinterested spokesman of the people and the Democracy and as such his actions could not abridge but only perfect democratic procedure.

Jackson fitted perfectly the popular American image of the man who need not follow accepted procedures because of the rectitude of his own character, which insured proper action in a world neatly segregated between the innocent and the guilty, the righteous and the monstrous. Jackson's popularity was rooted in his embodiment of the deepest American political myth: that man standing above the law was to be not a threat to society but its fulfillment. "Trust thyself. Every heart vibrates to that iron string," wrote Emerson in his exhortation to his countrymen to be truly self-reliant and hence to become truly representative men. And James Fenimore Cooper, intending to write a story glorifying the ways of his patrician father, created a subsidiary character who stole the novel and the affections of American and world readers. Natty Bumppo came into being as the representative of natural justice in contrast to the legal justice of the good Judge Temple, and Cooper intended to preach of the sad need for the latter to prevail. But the author himself, much less his democratic audience, had small enthusiasm for the formal dogma that Natty ought to be punished for illegally shooting a deer in a community where the respectable citizens killed maple trees for sugar and slaughtered passenger pigeons and fish for fun—legally, of course. And after Natty comes Henry David Thoreau and Huck Finn and William S. Hart and Gary Cooper and Humphrey Bogart and John Wayne and the Hemingway heroes—all men whose stature comes from their standing outside of society and the law in order to live by an individual code, which peculiarly does not threaten the social good but offers its best protection. "Self-interest rightly understood" was the term Americans used to suggest that there was no disjunction between individualism and social responsibility but rather perfect union, Alexis de Tocqueville reported—with great skepticism about how well this worked in fact.

The anarchistic implications of these tenets of Jacksonian democracy influenced but never seriously undermined that social force which most affected the lives of citizens, the legal system. Foreign observers agreed that the United States in the 1830s and 1840s was characterized less by anarchy than by a strong conformity to accepted standards and a general adherence to laws with little external pressure. Yet there were paradoxes here too: in the willingness of Americans to disregard law on particular occasions with no sense of striking at society itself, their frequent scorn of the legal process to which they had such frequent recourse, and their vehement dislike for lawyers, the "necessary evil" to which the populace nevertheless consistently gave political power.

Richard Rush wrote in 1815 that "here law is everything," and he explained that this was so because of "an alliance between an active and restless spirit of freedom and the comfortable conditions of all classes." This contentious sense of liberty and the widespread ownership and transfer of property described by Rush have generally been seen as the main impetus to law in American society. But these essentially stand as symbols for a larger truth: that as people move from a traditional society their relations must be controlled less by inherited patterns and more by formalized law. Roscoe Pound's seeing the origin of law in "codified tradition" is clearly correct, but equally important is the fact that it need be codified only when or in those areas where tradition itself is no longer strong enough to hold sway in disputes. In the United States both abundant resources and democratic traditions allowed the benefits of the new bourgeois order to be widely shared, and it also served, as did the nation's conglomerate population, to disintegrate traditional mores quickly. Tocqueville's study of the United States revealed to him essentially how democracy tended to destroy the traditional trammels, or human bonds, of aristocracy—the historical family, the permanent community, the established church, the inherited profession and social class—both to free man and to isolate him. Man in America, except for the network of voluntary associations with which he protected himself and the mass in general with which he identified, was man alone. Because of the identification with the mass, public opinion was an effective police force ensuring general compliance with accepted standards. But in subtler and especially commercial areas of human dealing, there were neither accepted familial, communal, religious, nor traditional authorities to settle disputes. A bourgeois society, as America fairly was by 1830, must elevate law both because of what it is creating and what it has to destroy.

Americans knew they needed law and even in frontier areas tended quickly to set up legal systems and generally to respect them. The *Spirit of the Times* reported, "One of the first wants of our new settlements is a regular administration of justice, for the privilege of litigation, so far as being considered, as a witty writer has termed it, an expensive luxury, is by our free and enlightened citizens regarded as one of the prime necessaries of life." Chaotic or ridiculous instances occurred in frontier law, but these were the exceptions rather than the rule and were cherished in American folklore and memory because they corroborated the illusion of freedom from oppressive technicalities. The heavy dependence of Americans on law stimulated a need to remember circumventions of it because the very use of the system denied the personal independence that was the American ideal.

Covert public dislike for the legal system commonly took the form of scorn of lawyers, the intellectual elite upon whom litigious Americans depended most directly. Timothy Walker's defense of the profession in his *Introduction to American Law,* long a textbook in American law schools, canvassed the common charges against lawyers. People complained of the undue complexity of the law, but Walker professionally exulted in it. "Whatever . . . may be my feelings as a man and as a citizen, as a lawyer, I am bound to rejoice in those difficulties which render our profession so arduous, so exclusive, so indispensable." Walker added "respectable" to his list of traits resulting from legal technicality, but he might better have included "profitable." The lawyer's function, Walker continued, was "to vindicate rights and redress wrongs," but in the next sentence he added, "The guilty and the innocent, the upright and the dishonest, the wronging and the wronged, the knave and the dupe, alike consult him, and with the same unreserved confidence." That guilty, dishonest, wronging knaves could place "unreserved confidence" in lawyers might for some confirm the idea that the profession delighted in chicanery and hired "out their conscience as well as their skill, to any client who will pay the fee." Of those charges, Walker told young law students, "I, for one, am willing to admit their truth to some extent. . . . We also take refuge behind the principle that supply corresponds to demand. If there were no dishonest or knavish clients there would be no dishonest or knavish lawyers. Our profession, therefore, does but adapt itself to the community." This adaptability, the moral ambiguity and sophistry, the seemingly purposeless complexity, the expensiveness charged to lawyers were all in truth a part of the legal system they represented. The attempts of legislators to make every man his own lawyer were as telling of social desires as they were futile.

Vice Unmasked, a book written in 1830 by P. W. Grayson, presents most coherently the intellectual structure of uneasiness with the law that ran through Jacksonian life. Little is known about Grayson except what he himself reveals in the book: that his criticism of lawyers is knowledgeable, he himself having been one before he repented. When the book was published, Grayson apparently had connections with the New York Workingmen's party; George Henry Evans published his book, and the *Working Man's Advocate* advertised it and reprinted a review of it from the *Daily Sentinel,* which judged *Vice Unmasked* an important study if "a little enthusiastic perhaps."

Grayson was unenthusiastic about law because he considered it the greatest obstacle to the realization of the promise of American life. That promise for Grayson, as for many Americans, had been to free man's potential by lifting from him the weight of the superstitions and repressive institutions of the past. The American government was the beginning of improvement, but progress was still slight, as the injustices and inequalities and unhappiness of America amply showed. What had gone wrong? Grayson's answer was simple: the United States had ended repressive government but had left untouched a legal system that impeded man's freedom and hence tarnished his natural integrity. Grayson fervently summarized the complaints against lawyers: they were a class of men who had a vested interest in fomenting and prolonging disputes; who were essentially social prostitutes willing to take any position that the highest bidder for their talents desired; who eschewed any concern for pursuing truth in order to pursue their client's interest; and who exulted in the complexities of their profession because these prevented honest men from acting in their own interests. Yet Grayson's prime target was not lawyers but the system that encouraged their moral degradation. The law itself was a jumble of old formulas inherited from feudal times, rarely suited to modern instances, and always more helpful in telling the cunning man how much he could get away with than in setting positive standards of human conduct. And whatever was done to improve it only changed its façade; one passed bankruptcy laws to protect the poor debtor, but the speculative stockjobber made use of them to defraud his honest creditors. Weaving together Thomas Paine's and a transcendental vision of man's potential, Grayson centered his indictment on the effects of law on the "moral essence of man," the way it debased man's sense of self and social responsibility by turning him from his high moral potential to a tricksy tailoring of conduct to avoid legal prosecution. In short, law was generally a tool of the cleverly vicious, a snare for the simply virtuous, and a burden on everyone, crippling human decency and progress.

Practically, Americans were not about to accept Grayson's program that law should deal only with instances of gross physical attack and in all other areas let man "seek, by the light of his own conscience, in the joyous genial climate of his own free spirit, for all the rules of his conduct." But Grayson's thinking paralleled that of many other Jacksonians. Indeed his major premise was perfectly correct: from a tough-minded point of view, law, as Oliver Wendell Holmes, Jr. argued later on, has much less to do with man's highest responsibilities than it does with telling bad men just how much they can get away with; in any legal system decisions must be based as much on technical requirements as on the unfettered pursuit of justice. "Law and right," wrote John Quincy Adams, "we know but too well by the experience of mankind, in all ages, including our own, are not convertible terms." Such was the paradox of legal development: the desire to be free from individual power and whim impelled rational man to set up a judicial structure that inevitably impeded almost as much as it promoted perfect justice. And so mankind's favorite myths of justice once again enthroned personal wisdom: the judgment of Solomon, Louis IX under the oaks, Cervantes' Sancho Panza, and any number of wise men ensuring the triumph of right in fairy tales or melodramas.

Both popular animus to the law and its importance in the lives of citizens helped to make the Jacksonian period, in Pound's phrase, "the formative era" of American law. The militant majoritarianism of Jacksonian rhetoric also spurred the efforts of conservatives to strengthen what seemed to be the only brake on untrammeled popular will. Francis Bowen wrote, "Here, nothing stands between the individual citizen and *his* sovereign—the majority of the people—but the majesty of the law and the independence of the courts." Conservatives like Joseph Story, Lemuel Shaw, Timothy Walker, and a host of lesser figures were so successful in increasing legal learning, dignity, and responsiveness to social needs that legal antipathy was never able to become programmatic. Even the codification issue, which drew on many of Grayson's ideas in "practical" form, was neutralized by conservative judicial skill and flexibility. Such efforts ensured that Jacksonian America became increasingly a government of laws not men, but democratic man was not entirely happy about it.

Within the legal structure, popular wariness about law appeared in the leniency with which juries tended to view offenders for whose crimes there were extenuating circumstances. Such legal actions, if technically irregular, often provided a kind of rough equity that the law could not formally incorporate. For instance, a St. Louis jury acquitted an actress who had stabbed her faithless lover to death in the theater one night. The argument that the man had a bad heart that might have given way before the knife got there was something of a blow to technical justice, but who knows if eternal justice would have been better served by a conviction? And one sympathizes with the California judge who concluded his charge to a jury: "Well, gentlemen, that's the law, but I don't really think it's God Almighty's justice, and I guess you may just as well find for the defendant." Democratic man admitted that a legal system was needed, but he had an active responsibility to see that it did not contradict the will of God Almighty, as interpreted by himself, of course.

This refusal to accept the sanctity of the law had its most disruptive manifestations in the long series of riots in the Jacksonian period. These were very diverse in origin and goal, but patterns do emerge about the structure of rioting, its social and psychological results, the type of person who rioted, and the problems of riot control in the period. A consideration of two incidents and of an ethnic category of riot suggests something of the nature of social violence in Jacksonian America and its implications for riot theory in general. The Bank Riot in Baltimore and the Snow Riot in Washington, D.C., took place within a week of each other in early August 1835. The Baltimore riot was highly unusual in that the mob attacked their social and economic superiors; partly for this reason information on it is unusually abundant. The Washington riot is more typical both in its direction and in the sketchiness of the material available on it. Together the two constitute an introduction to Jacksonian social violence.

Both riots took place in a climate of national near-hysteria. Instances of riot and lynching around the country filled the Baltimore and Washington newspapers throughout July and August. The same day that major rioting broke out in Baltimore, its leading periodical, *Niles' Register,* began with "a great mass of curious and important matter" showing that "the state of society is awful. Brute force has superseded the law, at many places, and violence become the 'order of the day.' The time predicted seems rapidly approaching when the mob shall rule." Niles blamed both lawless mobs and "fanatics who . . . have set their presses at work to spread desolation and death through the whole south" for the trouble. The most obvious precipitant of these "various excitements" was the growing effectiveness of abolition organization in the North and the sending of abolitionist literature southward. The South responded with fear and fury, claiming that these movements would create slave insurrection. The South threatened economic boycott against the North, and Northern commercial centers responded with huge public meetings condemning abolitionism and declaring that the North had no proper business even discussing slavery. Such declarations of sentiment failed to satisfy the South, which demanded "works" not "words"— specifically laws prohibiting the discussion of slavery and legal or illegal action to silence those promoting abolition. Laws curtailing freedom of speech or mobs seemed the only possible response to appease extreme Southern feeling.

The political situation of the nation further heated these passions. Martin Van Buren, running for the presidency as Jackson's chosen successor, was politically vulnerable in the South, while the leading opposition candidate, Jacksonian renegade Hugh Lawson White of Tennessee, had great strength there among both Jacksonians and Whigs. Since the South promised to be the central battleground for supremacy, the Whig and Democrat partisan press competed in rabid attacks upon the abolitionists. In many instances the press and leading politicians promoted proslavery mob action; more commonly they condoned them with open expressions of approval or quiet toleration. No Baltimore or Washington newspaper directly encouraged these particular riots, but even nonpartisan papers edited by men deeply disturbed by riot tended to print without comment incidents of proslavery violence or to deplore them while laying major blame on "those unprincipled incendiaries," the abolitionists who were their victims. Well over half of the riots in July and August of 1835 had no immediate connection with abolition, but they all sprang from a social climate with an extraordinary tolerance for riot. Circumstances allowed only a very few newspapers or public figures to take a strong stand against the best known of popular outbursts.

The Baltimore riot was an attack on those connected with the failure to settle the affairs of the Bank of Maryland, which had ceased operation almost a year and a half earlier. "Considerable numbers of people, 'good, bad, and indifferent' " congregated in Monument Square during the clear and pleasantly cool evenings between August 5 and 7. The general topic of conversation was the action of the trustees and the "secret partners" of the bank, and the mood was one of frustration and anger at the prolonged legal obstacles to settlement. On Friday afternoon Mayor Jesse Hunt called a public meeting, which pledged itself to keep the peace and try to discover the source of the inflammatory handbills posted on walls, but which also requested that the bank's books be immediately opened for public investigation. A crowd of ten thousand gathered on Friday night, but, aside from minor rock throwing, the peace was kept. On Saturday the trustees announced that the bank's books were impounded by the Harford County Court, and the mayor organized a citizens' guard armed with two-foot long poplar sticks. That evening the guard managed to keep the mob from their main objective, the home of the leading "partner," Reverdy Johnson, but were unable to prevent the sacking of the house of another "partner." When the crowd bombarded the guard with stones and brickbats and wounded several guards seriously, some of the guard's leaders demanded the right to use guns, and the mayor reluctantly consented. At least five people were killed, and some ten or twenty were wounded by shooting. Sunday morning the mayor announced that the firing had been done "against my will and advice," and the leaders of the citizens' guard decided that prudence dictated leaving town. The mob was left unopposed. That evening and night hundreds systematically sacked and damaged the homes of the mayor and of four men connected with the bank and did minor damage to property of certain leaders of the citizens' guard, while thousands watched. At about noon Monday, eighty-three-year-old Samuel Smith drove through the streets in a carriage flying an American flag to a large meeting where he effectively organized the citizens into an armed force to handle any further troubles. The destruction, which was still going on, immediately ceased, and the citizen patrols that guarded the city for well over a week met no opposition.

Federal troops were dispatched to Fort McHenry near Baltimore shortly after Smith and his fellow citizens had the situation under control, but most troops were quickly withdrawn to Washington, D.C., to overawe a riot that flourished between August 12 and 14 and sputtered on for several days thereafter. This riot resulted primarily in an attack on the property of free blacks. The mob congregated on Tuesday when it became known that abolitionist literature had been found in a trunk owned by Reuben Crandall, who was staying in Georgetown and was the brother of Prudence Crandall, already well known as a victim of riot when she had attempted to teach black girls in her school in Canterbury, Connecticut. Crandall was quickly arrested and arraigned in jail to prevent his falling into the hands of the mob, who then turned their attention to a restaurant, the Epicurean House, which was run by a mulatto, Beverly Snow. Before the mob arrived, Snow had wisely disappeared; after a fruitless search for antislavery writings, and some more successful drinking, the mob left. The next day they returned to "get Snow," but again he escaped. A search of the homes of other free Negroes resulted in finding some abolition newspapers in the house of James Hutton, who was hustled to jail to protect him from the mob. The crowd, after staging a public meeting the proceedings of which no newspaper reported, returned to Snow's to destroy his property, "not forgetting to crack a bottle of hock, 'now and then.' " That night, and intermittently during the next week, the crowd burned or stoned several black-owned buildings.

Such is the skeletal history of the two events. A closer examination of these two riots shows much not only about their own structure but about the nature of rioting in the Jacksonian period. The central question, of course, concerns what motivates riot. Seventy-five years ago Gustave Le Bon began the sociological study of crowd behavior with a discussion that can hardly be taken seriously today but that still informs much thinking about the problem. Man acting singly, Le Bon argued, acts rationally, but acting in groups—he lumps together such things as parliamentary bodies and riotous mobs—they revert to instinctual behavior; "bestial," "primitive," "childlike," "feminine" were Le Bon's favorite adjectives for it. Le Bon's explanatory devices are largely funny; the most irrational of crowds, Latin ones, he tells us, are so because they are "the most feminine of all." Yet his ideas have remained provocative because behavior within mobs suggests disruption more than continuity in the character of the participants, and aspects of his description are still convincing, particularly his emphasis on the emotive volatility, psychological release and anonymity, and the sense of total and totally justified power that comes from being part of a riotous crowd.

Sociologists have long raised questions about Le Bon's arguments, especially his emphasis on the irrationality of crowd behavior. Historians, particularly Eric Hobsbawm and George Rudé, first directly attacked the irrationality hypothesis in regard to riotous violence and suggested that rioters tend to act not irrationally but in ways made understandable by their social situation and related integrally to their social needs and desires. Certainly Rudé and Hobsbawm win the argument if rationality means simply an understandable response to a social situation that made people discontented. Such a criterion, however, excludes irrationality by definition, for no action can be wholly unrelated to man's unhappiness stemming from objective social experience; the lunatic who thinks he is Napoleon obviously does so because this illusion fulfills certain needs caused by real deprivations and traumas in his social history.

Jacksonian riots do not readily fall into categories of either "irrational" or "socially purposive" behavior. The mobs in Baltimore and Washington were not particularly wanton or vicious. In both cases the action taken was sensibly directed toward the social source of riotous anger—the financial manipulations of some rich men in one case and the pretensions to social dignity of blacks in the other. The Baltimore mob was particularly fastidious. They refused to sack houses of intended victims when they were informed that they were still officially owned by the contractor or were the property of the would-be victim's mother; they put out fires in houses that they were busy demolishing so adjoining property would not be endangered; they reprimanded some people for stealing rather than destroying property; and they voted by a slim majority not to burn a lumber yard because it threatened an adjacent one. (The minority had argued that it could be safely burned if the fire trucks were called out to keep the flames in bounds.) Their chief victims were rationally chosen: four men—Reverdy Johnson, John Glenn, Evan T. Ellicott, and Hugh McElderry—who had been "secret partners" in the Bank of Maryland and who had avoided settlement of the bank's affairs through legal prosecution of its former president and his relatives; John B. Morris, one of the trustees of the bank since its failure, who had steadily supported the nonsettlement policy; and Mayor Hunt, who was blamed for the firing into the crowd on Saturday. None was guilty of indictable offenses, and Hunt and Morris had not obviously profited from the situation, although the latter had lent himself to the delay and to the publication of a very inaccurate report of the bank's situation under the influence of his legal counsel, Reverdy Johnson. This unconscionable postponement worked a great hardship on the unusual number of people of modest means—"widows and orphans, small dealers and thrifty persons, mechanics and others"—who were the bank's creditors, while its debtors, including the partners, profiteered shamelessly. Given the complexity of the affairs of the Bank of Maryland, and judging by the mob's choice of victims, the Baltimore mob was not only rational but financially astute. Less is known about the specific mob actions in Washington, but there is evidence of similar restraint and selectivity. When told that the building and many of the furnishings of Snow's restaurant were actually owned by others, the mob confined itself to destroying the sign and a few things of minor value. And the property they attacked—black businesses, schools, churches, and homes—were those things most contributive to the free Negroes' sense of status and dignity, however tenuous, in the community.

Yet are selectivity and aspects of moderation incompatible with the idea that a riotous crowd unleashes elements of emotion that in important ways distort reality and allow individuals to act in a manner at variance with their usual behavior? The ablest defender of the Baltimore mob stressed its restraint and the justice of its social position: "fraud produced violence," and the people "operated upon the republican maxim 'resistance to tyrants is obedience to God.' " But he also stressed the emotive quality of the crowd situation. When the mob in Monument Square became active "every countenance was flushed with the spirit of destruction—reason had thrown down the reins and ungovernable fury had taken them up," and the retreat of the city guard led to Sunday's "anarchical desolation and mournful paralysis of reason." The handbills, which were sent through the mails and posted on the walls of Baltimore during the week preceding the riot, reveal this tying of highly irrational emotionalism to very real grievances:

> Arm! Arm! . . .—my Countrymen—Citizens of this Republic, and of this City, will you suffer your firesides to be molested—will you suffer your beds to be poluted—will you suffer your pockets to be riffled and your wives and children beggared. . . . Then arouse, and rally around the free and unbiass'd judge Lynch who will be placed upon the seat of justice and the people enmasse will be the members of the Bar, and these lions of the law shall be made to know that the people will rise in their majesty and redress their own grievances. . . . Have not the whole Bar and the judges linked in a combination together, and brow-beaten these very people out of their just rights, with a full determination to swindle and rob the industrious and poor part of the community out of their hard earnings. . . . Designing lawyers and lazy greedy peculators. . . , these smiling villains nearly all of them are building palaces and riding in their carriages with the very money taken from the poor laborer, orphans and honest hard working mechanics. . . . Want staring your poor heart broken wives in the face—your little children clinging around their mother, crying mother, mother a piece of bread—I say mother bread—O! mother give me some bread,— while these protected villains are roling in luxury and ease, laughing to scorn the people they have just robbed. These very villains stroll the streets with a bold and impudent assurance and pass for honest men—not satisfied with robbing you of your money, but treat you as Vassals to their noble lordships—to gratify their Venery desires hire pimps and procuresses to go polute your wives and prostitute your daughters—Gracious God!—is this our fair famed Baltimore—is our moral city come to this. . . . We have a remedy, my fellow citizens—Judge Lynch will be notified that he is at our head, and will take his place upon the bench—his maxims are Virtue, honesty, and good decent behavior—his remedies are simple, Tar and Feathers, effigys, gallowses and extermination from our much injured city—the victims that fall under this new law, I hope will be Johnson, Morris, Glenn, McElderry, Freeman and that dirty fellow Bossier etc., etc., etc.—
>   Let the warhoop be given . . . Liberty, Equality, Justice or Death!!!

Here a generalized social fury melted justified anger and real economic hardship into an amalgam of major democratic grievances and fears:

resentment at the deviousness and elitism of the law, a hatred of the powerful, the pretentious, the learned, the rich; uncertainties about economic status and the moral stability of the family. All these fears could be welded together and expressed because they resulted not from intrinsic flaws in society but from the machinations of specific villains—in this case five men and three etceteras. When Judge Lynch had those people "exterminated from the city," supposedly Baltimore and the United States could return to their "fair fame" and purity.

The talk in the circular of "Venery desires" shows how the anger of the mob also united wholly separate incidents. The inclusion of "Bossier" in the list of intended victims makes clear that the author joined a recent Baltimore scandal with the long-brewing Bank of Maryland controversy. Over a week before the riot, Joseph Bossière was assaulted by an irate guardian who found his ward in Bossière's house. Rumor had it that Bossière had seduced her and that the directress of the exclusive school where the girl boarded had acted as procuress. The moralistic anger over this incident, totally unconnected with the bank controversy, nonetheless merged with it in the minds of the rioters. The mob attacked the house where Bossière was staying, and to save it he gave himself up to the crowd; what was done to him was not reported.

In the Washington riot a similar event that had occurred about a week prior to the disturbance influenced the emotion of the mob. The slave of a prominent Washington widow entered her bedroom at night with an ax and drunkenly threatened to kill her. Newspapers soon had him spouting "abolitionist jargon" as he made the attack, and the conservative *National Intelligencer* labeled the story "The First Fruits." While the widow, convinced that the slave had simply been drunk, hid him in her home and tried to sell him to safety, the press flaunted the incident as proof of coming terrors if abolitionists were not muzzled. Hence Crandall's supposed activities could be seen as part of a plot threatening widows with violent death, and the attack on Negroes could then go forth in the guise of saving society from servile war. The purity of the family motif was also strangely tied to the attack on Snow. When no abolitionist literature was found in his restaurant, the official charge against him became that he had insulted the honor of mechanics' wives and daughters.

In addition to a triggering generalized moral fury, another emotional set characterized Jacksonian riots. Once action began, anger was replaced by joy and release if the mob was not seriously opposed. The few reports of the Washington mob suggest great good humor, almost Bacchanalia, as the crowd destroyed, partly by drinking, the contents of Snow's Epicurean House. The reports of the Baltimore riot trials give a vivid sense of their saturnalian quality. Several rioters were convicted largely because they had lustily bragged about their riot exploits. James Spencer, furious against Mayor Hunt because Spencer had had his "knuckles shot off" on Saturday, amused the crowd as he broke Hunt's dinnerware on the street: "Gentlemen, who wants to go to a tea party, but stop I'll go and get the plates." Particular care and delight was taken in burning Reverdy Johnson's law library. The mob emptied Johnson's and Glenn's wine cellars and referred to the wine they abundantly drank as "American blood," perhaps suggesting that it was squeezed from their townsmen's labors as well as evoking old rituals of saturnalia, in which the continuance of patterns of authority was made acceptable by their brief ritual cessation. One rioter on Monday, before order was restored, went around saying "damned if he wasn't Mayor of the city" and appointing various friends to official positions. Such precise parallels to saturnalia's mock king were doubtless rare, but the mood often suggested the joy that comes from the destruction of official authority and its brief bestowal on self. Fifes and drums played and crowds of thousands watched the destruction, laughing and cheering on the rioters. The moral or social issues that gave mobs life always circumscribed their action, but such restraints coexisted with a high degree of emotive fury and joy in power that transfigured social reality. Total self-righteousness, well or ill founded, joined with the unity and anonymity of the crowd to allow a saturnalia where social man's usual restraints could be shucked.

A bank clerk, witnessing a riot in 1843, was surprised that so little was done to protect the black victims:

> But the mob of Cincinnati must have their annual festival—their Carnival, just as at stated periods, the ancient Romans enjoyed the Saturnalia, and our city dignitaries must run no risk of forfeiting their "sweet voices" at the next charter election by any unceremonious interference with their "gentle violence"—their practical demonstrations of sovereignty.

The cross-examination of a Baltimore defense witness is telling. Asked if he had been in Morris's house, the reporter recorded the witness as saying, "Not sure—thinks he went in—don't know if he went upstairs, if he did he might have been insane—drank two or three glasses from a decanter—was 'pretty warm.' " Had he been at Hunt's? "Might have been in the house, didn't know—thinks he was sober—was a 'little warm,' might have been insane—a great many passions make a man insane beside liquor—excited to see so much property destroyed."

Most Jacksonian rioters were neither the "dregs of society," as Reverdy Johnson called the Baltimore mob, nor so much of a social elite as Richard M. Brown and Leonard Richards have found composing vigilante or antiabolition mobs. Of the twelve people convicted of riot in Baltimore, eight can be identified as to profession: three carpenters, two pavers, one blacksmith, one hatter, and one laborer. Of the ten people acquitted, four clearly did some rioting; two of these were carpenters, one a merchant, and one probably a farmer. Testimony revealed the names of nine other rioters, only two of whom were professionally identified, both as carpenters. Thus half of the fourteen rioters identified by job were carpenters and eleven (or 78.6 per cent) were "mechanics," that is workingmen with a particular skill. No ages were given, but in about one-third of the cases the rioter's youth was mentioned. The evidence is sketchy but corresponds with the usually even less certain data on other riots. Rioters were predominantly lower-middle-class people with a skill or some property and some position in the community; the majority also tended to be young, in their late teens or twenties, and to have ties with the Jacksonian equivalent of the modern urban gang, the fire companies.

In Washington twenty-some persons were arrested, but the press mentioned only two names: John Laub, a ship carpenter from the Navy Yard, and a "Mr. Sweeting, of Philadelphia," possibly of the same vocation. The diary of Andrew Shiner, a black worker at the Navy Yard, offers the most helpful clues about who participated. A large group of out-of-town workers had been hired to refurbish the frigate *Columbia.* Late in July one mechanic was caught stealing copper, and the commander of the Navy Yard, Commodore Isaac Hull, ordered that workers be barred from eating in the storeroom. Considering this order an assault on their honor, the workers went on strike and ten days later eased their offended dignity and relieved their enforced leisure by terrorizing blacks. At some points the mechanics considered attacking the Navy Yard, but prudence and the fortifications kept the riot racial. The strike explains how mechanics could spend Tuesday afternoon and all day Wednesday working at riot. The clearest evidence that the rioters were of this class grew from a meeting of "very respectable" mechanics called specifically to disavow such ties. The formal resolutions expressed resentment that mechanics should be thought involved with the riot and asked for the removal of federal troops from the streets, but several volunteer amendments, all adopted, revealed more than the meeting's sponsors wished. "Riotous" was changed to "excited," a resolution calling the presence of troops "an insult to freemen" was added, and finally the commander of the troops was damned "for stigmatizing those citizens of Washington who assembled . . . to inflict summary punishment on B. Snow as 'a set of ragamuffins.' " Little wonder that the Jacksonian journal, the *Globe,* an active sponsor of the meeting, had reservations about "the mode adopted to repel" those "unfounded" charges that mechanics had countenanced the riot.

The question of leadership of Jacksonian riots is even harder to answer. In the Snow Riot no evidence remains of leadership, although John Laub was labeled a "ring leader." Those arrested in Baltimore were also called ringleaders, but their trials made clear that only two of them might have been influential even in a secondary way. Yet certainly someone wrote the hundreds of handbills inciting to riot, and witnesses testified that the mob had clear leadership from time to time. The identity of "Red Jacket," "Black Hawk," and "the Man in the Speckled Hat"—names given to alleged leaders—is unknown; perhaps people thought they were leaders only because of their notable costumes. The riot testimony suggests that Leon Dyer was active in the crowd; he was not tried because of testimony that he helped prevent destruction at McElderry's. His doing this is not incompatible with being a leader; Benjamin Lynch, one of the convicted, reportedly said during the riot, "Gentlemen, we have gone far enough, if we go further we shall lose the sympathies of the people." Dyer, at any rate, was reported to have said, "I have got the party and can send them where I please," and to have bought drinks for the mob who worked destruction on the McElderry and Ellicott homes. A citizen of Baltimore much later identified "Red Jacket" as "Samuel M. . . , a cooper in Franklin street." This was Samuel Mass, a Jacksonian politician who had been president of the Maryland Executive Council the year before. Mass was arrested for leading a meeting, two days after the riot, of Tenth Ward Citizens who deplored the violence but also warned Reverdy Johnson that he would be deservedly driven out of Baltimore should he have the impudence to return. Dyer and Mass were leaders of the plebian wing of the Jacksonians; when Roger B. Taney went to Annapolis to urge an indemnity for the victims of the riot, Baltimore's Democratic representatives pointedly avoided calling on him, causing Taney to lament that they, like Baltimore's Jacksonian editor, should countenance the political leadership of Leon Dyer and his sort. The riot occurred because people were generally convinced of the exploitation by the bank's "partners" of the bank's creditors, but possibly the leaders and the most active rioters were lower-middle-class Jacksonians who found in the incident the perfect illustration of Jacksonian rhetoric about the people versus the monied interests, which they took considerably more to heart than did party leaders. When Henry Brown heard in the country that the people were rising up against the "monied aristocrats," he rushed to town, getting there in time to help sack at least John B. Morris's house. When an acquaintance chided Brown because Morris was "the poor man's friend," Brown said had he known that, he would not have hurt Morris's home, but went on railing against the "damned aristocrats."

This political situation would explain how Moses Davis, a town drunk, presumably, from the joking newspaper references to him as a "very *spirited* man," got one-fourth of the vote for mayor, to replace Hunt, who resigned. Davis' opponent was the law-and-order candidate, Samuel Smith, who was endorsed by the town's entire power structure from both parties. It would also explain why the vote declined one-third from the previous election despite strenuous attempts to get out the electorate for Smith to salvage "Baltimore's fair reputation." Benjamin C. Howard, one of the city's Democratic congressmen standing for reelection, ostentatiously avoided voting for Smith, despite his friendship for and earlier support of the riot victims. And the political situation would explain the unusual degree of emotive sincerity one senses in this riot's inflammatory handbills.

It is difficult to see much social purposiveness in Jacksonian riots. In Baltimore the riot resulted largely in reaction. The next legislature passed a law making local communities financially responsible for riot damage and an indemnity bill paying the victims of riot fully for their losses out of Baltimore's harbor funds. As the attorneys and leaders of the creditors—who desperately tried to prevent the riot—feared, the incident aided the exploiters by transforming the question of choosing between Johnson and Co. and the creditors to that of supporting Johnson and Co. or the mob. The victimization largely ensured the restored social position of Johnson, Glenn, E. T. Ellicott, and McElderry. None were elected to popular office, but all remained prominent and respected. Reverdy Johnson steered his election to the United States Senate as adroitly through the state legislature as he had his Indemnity Bill and became attorney-general of the United States under Zachary Taylor. But even had the riot succeeded in ruining or driving out its victims, it would in no way have promoted the relief of those people who lost heavily through the long-continuing trusteeship. The Washington rioters were more successful. Beverly Snow never returned to his nation's capital, no one even considered indemnifying blacks for their losses, and the city council made gestures toward meeting the rioters' demands for more stringent restrictions on free Negroes. The moral is one that runs through Jacksonian riots. Mobs often succeeded in their immediate goals but were in the long run counterproductive when directed against groups or institutions that had some social power. Mormons, Catholics, and abolitionists were all injured by riots, but more fundamentally drew much of their strength from these persecutions. Riots generally succeeded only when directed against the socially defenseless, particularly blacks.

The American Irish riots illustrate the problem in interpreting Jacksonian mobs as socially purposive. Certainly the Irish had much to be unhappy about, both before and after their coming to the United States. There was some prejudice against them, they had comparatively low-paying jobs, their housing was bad, and they had to send their children to schools tinged with Protestantism. And so Irish rioting could be seen as the just social response of an oppressed group. But as one looks more closely, these riots seem less against the injustices of the system than over traditional religious and clan rivalries and against groups less socially influential than they. Many of the so-called Irish labor riots on the canals, railroads, and aqueducts generally turn out to have been imported clan battles between groups of Irish Catholics from different areas of the old country. In an instance where they attacked management, records suggest that they were angrier about the foreman's Presbyterianism than his economic exploitation. It is significant that the

Irish participated in riots much more often in New York and Philadelphia where they were quickly welcomed into the political system than they did in Boston where they were given no political jobs prior to the Civil War. The Philadelphia riot case is illuminating. Philadelphia's first important postrevolutionary riot occurred in 1825 when a serious brawl broke out between Irish Catholics and Protestants just after they disembarked from the ship that brought them from Ireland; six years later a group of Irish Catholics attacked a parade of Orangemen celebrating the Battle of the Boyne, and a general brawl ensued. In 1829 the first of a series of eight Philadelphia riots against blacks and abolitionists occurred in which Irish names bulk large among those arrested, though they were obviously abetted by many home-grown rioters, especially in the antiabolition affrays. And the various antebellum railroad, weaver, nativist, fireboy, and antiprostitution riots seem to have had roots in the same ethnic animosities.

Had the oppressed Irish risen over their social hardships against the power structure, Rudé's conclusions about the crowd in history might apply to Jacksonian America, where, instead, riots featured Irish Catholics fighting Irish Protestants, Corkonions attacking Fardowners, and Irishmen harassing blacks and their supporters. Indeed favorite targets in some antiblack riots were Negro orphan asylums, homes for perhaps the most hapless of American citizens. The sad truth about the Jacksonian riots was that, though the performers had real grievances and fears, action was generally taken only when there was large promise of safety: by groups in situations and places where they had fairly broad political and social influence and against individuals and groups less popular than they.

Jeremiah Hughes's analysis of both the source and social effects of Jacksonian rioting was well taken:

> A radical error in democratic ethics begins to develope itself. The people have been told so often that all power, government, and authority of right belong to them and that they in fact are the only sovereigns here, that it is not to be wondered at that they occasionally mistake the true limit of that sovereignty, and undertake to exercise despotic powers. Who dare control the *People, a Free People?* Don't they make the government itself, and can't they rule it as they please? Such to a great extent is the political education of the day. . . . Governments are instituted mainly for the protection of the weak from the power of the strong. But for this they would not be endured. The majority are always powerful—they require no protection. To restrain an undue exercise of power against the weak is one great motive for which government is instituted.

Hughes's concern about the weak, about minorities, is very much to the point. Victims, more than rioters, were the oppressed, the unpopular, the unprotected.

The psychological effects of rioting are even harder to gauge than its social results. Mobs when unopposed clearly enjoyed themselves; two Baltimore rioters said that they got their $100 and $500 worth of enjoyment—presumably sums lost to the bank—out of their night's work. The amorphousness of bourgeois-democratic society and the constant Jacksonian stress on power belonging to the people made attractive the sense of group identity and invincibility that came from being part of what John Quincy Adams called "the mobility." A song recorded by a Campbellite minister and temperance lecturer who led the Hancock County anti-Mormon mob in Illinois caught some of the "togetherness" of the riotous crowd: "Hancock is a beautiful place/The Antis all are brothers./And when one has a pumpkin pie/He shares it with the others." Democracy's mythic heroes stand outside of society; most of the people who idolize them are enmeshed in it and, if Tocqueville and others are right, have strong desires to merge entirely with the mass. The psychological appeal of riot in democratic society is that the situation gives a sense of acting by a higher code, of pursuing justice and possessing power free from any structural restraint, and at the same time allowing a complete absorption in the mass so that the individual will and the social will appear to be one. To riot is to be Natty Bumppo in crowd, to be Randolph Scott en masse—and this is a kind of apotheosis for democratic man, fulfilling the official doctrine that power belongs to him and allowing him to escape the real system that attempts to share influence by making everyone powerless. The most famous rioter of the Jacksonian period was also the prime developer of the popular Western story. The permanent value of such mental satisfactions is less certain. Psychologically as well as socially, perhaps, people who associated themselves with groups victimized gained most from riot, if their groups were not permanently oppressed by it.

The problem of riot control in the Jacksonian period centered in a democratic sense of the limitations on the state's right to use strong physical force against the people. Five people died in Baltimore because the guard did get reluctant permission to fire, although many citizens felt that all trouble would have vanished if the guard had been properly armed in the first place and that fact had been made known. Total peace returned when Smith organized his heavily armed patrols, but by this time the use of force was supplemented by a revulsion of feeling against the mob, particularly when it was learned that a large list of additional victims had been designated. On the first day after the Washington riot began, the militia was seemingly instructed to try to awe the mob but not to interfere very actively if assaults were confined to black property. When Jackson returned to the city his strategy became one of conciliating the rioters while keeping enough troops around to prevent serious damage. Andrew Shiner was obviously repeating gossip but described Jackson's method accurately.

> When this great excitement commenced the Hon. Major General Andrew Jackson that wher president . . . wher absent from the City and when it got in it height the general arrived home and after he arrived home he sent a message to those gentelmen Mechanics to know what was the matter with them and if they were anny thing he could do for them in an Hon. way to promote their happiness he would do it.

When they complained of Negro actions, Jackson assured them "by the eternal god in this city" he would personally see that the blacks were punished if the mechanics had any disclosures to make about illegal activities, but he made clear, "by the eternal god the law must be preserved at the Risk of Hasards." Minor sporadic incidents occurred later, but in a couple of weeks Washington "was as quiet as a church and the laws wher all respected."

Outside of Washington, the multileveled character of American government kept riot control largely a local problem to be coped with by local officials. Such people, even more than Jackson, were often understandably sympathetic to their fellow citizen-voters or at least hesitant to attack any large group of them. Hence there was much truth to the frequent assertion that a greater show of determination on the part of authorities would have proved effective in stopping trouble. Some observers considered even a real show of determination an inadequate response to threatened violence. Roger Taney complained that the Baltimore bank mob ought to have been met by a "firm and free" use of guns at once, and Wendell Phillips accused the Boston mayor of being derelict in his duty for not having "ten men shot and sent to deserved graves" in the Garrison mob—this in a riot where the mayor acted with vigor and personal courage and where the total estimated damage was fifteen dollars. Even gross dereliction of duty was perhaps better than Phillips's emotive and moralistic approach, which could only feed the paranoiac self-righteousness rioters, actual and potential, possess. The heaviest loss of life tended to occur in two riotous situations: when authorities wholly acquiesced in a mob's destructive tendencies—as was the case with the Mormons in Missouri, with some groups of gentiles later in Mormon-controlled Utah, and in alleged abolitionist and slave conspiracies in the South; or when force was used to keep a mob from their ends. Elijah Lovejoy would not have been killed if he had let his press be removed from Alton as he had from St. Louis. No one died at the Ursuline Convent, which the mob burned unopposed; twenty were victims of the military when the mob was not allowed to fire a Philadelphia Catholic church. How weigh the five bodies in Baltimore against the property of the bank partners or that of men whose crime was answering a public call to aid in keeping the peace? How put Beverly Snow's small property and dignity in the balance with the lives that it might have cost to protect them? In some cases even human life may be less important than using force, if absolutely necessary, to allow unpopular faiths to be followed, unpopular people to be protected, unpopular ideas to be heard.

The clearest result of Jacksonian rioting was the development of professional police and fire companies in large cities. In the wake of the Baltimore riots there was a strong recognition of the lack of organized civil authority to cope with such problems. The only "republican solution" seemed to be organization of volunteer peace-keeping forces because a professional "army" to ensure order among the people was certainly a mark of despotism. City guards were formed in each Baltimore ward, and gout-ridden Henry Thompson headed a corps of City Horse Guards, but such organizations, without the stimulus of any very urgent business, quickly waned. At the same time, Sir Robert Peel's organization of the London police suggested that a professional police force need not be despotic and pointed to the solution that Americans would accept in the 1840s and 1850s. Riots, along with the increasing problem of crime, made clear in urban areas at least that the old voluntary principle could no longer handle social control among a people growing, and growing apart in economic status and ethnic diversity. American democracy, very reluctantly, came to accept that order and freedom required not only a legal system, but professionals specifically responsible for upholding it and forcing its dictates on recalcitrant fellow citizens. If Andrew Jackson was a political symbol for the mythic anarchic American ensuring the triumph of a higher code by his own strength and integrity in a world neatly divided between virtuous men and monstrous enemies, Abraham Lincoln came to represent the sadder side of the democratic psyche: the need to assert man's potential for freedom through accepting cruel responsibilities for using force in a world where the morality of all men was a mixed bag and where both sides prayed to the same God. Lincoln in his famous law-and-order speech of 1837 used recent riots to argue that only in unswerving respect for the law lay real protection from vicious disintegration and despotism. He and his nation in the Civil War proved their willingness to insist on their conception of law even if it had to be imposed by military force. In his *Battle-Pieces*, Herman Melville, the American who had most developed the theme of the heroically destructive potential of self-reliant individualism, noted how the Civil War marked society's tacit acceptance of his grimmer vision of man's fate—especially in a poem commenting on New York City's Draft Riot of 1863 where for the first time a professional police force was used not to control but to conquer "the Atheist roar of riot":

> Hail to the low dull rumble, dull and dead,
> And ponderous drag that shakes the wall.
> Wise Draco comes, deep in the midnight roll
> Of black artillery; he comes, though late;

In code corroborating Calvin's creed
And cynic tyrannies of honest kings;
He comes, nor parlies; and the Town, redeemed,
Gives thanks devout; nor, being thankful, heeds
The grimy slur on the Republic's faith implied,
Which holds that Man is naturally good,
And—more—is Nature's Roman, never to be scourged.

Still unshaken in their democratic convictions, Americans admitted in their prosecution of the Civil War and their growing resistance to rioters that the nation was in practice willing to temper the democratic myth of social responsibility through freedom with some of Draco's stern legalism and Calvin's harsh estimate of man's character and destiny. With a willingness, if you will, to use law not only to release human energy but to check and control it.

The Jacksonian experience suggests that riot is not antithetical to, or abnormal in, a democracy but the result of very basic tendencies and tensions within it. Because of these the riot situation poses in stark form many of the deepest dilemmas a democracy faces. To react harshly is to threaten groups who act within its bounds and in accord with some of its basic precepts; to react tolerantly is inevitably to make the state an accomplice in whatever is done. Riot crystallizes the paradox of vital democracy that must live in the shadow of twin totalitarianisms—that of total submission of all to the state's power and that of the tyranny of favored groups or individuals because of the state's weakness. And to avoid the ascendancy of either totalitarianism requires that democratic man live uneasily and creatively with the dangerous proclivities, potential and sometimes realized, in both his legalistic and anarchic myths.

Family Security in the Transition from Farm to City, 1750–1850

RICHARD L. BUSHMAN

The family farm in America has always had a tenuous existence. The wave of defaulting mortgages in the mid-1980s has its predecessors throughout American history. Yet the secure, self-sufficient farm has been the goal of many rural families since the settling of the North American colonies in the seventeenth century. The difficulties of establishing self-sufficiency, on the other hand, have contributed to the insecurity that has continually beset farm families.

The ownership of agricultural property has long been seen as the key to a successful and secure rural life. To own a farm free and clear from debt has been the life-long goal of farm families. At certain times in our history, this ownership was made possible by government land grants. For most farmers in the eighteenth and early nineteenth centuries, however, owning a farm meant paying for it, and in order to do this, a farmer needed cash. The only ways to generate cash were either to produce a surplus on the farm or to have a family member contribute a wage by holding a job off the farm. This wage could be earned by serving as a farmhand or by working at a job not directly related to agriculture—perhaps one in commerce or industry. Since the pattern of wage labor was usually unstable, the mortgage payments always remained in doubt.

As more and more farm families found it difficult to maintain their property, it became common in the nineteenth century for family members to work in industry, as well as on the farm. This changing pattern is the subject of the following essay by Richard L. Bushman (University of Delaware). In speaking of what he calls "family security," Bushman stresses the importance of land ownership not only in providing for day-to-day needs of the family but also in providing protection for family members in case of disability or old age. The lack of retirement benefits until the middle of the twentieth century made it necessary for aging individuals to provide security for themselves in some manner. The surest method of accomplishing this was through land and/or home ownership.

Later, as farm families moved to towns and cities, the possession of a house provided some of the same security. Even rented dwellings could provide the householder with income from boarders and subtenants. In the urban communities of the nineteenth century, houses were filled with as many people as possible. Some were family members, but others contributed to the family income by renting rooms or boarding. In this way, a measure of family security was provided as the shift from countryside to city took place.

I n the century after 1750, thousands of American families transferred their labors from farms in rural villages to factories in cities and small towns. At the time of the first federal census in 1790, only twenty-four places in the United States held more than 2,500 people. By 1850 there were 236 such places, and the population residing in them had risen from 202,000 to 3,544,000. Nearly as many people lived in cities and towns in 1850 as in the whole country in 1790. The magnitude of the move seems momentous when it is remembered that 80 to 90 percent of the population had lived on the land since the founding of the British colonies, and the lives of most families had been interwoven with fields, crops, and animals long before that.

What did the change mean for the hundreds of thousands of people who took work in towns? How were the schedules of daily existence altered, familiar roles strained, life plans disrupted? Much of the recent work has focused on the imposition of an industrial work discipline. The broken, irregular schedule of the annual agricultural cycle gave way to the demand for regular and coordinated production. But the rules of the industrial workplace were not all that was new about urban life. The most elemental change, affecting all who left the farm, shopkeep-

FAMILY SECURITY IN THE TRANSITION FROM FARM TO CITY, 1750–1850   By Richard L. Bushman, in *Journal of Family History*, Volume 6, 1981, pp. 238–52. Copyright 1981 by the National Council on Family Relations, 1910 West County Road, Suite 147, St. Paul, Minnesota 55113. Reprinted by permission.

ers and transportation workers as well as factory hands, was separation from the land. For the traditional peasant, land was a source of nearly every human need—nourishment, warmth, clothing. Landowners derived income from their property during illness and old age. Land was both subsistence and security. Planning for a season, a life, or for coming generations turned on the acquisition and use of land. The industrial work discipline may have disrupted familiar work rhythms, but separation from the soil jeopardized survival itself. Among many changes, the relation of land and family security is an aspect of the transition from farm to city deserving more attention.

The ends to which people put the soil has figured in a recent debate over the intensity and extent of profit-seeking among early American farmers. Were farmers oriented to the market and to what we loosely term individualism, or were their values family-centered and communal, aimed at self-sufficiency and continuation of the lineage? Whatever the exact nature of rural culture, a few simple propositions seem to be true, among them that the labor of a farm family could not provide for every need. Every farmer had to introduce a portion of his annual produce into the market economy in return for a few minimal necessities and cash for the payment of taxes. Were he to go in debt on a large scale, for a land purchase as contrasted to book debts with a storekeeper for example, the obligation to sell goods for money intensified. In their most primitive stage of development, Shenandoah Valley farmers, it is estimated, sent 10 percent of their goods to market. By 1820, Charles Danhof suggests, the average farmer sold 20 percent of his product. Among well-situated farmers the percentage rose much higher. As early as 1760, James Lemon argues, southeastern Pennsylvania farmers with 125 acres sent as much as 40 percent of their total product to market. Later in the nineteenth century big operators sold 80 to 90 percent of their production.

At least until the middle of the nineteenth century, however, increasing market production did not signal the end of home production. Even as farmers around 1840 gave up manufacture of cloth and then clothing, they continued to produce for themselves in other respects. Connecticut Valley farmers, for example, grew their own wheat up to the Civil War, despite more efficient production in the West. Nor was production for home consumption associated solely with poverty, and forgotten as one prospered. The reverse seems to be closer to the truth. Farmers at the bottom end of the scale were likely to be more dependent on trade than the well-to-do. The Joseph Smith, Sr. family, poor farmers in Manchester, New York (whom I refer to throughout as examples because so much is known of them) concentrated on maple sugar production after they first purchased a farm in 1818, to help meet the mortgage payments. Debt or lack of resources made small farmers cut back on family production in favor of the market. Small farmers' inventories show they lacked cheese presses, looms, spinning wheels, and even plows and oxen, the necessary resources to produce for themselves. Carville Earle's study of All Hallow's parish in seventeenth- and eighteenth-century Maryland shows the frequency of self-sufficiency implements rising markedly in the inventories as wealth increased. The richest planters were the most self-sufficient. Eventually in the eighteenth century great planters added shoemakers, weavers, and the rest of the required artisans to their plantation complement. Even nineteenth-century cotton planters continued to grow their own foodstuffs despite their commitment to an international market.

At some point a few eighteenth-century farmers crossed a line where commercial production brought sufficient returns to warrant a preponderant investment in market crops and the purchase of personal supplies. Caribbean sugar planters bought food, clothing, lumber, and horses from the North American mainland. Although they raised some corn and cattle, scarcity of land and the value of sugar induced them to put less acreage into food production than the demands of the plantation required. In the beginning of the eighteenth century, Carolina rice planters may have done the same, as the colony crossed over from the export to the import of provisions. But in the main, North American farmers in the eighteenth and early nineteenth centuries combined market production and self-support activities. Wherever one went land usage was mixed. One did not see broad wheat fields and nothing else in Pennsylvania, or uninterrupted acres of tobacco in Virginia. Orchards, corn fields, and hay fields were everywhere interspersed with market crops. Although perhaps exceptional in his diversification, Colonel Landon Carter sowed barley, spelt, peas, and oats along with tobacco, wheat, and corn. Cows and beef cattle grazed in southern pastures as commonly as in New England. Hogs were ubiquitous. A fully developed farm was conceived by husbandmen at all levels and in all sections ideally as a nearly comprehensive source of food, fuel, construction materials, and fiber.

Apparently most early American farmers subscribed to the advice of the U.S. patent office in 1852 that "as a general rule . . . it is better that the farmer should produce what he needs for home consumption. . . . The fulfillment of family needs ranked above income maximization as the primary principle of farm production. In the South in the early nineteenth century, small, slaveless farmers grew corn rather than cotton, despite the loss of income, in order to provide for their own needs and stay out of debt. The ruling idea of the small-holder everywhere was to achieve a "competence," by which was meant the capacity to provide for oneself in all circumstances, including illness and old age. Increasing participation in market production, even employment for some family members in village factories, did not dissipate attention to that goal.

In point of fact, few farmers achieved complete self-sufficiency in the sense of acquiring the capacity to produce all family needs from their own resources, save for the few items which had to be imported. To do so for a family of a certain size would have required a calculable amount of land, allotted in certain proportions to tillage, pasture, and woodlot, so as to produce food, fuel, and construction materials for the family, and summer and winter feed for the required number of animals. In addition, the family had to own the tools and implements necessary for harvesting, threshing, transporting, dairying, cooking, construction, spinning, and weaving.

Few achieved the perfect mix. Because of poverty, circumstances of inheritance, or unique opportunities, most farms lacked some essential elements or had to deal with an excess of others. The inventories of the planters in All Hallow's Parish in Maryland between 1760 and 1769, for example, consistently lacked basic items. Thirty-nine percent of plantation inventories did not name a plow or harrow, and 29 percent omitted any kind of plantation tools. Thirty-four percent of the inventories indicated no corn, and 74 percent no wheat. Fifteen percent had no hogs. Allowing for the inventory-taker's negligence, and the disappearance of items around the time of death, a large number of individuals who were thought of as planters still lacked the basics of plantation life.

The same is true in New England. On the tax valuation lists of 1784, in the central Massachusetts town of Brookfield, 78 percent of the taxpayers owned a house and some tillage. Of this group, 40 percent owned three acres of tillage or less, not enough to support both family and animals. Sixty percent of these farmers lacked a pair of oxen, and less than two-thirds owned a barn. Concord farmers were more prosperous, but one-third of them owned no oxen. Half of the farm inventories in nearby Marlborough, Groton, and Dedham lacked a plow.

In actuality, then, most farmers were dependent on their neighbors. People compensated for their deficiencies through exchanges of labor, goods, or land. They helped harvest corn in return for the use of oxen during spring plowing, or pastured a neighbor's animals to pay for trees cut on his woodlot. They laid walls, dressed beef, lent horses, got up wood, cleared brush. Young women worked at others' houses, breaking wool or flax, spinning, weaving, sewing, baking, and milking. When the census-taker visited the Joseph Smith household in 1820, none of the three older boys, Alvin, Hyrum, or Joseph, Jr., was listed as living there. They must have been laboring for someone else. By outside work, Alvin raised most of the $100 required for the annual payment on the farm. When Joseph, Jr. wanted a box for the gold plates, he dug a well for a woman in the next town.

Many of the exchanges involved labor from the poor and young in return for produce and equipment from the wealthy and established. The All Hallow's parish inventories in Maryland show that most instruments of self-sufficiency belonged to the richest planters. But the big planters were not isolated from communal exchange by virtue of their possessions. The plantation served as a center for store goods, milling services, shoemaking, tanning, and legal aid; and except for a few of the largest operations, the big planters needed the business of smaller farmers to make the acquisition of equipment and specialized workers profitable. The frequency of slave hiring from plantation to plantation suggests that the proper balance of workers and land was difficult to maintain, even among large owners. In New England rich and poor were of necessity constantly negotiating with neighbors for the rental of a pasture lot or the purchase of winter feed. The account books of wealthy farmers show them perpetually lending out a plow and team or hiring someone to harvest, fence, or thresh.

We must envision a network of exchanges covering each village or district, through which farm families produced their needs. Although they probably pursued the goal, few individual farmers achieved individual self-sufficiency. Subsistence was obtainable only through participation in the cummunal network. But subsistence was relatively secure because the required goods could be assembled through one's own labor within the boundaries of a barter economy. The farm family was not dependent on fickle prices or the fluctuations of available currency in the external economy to which they directed their market surplus. Farm property embedded within the district exchange system was a relatively sure foundation for domestic economy. From their own and their neighbors' lands, rural families could draw most of the supplies to sustain life.

One fortuitous consequence of this intricate exchange network was the creation of work for everyone. The complexity and flexibility of the village economy resulted in jobs, tasks, and opportunities suited to every level of ability and wealth. Returns were small, but laborers with little property nonetheless sustained themselves. The Smith family lost their Tunbridge farm in 1803 through a bad commercial investment, and for fifteen years rented land, peddled small items of their own manufacture, and hired out. During that fifteen-year period, Lucy Mack Smith bore six children; they sent one of their sons to a private school for a year; and the family migrated from Vermont to New York state. After eight years of tenant farming, as the family moved across the Connecticut River to New Hampshire, Lucy Mack Smith stated, "Here we settled ourselves down, and began to contemplate, with joy and satisfaction, the prosperity which had attended our recent exertions; and we doubled our diligence, in order to obtain more of this world's goods. . . ." The rural exchange network absorbed the labor of widows, eccentrics, and young single men and women without property, and provided at least a meager subsistence in return.

The system worked much better, however, for people with land. The most serious drawback of rural life without land was the lack of provision for illness and old age. Hector St. John Crèvecoeur's fictional

Hebridean immigrant to Pennsylvania worked with his family for wages for a year and earned $84. But then he sought a change of condition, explaining "that he was a man of middle age, and would willingly have land of his own, in order to procure him a home, as a shelter against old age; that whenever this period should come, his son, to whom he would give his land, would then maintain him, and thus live altogether." Lucy Mack Smith, with the same considerations in mind, commented when she was thirty-five and her husband forty, "We looked forward to the decline of life, and were providing for its wants, as well as striving to procure those things which contribute much to the comfort of old age." A freehold farm was equivalent to a retirement pension or a savings account.

A farm worker without land had no defense against old age, crippling illness, or accident. Amidst the intense physical exertion of farm and woodland, calamities occurred with grim regularity. Lucy Mack Smith's father, Solomon Mack, a French and Indian War veteran, lost 1,600 acres in Granville, New York, when he gashed his leg while felling trees and was unable to complete the required houses to claim the land. In 1777 a falling tree stripped the skin off his back and broke enough bones to keep him in bed for four months. While still lame from that accident, he fell on the waterwheel of the family saw mill and was crippled for life. The family carried on through these vicissitudes because they had land. The parts they could not work themselves they fed into the village exchange system in return for meat, milk, or grain. Solomon left his family for four years in the 1780s to work a coastal schooner sailing out of Halifax, and yet by management of their property in Montague, Massachusetts, his wife and children sustained themselves.

Farmers who escaped illness or accident in their prime working years could not escape the decrepitude of old age. Property and children were the only means of support when strength and health eventually failed. Society's only provision for the aged was some version of the poorhouse, and it was a symbol of degradation. A Lynn shoemaker, perhaps more proud than most, took his own life rather than become a helpless dependent in his old age. As late as 1890, 73.2 percent of the male population over age sixty-five were still working. For all the difficulties of sustaining oneself, less than 2 percent of the population over age sixty in the United States lived in poorhouses at any time in the nineteenth century. To avoid the humiliation of helpless poverty, fathers in seventeenth-century Andover, Massachusetts held on to their land to the last. The purpose was not control over progeny for its own sake, but for security and dignity in old age. Old men, widows, and underage children could rent out their land and derive an income when they themselves were unable to labor.

The intent always was to pass on the farm to the children eventually. The life plan of these people was to perpetuate a freehold down through the generations. A farm passing from father to son represented the equilibrium state in domestic economic life. A family did not achieve stability and permanence until it possessed an adequate freehold. Innumerable vicissitudes displaced families from that pattern and made them tenants, laborers, or city workers, but these expedients, however protracted, figured in their life plans as interludes while they saved to buy a farm. Though defeated by circumstances repeatedly, they strove as best they could to return to land of their own.

In actuality the rural economies of Britain and America were unable to provide farms for everyone. From the middle of the sixteenth century, English peasants were relentlessly squeezed off the land. In some sections the changeover to pasture reduced the number of laborers required and the amount of life-sustaining food produced. Part of the population had to leave or to take up new occupations, like weaving. More were driven off by debt. The costs of the enclosure commissions and of hedging fields, for one thing, forced many small owners to sell out.

American husbandmen were probably far more stable as a group. The original New England companies allotted huge town tracts to the first settlers. Most townships were at least thirty-six miles square, and in the seventeenth century the inhabitants attempted to reserve these blocks for as few as fifty families. The original settlers looked down the generations and sought to provide for all who were to come. Eventually, even these generous plots were taken up, but the worst that was required in the eighteenth century was removal to unsettled land fifty or a hundred miles away. The English author of *American Husbandry*, writing in the middle of the eighteenth century, claimed that the New England poor "aim at saving money enough to fix them into a settlement; their industry rarely fails of its end, so the evening of an industrious life is universally that of a little planter in the midst of all necessaries."

Life was not always so kind to everyone. The Smith family was among the large number of nineteenth-century New England families who failed to fare so well. Joseph Smith, Sr. was given a 100-acre farm by his father in Tunbridge, Vermont around 1796 which he worked until 1803 when he took up storekeeping to augment his income. Debts to Boston merchants and the failure of a ginseng venture led him to lose the land, and for fifteen years the Smiths were landless tenants moving from farm to farm. In 1818 they contracted for 100 acres in Manchester, New York when Joseph Smith, Sr. was forty-seven and Lucy Mack was forty-two. They made all the payments save one and found themselves overextended. They had contracted for the construction of a frame house in addition to the farm; and when the oldest son, a prime wage-earner, died of a calomel treatment for bilious colic, they could not meet the remaining payment. In 1825 they lost both house and farm and were once more landless tenants. The Smiths were not alone in their troubles. The upstate New York newspapers in the 1820s were filled with complaints about the overwhelming weight of mortgage debt. The land companies came to expect first owners to default and run off without completing payment.

Still the demand for farms remained high. The Smiths spent twenty-five years fruitlessly trying to acquire a farm free of a mortgage, and many others were just as determined. High prices (usually the land's capitalized earning power, virtually the maximum price that could be charged) failed to daunt aspiring farmers. For many midwestern farmers, tenantry provided an avenue to the desired goal. A tenant who provided seed and animals generally received one-third of the produce of the farm. A hard-working tenant could at least hope to accumulate enough for a downpayment. Approximately 2.3 million new farms were opened up between 1820 and 1880. Even in the northeast from Maryland to Maine, the number grew from 200,000 to 750,000. These must represent in part the successful efforts of some of the tenant population. Farm population shot up between 1790 and 1850, from 3.7 million to 19.6 million.

In the long run, of course, the cities won out. People pursued farms in the face of much higher income available from city work. Davis, Easterlin, and Parker estimate the labor income per worker in 1840 was three times as high for manufacturing employees as for agricultural employees, and workers were bound to share some of the benefits. When industrial wages in the Philadelphia iron industry fell between 1815 and 1830, the cost of living declined much more rapidly. Urban life had amenities a mean farm existence could not offer. Factory workers in Ohio said they preferred life in town where they could buy the little things they wanted.

The population in urban places grew 3.3 times faster than the rural population between 1790 and 1850. In 1800 about 84 percent of the workforce was in agriculture. In 1840 only 63 percent, and in 1870 just 52 percent worked on farms. Diane Lindstrom estimates that at least 30.5 percent of the 59,000 people who left the Philadelphia hinterland between 1821 and 1830 went to the city of Philadelphia itself. If nothing else, the fixed supply of land sooner or later forced a growing population to move.

But in interpreting the population figures, the sharp distinctions between rural and urban places, and between agriculture and non-agricultural workers can leave a false impression. The move from farm to city or farm to factory did not occur as abruptly as the numbers imply. In the 1790s manufacturing advocates envisioned factories as a supplement to farms not as a substitute. Alexander Hamilton insisted that manufacturing would enhance rural prosperity by "afford[ing] occasional and extra employment to farmers" in the off-season. Or they would send their wives and children to the factories when they could be spared.

"The husbandman himself experiences a new source of profit and support from the increased industry of his wife and daughters, invited and stimulated by the demands of the neighboring manufactories." Tenche Coxe commented on the benefit to all farmers, but particularly to the cattle and corn regions.

> This union of manufactures and farming is found to be very convenient on the grain farms; but it is still more convenient on the grazing and grass farms, where parts of every day, and a great part of every year, can be spared from the business of the farm, and employed in some mechanical, handycraft, or manufacturing business.

The village factory took its place in the rural exchange network alongside agricultural employments for casual labor like dairying, spinning, or well-digging. As small operators had always ranged the neighborhood and beyond for supplementary employment to compensate for deficiencies in their lands, animals, and equipment, so they now sent their wives and children to work in a nearby textile mill or even took a job themselves for a short period. Thirty percent of the workers at Slater's Oxford and Webster, Massachusetts mills between 1830 and 1840 were from the town. If New England followed the English pattern, most of the other workers were from ten to fifteen miles away. They did not have to go farther when cotton and woolen mills were dotted all across the landscape. Many of the workers at the Harper's Ferry Armory kept farms along with their industrial employment. They completed the monthly production quotas in two or three weeks and devoted the rest of the month to agriculture. Charles Danhof estimates that about one-quarter of northern and western farmers in 1850 were part-time. Farms continued to offer subsistence and security while industrial employment offered a new source of cash income.

It seems unlikely, then, that every farmer who took a job in a mill or moved to the city gave up farming and assumed the new identity of industrial worker. The very transience of the industrial population suggests a restless search for something beyond the factory. Forty-five percent of the employees of the Slater Mills in Massachusetts left within a year. At Rockdale, employees on the average stayed on the job just eleven months. City workers were no more stable. Virtually every study of residential mobility in the 1840s finds 40 to 60 percent of the urban population leaving the city within a decade. The poor, the young, and the single population especially, but many middle-aged married people as well, bounced from job to job, place to place, searching for better employment.

The causes of their discontent are not difficult to locate. Factory and city work were spasmodic. Bad weather, a delay in supplies, a sudden drop in prices, a breakdown in machinery could throw a whole shop out of work. Individual firms came and went as shopowners and entrepreneurs lost their shirts. A study of Massachusetts labor in 1877, a depression year, found that two-thirds of the workers had been out of work on the average of ninety-four days. Wages were uncertain, and they had one even greater fault: they were not enduring. They came in only while the worker worked. When sickness or old age struck him or her down, there was nothing. By the 1850s the agricultural journals, noting the flow of young people into the cities, acknowledged the superior wages, but stressed repeatedly the lack of security in times of personal or financial crisis.

People who had been raised in rural areas understandably strove to regain the form of security against decrepitude they knew best—land. Harriet Martineau saw this ambition as the archetypical pattern.

> An artisan works that he may die on land of his own. He is frugal that he may enable his son to be a landowner. Farmers' daughters go into factories that they may clear off the mortgage from their fathers' farms, that they may be independent landowners again.

A popular labor reformer between 1829 and 1850, George Henry Evans, believed the answer to the industrial worker's problems was free western land. He envisioned "Rural Republican Towns" where a home lot and a quarter section (and no more) were available to everyone without mortgage. He wanted enough artisans in each place to make every town self-sufficient through barter alone, without recourse to the fickle external economy. Evans and his many followers could imagine no other satisfactory solution to life's vicissitudes than the recreation of rural exchange networks based on land. The Morris family, whose fortunes A. F. C. Wallace traced from the Rockdale textile mills to an Ohio farm, may have been among the fortunate few, but their success was the goal of many whom adversity had pushed into the mills.

This army of transients, cut off from the land but still questing for it, provided the unskilled work force of early industrialization. Wives and children, young unmarried men, and a smaller number of families circled through the village mills. A somewhat different mix swelled the city population. They stitched the shoes, rolled the barrels, drove the carts, and clerked in urban shops. They were not, as a whole, skilled. The long apprenticeship necessary to acquire a skill appealed to few. Unlike many English urban workers, American laborers did not think of themselves as permanently removed from the land, and were unwilling to make the commitment to learn an industrial skill. They were content with jobs like those in textile mills which could be learned in a few weeks. Even though the wages for skilled labor in America kept rising, the mobile American laborer kept his hopes fastened on an independent farm, the preferred last resting place.

And yet cities and industrial towns eventually gained a permanent hold on an ever larger number of families. Superior wages overpowered the appeal of the land. Soils grew thin, costs rose, prices fell, and western lands receded farther and farther into the sunset. Immigrants and native Americans alike had to bear the shock of severance from the self-sufficient farm village, and erect defenses in their urban homes against layoffs, wage cuts, illness, and old age.

Through the nineteenth century very few could turn to public support or pension plans. Concern for support of the aged increased after the Civil War when a burgeoning urban population awakened people to the problem of aging in a nonagricultural society. Insurance companies devised old age annuities, benevolent and fraternal societies established old folks' homes, and a few retirement pension programs came into being. But few of the aged benefited. When interest was renewed around 1910, a survey of Massachusetts citizens, sixty-five and older, showed that 77 percent were independent of any form of public or organized relief. Of those who were dependent, three-fifths benefited from military pensions. Of the elderly population as a whole, only 2 percent were in almshouses, 1.5 percent in benevolent homes, 1.1 percent in asylums and hospitals. People hated anything that resembled the poorhouse. It was said of the Boston Irish, "they will sooner die in the streets" than go to Deer Island. Even after 1910 pension programs received little backing. From 1903 to 1929, 114 old age pension bills were proposed in the Massachusetts state legislature without a single one passing. There were only twelve private pension plans in the country in 1900, and yet not until 1930 did the American Federation of Labor support compulsory old age insurance.

Urban workers instead devised means to remain self-supporting. Their instinct was to bring the farm into the town. Town dwellers from the beginning of settlement wanted at least a plot for a garden and a barn or shed for animals, just as in England husbandry "was the most general by-occupation of townspeople of all classes. . . ." The first New England migrants called their settlements towns, and yet provided each inhabitant with a home lot of five to ten acres, enough for an orchard and pasture. These town plots probably represented an ideal. Boston settlers expected a half-acre at least for house and garden with rights to tillage and pasture in the town fields. William Penn's original plan for his "green country town" on the Delaware River would have assigned a hundred acres or more to each house, stretching back from a site overlooking the river. As it was, the space around each house shrank, but a barn and tiny garden was a conventional layout. The most urban of all American settlers, the Dutch, strove to own a little land in the fields outside the town. Henry Glassie has commented of the colonial town that it "consisted of rows of miniature farms . . ." just as English towns "had a profoundly rural visual quality." In 1760 most of the non-farmer taxpayers in Lancaster County continued to produce food for themselves.

That combination of food production and urban work continued as an ideal in the nineteenth century. In his 1819 statistical account, D. B. Warden said smiths, shoemakers, weavers, and tailors generally had one or two acres of land for a cow, fuel, and a garden. He may have been optimistic. Norman Ware claimed this was true of Lynn shoemakers, but Paul Faler found scarcely 10 percent of Lynn's adult males owned a pig, and less than 50 percent owned any real property. Ownership of a garden and a few animals may have been an aspiration more than a reality for most, although in Hamilton, Canada in 1861 between 20 and 25 percent of the inhabitants kept animals.

Certainly when they had the means, urban workers tried to get their hands on property. Sixteen of the twenty-two most upwardly mobile of Newburyport workmen between 1850 and 1880 purchased farm property on the edge of town. Two dozen others, who called themselves laborers, owned agricultural land and interspersed labor on it with work in town. To attract workers, iron manufacturers, who were generally in the countryside, offered their employees housing with sufficient land for garden plots and pasturage. The managers of Rockdale permitted workers to raise vegetables and keep animals on company land. City ordinances to impound stray animals reflected the small-scale agriculture going on in yards and side lots.

The meanest urban farm operations may have escaped the tax collector's scrutiny. Pigs were the principal public scavengers in the early years of Washington, D.C. Someone in town was raising animals on the city's refuse. A satirical cartoon in the February 11, 1860 *New York Illustrated News* showed a sow and suckling pigs in the mainroom of an Irish slum-dweller over the caption: "Backgrounds of Civilization—Interior of Mr. John Bradley's Cottage, His Family and Fellow-Lodgers." Along New York's east side from 42nd to 110th Street, Irish squatters lived in shanties with goats and pigs picketed nearby. By the late nineteenth century the poor and the desperate were associated with these remnants of urban agricultural subsistence.

The more permanent urban population of skilled artisans had banded together much earlier to protect themselves against illness and crippling accidents in another way. Long before commercial insurance was available to workers, unions and benefit societies provided small payments in times of sickness and paid funeral costs at death. These remained the most appealing aspect of union membership. In the organizational enthusiasm of the 1840s, paper organizations with auspicious plans sought to attract members by offering sickness and death benefits. The Lowell Female Labor League and the National Industrial Convention admitted their objectives were not sufficiently interesting to workers and added distress insurance as a lure. When the New York Typographical Union, a benefit society organized in 1809, revived itself in 1850, they wrote into their constitution sick benefits of $4 a week and death benefits of $20. The paternalistic Lukens Iron Company began the Wawasett Beneficient Society in 1870 for its workers, and the same features became a standard part of ethnic societies of the late nineteenth century. Workers may have failed to appreciate reform rhetoric about labor's true interests, but every working family knew the consequences of a crippling accident or the humiliation of a pauper's funeral.

More useful still to the urban family was their dwelling. The apartments or small houses of city workers played a far more important role in their domestic economy than mere provision of shelter. A dwelling served as a fly wheel to stabilize a family against the fits and starts of the urban economy and the vicissitudes of personal health. Its importance was partially measured by the exertions city workers made to acquire a house. Stephan Thernstrom found that two-thirds to three-quarters of the working-class men who remained in Newburyport for twenty years owned town property, usually house and lot. To acquire a house they sacrificed other amenities, including education for their children, and often entered into burdensome mortgages. Even the apparently least qualified workers strove to buy a house. In 1861 in Hamilton, Kingston, and London, Ontario, 29 percent of adult male illiterates owned their homes. The figures held for all ethnic groups, Irish Catholics, English Protestants, and Scottish Presbyterians. The percentages increased as a laborer rose in the wealth scale. Fifty-three percent of middle rank illiterate workers owned a house. Older workers were, of course, more likely to own than younger ones. The figures imply that home ownership was a goal sought as rapidly as time and means allowed. Immigrants purchased row houses in Philadelphia and triple-deckers in Boston, even when the entanglement of capital in a dwelling foreclosed more lucrative investments with greater long term benefits.

The size of the family made little difference in the likelihood of house purchase. In three Ontario towns, 29 percent of illiterate workers with zero to two children owned their homes, as compared to 30 percent of families with six or more children. A house significantly supplemented income no matter the size of the family. The Andrew Morris family, whom Wallace traced from Rockdale to a farm in Ohio, while working in the mills lived in a three-bedroom house with two children and four boarders. Andrew's income from the mills never exceeded $24 a month, while the boarders paid the family $35 a month. Without the additional income it is doubtful that the Ohio farm would ever have become a reality. Moreover, a dwelling was an independent source of income when the major breadwinner was ill or out of work. When his income failed, children, kin, and lodgers went on working and sustained the family with rents and contributions. The house enabled the wife and even small children to add to the family income.

City houses were stuffed with people. A quarter of the native-born household heads in Buffalo in 1855, whatever their age or wealth, took in relatives or boarders or both. In Rockdale between a quarter and a half of the workers' households contained boarders. In Richmond in 1850, 48.8 percent of households had boarders. The proportion varied with ethnicity, wealth, and age, but a substantial fraction of every group augmented their households. As children moved out, boarders moved in. In 1890 over 40 percent of native working-class families in Boston where the father was age fifty to fifty-nine took in boarders or lodgers. The reports of crowded housing in slum sections, with entire families in a single room, cannot be attributed solely to landlord greed. Renters of apartments in turn divided their small accommodations to squeeze income out of the space they controlled.

Many families needed the extra income just to meet day-to-day expenses. But during old age and periods of unemployment, the house was a lifeline. The house was an urban surrogate for the self-sufficient family farm. The house gave an owner access to a kind of urban exchange network comparable to the hiring of labor, tools, land, and animals, which enabled the rural village to sustain its poor and elderly. In a house, the aged and ill exchanged living space and meal preparation for part of the earning capacity of young men and women still active in the workplaces.

A city family did not need to purchase a house before taking in boarders and engaging in the urban exchange network. Renters subdivided and sublet their space. Rents were low enough to leave a comfortable margin, particularly if the lodgers took meals with the family. The Andrew Morris's house in Rockdale rented for $25 a year, while their four boarders each paying $2 a week contributed over $400 a year. But rental space did not satisfy urban families. The purchase of a house seemed to be a common goal. In Buffalo in 1855, less than a quarter of native-born household heads in their twenties owned real estate, while three-fifths of the household heads over sixty did. The extraordinary efforts to acquire property, even when the capacity to save was limited, suggests that families themselves saw a substantial advantage in home ownership.

The importance of ownership becomes clearer in light of the total situation of the elderly in cities. The aged in the nineteenth century supported themselves by maintaining independent households and continuing to work well past the conventional twentieth-century retirement age 65. The census attribution of occupation shows that only one in ten males over 55 in Essex County did not work in 1880, with a sharp drop by age occurring after age 75. All the while they retained their positions as heads of households. In a national sample from 1900, 73.4 percent of people ages 65 through 69 were heads of household or spouses of a head. In Providence, Rhode Island between 1860 and 1890, 85.1 percent of the men from 65 to 74 years were heads of households. The percentage dropped after that age, but nationally 52.9 percent over 75 were still heads of household or spouses; in Providence 72.1 percent of the men maintained that status. At this point, the family stepped in. Most of those who did not head households lived with children. Nearly all of the remainder lived with someone else. Only 12.3 percent of people over 75 lived alone.

We can imagine people in their older years, working, heading their own households as long as possible, and bringing in children, other relatives, and unrelated lodgers. At the end, many relinquished their roles as household heads, but continued to live with others. Through these last years, instead of a placid, simple family life, household members came and went, new configurations forming and reforming.

Ownership of a house may have been an advantage in the negotiations that accompanied the restructuring of households, as it was in the experience of one nineteenth-century household headed by a widow. Harriet Hanson Robinson was a middle-class housewife best known for her authorship of *Loom and Spindle*, a reminiscence about her life as a Lowell mill girl between 1835 and 1848. She left the mills when she married William Stevens Robinson, a well known but impecunious reforming newspaper editor in Concord, Lowell, and Boston. In 1866 the Robinsons purchased an eight-room house at 35 Lincoln Street in Malden, Massachusetts for $3,600, from which William commuted to work in Boston. Later the house was expanded and an inside toilet and a furnace added. Harriet intensively gardened the back yard and the unoccupied lot beside the house, planting cherry, apple, and peach trees, and feeding thirty hens, as well as raising the usual run of vegetables. In 1876 William died when Harriet was fifty-one, with three children at home and her aged mother to care for. She published her husband's writings and wrote two books herself, but the books brought little income. She never took employment. The three children were old enough to work and made contributions until they married and left home. But mainly Harriet supported herself from house rents. She confided to her journal at one point when showing the rooms, "O dear! I wish I did not have to rent rooms. No! I am thankful I have them to rent."

But besides financial support, the house was home base for all the Robinsons and enabled Harriet to function as a mother when all of the children were married. From rental income she eked out small amounts to send off to son and daughter in Colorado or Connecticut. More than that it was a haven in time of distress. "I am always glad that I have the house over my head," she wrote in 1884, "and shall never sell it unless I am obliged to while any of my children have not homes of their own."

Perhaps most important was an intangible value, expressed in a 1908 journal entry, the last year Harriet was to write: "My home is very pleasant and I can do just as I like in all things." The satisfactions of the independent householder contrast sharply with the feelings of her daughter Hattie, who did not own a house, but in old age lived with a niece, Martha. Martha married in 1935, and Hattie at 85 felt entirely superfluous. Unlike her mother she was a guest living at the pleasure of the owners. Irascible and demanding, she was forever offending Martha and her husband and regretting it. Despairing, Hattie set up rules for herself: "Ask no questions. Keep quiet, stay in own room, don't open door to kitchen (unless it is ajar)." And finally: "Will not do anything or touch anything unless I'm told I may." She fixed her own meals and ate in solitude. "I desire to be dead! But I must 'carry on.' "

The value of a house rested ultimately on its capacity for producing income and connecting the ill or aged with the work system of the city. But its worth enlarged as it became a bargaining chip in the intricate family negotiations for care and respect. Sentiment easily wrapped itself around thoughts of home. "I am so glad to flee it," Harriet wrote of Lincoln Street in 1884, "and hide my tired head and be at peace. Where papa and grandma lived and died and where I hoped my children can always come. Sure of welcome and rest." Such feelings attached them-selves more securely to an owned house than a rented dwelling.

Even for a person well above average in wealth and advantages like Harriet Robinson, an existence dependent on room rentals was meager at best. But interwoven with family support, house ownership worked for thousands of nineteenth-century families. Reform-minded investi-gators of the Progressive period complained of urban unemployment, desertions, drunkenness, filth, overcrowding, but found the condition of the elderly "comparatively good." Although fewer families owned houses in 1850 than farms in 1750, for the large number who had ac-quired real estate, the house was a practical answer to the challenges of the life course in the modern city.

Black Women, Work, and the Family Under Slavery

JACQUELINE JONES

In the middle of the nineteenth century, a cult of domesticity or "true womanhood" developed in America. This ideology suggested that the more gentle and fragile female character should lead women to restrict their lives to the private sphere, nurturing both the spiritual and physical lives of their families. It should go without saying that this ideology could have applied only to a few middle- and upper-class women. Certainly the lives of the working-class and the poor did not resemble this model. Probably the sharpest deviation from the desired pattern of "true womanhood" was found among slave women.

Since slavery was an economic and social system that was geared to derive the maximum production from its labor, it left no room for a cult of domesticity. The slaves, both men and women, were there to work, and to work hard. It comes as no surprise to the student that slaves had to work, but too often the literature describing the labor system focuses on the lot of the men.

The American slave system was unlike that in the Caribbean and Latin America, and it could not have developed the way it did without the efforts of slave women. The family unit was the basic component of slave life in the nineteenth-century United States. This meant that female slaves had two distinct institutions laying claim to their lives. They had to work as slaves, on the one hand, and be wives and mothers, on the other. They were required to contribute their labor to the productive process, and they voluntarily (for the most part) served in a domestic capacity for their families in the slave quarters. In this way, their work pattern resembled that of farm wives over the centuries, with the significant difference being that their labor outside the quarters was not free and, therefore, their efforts or skills did not work to enhance the economic position of their families. There was no profit in slavery for the slaves. Whatever enhancement to their lives their efforts generated came to them in the quasi privacy of their family lives. There they could nurture and care for their husbands and children within the limits of their time and inclinations.

The structure of plantation life as it affected slave women and children is the subject of the following essay by Jacqueline Jones (Wellesley College). She discusses the implications of the patterns that developed within the slave community for women's history in general, as well as for the subsequent development of Afro-American life.

"Ah was born back due in slavery," says Nanny to her granddaughter in Zora Neale Hurston's novel, *Their Eyes Were Watching God,* "so it wasn't for me to fulfill my dreams of whut a woman oughta be and to do." Nanny had never confused the degrading regimen of slavery with her own desires as they related to work, love, and motherhood: "Ah didn't want to be used for a work-ox and a brood-sow and Ah didn't want mah daughter used dat way neither. It sho wasn't mah will for things to happen lak they did." Throughout her life, she had sustained a silent faith in herself and her sisters that was permitted no expression within the spiritual void of bondage: "Ah wanted to preach a great sermon about colored women sittin' on high, but they wasn't no pulpit for me," she grieved.

Nanny's lament offers a challenge to the historian who seeks to understand American slave women—their unfulfilled dreams as well as their day-in, day-out experiences. Despite recent scholarly interest in the relationship between women's work and family life on the one hand and Afro-American culture on the other, a systematic analysis of the

BLACK WOMEN, WORK, AND THE FAMILY UNDER SLAVERY By Jacqueline Jones. Reprinted from *Feminist Studies*, Volume 8, no. 2 (1982): 235–69, by permission of the publisher, Feminist Studies, Inc., % Women's Studies Program, University of Maryland, College Park, MD 20742.

The author would like to acknowledge the helpful suggestions and comments provided by Rosalind Petchesky and other members of the *Feminist Studies* editorial board and by Michael P. Johnson. Research for this project (part of a full-length study of black women, work, and the family in America, 1830–1980) was funded by a grant from the National Endowment for the Humanities.

roles of slave women is lacking. In her pioneering article entitled "Reflections on the Black Woman's Role in the Community of Slaves" (published over a decade ago), Angela Davis made a crucial distinction between the work that women were forced to perform for a master and the domestic labor that they provided for their own families. But her emphasis on the political implications of nurturing under slavery has not received the in-depth consideration it deserves.

For example, a few scholars have explored the roles of the bondwoman as devoted wife and mother, physically powerful fieldworker, and rebellious servant. Herbert G. Gutman has illuminated the strength of kin ties within the slave community, and Eugene D. Genovese has furthered our understanding of black-white, male-female relations on the antebellum plantation. However, most historians continue to rely on the gender-neutral term "slave"—which invariably connotes "male"—and race supersedes sex as the focal point of their discussions. Consequently, questions related to the sexual division of labor under slavery and the way in which task assignments in the fields, the "Big House," and the slave quarters shaped the experiences of black women have largely gone unanswered—and unasked.

Moreover, historians primarily concerned with the status of American women have examined the effects of patriarchy on various classes and ethnic groups over time; in the process they have highlighted variations on the theme of women's distinctive work patterns as determined by changing economic conditions, combined with traditional cultural assumptions about women's domestic responsibilities. Yet within the context of current feminist scholarship slave women as a group remain for the most part neglected, perhaps because they existed outside the mainstream of the industrial revolution and (together with their menfolk) had few opportunities to put into practice their own ideas about appropriate work for women and men. According to this view, slave women were something of a historical abberation, a "special case" that has little relevance to current theoretical and methodological perspectives on women's work.

The purpose of this article is to suggest that the burdens shouldered by slave women actually represented in extreme form the dual nature of all women's labor within a patriarchal, capitalist society: the production of goods and services and the reproduction and care of members of a future work force. The antebellum plantation brought into focus the interaction between notions of women *qua* "equal" workers and women *qua* unequal reproducers; hence a slaveowner just as "naturally" put his bondwomen to work chopping cotton as washing, ironing, or cooking. Furthermore, in seeking to maximize the productivity of his entire labor force while reserving certain domestic tasks for women exclusively, the master demonstrated how patriarchal and capitalist assumptions concerning women's work could reinforce one another. The "peculiar institution" thus involved forms of oppression against women that were unique manifestations of a more universal condition. The following dis-cussion focuses on female slaves in the American rural South between 1830 and 1860—cotton boom years that laid bare the economic and social underpinnings of slavery and indeed all of American society.

Under slavery, blacks' attempts to maintain the integrity of family life amounted to a political act of protest, and herein lies a central irony in the history of slave women. In defiance of their owners' ten-dencies to ignore gender differences in making work assignments in the fields, the slaves whenever possible adhered to a strict division of labor within their own households and communities. This impulse was exhib-ited more dramatically in patterns of black family and economic life after emancipation. Consequently, the family, often considered by fem-inists to be a source (or at least a vehicle) of women's subservience, played a key role in the freed people's struggle to resist racial and gender oppression, for black women's full attention to the duties of mother-hood deprived whites of their power over these women as field laborers and domestic servants.

Interviewed by a Federal Writers Project (FWP) worker in 1937, Hannah Davidson spoke reluctantly of her experiences as a slave in Kentucky: "The things that my sister May and I suffered were so terri-ble. . . . It is best not to have such things in our memory." During the course of the interview, she stressed that unremitting toil had been the hallmark of her life under bondage. "Work, work, work," she said; it had consumed all her days (from dawn until midnight) and all her years (she was only eight when she began minding her master's children and helping the older women with their spinning). "I been so ex-hausted working, I was like an inchworm crawling along a roof. I worked till I thought another lick would kill me." On Sundays, "the only time they had to themselves," women washed clothes, and some of the men tended their small tobacco patches. As a child she loved to play in the haystack, but that was possible only on "Sunday evening, after work."

American slavery was an economic and political system by which a group of whites extracted as much labor as possible from blacks through the use or threat of force. A slaveowner thus replaced any traditional division of labor that might have existed among blacks before enslave-ment with a work structure of his own choosing. All slaves were barred by law from owning property or acquiring literacy skills, and although the system played favorites with a few, black females and males were equal in the sense that neither sex wielded economic power over the other. Hence property relations—"the basic determination of the sexual division of labor and the sexual order" within most societies—did not affect male-female interaction among the slaves themselves. To a con-siderable extent, the types of jobs slaves did, and the amount of regu-larity of labor they were forced to devote to such jobs, were all dictated by the master.

For these reasons the definition of slave women's work is problematical. If work is any activity that leads either directly or indirectly to the production of marketable goods, then slave women did nothing *but* work. Even their efforts to care for themselves and their families helped to maintain the owner's work force, and to enhance its overall productivity. Tasks performed within the family context—childcare, cooking, and washing clothes, for example—were distinct from labor carried out under the lash in the field or under the mistress's watchful eye in the Big House. Still, these forms of nurture contributed to the health and welfare of the slave population, thereby increasing the actual value of the master's property (that is, slaves as both strong workers and "marketable commodities"). White men warned prospective mothers that they wanted neither "runts" nor girls born on their plantations, and slave women understood that their owner's economic self-interest affected even the most intimate family ties. Of the pregnant bondwomen on her husband's expansive Butlers Island (Georgia) rice plantation, Fanny Kemble observed, "they have all of them a most distinct and perfect knowledge of their value to their owners as property," and she recoiled at their obsequious profession obviously intended to delight her: "Missus, tho' we no able to work, we make little niggers for Massa." One North Carolina slave woman, the mother of fifteen children, used to carry her youngest with her to the field each day, and "when it get hungry she just slip it around in front and feed it and go right on picking or hoeing . . . ," symbolizing in one deft motion the equal significance of the productive and reproductive functions to her owner.

It is possible to divide the daily work routine of slave women into three discrete types of activity. These involved the production of goods and services for different groups and individuals, and included women's labor that directly benefited first, their families, second, other members of the slave community, and third, their owners. Although the master served as the ultimate regulator of all three types of work, he did not subject certain duties related to personal sustenance (that is, those carried out in the slave quarters) to the same scrutiny that characterized fieldwork or domestic service.

The rhythm of the planting-weeding-harvesting cycle shaped the lives of almost all American slaves, 95 percent of whom lived in rural areas. This cycle dictated a common work routine for slaves throughout the South, though the staple crop varied from tobacco in the Upper South to rice on the Georgia and South Carolina Sea Islands, sugar in Louisiana, and the "king" of all agricultural products, cotton, in the broad swath of "Black Belt" that dominated the whole region. Of almost four million slaves, about one-half labored on farms with holdings of twenty slaves or more; one-quarter endured bondage with at least fifty other people on the same plantation. In its most basic form, a life of slavery meant working the soil with other blacks at a pace calculated to reap the largest harvest for a white master.

In his efforts to wrench as much field labor as possible from female slaves without injuring their capacity to bear children, the master made "a noble admission of female equality," observed one abolitionist sympathizer with bitter irony. Slaveholders had little use for sentimental platitudes about the delicacy of the female constitution when it came to grading their " hands" according to physical strength and endurance. Judged on the basis of a standard set by a healthy adult man, most women probably ranked as three-quarter hands; yet there were enough women like Susan Mabry of Virginia, who could pick four or five hundred pounds of cotton a day (one hundred and fifty to two hundred pounds was considered respectable for an average worker), to remove from a master's mind all doubts about the ability of a strong, healthy, woman fieldworker. As a result, he conveniently discarded his time-honored Anglo-Saxon notions about the types of work best suited for women, thereby producing many "dreary scenes" like the one described by northern journalist Frederick Law Olmsted: during winter preparation of rice fields on a Sea Island plantation, a group of black women, "armed with axes, shovels and hoes . . . all slopping about in the black, unctuous mire at the bottom of the ditches." Although pregnant and nursing women suffered from temporary lapses in productivity, most slaveholders apparently agreed with the (in Olmsted's words) "well-known, intelligent, and benevolent" Mississippi planter who declared that "labor is conducive to health; a healthy woman will rear most children." In essence, the quest for an "efficient" agricultural work force led slaveowners to downplay gender differences in assigning adults to field labor.

Dressed in coarse osnaburg gowns; their skirts "reefer up with a cord drawn tightly around the body, a little above the hips" (the traditional "second belt"); long sleeves pushed above the elbows and kerchiefs on their heads, female field hands were a common sight throughout the antebellum south. Together with their fathers, husbands, brothers, and sons, black women were roused at four A.M. and spent up to fourteen hours a day toiling out of doors, often under a blazing sun. In the cotton belt they plowed fields; dropped seed; and hoed, picked, ginned, and sorted cotton. On farms in Virginia, North Carolina, Kentucky, and Tennessee, women hoed tobacco; laid worm fences, and threshed, raked, and bound wheat. For those on the Sea Islands and in coastal areas, rice culture included raking and burning the stubble from the previous year's crop; ditching; sowing seed; plowing, listing, and hoeing fields; and harvesting, stacking, and threshing the rice. In the bayou region of Louisiana, women planted sugarcane cuttings, plowed, and helped to harvest and gin the cane. During the winter, they performed a myriad of tasks necessary on nineteenth-century farms of all kinds: repairing roads, pitching hay, burning brush, and setting up post and rail fences. Like Sara Colquitt of Alabama, most adult females, "worked in de fields every day from 'fore daylight to almost plumb dark." During the busy harvest season, everyone was forced to labor up to sixteen hours at a time—after sunset by the light of candles or burning pine knots. Miscellaneous chores occupied women and men around outbuildings regularly and indoors on rainy days. Slaves of both sexes watered the horses, fed the chickens, and slopped the hogs. Together they ginned cotton, ground hominy, shelled corn and peas, and milled flour.

Work assignments for women and men differed according to the size of a plantation and its degree of specialization. For example, on one Virginia wheat farm, the men scythed and cradled the grain, women raked and bound it into sheaves which children then gathered and stacked. Thomas Couper, a wealthy Sea Island planter, divided his slaves according to sex and employed men exclusively in ditching and women in moting and sorting cotton. Within the two gender groups, he further classified hands according to individual strength so that during the sugarcane harvest three "gangs" of women stripped blades (medium-level task), cut them (hardest), and bound and carried them (easiest). However, because cotton served as the basis of the southern agricultural system, distinct patterns of female labor usually transcended local and regional differences in labor-force management. Stated simply, most women spent a good deal of their lives plowing, hoeing, and picking cotton. In the fields, the notion of a distinctive "women's work" vanished as slaveholders realized that "women can do plowing very well and full well with the hoes and equal to men at picking."

To harness a double team of mules or oxen and steer a heavy wooden plow was no mean feat for any person, and yet a "substantial minority" of slave women mastered these rigorous activities. White women and men from the North and South marvelled at the skill and strength of female plow hands. Emily Burke of eastern Georgia saw women and men "promiscuously run their ploughs side by side, and day after day . . . and as far as I was able to learn, the part the women sustained in this masculine employment, was quite as efficient as that of the more athletic sex." In his travels through Mississippi, Olmsted watched as women "twitched their plows around on the headland, jerking their reins, and yelling to their mules, with apparent ease, energy, and rapidity." He saw no indication that "their sex unfitted them for the occupation."

On another estate in the Mississippi Valley, Olmsted observed forty of the "largest and strongest" women he had ever seen; they "carried themselves loftily, each having a hoe over the shoulder, and walking with a free, powerful swing, like *chasseurs* on the march." In preparing fields for planting, and in keeping grass from strangling the crop, women as well as men blistered their hands with the clumsy hoe characteristic of southern agriculture. "Hammered out of pig iron, broad like a shovel," these "slave-time hoes" withstood most forms of abuse (destruction of farm implements constituted an integral part of resistance to forced labor). Recalled one former slave of the tool that also served as pick, spade, and gravedigger: "Dey make 'em heavy so dey fall hard, but de bigges' trouble was liftin' dem up." Hoeing was backbreaking labor, but the versatility of the tool and its importance to cotton cultivation meant that the majority of female hands used it a good part of the year.

The cotton-picking season usually began in late July or early August and continued without interruption until the end of December. Thus for up to five months annually, every available man, woman, and child was engaged in a type of work that was strenuous and "tedious from its sameness." Each picker carried a bag fastened by a strap around her neck and deposited the cotton in it as she made her way down the row, at the end of which she emptied the bag's contents into a basket. Picking cotton required endurance and agility as much as physical strength, and women frequently won regional and interfarm competitions conducted during the year. Pregnant and nursing women usually ranked as half-hands and were required to pick an amount less than the "average' one hundred and fifty or so pounds per day.

Slaveholders often reserved the tasks that demanded sheer muscle power for men exclusively. These included clearing the land of trees, rolling logs, and chopping and hauling wood. However, plantation exigencies sometimes mandated women's labor in this area, too; in general, the smaller the farm, the more arduous and varied was women's fieldwork. Lizzie Atkins, who lived on a twenty-five-acre Texas plantation with only three other slaves, remembered working "until slam dark every day"; she helped to clear land, cut wood, and tend the livestock in addition to her other duties of hoeing corn, spinning thread, sewing clothes, cooking, washing dishes, and grinding corn. One Texas farmer, who had his female slaves haul logs and plow with oxen, even made them wear breeches, thus minimizing outward differences between the sexes. Still, FWP interviews with former slaves indicate that blacks considered certain jobs uncharacteristic of bondwomen. Recalled Louise Terrell of her days on a farm near Jackson, Mississippi: "The women had to split rails all day long, just like the men." Nancy Boudry of Georgia said she used to "split wood jus' like a man." Elderly women reminisced about their mothers and grandmothers with a mixture of pride and wonder. Mary Frances Webb declared of her slave grandmother, "in the winter she sawed and cut cord wood just like a man. She said it didn't hurt her as she was strong as an ox." Janie Scott's description of her mother implied the extent of the older woman's emotional as well as physical strength: she was "strong and could roll and cut logs like a man, and was much of a woman."

Very few women served as skilled artisans or mechanics; on large estates, men invariably filled the positions of carpenter, cooper, wheelwright, tanner, blacksmith, and shoemaker. At first it seems ironic that masters would utilize women fully as field laborers, but reserve most of the skilled occupations that required manual dexterity for men. Here the high cost of specialized and extensive training proved crucial in determining the division of labor; although women were capable of learning these skills, their work lives were frequently interrupted by childbearing and nursing; a female blacksmith might not be able to provide the regular service required on a plantation. Too, masters frequently "hired out" mechanics and artisans to work for other employers during the winter, and women's domestic responsibilities were deemed too important to permit protracted absences from the quarters. However, many young girls learned to spin thread and weave cloth because these tasks could occupy them during confinement.

The drive for cotton profits induced slaveowners to squeeze every bit of strength from black women as a group. According to the estimates of Roger L. Ransom and Richard Sutch, in the 1850s at least 90 percent of all female slaves over sixteen years of age labored more than 261 days each year, eleven to thirteen hours each day. Few overseers or masters had any patience with women whose movements in the field were persistently "clumsy, awkward, gross, [and] elephantine" for whatever reasons—malnutrition, exhaustion, recalcitrance. As Hannah Davidson said: "If you had something to do, you did it or got whipped." The enforced pace of work more nearly resembled that of a factory than a farm; Kemble referred to female field hands as "human hoeing machines." The bitter memories of former slaves merely suggest the extent to which the physical strength of women was exploited. Eliza Scantling of South Carolina, only sixteen years old at the end of the Civil War, plowed with a mule during the coldest months of the year: "Sometimes me hands get so cold I jes' cry." Matilda Perry of Virginia, "Use to wuk fum sun to sun in dat ole terbaccy field. Wuk till my back felt lak it ready to pop in two."

At times a woman would rebel in a manner commensurate with the work demands imposed upon her. "She'd git stubborn like a mule and quit." Or she took her hoe and knocked the overseer "plum down" and "chopped him right across his head." When masters and drivers "got rough on her, she got rough on them, and ran away in the woods." She cursed the man who insisted he "owned" her so that he beat her "till she fell" and left her broken body to serve as a warning to the others: "Dat's what you git effen you sass me." Indeed, in the severity of punishment meted out to slaves, little distinction was made between the sexes: "Beat women! Why sure he [master] beat women. Beat women jes' lak men." A systematic survey of the FWP slave narrative collection reveals that women were more likely than men to engage in "verbal confrontations and striking the master but not running away," probably because of their family and childcare responsibilities.

Family members who perceived their mothers or sisters as particularly weak and vulnerable in the fields conspired to lessen their work load. Frank Bell and his four brothers, slaves on a Virginia wheat farm, followed his parents down the long rows of grain during the harvest season. "In dat way one could help de other when dey got behind. All of us would pitch in and help Momma who warn't very strong." The overseer discouraged families from working together because he believed "dey ain't gonna work as fast as when dey all mixed up," but the black driver, Bell's uncle, "always looked out for his kinfolk, especially my mother." James Taliaferro told his father, who counted the corn rows marked out for aunt Rebecca ("a short-talking woman that old Marsa didn't like") and told her that her assignment was almost double that given to the other women. Rebecca indignantly confronted the master, who relented by reducing her task, but not before he threatened to sell James's father for his meddling. On another plantation, the hands surreptitiously added handfuls of cotton to the basket of a young woman who "was small and just couldn't get her proper amount."

No slave women exercised authority over slave men as part of their work routine, but it is uncertain whether this practice reflected the sensibilities of the slaveowners or of the slaves themselves. Women were assigned to teach children simple tasks in the house and field and to supervise other women in various facets of household industry. A master might "let [a woman] off fo' de buryings 'cause she know how to manage de other niggahs and keep dem quiet at de funerls," but he would not install her as a driver over people in the field. Many strong-willed women demonstrated that they commanded respect among males as well as females, but more often than not masters perceived this as a negative quality to be suppressed. One Louisiana slaveholder complained bitterly about a particularly "rascally set of old negroes"—"the better you treat them the worst they are." He had no difficulty pinpointing the cause of the trouble, for "Big Lucy, the leader, corrupts every young negro in her power." On other plantations, women were held responsible for instigating all sorts of undesirable behavior among their husbands and brothers and sisters. On Charles Colcock Jones's Georgia plantation, the slave Cash gave up going to prayer meeting and started swearing as soon as he married Phoebe, well-known for her truculence. Apparently few masters attempted to co-opt high-spirited women by offering them positions of formal power over black men.

In terms of labor-force management, southern slaveowners walked a fine line between making use of the physical strength of women as productive workers and protecting their investment in women as child-bearers. These two objectives—one focused on immediate profit returns and the other on long-term economic considerations—at times clashed, because women who spent long hours picking cotton, toiling in the fields with heavy iron hoes, and walking several miles a day sustained damage to their reproductive systems immediately before and after giving birth. For financial reasons, slaveholders might have "regarded pregnancy as almost holy," in the words of one medical historian. But they frequently suspected their bondwomen (like "the most insufferable liar" Nora) of shamming illness—"play[ing] the lady at your expense," as one Virginia planter put it. These fears help to account for the reckless brutality with which owners forced women to work in the fields during and after pregnancy.

Work in the soil thus represented the chief lot of all slaves, female and male. In the Big House, a division of labor based on both gender and age became more apparent, reflecting slaveowners' assumptions about the nature of domestic service. Although women predominated as household workers, few devoted their energies full time to this kind of labor; the size of the plantation determined the degree to which the tasks of cleaning, laundering, caring for the master's children, cooking, and ironing were specialized. According to Eugene Genovese, as few as 5 percent of all antebellum adult slaves served in the elite corps of house servants trained for specific duties. Of course, during the harvest season all slaves, including those in the house, went to the fields to make obeisance to King Cotton. Thus the lines between domestic service and fieldwork blurred during the day and during the lives of slave women. Many continued to live in the slave quarters, but rose early in the morning to perform various chores for the mistress—"up wid de fust light to draw water and help as a house girl"—before heading for the field. James Claiborne's mother "wuked in de fiel' some, an' aroun' de house sometimes. . . ." Young girls tended babies and waited on tables until they were sent outside—"mos' soon's" they could work—and returned to the house years later, too frail to hoe weeds, but still able to cook and sew. The circle of women's domestic work went unbroken from day to day and from generation to generation.

Just as southern white men scorned manual labor as the proper sphere of slaves, so their wives strove (often unsuccessfully) to lead a life of leisure within their own homes. Those duties necessary to maintain the health, comfort, and daily welfare of white slaveholders were considered less women's work than black women's and black children's work. Slave mistresses supervised the whole operation, but the sheer magnitude of labor involved in keeping all slaves and whites fed and clothed (with different standards set according to race, of course) meant that black women had to supply the elbow grease. For most slaves, housework involved hard, steady, often strenuous labor as they juggled the demands made by the mistress and other members of the master's family. Mingo White of Alabama never forgot that his slave mother had shouldered a work load "too heavy for any one person." She served as personal maid to the master's daughter, cooked for all the hands on the plantation, carded cotton, spun a daily quota of thread, wove and dyed cloth. Every Wednesday she carried the white family's laundry three-quarters of a mile to a creek, where she beat each garment with a wooden paddle. Ironing consumed the rest of her day. Like the lowliest field hand, she felt the lash if any tasks went undone.

Although mistresses found that their husbands commandeered most bondwomen for fieldwork during the better part of the day, they discovered in black children an acceptable alternative source of labor. Girls

were favored for domestic service, but a child's sex played only a secondary role in determining household assignments. On smaller holdings
especially, the demands of housework, like cotton cultivation, admitted
of no finely honed division of labor. Indeed, until puberty, girls and
boys shared a great deal in terms of dress and work. All children wore
a "split-tail shirt," a knee-length smock slit up the sides: "Boys and gals
all dress jes' alike. . . . They call it a shirt iffen a boy wear it and call
it a dress iffen the gal wear it." At the age of six or so, many received
assignments around the barnyard or in the Big House from one or more
members of the master's family. Mr. and Mrs. Alex Smith, who grew
up together, remembered performing different tasks. As a girl she helped
to spin thread and pick seeds from cotton and cockle burrs from wool.
He chopped wood, carried water, hoed weeds, tended the cows, and
picked bugs from tobacco plants. However, slave narratives contain descriptions of both girls and boys elsewhere doing each of these things.

Between the ages of six and twelve, black girls and boys followed
the mistress's directions in filling woodboxes with kindling, lighting fires
in chilly bedrooms in the morning and evening, making beds, washing
and ironing clothes, parching coffee, polishing shoes, and stoking fires
while the white family slept at night. They fetched water and milk from
the springhouse and meat from the smokehouse. Three times a day they
set the table, helped to prepare and serve meals, "minded flies" with
peacock feather brushes, passed the salt and pepper on command and
washed the dishes. They swept, polished, and dusted, served drinks and
fanned overheated visitors. Mistresses entrusted to the care of those
who were little more than babies themselves the bathing, diapering,
dressing, grooming, and entertaining of white infants. In the barnyard
black children gathered eggs, plucked chickens, drove cows to and from
the stable and "tended the gaps" (opened and closed gates). (In the
fields they acted as human scare crows, toted water to the hands, and
hauled shocks of corn together.) It was no wonder that Mary Ella
Grandberry, a slave child grown old, "disremember[ed] ever playin' lack
chilluns do today."

In only a few tasks did a sexual division of labor exist among children. Masters always chose boys to accompany them on hunting trips
and to serve as their personal valets. Little girls learned how to sew, to
milk cows and churn butter, and to attend to the personal needs of
their mistresses. As tiny ladies-in-waiting, they did the bidding of fastidious white women and of girls not much older than they. Cicely
Cawthon, age six when the Civil War began, called herself the mistress's "little keeper"; "I stayed around, and waited on her, handed her
water, fanned her, kept the flies off her, pulled up her pillow, and done
anything she'd tell me to do." Martha Showvely recounted a nightly
ritual with her Virginia mistress. After she finished her regular work
around the house, the young girl would go to the woman's bedroom,
bow to her, wait for acknowledgement, and then scurry around as or-

dered, lowering the shades, filling the water pitcher, arranging towels on the washstand, or "anything else" that struck the woman's fancy. Mary Woodward, only eleven in 1865 was taught to comb her mistress's hair, lace her corset, and arrange her hoop skirts. At the end of the toilet Mary was supposed to say, "You is served, mistress!" Recalled the former slave, "Her lak them little words at de last."

Sexual exploitation of female servants of all ages (described in graphic detail by Harriet Jacobs in Lydia Maria Child's *Incidents in the Life of a Slave Girl*) predictably antagonized white women. Jealousy over their husbands' real or suspected infidelities resulted in a propensity for spontaneous violence among many. Husbands who flaunted their adventures in the slave quarters increased the chance that their wives would attack a specific woman or her offspring. Sarah Wilson remembered being "picked on" by the mistress, who chafed under her husband's taunts; he would say, "'Let her alone, she got big, big blood in her,' and then laugh."

A divorce petition filed with the Virginia legislature in 1848 included a witness's testimony that the master in question one morning told his slave favorite to sit down at the breakfast table "to which Mrs. N. [his wife] objected, saying . . . that she (Mrs. N.) would have her severely punished." Her husband replied "that in that event he would visit her (Mrs. N.) with a like punishment. Mrs. N. then burst into tears and asked if it was not too much for her to stand." This husband went to extreme lengths to remind his spouse of slave-mistress Mary Chesnut's observation that "there is no slave, after all, like a wife." In the black woman the mistress saw not only the source of her own degradation, she saw herself—a woman without rights, subject to the impulses of an arrogant husband-master.

To punish black women for minor offenses, mistresses were likely to attack with any weapon available—a fork, butcher knife, knitting needle, pan of boiling water. Some of the most barbaric forms of punishment resulting in the mutilation and permanent scarring of female servants were devised by white mistresses in the heat of passion. As a group they received well-deserved notoriety for the "veritable terror" they unleashed upon black women in the Big House.

Interviews with former slaves suggest that the advantages of domestic service (over fieldwork) for women have been exaggerated in accounts written by whites. Carrying wood and water, preparing three full meals a day over a smoky fireplace or pressing damp clothes with a hot iron rivaled cotton picking as backbreaking labor. Always "on call," women servants often had to snatch a bite to eat whenever they could, remain standing in the presence of whites, and sleep on the floor at the foot of their mistress's bed (increasing the chances that they would sooner or later be bribed, seduced, or forced into sexual relations with the master). To peel potatoes with a sharp knife, build a fire, or carry a heavy load of laundry down a steep flight of stairs required skills and dexterity not always possessed by little girls and boys, and injuries were common. Chastisement for minor infractions came with swift severity; cooks who burned the bread and children who stole cookies or fell asleep while singing to the baby suffered every conceivable form of physical abuse, from jabs with pins to beatings that left them disfigured for life. The master's house offered no shelter from the most brutal manifestations of slavery.

For any one of all of these reasons, black women might prefer field-work to housework. During his visit to a rice plantation in 1853, Olmsted noted that hands "accustomed to the comparatively unconstrained life of the negro-settlement detest the close control and careful movements required of the house servants." Marriage could be both a means and an incentive to escape a willful mistress. Jessie Sparrow's mother wed at age thirteen in order "to go outer de big house. Dat how come she to marry so soon. . . ." Claude Wilson recalled many years later that "his mother was very rebellious toward her duties and constantly harassed the 'Missus' about letting her work in the fields with her husband until finally she was permitted to make the change from the house to the fields to be near her man." Other women, denied an alternative, explored the range of their own emotional resources in attempting to resist petty tyranny; their "sassiness" rubbed raw the nerves of mistresses already harried and high-strung. A few servants simply withdrew into a shell of "melancholy and timidity."

The dual status of a bondwoman—a slave and a female—afforded her master a certain degree of flexibility in formulating her work assignments. When he needed a field hand, her status as an able-bodied slave took precedence over gender considerations, and she was forced to toil alongside her menfolk. At the same time, the master's belief that most forms of domestic service required the attentions of a female reinforced among slave women the traditional role of woman as household worker.

The authority of the master in enforcing a sexual division of labor was absolute, but at times individual women could influence his decisions to some extent. In certain cases, a woman's preferences for either fieldwork or domestic service worked to her advantage. For example, the rebelliousness of Claude Wilson's mother prompted her removal from the Big House to the field, a change she desired. Similarly, masters might promise a woman an opportunity to do a kind of work she preferred as a reward for her cooperation and diligence. On the other hand, a slave's misbehavior might cause her to lose a position she had come to value; more than one prized cook or maid was exiled to the fields for "sassing" the mistress or stealing. A system of rewards and punishments thus depended on the preferences of individual slaves, and a servant determined to make life miserable for the family in the Big House might get her way in any case.

In the field and Big House, black women worked under the close supervision of whites (the master, overseer, or mistress) at a forced pace.

The slaves derived few, if any, tangible benefits from their labor to increase staple-crop profits and to render the white family comfortable (at least in physical terms). However, their efforts to provide for their own health and welfare often took place apart from whites, with a rhythm more in tune with community and family life. For slave women, these responsibilities, although physically arduous, offered a degree of personal fulfillment. As Martha Colquitt remarked of her slave grandmother and mother who stayed up late to knit and sew clothes "for us chillun": "Dey done it 'cause dey wanted to. Dey wuz workin' for deyselves den." Slave women deprived of the ability to cook for their own kinfolk or discipline their own children felt a keen sense of loss; family responsibilities revealed the limited extent to which black women (and men) could control their own lives. Furthermore, a strict sexual division of labor in the quarters openly challenged the master's opportunistic approach to slave women's work.

A number of activities were carried out either communally or centrally for the whole plantation by older women. On smaller farms, for example, a cook and her assistants might prepare one or all of the meals for the other slaves each day except Sunday. Similarly, an elderly woman, with the help of children too young to work in the fields, often was assigned charge of a nursery in the quarters, where mothers left their babies during the day. To keep any number of little ones happy and out of trouble for up to twelve to fourteen hours at a time taxed the patience of the most kindly souls. Slave children grew up with a mixture of affection and fear for the "grandmothers" who had dished out the licks along with the cornbread and clabber. Other grannies usurped the position of the white physician (he rarely appeared in any case); they "brewed medicines for every ailment," gave cloves and whiskey to ease the pain of childbirth, and prescribed potions for the lovesick. Even a child forced to partake of "Stinkin' Jacob tea" or a concoction of "turpentine an' castor oil an' Jerusalem oak" (for worms) would assert years later that "Gran'mammy was a great doctor," surely a testimony to her respected position within the slave community, if not to the delectability of her remedies.

On many plantations, it was the custom to release adult women from fieldwork early on Saturday so that they could do their week's washing. Whether laundering was done in old wooden tubs, iron pots, or a nearby creek with batten sticks, wooden paddles, or washboards, it was a time-consuming and difficult chore. Yet this ancient form of women's work provided opportunities for socializing "whilst de 'omans leaned over de tubs washin' and a-singin' dem old songs." Mary Frances Webb remembered wash day—"a regular picnic"—with some fondness; it was a time for women "to spend the day together," out of the sight and earshot of whites.

Much of the work black women did for the slave community resembled the colonial system of household industry. Well into the nineteenth century throughout the South, slave women continued to spin thread, weave and dye cloth, sew clothes, make soap and candles, prepare and preserve foods, churn butter, and grow food for the family table. Slave women mastered all these tasks with the aid of primitive equipment and skills passed on from grandmothers. Many years later, blacks of both sexes exclaimed over their slave mothers' ability to prepare clothing dye from various combinations of tree bark and leaves, soil and berries; make soap out of ashes and animal skins; and fashion bottle lamps from string and tallow. Because of their lack of time and materials, black women only rarely found in these activities an outlet for creative expression, but they did take pride in their resourcefulness and produced articles of value to the community as a whole.

Black women's work in home textile production illustrates the ironies of community labor under slavery, for the threads of cotton and wool bound them together in both bondage and sisterhood. Masters (or mistresses) imposed rigid spinning and weaving quotas on women who worked in the fields all day. For example, many were forced to spin one "cut" (about three hundred yards) of thread nightly, or four to five cuts during rainy days or in the winter. Women of all ages worked together and children of both sexes helped to tease and card wool, pick up the loom shuttles, and knit. In the flickering candlelight, the whirr of the spinning wheel and the clackety-clack of the loom played a seductive lullabye, drawing those who were already "mighty tired" away from their assigned tasks.

As the "head spinner" on a Virginia plantation, Bob Ellis's mother was often sent home from fieldwork early to prepare materials for the night's work; "She had to portion out de cotton dey was gonna spin an' see dat each got a fair share." Later that evening, after supper, as she moved around the dusty loom room to check on the progress of the other women, she would sing:

> Keep yo' eye on de sun,
> See how she run
> Don't let her catch you with you work undone,
> I'm a trouble, I'm a trouble,
> Trouble don' las' always.

With her song of urgency and promise she coaxed her sisters to finish their work so they could return home by sundown: "Dat made de women all speed up so dey could finish fo' dark catch 'em, 'cause it mighty hard handlin' dat cotton thread by fire-light."

In the quarters, group work melded into family responsibilities, for the communal spirit was but a manifestation of primary kin relationships. Here it is possible only to outline the social dynamics of the slave household. The significance of the family in relation to the sexual division of labor under slavery cannot be overestimated; out of the mother-father, wife-husband nexus sprang the slaves' beliefs about what women and men should be and do. Ultimately, the practical application of those beliefs (in the words of Genovese) "provided a weapon for joint resistance to dehumanization."

The two-parent, nuclear family was the typical form of slave cohabitation regardless of the location, size, or economy of a plantation; the nature of its ownership; or the age of its slave community. Because of the omnipresent threat of forced separation by sale, gift, or bequest, this family was not "stable." Yet, in the absence of such separations, unions between husbands and wives and parents and children often endured for many years. Marital customs, particularly exogamy, and the practice of naming children after the mother's or father's relatives (the most common pattern was to name a boy after a male relative) revealed the strong sense of kinship among slaves. Households tended to be large; Herbert G. Gutman found families with eight living children to be quite common. Out of economic considerations, a master would encourage his work force to reproduce itself, but the slaves welcomed each new birth primarily as "a social and familial fact." A web of human emotions spun by close family ties—affection, dignity, love—brought slaves together in a world apart from whites.

In their own cabins, the blacks maintained a traditional division of labor between the sexes. Like women in almost all cultures, slave women had both a biological and a social "destiny." As part of their childbearing role, they assumed primary responsibility for childcare (when a husband and wife lived on separate plantations, the children remained with their mother and belonged to her master). Women also performed operations related to daily household maintenance—cooking, cleaning, tending fires, sewing and patching clothes.

Fathers shared the obligations of family life with their wives. In denying slaves the right to own property, make a living for themselves, participate in public life, or protect their children, the institution of bondage deprived black men of access to the patriarchy in the larger economic and political sense. But at home women and men worked together to support the father's role as provider and protector. In the evenings and on Sundays, men collected firewood; made shoes; wove baskets; constructed beds, tables, and chairs; and carved butter paddles, ax handles, and animal traps. Other family members appreciated a father's skills; recalled Molly Ammonds, "My pappy make all de funiture dat went in our house an' it were might' good funiture too," and Pauline Johnson echoed, "De furn'chure was ho-mek, but my daddy mek it good an' stout." Husbands provided necessary supplements to the family diet by hunting and trapping quails, possums, turkeys, rabbits, squirrels, and raccoons, and by fishing. They often assumed responsibility for cultivating the tiny household garden plots allotted to families by the master. Some craftsmen, like Bill Austin's father, received goods or small sums of money in return for their work on nearby estates; Jack Austin, "regarded as a fairly good carpenter, mason, and bricklayer," was paid in "hams, bits of cornmeal, cloth for dresses for his wife and children, and other small gifts; these he either used for his small family or bartered with other slaves."

These familial duties also applied to men who lived apart from their wives and children even though they were usually allowed to visit only on Saturday night and Sunday. Lucinda Miller's family "never had any sugar, and only got coffee when her father would bring it to her mother" during his visits. The father of Hannah Chapman was sold to a nearby planter when she was very small. Because "he missed us and us longed for him," she said many years later, he tried to visit his family under the cover of darkness whenever possible. She noted, "Us would gather 'round him an' crawl up in his lap, tickled slap to death, but he give us dese pleasures at painful risk." If the master should happen to discover him, "Us could track him de nex' day by de blood stains," she remembered.

Hannah McFarland of South Carolina well remembered the time when the local slave patrol attempted to whip her mother, "but my papa sho' stopped dat," she said proudly. Whether or not he was made to suffer for his courage is unknown; however, the primary literature of slavery is replete with accounts of slave husbands who intervened, at the risk of their own lives, to save wives and children from violence at the hands of white men. More often, however, fathers had to show their compassion in less dramatic (though no less revealing) ways. On a Florida plantation, the Minus children often rose in the morning to find still warm in the fireplace the potatoes "which their father had thoughtfully roasted and which [they] readily consumed." Margrett Nickerson recalled how her father would tenderly bind up the wounds inflicted on her by a maniacal overseer; in later years, her crippled legs preserved the memory of a father's sorrow intermingled with her own suffering.

The more freedom the slaves had in determining their own activities the more clearly emerged a distinct division of labor between the sexes. During community festivities like log rollings, rail splittings, wood choppings, and corn shuckings, men performed the prescribed labor while women cooked the meals. At times, male participants willingly "worked all night," for in the words of one former slave, "we had the 'Heavenly Banners' (women and whiskey) by us." A limited amount of primary evidence indicates that men actively scorned women's work, especially cooking, housecleaning, sewing, washing clothes, and intimate forms of childcare (like bathing children and picking lice out of their hair). Some slaveholders devised forms of public humiliation that capitalized on men's attempts to avoid these tasks. One Louisiana cotton planter punished slave men by forcing them to wash clothes (he also made chronic offenders wear women's dresses). In *This Species of Property*, Leslie Howard Owens remarks of men so treated, "So great was their shame before their fellows that many ran off and suffered the lash on their backs rather than submit to the discipline. Men clearly viewed certain chores as women's tasks, and female slaves largely respected the distinction."

The values and customs of the slave community played a predominant role in structuring work patterns among women and men within the quarters in general and the family in particular. Yet slaveholders affected the division of labor in the quarters in several ways; for example, they took women and girls out of the fields early on Saturdays to wash the clothes, and they enforced certain task assignments related to the production of household goods. An understanding of the social significance of the sexual division of labor requires at least brief mention of West African cultural preferences and the ways in which the American system of slavery disrupted or sustained traditional (African) patterns of women's work. Here it is important to keep in mind two points. First, cotton did not emerge as the South's primary staple crop until the late eighteenth century (the first slaves on the North American continent toiled in tobacco, rice, indigo, and corn fields); and second, regardless of the system of task assignments imposed upon antebellum blacks, the grueling pace of forced labor represented a cruel break from the past for people who had followed age-old customs related to subsistence agriculture.

Though dimmed by time and necessity, the outlines of African work patterns endured among the slaves. As members of traditional agricultural societies, African women played a major role in producing the family's food as well as in providing basic household services. The sexual division of labor was more often determined by a woman's childcare and domestic responsibilities than by any presumed physical weakness. She might engage in heavy monotonous fieldwork (in some tribes) as long as she could make provisions for nursing her baby; that often meant keeping an infant with her in the field. She cultivated a kitchen garden that yielded a variety of vegetables consumed by the family or sold at market, and she usually milked the cows and churned butter.

West Africans in general brought with them competencies and knowledge that slaveowners readily exploited. Certain tribes were familiar with rice, cotton, and indigo cultivation. Many black women had had experience spinning thread, weaving cloth, and sewing clothes. Moreover, slaves often used techniques and tools handed down from their ancestors—in the method of planting, hoeing, and pounding rice, for example. Whites frequently commented on the ability of slave women to balance heavy and unwieldy loads on their heads, an African trait.

The primary difficulty in generalizing about African women's part in agriculture stems from the fact that members of West African tribes captured for the North American slave trade came from different hoe-culture economies. Within the geographically limited Niger Delta region, for example, women and men of the Ibo tribe worked together in planting, weeding, and harvesting, but female members of another prominent group, the Yoruba, helped only with harvest. In general, throughout most of sub-Saharan Africa (and particularly on the west coast) women had primary responsibility for tilling (though not clearing) the soil and cultivating the crops; perhaps this tradition, combined with work patterns established by white masters in this country, reinforced the blacks' beliefs that cutting trees and rolling logs was "men's work." In any case it is clear that African women often did fieldwork. But because the sexual division of labor varied according to tribe, it is impossible to state with any precision the effect of the African heritage on the slaves' perceptions of women's agricultural work.

The West African tradition of respect for one's elders found new meaning among American slaves; for most women, old age brought increased influence within the slave community even as their economic value to the master declined. Owners, fearful lest women escape from "earning their salt" once they became too infirm to go to the field, set them to work at other tasks—knitting, cooking, spinning, weaving, dairying, washing, ironing, caring for the children. (Elderly men worked as gardeners, wagoners, carters, and stocktenders.) But the imperatives of the southern economic system sometimes compelled slaveowners to extract from feeble women what field labor they could. In other cases they reduced the material provisions of the elderly—housing and allowances of food and clothing—in proportion to their decreased productivity.

The overwhelming youth of the general slave population between 1830 and 1860 (more than one-half of all slaves were under twenty years of age) meant that most plantations had only a few old persons— the 10 percent over fifty years of age considered elderly. These slaves served as a repository of history and folklore for the others. Harriet Ware, a northern teacher assigned to the South Carolina Sea Islands, reported in 1862, " 'Learning' with these people I find means a knowledge of medicine, and a person is valued accordingly." Many older women practiced "medicine" in the broadest sense in their combined role of midwife, root doctor, healer, and conjurer. They guarded ancient secrets about herbs and other forms of plant life. In their interpretation of dreams and strange occurrences, they brought the real world closer to the supernatural realm and offered spiritual guidance to the ill, the troubled, and the lovelorn.

For slaves in the late antebellum period, these revered (and sometimes feared) women served as a tangible link with the African past. Interviewed by an FWP worker in 1937, a Mississippi-born former slave, James Brittian, recalled his own "grandma Aunt Mary" who had lived for 110 years. A "Molly Gasca [Madagascar?] negro," she was plagued by a jealous mistress because of her striking physical appearance; "Her hair it was fine as silk and hung down below her waist." Ned Chaney's African-born Granny Silla (she was the oldest person anyone knew, he thought) commanded respect among the other slaves by virtue of her advanced age and her remarkable healing powers: "Ever'body set a heap of sto' by her. I reckon, because she done 'cumullated so much knowledge an' because her head were so white." When Granny Silla died, her "little bags" of mysterious substances were buried with her because no one else knew how to use them. Yet Chaney's description of his own mother, a midwife and herb doctor, indicates that she too eventually assumed a position of at least informal authority within the community.

As a little girl in Georgia, Mary Colbert adored her grandmother, a strong field hand, "smart as a whip." "I used to tell my mother that I wished I was named Hannah for her, and so Mother called me Mary Hannah," she recalled. Amanda Harris, interviewed in Virginia when she was ninety years old, looked back to the decade before the war when her grandmother was still alive: "Used to see her puffin' on dat ole pipe o' her'n, an' one day I ast her what fun she got outen it. 'Tain't no fun, chile,' she told me. 'But it's a pow'ful lot o' easment. Smoke away trouble, darter. Blow ole trouble an' worry 'way in smoke.' " Amanda started smoking a pipe shortly before her grandmother died, and in 1937 she declared, "Now dat I'm ole as she was I know what she mean." In the quiet dignity of their own lives, these grandmothers preserved the past for future generations of Afro-American women.

Within well-defined limits, the slaves created—or preserved—an explicit sexual division of labor based on their own preferences. Wives and husbands and mothers and fathers had reciprocal obligations toward one another. Together they worked to preserve the integrity of the family. Having laid to rest once and for all the myth of the slave matriarchy, some historians suggest that relations between the sexes approximated "a healthy sexual equality." Without private property, slave men lacked the means to achieve economic superiority over their wives, one of the major sources of inequality in the ("free") sexual order. But if female and male slaves shared duties related to household maintenance and community survival, they were nonetheless reduced to a state of powerlessness that rendered virtually meaningless the concept of equality as it applies to marital relations.

Developments during the turbulent postwar years, when the chains of bondage were loosened but not destroyed, made clear the significance of black women's work in supporting the southern staple-crop economy. They also revealed the connection between patterns of women's work and black family life—a connection that had, at least to some degree, remained latent under slavery. Black women did their part in helping to provide for their families after the war. Female household heads had a particularly difficult time, for under the "free labor" system, a mother working alone rarely earned enough to support small children who were themselves too little to make any money. Relatives in a better financial situation often "adopted" these children, or took the whole family under their care.

After the war, black women continued to serve as domestic servants, but large numbers stopped going to the fields altogether, or agreed
to work only in harvest time. Indeed, from all over the South came
reports that "the negro women are now almost wholly withdrawn from
field labor." Ransom and Sutch, in their study of the economic consequences of emancipation, estimate that between one-third and one-half
of all the women who worked in the fields under slavery provided proportionately less agricultural labor in the 1870s. This decline in overall
female productivity was the result of two factors: many wives stayed
home, and the ones who did continue to labor in the fields (like black
men) put in shorter hours and fewer days each year than they had as
slaves. Crop output in many locales dropped accordingly, and white
landowners lamented their loss, "for women were as efficient as men in
working and picking cotton."

In their speculation about the sources of this "evil of female loaf-
erism," whites offered a number of theories, from the pernicious influence of northern schoolteachers to the inherent laziness of the black
race. Actually, black women and men responded to freedom in a manner consistent with preferences that had been thwarted during slavery.
Husbands sought to protect their wives from the sexual abuse and physical punishment that continued to prevail under the wage system of
agricultural labor. Wives wanted to remain at home with their children, as befitted free and freed women; many continued to contribute
to the family welfare by taking in washing or raising chickens.

By 1867, freed people who wanted to assert control over their own
productive energies had reached what some historians term a "compromise" with white landowners anxious to duplicate antebellum crop levels. This "compromise" came in the form of the sharecropping system,
a family organization of labor that represented both a radical departure
from collective or "gang" work characteristic of slavery and a rejection
of the wage economy so integral to the (North's) fledgling industrial
revolution. Freed families moved out of the old slave quarters into cabins
scattered around a white man's plantation; they received "furnishings"
(tools and seed) and agreed to pay the landlord a share of the crop—
usually one-half of all the cotton they produced—in return for the use
of the land and modest dwelling. Under this arrangement, black husbands assumed primary responsibility for crop management, and their
wives devoted as much attention as possible to their roles as mothers
and homemakers. During the particularly busy planting or harvesting
seasons, a woman would join her husband and children at work in the
field. In this way she could keep an eye on her offspring and still put
to use her considerable strength and skills unmolested by white men.

The Reconstruction South was not the best of all worlds in which
to foster a new order between the races—or the sexes. Faced with persistent economic exploitation and political subservience within white-
dominated society, black men sought to assert their authority as protec-
tors of their communities and families. Outwardly, they placed a pre-

mium on closing ranks at home. This impulse was institutionalized in the freed people's churches ("Wives submit yourselves to your husbands" was the text of more than one postbellum sermon) and political organizations. One searches in vain for evidence of female participants in the many black conventions and meetings during this period, although this was perhaps in part attributable to the fact that women did not have the right to vote. Black women remained militantly outspoken in defense of their families and property rights, but they lacked a formal power base within their own communities. And in an atmosphere fraught with sexual violence, where freedwomen remained at the mercy of white men and where "the mere suggestion" that a black man was attracted to a white woman was "enough to hang him," a black husband's resentment might continue to manifest itself in his relations with those closest to him. A Sea Island slave folktale offered the lesson that "God had nebber made a woman for the head of a man." In the struggle against white racism this often meant that black women were denied the equality with their men to which their labor—not to mention justice—entitled them.

The sexual division of labor under slavery actually assumed two forms—one system of work forced upon slaves by masters who valued women only as work-oxen and brood-sows, and the other initiated by the slaves themselves in the quarters. Only the profit motive accorded a measure of consistency to the slaveholder's decisions concerning female work assignments; he sought to exploit his "hands" efficiently, and either invoked or repudiated traditional notions of women's work to suit his own purposes. In this respect, his decision-making process represented in microcosm the shifting priorities of the larger society, wherein different groups of women were alternately defined primarily as producers or as reproducers according to the fluctuating labor demands of the capitalist economy.

Within their own communities, the slaves attempted to make work choices based on their African heritage as it applied to the American experience. Their well-defined sexual division of labor contrasted with the calculated self-interest of slaveowners. Slave women were allowed to fulfill their duties as wives and mothers only insofar as these responsibilities did not conflict with their masters' demands for field or domestic labor. As sharecroppers, freed people sought to institutionalize their resistance to the whites' conviction that black women should be servants or cotton pickers first, and family members only incidentally. In working together as a unit, black parents and children made an explicit political statement to the effect that their own priorities were inimical to those of white landowners.

To a considerable extent, the freed family's own patriarchal tendencies—fathers took care of "public" negotiations with the white landlord while mothers assumed primary responsibility for childcare—resulted from

the black man's desire to protect his household in the midst of a violently racist society. The postbellum black nuclear family never duplicated exactly the functions of the white middle-class model, which
(beginning in the late eighteenth century) drew an increasingly rigid
distinction between masculine and feminine spheres of activity characteristic of commercial-industrial capitalism. Clearly, the peculiar southern way of life suggests that an analysis of black women's oppression
should focus not so much on the family as on the dynamics of racial
prejudice. However, black women and men in the long run paid a high
price for their allegiance to a patriarchal family structure, and it is important not to romanticize this arrangement as it affected the status and
opportunities of women, even within the confines of black community
life. Women continued to wield informal influence in their roles as
herb doctors and "grannies," but men held all positions of formal political and religious authority. Ultimately, black people's "preferences" in
the postwar period took shape within two overlapping caste systems—
one based on race, the other on gender. Former slaves were "free" only
in the sense that they created their own forms of masculine authority
as a counter to poverty and racism.

The story of slave women's work encapsulates an important part of
American history. For here in naked form, stripped free of the pieties
often used in describing white women and free workers at the time,
were the forces that shaped patriarchal capitalism—exploitation of the
most vulnerable members of society, and a contempt for women that
knew no ethical or physical bounds. And yet, slave women demonstrated "true womanhood" in its truest sense. Like Janie Scott's mother
who was "much of a woman," they revealed a physical and emotional
strength that transcended gender and preached a great sermon about
the human spirit.

Suggestions for Further Reading

General introductions to the history of immigration in the United States are M. A. Jones, *American Immigration** (University of Chicago Press, 1960), and Leonard Dinnerstein and David M. Reimers, *Ethnic Americans: A History of Immigration and Assimilation** (Harper & Row, 1975). On ante-bellum immigration in particular, the standard work is Marcus L. Hansen, *The Atlantic Migration, 1607–1860** (Harvard University Press, 1940). Catholic immigrants are treated in Jay P. Dolan, *The Immigrant Church: New York's Irish and German Catholics, 1815–1865** (Johns Hopkins Press, 1975); Kerby Miller, *Emigrants and Exiles: Ireland and the Irish Exodus to North America* (Oxford University Press, 1985); and Oscar Handlin, *Boston's Immigrants: 1790–1865** (Harvard University Press, 1941). The conflict between established settlers and Irish immigrants in Boston is discussed in Barbara Miller Solomon, *Ancestors and Immigrants** (Harvard University Press, 1956). Ray A. Billington, in *The Protestant Crusade, 1800–1860** (Macmillan, 1938), deals more generally with religious conflicts in the first half of the nineteenth century.

Several studies of violence in American history have appeared in recent years. A good collection of essays, many of them prepared for President Johnson's Commission on the Causes and Prevention of Violence, is Hugh Davis Graham and Ted Robert Gurr (eds.), *Violence in America: Historical and Comparative Perspectives** (U.S. Government Printing Office, 1969), also available in a paperback edition from Sage Publications. Leonard L. Richards, *"Gentlemen of Property and Standing": Anti-Abolition Mobs in Jacksonian America** (Oxford University Press, 1971) surveys one aspect of violence in this period. A recent study is Michael Feldberg, *The Turbulent Era: Riot and Disorder in Jacksonian America** (Oxford University Press, 1980).

The changes taking place in family life during this period are discussed in the following works: Nancy F. Cott, *The Bonds of Womanhood: "Woman's Sphere" in New England, 1780–1835** (Yale University Press, 1977), and Anthony F. C. Wallace, *Rockdale: The Growth of an American Village in the Early Industrial Revolution** (Norton, 1978). Agricultural developments having an impact on the family are traced in Clarence H. Danhof, *Change in Agriculture: The Northern United States, 1820–1870* (Harvard University Press, 1969).

For a general introduction to the lives of black women in this period, see Dorothy Sterling, *We Are Your Sisters: Black Women in the Nineteenth Century** (Norton, 1985). Deborah Gray White has

* Available in paperback edition.

published a study of slave women under the title *Ar'n't I a Woman: Female Slaves in the Plantation South* (Norton, 1985). A broader study of the black family in slavery and after can be found in Herbert G. Gutman, *The Black Family in Slavery and Freedom, 1750– 1925* * (Random House, 1976). For the picture from the other side of the racial barrier, see Catherine Clinton, *The Plantation Mistress: Woman's World in the Old South* * (Pantheon, 1982). Jacqueline Jones has expanded the essay reprinted in this collection and published *Labor of Love, Labor of Sorrow: Black Women, Work, and the Family from Slavery to the Present* * (Basic Books, 1985).

4

WESTWARD EXPANSION

Legacy of Hate: The Conquest of the Southwest

RODOLFO ACUÑA

By the middle of the nineteenth century, three nonwhite ethnic minorities had become inhabitants of the United States against their will—Afro-Americans, American Indians, and Mexican-Americans. The last of these groups traditionally has received the least attention by historians. The Mexican-Americans' story and place in American history has been seen as less dramatic and less consequential than that of either blacks or Indians. But they are here—and in rather large numbers. While Chicanos—as Mexican-Americans have recently begun calling themselves—make up less than three percent of the total American population, they constitute over ten percent of the population in the Southwest and are a majority in many small towns and rural counties from Texas to California.

From the beginning, they have been discriminated against on several counts: they are not considered white, they are of mixed (Spanish-Indian) ancestry, and they are predominantly Roman Catholic in religion. Any one of these characteristics would have led Mexican-Americans to be victimized by the dominant ideology of Anglo-Saxon expansionists. The attitude of many Americans was expressed by a famous Texas gunman who, when asked how many notches he had in his gun, replied, "Thirty-seven—not counting Mexicans."

As the theory of Manifest Destiny and the rigorous drive for national expansion thrust the United States government westward, it was clear that the American leadership was not concerned with "counting Mexicans." Once the conquest was complete, however, and the vast and potentially rich southwestern area was a part of the United States, there were the Mexicans, now residents on American soil, and many claiming hereditary property rights to land granted their families, and communities by the Spanish and Mexican governments. These property rights were not recognized by the laws of either the United States or the individual states that the Mexican-Americans found themselves subject to, and much of the political activity of Chicanos in recent years—particularly the Alianza movement in New Mexico—has called for a restoration of those rights or for reparations.

The existence of large numbers of these "alien" peoples in the territories of New Mexico and Arizona delayed statehood for those areas for decades, even after they had qualified constitutionally for admission to the Union. As the editor of *Harper's Weekly* wrote in 1876 after the Senate had passed a statehood bill, "New Mexico is virtually an ignorant foreign community under the influence of the Roman Church, and neither for the advantage of the Union nor for its own benefit can such an addition to the family of American States be urged."

In the second edition of his history of Mexican-Americans, Chicano historian Rodolfo Acuña (University of California at Northridge) has drawn on much recent scholarship to tell his story. In the selection from his work, reprinted here, Acuña describes the conquest of northern Mexico by the United States in the second quarter of the nineteenth century. He properly points out the role of slavery and racism in this struggle and indicates how some American historians have sought to justify the conquest in terms that show the continuing legacy of nineteenth-century racial and nationalistic attitudes.

T he tragedy of the Mexican cession is that most Anglo-Americans have not accepted the fact that the United States committed an act of violence against the Mexican people when it took Mexico's northwestern territory. Violence was not limited to the taking of the land; Mexico's territory was invaded, her people murdered, her land raped, and her possessions plundered. Memory of this destruction generated a distrust and dislike that is still vivid in the minds of many Mexicans, for the violence of the United States left deep scars. And for Chicanos—Mexicans remaining within the boundaries of the new United States—aggression was even more insidious, for the outcome of the Texas and Mexican-American wars made them a conquered people. Anglo-Americans were the conquerors, and they evinced all the arrogance of military victors.

LEGACY OF HATE: THE CONQUEST OF THE SOUTHWEST   From *Occupied America: A History of Chicanos*, 2nd ed., by Rodolfo Acuña (New York: Harper & Row, 1981) pp. 3–20. Copyright © 1981 by Rodolfo Acuña. Reprinted by permission of Harper & Row, Publishers, Inc.

BACKGROUND TO THE INVASION OF TEXAS

An integral part of Anglo rationalizations for the conquest has been either to ignore or to distort events that led up to the initial clash in 1836. To Anglo-Americans, the Texas War resulted because of a tyrannical or, at best, an incompetent Mexican government that was antithetical to the ideals of democracy and justice. The truth is that the roots of the conflict extended back to as early as 1767 when Benjamin Franklin marked Mexico and Cuba for future expansion. Filibusters* from the United States planned expeditions into Texas in the 1790s. The Louisiana Purchase in 1803 stimulated U.S. ambitions in the Southwest and six years later Thomas Jefferson predicted that the Spanish borderlands "are ours the first moment war is forced upon us." The war with Great Britain in 1812 heightened Anglo-American designs on the Spanish territory.

The U.S. experience in Florida set the pattern for expansionist activities in Texas. In 1818 several posts in East Florida were seized in unauthorized, but never officially condemned U.S. military expeditions. Negotiations then in progress with Spain finally terminated in the Adams-Onis or Transcontinental Treaty (1819) whereby Spain ceded Florida to the United States and the United States renounced its claim to Texas. The treaty set the U.S. boundary at the Sabine River, thereby excluding Texas. When the treaty was ratified in February 1821 Texas was part of Coahuila, a state in the independent Republic of Mexico. Many North Americans claimed that Texas belonged to the United States, pointing to Jefferson's contention that Texas's boundary extended to the Rio Grande and that it was part of the Louisiana Purchase. They condemned the Adams-Onis Treaty. The expanded boundary would have "put several key Mexican posts, notably San Antonio, Albuquerque and Santa Fe inside the United States." Therefore, Anglo-Americans made forays into Texas similar to those they had made into Florida. In 1819 James Long led an abortive invasion to establish the "Republic of Texas." Long, like many Anglos, believed that Texas belonged to the United States and that "Congress had no right or power to sell, exchange, or relinquish an 'American possession.' "

The Mexican government opened Texas, provided settlers agreed to certain conditions and for a time filibustering subsided. Moses Austin was given permission to settle in Texas. He died shortly afterwards, and his son continued his venture. In December 1821 Stephen Austin founded the settlement of San Felipe de Austin. Large numbers followed, many coming to Texas in the 1820s as refugees from the depression of 1819 and in the 1830s as entrepreneurs seeking to profit from the availability

---

* A *filibuster* is an adventurer who engages in insurrectionist or revolutionary activity in a foreign country.

of cheap land. By 1830 there were about 20,000 settlers, along with about 2,000 slaves.

Settlers agreed to obey the conditions set by the Mexican government—that all immigrants be Catholics and that they take an oath of allegiance to Mexico. However, Anglo-Americans became resentful when Mexico tried to enforce the agreements and Mexico became increasingly alarmed at the flood of immigrants from the U.S., most of whom retained their Protestant religion.

It soon became apparent that the Anglo-Texans had no intention of obeying Mexican laws. Many settlers considered the native Mexicans to be the intruders in the territory and encroached upon their lands. In a dispute with Mexicans and Indians, as well as Anglo-American settlers, Hayden Edwards arbitrarily attempted to evict settlers from the land before the conflicting claims could be sorted out by the Mexican authorities. As a result the authorities nullified his settlement contract and ordered him to leave the territory. He and his followers seized the town of Nacogdoches and on December 21, 1826, proclaimed the Republic of Fredonia. Mexican officials, who were supported by some Anglo-Americans (such as Stephen Austin), suffocated the Edwards revolt. However, many U.S. newspapers played up the rebellion as "200 Men Against a Nation!" and described Edwards and his followers as "apostles of democracy crushed by an alien civilization."

In 1824 President John Quincy Adams "began putting pressure on Mexico in the hope of persuading her to rectify the frontier. Any of the Texan rivers west of Sabine—the Brazos, the Colorado, the Nueces— was preferable to the Sabine, though the Rio Grande was the one desired." In 1826 Adams offered to buy Texas for the sum of $1 million. Mexican authorities refused the offer. The United States launched an aggressive foreign policy, attempting to coerce Mexico into selling Texas.

Mexico tried to consolidate its control over Texas, but the number of Anglo-American settlers and the vastness of the territory made it an almost impossible task. Anglo-Americans in Texas had already created a privileged caste, which depended in great part on the economic advantage given to them by their slaves. When Mexico abolished slavery on September 15, 1829, Texans circumvented the law by "freeing" their slaves and then signing them to lifelong contracts as indentured servants. Anglos resented the Mexican order and considered it an invasion of their personal liberties. In 1830 Mexico prohibited further Anglo-American immigration to Texas. Anglos were outraged at the restrictions. Meanwhile, Andrew Jackson increased tensions by attempting to purchase Texas for as much as $5 million.

Mexican authorities grew more nervous as the Anglo-Americans' dominance of Texas increased; they resented the Anglo-Americans' refusal to submit to Mexican laws. Mexico moved reinforcements into Coahuila, and readied them in case of trouble. Anglos viewed this move as a Mexican invasion.

Anglo-Texas colonists grew more defiant and refused to pay customs and actively supported smuggling activities. Armed clashes broke out. When the "war party" rioted at Anahuac in December 1831 it had the popular support of Anglo-Texans. One of its leaders was Sam Houston, who "was a known protégé of Andrew Jackson, now president of the United States. . . . Houston's motivation was to bring Texas into the United States."

In the summer of 1832 a group of Anglos attacked a Mexican garrison and were routed. A state of insurrection existed and Mexican authorities were forced to defend the territory. Matters worsened when the Anglo settlers met at San Félipe in October 1832. At this convention Anglos drafted resolutions sent to the Mexican government and to the state of Coahuila which called for more autonomy for Texas. A second convention was held in January 1833. Significantly, not one Mexican pueblo in Texas participated in either convention, many clearly branding the act sedition. Increasingly it became evident that the war party under Sam Houston was winning out. Sam Houston was elected to direct the course of events and Austin was appointed to submit the grievances and resolutions to Mexico City.

Austin left for Mexico City to press for lifting of restrictions on Anglo-American immigration and separate statehood. The slave issue also burned in his mind, Austin, anything but conciliatory, wrote to a friend from Mexico City, "If our application is refused . . . I shall be in favor of organizing *without it.* I see no other way of saving the country from total anarchy and ruin. I am totally done with conciliatory measures and, for the future, shall be uncompromising as to Texas."

On October 2, 1833, he wrote a letter to the *ayuntamiento* at San Antonio encouraging it to declare Texas a separate state. He later stated that he had done so "in a moment of irritation and impatience"; nevertheless, his actions were not those of a moderate. Contents of the note fell into the hands of Mexican authorities, who had begun to question Austin's good faith. Subsequently, they imprisoned him, and much of what Austin had accomplished in the way of compromise was undone.

Contributing to the general distrust were actions of U.S. Minister to Mexico Anthony Butler, whose crude attempts to bribe Mexican officials to sell Texas infuriated Mexicans. He offered one official $200,000 to "play ball."

In the autumn of 1834 Henry Smith published a pamphlet entitled *Security for Texas* in which he advocated open defiance of Mexican authority. The agents of Anglo land companies added to the polarization by lobbying in Washington, D.C., and within Texas for a change in governments. The Galveston Bay and Texas Land Company of New York, acting to protect its investments, worked through its agent Anthony Butler, the U.S. Minister to Mexico, to bring about the cooperation of the U.S.

According to Dr. Carlos Castañeda:

The activities of the "Land Companies" after 1834 cannot be ignored. Their widespread advertisement and indiscriminate sale of "landscrip" sent hundreds, perhaps thousands, to Texas under the impression that they had legitimate titles to lands equal to the amount of scrip bought. The Galveston Bay and Texas Land Company, which bought the contracts of David S. Burnet, Joseph Vahlein, and Lorenzo de Zavala, and the Nashville Company, which acquired the contract of Robert Leftwitch, are the two best known. They first sold scrip at from one to ten cents an acre, calling for a total of seven and one-half million acres. The company was selling only its permit to acquire a given amount of land in Texas, but since an empresario contract was nontransferable, the scrip was, in fact, worthless. . . .

The scrip would be worthless as long as Texas belonged to Mexico.

On July 13, 1835, a general amnesty released Austin from prison. While enroute to Texas, he wrote a letter from New Orleans to a cousin expressing the view that Texas should be Americanized even though it was still a state of Mexico, and indicating that it should one day come under the American flag. In this letter he called for a massive immigration of Anglo-Americans, *"each man with his rifle,"* whom he hoped would come "passports or no passports, *anyhow."* He continued: "For fourteen years I have had a hard time of it, but nothing shall daunt my courage or abate my . . . object . . . to *Americanize* Texans."

Anglos in Texas saw separation from Mexico and eventual union with the United States as the most profitable political arrangement. Texas-Mexican historian Castañeda notes:

> Trade with New Orleans and other American ports had increased steadily. This development was naturally distasteful to Mexico, for the colonists fostered strong economic ties with . . . the United States rather than with Mexico. Juan H. Almonte in his 1834 report, estimated the total foreign trade of Texas—chiefly with the United States—at more than 1,000,000 pesos, of which imports constituted 630,000 and exports, 500,000. He calculated the exportation of cotton by the settlers in 1833, as approximately 2,000 bales.

Colonel Almonte recognized the fundamental economic conflict reflected in these figures and his report recommended many concessions to the *Tejanos*, but also urged that "the province be well stocked with Mexican troops."

THE INVASION OF TEXAS

Not all the Anglo-Texan settlers favored the conflict. Austin belonged to the peace party, which at first opposed a confrontation with Mexicans. Ultimately, this faction joined the "hawks." Eugene C. Bar-

ker states that the immediate cause of the war was "the overthrow of
the nominal republic [by Santa Anna] and the substitution of centralized oligarchy," which allegedly would have placed the Texans more
strictly under the control of Mexico. Barker admits that "Earnest patriots like Benjamin Lundy, William Ellery Channing, and John Quincy
Adams saw in the Texas revolution a disgraceful affair promoted by the
sordid slaveholders and land speculators."

Barker draws a parallel between the Texas revolt and the American
Revolution, stating: "In each, the general cause of revolt was the same—
a sudden effort to extend imperial authority at the expense of local
privilege." In fact, in both instances the central governments attempted
to enforce laws that conflicted with illegal activities of some very articulate men. Barker further attempts to justify the Anglo-Texans' actions
by observing: "At the close of summer in 1835 the Texans saw themselves in danger of becoming the alien subjects of a people to whom
they deliberately believed themselves morally, intellectually, and politically superior. The racial feeling, indeed, underlay and colored Texan-
Mexican relations from the establishment of the first Anglo-American
colony in 1821." Therefore, the conflict, according to Barker, was inevitable and, consequently, justified.

Texas history is elusive—a mixture of selected fact and generalized
myth. Many historians admit that racism played a leading role in the
causes for revolt, that smugglers were upset with Mexico's enforcement
of her import laws, that Texans were upset about emancipation laws,
and that an increasing number of the new arrivals from the United
States actively agitated for independence. But despite these admissions,
many historians like Barker refuse to assign guilt to their countrymen.
Instead, Barker blamed it on the racial and cultural mistrust between
Mexicans and the colonists.

The antipathies of the Texans escalated into a full-scale rebellion.
Austin gave the call to arms on September 19, 1835, stating, "War is
our only recourse. There is no other remedy." Anglo-Americans enjoyed very real advantages in 1835. They were "defending" terrain with
which they were familiar. The 5,000 Mexicans living in the territory
did not join them, but the Anglo population had swelled to almost
30,000. The Mexican nation was divided, and the centers of power
were thousands of miles away from Texas. From the interior of Mexico
Santa Anna led an army of about 6,000 conscripts, many of whom had
been forced into the army and then marched hundreds of miles over
hot, arid desert land. Many were Mayan and did not speak Spanish. In
February 1836 the majority arrived in San Antonio, Texas, sick and
ill-prepared to fight. Although the Mexican army outnumbered the Anglo contingent, the latter were much better armed and enjoyed the
position of being the defenders. (Until World War I, this was a decided
advantage during wartime.) Santa Anna, on the other hand, had overextended his supply lines and was many miles from his base of power.

The defenders of San Antonio took refuge in a former mission, the

Alamo. In the days that followed, Texans inflicted heavy casualties on the Mexican forces, but eventually the Mexicans' sheer superiority in numbers won out. Much has been written about Mexican cruelty in relation to the Alamo and about the heroics of the doomed men. The result was the creation of the Alamo myth. Within the broad framework of what actually happened—187 Texans barricading themselves in the Alamo in defiance of Santa Anna's force and the eventual triumph of the Mexicans—there has been much distortion.

Walter Lord, in an article entitled "Myths and Realities of the Alamo," sets much of the record straight. Texas mythology portrays the Alamo heroes as freedom-loving defenders of their homes; they were supposedly all good Texans. Actually, two-thirds of the defenders had recently arrived from the United States, and only a half dozen had been in Texas for more than six years. The men in the Alamo were adventurers. William Barret Travis had fled to Texas after killing a man, abandoning his wife and two children. James Bowie, an infamous brawler, made a fortune running slaves and had wandered into Texas searching for lost mines and more money. The fading Davey Crockett, a legend in his own time, fought for the sake of fighting. Many others in the Alamo were men who had come to Texas for riches and glory. These defenders were hardly the sort of men who could be classified as peaceful settlers fighting for their homes.

The folklore of the Alamo goes beyond the legendary names of the defenders. According to Lord, it is riddled with dramatic half-truths that have been accepted as history. Defenders at the Alamo are portrayed as selfless heroes who sacrificed their lives to buy more time for their comrades-in-arms. As the story is told, William Barret Travis told his men that they were doomed; he drew a line in the sand with his sword, saying that all who crossed it would elect to remain and fight to the last. Supposedly all the men there valiantly stepped across the line, with a man in a cot begging to be carried across it. The bravery of the defenders has been *dramatized* in countless Hollywood movies.

In reality the Alamo had little strategic value, it was the best fortified fort west of the Mississippi, and the men fully expected help. The defenders had twenty-one cannons to the Mexicans' eight or ten. They were expert marksmen equipped with rifles with a range of 200 yards, while the Mexicans were inadequately trained and armed with smoothbore muskets with a range of only 70 yards. The Anglos were protected by the walls and had clear shots, while the Mexicans advanced in the open and fired at concealed targets. In short, ill-prepared, ill-equipped, and ill-fed Mexicans attacked well-armed and professional soldiers. In addition, from all reliable sources, it is doubtful whether Travis ever drew a line in the sand. San Antonio survivors, females and noncombatants, did not tell the story until many years later, when the tale had become well circulated and the myth was a legend. Probably the most widely circulated story was that of the last stand of the aging Davey

Crockett who fell "fighting like a tiger," killing Mexicans with his bare hands. This is a myth; seven of the defenders surrendered, and Crockett was among them. They were executed. And, finally, one man, Louis Rose, did escape.

Travis's stand delayed Santa Anna's timetable by only four days, as the Mexicans took San Antonio on March 6, 1836. At first, the stand at the Alamo did not even have propaganda value. Afterwards, Houston's army dwindled, with many volunteers rushing home to help their families flee from the advancing Mexican army. Most Anglo-Texans realized that they had been badly beaten. It did, nevertheless, result in massive aid from the United States in the form of volunteers, arms, and money. The cry of "Remember the Alamo" became a call to arms for Anglo-Americans in both Texas and the United States.

After the Alamo and the defeat of another garrison at Goliad, southeast of San Antonio, Santa Anna was in full control. He ran Sam Houston out of the territory northwest of the San Jacinto River and then camped an army of about 1,110 men near San Jacinto. There, he skirmished with Houston on April 20, 1836, but did not follow up his advantage. Predicting that Houston would attack on April 22, Santa Anna and his men settled down and rested for the anticipated battle. Texans, however, attacked during the *siesta* hour on April 21. Santa Anna had made an incredible blunder. He knew that Houston had an army of 1,000, yet he was lax in his precautionary defenses. The surprise attack caught him totally off guard. Shouts of "Remember the Alamo! Remember Goliad!" filled the air. Houston's successful surprise attack ended the war. He captured Santa Anna, who had no choice and signed the territory away. Although the Mexican Congress repudiated the treaty, Houston was elected president of the Republic of Texas.

The battle of San Jacinto was literally a slaughter of the Mexican forces. Few prisoners were taken. Those who surrendered "were clubbed and stabbed," some on their knees. The slaughter . . . became methodical: the Texas riflemen knelt and poured a steady fire into the packed, jostling ranks. . . . They shot the "Meskins" down as they fled. The final count showed 630 Mexicans dead versus 2 Texans.

It is commonly believed that after the surrender Texan authorities let Santa Anna off lightly, but, according to Dr. Castañeda, Santa Anna "was mercilessly dragged from the ship he had boarded, subjected to more than six months' mental torture and indignities in Texas prison camps."

The Texas victory paved the way for the Mexican-American War, feeding the growing nationalism of the young Anglo-American nation. Officially the United States had not taken sides, but men, money, and supplies poured in to aid fellow Anglo-Americans. U.S. citizens participated in the invasion of Texas with the open support of their government. Mexico's minister to the United States, Manuel Eduardo Gorostiza, vehemently protested the "arming and shipment of troops and supplies to territory which was part of Mexico, and the dispatch of United States troops into territory clearly defined by treaty as Mexican territory." General Edmund P. Gaines, Southwest Commander, had been sent into Western Louisiana on January 23, 1836; shortly thereafter, he crossed into Texas in an action that was interpreted to be in support of the Anglo-American filibusters in Texas: "The Jackson Administration made it plain to the Mexican minister that it mattered little whether Mexico approved, that the important thing was to protect the border against Indians and Mexicans." U.S. citizens in and out of Texas loudly applauded Jackson's actions. The Mexican minister resigned his post in protest. "The success of the Texas Revolution thrust the Anglo-American frontier up against the Far Southwest, and the region came at once into the scope of Anglo ambition."

THE INVASION OF MEXICO

The United States during the nineteenth century moved its boundaries westward. In the mid-1840s, Mexico was again the target. Expansion and capitalist development moved together. The two Mexican wars gave U.S. commerce, industry, mining, agriculture, and stockraising a tremendous stimulus. "The truth is that [by the 1840's] the Pacific Coast belonged to the commercial empire that the United States was already building in that ocean."

The United States's population of 17 million people of European extraction and 3 million slaves was considerably larger than Mexico's 7 million, of which 4 million were Indian, and 3 million Mestizo and European. The United States acted arrogantly in foreign affairs, partly because its citizens believed in their inherent cultural and racial superiority. Mexico was plagued with financial problems, internal ethnic conflicts, and poor leadership. General anarchy within the nation conspired against its cohesive development.

By 1844 war with Mexico over Texas and the Southwest was only a matter of time. James K. Polk, who strongly advocated the annexation of Texas and expansionism in general, won the presidency by only a small margin but his election was interpreted as a mandate for national expansion. Outgoing President Tyler decided to act and called upon Congress to annex Texas by joint resolution; the measure was passed a few days before the inauguration of Polk, who accepted the arrangement. In December 1845, Texas became a state.

Mexico promptly broke off diplomatic relations with the United States, and Polk ordered General Zachary Taylor into Texas to "protect" the border. The location of the border was in doubt. Texas contended it was at the Rio Grande, but based on historical precedent,

Mexico claimed it was 150 miles farther north, at the Nueces River. Taylor took his forces across the Nueces into the disputed territory, wanting to provoke an attack.

In November 1845, Polk sent John Slidell on a secret mission to Mexico to negotiate for the disputed area. The presence of Anglo-American troops between the Nueces and the Rio Grande and the annexation of Texas made negotiations an absurdity. They refused to accept Polk's minister's credentials, although they did offer to grant him an ad hoc status. Slidell refused anything less than full acceptance and returned to Washington in March 1846, convinced that Mexico would have to be "chastised" before it would negotiate. By March 28, Taylor had advanced to the Rio Grande with an army of 4,000.

Polk, incensed at Mexico's refusal to meet with Slidell on his terms and at General Mairano Paredes' reaffirmation of his country's claims to all of Texas, began to draft his declaration of war when he learned of a Mexican attack on U.S. troops in the disputed territory. He immediately declared that the United States had been provoked into war, that Mexico had "shed American blood upon the American soil." On May 13, 1846, Congress declared war and authorized the recruitment and supplying of 50,000 troops.

Years later, Ulysses S. Grant said that he believed Polk wanted and planned for war to be provoked and that the annexation of Texas was, in fact, an act of aggression. He added: "I had a horror of the Mexican War . . . only I had not moral courage enough to resign. . . . I considered my supreme duty was to my flag."

The poorly equipped and poorly led Mexican army stood little chance against the thrust of expansion-minded Anglos. Even before the war Polk planned a campaign of three stages: (1) Mexicans would be cleared out of Texas; (2) Anglos would occupy California and New Mexico; and (3) U.S. forces would march to Mexico City to force the beaten government to make peace on Polk's terms. And that was the way the campaign basically went. In the end, at a relatively small cost in men and money, the war netted the United States huge territorial gains. In all, the United States took over 1 million square miles of Mexican lands.

THE RATIONALE FOR CONQUEST

In his *Origins of the War with Mexico: The Polk-Stockton Intrigue*, Glenn W. Price states: "Americans have found it rather more difficult than other peoples to deal rationally with their wars. We have thought of ourselves as unique, and of this society as specially planned and created to avoid the errors of all other nations." In this vein, many Anglo-American historians attempt to dismiss the Mexican-American War by simply stating that it was a "bad war," which took place during the United States' era of Manifest Destiny.

Manifest Destiny had its roots in Puritan ideas, which continue to influence Anglo-American thought to this day. According to the Puritan ethic, salvation is determined by God. The establishment of the City of God on earth is not only the duty of those chosen people predestined for salvation, but is also the proof of their state of grace. This belief carried over to the anglo-American conviction that God had made them custodians of democracy and that they had a mission, that is, that they were predestined to spread its principles. As the young nation survived its infancy, established its power in the defeat of the British in the War of 1812, expanded westward, and enjoyed both commercial and industrial success, its sense of destiny heightened. Many citizens believed that God had destined them to own and occupy all of the land from ocean to ocean and pole to pole. Their mission, their destiny made manifest, was to spread the principles of democracy and Christianity to the unfortunates of the hemisphere. By dismissing the war simply as part of the era of Manifest Destiny the apologists for the war ignore the consequences of the doctrine.

The Monroe Doctrine of the 1820s told the world that the Americas were no longer open for colonization or conquest; however, it did not say anything about that limitation applying to the United States. Uppermost in the minds of the U.S. government, the military, and much of the public was the acquisition of territory. No one ever intended to leave Mexico without extracting territory. Land was the main motivation.

Further obscuring the issue of planned Anglo-American aggression is what Professor Price exposes as the rhetoric of peace, which the United States has traditionally used to justify its aggressions. The Mexican-American War is a study in the use of this rhetoric.

Consider, for example, Polk's war message of May 11, 1846, in which he gave his reasons for going to war:

> The strong desire to establish peace with Mexico on liberal and honorable terms, and the readiness of this Government to regulate and adjust our boundary and other causes of difference with that power on such fair and equitable principles as would lead to permanent relations of the most friendly nature, induced me in September last to seek reopening of diplomatic relations between the two countries.

He went on to state that the United States had made every effort not to inflame Mexicans, but that the Mexican government had refused to receive an Anglo-American minister. Polk reviewed the events leading to the war and concluded:

> As war exists, and notwithstanding all our efforts to avoid it, exists by the act of Mexico herself, we are called upon by every consid-

eration of duty and patriotism to indicate with decision the honor, the rights, and the interests of our country.

Historical distance from the events has not reduced the prevalence of this rhetoric. The need to justify has continued. In 1920 Justin F. Smith received a Pulitzer prize in history for a work that blamed the war on Mexico. What is amazing is that Smith allegedly examined more than 100,000 manuscripts, 120,000 books and pamphlets, and 200 or more periodicals to come to this conclusion. It is fair to speculate that he was rewarded for relieving the Anglo-American conscience. His two-volume "study," entitled *The War with Mexico,* used analyses such as the following to support its thesis:

> At the beginning of her independent existence, our people felt earnestly and enthusiastically anxious to maintain cordial relations with our sister republic, and many crossed the line of absurd sentimentality in the cause. Friction was inevitable, however. The Americans were direct, positive, brusque, angular and pushing; and they would not understand their neighbors in the south. The Mexicans were equally unable to fathom our goodwill, sincerity, patriotism, resoluteness and courage; and certain features of their character and national condition made it far from easy to get on with them.

This attitude of righteousness on the part of government officials and historians toward their aggressions spills over to the relationships between the majority society and minority groups. Anglo-Americans believe that the war was advantageous to the Southwest and to the Mexicans who remained or later migrated there. They now had the benefits of democracy and were liberated from their tyrannical past. In other words, Mexicans should be grateful to the Anglo-Americans. If Mexicans and the Anglo-Americans clash, the rationale runs, naturally it is because Mexicans cannot understand or appreciate the merits of a free society, which must be defended against ingrates. Therefore, domestic war, or repression, is justified by the same kind of rhetoric that justifies international aggression.

Professor Gene M. Brack, in the most recent of these works, attacks those who base their research on Justin Smith's outdated work: "American historians have consistently praised Justin Smith's influential and outrageously ethnocentric account."

THE MYTH OF A NONVIOLENT NATION

Most works on the Mexican-American War have dwelt on the causes and results of the war, sometimes dealing with war strategy. It is necessary, however, to go beyond this point, since the war left bitterness, and since Anglo-American actions in Mexico are vividly remembered.

Mexicans' attitude toward Anglo-Americans has been influenced by the was just as the United States' easy victory conditioned Anglo-American behavior toward Mexicans. Fortunately, many Anglo-Americans condemned this aggression and flatly accused their leaders of being insolent, land hungry, and of having manufactured the war. Abiel Abbott Livermore in *The War with Mexico Reviewed* accused his country, writing:

> Again, the pride of race has swollen to still greater insolence the pride of country, always quite active enough for the due observance of the claims of universal brotherhood. The Anglo-Saxons have been apparently persuaded to think themselves the chosen people, annointed race of the Lord, commissioned to drive out the heathen, and plant their religion and institutions in every Canaan they could subjugate. . . . Our treatment both of the red man and the black man has habituated us to feel our power and forget right. . . . The passion for land, also, is a leading characteristic of the American people. . . . The god Terminus is an unknown deity in America. Like the hunger of the pauper boy of fiction, the cry had been, 'more, more, give us more.'

Livermore's work, published in 1850, was awarded the American Peace Society prize for "the best review of the Mexican War and the principles of Christianity, and an enlightened statesmanship."

The United States provoked the war and then conducted it violently and brutally. Zachary Taylor's artillery leveled the Mexican city of Matamoros, killing hundreds of innocent civilians with *la bomba* (the bomb). Many Mexicans jumped into the Rio Grande, relieved of their pain by a watery grave. The occupation that followed was even more terrorizing. Taylor's regular army was kept in control, but the volunteers presented another matter:

> The regulars regarded the volunteers, of whom about two thousand had reached Matamoros by the end of May, with impatience and contempt. . . . They robbed Mexicans of their cattle and corn, stole their fences for firewood, got drunk, and killed several inoffensive inhabitants of the town in the streets.

There were numerous eyewitnesses to these incidents. For example, on July 25, 1846, Grant wrote to Julia Dent:

> Since we have been in Matamoros a great many murders have been committed, and what is strange there seemes [sic] to be very week [sic] means made use of to prevent frequent repetitions. Some of the volunteers and about all the Texans seem to think it perfectly right to impose on the people of a conquered city to any extent, and even to murder them where the act can be covered by dark.

And how much they seem to enjoy acts of violence too! I would not pretend to guess the number of murders that have been committed upon the persons of poor Mexicans and our soldiers, since we have been here, but the number would startle you.

On July 9, 1846, George Gordon Meade, who like Grant later became a general during the U.S. Civil War, wrote:

They [the volunteers] have killed five or six innocent people walking in the street, for no other object than their own amusement. . . . They rob and steal the cattle and corn of the poor farmers, and in fact act more like a body of hostile Indians than civilized Whites. Their officers have no command or control over them. . . .

Taylor knew about the atrocities, but Grant observed that Taylor did not restrain his men. In a letter to his superiors, Taylor admitted that "There is scarcely a form of crime that has not been reported to me as committed by them." Taylor requested that they send no further troops from the state of Texas to him. These marauding acts were not limited to Taylor's men. The cannons from U.S. naval ships destroyed much of the civilian sector of Vera Cruz, leveling a hospital, churches, and homes. The bomb did not discriminate as to age or sex. Anglo-American troops destroyed almost every city they invaded; first it was put to the test of fire and then plundered. *Gringo* volunteers had little respect for anything, desecrating churches and abusing priests and nuns.

Military executions were common. Captured soldiers and civilians were hanged for cooperating with the guerrillas. Many Irish immigrants, as well as some other Anglos, deserted to the Mexican side, forming the San Patricio Corps. Many of the Irish were Catholics, and they resented treatment of Catholic priests and nuns by the invading Protestants. As many as 260 Anglo-Americans fought with the Mexicans at Churubusco in 1847:

Some eighty appear to have been captured. . . . A number were found not guilty of deserting and were released. About fifteen, who had deserted before the declaration of war, were merely branded with a "D," and fifty of those taken at Churubusco were executed.

Others received two hundred lashes and were forced to dig graves for their executed comrades.

These acts were similar to those in Monterey when George Meade wrote on December 2, 1846:

They plunder the poor inhabitants of everything they can lay their hands on, and shoot them when the remonstrate; and if one of their number happens to get into a drunken brawl and is killed, they run over the country, killing all the poor innocent people they find in their way to avenge, as they say, the murder of their brother. . . .

As Scott's army left Monterey, they shot Mexican prisoners of war.

Memoirs, diaries, and news articles written by Anglo-Americans document the reign of terror. Samuel F. Chamberlain's *My Confessions* is a record of Anglo racism and destruction. He was only 17 when he enlisted in the army to fight the "greasers." At the Mexican city of Parras, he wrote:

> We found the patrol had been guilty of many outrages. . . . They had ridden into the church of San José during Mass, the place crowded with kneeling women and children, and with oaths and ribald jest had arrested soldiers who had permission to be present.

On another occasion, he described a massacre by volunteers, mostly from Yell's Cavalry, at a cave:

> On reaching the place we found a "greaser" shot and *scalped,* but breathing; the poor fellow held in his hands a Rosary and a medal of the "Virgin of Guadalupe," only his feeble motions kept the fierce harpies from falling on him while yet alive. A Sabre thrust was given him in mercy, and on we went at a run. Soon shouts and curses, cries of women and children reached our ears, coming apparently from a cave at the end of the ravine. Climbing over the rocks we reached the entrance, and as soon as we could see in the comparative darkness a horrid sight was before us. The cave was full of our volunteers yelling like fiends, while on the rocky floor lay over twenty Mexicans, dead and dying in pools of blood. Women and children were clinging to the knees of the murderers shrieking for mercy. . . . Most of the butchered Mexicans had been scalped; only three men were found unharmed. A rough crucifix was fastened to a rock, and some irreverent wretch had crowned the image with a bloody scalp. A sickening smell filled the place. The surviving women and children sent up loud screams on seeing us, thinking we had returned to finish the work! . . . No one was punished for this outrage.

Near Satillo, Chamberlain reported the actions of Texas Rangers. His descriptions were graphic:

> [A drunken Anglo] entered the church and tore down a large wooden figure of our Saviour, and making his lariat fast around its neck, he mounted his horse and galloped up and down the *plazuela,* dragging the statue behind. The venerable white-haired Priest, in attempting to rescue it, was thrown down and trampled under the feet of the Ranger's horse.

Mexicans were enraged and attacked the Texan. Meanwhile, the Rangers returned:

> As they charged the square, they saw their miserable comrade hanging to his cross, his skin hanging in strips, surrounded by crowds of Mexicans. With yells of horror, the Rangers charged on the mass with Bowie Knife and revolver, sparing neither age or sex in their terrible fury.

Chamberlain blamed General Taylor not only for collecting over $1 million (from the Mexican people) by force of arms, but also for letting "loose on the country packs of human bloodhounds called Texas Rangers." He goes on to describe the Rangers' brutality at the Rancho de San Francisco on the Camargo road near Agua Fria:

> The place was surrounded, the doors forced in, and all the males capable of bearing arms were dragged out, tied to a post and shot! . . . Thirty-six Mexicans were shot at this place, a half hour given for the horrified survivors, women and children, to remove their little household goods, then the torch was applied to the houses, and by the light of the conflagration the ferocious *Tejanos* rode off to fresh scenes of blood.

These wanton acts of cruelty, witnessed by one man, augmented by the reports of other chroniclers, add to the evidence that the United States, through the deeds of its soldiers, left a legacy of hate in Mexico.

THE TREATY OF GUADALUPE HIDALGO

By late August 1847 the war was almost at an end. General Winfield Scott's defeat of Santa Anna in a hard-fought battle at Churubusco put Anglo-Americans at the gates of Mexico City. Santa Anna made overtures for an armistice, and for two weeks negotiations were conducted. Santa Anna reorganized his defenses and, in turn, the Anglo-Americans renewed their offensives. On September 13, 1847, Scott drove into the city. Although Mexicans fought valiantly, the battle left 4,000 of their men dead with another 3,000 taken prisoner. On September 13, before the occupation of Mexico City began, *Los Niños Héroes* (The Boy Heroes) fought off the conquerors and leapt to their deaths rather than surrender. These teenage cadets were Francisco Márquez, Agustin Melgar, Juan Escutia, Fernando Montes Oca, Vicente Suárez, and Juan de la Berrera. They became "a symbol and image of this unrighteous war."

Although beaten, the Mexicans continued fighting. The presidency devolved to the presiding justice of the Supreme Court, Manuel de la Peña y Peña. He knew that Mexico had lost and that he had to salvage as much as possible. Pressure mounted, with U.S. troops in control of much of present-day Mexico.

Nicholas Trist, sent to Mexico to act as peace commissioner, had arrived in Vera Cruz on May 6, 1847, but controversy with Scott over Trist's authority and illness delayed arrangements for an armistice and hostilities continued. After the fall of Mexico City, Secretary of State James Buchanan wanted to revise Trist's instructions. He ordered Trist to break off negotiations and come home. Polk apparently wanted more territory from Mexico while paying less for it. Trist, however, with the support of Winfield Scott, decided to ignore Polk's order, and began negotiations on January 2, 1848, on the original terms. Mexico, badly beaten, her government in a state of turmoil, had no choice but to agree to the Anglo-Americans' proposals.

On February 2, 1848, the Mexicans agreed to the Treaty of Guadalupe Hidalgo, in which Mexico accepted the Rio Grande as the Texas border and ceded the Southwest (which incorporated the present-day states of California, New Mexico, Nevada, and parts of Colorado, Arizona and to the Anglo-Americans' proposals.

Polk was furious about the treaty; he considered Trist "contemptibly base" for having ignored his orders. Yet he had no choice but to submit the treaty to the Senate. With the exception of article X, which concerned the rights of Mexicans in the ceded territory, the Senate ratified the treaty on March 10, 1848, by a vote of 28 to 14. To insist on more territory would have meant more fighting, and both Polk and the Senate realized that the war was already unpopular in many sections. The treaty was sent to the Mexican Congress for ratification; although the Congress had difficulty forming a quorum, the agreement was ratified on May 19 by a 52 to 35 vote. Hostilities between the two nations were now officially ended. Trist, however, was branded as a "scoundrel," because Polk was disappointed in the settlement. There was considerable support and fervor in the United States for acquisition of all Mexico.

During the treaty talk Mexican negotiators were concerned about Mexicans left behind and expressed great reservations about these people's being forced to "merge or blend" into Anglo-American culture. They protested the exclusion of provisions that protected Mexican citizens' rights, land titles, and religion. They wanted to know the Mexicans' status, and protect their rights by treaty.

Articles VIII, IX, and X specifically referred to the rights of Mexicans. Under the treaty Mexicans left behind had one year to choose whether to return to Mexico or remain in "occupied Mexico." About 2,000 elected to leave; most remained in what they considered *their* land.

Article IX of the treaty guaranteed Mexicans "the enjoyment of all the rights of citizens of the United States according to the principles of the Constitution; and in the meantime shall be maintained and protected in the free enjoyment of their liberty and property, and secured in the free exercise of their religion without restriction." While Anglo-Americans have respected the Chicanos' religion, their rights of cultural integrity and rights of citizenship have been constantly violated. Lynn I. Perrigo in *The American Southwest* summarizes the guarantees of articles VIII and IX: "In other words, besides the rights and duties of American citizenship, they [the Mexicans] would have some special privileges derived from their previous customs in language, law, and religion."

The omitted article X had comprehensive guarantees protecting "all prior and pending titles to property of every description." When this provision was deleted by the U.S. Senate, Mexican officials protested. Anglo-American emissaries reassured them by drafting a Statement of Protocol on May 26, 1848, which read:

> The American government by suppressing the Xth article of the Treaty of Guadalupe Hidalgo did not in any way intend to annul the grants of lands made by Mexico in the ceded territories. These grants . . . preserve the legal value which they may possess, and the grantees may cause their legitimate (titles) to be acknowledged before the American tribunals.
>
> Conformable to the law of the United States, legitimate titles to every description of property, personal and real, existing in the ceded territories, are those which were legitimate titles under the Mexican law of California and New Mexico up to the 13th of May, 1846, and in Texas up to the 2nd of March, 1836.

Considering the Mexican opposition to the treaty, it is doubtful whether the Mexican Congress would have ratified the treaty without this clarification. The vote was close.

The Statement of Protocol was reinforced by articles VIII and IX, which guaranteed Mexicans rights of property and protection under the law. In addition, court decisions have generally interpreted the treaty as protecting land titles and water rights. Generally, the treaty was ignored and during the nineteenth century most Mexicans in the United States were considered as a class apart from the dominant race. Nearly every one of the obligations discussed above was violated, confirming the prophecy of Mexican diplomat Manuel Crescion Rejón who, at the time the treaty was signed, commented:

> Our race, our unfortunate people will have to wander in search of hospitality in a strange land, only to be ejected later. Descendants of the Indians that we are, the North Americans hate us, their spokesmen depreciate us, even if they recognize the justice of our cause, and they consider us unworthy to form with them one na-

tion and one society, they clearly manifest that their future expansion begins with the territory that they take from us and pushing [sic] aside our citizens who inhabit the land.

CONCLUSION

As a result of the Texas War and the Anglo-American aggressions of 1845–1848, the occupation of conquered territory began. The attitude of the Anglo, during the period of subjugation following the wars, is reflected in the conclusions of the past-president of the American Historical Association, Walter Prescott Webb:

> A homogenous European society adaptable to new conditions was necessary. This Spain did not have to offer in Arizona, New Mexico, and Texas. Its frontier, as it advanced, depended more and more on an Indian population. . . . This mixture of races meant in time that common soldiers in the Spanish service came largely from pueblo or sedentary Indian stock, whose blood, when compared to that of the plain Indians, was as ditch water. It took more than a little mixture of Spanish blood and mantle of Spanish service to make valiant soldiers of the timid Pueblo Indians.

In material terms in exchange for 12,000 lives and more than $100,000,000 the United States acquired a colony two and a half times as large as France, containing rich farm lands and natural resources such as gold, silver, zinc, copper, oil, and uranium which would make possible its unprecedented industrial boom. It acquired ports on the Pacific which generated further economic expansion across that ocean. Mexico was left with its shrunken resources to face the continued advances of the expanding capitalist force on its border.

Brigham Young Leads the Mormons into the West

LEONARD J. ARRINGTON and DAVIS BITTON

Of the many new religions that came out of New York State's "burned-over" district, none have been as successful as the Mormons, the Church of Jesus Christ of the Latter-day Saints. Joseph Smith, the founder of the group, claimed that an angel appeared to him and showed him where to find buried tablets of gold bearing miraculous revelations, which Smith was permitted to read by means of special eyeglasses. The revelations, set forth in *The Book of Mormon* in 1830, established the mission of the Latter-day Saints and granted them exclusive salvation.

In keeping with the communitarian religious ideals of the period, Smith organized his church as a cooperative theocracy with himself as the head bearing the title "First Elder." Thus, the Mormons were able to avoid a problem central to communitarianism—the problem of authority. The First Elder and his successors claimed divine authority and ruled autocratically. In a departure from strict communitarianism, Brigham Young, Smith's immediate successor, devised a judicious mixture of private and communal ownership of property, which helped to ensure the subsequent economic development of the Mormon state of Deseret, later incorporated into Utah. By the time the Civil War broke out, most of the communal religious groups that had flourished in New York and the old Northwest had died or were declining. The Mormons alone gathered size and strength.

As they developed their unique religious system, the Mormons met with continued opposition from their non-Mormon neighbors, whom they called gentiles. Harassment by the gentiles forced them to move from New York to Ohio, then to Missouri, to Illinois, and finally to the basin of the Great Salt Lake, an area so isolated and so forbidding that it discouraged other groups from settling there. Thus, the Mormons were free to live as they wished.

Much of the opposition to the Mormons was a reaction to three Mormon beliefs and practices. First was the select nature of the faith: believers were saved and nonbelievers, doomed. People have never taken lightly revelations of their own damnation, and the gentiles resented the Mormons' claim to exclusive salvation. Second was the authoritarian political organization of the Mormons, which seemed suspiciously un-American in an age of vocal democratic sentiment. Third was the practice of polygamy (plural marriage), a clear violation of a taboo observed in American society at large. This last practice brought the Mormons into conflict with the federal government, which would not agree to make Utah a state until polygamy was banned in the movement.

In 1979, Leonard J. Arrington (Utah State University) and Davis Bitton (University of Utah), both practicing Mormons, published a comprehensive history of Mormon life. The chapter from that work presented here describes what took place after the assassination of Mormon founder Joseph Smith. A critical moment occurs in any religious movement when the founder dies, and the Mormon religion was no exception. There were several claimants for the mantle of Joseph Smith, including one of his sons. Fortunately for the Mormons, Brigham Young assumed the leadership of the major part of the movement. Certifiably one of the organizational geniuses of American life, Young was able not only to hold the movement together but also to organize the mass exodus from Illinois to the Great Salt Lake basin, one of the most notable migrations in our history.

I have seen some sorrowful days since I left you and some happy ones. But I can tell you it is a sorrowful time here [Nauvoo] at present. Those that stood up for Joseph before his death are getting divided among themselves.

—Sarah Scott (1844)

We'll find the place which God for us prepared,
Far away in the West;
Where none shall come to hurt, or make afraid:
There the Saints will be blessed.
—William Clayton (1846)

The martyrdom of Smith plunged the church into a state of sadness and confusion. In addition to his religious role, Joseph had been the political, economic, and social mainstay

BRIGHAM YOUNG LEADS THE MORMONS INTO THE WEST   Originally published as "Dispersion and Exodus Under Brigham Young" in *The Mormon Experience: A History of the Latter-day Saints* by Leonard J. Arrington and Davis Bitton (New York: Knopf, 1979), pp. 83–105. Reprinted by permission of Random House, Inc.

of Nauvoo. The first impulse of the Saints in and around Nauvoo was to find a leader who could fill all of the dead Prophet's roles. But the means of orderly succession had not yet been clearly established.

As head of the Quorum of the Twelve Apostles, Brigham Young had shepherded the church through the exodus from Missouri. He had led the Twelve on their eighteen-month mission to England. Their success in that country—attended by healings, mass conversion, and innovations in proselyting and emigration—had welded them into a forceful, unified apostolic body. Impressed, Smith gave them additional duties and began to rely on Young's close association and counsel. Thus the Quorum, led by Young, assumed increasing importance. In Nauvoo its members were soon collaborating closely with Smith in both economic and ecclesiastical action. They further proved their mettle by a series of missions. The last of these, in 1844, was an assignment to travel throughout the East campaigning for Smith's candidacy for the American presidency—an effort apparently designed to disseminate Mormon political and religious views. It was while serving on this mission that Young learned of the assassination of Joseph and Hyrum Smith.

When Young arrived in Nauvoo from New England on August 6, he found that Sidney Rigdon had preceded him. Rigdon had been a counselor in the presidency of the church. Young met with the rest of the apostles at the home where John Taylor was recuperating and planned with them how to deal with this challenge for leadership of the church. On the following afternoon a general meeting of church members was held. Rigdon asserted that no one could take Smith's place but that he, as Joseph's counselor, would serve as the church's "guardian." Young answered with his own conviction that the Twelve held "all the keys and powers" for church leadership.

A dramatic general meeting was held the following day. Rigdon addressed the assembly at length but apparently gained little support. Then Young arose and dramatically reinforced his own and the Twelve's claim to preeminence.

> Attention all! . . . For the first time in my life, for the first time in your lives, for the first time in the Kingdom of God in the nineteenth century, without a Prophet at our head, do I step forth to act in my calling in connection with the Quorum of the Twelve, as Apostles of Jesus Christ unto this generation—Apostles whom God has called by revelation through the Prophet Joseph, who are ordained and anointed to bear off the keys of the kingdom of God in all the world.

After Young's speech and those of others supporting the Twelve, the Nauvoo congregation voted overwhelmingly to sustain him and the apostles as leaders of the church.

An earlier revelation had stated that the Twelve formed a quorum "equal in authority and power" to the First Presidency. The First Presidency having been dissolved by the death of Joseph and Hyrum Smith, only Rigdon was left to argue that he should take the reins of power. In pragmatic terms there was no viable alternative to direction by the tried and proven Twelve under the leadership of Brigham Young. Remembering another early revelation to the effect that church leaders were not ordained until after a vote of the church, most Latter-day Saints were satisfied after the August 8 meeting that Young was the choice of both God and the people. "Brother Joseph," concluded Young, "has laid the foundation for a great work and we will build upon it. There is an almighty foundation laid, and we can build a kingdom such as there never was in this world."

Many who were present at the August 8 meeting later remembered seeing in Brigham Young that day a new appearance and hearing from him a new voice—one that was very familiar, that of Joseph Smith. For them the "Mantle of Joseph" was given directly, miraculously, to Young. George Laub later recorded in his journal that that day Young's "voice was the voice of Br. Joseph and his face appeared as Joseph's face." Apostle Wilford Woodruff later remembered, "When Brigham Young arose and commenced speaking . . . if I had not seen him with my own eyes, there is no one that could have convinced me that it was not Joseph Smith."

Certainly most of the people wanted a legitimate successor, one similar to Smith, to fill the spiritual and emotional void caused by the death of their beloved Prophet. However social psychologists might explain the change of Young's voice and appearance at the August 8 meeting, he was in fact a Joseph Smith to those who accepted him—in some ways he became more. The next day, after the vote of confidence indicating the "common consent" of those assembled, he met with church leaders and proceeded with remarkable assurance to tighten up church organization. Such had not been necessary earlier, he explained, because of Smith's personal magnetic leadership: "I remarked that Joseph's presence had measurably superseded the necessity of carrying out a perfect organization of the several quorums."

A few selected entries from Young's holograph diary give the best indication of how his activities and sense of assurance developed over the next few months:

Sunday, August 18, 1844. I preached to the Saints in the morning. I had good liberty and by the help of the Lord I was enabled to satisfy the Brethren and unite them together so they will finish the Temple.

Friday, September 20. Went to the temple, called on Sister Evans, sealed her up to her husband; Horace, her oldest son, stood as proxy. Laid hands on Sister Hurley; the Lord is with me.

Sunday, September 22. I preached to the congregation of the Saints, had a good time. Told the Saints some new things.

Friday, January 24 [1845]. Brothers H. C. Kimball and N. K. Whitney was at my house; we washed and annointed and prayed. Had a good time. I inquired of the Lord whether we should stay here and finish the Temple. The answer was we should.

They did finish the temple. In fact, Young motivated the Nauvoo Mormons to do as much in the next eighteen months as had been accomplished in the previous three years. Here perhaps can be seen a quality in Young that distinguished him from Smith—not mere practicality, because Smith had that too, but a willingness, even a compulsion, to organize and *do,* to take Smith's plans and visions, even roughshod, and drive people to get things completed. Young moved directly ahead. He had his own style. These leadership qualities would come to fruition on the trek west and in the Great Basin. After the church's early surge of expansion and growth under Joseph Smith, Young led the church through a phase of consolidation, organizational strengthening, doctrinal clarification, and coming to grips with practical problems.

Brigham Young's early development was in many ways similar to Joseph Smith's, but it also contained the seeds of their differences. Like the Smiths, Young's family emigrated from New England to frontier New York in Brigham's boyhood. As he said much later, he was "brought up from [his] youth amid those flaming, fiery revivals so customary with the Methodists." He neither rejected nor fully accepted the strict, Methodist piety of his parents. Although he was interested in finding religious truth, he remained apart from the organized religion of his parents and friends. He did not find his answer in a vision. Young said that his prayer as a boy was "Lord, preserve me until I am old enough to have sound judgment, and a discreet mind ripened upon a good solid foundation of common sense."

Brigham's mother died in his fourteenth year. He was apprenticed out and soon became a skilled carpenter, painter, and glazier. Meanwhile he continued to seek religious satisfaction: "I used to go to meetings—was well acquainted with the Episcopalians, Presbyterians, New Lights, Baptists, Freewill Baptists and Reformed Methodists—lived from my youth where I was acquainted with Quakers as well as the other denominations." On the one hand, his concern for common sense was deeply offended by the revivalists: "Men were rolling and hollering and bawling and thumping, but [they] had no effect on me. I wanted to know the truth that I might not be fooled." On the other hand, his yearning for spiritual nourishment was not met by established churches with their doctrinal contentions and arid moralizing. His reaction to hearing the famous Methodist preacher Lorenzo Dow was restrained: "He could tell the people they should not work on the Sabbath day; they should not lie, swear, steal, commit adultery, etc. but when he came to teaching the things of God he was as dark as midnight." Young accepted traditional moral teachings, but his yearning for answers did not stop at that point.

Spirit and emotion but not to excess, common sense and good judgment but something more—such was the combination that haunted Young through his long quest for a religious "home." After his marriage in 1823 to Miriam Works, who had tuberculosis and slowly declined until her death in 1832, he tried mainly to be a moral, hardworking, and tender husband and father. But he also joined with various groups of independent "seekers" in the several towns in western New York where he pursued his carpentry and painting. When he moved in 1829 to Mendon, New York, where others of his family were also established, he joined with such a group, led by his brother Phineas, who described it thus: "We opened a house for preaching, and commenced teaching the people according to the light we had; a reformation commenced, and we soon had a good society organized." From such groups, as we have seen, came many of the early converts to Mormonism.

Young's conversion began with the Book of Mormon, a copy of which he saw, fresh off the press, in the spring of 1830. But he was not baptized until 1832. He said later, "I examined the matter studiously for two years before I made up my mind to receive that book. . . . I wished time sufficient to prove all things for myself." On another occasion he added, "I sought to become acquainted with the people who professed to believe that book. . . . I watched to see whether good common sense was manifest." Not that he rejected all spiritual gifts or manifestations. At a small branch of the church in Pennsylvania he first heard speaking in tongues—the glossolalia that had been mentioned in the New Testament. He also heard a missionary without eloquence or talent for public speaking say: "I know by the power of the Holy Ghost, that the Book of Mormon is true, that Joseph Smith is a prophet of the Lord." "My own judgment, natural endowments, and education," said Brigham, "bowed to this simple, but mighty testimony." Though he had earlier been repelled by the excesses of evangelical groups, Young found in Mormonism a counterpoise of rationality—"good common sense"—and a practical orientation that made the experience quite different.

The lay-priesthood dimension of Mormonism was especially satisfying to Brigham Young. He started keeping a diary the day after his baptism, which he described as follows: "Before my clothes were dry on my back Brother [Eleazer] Miller laid his hands on me and ordained me an Elder, at which I marvelled." He later remembered the elation that came from being called and authorized to *do* something. Soon he embarked on a series of proselyting missions throughout New York and up into Canada.

Anxious to meet Joseph Smith in person, Brigham and his brother Joseph found the Prophet chopping wood. After hours of intense conversation Young spoke in tongues their first evening together. But from what we can learn of Young's development in the church before he even met Smith, and of their subsequent relationship, it is probable that Young found in Smith the fullest human embodiment of the values he had already discovered for himself in Mormonism.

Young responded to Smith's call for the few hundred members of the infant church to gather at Kirtland in 1833. That winter he was especially diligent in learning from the Prophet and the other leaders in conversation and meetings. He volunteered for the Zion's Camp march to the aid of the church in Missouri that next spring. His faithful performance led to his being called, along with his closest friend, Heber C. Kimball, into the first Quorum of Apostles in 1835. Young later recalled that when two such relatively rough and untutored laborers were chosen, "some of the knowing ones marvelled . . . their looks expressed, What a pity." Indeed, it seems that Kimball and Young were more eagerly employed in finishing the Kirtland Temple for the 1836 dedication than in participating in the School of the Prophets, where Smith studied doctrine and languages with other church leaders. But as Smith later pointed out, among that original Quorum of the Twelve only Kimball and Young did not ever "lift their heel against me."

Young's loyalty to Smith had an emotional quality. Such fealty was crucial in Kirtland, where Smith's failed bank led to internal dissension. Young's fierce defense of Smith led to threats being made against himself, and he had to flee Kirtland for his safety, even before Smith himself was forced to leave in January 1838.

Over the next few years Young demonstrated not only tenacious loyalty but also the courage and competence to succeed in increasingly difficult assignments. He shepherded the migration from Missouri to Illinois; in mortal danger he returned with the Twelve from Illinois to Far West, Missouri, in order to fulfill to the letter Smith's revelation requiring them to take leave from the Saints at the temple site on April 26, 1839, for their mission to England; he led the apostles in England with a degree of success perhaps even beyond Smith's dreams. As a result of the confidence he developed during the mission, he went on more completely to establish the role of the Twelve when they returned. In 1844, as we have seen, most Mormons accepted Brigham Young as Smith's obvious successor.

During the year and a half after the martyrdom, Young marshaled the support of the badly shaken church. He told the beleaguered Nauvoo Saints, "I have traveled these many years, in the midst of poverty and tribulation, and that, too, with blood in my shoes, month after month, to sustain and preach this Gospel and build up this Kingdom." At times his forthrightness was costly. Although in some ways he admired Orson and Parley Pratt and Orson Spencer, he tended to be suspicious of smoothly articulate but "impractical" intellectuals. He was particularly distrustful of Sidney Rigdon. On September 1, 1844, a few days before being excommunicated for refusing to follow the Twelve,

Rigdon addressed a meeting. Young wrote in his diary: "His discourse was complicated and somewhat scattered. He said he had all things shone [shown] to him from this time . . . but he did not tell what the saints should do to save themselves." Young knew what the Saints needed to do to save themselves.

The members of the church had to come to grips with three questions: Who would assume Smith's prophetic mantle? What would be their attitude toward the new doctrines that had appeared in Nauvoo preceding Smith's death? And what should be the temporal role of the church? On the whole, the Nauvoo Saints under Young's leadership supported continuation of his predecessor's policies. Less comfortable with these policies and Young's leadership were a few Latter-day Saints who were geographically removed from Nauvoo and its "mysteries."

Predictably, the first dissenting body to organize after Young's assumption of leadership was headed by Sidney Rigdon. Upon his return to Pittsburgh, Rigdon called together a small group of followers and began publication of the *Latter-day Saints' Messenger and Advocate.* By the spring of 1845 the Church of Christ had voted Rigdon its president, denounced polygamy, and claimed that Joseph Smith had been a fallen prophet. By 1847 this small organization had virtually disintegrated, although Rigdon continued for another thirty years trying to rally support.

The most important of the splinter groups that formed immediately after Smith's death was led by James J. Strang, "prophet and king" of a group at Voree, Wisconsin. Brilliant but unstable, Strang had been baptized in Nauvoo in February 1844 by Joseph Smith himself, then sent to survey the Burlington area of Wisconsin as a possible new gathering place for the Saints in that part of the country. In May he wrote to Smith praising the Racine and Walworth county regions and asking for permission to establish a stake (a kind of diocese of several congregations) there. After learning of Smith's death, Strang claimed to have received a letter from the Prophet naming himself as prophet and president of the church and designating Voree as the new gathering place for the entire church. Strang showed the letter to a conference of elders in Florence, Michigan. Some were persuaded, others were not. The presiding elder excommunicated him. By the time word of the incident reached Nauvoo, the Twelve were firmly established as controllers of the church's interests. On August 26, 1844, they confirmed the excommunication.

Undeterred, Strang and his counselors proselyted throughout the Midwest and publicized a purported revelation in which Strang was ordained by an angel to be Smith's successor. During 1845 Strang and his followers gathered a small colony of believers at Voree. Eventually he won over two former apostles, William E. McLellin and John E. Page, who had lost their standing in the Nauvoo-based church, plus William

Smith, brother to Joseph, as well as William E. Marks, who had previously followed Rigdon, and other, less prominent members. Later that spring John C. Bennett joined Strang's movement.

The diverse group of former church leaders who gathered with Strang at Voree were not destined to harmonize. Dissension and excommunications forced Strang in 1847 to relocate his colony on Beaver Island in northern Lake Michigan. By 1849 most of the Voree Saints had gathered there, and in 1850, in an elaborate ceremony, Strang was crowned King of the Kingdom. But tragedy quickly ensued. On June 16, 1856, Strang was assassinated by alienated followers, and the next month his twenty-six hundred adherents were driven from Beaver Island. As late as 1977 there were three congregations and scattered families of Strangites totaling about four hundred members.

Strang's relevance to the Mormon dispersion arises from the fact that he succeeded in attracting a number of disgruntled former Mormon leaders. He secured his influence by patterning himself after Smith's career. Strang's professed angelic ordination, his claimed discovery of a buried record, his introduction of polygamy and a temporal kingdom, even his final martyrdom, seemed a replay of previous events. It was not surprising that some Mormons were attracted to a leader whose very eccentricities reminded them of their first prophet.

Prior to the exodus from Nauvoo, Strang and Rigdon offered the only organized alternatives to Brigham Young and the apostolic regime. With the disintegration of Rigdon's church and the Voree group, a number of scattered dissenters, all baptized Mormons, including some who had suspended judgment since Smith's death, remained aloof from any of the possible successors to Smith's seat. As the westward-looking Saints conducted the great migration and built a mountain-desert empire, these undefined collections of believers began to coalesce around certain centers. Each represented a different concept of Mormonism's nature.

The first trend was toward the founding of short-lived "personality cults," centered around striking, often bizarre, leaders. For instance, George J. Adams, a noted Boston actor, followed Strang for a short while but broke with "King James" when the Voree prophet would not extend the privilege of polygamy to his counselor (Adams). In 1861 Adams organized a tiny sect called the Church of the Messiah. When he attempted to move the cell to Palestine in 1865, he provided humorous grist for Mark Twain's *Innocents Abroad* (1869). Charles B. Thompson also left Nauvoo to join with Strang. One year later he was called to "lift up his voice" as "Baneemy, patriarch of Zion." Thompson-Baneemy acquired a retinue of fifty or sixty families, including that of William E. Marks, who had been Nauvoo stake president. In 1853 Thompson founded the Community of Preparation in southern Iowa. When the community broke up, Thompson moved to Saint Louis and continued publishing a newspaper there until 1888. In a similar manner James Brewster; Apostle Lyman Wight, who led a group to Texas; Alpheus Cutler; Francis Gladden Bishop, the oft-excommunicated Nauvoo member; and William E. McLellin, along with Martin Harris and David Whitmer, all established tiny religious edifices on the shakiest of foundations. A somewhat larger group than any of these, the Bickertonites, grew out of Sidney Rigdon's Pittsburgh apostasy. None of the ten or so such splinter groups was numerically consequential.

It was a later Reorganization movement that became a genuine rival to mainstream Mormonism. The milieu that spawned this Reorganization was most notable in the beginning for its diversity. Many Saints outside Nauvoo, as well as residents not privy to the doctrinal innovations of the period, had been surprised by the rumors that reached them after the death of Joseph Smith concerning secret temple rites, the plurality of gods, and especially plurality of wives. Such practices and beliefs immediately became linked, for them, with Brigham Young. Other Mormons, finding the rigors of travel and Young's strong hand on the march west unbearable, filtered back from Iowa or beyond to seek out old homes and comfortable ways. They sought shelter from the conflicts that had convulsed the preceding years of Mormon history.

The Reorganization began in Wisconsin among a small band of families that had outgrown the flamboyant pretenders of the immediate post-Nauvoo period. Among these unquiet spirits was Jason W. Briggs. Baptized in Potosi, Wisconsin, in 1841, Briggs and the branch he led renounced Brigham Young as a successor to Joseph Smith and at first joined with James Strang. Briggs soon found that "some of the doctrines of Strang did not suit me." Accordingly, his branch moved, practically as a unit, into the party of William Smith, brother of the Prophet, who claimed leadership in the movement by right of blood relationship. But the peripatetic Briggs again became dissaffected, perhaps by rumors that William Smith, like Young and Strang, favored polygamy.

His nostalgia for pristine purity drove Briggs to prayer in November 1851. "The elders whom I have ordained by the hand of my servant Joseph," the word of the Lord seemed to say, should fulfill their duty of preaching the restored gospel. In due time the Lord would call upon the seed of Joseph Smith and "bring one forth and he will be mighty and strong, and he shall preside over the high priesthood of my church; and then shall the quorums assemble, and the pure in heart shall gather, and Zion shall be reinhabited."

During the next several weeks Briggs and his friends revealed this "word of the Lord" to several nearby branches. Briggs had become convinced that Joseph Smith III, the Prophet's oldest living son, a nineteen-year-old boy, who remained in Nauvoo with his mother, was the promised "mighty and strong" heir to the presidency of the church. Over the next year and a half several other groups of Mormons seeking an alternative to Young's leadership joined the "Young Joseph" movement. The first conference of the Reorganizers convened on June 12, 1852. Those who assembled published a pamphlet entitled "A Word of Consolation to the Scattered Saints" and began a missionary effort. By April 1853 the movement was growing appreciably, but young Smith had still not stepped forward to take his place.

Soon another revelation came, this time to H. H. Deam. It called for a provisional president, seven apostles, and several other officers for the incipient movement. When read and accepted by the small flock of waiting Saints, it provoked several spiritual manifestations. Zenos H. Gurley (a former Strangite) and Deam were named senior apostles but declined the presidency, so the office went to Jason Briggs.

In the years immediately following, the Reorganized branches waited in vain for their new leader to take his place. Nevertheless, the movement gained momentum. Priesthood quorums were developed, a pamphlet was published, and some congregations that had failed to migrate with Young joined the cause. Still young Smith did not appear.

By 1860 he was at last ready to assume leadership. Two years earlier he had rejected the plan, but now, in Amboy, Illinois, he told the church:

> I came here not of myself, but by the influence of the Spirit. For some time I have received manifestations pointing to the position which I am about to assume. I wish to say that I have come in obedience to a power not my own, and shall be dictated by the power that sent me.

The twenty-eight-year-old man who accepted the call to head the Reorganized Church of Jesus Christ of Latter Day Saints probably played as great a role in forming its identity as did the teachings of his father. Joseph Smith III had grown up in Nauvoo with his mother, Emma, who trained her son in the Christian graces but taught him little about Mormonism. He was, as Alma Blair has characterized him, "open minded, slow to form opinions, logical with a sense of humor, able to see various sides to a question, but capable of coming to his own conclusions and holding to them." Charles Derry, who left the Utah church to join the Reorganized group, was impressed by his first meeting with Smith but added, "his appearance was more like that of a farmer than a church president."

Smith was faced with a difficult challenge. To prosper, the Reorganization had to forge for itself an identity based on something more than feelings of anti-Brighamism and antipolygamy. Its response was a conservative one. Eventually, Reorganized officials rejected virtually the entire Nauvoo experience. Its branch of Mormonism was redefined within the safer limits of Smith's earlier years. Polygamy, plurality of gods, baptism for the dead, temple ordinances, the literal gathering of the Saints, the establishment of an earthly kingdom—these and other subsequent additions by the founding Prophet to Mormon theology were progressively expunged from the faith. Thus the Reorganization came to occupy a stance between standard Protestantism and Utah Mormonism. It retained a belief in a reopened canon, but its doctrinal position edged closer to a socially conscious, conservative sort of Protestantism.

Difficulties with identity, however, have continued among Reorganized Saints. When the church in the West abandoned polygamy and emphasized the spiritual rather than the temporal Kingdom of God, the distance between sectarian America and western Mormonism appeared to diminish. The result has been to leave the Reorganization without a clearly defined role. It is no longer sufficient, Robert Flanders has pointed out, for members of the Reorganized movement to say, "We are not Mormons" or "We don't believe in polygamy." To maintain their identity a new footing is currently being explored. Flanders sees a possibility that increasing decentralization, pluralism, and "demythologization" will lead to "a new identity based on both early Mormon and modern ecumenical Christian principles."

Whatever their present situation, Reorganized Mormons were successful in the nineteenth century in welding together several remnants of dissident Mormonism, including some dissenters from the western church itself. Nourished by a small influx of converts from foreign and domestic missions, by the 1970s the Reorganization could claim some 220,000 church members, concentrated mainly in the Midwest. Headquarters are in Independence, Missouri. Relations between this group and the larger church, with its headquarters in Salt Lake City, are polite but not warm. Both accept Joseph Smith as a Prophet, but they draw different conclusions about the meaning of the Restoration.

For the majority of Saints, the death of their Prophet did not require such a searching reexamination of faith. They believed that the mantle of leadership and continuity had fallen upon the Twelve Apostles, led by Brigham Young. Thus the largest group of Mormons united under Young's leadership and, under the duress of continuing persecutions, reached westward for the long-sought dream of a Kingdom of God on earth.

But temporarily, for a year or two, they clung to Nauvoo. The murders of Joseph and Hyrum Smith had brought a short respite from the pressure of mob violence. During a period of relative peace, stretching through September 1845, Young and the Twelve Apostles moved ahead with a number of important tasks. First, they decreed that the vital missionary work in the eastern states and England should continue. "It is necessary," said Brigham Young in a general conference convened in October 1844, "that the Saints should also be instructed relative to . . . spreading the principles of truth from sea to sea, and from land to land until it shall have been preached to all nations." Young sent Parley P. Pratt to the East to reassert apostolic control over missions there. There Pratt found William Smith, George Adams, and Samuel Brannan leading rival factions of eastern members. He managed to impose some order and retain most of that vital missionary field for the Nauvoo Saints. Wilford Woodruff, the Welshman Dan Jones, and several other missionaries continued the work of the Twelve in the British Isles, which had long been the special preserve of the apostles. Contending "toe to toe and inch for inch for every bit of ground," in Jones's words, the Nauvoo missionaries converted more than six thousand Britishers in three years. Jones himself was responsible for thirty-six hundred baptisms in three and one-half years in Wales.

The second goal of the apostolic regime was to complete the Nauvoo Temple and share with as many members as possible the sacred rites performed only in that edifice. "You cannot obtain these things until that house is built," affirmed Young. More than two hundred laborers worked at cutting stone and wood for the temple. The Relief Society, a Nauvoo women's organization, had donated two thousand dollars to the project; Joseph Toronto, an Italian sailor, added twenty-five hundred dollars to the fund. By October 5, 1845, the ground floor of the temple was ready for use. Even before that date the upper sealing rooms were packed with faithful Saints who participated in sacred ceremonies under the direction of Young and other apostles. In the winter of 1845–46 they gave as much attention to the temple as to the preparations for the trek they knew was ahead of them.

A third objective of the Nauvoo leadership was to consolidate and strengthen the internal structure of the church. Young increased the number of the Seventies, a priesthood group under the Twelve, and charged them with conducting a vast missionary effort throughout the world. Missionary districts were established in each of the country's congressional precincts. By such efforts Young assured a steady influx of converts, minimized the possibility of further division in outlying branches, and institutionalized the loyalty the Saints had previously felt toward Joseph Smith.

Persecution began again in the fall of 1844, when Mormon homes in Illinois were subjected to "wolf hunts"—freewheeling raids. The mobs disbanded under pressure from a state militia unit, but the latter soon let it be known that it could not be counted upon to protect Nauvoo. In January 1845 the Nauvoo charter, which had granted such extraordinary powers as the right to have a militia, was repealed by the Illinois legislature. That spring, harassment of the leaders with legal writs recommenced. In September, after barn-burning and crop-burning attacks on surrounding settlements, harassed Mormons flocked into the city for protection. While they might have been able to defend their outlying settlements if they had earnestly tried, the hostility of those in control of the state and neighboring towns assured that such success would be short-lived, or at least very costly in lives. Young at first responded with tough language ("at the first sign of aggression . . .

give them the cold lead") and sent out a posse led by a sympathetic non-Mormon sheriff. But as soon as he saw bloodshed occurring, he began to negotiate.

By the end of September 1845 it was clear to the Saints that they would have to leave Nauvoo. In the years before his death Smith had discussed a number of colonizing projects in the West. He had looked to the Republic of Texas as a possible haven for the Saints. The Voree settlement in Wisconsin was part of the same expansive impulse. Early in 1844 he had planned an expedition to explore "Oregon and California" (terms then including practically the entire unexplored region of the present far western United States). Even earlier, some associates later remembered, he had prophesied in August 1842 "that the Saints would continue to suffer much affliction, and would be driven to the Rocky Mountains. . . . Some would live to go and assist in making settlements and building cities, and see the Saints become a mighty people in the midst of the Rocky Mountains."

Determined to find a haven well away from the increasingly populated Midwest, Brigham Young discussed the problem with his advisers in the fall of 1845, read John C. Fremont's *Report of the Exploring Expedition to the Rocky Mountains* (1845), and decided to send a party of fifteen hundred men to the Great Basin in the Rocky Mountains the next year. Almost immediately Nauvoo became a vast outfitting and blacksmith shop. Thousands of Latter-day Saint families struggled to sell their farms and homes and gather one good wagon, three yoke of oxen, two cows, two beef cattle, three sheep, one thousand pounds of flour, twenty pounds of sugar, one rifle and ammunition, a tent and tent poles, from ten to twenty pounds of seed, and some farming tools. Such an outfit was necessary, in Apostle Parley P. Pratt's calculations, to transport a family of five to the new gathering place. The departure was set for the spring of 1846, as soon as water was flowing and there was sufficient grass for the animals.

Rising persecution, and indictments charging Young and the apostles with counterfeiting and other crimes, accelerated the departure. Young also heard rumors that there would be federal military intervention to prevent their movement on the ground that the Saints were intent on setting up an independent commonwealth. On February 2, 1846, despite the continuing winter cold, Young and the Twelve decided it was time to leave. They were delayed several days by members who, anxious to experience the temple ceremonies, lined up from early in the morning until late at night, the apostles serving as officiators in the ordinances. Finally, on February 15, Young joined the growing camp in Lee County, Iowa, across the Mississippi. Intending that a small group led by the Twelve would move ahead to find a settling place and plant crops, he had advised the main body of Saints not to leave until they were well prepared. But a steady stream of Nauvoo Mormons left the city throughout the winter and spring, the flow of refugees swelling and ebbing with fluctuations in the pressure applied by non-Mormons. Despite the token prices paid for the Saints' property and the unready condition of many of the families, the evacuation of Nauvoo was virtually complete by September. Some Mormons later trickled back into the city, but in the fall of 1846 Nauvoo the Beautiful, the "City of Joseph," stood almost empty.

The exodus to the Far West, stretching as it did over several years and thousands of miles, is not easy to portray. It was not the movement of a single horde but rather a chain of sometimes loosely linked companies inching toward a destination at first ill defined. At one end of the chain, converts and refugees were continually beginning migration. At the other, almost immediately after the arrival in the Salt Lake Valley, they were dispersing into planned colonies throughout the Great Basin, that vast intermontane region whose waters drain toward the Great Salt Lake. The trek west added migration to the processes of conversion, gathering, and persecution in the Mormon panoply of formative experiences. It was a refiner's fire from which emerged tougher Saints.

Young and the other leaders compared the Mormon movement to the exodus from Egypt under Moses, calling the leading party the Camp of Israel. Biblical rhetoric was used to heighten the Saints' sense of leaving a place of persecution for a Promised Land and of being miraculously blessed and guided. Their safe crossing of the Mississippi on the ice, the flocks of quail that descended to feed the most ill-prepared group to be expelled when they were starving on the west bank, and the last-minute assistance from the federal government (in exchange for the Mormon Battalion volunteers) that tided them over the necessary eight-month delay in Winter Quarters, Nebraska—such experiences could not help but remind the Saints of Moses and the Children of Israel.

This biblical identification was given particular point in the leaders' emphasis that they, like the Children of Israel, were being continually tested in order to prepare a fit generation for that Promised Land. When his brother apostle at Winter Quarters warned that the advance company could not make the journey with the one hundred pounds of provisions available per person, Young replied that he "did not want any to go who had not faith to start with that amount." Moreover, they must learn to share: "Brother Perkins wanted to know something about our going west; I [Brigham Young] told him that those who went must expect to go on the apostles' doctrines and no man say aught that he has is his own, but all things are the Lord's; and we His stewards."

The earliest refugees crossed the Mississippi on rafts and flatboats in February 1846. Later the river froze, the ice permitting many families to walk their teams directly across to Iowa. On the other side of the river the refugees streamed into the Sugar Creek camp, some nine miles inland from the Mississippi. They camped there in the most primitive conditions, awaiting spring weather. Nine babies were born the first few days at Sugar Creek. As early as February 25, one group set out in ten-degree weather for the Des Moines River. On March 1, with refugees still streaming into the Sugar Creek camp, other wagons prepared to leave. Brigham Young departed from the camp late in the afternoon, traveled five miles, and camped with a party of more than a thousand.

The progress of the Camp of Israel across Iowa was less than steady. Many of the Saints were penniless: "We have sold our place for a trifle to a Baptist Minister," wrote Martha Haven. "All we got was a cow and two pairs of steers, worth sixty dollars in trade." As a result, most of the parties were continually on the lookout for employment in the many small Iowa towns through which they passed. The Mormons stopped over to earn what they could by building jails, courthouses, fences, and furniture, and by sending their band to play at funerals and wakes as far away as Saint Louis. Since many had crossed the Mississippi on foot, carrying their possessions in a handcart or box, they salvaged scraps of lumber and iron to piece together into wagons.

By June 22 five hundred wagons had reached the Missouri River above its union with the Platte. There, at Council Bluffs, Young established a temporary terminus for the migration. Behind him, twenty-five hundred wagons and perhaps as many as twelve thousand Saints were scattered across 120 miles of sparsely inhabited prairie. Despite the confusion that developed, organization was quickly reasserted. Prominent Nauvoo leaders such as Gen. Charles C. Rich, Apostle John Taylor, Bishop George Miller, Charles Shumway, and Brigham Young himself had each taken charge of companies of four to five hundred wagons. Within each camp a pyramidal organization grouped families into tens, fifties, and hundreds, provided leaders for each unit, and distributed specialized guards and pioneers evenly among the groups of fifty. When the leaders of the entire camp met in March at Shoal Creek, 100 miles out of Nauvoo, they reconstituted this organization (which had been scrambled in the rush out of Nauvoo) and approved regulations that would keep the Saints from bidding against each other for scarce supplies of grain and other foodstuffs in the surrounding country. Thus, early on, the special circumstances of the Mormons' overland migration enjoined a centralized organization quite unlike that of most travelers of the period.

During the fall and winter of 1846 several advance companies pushed past Council Bluffs. They spent the winter there on the Missouri, Platte, and Niobrara rivers. Young's group later backtracked three miles and established Winter Quarters, now part of Omaha, Nebraska. Mount Pisgah, Garden Grove, and Council Point, Iowa—these were the main way stations established to raise food for those following.

Life was difficult in the winter of 1846–47. Some two hundred people died at Winter Quarters alone—perhaps one in thirty. Petty quarrels frequently disrupted life in the camps. James Hemmick challenged Wilbur J. Earl to a duel and was expelled from the camp. Counterfeit money was circulated by a few in the community, leading to incidents with Indians as well as trouble in the camps. Although each succeeding party of pioneers planted or cultivated plots of public land to provision those following them, this food supply was sometimes insufficient. Many families survived on the charity of their neighbors.

Weather, varying degrees of unpreparedness, and human cussedness combined in such a way that it took four months to cross Iowa's three hundred miles. For comparison, it took the pioneer company only three months to cover the remaining one thousand miles to the Salt Lake Valley in 1847. Of course, that later company was designed for speed and provisioned and organized in the way Young had intended the first trail-blazing group across Iowa should be. But in 1846, despite the energy with which he threw himself against all obstacles, Young's plans repeatedly broke against human and physical reality. The epic journey he led the next year to the mountains was a dramatic achievement. It was in Iowa in 1846 that Young learned to be the Moses his people needed.

One example of Young's ability to land on his feet was his handling of the noted Mormon Battalion experience. Back in January, Young had instructed the church's leading authority in the East, Jesse C. Little, to "take every honorable advantage of the times you can" to get assistance from the national government for the destitute church in its migration west. He apparently hoped to obtain a contract to build a series of forts to protect the developing Oregon Trail. In May, Little met young Thomas Kane, a member of a prominent Pennsylvania family who had been reading sympathetically about the Mormons. Using Kane's connections in Washington, Little was able to obtain a series of interviews with President James K. Polk, who was naturally preoccupied with the recent declaration of war on Mexico. One suggestion was that the assistance take the form of enlistment of one thousand Mormon soldiers to march to California under General Stephen Watts Kearny and another one thousand to go by sea. By June 5 Polk had consulted with his cabinet and gave approval, but only for five hundred soldiers by land, apparently because of the opposition of Sen. Thomas H. Benton of Missouri, who impugned Mormon loyalty and persuaded the president that Mormons should constitute no more than one-third of Kearny's forces. Young was convinced by private informants that Benton was looking for a pretext to raise a military force in Missouri with which to pursue and disperse the whole body of Saints. This perception was recalled in an early speech in the Salt Lake Valley in 1847 when Young "damned President Polk for his tyranny in drafting out 500 men to form a Battalion, in order that the women and children might perish on the Prairies. [And] in case he refused their enlisting, Missouri was ready with 3,000 men, to have swept the Saints out of existence." Two days later, in an emotional welcoming-home ceremony for Battalion members just arrived from California, Young stated that, because of Benton's dangerous intentions, "the Battalion saved the people by going into the army."

Although the fear of being pursued by Missourians may have been exaggerated, Young was probably right that there was some kind of dirty work afoot. An intriguing letter from Thomas Kane on July 11, 1850, mentions the existence of some persons "besides the President who were willing to see you driven by force out upon the wilderness." The letter does not give further details, but Kane promised to write them up for the church to have from his executors when he died. (Such a document may exist among those still closed to researchers at Kane, Pennsylvania.) If Kane did learn of such a plot, it was only on his return to Washington in the fall of 1846, because he traveled out to Council Bluffs in June to assure the Mormons that Polk's overture was in good faith. Whether Young suspected anything at the time is not clear. At any rate, he could see that the Battalion provided opportunities that might indeed save the Saints. After moving from camp to camp, speaking before campfires and from wagon tongues, he accomplished the impossible by persuading five hundred Mormon boys and men to leave their families and enlist.

Young argued that sufficient men would remain to conduct the exodus and that the Battalion wages would be an indispensable source of "hard cash" income. Moreover, cooperation would guarantee government permission to camp on Indian lands and use grass and timber. In their extremity it was no small consideration that five hundred men would be transported to California at government expense, thereby assuring Mormon prominence in the new territory expected to be established there.

The Mormon Battalion left Council Bluffs on July 20 to march to Fort Leavenworth, Kansas. Outfitted there, they began what probably was the longest march of infantry to that date in American history. A year later they arrived on the Pacific Coast, where they disbanded after earning some seventy thousand dollars in wages and allowances.

During the winter, Young further strengthened the lines of internal organization and communication necessary to administer a church spread out over several thousand miles. He established an internal mail service to communicate between the camps. When word reached the Missouri of the miserable condition of the last Saints to leave Nauvoo, he sent a relief team to bring the stragglers to join the main body. To complete the lines of communication, he dispatched several apostles to England to oversee the missionary and emigration apparatus in that country.

On January 14, 1847, Young announced "The Word and Will of the Lord" to the Camps of Israel. The revelation reaffirmed the pyramidal organization of the previous summer and required the captains of each company to decide "how many can go next spring; then choose out a sufficient number of able-bodied and expert men, to take teams, seeds, and farming utensils, to go as pioneers to prepare for putting in spring crops." This document further required each company to care for its share of families of Battalion members, widows, and indigents and provided for extensive planting and building by those staying behind.

Early in April, Young and a party of "able-bodied and expert men" left Winter Quarters to scout the trail and establish a preliminary settlement in the Salt Lake Valley, which church leaders had already selected as the destination. As they commenced, some 143 men, 3 women, and 2 children, traveling in seventy-three wagons, comprised the company. The party traveled on the north side of the Platte River instead of the south side, which was the route for most groups heading west. As Wilford Woodruff later remembered, "We thought it best to keep on the north side of the river and brave the difficulties of burning prairies to make a road that should stand as a permanent route for the Saints independent of the then emigrant road, and let the river separate the emigrating companies that they need not quarrel for wood, grass, or water."

The first destination of the pioneer party was Fort Laramie, 543 miles up the Platte River from Winter Quarters. They arrived there on June 1, 1847. That leg of the journey was not extremely difficult, for there were few streams to be crossed, the terrain was flat, and the teams were in good condition. The pioneers did have a few mild encounters with Indians and often had difficulty finding forage for their draft animals.

At Fort Laramie the pioneers were pleased to encounter a group of Mississippi Latter-day Saints who had wintered in Pueblo, Colorado, with the Mormon Battalion and then headed north to join the main group. From that point the company traveled west along the North Platte to Devil's Gate, up the Sweetwater and over the South Pass, then diagonally south and west to Fort Bridger on the Green River. Along the way they met mountain men Jim Bridger, Moses Harris, and Miles Goodyear, who gave varying views of the Saints' prospects in different parts of the Great Salt Lake area. They took the rather new Sublette Cutoff down Echo and Weber canyons and then the trail made just the year before by the Donner-Reed company up East Canyon and through the mountains. Although aided by some of the clearing that had been done by the Donner-Reed party, the Mormon company made slow progress through the tortuous canyons. Young lagged to the rear owing to an attack of Rocky Mountain (tick) fever that nearly killed him. Orson Pratt and Erastus Snow, advance scouts, entered the Salt Lake Valley on June 21. Three days later Wilford Woodruff's carriage, in which Brigham Young lay, climbed the last incline before the valley. Young raised himself from the carriage floor and surveyed the new gathering place of the Saints. "The spirit of light," he later wrote in his journal, "rested on us and hovered over the valley, and I felt that there the Saints would find protection and safety." Erastus Snow recalled him as saying: "This is the place whereon we will plant our feet and where the Lord's people will dwell."

The pioneer company immediately began planting crops, laying out a stockade, and preparing for the arrival of the larger parties, which were en route to the valley. Characteristically, they dedicated the land to the Lord, prayed for rain, and built a dam for irrigation in case the rain failed to come. After setting the process of settlement in motion, Young and a large party of men left to return to the Missouri River Valley for the winter. As his band retraced the route of the migration, it passed each of ten companies heading west. Approximately seventeen hundred Saints traveled in these ten companies; these pioneers of 1847 formed the nucleus of the Mormon domain in the West.

Historians have called the Mormon migration the best-organized movement of people in American history. Unlike other contemporary journeys to the Far West, it was religiously motivated. The Mormons went without the guides and professional outfitters employed by most westering emigrants. A poverty-stricken band of people, in many cases unable to outfit themselves properly, the Saints were not frontiersmen; they were artisans, farmers, businessmen, and clerks. The organization and cohesion of the Mormons was in marked contrast to "the process of disruption [that] prevailed so generally" in overland trail movements. Unique to the Mormons were the planting and building for the benefit of those to come later, sending back from Salt Lake City relief and supply parties to aid others on the last and toughest part of the route, and establishing a Perpetual Emigrating Fund to finance the poverty-stricken so that they could make the journey and pay later. The entire community of Nauvoo, a whole culture, was transported to a completely uninhabited location. Other frontier communities either grew slowly, adding a few families at a time until local government and trade became possible, or materialized overnight in the boom-bust syndrome of the mining exploitation of the West. In contrast, Salt Lake Valley was, within three months of its settlement, home to nearly two thousand people and was well organized for trade and government.

Many of the characteristics of orderliness and obedience had previously been exhibited by the Saints, but the journey west reinforced them. Discipline, cooperation, and organization were essential; priesthood and camp leaders had authority to instruct members where and when to build fires, when to get up, when to stop, where to camp. One camp historian wrote that Brigham Young had instructed a company "not to abuse cattle but take care of them—not to yell & bawl or make any noise nor to be up at nights—but attend prayers & go to bed by 9—& put out the fires. It is best to tie up the cattle outside—horses inside—hogs & dogs to be tied up or shot—the sheep to be taken care of &c." In large measure the people recognized Young's authority as necessary, and the exigencies of the trip and his successful leadership further strengthened his influence.

In addition, a certain resiliency, a feeling of having undergone the worst, grew in the Saints. "Mother, these western moves are hard on cattle," wrote Martha Haven, acknowledging that the move was also hard "on the people." Toughness led to pride. Martha Haven's letter concludes: "Truly, we have no abiding City. The ensign is to be reared upon the mountains and *all* Nations to flow unto it. We are not going to a remote corner of the earth to hide ourselves far from it." And early in the migration William Clayton penned the anthem of a generation of Utah Mormons:

> Come, come ye Saints, no toil nor labor fear;
> But with joy wend your way.
> Though hard to you this journey may appear,
> Grace shall be as your day.
> 'Tis better far for us to strive,
> Our useless cares from us to drive;
> Do this, and joy your hearts will swell—
> All is well! All is well!
>
> Why should we mourn or think our lot is hard?
> 'Tis not so; all is right.
> Why should we think to earn a great reward,
> If we now shun the fight?
> Gird up your loins, fresh courage take;
> Our God will never us forsake;
> And soon we'll have this tale to tell—
> All is well! All is well!
>
> We'll find the place which God for us prepared,
> Far away in the West,
> Where none shall come to hurt or make afraid
> There the Saints will be blessed.
> We'll make the air with music ring,
> Shout praises to our God and King;
> Above the rest these words we'll tell—
> All is well! All is well!
>
> And should we die before our journey's through,
> Happy day! All is well!
> We then are free from toil and sorrow too;
> With the just we shall dwell!
> But if our lives are spared again
> To see the Saints their rest obtain,
> O how we'll make this chorus swell—
> All is well! All is well!

Having traveled back to Winter Quarters, Young reiterated his leadership by calling a general conference in December to sustain him as president of the church, with Heber C. Kimball and Willard Richards as counselors. Then, during the winter of 1847–48, Young and his fellow leaders organized five emigrating companies that would transport twenty-five hundred more Saints to their new home during the following summer.

For those in the Salt Lake Valley, the chief task was to survive the winter and then prepare for the flood of new immigrants expected the next summer. In addition to the pioneer companies, the Mississippi Saints and a number of ex-Battalion members swelled the settlement's population. In Young's absence during the first winter in the valley, government was in the hands of a stake presidency composed of John Smith (uncle to Joseph Smith), Charles C. Rich, and John Young. Under this leadership the Saints were organized into teams to construct a stockade lined with individual cabins; to plow, plant, and irrigate as much land as possible; to lay out a city; to bring in timber from nearby canyons; and to explore and hunt through the whole area.

On July 25 and 28, 1847, Young had preached sermons that, like John Winthrop's sermon aboard the *Arbella,* established the guidelines for the new community:

> Those that do not like our looks and customs are at liberty to go where they please. But if they remain with us they must obey the laws sanctioned by us. There must be no work done on the Sabbath. As soon as we select a place of permanent location we shall take the compass and chain and lay out a city, and every man shall have his inheritance therein. We shall also lay out ground for cultivation, and every man shall have his inheritance and cultivate it as he pleases. Only he must be industrious. We do not intend to buy any land or sell any. . . .
>
> We propose that the streets will be 88 feet wide, sidewalks 20 feet, the lots to contain 1¼ acre, eight lots in a block, the houses invariably set in the center of the lot, 20 feet back from the street, with no shops or other buildings on the corners of the streets. . . .

From the beginning, Young sought to eliminate the divisive influences that had speeded the destruction of Nauvoo. Speculation, private ownership of natural resources, trade with Gentiles, and in fact almost all contact with the outside world were abjured. This Zion was to stand alone. That, at least, was the hope, the ideal.

By winter the pioneers had enclosed three blocks within a crude adobe wall, circled the city with eleven miles of fence and ditch, and prepared more than 5,000 acres for spring planting. Some 872 acres were sown in the fall with winter wheat. Captain James Brown of the Mormon Battalion was dispatched to California to collect Battalion pay and to purchase cattle and wheat and other seed. Roads, bridges, sawmills, and flour mills appeared as the council allocated public labor and directed private individuals in the task of preparing the valley for habitation.

Although the seventeen hundred Saints in the valley did not falter in their concerted efforts, a food shortage developed early in the winter. Too many poorly provisioned families had followed the pioneer company into the valley. The crops planted on July 24 had barely sprouted before untended animals grazed them to the ground. Indians and wolves decimated the livestock herds. The 1847 harvest consisted of a meager quantity of marble-sized potatoes. By winter the high council was asking for donations "in behalf of the destitute" and had inaugurated a voluntary rationing system. By spring the hungry farmers were reduced to eating crows, wolf meat, tree bark, thistle tops, sego lily bulbs, and hawks. Priddy Meek's dilemma was typical: "I would dig until I grew weak and faint and sit down and eat a root, and then begin again. I continued this until the roots began to fail."

Just when the prospect of an abundant spring harvest in 1848 lifted pioneer spirits, hordes of crickets—"wingless, dumpy, black, swollenheaded, with bulging eyes in cases like goggles, mounted upon legs of steel wire, . . . a cross of the spider on the buffalo"—swarmed over the sprouting grain. Neither fire nor water nor broomsticks could halt the invasion. At the height of the plague Charles C. Rich cautioned the pioneers not to dismantle their wagons "for we might need them." He may have been contemplating a move to California. At this point flocks of sea gulls from the Great Salt Lake appeared over the fields and began devouring the crickets. Many witnesses saw the intervention as providential; a remnant of the harvest was preserved, encouraging the Saints to remain in the valley. A Salt Lake City monument now commemorates the timely intervention of the birds.

In 1848 the arrival of twenty-four hundred immigrants more than doubled the new colony's population. Some of them were put up in the "old fort" erected by the pioneer company of 1847, others were located in log cabins, tents, and wagons in blocks laid out around the projected site of the temple. The Mississippi Saints were located in Cottonwood, an irrigable farming region ten miles southeast of Salt Lake City. Under Brigham Young's direction the Council of Fifty replaced the high council as the de facto governing body of the colony. Under the council's close supervision food was rationed through another winter, more stringently than during the previous one. Cooperation was enjoined; speculation and private monopoly were denounced. "Natural feelings would say let them and their cattle go to Hell," exclaimed Young when some refused to join their cattle with the community herd, "but duty says if they will not take care of their cattle, we must do it for them." Of the surplus of those reluctant to share, Young said, "We will just take it and distribute among the Poors, and those that have and will not divide willingly may be thankful that their heads are not found wallowing in the Snow." If the Saints' natural inclinations did not lead them to cooperation, the exigencies of their environment did.

During the winter Young established a court system, formed a provisional government for "the State of Deseret," distributed city lots and five- and ten-acre farming plots to nine hundred applicants, appointed trustees for natural resources, started several public works projects, coined several thousand gold pieces from dust brought by Battalion members returning from the California gold fields, and instituted a tax for public improvements.

Despite their industrious labors and careful planning, the Saints faced a gloomy future in the winter of 1848–49. In their two years in the valley the settlers had yet to reap a decent harvest. As reports of the gold strike in California trickled in, even the most loyal Saints began to wonder at their leaders' wisdom in choosing the inhospitable Great Basin for settlement. A few departed for the gold fields; others returned to the East. Brigham Young and the bulk of the church stood fast, but when Heber C. Kimball rose before them that spring to prophesy that the Saints would soon be able to buy eastern goods cheaper on their own streets than they could in the East, even the most faithful shook their heads. "I don't believe a word of it," declared stolid Apostle Charles C. Rich. But within weeks thousands of forty-niners began to pass through the Salt Lake Valley on their way to the gold fields of California, leaving a wake of abandoned or cheaply traded goods and wagons. A fluke of fortune—or, as the Mormons interpreted it, a special blessing of Heaven—at once fulfilled prophecy and combined with a good harvest and Mormon self-help to guarantee survival and make the continuing colony viable. Over the next half-century the settlement would grow to a network of nearly five hundred communities housing tens of thousands of Latter-day Saints.

The Indian Frontier
During the Civil War

ROBERT M. UTLEY

After the Europeans arrived in the western hemisphere, different Indian groups went through cultural changes as they struggled to preserve their identity and their lands. Perhaps the most impressive of the Indians' adaptations to the white presence on the American continent was the elaborate culture that evolved among the nomadic tribes of the Great Plains once they acquired the Europeans' animal—the horse.

When the Indians of Latin America first saw the conquistadors astride the horses they had brought from Spain, they thought the two were a single creature (a mistake that also may account for the mythical centaur). The Indians soon learned, however, that man and horse were separable and that the latter could be domesticated to great advantage. The Spaniards introduced horses into Mexico in the sixteenth century, and herds of the animals spread northward over the plains. Late in the seventeenth century, North American Indians began to breed Spanish horses. When white settlers reached the Great Plains over a century later, they met the first mounted Indians ever to be seen—the prototypes of the fierce, proud Indians seen today in Westerns.

By the time they encountered the whites, the Plains Indians were well on their way to developing a complex culture that centered on the horse and the buffalo. The buffalo was a prolific native of the plains that the Indians relied on for food, shelter, and clothing. The horse had transformed their lives by dramatically increasing their mobility and giving them greater effectiveness in waging war and hunting the all-important buffalo.

By the outbreak of the Civil War, more than two-thirds of the Indians that remained in the United States belonged to the Great Plains civilization. As Americans began to flood into the West, the Indians of the western territories took violent action to protect their diminishing homelands. The United States Army in turn developed a policy of eliminating this Indian threat through military activity. During the early 1860s, the army engaged in two wars at the same time: one against the Confederacy and one against the Indians on the frontier. From the Mexican border to the Canadian, the army found itself involved with an elusive and dangerous foe in the West.

In his book on the end of the Indian frontier, Robert M. Utley (Historian, National Park Service) describes how the military solution failed to eliminate the conflict between the Indians and the United States. Even though the U.S. Army won many of the engagements with Indian forces, conventional warfare did not settle affairs. In the late part of the nineteenth century, a combination of new governmental land and reservation policies, along with a renewed military effort, finally "pacified" the western Indians and opened the West to relatively peaceful white settlement.

M angas Coloradas (Red Sleeves) and Cochise towered above all other Apache leaders. Tall, muscular, gifted with uncommon intellect, and dynamic and forceful leaders possessed of warrior skills honed to perfection in countless raids on Mexican settlements, they held unchallenged dominion over their people. Mangas Coloradas and his Mimbres Apaches lived in southern New Mexico, ranging southward from densely forested mountains around the head of the Gila River across deserts studded with barren peaks and dry salt lakes, and into Mexico. Cochise and his Chiricahua Apaches occupied rocky mountain chains immediately to the west, in what would soon become the southeastern corner of the Territory of Arizona.

If Mangas Coloradas and Cochise did not themselves watch the strange actions of the American soldiers as the summer's furnace heat pounded the deserts in July 1861, some of their followers assuredly did, for few activities of the white people went unobserved by the Apaches. At Forts Buchanan and Breckinridge in Cochise's domain and Fort McLane in Mangas's, the soldiers burned the buildings along with all the stores they could not carry and marched eastward to Fort Fillmore, on the Rio Grande. The chiefs drew the obvious conclusion. They had whipped the soldiers and driven them from the country.

For these two chiefs, war had come but recently. Throughout the

THE INDIAN FRONTIER DURING THE CIVIL WAR   From *The Indian Frontier of the American West, 1846–1890* by Robert M. Utley (Albuquerque: University of New Mexico Press, 1984), pp. 65–98. Reprinted by permission of the University of New Mexico Press.

1850s, as other Apaches fought the American newcomers, Mimbres and Chiricahuas gave them little trouble. Occasionally a small party might rob or kill in the settlements scattered down the Rio Grande Valley and clustered around the adobe village of Tucson, but these were nothing compared with the devastation unrelentingly visited on Mexicans in Chihuahua and Sonora. The Apaches allowed travelers to move in relative safety on the road between the Rio Grande and Tucson and offered no opposition to the Butterfield stagecoaches that appeared on this road in 1858. Cochise and his followers even supplied firewood to the stage station in Apache Pass.

The uncertain peace ended abruptly in 1860–61. For both chiefs the cause was intensely personal. In May 1860 prospectors discovered gold near the old Spanish copper mines at the southern edge of the Mimbres Mountains, the heart of Mangas Coloradas's homeland. By autumn the teeming camp of Pinos Altos claimed seven hundred miners. Mangas Coloradas went among them—in a spirit of friendship, said the Indians, to deceive them into going elsewhere, said the whites, somewhat lamely. Whichever, as an Apache later described it, "The White Eyes bound him to a tree and lashed him with ox goads until his back was striped with deep cuts. He crept away like a wounded animal to let his wounds heal. . . . Never before had anyone struck him, and there is no humiliation worse than that of a whip."

For Cochise the collision occurred in February 1861, when a party of soldiers arrived in Apache Pass and asked to talk with him. He went into the soldier chief's tent. Through an interpreter the young officer, Lieutenant George N. Bascom, accused him of a raid on a ranch near Fort Buchanan, in which he had allegedly stolen stock and kidnapped a boy. Cochise explained that Coyotero Apaches had done this, not Chiricahuas. The officer would not believe him. Finally he declared that Cochise was under arrest. Enraged, the chief drew a knife, slashed his way through the tent wall, and sprinted to safety amid a volley of musket balls. At the same time, however, the soldiers seized five of his relatives who had been waiting outside the tent. In turn, Cochise seized a Butterfield station attendant and two travelers on the road through Apache Pass. These he tried to exchange for his relatives. The officer refused. Cochise struck back. His men massacred the drovers of a small freight train making its way through the pass, waylaid but failed to stop a stagecoach, and attacked soldiers watering stock at Apache Springs. After a week's standoff, Cochise cut out for Mexico, leaving beside the road in the pass the horribly butchered remains of the white hostages. In retaliation, the soldiers hanged their hostages from the limbs of a scrub oak tree. The bodies dangled there for months afterward.

Mimbres and Chiricahua lashed back at the whites. The withdrawal of the soldiers inspired them to even greater aggression. Both travelers and settlers suffered. Pinos Altos withstood a direct assault, and then a siege that flushed most of the miners out of the country. The handful of Confederate soldiers that trooped across the desert to occupy Tucson made no attempt to fight back. The raiders easily eluded the "Arizona Rangers" mobilized by the miners in self-defense.

Then in June 1862, as summer again dried the desert water holes, the Apaches saw soldiers coming from the west in great numbers. The Confederates hastily retreated to the Rio Grande. Cochise and Mangas Coloradas gathered their warriors on the slopes of Apache Pass to ambush the invaders. The first contingent reached the pass on July 15. Thrown back by rifle fire, the soldiers regrouped and fought their way through the pass to Apache Springs. The Indians posted themselves behind rocks on the slopes above to keep them from the vital water. But the soldiers wheeled up big guns and opened fire. Explosions that filled the air with deadly flying metal scattered the Apaches. Next day they tried again, only to be driven off again by bursting shells. "We would have done well enough," one later told an officer, "if you had not fired wagons at us."

The mettle of these new soldiers became even clearer the following winter. Mangas Coloradas had been shot in the Apache Pass fight. His men had borne him southward to Janos, Chihuahua, and forced a Mexican doctor to dig the bullet out of his chest. Soon he was again leading his men against the Pinos Altos miners. On January 17, 1863, however, he allowed himself to be lured by a white flag to a parley with a soldier chief, who promptly seized him as a prisoner. That night, as he tried to sleep next to a campfire, the guards heated bayonets and touched them to his feet. Rising in angry protest, he was instantly cut down by a volley of musket balls—killed, reported his captors, while attempting to escape.

Like Mangas Coloradas and Cochise, Indians all over the West in 1861 watched the curious spectacle of white soldiers marching away to the east. In Texas, Indian Territory, and southern New Mexico the soldiers pulled out altogether. Elsewhere they left a few of their number behind to hold the forts. Some of the Indians joined the Apaches in supposing that they had frightened the white soldiers away. Others knew more or less about the white people's quarrel that, like their own wars, had grown so intense that they had begun to fight among themselves. Soon, however, these people also discovered, with Mangas and Cochise, that a new day had not dawned. Soldiers came back in greater numbers than ever. And as the fate of Mangas Coloradas demonstrated, they approached their task with uncharacteristic directness, vigor, and combativeness.

The firing on Fort Sumter in April 1861 had immediately drained the West of all the regulars who could be spared, and for a time the frontier settlements and travel routes lay perilously exposed to Indian attack. At once, however, the federal government mobilized for the war against the Confederacy. Between 1861 and 1865 two million men sprang to the defense of the Union. The overwhelming majority served in volunteer regiments rather than the regular army, which shrank to a feeble skeleton. Many of these men discovered that they had volunteered for duty against enemies clad in breechclout and feathers rather than Confederate gray. By 1865 almost twenty thousand soldiers, mostly volunteers, served in the West, about double the 1860 figure. In Texas, settlers looked to Confederate units numbering between one and two thousand for frontier defense.

The volunteers made effective fighters. They tended to be better educated and more energetic than the regulars; they wanted to get the job finished and go home. Those from the western states and territories brought to their task a harsh, uncompromising view of the Indian and usually preferred extermination to negotiation. They followed some tough and aggressive generals. Steely eyed "General Jimmy" Carleton and the fiery Irishman Patrick Edward Connor went about Indian fighting with gusto, persistence, and little compassion for the enemy. Henry H. Sibley, Alfred Sully, and the veteran George Wright all displayed notable leadership.

It was Carleton who led the "California Column," eighteen hundred strong, across the Southwest in 1862, his mission to head off a Confederate invasion of New Mexico. By the time he reached the Rio Grande, Colorado Volunteers had driven back the Confederates, and Carleton's California and New Mexico Volunteers spent the war years fighting Apaches and Navajos. It was the advance guard of Carleton's army that clashed with Mangas Coloradas and Cochise in Apache Pass in July 1862. It was Carleton's subordinates, too, who in January 1863 saw to it that Mangas Coloradas would never again interfere with the development of the Pinos Altos mines.

Connor, Carleton's fellow Californian, also led California units eastward, to garrison the central overland route and to war with Indians who threatened California's tenuous link with the East. On the frozen battlefield of Bear River, Utah, he showed himself a practitioner of Carleton's no-nonsense brand of Indian fighting. Here, in January 1863, Connor and his men smashed the village of Shoshoni Chief Bear Hunter and left the snowy ground littered with the bodies of the chief and more than two hundred of his people. From headquarters in Salt Lake City, Connor passed the remaining war years in similarly ruthless operations against Indians of Utah, Nevada, and Idaho, and he found time in addition to wage a vituperative feud with Brigham Young and the Mormon hierarchy.

The diversion of such military strength to the West when troops were so desperately wanted in the South revealed the measure of Abraham Lincoln's need for western gold and silver and western political support for the prosecution of the war. It also dramatized how little the war slowed the pace of the westward movement.

The West's mineral wealth continued to attract fortune-seekers. The

Cherry Creek strikes of 1858 triggered the Pike's Peak rush and led to the founding of Denver and a proliferation of camps in the front range of the Rockies. On the eastern flank of the Sierra Nevada, discovery of the Comstock Lode in 1859 set off a rush that carried into the 1860s, gave rise to Virginia City, and sent prospectors north and south along the Sierra foothills. In the Pacific Northwest, the Colville strikes of 1855 were followed in 1858 by the Fraser River rush. In 1860 goldseekers pushed into the Nez Perce country and found color in the Clearwater River. Others who followed opened mines on the Salmon, the Boise, and the tributaries of the Snake River heading in Oregon. Beginning in 1861, prospectors turned up riches on the headwaters of the Missouri River, loosing an influx that built another Virginia City and swelled Montana's population to nearly thirty thousand by 1864. Gold deposits brought miners flocking to the lower Colorado River and the mountains bordering it on the east.

As population grew and spread, so did the transportation and communication network. The telegraph linked California to the Union in October 1861. Denied its southern route by the secession of Texas, the Butterfield Overland Mail moved northward, paralleling the telegraph wire on the central route. In 1862 Ben Holladay bought the enterprise and ultimately built a stagecoach empire that spanned the West and tapped the mining camps on each side of the trunk line as well. Stage lines also reached out from Leavenworth to Santa Fe and up the Smoky Hill to Denver. And with the opening of the Montana mines, steamboats in growing numbers ascended the Missouri River to Fort Benton, the head of navigation.

The political map of the West responded to the surge of activity: Dakota, Colorado, and Nevada territories were created in 1861, Idaho and Arizona territories in 1863, and Montana Territory in 1864. Silver-rich Nevada gained statehood in 1864.

For the Indians, the mounting tempo of westward expansion, the invasion of new areas of their homeland, the unsettling effect of the white man's Civil War, and the sudden appearance of a larger and more warlike military force combined to create new tensions and fears and new situations fraught with explosive potential. With the coming of the Civil War, many of the tribes entered a new and more traumatic phase of their relations with the white people.

No Indians experienced more trauma than the Five Civilized Tribes of Indian Territory. Many of these people owned slaves and felt a natural affinity for southerners. Also, geographical proximity gave the Confederacy an edge over the Union. The Choctaws and Chicasaws went overwhelmingly with the South. The Cherokees, Creeks, and Seminoles split, shattering the unity so painstakingly restored since the internal conflicts of the removal period. For all, the Civil War proved a calamity of far-reaching, long-lasting consequence.

The Confederate government moved swiftly in the spring of 1861 to embroil the populous Five Tribes in the conflict with the North. Albert Pike, Arkansas' noted poet-politician, appeared in Indian Territory as Confederate commissioner charged with concluding treaties and enlisting the various Indian groups in the war. Holding forth more liberal treaties than the United States had ever offered, Pike signed up Choctaws, Chickasaws, Seminoles, and Creeks. The last two agreed less than unanimously. Such chiefs as Chilly and Daniel McIntosh and Motey Canard led most of the Creeks into the pro-Confederate "United Nations of Indian Territory." But the respected Opothleyahola organized several thousand Union Creeks and Seminoles, and a scattering of like-minded people from other tribes, to stand firm for the North.

In the Cherokee Nation, the wise and able John Ross, long the Principal Chief, spoke eloquently for neutrality. "I am—the Cherokees are—your friends," Ross told Confederate proselytizers, "but we do not wish to be brought into the feuds between yourselves and your Northern Brethren. Our wish is for peace. Peace at home and Peace among you." War among the whites distressed Ross, but war at home tormented him with visions of strife within and devastation from without should his people take sides. Yet he was helpless to stave off a revival of the old removal factionalism in which he himself had figured so prominently. Those who had opposed removal now lined up behind Ross's rivals, chief of whom was Stand Watie. Not only did Watie agitate for Cherokee adherence to the Confederacy; he also raised a Cherokee regiment for service in the Confederate army.

At last, despite his strong convictions, Ross had to give in. In August 1861 the Confederate victory at Wilson's Creek, Missouri, gave the South strength and prestige in this part of the country and made it unlikely that the North could back the Cherokees meaningfully even if they remained loyal. Moreover, the Confederate victory greatly enhanced Watie's position in the tribe, for he and his Indian troops had fought well in the battle. Fearing a Cherokee civil war if he held out longer, less than two weeks after Wilson's Creek Ross sorrowfully brought the Cherokees into alliance with the Confederacy.

Ross's defection stunned Opothleyahola and left him and his Union followers isolated. The civil conflict that Ross had feared occurred as Indian troops in Confederate service went after them. In three armed clashes, in November and December 1861, they inflicted heavy casualties and scattered the loyalists, bereft of their stock, wagons, and other possessions, across a frozen, snow-covered land. Later the refugees reassembled in Kansas, to live precariously on government charity and to furnish recruits for federal regiments.

In Indian Territory, the bright hope offered by the Confederates began to dim. All the tribes contributed troops—three Choctaw-Chickasaw regiments, a Creek regiment, a Creek-Seminole regiment, and two Cherokee regiments, including Stand Watie's. They fought at Pea

Ridge, Arkansas, in March 1862, where both sides accused all but Watie's men of undisciplined excesses. The Union victory at Pea Ridge, moreover, opened the way for a Union drive into Indian Territory from Kansas. Cherokees, betraying their true sentiments, defected by the hundreds. But Ross's high sense of honor kept him firmly in the Confederate camp until Unionists settled the question by taking him prisoner. For the rest of the war, from a base in Philadelphia, he served his nation well as head of the government in exile and as emissary to the U.S. government. In Washington he formed a close friendship, based on mutual respect, with Abraham Lincoln.

At home the war dragged on, the fortunes of the Confederates and their Indian allies now in decline. In July 1863 the Battle of Honey Springs dealt them a decisive defeat. Confederate Cherokees, Creeks, and Seminoles fled southward to the Choctaw-Chickasaw country and even to Texas, forming camps of suffering refugees matching those of the loyalists in Kansas. Everywhere desolation reigned—fields untended, stock running loose, homes empty or burned, and Indian fighting Indian as Cherokee, Creek, and Seminole pursued civil wars of their own. Each of these nations had two governments, one Union and one Confederate, with each claiming legitimacy. After Ross's departure, Stand Watie set up a rival Cherokee government with himself as chief. Watie also continued to compile a war record that won high praise from Confederate authorities but also drew allegations of guerrilla atrocities. In 1864 the Confederates made him a brigadier general, the only Indian to hold such high rank, and in 1865, more than two months after Appomattox, he was the last Confederate general to surrender his forces.

With war's end the Five Tribes faced a disheartening prospect. Like white southerners, the people had to rebuild their homes and eke out a living. They had to repair the divisons of war, compose the differences that had set them violently one against another, and suppress the bitter factionalism that the war had revived and so disastrously aggravated. And they had to brace themselves for the retribution an outraged North would be sure to loose upon them as punishment for siding with the Confederacy.

The Eastern Sioux of Minnesota grew hungrier and angrier as July and August 1862 slipped by without the annual distribution of their annuities. The agency warehouse contained stores of food and other goods, but the agent would not make the issue until the cash portion of the annuity arrived too. This made no sense to the Indians, especially as the traders would claim most of it to satisfy credit they said, and nobody could disprove, had already been extended.

Little Crow argued with the white officials. The leading chief, he was a man of oratorical ability and persuasive power, although his authority had come under increasing challenge from more militant chiefs who regarded him as a tool of the whites, a charge given substance by his part in the treaties that had compressed the Eastern Sioux into a ten-mile-wide reservation extending 150 miles up the south side of the Minnesota River. Even Little Crow, the friend of the whites, could not get the warehouse doors opened. The attitude of the whites was conveyed in a remark by trader Andrew Myrick that, summing up the grievances of a decade, furnished a rallying cry for revolt: "So far as I am concerned," said Myrick, "if they are hungry let them eat grass or their own dung."

The Eastern Sioux—Mdewakanton, Wahpekute, Wahpeton, and Sisseton—had once roamed the expanse of forest and lake drained by the upper Mississippi River, sharing its bounty with Winnebagos and contesting it fiercely with Chippewas. In the 1840s, however, the white frontier of settlement crept up the Mississippi. Minnesota became a territory in 1849. The census of 1850 showed a population of six thousand whites and more than twice as many Indians. By 1858 whites numbered more than 150,000 and Minnesota gained statehood. Methodically, treaty commissioners negotiated with the tribes of Wisconsin and Minnesota for cession of the lands into which lumbermen and farmers were moving. For the Sioux, treaties in 1851 and 1858 extinguished title to 28 million acres in exchange for annual annuities and the reservation on the Minnesota River. Little Crow played a prominent role in persuading the Sioux to accept these treaties.

Reservation life had not been happy. Some Indians, including Little Crow, cut their hair, moved into log cabins, and tried to learn farming. Others did not. Discontent deepened as more and more whites, mostly German and Scandanavian immigrants, surrounded the reservation and as less and less of the annuities promised in the treaties found their way to the Indians. By one means or another, the money due the Sioux always seemed to end up in the pockets of traders and other claimants. More than any other factor, this pattern, repeated year after year, kindled in the Sioux a dangerously volatile temper.

In fact, Minnesota in the 1850s afforded a classic example of the corruption of the federal Indian system, especially after statehood provided voting representation in the Congress. Senators and representatives dictated the appointment of their friends and supporters to the Indian Bureau's field posts back home and exerted their influence to keep federal appropriations flowing to the reservations back home. The local officials, in league with traders and contractors, plundered the annuities and other appropriations to the personal enrichment of all. Profits and patronage also oiled local party machinery and forwarded the political fortunes of candidates for state and national office.

Minnesota's leading public figures came out of this tradition. Among the negotiators of the Sioux treaty of 1851 were Agent Alexander Ramsey and trader Henry H. Sibley. Of $475,000 the Indians were to receive when they moved to their new reservation, Sibley claimed $145,000 as overpayments his firm had made to them for furs. Agent Ramsey allowed this and other claims amounting to two-thirds of the total due the Sioux. Again, in 1858, Sibley and other traders entered claims against the $266,880 the Sioux were to get for selling half their Minnesota Valley reservation, and only $100,000 found its way to the Indians. Sibley became the state's first governor, Ramsey the second.

Critics condemned the system and cried in vain for reform. In 1860, urging reform on President James Buchanan, Minnesota's Episcopal Bishop Henry B. Whipple warned that "A nation which sowed robbery would reap a harvest of blood." Exemplifying all the evils of the Indian system, Minnesota provided the setting for the fulfillment of the bishop's prophecy.

On August 17, 1862, four Sioux youths hunting north of Redwood Agency murdered five white settlers. The deed had not been planned. One had dared another to prove his courage. But for the Sioux the issue of whether or not to stand behind the boys provoked a stormy scene in which the gathering wrath of a decade boiled over. Militant chiefs, bolstered by a riotous mob of young men shouting for blood, won the pledge of a reluctant Little Crow to lead them in war against the whites.

At dawn on the next day Indians swept through Redwood Agency, killed the men, took the women and children captive, and put the buildings to the torch. In wide-ranging parties they spread over the countryside, killing, raping, pillaging, and burning. Surprised, unequipped for defense, unversed in frontier life, the farmers fell by the score, dispatched with a savagery rarely equalled in the history of Indian uprisings. By evening some four hundred whites had been slain, and hundreds more flew in panic toward Fort Ridgely.

Nothing, it seemed, could prevent the onslaught from engulfing St. Paul itself. But divided counsel overtook the Indians. Little Crow and part of the rebels attacked Fort Ridgely. The rest of the Sioux rode against the town of New Ulm. In desperate fighting at both places, the defenders turned back the assaults.

Governor Ramsey called on his old associate Henry Sibley to organize the relief. Commissioned colonel in the state militia, Sibley led some fifteen hundred men up the Minnesota River against the foe. "My heart is steeled against them," he told Governor Ramsey, "and if I have the means, and can catch them, I will sweep them with the besom of death." The scenes of carnage and desolation along the march only intensified the spirit of revenge. At Redwood Agency Andrew Myrick's mutilated corpse lay outside his store, mouth stuffed with blood-caked grass in gruesome rejoinder to his callous remark about hungry Sioux.

Their leaders quarreling among themselves, the Sioux fell back before Sibley's advance. On September 23 they rallied enough to stage an ambush at Wood Lake. Sibley's troops easily drove them from the field in an action that proved decisive. After Wood Lake many of the fugitives scattered westward into Dakota and northward into the British possessions. Some two thousand, however, fell captive or surrendered to military patrols scouring the countryside. With no more battlefields to sweep with the besom of death, Sibley turned to the courtroom. A military commission found 303 Sioux guilty of various offenses, most on the flimsiest of evidence, and condemned them to die by hanging. President Lincoln called for the trial records, however, and over the vehement protests of Minnesota authorities reduced the list to thirty-eight. On a frosty December day they died on the gallows.

The Minnesota bloodbath cost the Sioux their reservation—and the innocent Winnebagos theirs, too—for Lincoln could not resist the demand of Minnesotans for their removal westward to new homes in Dakota Territory. Some settled on a reservation on the Missouri River. Others scattered over the Dakota prairies or mingled with the Teton Sioux. Picking berries on a farm near Hutchinson, Minnesota, the following summer, Little Crow was gunned down by the owner. The state legislature voted him a $500 reward.

The coming of the Civil War heightened the complexity of the Navajos' relationship with one another and with the Hispanic population of New Mexico. Indians and New Mexicans had always alternated raid and counterraid with friendly intercourse and trade. In 1861, with the departure of the regulars, New Mexicans donned blue uniforms and took their places in the forts, thus adding to the usual ambiguity of the war-peace relationship.

Compounding the ambiguity, most Navajos fell into one of two categories, *ladrone* or *rico,* the former poor in sheep and other possessions by which the latter measured their wealth. The raiders who preyed on New Mexican settlements usually came from the ranks of the ladrones, while New Mexican retaliation usually fell on the peaceably disposed ricos, whose abundance of sheep, horses, and orchards made them more tempting as well as more convenient targets. As the tempo of military activity in the Navajo country quickened in the late 1850s, rico and ladrone became synonymous with peace party and war party. Progressive impoverishment by Hispanic raiders transformed ricos into ladrones, proportionately swelling the war party and shrinking the peace party.

As the bluecoats abandoned their forts and concentrated to meet the graycoats, Navajo raiders struck fiercely at New Mexican settlements. By the middle of 1862, however, the Confederates had been repulsed and new bluecoats had come from the west to join with the New Mexicans in fighting Indians. They built a new fort, Wingate, at the edge of the Navajo country. Word came that they were badly whipping the Mescalero Apaches east of the Rio Grande.

Worried, eighteen Navajo ricos journeyed to Santa Fe in December 1862 to talk with the new soldier chief. He dealt with them brusquely, without the ceremony usual for such meetings. He told them to go home and to tell their people he would need more than mere words before he would grant peace.

Actually, General Carleton's lack of specificity reflected his current preoccupation with the Mescalero Apaches, even then verging on collapse. Leading his troops in the field was an old friend—mountain man, fur trapper, scout, and now colonel of New Mexico Volunteers, Kit Carson. By the spring of 1863 most of the Mescaleros had surrendered to Carson's columns. Carleton had them moved from their mountain homeland to a barren stretch of the Pecos River Valley in eastern New Mexico called Bosque Redondo, "round grove of trees." Here he built Fort Sumner to watch over them. Now he was ready for the Navajos.

In April 1863 two peace chiefs, Barboncito and Delgadito, met with General Carleton near the edge of their home country. Again he talked bluntly. All Navajos who wanted to be friends, he said, must go live at Bosque Redondo. Stunned, the chiefs said no, but two months later he repeated his ultimatum in unmistakable terms. "Tell them," he directed the commander of Fort Wingate, "they can have until the twentieth day of July of this year to come in—they and all those who belong to what they call the peace party; *that after that day every Navajo that is seen will be considered as hostile and treated accordingly*; that after that day the door now open will be closed."

This was no idle threat. The Navajos suddenly discovered Kit Carson and his soldiers thrusting deep into their homeland—north around Canyon de Chelly, west to the Hopi mesas, and south to the Little Colorado. On each sweep the troops killed Indians whenever they could, but mainly they seized stock and destroyed crops. Other Indians—Utes, Pueblos from Jemez and Zuñi, and even the normally mild Hopis—scented plunder and joined the fray, as did the ubiquitous citizen units that had always used Indian defense as a cloak for private gain. By the close of 1863, the Navajos had lost 78 people killed and 40 wounded and at least 5,000 head of sheep, goats, and mules.

The final blow, in January 1864, was Carson's defiant march the length of Canyon de Chelly, long the most forbidding Navajo citadel. As shouting, cursing Indians rained arrows from the rims of the sheer red sandstone walls, the troops, negotiating the sandy bottoms far below, corralled two hundred sheep and methodically destroyed fruit orchards. Sixty Navajos promptly surrendered with the admission, as Carson informed Carleton, that "owing to the operations of my command they are in a complete state of starvation, and that many of their women and children have already died from this cause."

These were harbingers of a flood of Navajos driven by hunger and demoralization to surrender. By the middle of March 1864, six thousand camped around Forts Canby and Wingate awaiting the threatened deportation. The soldiers organized a Long Walk, the eastward equivalent of the Trail of Tears by which Cherokees and others had journeyed westward to the Permanent Indian Frontier a generation earlier. In contingents of hundreds, the Navajos made their painful, sometimes fatal way under the guns of the soldiers across the territory to the Bosque Redondo. By late 1864 more than eight thousand people, three-fourths of the tribe, had been moved to their new home on the arid Pecos bottom. "The exodus of this whole people," observed an officer, "men, women, and children, with their flocks and herds, leaving forever the land of their fathers, was an interesting but a touching sight."

Carleton looked on Bosque Redondo as a testing ground for the reservation policy, and, employing his wartime powers to the limit, he set forth to show the Indian Bureau how the army could make it work. Far from their homes, he believed, the Navajos could be taught to farm, their children instructed in reading and writing, and all given "the truths of Christianity." Gradually the old people would die off, taking with them "all latent longings for murdering and robbing." The young would replace them without such longings. In ten years the Navajos would form "the happiest and most delightfully located pueblo of Indians in New Mexico—perhaps in the United States." The Navajo Wars would be a thing of the past.

For the Navajos, life at Bosque Redondo turned out to be not so idyllic. There was not enough tillable land for so many Indians, and the crops they did grow fell victim to flood, drought, hail, and insects. The sheep and goats could not find enough grass, and Kiowas and Comanches from the plains to the east raided the herds. Government rations barely held off starvation. Government clothing did not hold off the winter cold. Weakened by malnutrition and exposure, the Indians succumbed to pneumonia, measles, and other diseases. They quarreled endlessly with their old enemies, the Mescalero Apaches, who shared the reservation with them, until the Mescaleros stampeded back to their mountain homes late in 1865.

Despite overwhelming evidence, Carleton refused to admit failure. And of one result he could boast: he had ended the Navajo Wars. Symbolizing this reality, in September 1866 Manuelito finally surrendered. Since 1855 this young spokesman for peace, on whom had fallen the mantle of Zarcillos Largos at the Laguna Negra council, had matured into the foremost Navajo war leader. With a diehard remnant of the tribe, he had withdrawn far to the west rather than yield to Carleton. His surrender marked the final triumph of the military campaign, and en route to Bosque Redondo Carleton had him paraded as a prisoner through the streets of Santa Fe.

Gentle, wise, wrinkled by sixty plains winters, Black Kettle personified the Cheyenne peace spirit. He believed accommodation with the whites more likely than war to preserve his people's freedom to follow the buffalo. War spirit fired the Cheyennes, too, especially the ever belligerent Dog Soldiers; and even in Black Kettle's own band, the young men now and then stole and killed along the Santa Fe Trail. Many, perhaps most, Cheyennes thought him too willing to do the white man's bidding, but enough shared his basic viewpoint to keep him constantly in the top ranks of tribal leadership.

Not surprisingly, then, Black Kettle's name headed the list of Cheyenne chiefs who, along with a handful of Arapahos, signed the Fort Wise Treaty of 1861. This treaty addressed the perennial issue of Indian land "title." The Cheyennes and Arapahos ranged the High Plains approaches to the Rocky Mountains, now teeming with "Pike's Peakers" seeking fortunes in gold, and thus occupied a considerable portion of the newly created Territory of Colorado. At Fort Wise the chiefs agreed to a reservation south of the Arkansas River in exchange for all other lands identified as theirs in the Fort Laramie Treaty of 1851.

The compact suffered the defects of most such treaties. The Indians did not understand what they had promised. Only a handful of Southern Cheyenne and Southern Arapaho chiefs had signed. The document bore the mark of not a single Dog Soldier, most powerful of the Southern Cheyenne divisions, nor that of any representative of the Northern Cheyennes and Northern Arapahos, whose occupancy of this country also drew sanction, in the white scheme of things, from the Treaty of 1851. Territorial Governor John Evans labored diligently but vainly to sign up these other Indians, a tacit admission that the Fort Wise Treaty, despite official rhetoric, had not freed eastern Colorado of Indian title. In seeming vindication of his pacific course, Black Kettle and his band continued to wander the plains, occasionally pausing at the Upper Arkansas Agency to receive annuities from an agent more occupied with graft than with treaties and land titles.

The failure of the Indians to grant a ready solution to Colorado's land problems sorely vexed Governor Evans. A conscientious and ambitious man, friend of President Lincoln, he nurtured a grand vision of Colorado's destiny and his own contribution to shaping it. The Indians stood in the way, maddeningly unresponsive to his efforts to gain land titles and settle them as farmers on the arid reservation defined in the Fort Wise Treaty. In the Indians' lack of cooperation Evans perceived sinister intent, and he readily credited reports that the tribes planned to go to war in the spring of 1864.

These reports drew plausibility from events on the northern Plains. Shock waves from the Minnesota uprising of 1862 rolled westward. In the summer of 1863 Generals Henry H. Sibley and Alfred Sully had led armies into Dakota Territory against the Minnesota fugitives and had also collided with the Teton Sioux of the upper Missouri. The generals planned another combined offensive against the Sioux in the summer of 1864. Also, along the Platte and the Arkansas, other Indians perpetrated scattered outrages, hardly enough to presage war but enough to sustain Evans's fears. One of Colorado's two volunteer regiments kept busy guarding the Santa Fe Trail, but as a measure of the tranquillity in Colorado itself, the other, the First, had stagnated at Camp Weld, near Denver, since its triumph over invading Confederates in New Mexico in 1862.

Governor Evans drew like-minded support from the military commander in Colorado. A man of impressive physique as well as enormous ego and ambition, Colonel John M. Chivington had forsaken the Methodist ministry to earn fame as Colorado's "Fighting Parson" in the New Mexico campaign. Now, as Congress authorized Colorado to apply for statehood, he harbored political ambitions that further military exploits could be expected to promote.

Whether Evans and Chivington cynically provoked an Indian war to advance their personal ambitions or simply were so certain of one that expectation proved self-fulfilling, the result was the same. No alliance of tribes materialized, although as usual the spring grasses stirred youthful energies, and stock herds and other white property suffered. To these offenses, real and imagined, Chivington's soldiers responded with heavy-handed violence. "Burn villages and kill Cheyennes whenever and wherever found," ordered one of his field officers.

Like other Cheyennes, the war burst on Black Kettle with painful suddenness. He and Lean Bear with their people, about four hundred in all, had spent the winter near Fort Larned, Kansas. Moving north in mid-May to hunt buffalo, they encountered some of Chivington's soldiers on the Smoky Hill River. Lean Bear rode out to show them papers given him during a visit to Washington, signed by Abraham Lincoln, telling of his friendly character. The soldiers shot him and his companion from their ponies, then opened fire with howitzers. The Indians returned the fire for a time until Black Kettle rode up. "He told us we must not fight with the white people," recalled one, "so we stopped." The soldiers retreated; twenty-eight Indians lay dead.

The war anticipated by the Colorado officials had now broken over the Platte and the Arkansas. It featured but a few scattered raids in June and July, then built to a destructive peak in August. Fed by sensational newspaper accounts that multiplied and magnified actual depredations, hysteria gripped Denverites throughout the summer. Few doubted the governor's repeated declarations to Washington that the alliance he had forecast in 1863 now threatened to wipe out the Colorado settlements.

Coloradoans had another preoccupation that summer of 1864, secondary to the Indian war but not unrelated. A fierce political battle raged between Republican champions of statehood and Democratic opponents. As Lincoln's appointee, Evans led the statehood forces and, in the event of victory, aspired to a seat in the U.S. Senate. Chivington sought election to the House of Representatives. The voters would decide on September 13. Meantime, the Indian question became a central issue in the confused and bitter campaign.

Evans appealed to Washington for authority to raise more troops for Indian duty, and at last, on August 13, he received permission to recruit another regiment, the Third Colorado Cavalry, to serve for one hundred days. Unlike the other two Colorado regiments, called into federal service by the demands of the Civil War, the "Hundred Dazers" had but one purpose—to fight Indians.

With winter approaching, however, the war ardor of the Indians began to cool. Late in August Black Kettle sensed the time auspicious for a peace feeler. Not all the chiefs favored this course. The whites had started the war, and the raids on the Platte and Arkansas, and against the isolated homesteads of eastern Kansas, continued to yield plunder and captives. But Black Kettle gambled that he could bring all into line. Mixed-bloods framed a letter for him that asked for peace talks and, as earnest of sincerity, offered the release of white captives. At great peril a small party of Indians rode south with this letter. Fortunately they fell into the hands of an unusually sensitive and compassionate officer, Major Edward W. Wynkoop, commander of Fort Lyon. Also at great peril, and with grave misgivings, Wynkoop and a small command set forth to test the Cheyenne initiative.

Against large odds, Black Kettle and Wynkoop came to terms. The confrontation of 130 scared soldiers with more than 500 shouting, well-armed Indians almost ended in violence before talks could get started, and several times thereafter mutual suspicion, taut nerves, and dissent in both camps came close to precipitating armed collision. But in the end the white major and the Cheyenne peace chief prevailed. Black Kettle turned over four white captives to the soldiers, and Wynkoop, on September 18, wrote jubilantly to Governor Evans that he was on his way to Denver with Black Kettle and other chiefs for peace talks.

The news hardly elated the governor. Although the electorate had rejected statehood on September 13, political considerations still ruled. The Third Regiment had been called up to fight Indians. The recruits expected to. The citizens expected them to. Washington officials and Chivington's superiors at Fort Leavenworth expected them to. After emitting cries of alarm all summer and finally winning authority to form the Third Regiment, Evans could not concede peace without severe loss of credibility in all quarters. Besides, the issue of peace or war lay chiefly with the army, as General Samuel R. Curtis, Chivington's superior, made clear on September 28. "I want to peace till the Indians suffer more," he telegraphed. "No peace must be made without my directions."

Yet here on this very day came Black Kettle, Bull Bear, White Antelope, and other Cheyenne and Arapaho chiefs, under escort of one of Chivington's own officers, to talk peace. It posed a genuine dilemma for both the governor and the military commander, and they met it with dissimulation. After hours of verbal sparring, Chivington declared: "My rule of fighting white men or Indians is to fight them until they lay down their arms and submit to military authority. They are nearer to Major Wynkoop than anyone else, and they can go to him when they get ready to do that." Whatever Chivington meant by that, if indeed it was anything more than an artful attempt to straddle the dilemma, Black Kettle and his fellow chiefs took it at face value. They could have peace by surrendering to Major Wynkoop.

With full trust in Wynkoop, Black Kettle and Little Raven moved swiftly to do just as Chivington had instructed. Little Raven and 113 lodges of Arapahos arrived at Fort Lyon in mid-October, and Wynkoop issued them army rations. Early in November Black Kettle and a party of followers rode in, having left their village of 115 lodges on Sand Creek about thirty-five miles northeast of the fort. To his dismay, Black Kettle discovered "Tall Chief" Wynkoop about to leave. He had been summoned eastward to explain to General Curtis his curious behavior in feeding hostile Indians. Major Scott J. Anthony had taken his place. The two majors explained the situation to Black Kettle. The army lacked sufficient rations to feed so many Indians, and official permission to accept them as prisoners would have to be obtained. Meantime, the Arapahos should move out to hunt, and the Cheyennes should remain on Sand Creek and also hunt.

Through October and November 1864 Colonel Chivington bore mounting abuse from the Colorado press, which ridiculed him and the "Bloodless Third" for their inactivity. He considered leading an expedition to the upper Republican River, where plenty of indisputably hostile Sioux and other Indians camped. But this would be chancy at best, especially with the Third's hundred-day enlistment running out. In Chivington's mind the Cheyennes and Arapahos near Fort Lyon were equally guilty of outrages against whites, just as surely deserved punishment, and were technically still "hostile Indians." They were also much easier to get at. With great secrecy, he concentrated his troops at Fort Lyon, where he found an eagerly cooperative Major Anthony.

At daybreak on November 28, 1864, Chivington deployed his column of seven hundred men and charged into Black Kettle's sleeping camp, which sheltered about five hundred Indians. Black Kettle hoisted an American flag and a white flag over his lodge and tried to calm his startled people. White Antelope ran toward the soldiers waving his arms and was shot down in the first volley. Frantically the Cheyennes fled, seeking cover, as the cavalrymen cut them down. They had no chance to organize resistance, and for several hours after the opening charge the troopers ranged the village and surrounding country, honoring their colonel's intent that no prisoners be taken. Men, women, children, and even infants perished in the orgy of slaughter, their bodies then scalped and barbarously mutilated. At day's close some two hundred Cheyenne corpses, about two-thirds women and children, littered the valley of Sand Creek.

"Colorado soldiers have again covered themselves with glory," exulted the *Rocky Mountain News* as the victors of Sand Creek paraded triumphantly through Denver's streets to the cheers of her citizens. Theater patrons applauded a display of Cheyenne scalps, some of them of women's pubic hair, strung across the stage at intermission. The "Bloody Thirdsters," and Chivington too, were mustered out of the service acclaimed as heroes by their admiring fellow citizens.

By 1865 military force as the solution to the Indian problem had achieved virtually unchallenged supremacy. In Indian matters President Lincoln had shown himself a humanitarian, but the struggle with the Confederacy ruled his White House years and he left Indian affairs almost entirely to Congress and the Indian Bureau. Commissioner of Indian Affairs William P. Dole skillfully promoted traditional civil policies—reservations, Christianity, "civilization"—but the Civil War so consumed public and official attention that he made little headway. In the Congress he encountered Indian committees dominated by westerners. In the West his agents found themselves powerless against military potentates such as Carleton, Connor, Curtis, Sibley, and Sully. Backed by regiments full of warlike westerners, supported by western public opinion, and unrestrained by a national authority preoccupied with saving the Union, the generals almost by default had made U.S. Indian policy overwhelmingly a military policy.

No general believed more fervently in the military solution, or held the civil agents in greater contempt, than John Pope. Pompous, bombastic, quarrelsome, and verbose, he had been exiled to Minnesota after losing the Battle of Second Manassas in 1862. In directing the operations of Generals Sibley and Sully on the northern Plains, however, Pope had done so well that, late in 1864, General Ulysses S. Grant placed him in charge of a huge new command extending from the ninety-fifth meridian to the Rocky Mountains and from Confederate Texas to the British possessions. As the spring of 1865 opened, Pope organized the biggest offensive ever mounted against the Plains Indians.

Pope and his officers classed all the Plains Indians as hostile. Many in fact were, thanks in no small part to Colonel Chivington. Predictably, Sand Creek had touched off an explosion. As the surviyors of Chivington's strike straggled into the other Cheyenne camps on the Smoky Hill, runners bore war pipes to all the Sioux, Cheyenne, and Arapaho bands of the central Plains. Throughout January and February 1865, they spread death and destruction along the overland route, burning virtually every ranch and stage station on the South Platte, twice sacking the town of Julesburg, ripping up miles of telegraph wire, plundering wagon trains, running off cattle herds, and completely cutting off Denver from the East. Then, abruptly, the war ended. In council the chiefs had decided to cast their fortunes with their brethren to the north. Troops struggling desperately through snow and mud to confront the raiders found them all moving rapidly northward.

On the northern Plains, Teton Sioux, Northern Cheyennes, and Northern Arapahos had not been as directly provoked as the kinsmen who came among them with stories of Sand Creek. But some had fought General Sully on the upper Missouri the previous summer, and all were distressed by the growing traffic of whites to the Montana mines. Some of the goldseekers went by steamboat up the Missouri River. Others, more ominously, traveled overland by an increasingly popular route that ran northwest from Fort Laramie. Known as the Bozeman Trail, it cut through the very heart of the Sioux buffalo ranges in the Powder River country.

South of the Arkansas River, the Kiowas and Comanches were also classed as hostile. In the summer of 1864 they had endangered the Santa Fe Trail, the supply line to General Carleton's army in New Mexico. He had reacted with customary vigor by sending Colonel Kit Carson to deal with these tribes as he had with Apaches and Navajos. On November 25, 1864, at Adobe Walls in the Texas Panhandle, Carson and his New Mexico Volunteers had a hard fight with Kiowas. The Indians suffered losses, but Carson escaped disaster only under cover of artillery fire. Although the Kiowas and Comanches may not have regarded the conflicts of 1864 as placing them among the hostiles of 1865, General Pope and his campaign planners did.

Pope's Plains operations of 1865 represented the most extensive test ever of the military solution. In regiments and brigades rather than in companies and battalions, the army marched against the Indians. In all, six thousand troops took the offensive, while thousands more defended the travel routes and settlements. South of the Arkansas, General James H. Ford tried to bring the Kiowas and Comanches to battle. In the north General Sully campaigned once again on the upper Missouri, and General Connor launched three heavy columns into the Powder River country.

The offensive dramatized the limitations of the military solution and ended in a failure so complete that the generals could not gloss it over. They discovered that big columns operating in an inhospitable country far from their bases required massive logistical support and had to devote themselves almost entirely simply to keeping themselves provisioned. Some of Connor's units came close to disaster when bad weather wiped out horse and mule herds weakened by starvation and almost did the same to soldiers in similar condition. Also, big columns trailing long supply trains moved so ponderously that only the most careless Indians failed to get out of the way. In addition to such obstacles inherent in large-scale operations, the generals confronted other difficulties. Appomattox had ended the Civil War. The volunteers, hitherto such aggressive fighters, wanted to go home. Sent instead to chase Indians, they approached their task sullenly, even mutinously. Whole units melted away in desertion. Supply costs skyrocketed, moreover, at the very time the public demand for drastic curtailment of military expenditures hit the War Department. At the close of the season, the armies dissolved, beaten not by the Indians but by terrain, distance, weather, logistics, morale, and the miscalculations of the generals.

But the generals had also fallen victim to forces beyond the purely military, for the armies had marched against a rising tide of peace sentiment. Sand Creek had momentarily distracted public attention from the Civil War and sent waves of revulsion across the land. Three separate official investigations got under way, although civilian immunity now shielded Chivington and his lieutenants. In this climate voices of peace, hitherto drowned by the clash of arms, could be heard again. Before adjourning in the spring of 1865, Congress created a joint committee to investigate "the condition of the Indian tribes and their treatment by the civil and military authorities of the United States" and also authorized a treaty commission to approach the Sioux of the upper Missouri. These two commissions, beaming peace signals at the Plains Indians in the midst of a military offensive, contributed to the array of setbacks that dashed the hopes of the military strategists.

The two congressional enactments of March 1865 marked the first tentative steps toward a different kind of Indian policy, one that when fully matured would be described as "conquest by kindness." Both efforts reflected uncertainty among most civil and military authorities over what approach to take; war and peace factions had yet to polarize. Both efforts, too, reflected a pattern of motivation that would increasingly characterize federal measures toward the Indians, a pattern that rooted Indian policy in a strange mixture of genuine humanitarianism and crass self-interest.

The Dakota project rested on a large measure of self-interest. It germinated in the fertile brain of Territorial Governor Newton Edmunds. In Dakota, curiously, politicians and newspapers damned the generals and called on Congress to make peace. Actually, Dakotans had not suddenly acquired a sympathy for the Indians. For one thing, they were outraged that General Pope's quartermasters bought supplies for General Sully's expeditions in Sioux City, Iowa, rather than Yankton, Dakota. But the principal explanation for the new pacifism lay in the public image of Dakota as a war-torn territory; not only had immigration ceased, but settlers were packing up and leaving. So people had to be shown that they did not risk their scalps by settling in Dakota. In October 1865 the Edmunds Commission journeyed to the upper Missouri, signed up some chiefs of the "stay-around-the-fort" bands, and proclaimed peace. It was a brazenly cynical tactic, for as the governor and his associates well knew, not a single chief of the Sioux with whom Generals Sully and Sibley had been fighting for three years had even talked with the commissioners, much less touched the pen to their treaty. Yet the public perception fostered by the Edmunds Commission made it an influential force in the evolution of a peace policy.

A similar contribution to policy sprang from a treaty negotiated at the same time with the Kiowas and Comanches on the Little Arkansas River in Kansas. This treaty owed much to Senator James R. Doolittle, chairman of the Senate Committee on Indian Affairs and author of the measure that sent three congressional groups to the West in the summer of 1865 to inquire into "the condition of the Indian tribes." Doolittle and two colleagues made up one of the groups. In Kansas, working with Kiowa-Comanche Agent Jesse H. Leavenworth, they successfully blocked General Pope's offensive against the Indians south of the Arkansas River and laid the groundwork for the peace initiative that culminated on the Little Arkansas in October. Throughout the tortured sequence of events that turned a military offensive into a peace offensive runs a mostly hidden thread of private gain. High officials in Washington as well as Kansas, both civil and military, had interests in the railroads that now, with the Civil War's end, would begin building across Kansas. Indian hostilities would scarcely promote either the financing or the settlement on which their progress depended. Although characterized by General Pope as "not worth the paper it is written on," the Little Arkansas Treaty, like the Edmunds Treaty, created the momentary illusion of peace and thus strengthened the drive for an overall peace policy.

The military debacle on the northern Plains in 1865 signaled the end of a distinct phase of U.S. relations with the western Indians. Although not repudiated, the purely military solution had been severely discredited. Now proponents of other approaches could at least gain a hearing. The autonomy enjoyed by frontier commanders during the war years vanished with the volunteer armies.

One who may have drawn satisfaction from helping to stimulate the peace sentiment among the white people was Black Kettle. Chivington thought he had killed the Cheyenne peace chief at Sand Creek. But, with other survivors of his band, he had fled to the Smoky Hill. When his fellow chiefs resolved to go north and enlist their brethren in the fight, Black Kettle led his people south of the Arkansas to escape the hostilities. Not surprisingly, in October 1865 he turned up with his band at the treaty council on the Little Arkansas.

With what emotions Black Kettle made his mark on the Little Arkansas Treaty can only be surmised. On the one hand, he surely saw a measure of vindication in its express repudiation of "the gross and wanton outrage" perpetrated by U.S. soldiers at Sand Creek. On the other hand, he may have puzzled over the reparation awarded him personally—a grant of 320 acres of patented land to be carved from a reservation in turn to be carved from those vast reaches of High Plains that he and other Cheyennes still looked upon as their birthright.

The Chinese
Discover America, 1784–1879

MICHAEL H. HUNT

Too often the study of immigration in American history deals only with the Atlantic migration and overlooks the fact that several waves of immigration came from East Asia. The first major wave was a large-scale migration from the Pearl River Delta area of China to California and the West during the gold rush, beginning in 1848. The second wave was an influx of Japanese settlers on the West Coast around the turn of the twentieth century.

Toward the middle of the nineteenth century, political unrest in China displaced many peasants and urban poor. Many of these people migrated to Latin America and the American tropics under a system of contract labor much like indentured servitude. There they sometimes replaced African slaves, whose numbers were dwindling with the abolition or suppression of the Atlantic slave trade. These Oriental laborers were called "coolies." In China this term meant merely unskilled laborers, but in the western hemisphere, it soon acquired the connotation of bound, or involuntary, laborers. Very few of the Chinese immigrants to the United States were coolies in this latter sense of the word, even though they were under the strict control of the Chinese organizations that had arranged for their passage, the Six Companies being most notorious. Most of these immigrants had belonged to the free peasantry in China and thus had roots in the same class that produced the Irish and German immigrants of the period.

If it was difficult for white European immigrants to find a place in the relatively stable East Coast society at mid-century, it was even more difficult for East Asians to move into the highly fluid, rapidly changing, rambunctious society of California. Next to the blacks, the Chinese were the immigrant group most different from the dominant whites. Their physical appearance was distinctive, and they tended to preserve their language, religion, customs, and culture. Over half of the immigrants were married men who had left their families in China and who needed to work hard and live extremely frugally in order to send money home, to visit their families in China, or to return to China permanently. All these factors set the Chinese apart from white America, even though by 1852 the Chinese in California alone numbered 25,000 and make up ten percent of the state's total population.

As early as 1852, attempts were made to deny the Chinese admission to the West Coast, and in 1882, anti-Chinese sentiment culminated in the passage of the Chinese Exclusion Act. Although this law was intended to halt immigration only for a ten-year period, it virtually stopped the Chinese migration to the United States. Ironically, it had the effect of opening the West Coast to Japanese immigration: the expanding economy needed laborers for the jobs that earlier had been filled by the Chinese.

Michael H. Hunt (University of North Carolina at Chapel Hill) has written about the developing relationship between the United States and China in the nineteenth century. In the chapter from his study reprinted here, Hunt explores the beliefs about the United States that China's elite held in the early nineteenth century and the relationship between these attitudes and the beginning of the Chinese migration to America at mid-century. The selection goes on to describe the activities of the Chinese "sojourners" in the West and Americans' reactions to them.

By the middle of the nineteenth century the United States had come to hold a special attraction to some Chinese, just as China had come to hold a special promise to a select group of Americans. The United States first came onto the Chinese horizon through the work of scholar-officials seeking to understand the Western powers whose intrusions had begun to unsettle their world. As problems of foreign policy along the China coast became more acute from the 1830s onward, investigations into the origins and interests of the Americans assumed a pressing, practical character. In the 1850s, at the very time the United States was becoming for the first time an important point of reference in Chinese foreign policy, the trans-Pacific odysseys of the men of the Canton delta, drawn to the "mountain of gold" by

THE CHINESE DISCOVER AMERICA   From *The Making of a Special Relationship: The United States and China to 1914* by Michael H. Hunt. (New York: Columbia University Press, 1983), pp. 41–79. Copyright © 1983 Columbia University Press. Reprinted by permission.

economic opportunities, introduced the United States to Chinese in a second way. These Chinese emigrants did not go as permanent residents intent on assimilating into American society, but as sojourners. They would in time set off a "native" opposition on the Pacific slope that bears at points a striking similarity to the hostility Americans encountered in China. By the 1870s this conflict between Chinese emigrants and their American opponents had grown to such proportions that it occupied a central place in Sino-American relations.

THE AMERICAN INFATUATION

With the arrival of the *Empress of China* in Canton in 1784, the United States as a separate country began to intrude on the Chinese consciousness, but even then Americans occupied a decidedly marginal place in thinking on maritime affairs, itself a topic of only peripheral concern to Chinese intellectuals and officials until the 1830s. During those early decades the dominant Chinese tendency, well established before the first direct Sino-American contact in the 1780s, was to lump Westerners ("ocean barbarians") together as a single undifferentiated tribe. The contempt for outside cultures, which sustained the simple vision and which militated against exploring its diversity, was itself deeply rooted in cultural tradition. "If he be not of our kin," the *Tso-chuan* reminded generation after generation of exam-bound Chinese students, "he is sure to have a different mind." These foreigners, who came from across the "western ocean," were thought to have animal-like natures, more like sheep and dogs than men. The very written characters selected to name these people reflected this sharp distinction drawn between civilized Chinese and the wild barbarian. For example, the general term for those who arrived by sea, the Americans included, was represented by the character for sheep with the sign for water added alongside. In general, foreign names, both national and personal, were transliterated or translated well into the nineteenth century in ways intended to demean and give unsavory connotations.

The dim early perceptions of the Americans derived in large measure from Chinese observation of the dominant British community in Canton. Since the Americans spoke the same language, sought out the company of the British, and shared with them a seemingly unrestrained devotion to trade, it was natural for some Chinese to classify the Americans as merely a subgroup of the English tribe. Others, less sophisticated, simply took the Americans as another kind of "sea-going barbarian," a type whose essential traits had been previously defined by watching the British. Time and again reports coming out of Canton intoned, "The sole object of the foreigners is to trade. . . ." They warned that their minds were essentially "inscrutable," and that their daily behavior revealed a great craftiness in pursuit of profit. Some few observers took note of the mechanical ingenuity of these newcomers and their essentially frivolous creations. With the onset of Sino-British tensions in the 1830s the image of the foreigner in Canton began to take on darker coloring. As Chinese authorities sought to "rein in," the foreigners became even more unreasonable. The British as the quintessential foreigners then impressed Chinese more and more with their violent side, the fearful destructiveness of their weaponry, and their ability to draw Chinese traitors to their side.

Chinese geographers knew of the existence of the North American continent from Jesuit works of the late seventeenth century. And in 1787, four years after independence, Americans as a people distinct from the English appeared for the first time in the Chinese record. Even this brief delay may have been more attributable to the desire of the first American traders in Canton to be counted as English to avoid various exactions than to any indifference on the Chinese side. Then and in subsequent years the Chinese would refer to the United States as the "flowery flag country" (*Hua-ch'i kuo*) after the picturesque national banner whose stars appeared to the Chinese as flowers, by various literal translations of "United States" (e.g., *Lien-pang kuo*), by a considerable range of transliterations of "America," or even some combination of these, before ultimately settling on *Mei-kuo* ("beautiful country") as the standard term. The surviving early references are, however, few and terse, suggesting miniscule interest and no knowledge of the United States beyond the fact that it was a trading nation at Canton with "numerous" ships. By the 1810s the conception of the United States had expanded to a nation at odds with the British. The two have, the governor general in Canton noted in 1814, "engaged in plundering each other's goods and money." Three years later that same official further observed that the American barbarians were "most respectful and submissive to us." They had, strange though it seemed, no king, and instead selected a chief by lots to serve a four-year term. Two published works from the early 1820s added little to this picture. A geography from that time identified the United States as a somewhat narrow and isolated island, about ten days to the west of England, which had once controlled it. Americans followed customs similar to those of the English (including monogamy), and traveled about in steamships which they were adept at building. Governor general Juan Yüan included an entry on the United States in one of his many scholarly compilations, a work on the "outer barbarians" completed in 1822 (his fifth year in Canton and the year after disposing of the Terranova affair). It simply indicated that the Americans, whose ships in Canton had become as numerous as those of the English, occupied a part of the "vast territory" of the North American continent. Seven years later Juan's successor claimed that the Americans, "although not docile and submissive," were seldom as "rascally" as the British (a distinction that some officials writing at about the same time openly questioned).

From the late 1830s onward Chinese observers labored to bring the United States into sharper focus. An aggressive British policy made imperative a fuller understanding of the foreign troublemakers and helped bring the United States out of the haze. Ch'i-ying, who was to negotiate the American treaty with Cushing, observed succinctly in an 1842 memorial to Peking that "to control barbarians, one must first know their nature."

Americans in Canton, both by their actions and by the information they conveyed, also played a pivotal role in this growing Chinese appreciation of the United States. Merchants left their mark chiefly by demonstrating the national devotion to trade. The far less numerous and late-arriving American diplomats sent confusing signals. On the one hand, they stressed the fiercely independent attitude of the United States toward Britain and a deep concern over equitable commercial opportunity, whereas on the other hand their behavior often suggested dependence on—if not outright collusion with—the British. The missionaries exercised an influence all out of proportion to their numbers by using their Sinological skills to celebrate the achievements of the West generally and the United States in particular. As a byproduct of their effort to shake Chinese arrogance and resistance to the Christian message, missionary informants, preachers, and translators imparted much of the basic cultural and historical information that gave nuance and depth to early Chinese commentary on the United States. The most important of these was without question Elijah C. Bridgman, whose full Chinese language account, "A brief guide to the United States of America" (Mei-li-ko ho-sheng kuo chih-lüeh), appeared in Singapore in 1838 and subsequently circulated along the China coast.

This search for more information on the United States centered naturally enough in Canton, where both the crisis and the Americans were to be found. Liang T'ing-nan, a native scholar and counselor to a succession of governors general, was one of a growing number of Chinese guided by the premise that understanding the foreign danger was the precondition for meeting it. Liang's first published notice of the United States in 1838 was no more than a reproduction of Juan's simple sketch of 1822. But several more years of investigation and the discovery of Bridgman's study enabled him to describe for his readers the course of English settlement of the thirteen colonies and the dispute over taxation that led to conflict and American independence (in 1788!) under the leadership of George Washington. Liang also touched on such diverse topics as the topography of the United States, its climate, social and political institutions, and commerce. The pioneering works by Liang as well as Bridgman were in turn to shape the other notable study touching on the United States that dates from this period, Lin Tse-hsü's

"Guide to the four continents" (*Ssu-chou chih*). Lin, who arrived in Canton in 1839 as the imperially appointed commissioner charged with closing down the opium trade, hastily embarked on gathering as much information as was available on the barbarians he had been sent to manage. The resulting compilation provided detailed treatment of the establishment of the American colonies and states, the structure and operations of the government, the topography, and the population (including prominently blacks and Indians). This highly descriptive work, weighted down with dates and statistics, nonetheless had a clear message for the attentive reader: the United States, after only sixty years as a nation, had already become a "major power" and a rival to the English. Lin's account held up for particular praise the extensive system of schooling, the unmatched skill of the Americans at putting the steam engine to practical use, and the responsiveness of the government to the people ("no different than the rule of worthy emperors").

In the relatively placid period between the end of the Opium War and the turmoil of the 1850s two works appeared which finally supplied the first coherent picture of the United States and struck the central themes that were to resonate in later works. The first of these works was Wei Yüan's "Treatise on maritime kingdoms" (*Hai-kuo t'u-chih*) of 1844. Wei, born in 1794 in the inland province of Hunan, had already established himself as a widely respected scholar before developing an interest in the late 1830s in the problem of "maritime defense." That interest grew in intensity as a result of firsthand exposure to the British threat along the coast and an encounter in 1841 with his friend Lin Tse-hsü, then on his way from Canton into exile after his attempt to bring the British opium traffic under control had miscarried. Lin left behind a copy of his "Guide to the four continents," and Wei set to editing and supplementing it. The first results of his research appeared in print in 1842 under the title "Chronicle of imperial military campaigns" (*Sheng-wu chi*), a work already in progress before his meeting with Lin. Two years later the full scope of his investigations became public in the "Treatise on maritime kingdoms." This latter, full-scale study of the foreign problem was guided by starkly utilitarian concerns. Wei offered his work as a textbook on how to handle the unprecedented barbarian threat confronting China. He wanted to correct misconceptions and supply fuller information, the better "to use barbarians to attack barbarians, to use barbarians to soothe barbarians, and to study the barbarians' superior techniques to master barbarians." While urging a better understanding of these foreigners, Wei maintained an unshaken sense of Chinese cultural superiority evident in his consistent use throughout his writing of the condescending term "barbarian" (*i*) and his belief that China was obliged to show generosity and solicitude for those respectful and obedient outsiders who came to China to make their livelihood.

Out of these preoccupations and biases came a surprisingly sympathetic portrait of the United States. Wei's account traced the emergence of a new country into a rapacious world of international rivalry. The struggle for the East Coast of North America ended with the aggressive British in control and the French deeply embittered over the loss of their settlements there. Britain's bullying was, however, to prove her undoing. "The British barbarians levied numerous and heavy taxes which caused the thirteen parts of America to start a righteous revolt to drive them out. At the same time the Americans asked France to help them. . . . The Americans cut the British supply lines. The British soldiers were in hunger and distress, and the British ceded territory and asked for peace." In gaining their independence and "recovering [sic] the twenty-seven parts [states] of their original land," Americans demonstrated martial virtues. In drawing on France to defeat Britain, they showed themselves clever. They subsequently constructed a sound political system and made their country rich, so that by the 1830s the United States had come to stand, as Wei understood it, alongside France as one of the "powerful countries of the West." Yet the United States, despite its wealth and power, "did not bully small countries and did not behave arrogantly toward China." Those Americans who came to Canton to trade were, along with the French, "the most amicable and obedient" of the foreigners, and they naturally resented the British, "the most fierce and arrogant of people," for attempting to dominate China's trade. Old rivalries of the West, Wei's account told his readers, lived on, even along the China coast.

Wei's "Treatise" remained the definitive Chinese account of the United States for only a few years. It was overtaken in 1849 by a more detailed and cosmopolitan work, "Brief survey of the maritime circuit" (*Ying-huan chih-lüeh*), by Hsü Chi-yü, an official one year Wei's junior and one of a small but growing group of Chinese experts on the West. Hsü's "Brief survey" had much in common with Wei's "Treatise," both in genesis and themes. Like Wei, Hsü hailed from the interior (in his case, landlocked Shansi in the north). He had not become involved in the barbarian crisis until 1840, the beginning for him of a decade of service in a variety of posts in the southern coastal provinces of Kwangtung and Fukien (where he ultimately held the post of governor). After one local defeat during the Opium War, Hsü in his agitation over the English peril had complained, "I can neither eat nor sleep, trying to think of ways to help." Hsü, now aroused, set himself the same task Wei had undertaken—to search out new information that might shed light on these "intractable" and seemingly "unfathomable" intruders and thereby suggest solutions to China's foreign crisis.

In the five years between 1843 and 1848, a relatively tranquil period in Sino-foreign relations, Hsü devoted to the project what time he could spare from his official duties. He built on Wei's "Treatise" just as Wei had drawn from Lin's "Guide." But directed by genuine curiosity as well as his utilitarian concerns, Hsü also gleaned information from

Chinese travelers and barbarian experts, foreign informants, and foreign printed sources to add substantially to and amend the work of his predecessors. For his account of the United States he consulted David Abeel, an American missionary in Amoy. (Abeel found to his disappointment that his interlocutor was "far more anxious to learn the state of kingdoms of this world, than the truths of the kingdom of heaven.") Hsü also consulted Bridgman's account of the United States. Finally, he talked with an American doctor in Amoy, and he may have sampled a periodical published in Chinese by the Anglo-American missionary organization, the Society for the Diffusion of Useful Knowledge. The result, consistent with the spirit and breadth of Hsü's inquiry, was a study of genuine intellectual sophistication whether compared to extant Chinese accounts of the United States or even to guides to China prepared by contemporary Americans. Hsü in effect invited his countrymen to think of foreigners in a less stereotyped, more open-minded way by avoiding the more blatant forms of condescension (such as using the term "barbarian") that had marred the work of his predecessors and by suggesting that the world was diverse and that the Chinese could learn from it.

On close examination the Americans revealed themselves to Hsü, as they had to Wei, as an admirable people—"docile, good-natured, mild, and honest"—yet also possessed of "wealth and power." Hsü was particularly intrigued by the success of the Americans at repelling the domineering British and at making their country strong and rich in a short time. Because of the obvious relevance of such achievements to China's contemporary plight, Hsü gave more attention in the "Treatise" to the United States than to any other single country, even more than to the formidable and overbearing British. Hsü told part of the American success story in terms of the rapid development of unsettled land. Americans, who once hugged the Atlantic Coast, managed in two hundred years to possess the heartland of North America where "the favorable climate and fertile land are almost as good as China's," and to achieve "a prosperity which has overflowed into the rest of the world." With scarcely concealed admiration, Hsü traced the process: "Cities were laid out along the coast. . . . Trade flourished and gradually became very abundant. Because of this, wealth and power were achieved."

Hsü recognized that development continued even as he wrote. Americans had extended their landholdings across the continent, ousting the "aborigines." He was particularly impressed by the way Americans applied their technical skills to integrate a once wild frontier into the national political and economic system. They built canals linking many small rivers into a transportation network. "They also build fire-wheel carts [steam locomotives], using rocks with melted iron poured on them for the road in order to facilitate their movement. In one day they can travel over three hundred *li* [about a total of one hundred miles]. Fire-wheel ships [steamers] are very numerous. They move back and forth on the rivers and seas like shuttles. . . ." Here was a pattern of settlement, without counterpart in China's own frontier experience, in which technology imparted a marvelous speed and prosperity and consolidated political loyalties.

Hsü depicted as no less a marvel the social and political order of this newly developed land. The marvel in this case was not (as might be anticipated) its foreignness but rather its startling similarity at many points to Chinese ideals. The American society, as Hsü described it, was divided into categories familiar to his readers. Scholars (including clergy, doctors, and lawyers) were at the top, followed by peasants (meaning farmers), laborers, and merchants. Hsü took the parallel between the two countries a step farther by picturing Americans as lovers of education and learning. They were also, like the Chinese, a homogeneous people. Although somewhat less than half came from non-English stock, all were Christians and English-speaking. Even his account of the American political system, described as "a wonder" and unprecedented either "in ancient or modern times," emphasized patterns of behavior that strikingly paralleled Confucian ideals of civic virtue.

Hsü largely credited American political achievements to George Washington. Compared by Hsü to the mythic sages of Chinese antiquity, the American leader was to become through this account and others influenced by it a familiar figure to Chinese interested in foreign learning and an especially important one to a subsequent generation of Chinese nationalists. Hsü's Washington fit the archetype of the dedicated national leader devoted to the people and the state rather than personal or family power. Sketched out according to the conventions of Chinese biography, Hsü's Washington emerges more Chinese than foreign. Raised by his widowed mother, he displayed as a child a natural talent for civil and military affairs and from an early age had great ambitions. "His bravery and eminence surpassed all others." Although the British rulers withheld the recognition he deserved, not so "the people of his native place." When they rebelled against oppressive British taxation, they called Washington out of retirement, and with his "patriotic zeal" he led them through eight years of bloody war to victory. Though Washington then "desired to return to his fields," he could not set aside the popular mandate. He thereafter "governed his state with reverence and respected good customs. He did not esteem military achievements; he was very different from [the rulers] of other states." Hsü was particularly impressed by Washington's encouragement of agriculture and commerce and his belief that "it was selfish to take a state and pass it on to one's descendants; he said it was better to choose a person of virtue for the responsibility of governing. . . ."

Washington's political legacy thus was a state operating in accord with Chinese political ideals in which the educated and virtuous ruled while remaining attuned to the needs of the people. To narrow the distance between ruler and ruled, officials were elected by vote of the common people (a device invented by Washington!), subject to popular recall, and expected to return to the ranks of the people after a term of service. There was no room in this system for political privilege or hereditary rank or rule. The government was kept properly simple. The "gentry" of the nation gathered in the capital named in Washington's memory. There the "virtuous scholars" of the Senate attended to domestic and foreign affairs with the aid of the men "distinguished in ability and knowledge" of the House. The head of state was a "general commander" chosen from among the "commanders" of each of the states for a four-year term. To avert clashes between central and local power, the Americans had developed a balanced and cooperative relationship between the federal government and the states. Taxes were admirably light. The government supported few soldiers (regarded by the Chinese as a scourge) and instead depended on a militia system made up of all the citizens except scholars and strikingly similar to one that had prevailed in ancient China. It had proven sufficient to keep the country safe, respected, and at peace.

By contemporary Chinese standards, Hsü's America was something of a utopia. The attractiveness of the picture was due in part to the nationalistic biases of his American sources and the desire of missionary informants to impress the Chinese by catering to their social and political prejudices. But probably even more it was due to Hsü's own desire to stir his readers by suggesting how far contemporary China itself had declined from a golden age of virtue. Chinese suffered rebellion and privation, while Americans, having succeeded in linking ruler to ruled, enjoyed order and plenty. China faced a mounting foreign threat, while the United States had enjoyed peace and security since independence. (Hsü was apparently unaware of the crises the United States had faced during the Anglo-French struggle between 1793 and 1814 or of the Mexican War, in progress even as he prepared his study.)

The vision of the United States advanced by Wei and polished by Hsü was to prove seductive to other Chinese intellectuals, who imbibed the infatuation with the United States either directly from the source or through later works which repeated Wei and Hsü uncritically. Hung Jen-k'an, called to serve as prime minister of the Taiping rebels in 1859, prepared a report depicting the United States as righteous, wealthy, and powerful and endowed with model political and social institutions. The Americans, Hung observed, though originally English, had thrown off oppressive British rule, and unlike the British "do not invade or bully neighboring countries." Huang En-t'ung, an aide to governor general Ch'i-ying during the Cushing talks, made the same points in an 1865 work on "barbarian management." Both a geography of 1876 and a work prepared by the reformer Wang T'ao about that same time (but now lost) celebrated Washington's pivotal role as founding father and the economic, political, and social achievements of the country he founded. The scholar-diplomat Huang Tsun-hsien, writing in 1880, also made much of "the great founder" Washington who overthrew "the tyrannical rule of England" and whose "moral teachings" led his countrymen on the path of "propriety and righteousness." The Americans, Huang reported, conducted the most admirable of foreign policies. "They do not infringe upon other lands or people, and they do not interfere with other governments." Although possessed of greater strength and wealth than the Europeans, the United States "always helps the weak, supports universal righteousness, and thus prohibits the Europeans from doing evil."

Wei's and Hsü's writing on the United States also carried an important message to policy makers looking for help in barbarian management. Both Wei and Hsü had approached their research with a pragmatic concern for solving China's crisis with Britain, and Wei at least was bold in making explicit his strategy for dealing with it. Wei contended that contradictions existed between the United States and Britain that China could turn to her advantage. But exploiting those contradictions was only one element in a larger strategy of Wei's devising. To slow the enemy's advance, China should stimulate the resistance to Britain by Russia, Nepal, Burma, Thailand, and Vietnam. Closer to home, China should make adroit use of commercial concessions to align the French and Americans against their old enemy, the English, and to secure from them assistance in building up China's naval and coastal defenses and helping ward off any renewal of British aggression. The history of Anglo-American conflict emphasized by Wei as well as Hsü lent plausibility to this strategy of enlisting "respectful and obedient" American barbarians against the overbearing English. Wei sought to support his argument by reference to the recently concluded Opium War, when the Americans and French had indeed shown their resentment of British ascendance and had even brought in their own warships. Had China then held out to those two discontented powers the lure of commercial advantage, they might have lined up in opposition to Britain. Hsü, though reticent in arguing explicitly for any particular policy, went even further than Wei in building up the United States as a new center of world power that Chinese officials might enlist to offset the Europeans.

TESTING POLICY IMPLICATIONS

As Wei and Hsü intended, officials charged with devising China's response to the new foreign threat began to allot to the United States a part in "barbarian management." Pioneering studies, of which Wei's may have been the most important because of its early publication and its pointed message, may have moved some officials. But it is equally possible that many drew directly from the same body of ideas and experiences that inspired Wei and Hsü. The impulse to make diplomatic use of the United States—which asserted itself intermittently through the nineteenth century and well into the twentieth—was in turn to provoke critics to ask if Americans were really as different as they claimed to be or if they were not in fact a part of the larger foreign threat. Their doubts echo in the pidgin English observation supposedly made by a merchant on his first contact with Americans in 1784: "All men come first time China very good gentlemen, all same you [but] two three times more you come Canton, you make all same Englishman too."

The temptation to test the alleged strength and independence of the Americans appeared naturally enough earliest and strongest among officials along the South China coast during the Opium War and its immediate aftermath. Lin Tse-hsü, the commissioner despatched to Canton by the Emperor to bring an end to the opium trade, was the first to take a serious, albeit minor, interest in the Americans as a makeweight in Chinese policy. In March 1839, shortly after his arrival, Lin demanded that foreign suppliers surrender their opium stocks and promise not to resume trade in that drug. Lin rewarded the compliant Americans by granting them permission to stay on in Canton and trade, while he excluded the uncooperative British. He hoped thereby (as he later explained) to keep the foreigners divided. Conceivably China might even stimulate the envy and dislike felt for the English by the Americans as well as the French and thus encourage the two countries strong enough to contend with Britain to play a more active role to China's advantage. To put the Americans in the same category as the British and deprive them both of trade would, on the other hand, be self-defeating, for it would drive the Americans to make common cause with China's enemy.

The court was to cashier Lin in August 1840 after he had plunged China into a one-sided war with the British, but his vision of exploiting the divisions among the foreigners was kept alive as China suffered a series of military reversals. Late in 1840 Juan Yüan, having deepened his acquaintance with the United States, wrote from the capital urging Lin's successor to consider the possibilities of pitting the "peaceable" and powerful Americans against the "obstinate" British. "If we treat the American barbarians courteously . . . and also take the trade of the English barbarians and give it to the American barbarians, then the American barbarians are sure to be grateful for this Heavenly Favor and will energetically oppose the English barbarians. . . ." Kiangsu governor Yü-chien echoed both Juan's estimate of American strength and his emphasis on playing on American commercial interests. Within Canton itself P'an Shih-ch'eng, a wealthy merchant with official standing, suggested that China might also make practical use of the Americans in the midst of war by borrowing their technological expertise, an idea he himself acted on.

Even after the war, Ch'i-ying, who came to Canton as governor general in mid-1843, continued the search for ways to manage the Americans. Anticipating Wei and Hsü, he described them as a recently established people, industrious and rich in land. "With England [the United States] is outwardly friendly but actually resentful." Initially, through 1843, he sought to win American gratitude by no more than a grant of trade "privileges" along the lines of those treaty rights already secured by Britain. Peking agreed (so long as no complications with the English resulted), and in November 1843 confirmed Ch'i-ying's promise of equal commercial opportunity with an edict meant to display the Emperor's "tranquilizing purpose." But the Americans were neither tranquilized nor grateful. Cushing soon demonstrated that Americans could be obstinate and pushy and that they esteemed national prestige no less than profitable commerce. If the British concessions were embodied in a treaty, Cushing would have the same for the United States and not be fobbed off with promises of mere "privileges." Moreover, he wanted to travel to Peking, a demand (Ch'i-ying guessed) that Cushing either had cooked up with the British or meant to use to surpass them. Carefully reining in this headstrong foreigner, Ch'i-ying made clear that he was prepared to conclude a generous commercial treaty, but only on the condition that Cushing give up his audacious dreams of a journey to Peking. As late as 1846 Ch'i-ying seems to have still been interested in ways he might use the United States to check the "proud and domineering spirit" of the British, but other officials now only occasionally referred to the Americans as "respectful and obedient," and none seriously regarded the United States as an offset to the British.

The advance of the Taiping on Shanghai in 1853 reawakened interest in the United States, though now not as a makeweight against the powers but rather as a source of assistance against the rebels. The chief advocate of this revised approach was Wu Chien-chang, a Shanghai merchant who had once been a part of the old cohong system and now was active in the city government. His view of the United States, in line with Wei's and Hsü's, was of "a rich country, strong militarily, most respectful and obedient" in its dealings with China. In contrast to the English, who were not only in general "overbearing and cunning and only concerned with gain" but also of late in close touch with the Taiping rebels, Americans trading with the Taiping were few in number, and American diplomats were moderate. Attempts in 1853 to secure American assistance for the imperial cause were, however, to founder. The American commissioners, Marshall and McLane, insisted on an unacceptable quid pro quo, and in any case American warships were not available, and ranking officials in the area opposed drawing on the support of any of the barbarians, who were all "by nature deceitful."

The hostile reaction Wu encountered among his official colleagues reflected widespread resistance within the Ch'ing bureaucracy to the American infatuation. The oldest and most pervasive source of opposition came from the militant view on foreign affairs, a compound of traditional assumptions about China's central place in a hierarchical world order and of ignorance about the new Western challenge to that order. Some officials turned a blind eye to treatises such as Wei's and Hsü's, regarding as dubious if not foolish the proposition that there was something to be learned from studying foreigners. What educated man had not heard—indeed memorized in childhood—the lines from Mencius (and others like it): "I have heard of men using the doctrine of our great land to change barbarians, but I have never heard of any being changed by barbarians." Drawn to China by their need to trade, these men of inferior culture were supposed to be dazzled by the richness of the civilization they found. As the superior, China was obliged to show condescending kindness, display no favoritism among them, and at times indulge violent and unreasonable behavior. The phrase "nourishing men from afar" (*huai-jou yang-jen*) reflected the tendency to view foreigners as pitiable mendicants. Though increasingly overwhelmed by power realities as the nineteenth century progressed, this rhetoric affirming Chinese superiority persisted, even in adversity, in official thinking and imperial pronouncements, indeed down to the very end of the dynasty.

The militant outlook was sustained by the widespread confusion and misinformation about foreigners that resulted from chance contacts and carelessly assembled snippets of random information. The "white devils are fond of women; the red devils are fond of money; the black devils are fond of wine" was taken by the Tao-kuang Emperor for keen analysis. Officials on Taiwan in 1842 concluded from an interrogation of two shipwrecked sailors that America might once have been "in England," that a man might be able to "walk from London to America in a week," and that London might be as large as America. Intentionally false reports from provincial officials worsened the problem. Pandering to the known prejudices of their superiors, even those who knew better soothingly described foreigners as contemptible barbarians, minimized the threat they posed, and exaggerated China's strength. Ch'i-ying in his official communications noted how "ignorant" and uncultured Americans were, while Hsü Chi-yü's memorials to court employed derogatory terms carefully excluded from his "Brief survey."

The militant outlook on foreign policy found a home at court in the 1850s. The Hsien-feng Emperor (1850–1861) reversed the policy of appeasement followed since the Opium War, cashiered the leading officials tainted by it (including Hsü Chi-yü), and redirected policy along lines of increased resistance to foreign pressure along the coast. Militants at court and in the provinces fought off demands for treaty revision and played up the dangerous symbiotic relationship that had developed between foreigners in search of profit and rebels in need of aid. Under the new dispensation the powers were at first regarded as one in cunning and covetousness; differences among them were not worth troubling over. The United States—its diplomats joining the cry for treaty revision, its missionaries spreading heterodox ideas that inspired rebellion, and its merchants supplying rebels arms and provisions—seemed in the 1850s no exception and hardly benign.

The militants found their champion in the provinces in the person of Yeh Ming-ch'en, the governor general of Kwangtung-Kwangsi, who struggled to keep the British out of Canton between 1853 and 1857. Increasingly aroused by foreign incursions and aware of China's military vulnerability, Yeh promoted a strategy of popular resistance. In a protracted war on Chinese soil against a united and aroused populace, an invader would ultimately find himself overextended, outnumbered, and demoralized. Yeh saw little incentive for making (or attempting to exploit) subtle distinctions within the enemy camp since such a policy would almost certainly sow popular disaffection and confusion that would in turn undermine a policy of resistance. But in addition Yeh looked upon appeals for assistance from the deceitful foreigners as a dangerous confession of China's weakness and an intolerable blow to her prestige.

The diplomatic infatuation with the United States was to encounter a second, new source of opposition in the 1850s from an unexpected quarter—officials who took the new literature on foreign affairs and the study of foreigners seriously. Their investigations had led them to doubt the diplomatic value of the United States to China. Ho Kuei-ch'ing, the governor general of Kiangsi and Kiangsu and imperial commissioner in charge of foreign affairs (1858–1860), emerged as the most consistent and forceful exponent of this view. American enmity for Britain, he argued, was much exaggerated. But even if China should manage to pit Americans against the British, the strength of the Americans (even reenforced by the Russians) was not sufficient to deter Britain. Rather than a weak China trying to manipulate stronger foreign countries, Ho preferred to accommodate all the Western powers and avoid a war dangerous to China's security. The "fuel under the pot" of Sino-foreign relations was, in his view, the dissatisfactions of foreign merchants. Meet merchant demands and they would emerge as a check on foreign diplomats with their love of prestige and their taste for disruptive wars and displays of force.

Debunked by those knowledgeable in international affairs, the American infatuation was now taken up by the less well versed. The twin evils of internal rebellion and foreign aggression in the late 1850s forced the beleaguered militants at court and in the provinces—in an ironic reversal—to try their own hand at manipulating the Americans. Apparent American restraint during the renewed Anglo-Chinese conflict between 1856 and 1860 in particular shook the court's view of the Americans as simply another inconstant and unscrutable breed of barbarian and awakened interest in the diplomatic implications of American commercial greed and jealousy of Britain. Now the court watched and occasionally courted the United States (as well as Russia after France went over to the British side in 1857) not so much as a potential ally but as an intermediary to be kept neutral and used to calm the British in defeat and restrain them in victory. At times the court's policy amounted to no more than the practical recognition that American assistance was a straw worth grasping for after all else had failed.

During the first phase of the Hsien-feng Emperor's policy of resistance, Peking had watched with admiration and approval as Yeh held the British at bay outside Canton. Then in January 1858 British forces, reinforced by the French, stormed the city, seized Yeh, and carried him off to imprisonment in India. In the early stages of the confrontation, Yeh had sought to isolate the British from the Americans by opening the Canton trade only to the latter. He was in turn encouraged by the decision of the U.S. government to recall Peter Parker (a "crafty" troublemaker in Yeh's view). He interpreted Parker's replacement by William Reed in November 1857 as a welcome repudiation by the U.S. government of an aggressive policy. So when Reed arrived, Yeh agreed with uncharacteristic promptness to talk (though without making any of the concessions on treaty revision that the American wanted). With open warfare with the British looming, Yeh in a show of solicitude persuaded the American residents to evacuate Canton for their own safety and, once fighting began, made sure they understood that the British were responsible for the resulting disruption of trade. Yeh even let pass the highly partisan, indeed belligerent, conduct of the local American consul and naval commander during the conflict.

Once Canton fell and the Allies made ready to go north to demand treaty revision at gunpoint, the Emperor and his advisers would now themselves try to bring the United States to serve China's cause. The groundwork had already been laid by Yeh's reports stressing the resentment felt by the Americans toward the unreasonable British. Consequently, after Yeh's loss of Canton the court had condemned his failure to take advantage of what it incorrectly regarded as an American offer of good offices, while the Emperor himself had brushed aside reports implicating Americans in the attack on Canton as "misinformation" spread by the British in order to veil their own aggression. In April 1858 British and French forces arrived off the northern coast. Peking would not yield on treaty revision, but wanting to provide them a way to back down, asked Minister Reed, who had accompanied the Allied expedition north, to serve as mediator and help avert a collision. On May 20, as the naval bombardment of the Chinese forts began, the court again appealed to Reed to set a good example by continuing his own negotiations with China and to use his good offices to secure a three-day truce and keep the lines of communication with the Allies open. On both occasions Reed demurred.

All this came as no surprise to T'an T'ing-hsiang, the governor general of Chihli and the militant official to whom the court had entrusted the direct supervision of developments along the coast. He regarded the foreigners as "all in one category in their insatiable greed," and wanted to substitute for diplomatic wrangling an all-out military effort against them. But T'an's strategy for barbarian management crumbled along with his coastal defenses, and by the end of May he too wished to invoke American assistance in bringing the fighting to an end while avoiding talks with the Allies. He now reasoned that even though the Americans and Russians "are sure to make insatiable demands, still, compared to fighting, this has its advantages." The court agreed to this plan to win time; however, mounting Allied pressure forced the court in June to give in and engage in substantive talks. The two high officials, Kuei-liang and the veteran Ch'i-ying, appointed to handle negotiations twice invoked American aid in softening Allied demands, and both times came away empty-handed. Kuei-liang after the first attempt reported Reed's party insolent, querulous, and exigent, while the court dismissed as "presumptuous" their request for diplomatic residence in Peking. Under threat of force, the Chinese now bowed to British and French demands for treaty revision. To maintain the good will of the American and Russian neutrals, the Chinese agreed to revise their treaties as well. By the end of the second try—an emotional performance in which Kuei-liang invoked the clause that he himself had had inserted in the new American treaty providing for good offices in times of trouble—he was convinced that the Americans and Russians were no different from the British and French. "To get them to intercede could hardly be of any advantage."

Chagrined and a bit wiser, officials in the north seem to have moved toward Ho's view that the United States was not a useful auxiliary to Chinese policy. As a halfway measure the court did agree to diplomats visiting Peking. They had, however, to reconsider when in June 1859 a second Allied expedition came north, accompanied once more by an American diplomat, and again a clash of arms resulted, due on this occasion to a dispute over what route Allied diplomats would take from the coast to Peking, where an exchange of the new treaties was supposed to take place. Now it was the Chinese turn to win, and American assistance was needed to soothe the British. But when the court and the chief Chinese negotiator Heng-fu actually turned for assistance, Ward responded that he would speak to the British only after he had completed his own projected trip to Peking. The court was not happy about receiving any foreign diplomat, particularly one so cool to Chinese appeals. Enthusiasm for Ward's visit was further dampened by reports from the victorious general Senggerinchin (Seng-ko-lin-ch'in) that the Americans, British, and French were "all fellow conspirators." The Ward visit went ahead, but not under conditions likely to consolidate ties with the United States.

By mid-1860 the Chinese faced the third foreign expedition in as many years. The Chinese government, determined to fight rather than make further concessions, faced an Allied force intent on revenge for the past year's defeat. As usual, an American representative tagged along, and once again, the analysis from Shanghai suggested that while the American Ward "has no desire to do harm, he cannot exert himself on our behalf." All the major foreign powers were banded together, so Shanghai concluded. Senggerinchin, awaiting the military rematch on the northern coast, agreed. But in early August, after foreign warships had massed offshore and Allied forces had begun to move on Peking, the court snapped up an offer by Ward to act as intermediary only to see him withdraw his offer once fighting began a few days later. Now in desperation, it instructed its commanders to screen foreign prisoners for Americans who might be used as diplomatic intermediaries.

Peking's fall to Anglo-French forces early in the autumn and the flight of the court brought to an end one era of Chinese resistance to foreign encroachment but not to spasmodic efforts to find a way to translate the supposedly helpful attitude of the United States into some tangible benefit to China. Indeed, hardly had the invading Allied force withdrawn than Tseng Kuo-fan, one of the major architects of the restoration of imperial authority that lay ahead, revived the clichéd view of the Americans as "pure-minded and honest" and "long recognized as respectful and compliant toward China." Why not find a way to draw them still closer to China and ensure they did not ally with the "most crafty" English and the French? Tseng wondered.

The good offices provision written into the 1858 treaty by Kuei-liang still encouraged Chinese policy makers to believe that the United States occupied a special position as mediator between China and the powers. Thus when the newly established foreign office, still without its own missions abroad, decided in the late 1860s to have a foreigner carry China's case for diplomatic restraint directly to the capitals of the powers, Anson Burlingame, the first American minister to reside in Peking, was its choice. He was not only able, sincere, sympathetic to China's plight, and eager to add to his reputation, but also a citizen of "the most tranquil" of the powers, so Prince Kung reported as head of the foreign office in late 1867. Seven years later the benign image and the treaty pledge of good offices led Li Hung-chang, Tseng's junior associate, to appeal to one of Burlingame's successors, the "prudent and sincere" Benjamin Avery, for help in averting a conflict with Japan over Taiwan, where the Japanese had landed a punitive expedition following attacks on their Luichiu "subjects" by aborigines there.

Americans could also be useful in fighting rebels. Frederick Townsend Ward, whose force of foreign adventurers (known as the Ever-Victorious Army) battled the Taiping in the lower reaches of the Yangtze in the early 1860s, came to be valued by Li as a man of "ability, sagacity, and willingness to attach himself to the Chinese cause. . . ." Ward's death in battle in September 1862 led Li to look for another equally reliable American as a successor. The nod went to Henry Burgevine, a North Carolinian who had served under Ward. Finally, the

United States occupied a favored position as a place where Chinese might master the skills that made the West strong. Tseng and Li arranged to send young Chinese (between ten and fifteen years of age) for a prolonged course of study abroad. In 1872 the first group was selected and set off for the United States to settle along the Connecticut River valley. There under the supervision of Yung Wing, an 1854 graduate of Yale, their sponsors expected them to master military and naval skills, surveying, manufacturing, and mining, all desperately needed in China's own development.

The outcome of this reliance on the United States once again fell far short of what the positive image had led Chinese officials to expect. Burlingame violated his formal instructions—to the annoyance of the foreign office—without making any noticeable dent in the policy of the powers. Avery, though exceedingly sympathetic to China's position on the Taiwan case, lacked the influence to effect its outcome or even to restrain an American, Charles LeGendre, who much to Li's annoyance had been assisting the Japanese as a Taiwan expert. Burgevine quickly proved himself to Li a "shady character" and "very obstinate," and so after only three months Li had him replaced. For the following three years Burgevine made trouble (including a short stint serving the Taiping) until Li finally lost patience and arranged an "accidental" drowning (to the evident relief of the almost equally exasperated American diplomats).

The educational mission, still another disappointment, secured none of the immediate benefits its sponsors expected because the students seem to have spent as much time on baseball and Latin as on practical subjects. The mission, moreover, proved expensive ($1,200 for each of the 120 students sent out by 1875). Yung Wing and his colleagues, who had a more traditional outlook, were like oil and water, an impossible mix. And the students themselves were becoming culturally deracinated (with some even refusing to return home). Li at last gave in to the critics within the bureaucracy, who charged that the mission "wastes money, breeds corruption, and will show little result," and to his own growing doubts and had the mission terminated in 1881. When he sought access to U.S. military academies where more mature students might derive more immediate benefit, Washington turned him down. Yet despite all these disappointments and reverses, the benign image of the United States persisted, providing a basis for a renewed policy interest in the United States in the decades ahead as the imperialist powers began to close in on China's frontiers.

FROM CANTON TO CALIFORNIA

Chinese emigration to the United States was but a small part of a greater movement of Chinese abroad that gained impetus in the 1840s and continued well into the twentieth century. The half a million or so Chinese who journeyed to the United States between 1850 and 1900 represented a fraction, certainly no more than a tenth, of all the Chinese who left south coastal China over those years to find employment abroad. Although frequently stereotyped as a people bound to home and hearth, the Chinese had not only responded at home to the lure of underpopulated frontier regions or long-settled areas suddenly decimated by natural disaster or war, but had also ventured off to Southeast Asia as early as the fourteenth century to establish permanent communities. By the mid-nineteenth century the trickle of emigration from South China became a flood as difficulties at home coincided with a high demand for labor and mercantile skills in Southeast Asia and the Americas. Records on departures from Macao alone show half a million Chinese responding to the new opportunities which Western trade, capital, and technology had created in the mines, railways, and commercialized agriculture of those regions. The flow of emigrants climbed dramatically higher from the 1870s onward.

Emigrants to the United States issued almost exclusively from a 4,000 square mile region embracing Canton (the capital of the province of Kwangtung) and the immediately adjacent provincial districts to the south. This area was divided into three culturally and geographically distinct regions. One of these, the three districts known as *San-i* (or in Cantonese *Sam Yup*) surrounding Canton, lay on rich delta land and boasted the highest level of culture and prosperity. A second area made up of four districts (literally *Ssu-i* or, in Cantonese, *Sze Yup*) located just to the southwest of Canton was a hilly region where much of the land was marginal. Relative poverty, a distinct dialect, and a sense of social inferiority set the people of Sze Yup off from their Sam Yup neighbors. The third district zone was Hsiang-shan (Hueng-shan in Cantonese; later renamed Chung-shan) district, sandwiched between Sam Yup to the north and Portuguese Macao to the south. It enjoyed a diversified economy of farming, fishing, and handicrafts as well as some claim to the cultural refinement of Sam Yup. Overlaying these territorial distinctions was a basic ethnic line that divided Chinese, who had long lived in the Delta, from the Hakkas (literally, "guest people"), who had begun to move from central China as early as the fourth century A.D. and continued southward by stages through the nineteenth century. The settlement by Hakkas on the marginal land of Sze Yup created tensions between peoples already divided by language and social customs.

By the middle of the nineteenth century the impulse to emigrate had become intense. The basic impetus came from demographic pressures. In the six decades before 1850 population density in the whole of Kwangtung increased nearly 80 percent with the result that by mid-century an average of 284 people had to live off one square mile of land. In the Canton delta generally population must have pressed perilously close against the productivity of arable land, diminished by wetlands, waterways, and mountains. Sze Yup in particular, with its high proportion of marginal land, must have felt these pressures acutely as the influx of Hakkas added to the natural increase of the local population. A dismaying succession of floods and droughts accompanied by banditry, rebellion, and foreign intrusion further disrupted the delta economy, already straining to support its population. Although the great Taiping Rebellion of 1850–1864 bypassed the region, it set off local shock waves, precipitating conflicts among clans, secret societies, and ethnic groups that a weakened dynastic authority found difficult to control. Sze Yup witnessed the most intense internal conflict: a fourteen-year struggle (1854–1867) between Hakkas and the more numerous and prosperous older settlers which produced hundreds of thousands of casualties; and a major uprising by the Red Turban secret society, which ended in bloody suppression. Sam Yup bore the brunt of foreign conflict between 1839 and 1860 with Canton itself subjected for a time to British occupation. The new treaty system that the British set in place opened the way for an influx of imported manufactured goods which supplanted peasant handicrafts, sped the unsettling trend toward commercial agriculture, and tied local prosperity to developments in the international economy. The simultaneous rise of Shanghai as the major entrepôt for foreign trade further deepened the economic crisis in the Canton region.

The impulse to flee a society thus rendered insecure must have been strong. The livelihood of the rural poor—peasants, craftsmen, peddlers—in particular suffered in the face of a combined threat from rebels and bandits, government troops, landlords, tax collectors, and vagaries of the market. The unfortunate grasped at emigration as a means of survival in a time of adversity. For the losers in the mid-century conflicts—the Hakkas, the hunted adherents of secret societies, and members of weak clans—the choice was probably often a precipitate one made in the face of deprivation or death at the hands of their enemies. But many, perhaps most, approached the decision to go abroad to work as a carefully calculated family affair. A son who could not find profitable employment, or a husband no longer able to care for his dependents would find employment overseas that would permit him to support himself and send regular remittances home to support his family. Any surplus was invested locally, usually in land. In some cases families would send a member from each generation abroad, a practice that in some areas went back to the seventeenth century. Those who left early would establish themselves and prepare the way for the arrival of younger relatives. In time the emigrant himself would more likely than not return. Of the roughly 4.8 million emigrants known to have left south coastal China between 1876 and 1901, some 4 million came back. Migration thus served in effect as a local industry, an economic lifeline for the people of an entire region.

News of the California gold rush reached Hong Kong in the spring of 1848 and filtered out into the countryside, stimulating the first stream of emigration to the United States. Although the gold fields were to play out in a little over a decade, California's developing but labor-short economy remained a distant magnet to the Chinese. Those at home measured their opportunities through the letters sent home by the pioneers and the size of the accompanying remittances. Vivid testimony would come after a time with the first homecomings, when the successful emigrant would treat his neighbors to a sometimes resplendent celebration. As if to fix an alluring image in the prospective emigrant's mind, California came to be known as "the mountain of gold." To help convert fantasy to reality, foreign shipping companies and Chinese emigration agents circulated promotional literature testifying to opportunities abroad that surpassed anything at home and offering assistance in making the journey. Finally, the prospective emigrant might incline to California knowing that guests of the golden mountain ran small risk of falling into the ill-reputed coolie trade. The Chinese had aptly named it the "pig trade" and called "piglets" those unfortunates who sold themselves, frequently under coercion or deception, for a fixed period of labor abroad. At its worst, as it was conducted in Cuba and Peru through the mid-1870s, only one coolie in ten survived the perils of the voyage and the abuses of employment to return home. But in Hong Kong, the principal point of departure for the United States, British regulations protected the emigrant from the unscrupulous coolie brokers. And in the United States the courts would not enforce—and public opinion decried—labor contracts.

The mechanism of emigration developed considerable speed and efficiency as the nineteenth century progressed. In the days of sail the ocean voyage alone took two or three months, but with the advent of regular steam service in the mid-1860s a peasant could make the transition from the rice fields of his semitropical home to the gold fields of California or to the snow-covered Rockies and a railway construction gang in a matter of weeks. Brokers played a pivotal role in making the system work. An emigrant headed for the United States would deal directly with a broker based in Hong Kong who dealt exclusively with emigrants from his own home area. These brokers would rely on their local reputation, personal contacts, advertising circulars, and command of current information to draw prospective travelers to them. For the indigent they would arrange travel loans from merchants, and for those who could not stay with relatives or kin in Hong Kong while awaiting departure, they provided inexpensive accommodations in dormitories, which usually served as the brokers' headquarters and as a message center. To obtain his ticket the emigrant would have to work through a second broker, a Chinese who acted as sales agent for foreign shipping firms. These various brokers enjoyed within their particular spheres a virtual monopoly protected by their guild organizations. On each emigrant the broker made a commission, and on a large volume of departures they built substantial fortunes.

Dialect and place directed the emigrant from the moment he left home until he found employment abroad. They separated men who could not easily communicate with each other and drew together those of common dialect, customs and traditions, and perhaps even kinship. At the outset, the prospective emigrant gained his most reliable information from his neighbors with experience overseas or from brokers from his area. Once in Hong Kong he would stay either in private homes or in dormitories run and occupied by men from his own locale. In organizing his life abroad the emigrant would place no less emphasis on dialect/place loyalties. On arrival in San Francisco the emigrant would emerge from steerage to the greetings of men who shared a common surname, common background (in the case of Hakkas), or common place of origin. They would escort him through the official inspection, past the assembled white rowdies, and on to lodgings occupied by other men like him. In finding his first job and in joining social and benevolent associations, the newcomer depended on the aid and company of these fellows.

The merchant played a crucial role in emigration as financier, supplier, and trans-Pacific liaison. The dominant Sam Yup merchants were the chief source of travel funds for emigrants, the bulk and certainly the poorest of whom were from Sze Yup. Organized by guilds and linked by close personal and old business ties, these Sam Yup firms formed a network that extended from Canton to Hong Kong and on to San Francisco. Chinese merchants in the United States (perhaps 4 or 5 percent of the total Chinese population) would collect travel loans made initially on their own account or on the account of agents or associates in China. Those same merchants would retail to Chinese workers throughout California supplies brought in from China. Their shops also served as employment offices to which white employers came to hire labor gangs. The merchant maintained contact with home. He kept brokers in Hong Kong appraised of the employment situation. On the occasions such as in 1853–1854, 1876, and 1886 when economic depression and anti-Chinese agitation made jobs difficult to find and travel debts hard to pay off, merchants in San Francisco signaled a temporary halt to emigration. The merchant's shop provided for the bulk of the community a link to home. In his guise as postman and banker the merchant would receive letters from China, dispatch the reply, arrange the accompanying remittances (at a 2–10 percent commission), hold savings in safekeeping, and offer goods on credit. As a result of the multiple services he performed, the merchant built up within the emigrant community a network of clients—laborers, petty craftsmen, and small shopkeepers indebted literally and figuratively for past services and dependent for future assistance. In the absence of both officials and the scholar gentry who in China made up the local elite, the merchant patron emerged as the natural leader of the community. Not only had he helped transplant and maintain a piece of South China overseas, but his economic successes epitomized the ambitions of a community oriented essentially toward money-getting.

The particularistic loyalties of the emigrant and the leading role played by the merchant fused in the variety of associations which gave social coherence and cultural continuity to the life of the overseas Chinese. These associations had their origins in Chinese society but had evolved to better meet the needs and conditions encountered abroad. The emigrant's deepest attachments were to lineage organizations. These common descent groups (or clans) flourished in Kwangtung and Fukien as nowhere else in China. Respected elders directed their affairs, fulfilling group ceremonial obligations, redressing injustices and insults, and resolving internal disputes. The more developed and affluent lineages maintained an impressive temple where homage was paid to prominent forebears (thereby consolidating group solidarity and prestige) and held income-producing property which might be used to support the indigent or educate the worthy poor from within the lineage. The lineages which existed overseas were in some cases extensions of the actual lineage to which the emigrant had belonged at home, but in other cases, where there was an insufficient number of relations to form a lineage offshoot, emigrants contrived new lineage groups based on a fictitious common ancestor. Either way, lineage members ensured mutual support and group solidarity that might find its application in job hunting, social life, and personal welfare. The lineage in the United States, however active it might be, could not help but be a pale reflection of those strong lineages which dominated the rural scene in South China through gentry leadership and the control of common lineage land and the incomes they produced. Deprived of these sources of political and economic power, the lineage in the overseas community had to make room for (though usually not ceding primary loyalty to) place associations, occupational guilds, and secret societies.

The place association, whose institutional development went back over five hundred years, served in China as a lodging and gathering place for officials, examination candidates, merchants, and craftsmen of a particular region visiting in the capital or in one of the chief commercial centers. The place association, perfectly suited to the needs of emigrants, proliferated in San Francisco. The people of Sze Yup organized three different associations reflecting the chief divisions within their ranks. The people of Hsin-ning district constituted the largest of these Sze Yup associations, while several powerful Sze Yup lineages formed another. Sam Yup, with its prominent merchant element, predictably boasted the wealthiest of the place associations. To make themselves heard and to preserve their interests, the people from Hsiang-shan district as well as the Hakkas formed their own separate groups. From the time of their formation in the early 1850s, the number of associations ranged upward from five, depending in the main on the splits and consolidations that occurred within the ranks of Sze Yup. Each association aided the emigrant from his arrival in the United States up until his departure or death. Like the lineage and the other associations, place associations offered lodgings, help with employment, support through periods of disability or unemployment, assurances of burial in home soil, arbitration of disputes, and legal assistance before American authorities.

Occupational guilds, yet another form of association carried over from China, brought together in each case emigrants from a particular town or district and sought to secure a monopoly over a particular occupational specialty, perhaps one to which its members were suited by previous experience, and to protect it against interlopers, particularly Chinese from other regions or other ethnic backgrounds. For example, Sam Yup controlled the butcher trade and portions of the garment industry; Sze Yup dominated in the laundries, retail stores, and restaurants; and Hsiang-shan stood preeminent in the retail fish business, flower growing, and sections of the garment industry. Other important guilds represented Chinese in the shoe and cigar factories. The occupational guild, which might count Chinese employers as well as workers among its members, also sought to put a stop to abuse by whites, settle internal disputes, and act as an employment agent. To keep wages and prices up, the guilds resorted to strikes against white employers, price-cutting and social ostracism against intruding retail or laundry firms, and violence against nonunion workers.

Even secret societies in the United States were oriented toward place of origin. They had sprung from the Triads, a secret society which flourished among deracinated and insecure groups along the southern coastal provinces and the Yangtze Valley. While retaining the organization and secret oaths and rituals of the old world organizations, secret societies in the United States sloughed off their traditional anti-Manchu ideology and instead operated openly in the service of the economic and social needs of their membership, largely, if not exclusively, the men of Sze Yup, especially the poor, the itinerant, and those without strong lineage ties. By the late nineteenth century, and perhaps even earlier, 70 to 80 percent of the Chinese in the United States held membership at least nominally. In the larger Chinese communities the societies provided an alternative to, or even a refuge against, powerful lineage or place associations, while in Chinese communities too small to support lineage or place associations secret societies served as flexible, all-purpose organizations. Each society and its affiliates provided the expected services—lodging to traveling members, help in dealing with American authorities, arbitration of disputes between members, protection against wrongs by outsiders, and assurance of proper burial. Societies seem to have dominated prostitution and gambling within the larger Chinatowns, either by exercising direct control or by offering "protection" to those who did, and on occasion tried to assert control of mining rights against other Chinese.

In San Francisco's China Association (Chung-Hua hui-kuan) the merchant leaders of the community's various organizations came together. Popularly known as the Six Companies, this umbrella association came into existence in 1862. It was made up initially only of the original place associations and later of their splinter groups. Because these place associations incorporated the strong lineages as well as the Hakkas, all elements in the community were represented (except for the secret societies during the Six Companies' first two decades). The heads of the place associations guided the affairs of the Six Companies and rotated the presidency among their own rank. Through the Six Companies the diverse elements of the community were able to discuss problems of common concern and to speak with one voice both to China and American authorities. The Six Companies adjudicated disputes between constituent organizations and relied on its prestige and community pressure, or on some occasions appeal to America courts, to secure acceptance of its decisions. The Six Companies, unlike the secret societies, did not use force against the recalcitrant.

To handle their relations with the host culture, each of the associations put forward an intermediary, generally known as the "interpreter." The title is something of a misnomer since usually an interpreter's duties went beyond mere translation, whereas his actual command of English, usually picked up in commerce or church schools, was more often than not rudimentary. The interpreter was primarily charged with representing and defending his group's interests. An occupational guild might employ him as foreman in a white-owned shoe factory. A secret society might send him out as the head of a railway work gang made up of society members or dispatch him to court to help defend a "highbinder" accused of murder. Or a place association might rely on the interpreter to extricate a newcomer enmeshed in customs difficulties. To assist the interpreter in his errands, the associations and especially the Six Companies would often engage the services of American lawyers and publicists.

These self-imposed exiles, who labored to support distant dependents and in moments of leisure dreamed of homecoming, needed industry, a frugal lifestyle, and even luck to manage a return home in less than ten years. Prospective emigrants who could not obtain $40 to $50 for travel money from friends or relatives or by the mortgage or sale of personal property had to borrow. They would arrive in the United States with a debt of about $100. The newcomer might go to work on the railways or in industry at about $30 a month. After covering his living expenses, the emigrant would have left at the end of each month $10 more or less that he could apply against his travel debt and then later, once it was paid off, send home as remittances or retain as savings. After seven years of steady work under ideal conditions (more likely to obtain into the 1870s than after), an emigrant might have accumulated the $300 in savings considered a near minimum for a return home.

With that money he would celebrate his homecoming with relatives and neighbors, and retire comfortably to live on the earnings of the land that his remittances and savings had purchased.

But this story gilds the edges of the emigrant experience. The loneliness and anticipation was legendary even for those who made it back within a decade. A Hsin-ning verse couched in the voice of the emigrant's wife caught the melancholy associated with long-deferred homecoming:

Grey hair dressed and piled high received flowers worked with the feathers of kingfishers;
Yesterday the husband who went abroad came home;
For the ten years that I had not seen his face;
I passed the evenings with bitter memories twisting threads before the lamp.

Homecoming for some was delayed beyond ten years; for others it never came because of economic setbacks, gambling losses, high living, or simply a loss of drive as the youth became an old man. Many lived out their lives in the community they had come to know best, supported by savings, odd jobs, or charity. Even those who made it back home did not always stay. They might be fleeced in Hong Kong by con men on the lookout for country boys with money in their pockets. They might invest their savings unwisely or find the demands of family and relatives exceeded both their expectations and their purse. Or they might simply go abroad again for the very reason they had left in the first place—a man's labor was better rewarded abroad than in the delta.

The community these hopeful emigrants made up was nearly all male. Emigrants did not bring wives with them, for to do so would have added to the costs of transportation while at the same time disrupting the fabric of the family that emigration was supposed to preserve in the first place. The proportion of women in the Chinese community climbed as high as 8 percent in 1870, but subsequently fell and was nowhere near that again until 1910. Among the women in the Chinese community, some came as legitimate wives or concubines, but these were too few to produce that native-born second generation that for other immigrant groups in the United States was the key to assimilation. Aside from the wives of affluent merchants, women in Chinatown were an important part of its economy. In 1870 well over half of them labored in Chinatown's most prosperous industry: prostitution. Many came from poor families unable to afford to raise a daughter, who would not perpetuate the family line and who, once married, would serve her husband's family and not her own parents. "When you raise girls, you're raising children for strangers," was one way of looking at the problem. "It is more profitable to raise geese than daughters," was another. Some women had thus been sold as children into service and others were deceived in later life, for example by "marriages" that delivered them into the hands of madams in the United States. What began in the early 1850s as a business conducted in the main by free agents soon fell under the control and protection of Chinese males who recognized the money to be made in organized prostitution. Although the prostitute's life in Chinatown was probably no harder than that in Canton, the comparison would have been of little consolation to those doomed to the ravages of venereal disease after roughly a decade of work. The more fortunate escaped or worked out a contract period of four to five years and then found a husband.

In the main the overwhelmingly male work force demonstrated striking geographical and even some occupational mobility. During the period of free immigration the laborer often worked for good wages, only somewhat below that of his white counterpart, and on occasion when he thought the pay too low or working conditions unsatisfactory, he went on strike. A newcomer in the 1850s might begin in gold mining, move on to railway construction, shift to underground mining (where he could apply tunneling techniques learned on railways), or take up work in agriculture or in an urban industry. The search by laborers and merchants for remunerative employment and relief from Western hostility from the 1880s onward resulted in a steady eastward spread of the Chinese population. As the community scattered, the Chinese became regular patrons of the railways, moving from city to city, keeping in touch with friends and relatives, looking for new jobs, or attending to the business of community associations. A Chinese of this time whose life story has been documented, offers an example of this mobility. He arrived in San Francisco, followed a railroad construction crew east, and lived in Detroit before finally settling in New York. In the process he went through three occupations—servant, laundryman, and general merchandiser.

The generalizations thus far advanced about the early emigrant community apply best to San Francisco, but many of the characteristics of San Francisco were reproduced by the smaller Chinese communities up and down the West coast and at points inland, and were subsequently retained as prominent features of late nineteenth-century Chinatowns across the country. As outside observers repeatedly noted, these Chinese communities—whether large or small—were merchant-led and made up primarily of bachelors whose orientation toward China was expressed culturally by their associations and economically by the flow of savings back to families in China.

Although at best a flawed reproduction of life in the Canton delta, Chinatown did perpetuate in microcosm the linguistic, territorial, and ethnic fissures of home and perhaps even exacerbated those old tensions by throwing peoples of differing backgrounds into an unprecedently close relationship. The feud between Hakkas and older settlers carried over to California, as did clan antagonisms. But the most important division, high in its potential for friction and conflict, was that between the poor but numerically dominant emigrants from Sze Yup and the fewer but economically powerful representatives of Sam Yup. The Sze Yup share of the population in California, the focus of early Chinese settlement, climbed from roughly two-fifths (16,000) in the mid-1850s to four-fifths (124,000) by the mid-1870s. At the same time the Sam Yup numbers fell from a bit below one-fifth (roughly 10,000) to less than one-tenth (11,000). Sze Yup controlled three of the Six Companies in San Francisco's Chinatown, while Sam Yup controlled but one.

On the whole, the men of Sze Yup arrived with empty pockets and little education. Less indoctrinated in Confucian values and made to feel socially inferior in the Chinese context by the presence of the men of Sam Yup, they were to go the farthest in picking up American ways. For example, the converts Protestant missionaries made in Chinatowns came mostly from this group. On the other hand, Sam Yup emigrants boasted greater wealth, better education, and closer contacts with home through business, flourishing lineages, and officials in the provincial capital. The Sam Yup people, constituting a large proportion of the merchant population, congregated—perhaps in the interest both of business as well as of social solidarity—in San Francisco, the largest Chinese community and the one in most intimate contact with China. Unlike Sze Yup, Sam Yup found the smaller settlements less hospitable and American culture less alluring. They appear to have regarded the secret societies with distaste, in part perhaps because the societies in the old country were associated with unsavory types—the déclassé, desperadoes, and social bandits. More to the point, however, was fear that these Sze Yup dominated societies were a potential threat to Sam Yup interests.

THE SINOPHOBIC REACTION

Overseas Chinese communities, such as the one in San Francisco, initially maintained the values and institutions of the homeland. But once established, the community's subsequent development from decade to decade depended in large measure on the response of the host country to this foreign presence. In some cases in Southeast Asia and Latin America tolerance had led to intermarriage and the decline of a distinct Chinese community as its inhabitants either assimilated or participated in a hybrid culture neither entirely Chinese nor native. In other cases, especially in Southeast Asian states struggling for independence and identity, native nationalists have attacked the Chinese as an economic and cultural threat. The Philippines, Thailand, and Indonesia each offer an instance of an indigenous culture giving up its accommodating attitude toward resident Chinese in favor of Sinophobic nationalism in the late nineteenth or early twentieth centuries. California's mid-nineteenth century reaction to the Chinese holds parallels with these latter cases where Sinophobic nationalism has turned against Chinese settlement. And not surprisingly, to carry the comparison further, the Chinese in California did what other overseas Chinese have done when placed under external pressure. They maintained or, for those who had already begun participating in the host society, recreated a tightly knit, autonomous community where they could preserve their cultural identity and insure physical security through group solidarity. But rather than lessen tensions, the development of these compact Chinatowns living a life of their own instead served to accentuate Sinophobia by veiling these strangers in mystery.

Sinophobia in California was couched in an idiom familiar to the economic and cultural nationalists of Southeast Asia. Economically the Chinese were seen as a peril to free American labor. The Chinese, to be sure, possessed virtues esteemed by Americans. Even Sinophobes aghast at "the swarm of Chinese" entering the United States grudgingly conceded admiration for "their wonderful manual skill, their highly developed and intelligent imitative faculties, their tireless industry, and their abnormal frugality." But the "servile labor contracts" and the inherent constitutional indifference of the Chinese to material comforts perverted these virtues and gave them the power in a racial struggle for survival to drive out the whites. The Chinese were also thought to be a constant drain on the national wealth because their earnings in the United States went back to China to support their families or to purchase the Chinese produce that they favored. Finally, American Sinophobes stressed the peril the Chinese posed to the American culture. His refusal to assimilate by becoming a good Christian and citizen signaled his rejection of national religious and democratic ideals or at least an indifference that put in doubt the transforming power of American culture and the related myth of American mission. By clinging instead to his old culture, the Chinese not only established his unworthiness to participate in the American dream but posed a palpable threat. Sinophobes conjured up a stereotype of Chinatown as a fire hazard and a sink of immorality and filth. It polluted those whom it touched and threatened the health and safety of the larger community. Here was an invitation, if not an injunction, to eliminate the Chinese presence.

The Sinophobic argument developed out of a strange mixture both of popular misconceptions and of fascination and fear that long retained its vitality with serious consequences for the immigrant and many of his descendants. It assigned the Chinese mysterious qualities—the ability to work longer and harder than whites on only small quantities of the worst food, all while living in dirty, disease-ridden subterranean chambers and indulging in vices of the worst kind. The total sexual power Chinese men exercised over prostitutes was a particular and recurrent source of wonder and comment by Sinophobes, while the supposed vulnerability of white women and girls to that power was a persistent cause for alarm. The seeming lack of freedom by both men and women in the Chinese community was the fault of cunning and unscrupulous merchant leaders. They commanded an invisible and mysterious network of despotic control that enabled them to direct and profit from the lucrative and sordid vice business as well as the labor of ordinary immigrants. They had in effect created a state within a state. Chinatown, a foreign transplant that had taken root in American soil, not only threatened to subvert liberal institutions and overwhelm free labor, but might also by its mere presence scare away desirable immigrants from other parts of the world and in time claim North America as an exclusive preserve of the Chinese.

The Chinese were a threat to national dreams, particularly as they were to be realized in the context of the special California frontier. There Americans, whether of old stock or new, pursued a personal quest for freedom and economic opportunity. On a larger canvas their efforts were seen as a contribution to fulfilling the nation's destiny—the last, most brilliant movement in the westward march of civilization. But reality seldom coincided with the ideal. For the European-born, who constituted slightly over a third of California's work force in 1870, the contrast between promise and performance gave rise to particularly strong discontents. Like the native-born (40 percent of that work force), they had to bear the buffeting of a boom and bust economy. They too had to get along in a raw, violence-prone society. They, however, bore the additional burden of being themselves people in cultural transition and under nativist suspicion for their own lingering foreign ways. Especially the Irish, with their papist associations and their own secret societies, provoked criticism on this count. The anti-Chinese struggle became a way for white Californians to vent frustrations, assuage disappointments, work for a better future, and secure the comforts of group solidarity. For the recent arrival from Europe the Chinese also served as a foil. By attacking the Chinese menace he could demonstrate his own impugned loyalty and enhance his sense of self-worth.

Sinophobia found its home in and provided an ideological glue for California's embryonic labor movement. Labor saw as its enemies the Chinese and the "capitalist monopolies" that controlled the railways, large landholdings, and mines. Though big capital was arguably the greater threat, labor came to concentrate its fire on the Chinese, and for good reasons. An attack on the Chinese (and only incidentally on the capitalists purportedly standing behind them) founded on broad nationalist grounds brought valuable allies to the side of organized labor including independent miners, small businessmen, some farmers and politicians, while a stark appeal to divisive class interests carried with it the risks of political isolation and possible defeat. The pattern of hostility and violence began to develop in California soon after the arrival of the first Chinese and moved spasmodically toward a climax nearly two and a half decades later. Sporadic attacks against the Chinese venturing out into the gold fields occurred in the 1850s, especially be-tween 1852 and 1854. In the following decade the conflict carried over into newly opened underground mines where both Chinese and white wage earners worked. The anti-Chinese violence also began to build in an urban context. Rowdies, transients, merrymakers, and the unem-ployed had earlier made city life difficult for the Chinese. The rise of a class of wage earners in the 1860s gave a new complexion to the agi-tation, particularly in San Francisco, California's premier city with a quarter of the state's population. In 1862 the first anticoolie club ap-peared there, and in 1867 and again in 1869 it launched sharp attacks against the Chinese and made their presence a central issue in state politics. In the 1870s urban agitation turned violent, most dramatically in riots in Los Angeles in 1871 and in San Francisco in 1877.

Precipitants were needed to convert the hostility of Sinophobes into violence. Downswings in the local economy appear to have been one cause. The incidents of 1854 followed the end of the surface-mining boom. Those in 1867 and 1869 coincided with brief economic down-turns. The 1877 riots in San Francisco came one year after California had absorbed the full impact of the national depression originating in the East. The unemployed flocked into the city. More than 4,000 men applied for relief in San Francisco over a three-month period in 1877 and an estimated 30,000, perhaps 15 percent of the city's total popu-lation, went without work that year. Major influxes of "orientals," ad-ditions to an already highly visible Chinese community, also appear to have helped touch off attacks (as in 1852, 1854, 1869 and 1877). By 1870 the Chinese constituted one-twelfth of California's population and one-quarter of her work force. Spreading word of massive new additions to the Chinese population must have induced a sense of desperation and alarm that loosened normal restraints and opened the way for mob violence.

Feeling against the Chinese in the 1870s was aggravated by the failure to administer a deadly blow to them despite the considerable political progress Sinophobes had made on home ground. They had first won the California Democratic party. By 1875 the state Republicans had also assumed a sympathetic stance out of political necessity if not conviction. In 1877 the Workingmen's party under the leadership of the Irish immigrant Denis Kearney emerged as the primary vehicle for Sinophobia, momentarily depriving the state Democrats of that role. The next year the Workingmen's party, then at the peak of its power, put together a new state constitution peppered with anti-Chinese clauses. These clauses together with other measures dating back to the 1850s put the Chinese under occupational disabilities, imposing special licenses, fees, and regulations on Chinese laundrymen, fishermen, miners, and peddlers and excluding Chinese labor from employment on publicly funded projects or by corporations registered in California. They de-prived Chinese of the right to become naturalized citizens, to testify in court against whites, or to attend white public schools. Local courts offered little justice to the Chinese when, as was frequently the case, both judge and jury shared community prejudices against them. Municipal authorities added to the burdens of the Chinese by applying, often to them alone, special regulations concerning health, prostitution, opium smoking, and gambling. Finally, the Sinophobes sought to solve the Chinese problem by blocking the arrival of new immigrants. One approach was to require transport companies to pay taxes or post bonds set at prohibitively high levels. The simpler alternative was a flat denial of the right of "Mongolians" to land in the United States. But of this array of state and local measures, part had simply proven unworkable, and much had been struck down by the higher courts, initially as violations of the equal protection clause of the Fourteenth Amendment. The conclusion of a treaty with China in 1868 guaranteeing the right of free immigration and the passage of the civil rights measures between 1868 and 1870 gave state and federal courts new and broader grounds for nullifying these regional solutions to the Chinese problem and added to the frustrations of Western Sinophobes.

Finally California, with the support of other western states, took its problem to Congress with the intention of securing federal legislation, silencing the courts, and abrogating the offending 1868 treaty. The campaign in Congress, led by California's own Senator Aaron A. Sargent, began auspiciously. The Senate agreed in 1876 to an investigation, if for no other reason than to put off the West Coast delegation's call for the more drastic course of treaty revision ending immigration. In reporting the results of the joint House-Senate inquiry the next year, Sargent ignored the balance of the testimony sympathetic to the Chinese and instead stressed the "great and growing evil" of Mongolian immigration and warned that unless checked it would overwhelm "republican institutions" and "Christian civilization" on the Pacific Coast. But the best the western states could get in their first two years of effort in Washington was the passage of a mildly worded request that the President find some way to modify the objectionable provisions of the 1868 Burlingame–Seward treaty guaranteeing the right of free immigration to Chinese. Neither national political party had yet wholeheartedly embraced their cause; and the Republicans in the White House, while paying some lip service to the plaint of the anti-Chinese forces, took no concrete steps to undo the controversial 1868 treaty or to move Congress to action.

In their political drive, Sinophobes had already by 1876 overcome the pro-Chinese forces in California and elsewhere in the West. The debate between them had turned on the role of Chinese labor in the local economy and the nature of the Chinese community. Farmers, manufacturers, and railway builders as well as missionaries had come to the defense of cheap Chinese labor as a major contribution to regional development and to the competitiveness of California's light industry.

In general, the Chinese did not supplant white labor but rather supplemented it and increased regional prosperity, so they argued to the catcalls of the unemployed who followed Denis Kearney and found in the Chinese a scapegoat for the blows administered by unseen economic forces. To counter the charges that the Chinese were unassimilable and hence a social danger, these opponents of exclusion compared the orderly, peaceful, and industrious Chinese laborers to the riotous sandlot Irishmen and the corrupt, irresponsible politicians who went along with them. The Chinese Six Companies were not despotic but voluntary associations and Chinese labor not enslaved but free and a far sight less dangerous than the nascent labor unions with their monopolistic designs to control the terms of employment. With the passage of time and an end to discriminatory treatment, the Chinese would embrace Christian and democratic ideals, and many would return to China to spread civilized ways and thereby contribute to "the rejuvenation of a nation." Missionaries were predictably the most persistent opponents of exclusion, continuing undaunted to press the case for the Chinese in the press, pamphlets, public hearings, and lectures long after business interests in California had taken refuge in a prudent silence.

Sinophobia in the West met and mastered these opponents of exclusion obviously because it enjoyed popular support in the region but also because the defenders of the Chinese seemed to place their narrow, personal interest in the Chinese as converts, customers, and workers ahead of the white workingman's welfare. However, outside the West and especially in Washington, Sinophobes found themselves not only bereft of a broad base of political support but also confronted by a new set of arguments less easily neutralized by charges of self-interest. Exclusion, so its national critics responded, would violate treaty rights, undercut the national tradition of free immigration, and damage American commercial, diplomatic, and missionary interests in China. In all these ways a narrow sectional demand jeopardized broad national interests. The exclusionists thus went into 1879 still faced with the task of moving Congress to act on the Chinese problem and of convincing the major parties of the political risks they would run by neglecting it.

The Last of the
Old-Time Mining Camps

ROGER D. MCGRATH

Frontier violence in the Old West provides some of the most enduring myths in American culture. Pulp novels, movies, and television programs have filled the West with crazed killers, bank and stagecoach robbers, gun duelists, and cowed townspeople. The reality of western life, however, has been elusive. Scholars, as well as popular writers, have tended to focus on the more dramatic, particularly more violent, episodes of western history. The gunfight at the O.K. Corral has always had more appeal to the reading and viewing public than the slower, relatively peaceful process of community building.

Roger D. McGrath (California State University at Long Beach) has attempted to assess the nature and extent of western violence by studying in detail two mining communities in the trans-Sierra country on the California-Nevada border. The towns of Aurora and Bodie typify the settlements that grew rapidly as the gold and silver fever hit the western United States in the middle of the nineteenth century. The discovery of rich ore-bearing "lodes" caused the ever-hopeful prospectors to hastily establish claims. Shortly thereafter, towns came into being, as those prepared to provide the commercial and service necessities for the miners appeared and set up shop. Many of the violent episodes of the western myth occurred in such places.

As a result of his research, McGrath concludes that certain aspects of the frontier myth are true and others are greatly overstated.

> The trans-Sierra frontier was unmistakably violent and lawless, but only in special ways. Whereas bank robbery, rape, racial violence, and serious juvenile crime seem not to have occurred, and robbery, theft, and burglary occurred relatively infrequently, shootings and shoot-outs among toughs, badmen, and miners were fairly regular events. . . . The old, the

young, the unwilling, the weak, and the female—with the notable exception of the prostitute—were, for the most part, safe from harm. (p. 247)

The chapter from McGrath's book reprinted here does not focus on a particular aspect of frontier violence but, rather, deals with the establishment of and the daily life in the town of Bodie. In this selection, we can see at work the forces that contributed both to the violence of frontier life and to the continuity and stability of those settlements that survived the mining era.

Eight miles southwest of Aurora lay Bodie. Although gold was discovered there in 1859, a year before the Esmeralda strike, little excitement was generated until a real bonanza was struck in 1877. Then, during the next six years, Bodie produced nearly $15 million worth of gold and silver bullion. Total production eventually surpassed $20 million. Among the mining towns of the Great Basin, only Virginia City produced more bullion. Ironically, the discoverers of Bodie's wealth never shared in it.

During the summer of 1859 reports of rich strikes in the trans-Sierra country began to reach California. The fabulous Ophir vein of the Comstock Lode was discovered in June by Peter O'Riley and Patrick McLaughlin, and in July new strikes were reported around Dogtown and Monoville. Prospectors were soon trekking eastward across the Sierra to these new El Dorados. Among the dozens of prospectors who followed the Sonora Pass trail that summer into the trans-Sierra were Terrence Brodigan and W. S. Bodey. Their backgrounds were radically dissimilar, yet their quest was the same.

As a young man Brodigan had emigrated from his native Ireland to Australia, where instead of prospecting for gold he raised sheep. The gold rush brought him to California, and he eventually settled in Sonora. There he became the proprietor of a hotel and a livery stable, while continuing to prospect now and then. New York-born Bodey, an occasional resident of Brodigan's hotel, was making his living as a tinsmith in Poughkeepsie when he caught the gold fever in 1848. Leaving behind a wife and six children, he booked passage on the *Matthew Vassar* and sailed around the Horn to California. He spent the next ten years working the placer deposits of the Mother Lode. Although he

THE LAST OF THE OLD-TIME MINING CAMPS From *Gunfighters, Highwaymen, and Vigilantes* by Roger D. McGrath (Berkeley: University of California Press, 1984), pp. 102–123. © 1984 The Regents of the University of California. Used by permission of the University of California Press.

never had more than modest success, he was able to send money home regularly to support his wife and children. He persevered because he knew he would strike it big somewhere up the next gulch.

Brodigan and Bodey crossed into the trans-Sierra separately, but joined forces at Monoville. Together with Patrick Garrity, William Doyle, and E. S. Taylor, they left the Mono diggings and, under Brodigan's leadership, worked their way north and northeast, leaving the ground behind them pockmarked with prospect holes. At Esmeralda Gulch a threatening band of Paiute forced them to turn back to the south. Brodigan led the prospectors over a high, sagebrush-covered ridgeline and into a shallow valley. Liking the appearance of the land, they brought their burros to a halt. Bodey picked a likely spot and began to dig yet another prospect hole. He turned over a shovelful of dirt, then another, and another. Suddenly he straightened up and exclaimed, "This looks like pay dirt at last, and if it is, you know and I know we came a hell of a ways to find it."

All hands now fell to work, and well into the evening the prospectors feverishly dug and washed the pay dirt. Yellow bits of metal kept turning up. Finally, Doyle shouted, "Come on, boys, we can't do any less than drink the last part of the bottle. We'll take our chances on a snake bite to drink a toast to Bodey, and the best showing we've seen on the Eastern slope of these Sierra Nevada Mountains." Winter was fast approaching, however, and the prospectors realized that serious working of the claim would have to wait until spring. They built a small cabin at the discovery site and returned to Monoville for supplies. There it was decided that Bodey and Taylor would return to the cabin, and that Brodigan, Garrity, and Doyle would cross the Sierra to Sonora for the winter.

Brodigan gave Bodey his parting blessing, and the two parties headed off in opposite directions. Although neither party knew it, a blizzard had hit the Sierra and was moving east with frightening speed. Brodigan, Garrity, and Doyle were beginning the climb up to Sonora Pass when the storm roared down on them. Fighting blinding snow and howling winds, they retraced their steps out of the mountains and eventually reached Sonora by way of the Carson Valley and the Placerville Road.

Bodey and Taylor were more than halfway up Cottonwood Canyon, less than four miles from the cabin, when the blizzard caught up with them. If they were to live, they would have to reach the cabin. Snow, driven by howling winds, quickly piled up in great drifts. Each step the prospectors took became a struggle. To lighten their loads, they abandoned pack after pack of supplies until they carried only the barest essentials. Bodey's strength finally failed him, and he fell exhausted into the snow. Taylor, a part-Cherokee veteran miner who was less than five feet tall, lifted Bodey onto his back and staggered forward another hundred yards before he, too, fell from exhaustion.

Leaving Bodey wrapped in a blanket, Taylor again pushed onward. The blizzard was now so intense that he could see no more than a few feet ahead. A half mile of struggling brought him to a rocky, black bluff which he recognized as the bluff that rose behind the cabin. Heading in what he thought must be the direction of the cabin, he stumbled into the crude structure. There he warmed himself by a fire and gulped down several cups of hot coffee before setting out to rescue Bodey. He returned to what he thought must be the spot where he left Bodey, but could find no trace of his partner. In the face of the blizzard, he searched for several more hours without any luck.

The storm continued unabated for the next two days. When the skies finally cleared, Taylor again ventured out to search for Bodey. Snow lay several feet deep on the ground and was piled into great drifts in areas exposed to the wind. In those conditions, Taylor's efforts were doomed to failure. Conditions did not improve. Storm after storm hit the trans-Sierra country that winter. Mining operations were shut down for several months, and travel was nearly impossible. During one period all communication between Gold Hill and Virginia City was inter-rupted, although the two towns were but a mile apart.

Taylor, alone in the cabin, was haunted by thoughts of Bodey throughout the winter. There were nights when he swore that he could hear his partner calling for help. Time passed slowly. When the snows finally melted in the spring, Taylor discovered Bodey's body, less than a mile from the cabin. Coyotes had gotten there first. Only naked bones, a bowie knife, a revolver, and the blanket that Taylor had originally wrapped Bodey in remained. Taylor now wrapped the bones in the blanket and buried them on the spot. Bodey was gone, but his name would remain.

During the summer of 1860 the Bodey mining district was orga-nized. To avoid mispronunciation, the name was soon being spelled Bodie. Edmund Green was elected president of the new district, A. D. Allen, secretary, and Jeremiah Tucker, recorder. Some twenty claims, all located on Bodie Bluff and a lower ridge that extended southward from it, were officially recorded by the end of July. Bodie Bluff reached an elevation of nine thousand feet. Six hundred feet lower, at the base of the bluff, the town of Bodie developed. The climate, terrain, and vegetation were nearly identical to what miners found at Aurora, only a two-hour ride to the northeast. However, since Bodie was almost a thousand feet higher than Aurora, winters at Bodie were even more severe. Sam Clemens claimed there were only two seasons in the area: the breaking up of one winter and the beginning of the next. "So un-certain is the climate in Summer," said Clemens, "that a lady who goes out visiting cannot hope to be prepared for all emergencies unless she takes her fan under one arm and her snowshoes under the other. When they have a Fourth of July procession it generally snows on them, and they do say as a general thing when a man calls for a brandy toddy there, the barkeeper chops it off with a hatchet and wraps it up in paper, like maple sugar. And it is further reported that the old soakers haven't any teeth—wore them out eating gin cocktails and brandy punches."

The mines at Bodie developed slowly because of the far more spectacular strikes at Aurora and Virginia City. Bodie's ore, at least that which had already been discovered, paled in comparison. Most of the original locators at Bodie drifted off to other towns: Terrence Brodigan to Virginia City; Patrick Garrity, Edmund Green, and A. D. Allen to Aurora; and E. S. Taylor, after a stay in Aurora, to Hot Springs (present-day Benton). Taylor never got over Bodey's death and spent much of his time prospecting alone. Early in 1862 a band of Paiute found him alone in his cabin at Hot Springs. As soon as the sun set, the Paiute attacked. The half-Cherokee Taylor fought back fiercely and killed several Paiute before he was finally overpowered and killed. His bullet-riddled body and his severed head were later found by a group of Aurorans on their way to fight the Paiute in the Owens Valley. Taylor's head was saved and was later passed around Aurora and Bodie as a grisly souvenir of the Indian War. Of the discoverers of the ore, only Brodigan would one day return to Bodie. During the town's heyday, he bottled spring water and delivered it to hotels and restaurants. One of his sons served as a deputy constable in Bodie and another became the secretary of state of Nevada.

The development of the mines at Bodie was retarded, not only by prospectors rushing off to more promising strikes at Aurora and Virginia City, but also by the lack of investment capital; it, like the miners, had gone to those other strikes. In an attempt to attract investment capital, several mines merged early in 1863 to form the Bodie Bluff Consolidated Mining Company. No less a figure than Leland Stanford, the governor of California, was made president of the company. The Bodie Bluff proffered over 11,000 shares of stock and set its worth at more than a million dollars. Stock certificates featured a rendering of the bluff, a score of mines, and the Isabella tunnel. This work of art did little to impress potential investors, however, and the next year another consolidation occurred. The new company, the Empire Company of New York, controlled over 38,000 shares of stock, several mill sites, tunnel rights, and numerous buildings. The Empire set its worth at $10 million and, to entice investors, prohibited assessments. (It was common practice in those days to "assess" stockholders for the cost of mining operations until the mine could pay for itself.)

By 1864 Bodie contained a boarding house and some twenty wood and adobe houses. The town was laid out along Bodie Creek in the shadow of Bodie Bluff. Only sagebrush and bunchgrass decorated the bluff and the other mountains that surrounded the town, "presenting even to the eye of a traveler who had just been surfeited with the deserts of Arizona a wonderfully refreshing picture of desolation."

Nevertheless, there were precious metals in those hills, and with the formation of the Empire Company the town was on the upswing. Streets were being surveyed and marked with stakes, and real estate speculation was vigorous. Real estate promoters spoke of the brilliant future of Bodie and offered "choice" lots for sale. The promoters failed to mention that the lots had not been surveyed or staked. The population of the entire district probably did not exceed fifty. Two miners had their wives with them, but the rest were without women. One visitor to Bodie thought this a blessing:

> These jolly miners were the happiest set of bachelors imaginable; had neither chick nor child, that I knew of, to trouble them; cooked their own food; did their own washing; mended their own clothes, made their own beds, and on Sundays cut their own hair, greased their own boots, and brushed their own coats; thus proving by the most direct positive evidence that woman is an unnecessary and expensive institution which ought to be abolished by law. . . . True, I must admit that the honest miners of Bodie spent a great deal of their leisure time in reading yellow-covered novels and writing love-letters; but that was probably only a clever device to fortify themselves against the insidious approaches of the enemy.

Over the next four years, the Empire Company poured several hundreds of thousands of dollars into its mines on Bodie Bluff. The company also bought the Fogus quartz mill at Aurora, moved it to Bodie, and increased the number of its stamps from twelve to sixteen. Despite these heavy capital expenditures, the Empire Company never struck ore worth much more than the cost of processing. The venture was a bust. In 1874 the Fogus stamp mill, which the company had purchased for $45,000 a decade earlier, was sold for delinquent taxes for $450. Independent mines suffered much the same fate as the Empire Company. Although they all struck ore, none of the ore was rich enough to make their operations profitable. Many of them were abandoned, then relocated, then abandoned again.

In 1875 the Bunker Hill mine, which was first located in 1861 and was subsequently sold and relocated three or four times, struck a rich vein. The vein was exposed by a cave-in just when the two new locators of the Bunker Hill were about to abandon the mine. Over the next year or two they mined and milled gold and silver ore that netted them $35,000, and then they sold out for twice that much to a mining syndicate based in San Francisco. The mine was renamed the Standard, and 50,000 shares of stock went on the trading block. New shafts were sunk, and several drifts and crosscuts were run. Each new tunnel exposed rich veins of quartz bearing both gold and silver, some of the ore assaying as high as $6,000 per ton. Bodie's bonanza had finally been struck.

San Francisco money now began to pour into Bodie. During 1877 no fewer than a dozen mining companies were incorporated, including the Standard, the Bulwer, and the Bodie. These three mines, together with the Noonday, which was incorporated early in 1878, yielded the bulk of Bodie's gold and silver. In 1877 nearly $1 million worth of bullion was shipped out of Bodie, over $2 million in 1878, $2½ million in 1879, and over $3 million in both 1880 and 1881. Then bullion shipments dropped to slightly more than $2 million in 1882 and less than $1 million in 1883.

By 1883 the majority of Bodie's mines had ceased operations. Although the district had by then produced some $14 million worth of bullion, only the Standard and the Bodie had consistently operated at a profit. The Standard continued to mine gold profitably well into the twentieth century. Bodie's total bullion production has been estimated at some $21 million. The Standard accounted for about $14 million of this, the Bodie for $4 million, the Noonday for $1 million, and the Bulwer for a half million.

During the late 1870s and early 1880s, there were over thirty Bodie mining properties on the San Francisco Stock Exchange. Stock quotations were telegraphed to Bodie daily, and nearly everyone speculated in the market. One resident asserted that the most popular expression in Bodie after "Let's take a drink" was "How are the stocks today?" The price of a share of any particular stock fluctuated daily, and oftentimes the fluctuation was extreme. During the summer of 1878 a share of Bodie rose in value from $0.50 to over $50.00. The same share sold for $5.50 in March 1879 and then for $48.00 in May. Other stocks experienced fluctuations only slightly less radical. Fortunes—on paper—were made and lost and made and lost again with surprising regularity. A speculator who had lost his entire savings in a stock venture commented, "Nearly everybody in Bodie, at one time or another, had a good deal of money, but almost everybody left the camp broke when the bottom dropped-out."

Because of the fabulously rich strikes of the Standard and the Bodie, however, it seemed that investment in mining stock was a good gamble. It was only a matter of time, thought many a Bodieite, before the other mines hit the rich ore also. The Mono mine, for one, had operated at a loss during 1879 and 1880. Yet, since it was adjacent to the Bodie, there was hope that the Bodie vein would one day be found to extend into the Mono. By 1881 over a half million dollars had been poured into the Mono by its stockholders, and still no Bodie vein. From a high of $14.50 a share in 1879, Mono stock dropped to a low of $0.30 in early 1881.

The principal stockholders of the Mono, mostly wealthy San Francisco speculators, now hatched a plot, not only to save their original investments but also to reap large profits. They began to buy Mono stock and subtly spread the rumor that the Mono had struck the Bodie vein. "Hundreds of people," recalled a former Bodieite, "who thought they alone had received this 'inside information' eagerly bought the stock. My mother heard the rumor, eagerly invested her savings account of $1,500, and advised me to do likewise with the $600 that I had saved for my education. As soon as 'the insiders' had unloaded all the stock they could on the public, the shares began to fall rapidly in price; they dropped from $12 to practically nothing in a short time."

By 1882 most people in Bodie had come to the realization that none of the mines in the district, except the Standard and the Bodie, had made any real profits. Moreover, it had also become apparent to Bodieites that for the most part, their speculation in stocks was enriching only the wealthy stock manipulators in San Francisco. Consequently, the value of most stocks plummeted to near nothing during 1882, and all but four or five mines were shut down. Bodie's mining boom, much of which consisted of paper profits and hope, was over.

The town of Bodie itself boomed and declined in step with the mines. During the summer of 1877 Bodie began to expand rapidly. By fall, Frank Kenyon, one of the West's pioneer newspapermen, began to publish the *Bodie Standard*. The newspaper, which would be printed in Aurora until its presses were moved to Bodie in May 1878, announced in its sixth edition:

> But a few short months ago, Bodie was an insignificant little place. Now, she is rapidly growing in size and importance; and the people are crowding in upon her from far and near, and Why? Because of rich discoveries in GOLD, yellow glittering precious Gold. The baseness of man, and yet his antidote, his blessing and his curse. His happiness and his misery. His solace and his affliction. The forger of change, and manumitter. The pastor and the prison, and the releaser. The richman's strength. The poorman's weakness.

People flocked to Bodie from everywhere in the West: from Virginia City and Grass Valley, from Sacramento and San Francisco. The first stagecoach arrived in Bodie in late December 1877 loaded with passengers. By February 1878 the town had a population of about fifteen hundred, over a third of whom had no employment. Nevertheless, new arrivals were averaging ten a day. There were only four lodging houses and some two hundred cabins and houses to shelter all these people. The real necessities of life, however, had been provided for: Bodie was already home to seventeen saloons and fifteen brothels. The town also boasted six restaurants, five general stores, a Wells, Fargo & Company express office, and two stage lines. Lumber was expensive at ten cents a board foot, and lots were selling for a hundred to a thousand dollars apiece. Building was progressing at a frantic pace, despite howling winds, drifting snow, and temperatures that rarely rose above freezing.

During May 1878 a telegraph line was completed to Bodie, and the citizens sent their first dispatch: "Bodie sends greetings and proclaims to the mining world that her gold mines are the most wonderful yet discovered." The frantic pace of construction increased with the coming of spring, and new mining claims were being recorded daily. In July the United States Land Office was moved from Independence in the Owens Valley to Bodie to meet the demand for its services. So many men came into Bodie during the summer and fall of 1878 that most of them went without accommodations and were forced to sleep on billiard tables and saloon floors.

Traffic on Bodie's streets was regularly congested with wagons of all varieties. There were large freight wagons drawn by twenty-mule teams, ore wagons hauling rock to be crushed in the mills, wood wagons bringing in firewood, hay wagons headed for livery stables, and lumber wagons on their way to construction sites. Materials and supplies were stacked alongside Main Street, Bodie's principal thoroughfare, for its entire length. Through this traffic came men on foot and men on horseback, and six-horse stagecoaches "filled with passengers from deck to keel. Sixteen is an average load; but, as a stagecoach or streetcar is like a can of sardines, there is always room for just one more." By the end of 1878 Bodie's population had swelled to about four thousand, and new arrivals were said to be coming into town at the rate of thirty a day. The number of saloons now surpassed forty and there were some eight hundred structures of all types, all built of wood. Early in 1879 O'Day and Fraser opened a brickyard, and soon a number of brick buildings were under construction.

Bodie's boom continued throughout 1879 and peaked in 1880. The federal census of 1880 counted 5,373 persons in Bodie. Nearly half were foreign born: approximately 850 Bodieites had been born in Ireland, 750 in Canada, 550 in England and Wales, 350 in China, 250 in Germany, 120 in Scotland, 100 in Mexico, 80 in France, and 60 in Sweden and Norway. Of the native-born Americans, about 900 had been born in California and 550 in New York. With the exception of 350 or so Chinese, a few dozen Indians, and 19 "colored," Bodie was all white. Women, many of whom were prostitutes, accounted for only about 10 percent of the population, and there were probably no more than 150 children.

A goodly number of Bodie's residents were what was known as "mining-camp men." These were men who had come to California during the gold rush, or shortly thereafter, and had been rushing to each new excitement ever since. By Bodie's time they were a dying breed, who made Bodie the "last of the old-time mining camps." They were not only prospectors but also professional men, gamblers, businessmen, and badmen. "These men," commented one Bodieite, "were virile, enthusiastic, and free livers; bound by few of the rules of conventional society, though with an admirable code of their own: liberal-minded, generous to a fault, square-dealing, and devoid of pretense and hypocrisy. While the mining camps were not entirely composed of men of this type, it was they who gave the camps their distinctive flavor."

With a population of well over five thousand, Bodie had become a sprawling metropolis. Main Street, which ran generally north and south and paralleled Bodie Creek, was the principal thoroughfare. It was intersected by King, Union, and Green streets and paralleled by Fuller, Prospect, Bonanza, and Wood streets. Several smaller streets connected these major arteries. The intersection of Main and King was "downtown" Bodie. No less than 450 businesses lined the streets of Bodie, and seven quartz mills were perched on the hillsides. There were two banks, the Mono County Bank and the Bank of Bodie, a postoffice, a telegraph office, a United States Land Office, four livery stables, a dozen hotels, six general stores, and numerous restaurants, markets, barbershops, and other small businesses. Two stage lines made daily runs to Carson City and Virginia City, and three daily newspapers and one weekly kept Bodieites abreast of local, national, and world affairs.

Linking Bodie to the outside world were several privately owned toll roads. These roads were built under country franchises, and their toll rates were regulated by the county. The most traveled toll road was the Big Meadows and Bodie Road, operated by J. C. Murphy. The road ran west from Bodie through Murphy Springs, Mormon Meadows, and Dogtown, and then north to Big Meadows (present-day Bridgeport). There the road connected with the Sonora and Mono Road, a county highway which crossed the Sierra by way of Sonora Pass. Over this route came the finest goods that San Francisco had to offer, including the latest inventions. One day the first shower stall, complete with overhead sprinkler, arrived in Bodie and was placed on display at Gillson and Barber's general store. The new contraption, commented the *Bodie Standard* on 25 September 1878, "consists of a closet and looks like a 'sweat-box' formerly used as a means of torture." Delicacies also came to Bodie through Sonora Pass. George Callahan's Can Can restaurant, reputed to be Bodie's finest, featured oysters from San Francisco Bay as well as fresh duck from Mono Lake and fresh trout from the Sierra.

Bodie, like Aurora, was home to an extraordinary number of saloons. Much of Main Street was lined with saloons, nearly fifty in all, or about one for every hundred Bodie men. The *Bodie Standard,* on 19 October 1879, said it believed that the street "has more saloons in a given length than any thorofare in the world." Their names indicated that Bodie was, indeed, an old-time mining camp: American Flag, Argonaut, Assessment, Aurora, Bank Exchange, Bonanza, Caledonian, Carson, Comstock, Delta, Dividend, Empire, Gold Brick, Headquarters, Oasis, Occidental, Oriental, Parlor, Parole, Pioneer, Reno, and Shamrock.

The better Bodie saloons, such as Patrick Gallagher's Shamrock or Dick McAlpin's Parlor, occupied a room some thirty feet wide and seventy-five or a hundred feet deep. A bar abutted one wall, and a "chop stand," specializing in fried chops, steaks, and ribs, ran along the other. At the rear of the saloon or in an adjoining room were located the gambling tables. Faro, twenty-one, red and black, draw poker, and roulette were the favorite games. A billiard table or two could also be found in many saloons.

The saloon was the most important social institution in Bodie. Bodie's saloons were crowded with men—women, including prostitutes, almost never ventured into the saloons—every night of the week. One Bodieite recalled that "nearly everybody drank, nearly everybody gambled." Besides serving imported "whiskies from Cork City, Ireland," as did Patrick Fahey's Mono Brewery, the saloons also served Bodie's own powerful home brew: a whiskey said to be made "from old boots, scraps of iron, snow-slides and climate, and it only takes a couple of 'snorts' to craze a man of ordinary brainpower."

The fame of Bodie's whiskey soon spread to San Francisco, where the newspapers printed tongue-in-check reports of the fluid. When a visiting Bodieite asked for a drink at a Market Street saloon, a local paper reported that the barkeeper served him a mixture of alcohol, turpentine, Perry Davis pain-killer, Jamaica ginger, and pepper sauce. The Bodieite downed the concoction without batting an eye and exclaimed, "Young man, that's whiskey. I ain't tasted nothin' like it since I left Bodie two weeks ago today. That's real genuine licker, kinder a cross 'tween a circular saw and a wildcat, that takes holt quick, en hols on long. Jus' you go to Bodie and open a saloon. And with that whiskey you might charge 4 bits a glass for it and the boys 'ud never kick."

Bodie's drinking stories are legion. There was the old alcoholic named Midson, who one winter night was thrown out of a saloon into the street. He toppled over into a snowbank and passed out. There he lay until some passerby discovered him the next morning. By then he was frozen solid and showed absolutely no signs of life. Some friends placed his rigid figure next to a fire and literally thawed him out. Miraculously, Midson revived and with his first breath asked for a drink. Doctors commented that any ordinary man would have died from exposure. Midson did not even catch pneumonia. John Peters was as lucky as Midson. After a night of hard drinking, Peters was groping his way home in the dark. Thoroughly drunk, he wandered off the trail and fell a hundred feet down a mine shaft. When discovered the next day, he was perfectly well except for a few bruises.

Just as puzzling to local physicians was the remarkable case of a Bodieite who became drunk without drinking. The man in question woke up perfectly sober the morning after a drunken night in the saloons. By midday, however, he felt himself growing gradually more intoxicated until by late afternoon he was roaring drunk again. Witnesses swore that he had not touched a drop of liquor that day. A story that stretches credulity even further tells of an "old stiff," renowned for his erudition in drinking matters, who was challenged to identify every drink put to his lips while he was blindfolded. Different types of whiskey, brandy, gin, rum, and wine were all given to him. He identified every one. Then he was given a glass of water. He tasted it, smacked his lips, swirled it around in his mouth, and swallowed it. He did this several more times. Finally, he gave up in despair and admitted that the boys had stumped him; he could not identify the drink.

Occasionally, quantity rather than quality was the criterion involved in the challenge. A big, strong woodchopper named Logart, reputed to be a "hard-drinker," was challenged to the feat of downing three gills (nearly a pint) of whiskey without stopping. Bets were placed, and the contest began. Logart drank the whiskey down with apparent ease, but then was seized with convulsions and fell to the floor. He vomited and writhed in pain and "his face grew perfectly blue and white alternately." Medical aid was summoned, but the doctors were of little help. Logart lay insensible for another two hours before he finally recovered.

There were those in Bodie who frowned on the drinking exploits of the "boys." One fall evening in 1881 a temperance lecturer, Colonel C. M. Golding, delivered a stirring speech before a packed house at the Miners' Union Hall. Ironically, most of the men in attendance were hard drinkers who had come to the lecture to relieve the "monotony and dullness of the times." Golding excoriated Bodie's liquor dealers and saloonkeepers, many of whom were in the audience. The proprietor of the Bank Exchange saloon, Joe McDermott, thought that "the lecture is good, possessed of argument and no man in Bodie could pass a more pleasant and edifying hour than by listening to it, but if they think they can deliver more temperance lecturers than I can sell whiskey, why just let them keep it up." Nevertheless, the temperance people won a small victory when the Mono County supervisors enacted a law that prohibited saloons from opening on Sundays. Just one month later, the Mono County district attorney announced that he was discontinuing prosecution for violation of the Sunday-closing law. Wholesale violation had made the law impossible to enforce.

By 1879 some fifteen Bodie saloons had gambling rooms, and dozens of professional gamblers had taken up residence in the town, an indication of Bodie's prosperity. Mining towns were judged successful only when they could claim large numbers of "sports" or "genteel loafers," as the professional gamblers were known. The sports spent most of their time in the saloons or brothels. "Their chief delights," said Bodie's *Daily Free Press*, "are wine, women and billiards; their occupation is faro, and occasionally a game of 'draw'."

The sport was cool and confident, usually "a man of education," a good judge of human character, and "in spite of his calling," said the *Bodie Standard*, "preserves a dignity, a strength of character recognized by all classes and is ever ready to defend his manhood against any encroachments." He wore snow-white shirts, tailored suits, polished boots, and fine jewelry. This sartorial splendor was not all for show: if he ever went broke, he could use his expensive outfit as collateral for a stake. The sport's credit was invariably good because he always promptly paid his debts when he won. His greatest delight was to entice several hard-working miners into a game of cards just as payday dawned. "That he will win," commented the *Daily Free Press,* "is as sure as death and assessments, unless he is completely out of luck; and even then his su-perior sagacity is usually sufficient to pull him through.

In a day when the average miner earned only about $25 for a sixty-hour workweek, some of the stakes were enormous. Jack Gunn won nearly $4,000 one night playing faro against the house in the Parole saloon. Another gambler came away from a seven-up game in the Tem-ple saloon with $1,300. And a Mexican "played his wife off at a game of poker, and she went off perfectly satisfied with her new liege."

A distant second to the saloon as a social institution in Bodie was the brothel. Brothels were concentrated along Bonanza Street, also known as Virgin Alley or Maiden Lane. Bonanza ran from King Street north-ward to the edge of town, and was just west of and parallel to Main Street. Brothels and dance houses, which lined both sides of the street, were separated by a number of small cabins in which the "girls" lived. Several saloons that fronted on the west side of Main Street opened in the rear onto Bonanza Street. Prostitutes rarely ventured into the sa-loons, but they did spend many working hours in the dance houses. There they would waltz drunken miners dizzy, being certain that the miners stopped now and then to purchase more drinks at the bar. If the men had any money left at the end of the evening, the prostitutes would lead them away to private rooms.

Bodieites also found time to participate, as contestants and specta-tors, in a variety of sports. Wrestling was by far the most popular sport, but foot racing and horse racing, animal fights, hunting, and target shooting also had their devotees. Wrestlers usually fought in one of three styles: collar-and-elbow, Cornish, or Greco-Roman. For a time Rod McInnis dominated the main event, then came James Pascoe, Harry and Frank Gallagher, Dan McMillan, and H. C. Bell. These men fought for a predetermined purse—sometimes as much as $500—and a per-centage of the gate. Although thousands of dollars were wagered on the matches, and spectators regularly numbered in the hundreds, only one serious disturbance ever occurred at the matches.

Before a packed house at the Miners' Union Hall in August 1880, Rod McInnis met Eugene Markey for the collar-and-elbow heavyweight title of Bodie. McInnis, a miner at the Standard, was supported by the working men of Bodie; Markey, a former police officer who spent most of his time in saloons, was backed by the local sports. Both groups had bet heavily on their favorites, and the match was considered even money. As soon as the three-fall match began, however, it became obvious that

McInnis was the better wrestler. Markey, knowing that he could not throw McInnis, fought defensively. For several minutes the two men struggled and then, with a quick movement, McInnis threw Markey to the canvas. The sports, with several thousands of dollars riding on Markey, were thoroughly shaken. Then McInnis threw Markey a second time, but referee Johnny Riordan disallowed the throw.

The sports now knew it was only a matter of time before Markey went down again. To save themselves, they had two of their men, special officers Dave Bannon and Robert Whitaker who were supposed to be responsible for preventing disturbances in the hall, stage a fight. Bannon and Whitaker drew their revolvers and began waving them wildly and exchanging epithets. "The immense crowd," reported the *Daily Free Press,* "made a rush for the sidewalk, carrying the doors along with it. Lights were put out, chairs thrown about, windows and lamps broken."

During the stampede referee Riordan was carried into the street and told by several armed men not to return to the hall if he valued his life. Gradually, the spectators drifted back into the hall. Riordan was not among them and could not be found. McInnis's backers were furious. The next day Riordan surfaced and announced that the match would continue that evening. Markey failed to appear at the appointed time, and McInnis was announced the winner. Whether the sports paid off their debts is not known.

Numerous foot races, both walking and running, were also held in Bodie. Most of these were long distance-affairs; a few of them covered a hundred miles or more. In one grueling seventy-two-hour walking match conducted in the Miners' Union Hall, George Wilcox completed 230 miles to W. H. Scott's 229 miles. Scott was a veteran professional from San Francisco, but he could never quite catch the young Bodieite Wilcox, who was thoroughly acclimated to the altitude of over eight thousand feet. Wilcox walked away with the winner's purse of $500. It was a walking match also that saw the only appearance of female athletes in Bodie. Daisy Livingstone and Kitty Franklin, two prostitutes, strode a ten-miler before a large audience in Bodie's gymnasium one winter evening. Daisy won by over nineteen laps.

Shorter races were usually run only during Bodie's Fourth of July celebrations, but there were exceptions. One summer evening Harvey Boone and Ben Eggleston met in a seventy-five-yard race held on Main Street. When Boone arrived at the starting line, attired only in a suit of long, red-flannel underwear and red socks, the more than five hundred spectators roared their approval. Moments later Eggleston jogged up to the line "in high-toned white lamb's wool undershirt and drawers, with stockings to match," and the crowd wildly applauded and roared again. Although Eggleston took an early lead in the race, Boone pulled even at the midway mark and went on to win by a yard.

Horses were occasionally raced at Booker Flat on the south edge of town. Charles O'Malley's mare Nellie was generally considered the fastest horse in the county. Animal fights were also not uncommon. Usually dogs were pitted against each other or other animals, including badgers, bobcats, and bears. There were also Bodieites who hunted animals. One expedition to the Mono Lake region brought back 3 deer, 1 black bear, 2 mountain lions, 300 ducks, 164 geese, and 91 rabbits. It took a couple of ore wagons to haul the kill to town. For Bodieites who did not have the time to enjoy the hunt, there was the Bodie Rifle Club, which held shooting matches every Sunday near the Red Cloud mine and a turkey shoot each Thanksgiving. Pistol practice could be taken each afternoon at the town gymnasium, and there were always dozens of men on hand attempting to win the daily pool.

Unlike Aurorans, Bodieites generally paid little attention to national politics and almost none to local politics. On the morning of 23 June 1878 when election judges Pat Kelley and J. McGrath opened the polls for the election of delegates to the state constitutional convention, there was no one there to vote. Only a few voters straggled in during the next several hours, and there was a brief flurry of activity at lunchtime and again around dinnertime. Total ballots cast numbered only 176, out of a population of nearly 2,000. "This was the most important election which has been held for many years in California," commented the Bodie Standard on 26 June, "and it is to be deeply regretted that so little interest was manifested."

The presidential and congressional election year of 1880 saw considerably more political activity. Several Republican and Democratic rallies were held during September of 1880, in which hundreds participated. Nevertheless, in the November election only 1,200 votes were cast for president (the Republican, James Garfield, won over the Democrat, Winfield Scott Hancock, 640 to 553)—and Bodie contained well over 5,000 residents. Even in this presidential election Bodie's political apathy was apparent. In Aurora the Civil War and the California-Nevada boundary dispute had caused bitter political divisions, large voter turnouts, election frauds, duels, and assassination attempts, but in Bodie barely 20 percent of the residents, most of whom were eligible to vote, bothered to cast ballots.

The only political issue that consistently aroused Bodieites, or at least Irish Bodieites, was England's continued occupation of Ireland and her oppression of the Irish. Bodie boasted a local chapter of the Land League of Ireland, which was devoted to placing the Irish tenant farmer back "in possession of the land which rightfully belongs to him." The Land League had been founded during the fall of 1879 at Castlebar, County Mayo, Ireland, after the failure of more than a dozen legislative attempts to amend oppressive English land law in Ireland. The league aided the Irish tenants and organized protests against English landlords. The term "boycott" was coined during this period when Irish tenants refused to work lands overseen by Charles Boycott for an English landlord. The repressive measures—including the demolition of thousands of homes and, in one instance, the bayoneting of women and children—that the English took against Irish tenants throughout Ireland gave the movement its momentum.

Newspapers and journals in the United States, such as Patrick Ford's *Irish World* and John Boyle O'Reilly's *Boston Pilot*, enlisted the support of Irish-Americans for the Land League. Charles Stewart Parnell, the president of the league, made a trip to the United States and addressed Congress. Within months, local chapters of the league sprang up across America, and money began to flow to Ireland to support families—some twenty thousand a year—evicted from their farms by English landlords. Money also went to finance the defense of Land Leaguers, including all of the league's officers, who were arrested by the English.

The Bodie chapter of the Land League was established on the Wednesday evening of 22 December 1880. "For seven centuries," said Judge Thomas Ryan in the chapter's first meeting, "Ireland has been fighting for liberty. . . . Those who have gathered here to-night should not respond as Irishmen, merely, but as citizens of the leading republic of the earth and aid in liberating the oppressed people from English rule." Weekly meetings of the chapter regularly filled the Miners' Union Hall to overflowing. Speeches, music, songs, and fund raising highlighted the meetings. Featured speakers included chapter presidents Thomas Ryan and John F. McDonald and such prominent Bodieites as Judge John McQuaid, Patrick Reddy, J. C. McTarnahan, and Father John B. Cassin.

If Bodieites, with the special exception of the Land League, were less than enthusiastic about politics, they were downright apathetic about organized religion. Although John B. Cassin, a Catholic priest, and G. B. Hinkle, a Methodist Episcopal minister, both arrived in Bodie during 1878, neither of them had a church until late 1882. Before then the Miners' Union Hall was used for Sunday services; Catholics met at ten o'clock in the morning, following by Methodists at two in the afternoon. Fund-raising events were held now and then by the women of Bodie for the building of churches for both denominations. One benefit during the summer of 1880 raised over a thousand dollars for Father Cassin.

Nevertheless, not until July 1882 was construction begun on a Catholic church. Two months later the church was completed, and on 10 September Father Cassin dedicated it to Saint John the Baptist. A Methodist church had also been under construction during the summer of 1882, and its doors were opened only a week after those of the Catholic church. Now that Bodie finally had two churches, the need for them was rapidly diminishing. During 1882 the majority of Bodie's mines closed, and two-thirds of its population drifted away to other camps.

School was another institution of little significance in Bodie. In early January 1878 the first term of the first public school in Bodie commenced in the home of Annie Donnelly. Although in 1878 there were some forty or more school-age children in Bodie, only fourteen showed up for classes. Donnelly appealed to the parents of Bodie to send their children to school. Enrollment increased gradually until Donnelly's house could no longer accommodate the students. The summer term was postponed because no school facility could be found.

Classroom space was eventually leased in the Cary Building on Main Street, and a special tax was levied to provide funds for the construction of a schoolhouse. By late February 1879 a schoolhouse, complete with cupola, had been erected on Green Street, and Mrs. Donnelly was expecting to greet some eighty students for the spring term. Truancy remained a problem in Bodie, especially among the town's older boys. The lessons they learned in the classroom paled in comparison with those they learned on the streets of the West's wildest mining town in 1879.

Institutions of law enforcement and justice in Bodie were similar to those in Aurora. Bodie, however, was not the county seat of Mono County as Aurora had been. Therefore, the county sheriff, county jail, district attorney, and superior court were located not in Bodie but in Bridgeport, some fifteen miles away, over a twisting mountain road. Law enforcement in Bodie was left to a town constable and his deputies, or police officers, as they were commonly known, and a justice of the peace held court.

Serving as constable for several terms during Bodie's boom years was John F. Kirgan. Kirgan originally came to California in 1848 after serving in the Mexican War, where he won decorations for bravery at Monterrey and Buena Vista. He was sergeant at arms during California's first constitutional convention and again during the first meeting of the state legislature at Vallejo. Elected Bodie town constable in 1878, Kirgan served on and off until March 1881, when his sulky overturned on Main Street and he was fatally injured. Kirgan was highly respected and well liked. Others serving as Bodie town constable included S. G. Stebbins and James S. Herrington. Kirgan also served as jailer of the Bodie jail during the town's heyday. The jailer was appointed by the county sheriff and carried the title of deputy sheriff. Much of the time Kirgan held the jobs of constable and jailer simultaneously. The first Bodie jail was built late in 1877 and contained only two small, poorly ventilated cells. Within a year or two it could no longer accommodate the steadily increasing number of prisoners, and Kirgan was forced to lodge some of the men in a cabin next door.

A new jail was finally built in August 1880 and "furnished with all the articles for comfort that can be found in any jail on the coast." From a front office a hallway led to four cells, two on each side, and through a heavy rear door to an exercise yard surrounded by a high planked fence. All doors were reinforced with iron, and each cell had an iron-grated front and "the latest improved locks." Ironically, just two months after the new jail was completed, Bodie's first and only jailbreak occurred. While Kirgan was away, two prisoners somehow managed to slip into the exercise yard and scale the fence to freedom. The *Daily Free Press* thought that the prisoners must have "had pressing business on the outside."

Kirgan always kept the jail clean and orderly and personally supervised the preparation of all meals. The *Daily Free Press* called Kirgan's jailhouse food "wholesome and ample," and the *Bodie Standard* thought that "not the better quality of food is found on any table in the county." Meals were served twice a day at a daily cost of less than a dollar per man. Kirgan put on a special affair each Thanksgiving. The prisoners were moved to write the *Bodie Standard:* "We, the boarders of the 'Hotel de Kirgan,' express our heartfelt and sincere thanks and gratitude to the proprietor of said institution for the courteous manner and bountiful feast of which we partook for Thanksgiving Dinner. The table was complete in every particular. . . . Hoping that Kirgan may live to enjoy the good of this world and Thanksgiving dinners for many years, we remain, Respectfully, 'The Boarders.' " Very few western lawmen ever received such a tribute from their prisoners.

Although Bodieites petitioned the state legislature for the appointment of a superior court judge who would sit in Bodie, only justices of the peace ever held court in the town. Participants in superior court cases were forced to travel to the Mono County courthouse in Bridgeport. Jurors were especially annoyed by this inconvenience. When a large number of jurors were summoned one July to hear a number of murder cases, the *Bodie Chronicle* commented, "We presume the road to Bridgeport will be perfectly blue from the 'cussing' that will be indulged in by those meandering towards the Capital of Mono." Bodieites were exceptionally adept at inventing excuses to free themselves from jury duty. A deputy sheriff often spent several days attempting to round up the requisite number of jurors.

Fortunately for Bodieites, most cases were handled by local justices of the peace. Justice court was held in a room above the Rosedale saloon on Main Street, and court was often adjourned so that the liquid refreshment served downstairs could be enjoyed. Justices paid themselves and the officers of the court out of the fines they levied. "This practice is demoralizing," said the *Daily Free Press* on 17 July 1880, "and an inducement to the imposition of heavy fines." A half a year later, when a new justice of the peace was installed, the newspaper commented, "The new machine has been oiled up, Justice has had her eyes properly bandaged, and everything is ready for business." Justices of the peace during Bodie's heyday included R. L. Peterson, Thomas Newman, A. M. Phlegar, and D. V. Goodson.

Bodie also boasted its own National Guard company. The guards met at the fire station, usually on Tuesday evenings, and held rifle practice on a range near the Queen Bee Hill on Sundays. The company could have passed for a unit of the Fenians, the nineteenth-century precursor of the Irish Republican Army. Nearly every member of the company carried an Irish name. The officers included Callahan, Kelly, and McPhee; the noncommissioned officers, Fahey, Kearney, Markey, and O'Brien; and the privates, Boyle, Carroll, Costello, Finnegan, Lyons, McGrath, Mullin, O'Donnell, O'Keeffe, Phelan, Shea, Thornton, Tobin, and Whelan.

The legal profession was well represented in Bodie by attorneys Patrick Reddy, John McQuaid, Thomas P. Ryan, John Kittrell, Frank Owen, R. S. Minor, and more than a dozen others. Reddy, both literally and figuratively, stood head and shoulders above his colleagues. He was, as one Bodieite recalled, "easily the most striking figure in town." Reddy was large, powerfully built, and handsome. He had a commanding personality and was a born fighter and leader of men. His origins were humble. He was born in Woonsocket, Rhode Island, in 1839, shortly after his impoverished parents arrived in the United States from County Carlow, Ireland. Like many other Irish-Americans of that era, although he was born in America he had been conceived in Ireland.

Reddy came to California in February 1861 and worked as a laborer in Contra Costa County and as a miner in Placer County, before he crossed into the trans-Sierra country in 1863. Virginia City, Aurora, Darwin, and Montgomery were some of the mining camps he lived in. His years in those camps were said to have been nothing less than wild and reckless: one contemporary went so far as to call him the "terror" of Aurora in 1863. The next year he was shot in the arm by an unknown assailant while walking down B street in Virginia City. He lost the arm as a result of the wound, but he never lost his fighting spirit. Thirty-three years later, when he was nearly fifty-eight years old, he emerged from the state supreme court in Sacramento to see a number of people rushing out of the post office nearby. When one of those fleeing the building told Reddy that there was an armed man inside threatening to kill a woman, Reddy ran into the post office. He found the man, later identified as Peter Hulsman, standing over a woman and brandishing a revolver. One-armed Patrick Reddy lunged for the gun and grabbed it before Hulsman could fire. Another man then jumped on Hulsman's back. Hulsman, in a last desperate effort, tried to turn the gun on Reddy and fire. But Reddy jammed his thumb between the hammer and cylinder of the revolver as Hulsman cocked it and, when Hulsman pulled the trigger, the hammer fell on Reddy's thumb. Reddy and the other man then wrestled Hulsman to the floor. After the police arrived, Reddy had his thumb, which was bleeding profusely, bandaged and, as the *San Francisco Call* put it, "continued on down the street as if nothing unusual had happened."

Shortly after Reddy lost his arm—he would later call it a blessing in disguise—he married and began to study law. In 1867 he was admitted to the bar and began to practice law in Independence, a location that enabled him to attract business from the entire southern trans-Sierra region. Responding to the great boom at Bodie, he moved his practice there in April 1879 and by 1880 his law office occupied the entire top floor of the Molinelli Building on Main Street. The *Bodie Standard* called it "the most imposing law office outside of San Francisco." Although Reddy's dark auburn hair was beginning to turn white and he was gaining an ever more dignified appearance, he occasionally went on a spree. Then he would proceed from saloon to saloon, ordering drinks for everybody and challenging Bodie's strongest men to arm-wrestling matches.

Reddy dominated both the justice court at Bodie and the superior court at Bridgeport. He prepared his briefs carefully, had almost total recall, and captivated judge and jury with a commanding voice, beautiful diction, and a lilting Irish brogue. Years later in San Francisco, law students would crowd into the courtroom to watch him perform. In Bodie, Reddy won the reputation of supporting the underdog. He donated his services to dozens of Bodieites who could not afford to pay him, while his wealthy clients were charged reasonably high fees. He was known to occasionally slip $20 gold pieces into the hands of destitute miners and to treat them to elegant dinners. Reddy was also active in politics. He was a founding member of the Bodie chapter of the Land League of Ireland, a Mono and Inyo county delegate to the state constitutional convention in 1878–1879, and a state senator from 1883 to 1887. Although Reddy stopped prospecting and mining when he lost his arm, he never stopped dabbling in mining stock. He was a part-owner of several mines, including the Yellow Aster, which made Randsburg famous. The name of his favorite mine, the Defiance, symbolized his character.

In 1881 Reddy opened a law office in San Francisco, while maintaining his practice in Bodie for another two years. Within a few years and with the addition of junior partners William H. Metson—whom Reddy trained earlier in Bodie—and J. C. Campbell, Reddy had established one of San Francisco's most prominent law firms. His firm represented clients from throughout the Far West, including Alaska, and, as in Bodie, the clients were often underdogs. When the mine owners of the Coeur d'Alene district in Idaho, with the support of state and federal troops, tried to destroy the miners' union during the 1890s by hiring strikebreakers, shooting union leaders, and imprisoning hundreds of miners in bullpens, Reddy rushed to the scene to aid the miners. "He distinguished himself," noted the San Francisco *Bulletin*, "against the best legal talent of the Northwest in the numerous cases which grew out of those labor troubles." During the 1890s Reddy was also bold enough to publicly support women's suffrage.

Reddy died at his home on Pacific Avenue in San Francisco early on the morning of 26 June 1900, after a month-long battle with Bright's disease, complicated by pneumonia. Among those at his bedside were his wife of thirty-six years, Emma, and his younger brother, Edward "Ned" Reddy, who had come to California with him in 1861 and who had shared many of his experiences in the mining camps of the trans-Sierra. They said that the famed attorney died with a smile on his face. Later that morning, when lawyer James G. Maguire announced in the United States Circuit Court in San Francisco that Patrick Reddy had died, the judge ordered the court adjourned for the day as a tribute to Reddy.

Reddy left an estate valued at over a quarter-million dollars, a substantial sum in 1900, yet it was only a small portion of what he had made in his lifetime. Oliver Roberts, a lifelong friend of Reddy, said shortly after Reddy's death, "Senator Reddy earned more than a million dollars in his profession as a lawyer, and if he dies a comparatively poor man, it is because he had given most of it away. He knew everybody in the mining regions of California, and he seldom came back from a trip without bringing with him one or two of the old boys who were crippled by accident or disease, and as soon as they were able to get out of the hospital he would grub stake them and send them back to whatever camp they wanted to go. Many an old-timer will miss Pat Reddy. He was a big man, Pat was, and his heart was as big as his body."

Reddy's presence in Bodie, as a mature attorney of unusual ability, added something very special to the town. Bodie was otherwise a town much like other western mining towns, especially Aurora. Bodie, like Aurora, had a mostly white and male population of over five thousand, numerous saloons and brothels, conventional institutions of law enforcement and justice, a brief but spectacular boom period, and mines that produced millions in bullion. And, of course, Bodie was located just eight miles away from Aurora at approximately the same elevation; the two towns shared the same climate, terrain, and vegetation. Nevertheless, there were important differences. Whereas Aurora's politics had been superheated by the Civil War and the California-Nevada boundary dispute, Bodie's political life was uninspired and mundane. Also, the Owens Valley Indian War, occurring during Aurora's boom, was only a memory by the time of Bodie's strikes in 1877 and 1878. The war had ended organized Indian resistance to white encroachment, and Bodieites traveled the trans-Sierra country with no fear of Indian attack. Finally, Bodie did not enjoy full employment as did Aurora, where jobs often went begging. A good number of Bodieites spent much of their time unemployed.

Suggestions for Further Reading

Several books deal in general fashion with the westward movement of settlers in North America. The standard work is Ray A. Billington, *Westward Expansion* (rev. ed.; Macmillan, 1967), but more relevant here is his *The Far Western Frontier, 1830–1860* * (Harper & Row, 1956). See also *The New Country: A Social History of the American Frontier, 1776–1890* * (Oxford University Press, 1974) by Richard A. Bartlett. The basic studies of Manifest Destiny are A. K. Weinberg, *Manifest Destiny* * (Johns Hopkins Press, 1935), and Frederick Merk, *Manifest Destiny and Mission in American History: A Reinterpretation* * (Knopf, 1963).

An old but still useful survey of Mexican-American history is Carey McWilliams, *North from Mexico: The Spanish-Speaking People of the United States* * (Lippincott, 1949). See also Matthew S. Meier and Feliciano Rivera, *The Chicanos: A History of Mexican Americans* * (Hill & Wang, 1972). Regional history is stressed in Ernesto Galarza, Herman Gallegos, and Julian Samora, *Mexican Americans in the Southwest* * (McNally and Loftin, 1969). An important study of the conquest of the Mexican territory is Robert W. Johannsen, *To the Halls of Montezuma: The Mexican War in the American Imagination* (Oxford University Press, 1985).

The origins of Mormonism are treated in Richard L. Bushman, *Joseph Smith and the Beginnings of Mormonism* (University of Illinois Press, 1984). Thomas F. O'Dea's *The Mormons* * (University of Chicago Press, 1957) is an excellent survey of Mormon belief and practice. The migration to the Great Salt Lake is described in Wallace Stegner, *The Gathering of Zion: The Story of the Mormon Trail* (McGraw-Hill, 1964). Two recent works that deal with aspects of the Mormon tradition are Klaus Hansen, *Mormonism and the American Experience* * (University of Chicago, 1981), and Jan Shipps, *Mormonism: The Story of a New Religious Tradition* (University of Illinois, 1985). On the development of the Mormon community in Utah, see Nels Anderson, *Desert Saints: The Mormon Frontier in Utah* * (University of Chicago, 1942).

An exhaustive survey of United States policy in Indian affairs has appeared in Francis Paul Prucha, *The Great White Father: The United States Government and the American Indian*, 2 vols., (University of Nebraska, 1984). Two basic anthropological studies of the Plains Indians are E. A. Hoebel, *The Cheyennes: Indians of the Great Plains* * (Holt, Rinehart and Winston, 1960), and R. H. Lowie, *Indians of the Plains* * (McGraw-Hill, 1954). For the impact of the horse on Indian culture, see F. G. Roe, *The Indian and the Horse* (University of Oklahoma Press, 1955).

* Available in paperback edition.

The first modern study of Chinese-American history is by Gunther Barth, *Bitter Strength: A History of the Chinese in the United States, 1850–1870* (Harvard University Press, 1964). Attitudes toward the Chinese immigrants are described in Stuart C. Miller, *The Unwelcome Immigrant: The American Image of the Chinese, 1785–1882* * (University of California Press, 1969), and Alexander Saxton, *The Indispensable Enemy: Labor and the Anti-Chinese Movement in California* * (University of California Press, 1971). See also Victor Nee and Brett de Bar Nee, *Longtime Californ': A Documentary History of an American Chinatown* * (Pantheon, 1973).

On American violence in general, see the work by Hugh Davis Graham and Ted Robert Gurr (eds.), *Violence in America: Historical and Comparative Perspectives* * (U.S. Government Printing Office, 1969). Frontier violence is a thing of myth and legend. Two attempts by historians to put matters in perspective are Richard Maxwell Brown, *Strains of Violence: Historical Studies of American Violence and Vigilantism* * (Oxford University Press, 1975), and W. Eugene Hollon, *Frontier Violence: Another Look* * (Oxford University Press, 1974).

A 6
B 7
C 8
D 9
E 0
F 1
G 2
H 3
I 4
J 5

JE 3 '02 DATE DUE

GAYLORD   #3523PI   Printed in USA